Outlook 2002:
The Complete Reference

Outlook 2002:
The Complete Reference

Thomas E. Barich

Osborne/**McGraw-Hill**

New York   Chicago   San Francisco
Lisbon   London   Madrid   Mexico City
Milan   New Delhi   San Juan
Seoul   Singapore   Sydney   Toronto

Osborne/**McGraw-Hill**
2600 Tenth Street
Berkeley, California 94710
U.S.A.

To arrange bulk purchase discounts for sales promotions, premiums, or fund-raisers, please contact Osborne/**McGraw-Hill** at the above address. For information on translations or book distributors outside the U.S.A., please see the International Contact Information page immediately following the index of this book.

Outlook 2002: The Complete Reference

234567890 FGR FGR 01987654321

ISBN 0-07-213274-4

Publisher
    Brandon A. Nordin

Vice President & Associate Publisher
    Scott Rogers

Acquisitions Editor
    Gretchen Ganser

Project Editor
    Lisa Wolters-Broder

Acquisitions Coordinator
    Alissa Larson

Technical Editor
    Will Kelly

Copy Editors
    Mike McGee and Jan Jue

Proofreaders
    Stefany Otis and Brian Galloway

Indexer
    Claire Splan

Computer Designers
    Carie Abrew and Lauren McCarthy

Illustrators
    Michael Mueller, Alex Putney,
    Lyssa Sieben-Wald, and Beth Young

Series Design
    Peter F. Hancik

This book was composed with Corel VENTURA™ Publisher.

About the Author

Thomas E. Barich is a computer consultant, CD-ROM developer, and author of a number of titles on a variety of computer software applications, including Microsoft Outlook, Microsoft Office, Symantec's ACT!, and others.

Dedication

This book is dedicated to Mary Kelly, who, in addition to being one of the nicest people I know, also happens to be my all-time-favorite aunt.

Contents

Part I

Outlook Basics

Part II

Communicating With E-Mail

Part IV

Managing Time and Details

Part VII

Building Outlook Applications

Part VIII

Appendixes

Introduction

Computer book introductions usually attempt to convey three things to the reader–what the book is about, for whom the book is written, and how to understand the conventions that are used in the book. While I think these objectives are worthy, the typical approach generally falls short of the mark. Therefore, I propose to make this introduction less typical and more helpful.

To give you a sense of what the book is about, the typical computer book introduction provides a synopsis of what each part covers. There's nothing wrong with that, but it's no match for the table of contents. If you really want to know what kind of coverage this book contains, head for the table of contents. It's clear, concise, and informative.

Who is this book written for? That's easy. It's written for anyone who wants to learn about Outlook, and who wants a handy reference book to help solve problems when they arise. Other than that, the onus of deciding whether this book is right for you falls, naturally, on your shoulders. The only way you can decide is by making sure the coverage is appropriate and that the style is easy to read and understand. Therefore, I recommend you review the table of contents, read random sections of the book, and skim through the index.

The third thing that most computer book introductions explain is the conventions used throughout the book. Because the icons and text formatting used in this book to mark special items, such as Tips, Notes, and MOUS coverage, are clear and unambiguous, there's no reason to belabor the issue. I'm sure you know that each time you see an icon that says Tip, it means the associated text is actually a bit of helpful advice.

Now, on to the really important stuff. Stop wasting time and get to work!

The
Complete
Reference

Outlook 2002

Part I

Outlook Basics

The Complete Reference

Chapter 1

Exploring Outlook

Outlook 2002 can greatly enhance your productivity by helping you get organized and keeping you organized. Unfortunately, as good as Outlook is, it can't do it alone. So you're going to have to roll up your sleeves and do some of the work yourself. Since the first order of business is to become familiar with the program and the way it functions, this chapter is going to take you on a tour of Outlook 2002. Here you'll get a good look at what exactly Outlook 2002 is and what it can do for you. You'll discover the convenience and flexibility Outlook provides in helping you communicate, delegate, schedule, track, and otherwise organize your day, your work, and your life. You'll learn about the program's main features and tools, how to open, close, and find your way around the program, and how to get additional help when you need it.

Introducing Outlook

Outlook 2002 is the Swiss army knife of personal information managers (PIMs). It provides you with all the tools you need to send and receive e-mail, keep track of your schedule, stay in touch with your contacts, and even manage your to-do lists. In addition, it integrates with other applications to enable you to compose form letters, send faxes, access the Internet, collaborate and exchange documents with others, and more.

Send and Receive E-mail, Faxes, and Documents

Although Outlook is a full-featured PIM, its e-mail management feature is, by far, its most popular. Some folks use Outlook for nothing else. Not only can you send and receive e-mail from any number of corporate or Internet mail addresses, you can also send documents and files, sort messages in a variety of ways, and even organize your messages automatically with the Outlook Rules Wizard. Because Outlook is Internet-savvy, you can send messages in the HTML format, which enables you to include colorful text and graphics. Depending on your configuration, you also can send faxes directly from Outlook. As you can see in Figure 1-1, the Inbox holds all your incoming mail, shown in the right pane, until you either store it or delete it.

Schedule Meetings and Appointments

For keeping track of your schedule, Outlook provides a powerful set of features to ensure you never miss another appointment or important engagement (unless, of course, you want to!). Corporate users on a network running Microsoft Exchange Server can schedule complex meetings with ease down to the last detail. Just enter the names of everyone you want to invite to the meeting, then ask Outlook to find a time at which everyone is available. You can even include a conference room or a resource (such as an overhead projector) by inviting the resource just as you would another meeting participant. Of course, the resource must have its own mailbox setup on the server before it will appear in the Select Attendees and Resources dialog box.

OUTLOOK BASICS

Figure 1-1.   *The Outlook Inbox helps you manage all your e-mail*

Need an online meeting instead? No problem—Outlook works with Microsoft NetMeeting to connect you with users anywhere on the planet for a live, real-time conference.

Even home users will find dozens of ways to use the Calendar folder: you can keep track of birthdays, holidays, and other special occasions; plan trips and vacations; or be reminded about next week's doctor's appointment (see Figure 1-2).

Manage Your Contact List

After you learn to use Outlook's contact management features, you can throw away your Rolodex, your little black book, *and* that unruly stack of business cards (not to mention the cocktail napkins and matchbook covers scribbled with names and numbers). The Outlook Contacts folder (shown in Figure 1-3) provides the room to store virtually any kind of information about each and every important person in your life, whether it's the company CEO, the potential client you met at a trade show last month, or your long-lost nephew in Sheboygan. However, the best part of using the Contacts folder is the ability to retrieve your contact information with just a click of your mouse.

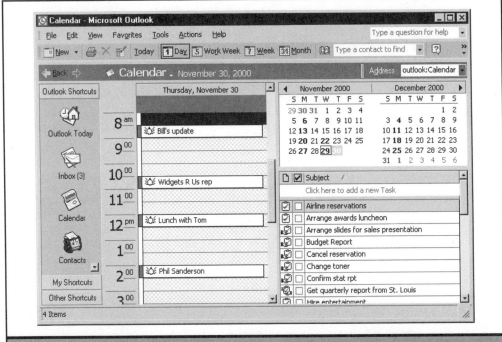

Figure 1-2.   *The Calendar folder provides all the tools you need to stay on schedule*

Track and Delegate Tasks and Projects

As you can see in Figure 1-4, the Tasks feature in Outlook provides everything you've always wanted in a to-do list, and more. In addition to managing your own to-do lists, you can assign tasks to other users, set due dates and reminders, even get automatic progress reports at specific intervals. You can also use the Tasks feature for personal reminders, such as paying bills, remembering the kids' games, and *not* forgetting to pick up an anniversary present for your spouse.

Log Journal Entries and Keep Notes

The Journal is a convenient way to keep track of what you did, when you did it, and how long it took (see Figure 1-5). If you bill hourly for your work, you'll certainly appreciate this feature. Start the timer before beginning work on a task to log time spent. Jot down notes from your phone call while it's happening (and use the timer to track the length of the call). Use contacts and categories to sort journal entries by clients or jobs. While not designed for complex project management, the Journal can handle everyday projects with ease.

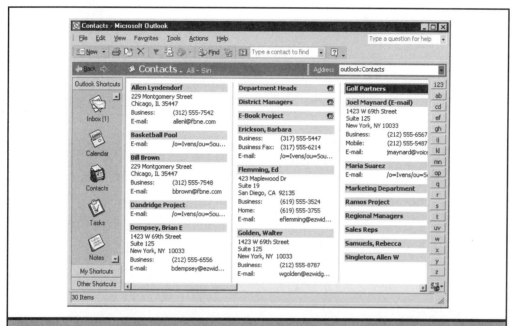

Figure 1-3. *Accessing contact information is a breeze with the Outlook Contacts folder*

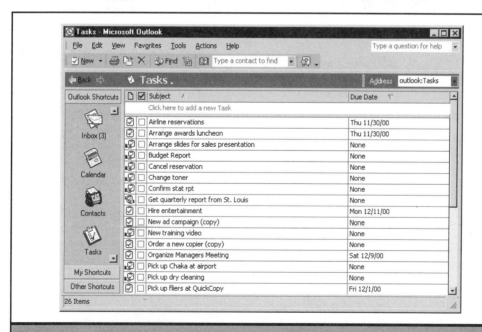

Figure 1-4. *Managing your to-do list was never this easy*

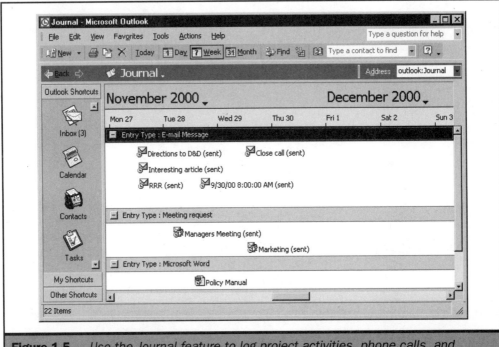

Figure 1-5. *Use the Journal feature to log project activities, phone calls, and documents*

Access Web Sites and Newsgroups

Outlook makes your Internet access complete by acting as a Web browser and by working with Outlook Express, the e-mail client and newsreader program that comes with Internet Explorer, to give you access to newsgroups (see Figure 1-6). You can even configure Outlook to open a particular Web page each time you click a folder. Of course, in order to take advantage of the Web and newsgroup features, you must have an Internet connection, either through your network or a modem.

If you select View | Go To | News, and Outlook Express opens instead of the Microsoft Outlook Newsreader, it means that Outlook Express and not Outlook is designated as your default newsgroups software. To use the Outlook Newsreader, Outlook must be your default newsgroups program. See Chapter 22 for details on how to make Outlook your default newsgroups software.

OUTLOOK BASICS

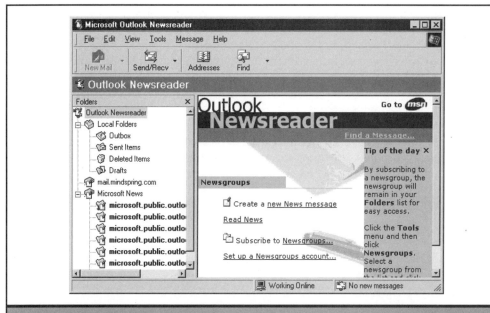

Figure 1-6.   *Outlook integrates with Outlook Express to give access to Internet newsgroups*

Is Your Computer on a Network?

If you're using Outlook at work, you're probably connected to a network. A network consists of two types of computers: servers and workstations. The servers are those computers, locked in the closet on the fourth floor, that receive, warehouse, and distribute information to the workstations, or clients. The workstations are the computers sitting on everyone's desk (including yours).

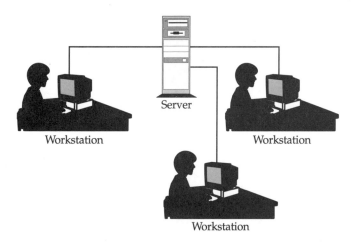

It's also likely that a program called Microsoft Exchange Server is running on that network. Exchange Server is a popular network server-based messaging and groupware system that manages large volumes of mail to a multitude of users' computers. Microsoft Outlook is a client mail program that runs on individual users' computers (workstations). You may have another mail system, such as Lotus cc:Mail or Microsoft Mail instead of Exchange Server. No problem—Outlook works with those too. If you're not sure about which mail system your company uses, check with your network administrator.

The details of how networks and Exchange Server work are not necessary for an understanding of Outlook. The main things you need to know are whether or not you're on a network and, if so, whether it is running Exchange Server.

Note   *You'll learn more about the benefits you get from using Outlook with Exchange Server in Part V.*

Unlike previous versions of Outlook, the latest version does not have different configurations depending on whether you're using Outlook on a network or as a stand-alone program. It's a change for the better. Now, you merely set the program up to work the way you work.

Starting Outlook

Outlook, like most Windows programs, plants a shortcut on the Start menu during installation. And as is the case with other Windows programs, you can count on having more than one way to do the same thing. With that in mind, here are a few ways you can launch Outlook:

■ **From the Start menu**   Click Start | Programs | Microsoft Outlook.

■ **From the desktop**   Double-click the Outlook icon on the desktop.

■ **From the Quick Launch bar (Windows 98/2000)**   Although, by default, Outlook does not put a shortcut on the Quick Launch bar — initially located at the lower left corner of your screen on the status bar — it is an easy task to put one there. The simplest method is to click Start | Programs and locate the Outlook shortcut. Then right-click the shortcut and drag it to the Quick Launch bar. Move your mouse pointer to a place on the bar to the right or left of an existing shortcut and release the right mouse button when your cursor turns into a dark I bar. Select Copy Here to create a new shortcut on the Quick Launch bar. After that, all you have to do is click the icon to launch Outlook.

■ **From the Office Shortcut bar**   If you regularly use the Office Shortcut bar, you'll find a variety of Outlook-related buttons here. You can use the shortcut bar to go directly to a new message, appointment, task, contact, journal entry, or note. Outlook will present you with the blank item you requested. If Outlook isn't running, only the form appears. Complete it and click Save and Close or Send to store or send it. You can display the Office Shortcut Bar by choosing Start | Programs | Microsoft Office Tools | Microsoft Office Shortcut Bar from the Windows taskbar.

If you have multiple profiles set up and you enable the Prompt For A Profile To Be Used option, Outlook asks you to select the profile you want to use each time you start the program. With the option disabled, Outlook starts with the profile selected in the Always Use This Profile option. Profiles are groups of individualized settings that determine which services are available to each user and how those services are configured. You'll learn more about creating your own profile in Chapter 2, "Working with Profiles."

After you choose which profile to use, Outlook will begin loading the files and settings last used in that profile. Unless you've changed the default settings, Outlook opens to the Inbox (see Figure 1-7).

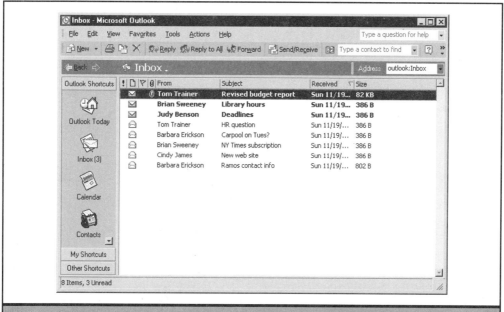

Figure 1-7. *If you're like most users, you'll be a frequent visitor to the Inbox*

Exploring the Outlook Interface

In order to harness the power Outlook offers, you must understand the different components, how they work, and how they integrate with each other. To make that task a little easier, familiarize yourself with some of the basic features common to all Outlook components.

Figure 1-8 identifies the main Outlook screen items. You'll recognize some of them from other Microsoft or Windows applications; others will be discussed in more detail later in this chapter:

- **Title bar**   Check here if you forget where you are. Click and drag here to move the window on the screen, or double-click to maximize or restore the window size.

- **Menu bar**   Click a menu topic to reveal a list of available commands and submenus, then click the desired command.

- **Status bar**   Look here for statistics on the current view, such as total number of items in the selected folder.

- **Toolbars**   Toolbars are the button bars at the top of the window, containing a variety of common commands. The toolbars and the buttons they include vary depending on which component you are using.

- **Folder List**   The Folder List provides a Windows Explorer-like view of your Outlook folders. To activate the Folder List, select View | Folder List from the Menu bar. You can also open the Folder List by clicking the current folder's title in the Folder banner.

- **Folder banner**   The Folder banner displays the name of the folder in which you're currently working. Unlike its predecessors, the Outlook 2002 Folder banner contains Back and Forward buttons and an Address box for easy navigation both in Outlook and on the Web.

- **Outlook Bar**   The Outlook Bar provides a quick and easy way to navigate around Outlook. You'll find shortcuts to the main Outlook components as well as your system files on the Outlook Bar. Click a shortcut to switch to the associated folder. As you can see in Figure 1-8, the Outlook Bar is composed of three shortcut groups – Outlook Shortcuts, My Shortcuts, and Other Shortcuts. You'll learn how to add and remove shortcuts and shortcut groups from the Outlook Bar in Chapter 24.

- **Information viewer**   The Information viewer is the main viewing area of the Outlook window. It displays the contents of the currently selected folder. For example, in the Inbox, the Information viewer displays a list of your received e-mail messages. Switch to Calendar, and the Information viewer displays today's appointments along with the Date Navigator and the TaskPad.

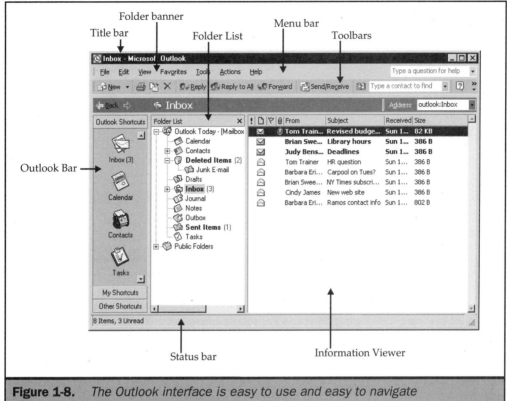

Title bar
Folder banner
Folder List
Menu bar
Toolbars
Outlook Bar
Status bar
Information Viewer

Figure 1-8.   *The Outlook interface is easy to use and easy to navigate*

What Is Outlook Today?

As you can see in Figure 1-9, Outlook Today is a handy one-screen summary of your day. At a single glance, you can see today's date, your upcoming appointments, the number of unread messages in your Inbox, and the current items on your Tasks list.

If you need a little more detail, simply click an item to display the form (appointments and tasks) or the folder (messages) associated with it. You can even mark tasks as completed by checking them off in the Outlook Today view.

If you like the idea of getting a quick overview of your day each morning, you can elect to have Outlook open to Outlook Today each time you start the program. See Chapter 24 for details.

Figure 1-9.   *Outlook Today provides a quick overview of appointments and tasks*

Using the Information Viewer

Since the Information viewer is the display area for the currently selected folder, your options for manipulating it are limited to those involving the viewing of information. You can resize it by changing the size of (or hiding) the Outlook Bar. Depending on the folder you're in, you can split the Information viewer by activating the Preview Pane, and you can open the Folder List by clicking the folder name in the Folder banner. You can also access shortcut menus by right-clicking the Folder banner or the display area of the Information viewer itself.

To allow more room in the Information viewer, keep the Folder List closed. You can click the folder's title on the Folder banner to briefly reveal the Folder List. Choose the folder you want to see next; the Folder List will close again, leaving your Information viewer uncluttered.

Getting Around in Outlook

There are a number of ways to move around in Outlook, but you'll find there are two traditional methods that provide easy navigation of the program. They are the Outlook Bar and the Folder List. There's also a third, non-traditional (at least for Outlook and other Office applications right out of the box) method, issuing voice commands.

Using the Outlook Bar

The Outlook Bar shown in Figure 1-10 is the primary navigation tool in Outlook. It's loaded with shortcuts to the main Outlook components as well as your system files and folders. Click a shortcut icon to open the associated folder.

By default, the Outlook Bar contains three shortcut groups:

- **Outlook Shortcuts**   This group contains shortcuts to the most commonly used Outlook folders.

- **My Shortcuts**   Here you'll find some of the less frequently used Outlook shortcuts.

- **Other Shortcuts**   The Other Shortcuts group provides access to your system files and folders (My Computer) as well as your My Documents and Favorites folders.

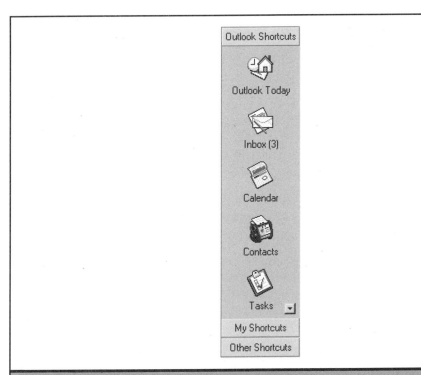

Figure 1-10.   *After using the Outlook Bar, you'll wish every Windows program had one*

Navigating with the Outlook Bar

Now that you understand the theory, it's time for a little practical application. Why not take the Outlook Bar for a test drive and see what it can do? To begin with, click any shortcut and open the associated folder. You'll note that not only does the content of the Information viewer change but also the commands on the toolbar. If you check the menus, you'll find differences there as well. Spend a little time moving around Outlook using the Outlook Shortcuts. Here's a list of the places you can go using the shortcuts found in the Outlook Shortcuts group:

- **Outlook Today** As discussed earlier in this chapter, Outlook Today provides a quick overview of your daily activities and unread messages.

- **Inbox** The Inbox is the heart of your e-mail system. It's where all your incoming mail resides until you decide what to do with it.

- **Calendar** The Calendar folder contains the appointment calendar, the Date Navigator, and the TaskPad. You can schedule appointments and meetings, look up dates, and even record tasks on your to-do list.

- **Contacts** The Contacts folder is the receptacle for all your contact information. In addition to storing and manipulating your contact data, the Contacts folder can also double as an Outlook address book.

- **Tasks** The Tasks folder is a to-do list on steroids. It provides all the tools you need to track and manage your past (in case you're just a little behind), present, and future tasks.

- **Notes** Can't figure out what to do with a miscellaneous scrap of information you know you should hold on to? Create an Outlook note! The electronic equivalent of sticky notes, Outlook notes let you record and organize bits and pieces of data that don't seem to fit anywhere else.

- **Deleted Items** When you delete an Outlook item, it gets dumped in the Deleted Items folder. However, be sure not to confuse Deleted Items with the Windows Recycle Bin. They have nothing to do with one another, and they do not collaborate. Items moved to the Deleted Items folder remain there until you empty the folder, at which time they are removed permanently from your hard disk. They do *not* go the Windows Recycle Bin.

Depending on your screen resolution and the state of your Outlook window, you may not be able to view all the shortcuts in My Shortcuts at one time. If you see a down arrow button in the bottom right corner of the Outlook Bar it indicates the presence of additional shortcuts.

Click the down arrow button to bring the additional buttons into view. Once you do that, you'll notice that the shortcuts at the top of the Outlook Bar have now disappeared, and an up arrow button appears in the top right corner. As you've undoubtedly figured out by now, the buttons are scroll buttons and you simply click them to move the missing shortcuts into view.

If you're ready to move on and try something new, click the My Shortcuts button to display the secondary set of Outlook shortcuts (see Figure 1-11).

Even if you don't use these shortcuts often, it's nice to know where they are when you need them:

- **Drafts**   Did you ever write an e-mail in haste and hit the Send button, only to realize that you forgot something, or even worse, that you never should have sent the message at all? Use the Drafts folder to save unfinished or questionable messages for later review.

- **Outbox**   The Outbox is a way station for messages you send. On a Microsoft Exchange server network the server sweeps the Outbox at regular intervals and picks up your outgoing mail automatically, so messages spend little time there

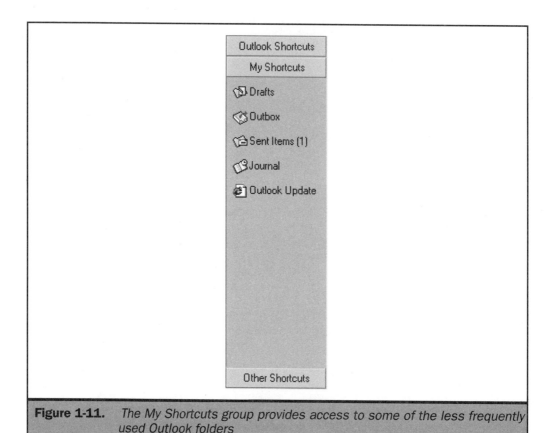

Figure 1-11. *The My Shortcuts group provides access to some of the less frequently used Outlook folders*

when you're logged on to the network. If, however, you're working offline, messages stay in the Outbox until you log back on. The Outbox also gets used if you have an Internet e-mail account and choose not to have outgoing messages sent automatically. They are stored in the Outbox until the next time you manually send mail using your Internet account.

■ **Sent Items**   When you get the urge to review messages you've sent (or when a question arises that may be answered in a previously sent message), you'll find the Sent Items folder quite helpful. By default, Outlook is configured to save a copy of all outgoing messages in the Sent Items folder.

■ **Journal**   The Outlook Journal provides a place for you to track phone calls, e-mail messages, tasks, and even Office documents.

■ **Outlook Update**   If you're connected to the Internet, either through your network or through a modem, the Outlook Update shortcut opens the Outlook section of the Microsoft Office Update Web site right in your Information viewer.

The third and final shortcut group, Other Shortcuts, provides access to your computer and your system files:

- **My Computer**   This shortcut is identical to the My Computer icon on your Windows desktop. It displays your Windows environment in the Outlook Information viewer.

- **My Documents**   For quick and easy access to the My Documents folder on your hard disk, click this shortcut icon. The contents of your My Documents folder appear in the Outlook Information viewer.

- **Favorites**   The Favorites shortcut, as you've probably guessed, opens your Favorites folder and displays the contents in the Outlook Information viewer.

 You can add your own groups and shortcuts to the Outlook Bar, which you'll learn more about in Chapter 24.

Drag and Drop Items on the Outlook Bar

Not only is the Outlook Bar a great tool for getting around in Outlook, it also provides a quick and easy way to move and copy information. In addition, it enables you to easily create one kind of Outlook item from another, such as creating messages from notes, contacts from appointments, and even appointments from tasks.

For example, suppose you've got a task on your to-do list to make a doctor's appointment. Once you stop procrastinating and get around to making the appointment, there are a couple of ways you can add it to your calendar. You can delete the task from the Tasks list (or mark it completed), open the Calendar folder, and finally create a new appointment—or you can save yourself some trouble and use the Outlook Bar. Simply drag the item from your Tasks list and drop it on the Calendar shortcut on the Outlook Bar. A new appointment form opens immediately with all the available information from the Task list already included. All you have to do is fill in the date and time, set a reminder, and click Save and Close.

 For more information on working with tasks and appointments, see Chapters 11 and 13.

Hiding and Restoring the Outlook Bar

One nice thing about the Outlook Bar is that if you don't like it you don't have to look at it. Even if you do like it, you may decide you need more room for the Information viewer. In either case, you can hide and display the Outlook Bar at will. You can even change its size if you like.

If the Outlook Bar is visible, you can hide it by right-clicking a blank spot on the Outlook Bar and selecting Hide Outlook Bar from the shortcut menu. You can also open the View menu and click Outlook Bar to remove the check mark that appears to the left. To restore a hidden Outlook Bar simply return to the View menu and click Outlook Bar to add a check mark.

Using the Folder List as a Navigational Tool

The Folder List is a tree-like structure that provides you with a simple way to view, navigate through, and utilize your Outlook folders. If you're at all familiar with Windows Explorer, you'll feel right at home using the Folder List (see Figure 1-12).

Using the Folder List to get around in Outlook is easy. From any folder, choose View | Folder List to display the Folder List in the Information viewer. You can also display the Folder List by clicking the folder name on the Folder banner, which assumes the appearance of a button as soon as you move your mouse pointer over it. The folder name is located at the left side of the Folder banner and contains a small down arrow indicating the presence of a drop-down window.

 Clicking the folder name only opens the Folder List temporarily. As soon as you make a selection in the Folder List, or take any other action in Outlook, the Folder List closes automatically. You can keep it open permanently (or at least until you elect to close it) by clicking the yellow pushpin icon located in the top right corner of the Folder List.

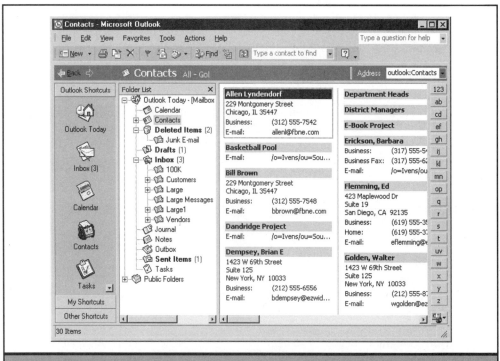

Figure 1-12.   *The Folder List provides the same ease of use found in Windows Explorer*

Once you've got the Folder List open, all you have to do is click the folder to which you want to move. Immediately, you're transported to the selected folder. If you used the Folder List command on the View menu, or if you clicked the yellow pushpin, the Folder List remains open, enabling you to keep moving whenever the urge strikes.

In addition to providing you with another navigation tool, the Folder List also gives you another means of creating Outlook items by dragging the item and dropping it on a folder in the list. As soon as you drop the item, a new form of the type used in the folder on which you dropped the original item opens, containing the data from the dropped item. For example, if you drop an appointment item in the Notes folder, a new Notes form opens, containing the appointment information. It's the same as dropping items on the Outlook Bar shortcuts, except that you have more options (unless you've customized the Outlook Bar) with the Folder List.

Using the Toolbars

Toolbars are those handy little devices you find hanging out on most Windows programs. They contain buttons for accessing the most commonly used features of the program. Outlook follows the tradition and has a great set of toolbars (see Figure 1-13), and a wealth of toolbar options. In addition to providing you with three main toolbars (four if you count the Menu bar, which is technically a toolbar) and four subsidiary toolbars (found only in certain Outlook forms), Outlook also enables you to modify existing toolbars and even create your own custom toolbars.

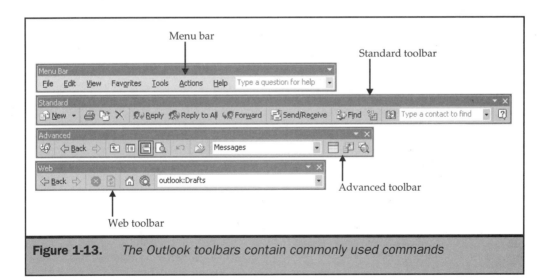

Figure 1-13.   *The Outlook toolbars contain commonly used commands*

When you open the Customize dialog box, you'll see the Menu bar listed under toolbars. Technically this is accurate, since the Menu bar is nothing more than a toolbar that contains menus instead of command buttons. However, for the sake of clarity, this book treats toolbars and menus as different devices.

The primary Outlook toolbars include the following:

■ **Standard** This is your "meat and potatoes" toolbar. It contains the standard commands you find in most Windows programs, such as New, Print, and Find, plus the basic commands for the Outlook component you currently have open.

■ **Advanced** The Advanced toolbar sports a collection of command buttons that let you perform Outlook tasks such as changing views, showing and hiding the Folder List, undoing the last command, and so on. As with the Standard toolbar, the Advanced toolbar changes depending on the Outlook folder currently open.

■ **Web** When you use Outlook to view Web pages on the Internet or your company's intranet, the Web toolbar appears. If you understand Back, Home, Refresh, and Stop, you shouldn't have much trouble figuring out this one. (See "Using Outlook as a Web and File Browser," later in this chapter.)

The secondary toolbars are found only in Outlook forms, such as the appointment form, the message form, the contact form, and so on:

■ **Formatting** If you use a word processor, the Formatting toolbar should be a familiar sight. It provides the basic commands for manipulating and dressing up your text. The Formatting toolbar is available in any form that accepts text in a message or note field.

■ **Clipboard** This Office Clipboard, which Outlook uses, enables you to cut and paste up to 12 different items in any one session. The Clipboard toolbar gives the option to select which item to paste, to paste all items on the clipboard, or to clear the entire Office Clipboard. Like the Formatting toolbar, the Clipboard toolbar is available in all forms that accept text entry in a message or notes field.

■ **Form Design** This toolbar provides you with commands used in designing and customizing forms. Although the Form Design toolbar appears on the Toolbars tab of the Customize box when accessed from any form, it can only be activated in the design mode.

■ **Response** This toolbar is available only when viewing e-mail messages you receive that contain voting buttons.

One last thing to remember. If you have Microsoft Word installed, Outlook uses Word as the e-mail editor by default. Therefore, when you right-click a toolbar in a message form, you'll see a host of available toolbars. These are Word toolbars, not Outlook toolbars.

Showing and Hiding Toolbars

The first time you run Outlook, the Standard toolbar is the only one that appears in most Outlook folders. You can access additional toolbars by right-clicking anywhere on a visible toolbar and selecting from the shortcut menu that appears. Toolbars with check marks are already visible. Toolbars without check marks are currently hidden. To hide a visible toolbar, right-click and deselect the toolbar you want to eliminate.

 You can open the Customize dialog box by double-clicking a blank area on any toolbar.

Repositioning Toolbars

Since not everyone works the same way, you'll be pleased to discover you're not locked into using the Outlook toolbars where they fall. Each toolbar can be moved from its original position and placed anywhere you fancy in the Outlook window. While you can locate the toolbars wherever you want, there are two toolbar states that you should be aware of: docked and floating. As you can see in Figure 1-14, a docked toolbar is one that is securely planted along one of the four edges (or adjacent to a toolbar on the edge) of the Outlook window. A floating toolbar, on the other hand, is one that is just hanging out in any random spot on the window.

To move a docked toolbar, grab its handle (the raised vertical bar at the left edge of the toolbar), drag it to the new location, and drop it. To move a floating toolbar, grab it by the title bar, drag it to a new location, and drop it. To dock any toolbar, move it to the desired edge of the Outlook window until it automatically positions itself against the window edge or against an existing docked toolbar. To float a toolbar, move it into the Outlook window and drop it wherever you want it. You can also resize floating toolbars by dragging any of the four sides to enlarge or reduce the length or width of the toolbar.

 If you double-click the title bar of a floating toolbar, it will automatically return to its last docked location.

Customizing Toolbars

You can add and remove buttons on existing toolbars, change the order in which the buttons appear, and even create your own toolbar from scratch. For more information on these procedures, see Chapter 24.

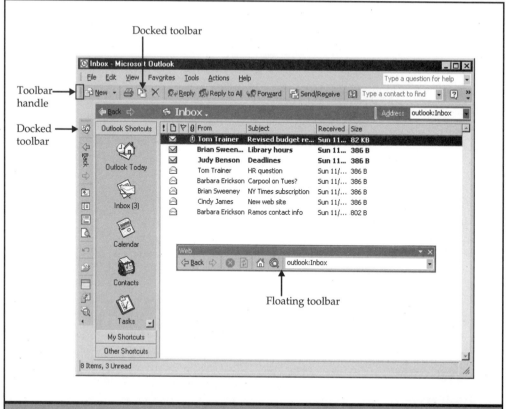

Figure 1-14.   *Outlook lets you customize your work environment to suit your needs*

Working with Multiple Outlook Windows

Despite its power and flexibility, there are a few things Outlook can't do that many users wish it could. You can't, for example, view different components at the same time in the same session of Outlook. So, what do you do if you're responding to a ton of e-mail requests to set up meetings over the next several months and you want to view both your Inbox and your Calendar window at the same time? Simple: start a new Outlook session, then position both windows so you can see as much as you can of both. If you have a large monitor (17" or more) and run at a high screen resolution, you can really pack a lot of information on one screen.

You can run as many sessions of Outlook or any other application(s) as your computer can handle. If performance deteriorates, it's probably because your computer is running low on available memory (RAM). In this case, you may have to close one or more open windows, documents, or sessions before proceeding.

To run multiple sessions of Outlook and arrange them neatly onscreen, follow these steps:

1. With one Outlook session already running in any view, minimize all open windows. If you're using Windows 98 or later, just click the Show Desktop button on the Quick Launch bar. Otherwise, right-click anywhere on a blank area of the Windows taskbar and choose Minimize All Windows.

2. Double-click the Outlook icon on the Windows desktop to open a second session.

3. Click the original Outlook session's taskbar button to restore it. You now have two Outlook sessions visible; if any other applications are running, they are minimized.

4. Right-click the taskbar and choose Tile Windows Vertically. The windows will be evenly sized, the currently selected windows filling the left half of the screen, the other filling the right half, as shown in Figure 1-15.

5. If you'd prefer to have the windows lined up one on top of the other, right-click the taskbar and choose Tile Windows Horizontally. The windows will be evenly sized, the currently selected window filling the top half of the screen, the other filling the lower half.

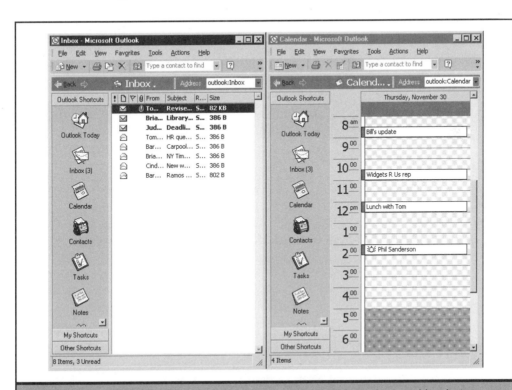

Figure 1-15.   *Placing both Outlook sessions side by side makes working in two folders at the same time a snap*

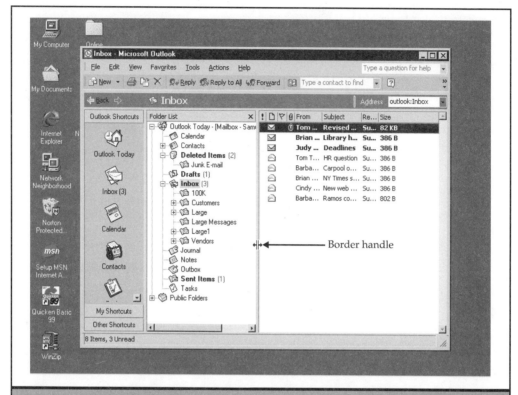

Figure 1-16.   *Drag interior and exterior borders to make the Outlook environment fit your needs*

Most of the interior borders within the Outlook window can be adjusted by dragging them elsewhere (see Figure 1-16). With a large monitor, a speedy computer, and some creative resizing, you can view several Outlook components at once and still have room to work on a word processing document or other window on the desktop. Don't overdo it though—it doesn't take much to drain your computer's memory resources.

Using Outlook as a Web and File Browser

Because the Office 2002 suite of applications is so closely integrated with the Internet, it's no surprise that the "don't use a hammer to drive a screw" rule doesn't always apply: now you can create Web pages with Excel, you can create graphics in Word, and you can use Outlook as a browser.

OUTLOOK BASICS

The rising popularity of corporate intranets has made this feature even more popular. Employees now can use a single application to access e-mail, schedule meetings, manage files, order supplies, update their personnel information, receive company news and information, and more, all from the same application. What's more, Outlook reads and creates electronic forms in HTML (Hypertext Markup Language, the language used to compose Web pages), so gathering information from employees, customers, and others is now as simple as sending e-mail. Home users might like to view their favorite Web page while their e-mail downloads. Because of this nearly seamless integration, the possibilities are endless.

Technically, Outlook Today is a Web page, too—it's just one that's built into Outlook rather than posted on the Net. When you view Outlook Today, you're really using Outlook as a browser.

Setting a Home Page for an Outlook Folder

If you have a particular Web site or intranet page you visit frequently, you can tell Outlook you want to view that page each time you go to a particular folder. A Web or intranet page designated in this way is called a folder home page. In fact, your network administrator may have already set a home page for some or all of your folders. To designate a home page for a folder, follow these steps:

1. Right-click the desired folder shortcut in the Outlook Bar and choose Properties from the shortcut menu that appears. The Properties dialog box is displayed.

2. Click the Home Page tab to display the setting for the folder Home Page (see Figure 1-17).

3. Enter the URL of the page you want to set as the folder home page. The address can be a Web page on the Internet or your corporate intranet, a file on your local hard drive, or even another folder within Outlook.

4. If you want the page to display automatically every time you open that folder, click Show Home Page By Default For This Folder.

5. Click OK to save the settings.

If you set a Web page as the folder Home Page, you must be connected to the Internet to view it.

Using Outlook to Browse System Folders

The programmers at Microsoft have been diligently working to make Outlook an all-encompassing work environment. To that end, they've provided the functionality of Windows Explorer within Outlook. The Other Shortcuts group on the Outlook Bar contains three shortcuts that give you complete access to your system folders, files, and

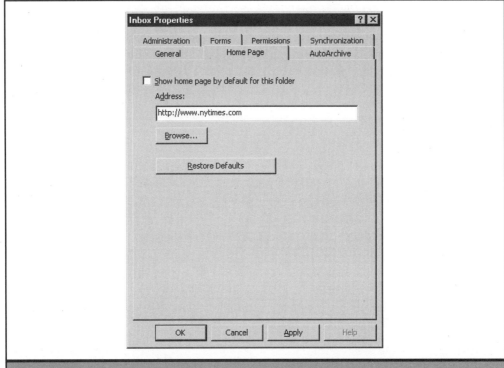

Figure 1-17. *Outlook has a variety of settings you can use to customize each folder*

drives without ever having to leave Outlook. Click the Other Shortcuts button in the Outlook Bar to display the available shortcut icons. Then click the desired shortcut, and the associated windows environment (My Computer) or system folder (My Documents or Favorites) appears in the Information viewer. As you can see in Figure 1-18, the Information viewer adopts the Windows Explorer appearance by displaying drives and folders in the left pane and their contents in the right pane.

Whether you're a novice or an expert, there are going to be times when you run up against something in Outlook that has you totally stumped. When that time comes, don't panic; there's plenty of help at hand. Fortunately, Outlook has a very thorough Help system that offers information on a variety of Outlook subjects and features. You'll even find troubleshooting guides that cover frequently encountered problems, and offer solutions.

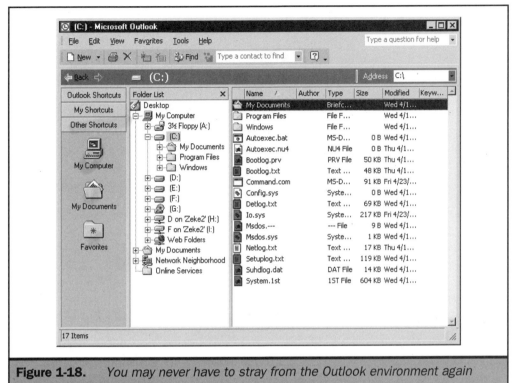

Figure 1-18. *You may never have to stray from the Outlook environment again*

Getting Quick Help

Outlook 2002 has a new help feature that provides quick and easy access to Outlook help. It's called Ask a Question and it's located on the Menu bar.

Ask a Question

All you have to do is type a question or keyword into the Ask a Question text box and press the ENTER key. Immediately a drop-down list of possible help topics appears below the text box. Select the appropriate topic to display the related help topic page.

Using the Office Assistant

The Office Assistant was first introduced in Office 97 as a way to make the Help system more user-friendly. The Office Assistant is an animated onscreen character that interacts with the user. You tell it, in plain English, what you want to know, and it offers several Help topics it thinks may help.

The Office Assistant works fairly well and can be helpful if you're new to the program. It can also be customized, enabling you to change the way it works and the way it looks (by selecting a different animated character). If, as you become more experienced, the little critter starts to drive you crazy, you can always hide it or terminate it permanently by uninstalling it.

To show the Office Assistant, choose Help | Show the Office Assistant or click the Microsoft Outlook Help button on the Standard toolbar. To hide it, return to the Help menu and choose Hide the Office Assistant.

To get help from the Office Assistant, follow these steps:

1. Click the Microsoft Outlook Help button (the question mark) on the Standard toolbar to activate the Office Assistant. The animated character (Clippit, by default) appears on the screen and asks you what you'd like to do (see the previous illustration).

2. Enter a question or keywords related to the subject. The current text in the text box is highlighted so you can start typing immediately. You can enter keywords (**print**, **messages**, and so on) or complete questions, such as **how do I a print a message?** There's no need to worry about proper casing or punctuation, since the Assistant ignores both.

3. Click Search. The Office Assistant presents a short list of topics that match your sentence or your keywords.

4. Click the topic that seems most likely to supply the answer to your question. The Outlook Help application opens to the appropriate page and provides detailed information on the topic (see Figure 1-19).

5. When you're finished with Help, click the Close button.

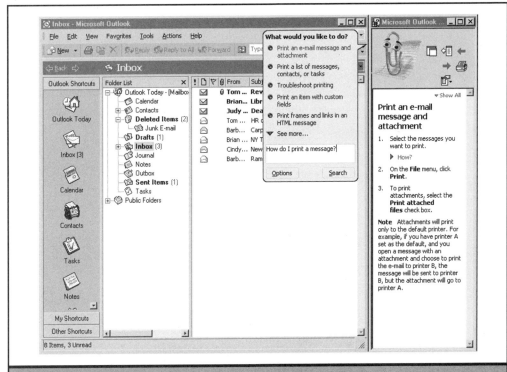

Figure 1-19.   *The Office Assistant is your guide through the Outlook Help system*

Customizing the Assistant

By default, the Office Assistant appears in the guise of Clippit, an animated and
(according to some users) cute paper clip. However, there's no accounting for taste,
and consequently some folks find him more annoying than cute. If you're among that
number, you might want to select a different character, also referred to as an *actor*. You
can choose another actor at any time. However, you may need your Office 2002 disks if
the optional actors were not installed during the initial installation. Each assistant has a
unique look and personality, but you always get the same information. In addition to
changing the actors, you can also set a variety of other options.

Choosing a new actor is easy:

1. Right-click the Office Assistant and select Choose Assistant from the shortcut
   menu to display the Office Assistant dialog box. Unless you've changed actors
   before, the first actor you see is Clippit (see Figure 1-20).

2. Click Next to see the next actor, The Dot.

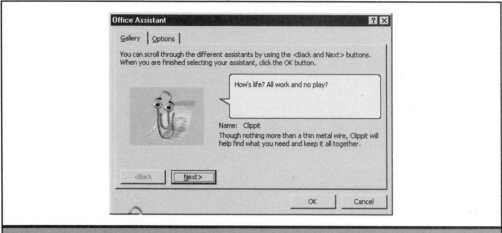

Figure 1-20. *The Gallery contains the available Office Assistant actors*

3. Continue clicking Next until you find the actor of your choice. Click Back if you want to review earlier actors. Click OK when you find one you want to use.

4. If the additional actors are installed, you're returned to the active window and the new actor replaces Clippit. If, however, the actor you've chosen is not available, Clippit informs you and asks if you would like to install it now.

5. If you want to install the other actors, insert the Office 2002 CD (or Outlook 2002 CD) in your CD-ROM drive and click Yes; otherwise click No to return to Outlook and stick with Clippit.

Thankfully, the Office Assistant's actors are not the only thing you can customize. You can also change a variety of settings that control the way the Office Assistant operates.

To set the Office Assistant options, follow these steps:

1. Right-click the Office Assistant and choose Options to display the Office Assistant dialog box (see Figure 1-21).

2. Set the desired Office Assistant options. To enable an option, click it to add a checkmark. To disable an option click it to remove the checkmark. The options are

   ■ **Use the Office Assistant** This is the option to use if you want to turn the Office Assistant off. Clear this option, and Clippit and his little buddies will stay out of your hair while you're working. To bring the Office Assistant back to life, select Help | Show the Office Assistant from the Menu bar.

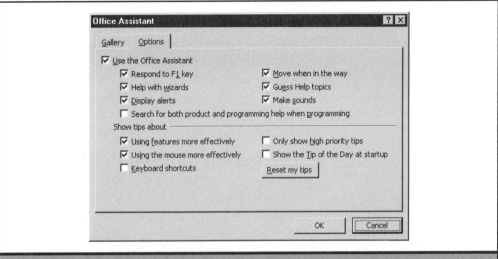

Figure 1-21.   *You can practically make the Office Assistant jump through hoops with all these options*

- **Respond to F1 key**   In most Windows programs, pressing the F1 key brings up the Help system. With this option enabled, the Office Assistant appears in Outlook when you press F1.

- **Help with wizards**   If you want the Office Assistant to offer unsolicited help when you use the Rules Wizard, check this option.

- **Display alerts**   To display messages from the Office Assistant, enable this option.

- **Search for both product and programming help when programming**   If you're using Visual Basic for Applications (VBA), enabling this option causes the Office Assistant to search both the Outlook Help system and the VBA Help system when responding to a Help question.

- **Move when in the way**   Always keep this option enabled when using the Office Assistant. Since he's programmed to stay on top of all windows, he'll get in your way when you open a form or dialog box unless you check this option and tell him to move out of the way while you work.

- **Guess Help topics**   In an effort to anticipate your needs, the Office Assistant will attempt to guess which Help topics you'll need, depending on the task you're working on. While this can be helpful occasionally, it can also be very annoying to have the Office Assistant constantly popping up and offering his two cents without having been asked.

■ **Make sounds** If you'd like the Office Assistant to use sounds, check this option.

■ **Show tips about** The remaining options determine the type of tips the Office Assistant offers. Enable the tips you think will be helpful and disable those you don't need.

■ **Reset my tips** After you've been using Outlook for a while, you may exhaust the supply of tips, since they're not repeated. Click the Reset My Tips button to start over and enable the Office Assistant to display previously viewed tips.

3. Click OK to save your new settings and return to the active window.

If hiding the Office Assistant isn't enough, you can permanently disable it by uninstalling it. You'll need your Office 2002 CD (or Outlook 2002 CD) to perform the uninstall. If you're using Outlook at work, you may have to talk to your network administrator about removing the Office Assistant.

The Outlook 2002 Help System

As the name implies, the Office Assistant is not an essential part of the Outlook Help system, merely an "assistant." Therefore, if you decide to disable or uninstall the Office Assistant, you can still use all the features of the Help system. Outlook Help includes four different components to ensure you get the help you need quickly and easily:

■ **Microsoft Outlook Help** Here you'll find definitions, step-by-step instructions, and cross-references to related topics. After you disable the Office Assistant, you can access Outlook Help by clicking the Microsoft Outlook Help button on the Standard toolbar, pressing F1, or selecting Help | Microsoft Outlook Help from the Menu bar.

■ **ScreenTips** Not quite sure what a particular button does? No problem, take advantage of ScreenTips, by pointing to the toolbar button in question. After a brief delay, a short description of the button appears in a text bubble.

■ **What's This?** For those times when all you need is a quick description or explanation of an item, use the What's This? feature. To use What's This?, choose Help | What's This? from the Menu bar. When your mouse pointer turns into a question mark, point to the item you want more information on and click. An information box pops up with an explanation unless there is no Help on that particular item, in which case a message displays informing you of the fact. Press ESC to close the box when you're finished.

■ **Office on the Web** If you're connected to the Internet, this Help feature whisks you away to the Outlook section of the Microsoft Office Update Web site, where you'll find information, updates, and news items about Outlook.

Browsing Microsoft Outlook Help

Microsoft Outlook Help provides access to a large store of useful information regarding the use and troubleshooting of most of the Outlook features. As you can see in Figure 1-22, Microsoft Outlook Help provides three methods of locating the information you need:

- **Contents**   A hierarchical listing of Help topics, each of which can be expanded by clicking the icon to the left.

- **Answer Wizard**   Enter keywords or questions and search for related information.

- **Index**   An alphabetical listing of topics covered in the Help file.

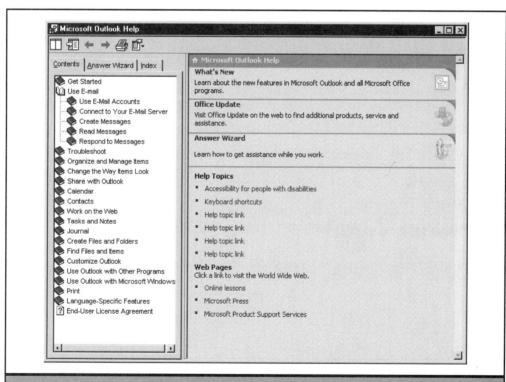

Figure 1-22.   *The Contents tab provides an easy-to-navigate table of contents of the available Help topics*

To view the Help contents with the Office Assistant disabled (or the Respond to F1 Key option disabled), follow these steps:

1. Press F1 to open the Microsoft Office Help window, seen in Figure 1-22. If the Contents pane is not visible, click the Contents tab to display it.

If you think you've disabled the Office Assistant, but it still appears when you press the F1 key, it's probably only hidden, not disabled. To disable the Office Assistant, call it up, click Options, and deselect Use the Office Assistant. If you want to keep the Office Assistant, but still be able to access the Microsoft Outlook Help window, only disable the Respond to F1 Key option.

Note

If only one pane of the Help window is visible, click the Show button on the toolbar to display both panes.

2. Click the icon to the left of a topic to display its subtopics. Book icons represent topic headings and question mark icons represent the actual topics.

3. Find and click the topic on which you need help to display the topic contents in the right pane.

4. When you're finished, click the close button (the small X in the upper-right corner of the Help window) to close the Help file and return to the active window.

As you're viewing Help information in the right pane of the Help window, you may notice blue underlined text which resembles links you see on Web pages. It just so happens that they are links—not to Web pages, but to other, related Help topics. To view the related topic, click the link.

Using the Answer Wizard

The Answer Wizard provides the same type of assistance offered by the Office Assistant, without the antics. Simply type your question or enter keywords in the What Would You Like To Do? text box, click Search, and then click the topic that looks like it will provide the help you're looking for. The topic appears in the right pane.

Using the Help Index

The third component of the Microsoft Outlook Help window is the Index. Like any other index, it contains an alphabetical listing of the most commonly sought-after words and phrases in the body of the document. To make it even easier to use, a search option is provided so you don't have to scroll through the list looking for a particular topic.

1. Press F1 to open the Microsoft Outlook Help window. Remember, this only works if you've disabled the Office Assistant.

2. Click the Index tab to display the Index page.

3. Enter a keyword in the Type Keywords text box and click Search to display a list of topics related to the keyword. You can also scroll through the keyword list and click a keyword to display the associated topics.

4. Click the desired topic in the Choose a Topic list to display the topic contents in the right pane.

5. Click Close to exit the Microsoft Outlook Help window.

Unfortunately, the Microsoft Outlook Help system does not contain a full text search that includes every word in the Help files. Therefore, any searches you perform must be done using the Answer Wizard or the Index. Since the Index is rather limited, you may get better results using the Answer Wizard to search for keywords.

Getting Help Online

If you can't find what you're looking for in the Microsoft Outlook Help files, there's another Help feature you can try. It's called Office on the Web. Here you'll find important security updates, general announcements, technical support pages, a searchable information database, and more. To visit the Office Update Web site, click Help | Office on the Web. After establishing a connection, Outlook will open your default Web browser and display the Outlook section of the Microsoft Office Update Web site. From there, you're free to explore all the tools available.

 One of the most useful resources on the Microsoft Web site is the Knowledgebase. It contains a vast database of questions (and answers) posed to the Microsoft technical support department.

Closing Outlook

If you can afford the RAM, you may want to launch Outlook as part of your daily startup and leave it open the entire time you're at your computer. If you use reminders for meetings and tasks, this is even more important, since Outlook can't remind you unless it's running. When you decide to shut down the program, be sure to save any unfinished work and close any open items. (If an individual message or other item is still open, Outlook can't finish shutting down until you close that item.)

To close Outlook, just click the Close button on the Title bar, press ALT+F4, or choose File | Exit from the Menu bar.

The
Complete
Reference

Outlook
2002

Chapter 2

Working with Profiles

One of the handy features Outlook provides is the ability to create and use multiple profiles. Profiles are the basic settings that enable each user to save his or her customizations of Outlook. In addition to making it easy for different users to share the same machine, profiles enable a single user to establish different Outlook configurations containing different services and different settings. This chapter takes you through the necessary steps to create and customize profiles. You'll also learn to add e-mail accounts to a profile as well as set delivery and addressing preferences.

Creating a Profile

Profiles are Outlook's way of remembering the e-mail accounts, data files, preferences, and option settings for individual users. No matter how a user customizes Outlook 2002, all changes to the settings are retained in the profile being used at the time the changes are made.

Note   *Users who log on from different computers can have their profiles available no matter which computer they're using. However, the profiles must be created by the network administrator and stored on the server. Each time the user makes a change, it's saved before logging off the server.*

Unlike previous versions, Outlook 2002 does not automatically create a default profile. Therefore, you'll have to create one for yourself before you can log on to Outlook. You can either create one from scratch, or if another profile has already been created, make a copy of it and customize it to suit your needs.

Creating a New Profile from Scratch

If there are no existing profiles in your Outlook configuration, or you need to create one considerably different from the existing ones, you'll need to start at the beginning. To create a new profile from scratch, follow these steps:

1. Choose Start | Settings | Control Panel to open the Control Panel window.

2. Double-click the Mail (Mail and Fax if you have faxing installed) applet icon to open the Mail Setup - [current profile name] dialog box.

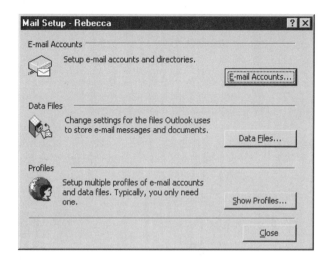

3. Click Show Profiles to open the Mail dialog box (shown in Figure 2-1), which displays all existing profiles on this computer.

4. Click Add to open the New Profile dialog box.

5. Now, enter a name for the new profile and click OK to display the E-mail Accounts dialog box seen in Figure 2-2.

When you reach this point, you have several choices. You can either add an e-mail account, a directory or an address book, or you can simply close the dialog box (click Close) and create an empty, named profile. It will contain no accounts, directories, or address books, but you can return at any time and add them then. If you elect to close the E-mail Accounts dialog box, the profile is created immediately. If you choose to continue and add an account, the profile is created after you finish setting up the account.

Adding E-mail Accounts

Since the most commonly used feature of Outlook is its e-mail client, it's fairly safe to assume that most users will want to set up one or more e-mail accounts. There are a number of different ways this can be done:

■ During the creation of a profile (as described in the previous section).

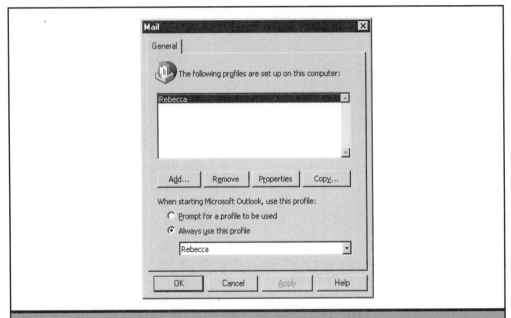

Figure 2-1. The Mail dialog box enables you to add, remove, and modify Outlook profiles

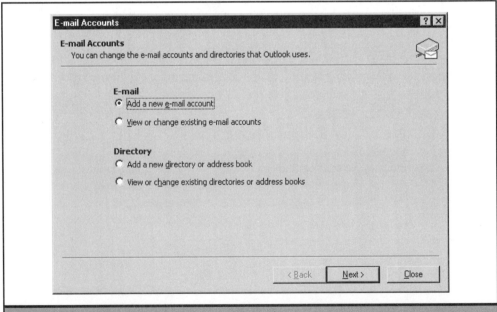

Figure 2-2. At this stage of the game you can set up e-mail accounts or data files

- By opening the Mail (Mail and Fax) applet in the Control Panel, double-clicking an existing profile to display its Mail Setup dialog box, and then clicking the E-mail Accounts button.

- From anywhere in Outlook, choose Tools | E-mail Accounts from the Menu bar to open the E-mail Accounts dialog box for the current user.

No matter which method you choose, the process is identical. In the E-mail Accounts dialog box (see Figure 2-2), select Add A New E-Mail Account and click Next. This displays the Server Type screen, which provides a number of choices for types of e-mail account servers.

- **Microsoft Exchange Server**   This is Microsoft's e-mail and folder management system used by many companies. If you're connecting to Microsoft Exchange, you'll need to know the name of the server and the name of your mailbox on the server. Your system administrator will have both pieces of information.

- **POP3**   This is the most common type of Internet e-mail account currently in use. For this you'll need an outside connection, either through a local area network (LAN) or a modem to connect to your Internet service provider (ISP). For this type of account, you'll need to know your e-mail address, your incoming (POP3) and outgoing (SMTP) mail servers, and your username and password. This information should be available from your Internet service provider (ISP) or system administrator.

- **IMAP**   Similar to a POP3 server, the IMAP server is also for Internet e-mail. While IMAP servers provide more robust e-mail features, they are less widespread, and therefore, less frequently used.

- **HTTP**   If you have a Hotmail, or other Internet-based e-mail service, use this account type. Here, you'll need your e-mail address, username, password, and server URL (Internet address).

- **Additional Server Types**   At the time of this writing, no additional server types were available. By the time you read this, however, Microsoft may have made a last minute change and included one or more server types. Prior versions of Outlook supported both Microsoft Mail and CC:Mail.

From this list of server types, select the appropriate one and click Next. What you encounter depends, of course, on the type of server you selected. The remainder of this exercise covers the addition of a Microsoft Exchange Server account. For any other account type, follow the instructions on the screens that appear, clicking Next until you reach the end.

After you select Microsoft Exchange Server, click Next to display the Exchange Server Settings screen seen in Figure 2-3.

Enter the name of the Microsoft Exchange Server (the computer that is running Microsoft Exchange Server software). If you don't know the name, ask your network administrator.

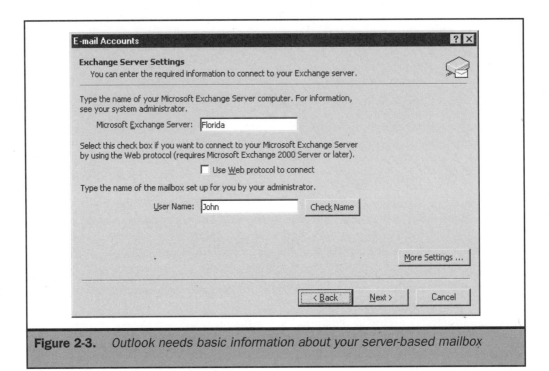

Figure 2-3. *Outlook needs basic information about your server-based mailbox*

 Check the properties of existing profiles to see if any have Microsoft Exchange Server services installed. If so, select Microsoft Exchange Server and click the Properties button to find the Microsoft Exchange Server name.

If you're on a Microsoft Exchange 2000 Server, you can connect using the Web protocol. Check the Use Web Protocol To Connect option. Unless you know that you're on a Microsoft Exchange 2000 Server and you have a need to use the Web protocol, leave this option unchecked. Finally, enter the name of the Microsoft Exchange Server mailbox you want to use for this profile. Unless you know it, you'll have to get this name from your network administrator, since each user has a unique mailbox.

You can click the Check Name button to see if the name you've entered actually corresponds to an existing mailbox on the server. However, even if you fail to click the Check Name button, Outlook automatically checks when you click Next. If it can't find the mailbox, it alerts you and gives you the opportunity to change the name in the Microsoft Exchange Server dialog box.

The last option on the Exchange Server Settings screen, the More Settings button, provides additional options for working offline, adding other mailboxes to this account, configuring remote mail, and more. See Chapter 17 for additional information on using these advanced settings.

Click Next to add the new e-mail account. As noted earlier, if Outlook can't find the mailbox you've indicated, it will prompt you to change the name. The same is true of the Microsoft Exchange Server. If you've entered an invalid server name, Outlook now alerts you to that fact and displays the Microsoft Exchange Server dialog box, wherein you can make the necessary change.

Outlook does not check either the server name or the mailbox name in the Microsoft Exchange Server dialog box. Therefore, if you enter invalid names for either (or both) Outlook will blindly accept them, seeming to confirm their existence. However, when you attempt to log on, you'll be notified that either the server or the mailbox does not exist.

Click Finish to complete the e-mail account setup and return to the active window or dialog box.

You can modify the properties of the new profile at any time by returning to the Mail dialog box, selecting the profile and clicking Properties. However, you cannot change the Microsoft Exchange Server name or the mailbox name of a profile that is in use. Once you switch profiles or close Outlook, you can change either.

Setting the E-mail Account Processing Order

If you add multiple e-mail accounts that support the same mail type, you'll want to be sure to set the processing order of the accounts. If, for example, you have both an Internet e-mail account and a Microsoft Exchange Server account, each of which support Internet addresses (Simple Mail Transfer Protocol, or SMTP), you could elect to have the SMTP mail processed by either account. The order of the processing list determines which account takes precedence.

To set the processing order, choose Tools | E-mail Accounts from the Menu bar to open the E-mail Accounts dialog box, which contains a display listing of all the installed e-mail accounts. The processing order is determined by the e-mail account's placement in this listing. The topmost account is processed first, followed by the next one, and so on. To change, select the account you want to relocate and use the Move Up or Move Down button to make the change. To move any account immediately to the top of the list and make it the default account, use the Set As Default button. Click Finish when you're done to save the changes and return to the active Outlook window.

Copying an Existing Profile

When several users access the same computer, it's likely that the services and settings for one user's profile will be similar to others'. You can save a lot of time by making a copy of an existing profile, and then making the necessary adjustments for the new user.

To create a new profile from an existing one, follow these steps:

1. Open the Control Panel and double-click the Mail (Mail and Fax) icon to open the properties dialog box of the default profile.

2. Click Show Profiles to display the Mail dialog box.

3. Select the existing profile to use as the basis for the new profile, and click Copy. Outlook will prompt you to name the new profile.

4. Enter a name for the new profile and click OK. The profile will be added to the list.

5. Select the profile you just created and click Properties to view the Mail Setup dialog box for the new profile.

You can display a profile's Mail Setup dialog box by double-clicking the profile name in the list of existing profiles.

6. Review the existing e-mail accounts, directories and data files, and make the necessary changes for the new user. Delete any services that aren't needed, such as the original user's personal folders, address books, or Internet e-mail account.

If the profile being copied contains a Microsoft Exchange Server e-mail account, be sure to verify the server name and change the mailbox name to match the new user. The new user will not be able to log on to Microsoft Exchange Server if the server and mailbox name do not match his or her user profile on the network server.

7. Click OK to return to the Mail dialog box.

Adding profiles by copying existing profiles is quick and easy. However, the ability to copy personalized information means that care should be taken to ensure that the feature is not abused. One way is to password-protect personal folders on all profiles. That way, even if the personal folders are copied, they cannot be accessed unless the new user knows the password.

Choosing a Startup Profile

Each time Outlook loads, it uses one profile that has been designated as the default profile. If you only have one profile on your computer, it automatically becomes the default profile. If, however, you have multiple profiles on a single computer, you have to decide which profile is loaded by default when Outlook starts. Obviously, you will choose the profile you use most frequently.

To select a default profile, follow these steps:

1. Choose Start | Settings | Control Panel to open the Control Panel.

2. Double-click the Mail applet to open the properties dialog box for the current default profile.

3. Click Show Profiles to display the Mail dialog box.

4. If you would like a choice of profiles each time you log on to Outlook, select the Prompt For A Profile To Be Used option. If you would prefer that Outlook start

OUTLOOK BASICS

with a particular profile instead, choose the profile to use as the default from the When Starting Microsoft Outlook, Use This Profile drop-down list.

Tip

Setting a default profile presents a problem when the user logged on to the network is not the owner of the default profile. Each time a user logs on to the network, he signs on with his network logon name, which is associated with a specific mailbox on the Microsoft Exchange Server. If the mailbox associated with the default profile isn't the same as the one associated with the network logon name, Outlook will not start. Therefore, unless all the profiles belong to the same network user, you're better off letting Outlook prompt for a profile on start up.

5. Click OK to save the new setting and return to the active Outlook window.

If you elect to have Outlook prompt for a profile, the next time *any* user starts Outlook, the Choose Profile dialog box appears, asking for the name of the profile to be used for the current session of Outlook.

In addition to providing a choice of profiles to use, the Choose Profile dialog box contains several options. Clicking the New button opens the New Profile dialog box, which enables you to create a new profile on the spot. In addition, the Choose Profile dialog box contains an Options button, which, not surprisingly, displays more options when clicked.

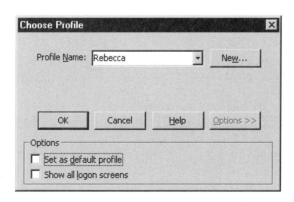

The last two options in the Choose Profile dialog box are:

- **Set as default profile**   This sets the currently selected profile name as the default profile. Don't worry, it does not return Outlook to the practice of automatically opening with the default profile. It simply makes the currently selected profile the one that appears in the Profile Name box each time the Choose Profile dialog box is displayed.

- **Show all logon screens**   With this option enabled, the properties dialog box for each information service (e-mail accounts, data files, address books, and so on) in the selected profile appears, and must be approved (click OK) before Outlook opens. It ensures that you have, indeed, selected the correct profile, and it offers an opportunity to make changes to each service before you start Outlook. However, unless you can't remember your profile name or you modify your information services constantly, this is a bit of overkill and should probably be left unchecked.

After you set the desired options, click OK to launch Outlook. If at some point in the future you find yourself with a single profile and no need for the Choose Profile dialog box, return to the Mail dialog box and enable the Always Use This Profile setting.

Deleting a Profile

If you've been using multiple profiles and one of the profiles is no longer necessary, you can do a little housekeeping and remove the unneeded profile. The truth of the matter is, anyone with access to your computer can delete any of the profiles on the computer. However, that's not quite as bad as it sounds since none of your data is lost. But, on the other hand, it can be annoying if you've done extensive customization of your Outlook settings and options. They, unfortunately, *will* be lost.

If your profile is deleted accidentally or intentionally before you're ready to give it up, you may be able to avoid recustomizing the new profile you create by copying an existing profile that has the same or similar settings to those in the deleted profile. See the section on copying profiles earlier in this chapter.

If you're bound and determined to delete an existing profile, here's all you have to do:

1. Choose Start | Settings | Control Panel to open the Control Panel window.
2. Double-click the Mail (Mail and Fax) applet to open the Mail Setup dialog box for the default profile.
3. Click Show Profiles to display the Mail dialog box (see Figure 2-4).
4. Select the profile you want to delete.

OUTLOOK BASICS

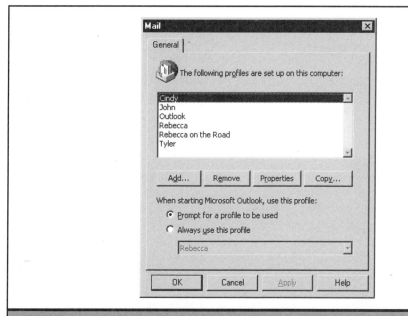

Figure 2-4. *The Mail dialog box enables you to add, copy, and remove profiles as well as view their properties*

5. Click Remove, and when Outlook asks if you're sure, click Yes to delete the selected profile.

6. Click OK to exit the Mail dialog box and return to the active window.

In the event you change your mind after you click the Remove button, you'll have no recourse but to create a new profile to replace it. Deleted profiles are *not* placed in the Windows Recycle Bin or any other place from which they can be resurrected.

Setting Delivery Preferences

If you have both a server-based mailbox and one or more data files added to your profile, you can choose one of them as the delivery location for your e-mail. Actually, "delivery location" is somewhat misleading since it includes both the incoming and outgoing messages. If you select the server-based mailbox as your delivery location, all incoming mail is deposited in the Inbox subfolder of the main Mailbox folder, and copies of sent mail (if you have enabled the Save Copies of Sent Mail option) are retained in the Sent subfolder of the main Mailbox folder. If you choose Personal

Folders as your delivery location, the Inbox and Sent Items subfolders of Personal Folders are used. By choosing a data file, you are electing to have your e-mail stored on your local computer and not on the server.

Unless you're meticulous about backing up your personal folders every day, you should set the delivery location to the server-based mailbox even if you have personal folders. The reason is simple: most administrators back up all the information stored on the server nightly.

The best use of personal folders is for storing messages you want to retain if your network administrator imposes any size limitations on the server-based mailbox. When your mailbox on the server reaches the maximum capacity, you may lose some of your e-mailing privileges until you clean up your mailbox. When that time comes, you'll want to transfer the more important messages to a data file on your local computer.

To set the default delivery location, choose Tools | E-mail Accounts to open the E-mail Accounts dialog box. From the Deliver New Mail To The Following Location drop-down list, select the location where you want your mail delivered. If you want to use a data file but don't have one installed, you can create a new data file by clicking the New Outlook Data File button. When you're done, click Finish to save the new location and return to the active Outlook window. As soon as you click Finish, Outlook alerts you that you've changed the default delivery location and that you'll have to restart Outlook before the changes will take effect.

Setting Addressing Preferences

Outlook address books are the electronic equivalent of the old paper-based address books and Rolodexes that have populated desktops for eons. They contain the basic information you need to get in touch with those individuals with whom you communicate regularly. Although all the Outlook address books can hold a variety of information, for the purposes of this discussion, the only important piece of information is the e-mail address. Fortunately, all three of the different Address Book types available in Outlook are capable of handling e-mail addresses:

■ **Outlook Address Book**   The Outlook Address Book is installed automatically when you add a Microsoft Exchange Server e-mail account to a profile. It utilizes the e-mail information found in the Contacts folder. However, contact information is not stored directly in the Outlook Address Book, but rather in folders displayed as e-mail address books. By default, the Contacts folder appears as an Outlook Address Book. If you open the Contacts Outlook Address Book, you'll see a listing of all your contacts and their respective e-mail addresses and/or fax numbers. Contacts that have neither do not appear in the Contacts Outlook Address Book.

■ **Global Address List**   This is the company-wide listing of internal e-mail addresses maintained on the Microsoft Exchange Server. If most of your e-mail communication is internal, you'll probably want to use this as your default address book. You must, of course, be on a Microsoft Exchange Server network to take advantage of the Global Address List. If you're running a stand-alone version of Outlook, you will not see the Global Address List.

■ **Personal Address Book (PAB)**   If you communicate with people you don't want to add to your Contacts database, you can create a Personal Address Book that is stored locally on your computer and contains only those names you choose to enter.

For more information on creating and using address books, see Chapter 7.

Outlook enables you to customize the way address books are used. You set a default address book to use when you employ the Address Book command or each time you address an e-mail. You can also indicate the address book in which you want to keep your personal addresses, and set the order in which address books are used to check names added as recipients to e-mail messages.

To set the addressing options, you must first access the address book Addressing dialog box. Begin by opening the Address Book. Fortunately, getting to the Address Book is relatively painless. You can click the Address Book button on the Standard toolbar, press CTRL+SHIFT+B or choose Tools | Address Book from the Menu bar. Whichever method you use, the Address Book dialog box is the result.

Now choose Tools | Options from the Address Book dialog box Menu bar to display the Addressing dialog box.

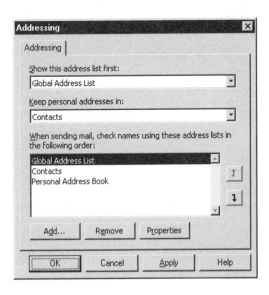

From the Show This Address List First drop-down list, select the address book you want designated as the default address book. This is the address book that appears automatically when you use the Address Book command, or when you click the To, Cc, or Bcc buttons on a new e-mail message form. From the Keep Personal Addresses In drop-down list, select the address book in which you want names you add to the address book stored. By default, Outlook uses the Outlook Address Book.

Since only administrators can add names to the Global Address List, your choices are going to be limited to the Outlook Address Book and the Personal Address Book, even if you have all three address books installed.

The next step is to set the order in which the name-checking feature searches the installed address books. Use the arrow buttons to the right to move the address books up or down on the list. If the address book you want to use for name checking doesn't appear on the list, click Add to open the Add Address List dialog box.

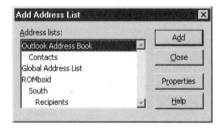

Select the address book from the list and click Add. If you want to add more address books, repeat until you're finished, then click Close to return to the Addressing dialog box. If necessary, adjust the position of the newly added address book in the list. Now, click OK to save your settings and return to the Address Book. Press F4 to close the Address Book and return to the active Outlook window.

The Complete Reference

Outlook 2002

Part II

Communicating With E-Mail

The Complete
Reference

Chapter 3

Composing and Sending Messages

W hile Outlook can help you with any number of organizational tasks, its primary and most popular function is handling e-mail. Outlook includes a full-featured e-mail client that can create, format, spell check, and even grammar check (if you use Microsoft Word as your e-mail editor) your e-mail before sending it on its way. This chapter provides you with everything you need to harness the power of the Outlook e-mail engine for composing and sending e-mail messages.

Navigating Outlook E-mail

Getting around the Outlook e-mail component is actually pretty easy. The first thing to do is familiarize yourself with the various folders that make up the e-mail component and the way they work.

The mail folders include:

- ■ **Inbox**   The Inbox folder is the receptacle for all incoming mail. As mail arrives, it is deposited in the Inbox where it remains until you move it or delete it, either manually or by applying a preestablished message-handling rule. For more information on automating message handling, see Chapter 5.

- ■ **Outbox**   The Outbox folder is a way station for outgoing mail. However, since the default settings are to send immediately, messages may spend little or no time there. In an Exchange Server environment, messages are held in the Outbox only until the Microsoft Exchange server makes its periodic sweep to pick up mail. If you're sending Internet e-mail, the messages are sent immediately if you're connected, or the next time you establish a connection.

- ■ **Sent Items**   By default, a copy of each message you send is stored in the Sent Items folder. Any time you need to verify that information was sent, just check this folder.

- ■ **Drafts**   When the phone rings or somebody knocks on your door while you're in the middle of composing an e-mail message, the Drafts folder provides a safe haven for the partially completed message. Rather than risk losing it, you can click the Save button to send it to the Drafts folder. If you forget to save it, don't worry, you'll probably still be okay. Every three minutes, Outlook automatically saves unsent messages to the Drafts folder (unless you've disabled the default setting).

Once you've got the hang of which folder does what, the rest is a snap. Use the Outlook Bar or Folder List to open the desired mail folder and display any messages it contains in the Information viewer (see Figure 3-1).

To use the Outlook Bar, click the shortcut associated with the mail folder you want to open. The folder opens and its contents appear in the Information viewer. By default, you'll find the Inbox shortcut in the Outlook Shortcuts group, and the Outbox, Drafts, and Sent Items shortcuts in the My Shortcuts group.

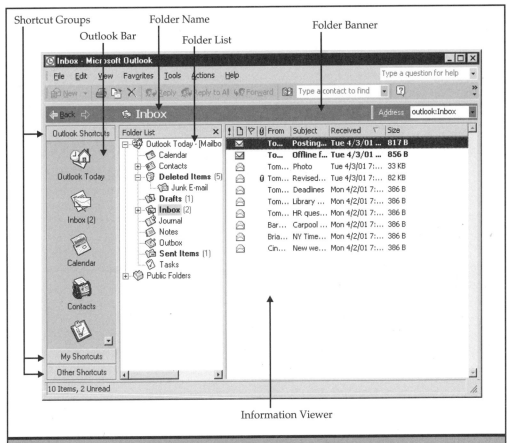

Shortcut Groups · Outlook Bar · Folder Name · Folder List · Folder Banner

Information Viewer

Figure 3-1. *Use the Outlook Bar or Folder List to navigate the mail folders*

Tip *If you only use Outlook for e-mail, or if you find yourself accessing the Outbox, Drafts, or Sent Items folders frequently, you may want to move their shortcuts from the My Shortcuts group to the Outlook Shortcuts group. See Chapter 24 for more information on modifying the Outlook Bar.*

The Folder List displays a tree-like listing of all your Outlook folders, enabling you to navigate between mail folders the same way Windows Explorer enables you to navigate your system folders. To display the Folder List, click the folder name that appears in the Folder banner or choose View | Folder List. Then click the folder you want to open. Folders designed to hold mail items (Inbox, Outbox, and so on) that contain unread or unsent mail appear in bold with a number in parentheses to the right of the folder name. The number indicates how many unread or unsent messages the folder contains.

If you open the Folder List by clicking the folder name, it (the Folder List) closes after you select a folder. If you want it to stay open permanently (or at least until you decide to close it), click the pushpin in the top right corner of the Folder List window. When you're tired of looking at it, click the X in the top right corner of the Folder List to close it.

After you open the desired mail folder, the next step is to open and read the messages. Nothing could be simpler. Double-click a message to open it in its own window.

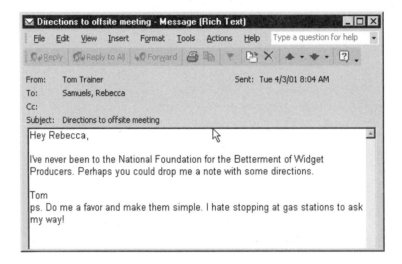

There are a couple of viewing options that make it even easier to read your e-mail. As a matter of fact, if you use them, you don't even have to open your messages. These options are AutoPreview and Preview Pane, seen in Figure 3-2.

■ **AutoPreview**   As you can see, AutoPreview displays the message header information and the first line or two of the message. This comes in handy for quickly reviewing an onslaught of incoming mail to see which messages should be read immediately, and which ones can languish in the Inbox until you have nothing better to do.

■ **Preview Pane**   The Preview Pane creates a small window within the Information viewer in which the contents of the selected messages are displayed. Using the Preview Pane is rather convenient since, unlike opening each message in its own window, there's nothing to close after you read the message. As trivial as it may sound, you'll actually save a noticeable amount of time and energy by taking advantage of these productivity aids Outlook offers—especially if you receive a lot of e-mail each day.

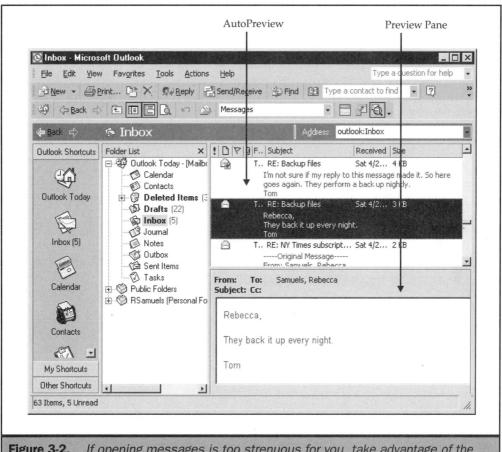

Figure 3-2.   *If opening messages is too strenuous for you, take advantage of the preview options Outlook affords*

After you've familiarized yourself with the Outlook mail components, the next step is to start putting them to work.

Choosing an E-mail Editor

Outlook is a stand-alone program, which means it needs no other software (other than the operating system) to function. However, it is also part of the Microsoft Office suite, and as such, takes advantage of the relationship. One of the ways in which Outlook uses the other Office applications is by integrating Microsoft Word as an optional e-mail editor.

If you have Microsoft Word installed, Outlook automatically uses it as the default e-mail editor. The advantage of using Microsoft Word as your e-mail editor is the simple fact that you get almost all the additional functionality Word offers, including the thesaurus, the grammar checker, AutoCorrect, a wealth of formatting options, and a lot more. However, if you prefer simplicity (especially if you plan to use text-only e-mail), you may prefer to use Outlook's built-in e-mail editor. In either case, you can change from one to the other (as long as Word is installed) with ease.

To change your e-mail editor, follow these steps:

1. Choose Tools | Options to open the Options dialog box.

2. Click the Mail Format tab to view the options for formatting e-mail messages (see Figure 3-3).

3. Enable (add a check mark) the Use Microsoft Word To Edit E-mail Messages to use Microsoft Word as your e-mail editor. Disable (remove the check mark) this option to use Outlook's built-in editor.

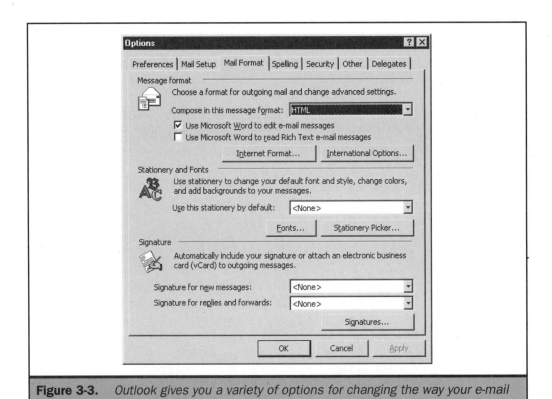

Figure 3-3. *Outlook gives you a variety of options for changing the way your e-mail messages appear*

If the Use Microsoft Word To Edit E-mail Messages option is unavailable, it means you don't have Microsoft Word installed.

4. Click OK to save the change and return to the active Outlook window.

As you can see in Figure 3-4, using Word as your editor causes a number of changes to the new message form used to compose e-mail messages. The message window title bar now indicates that Microsoft Word is the editor. The Actions menu is gone and in its place are the Table and Window menus. Some new toolbar buttons have been added, while some existing buttons have been relocated.

Using Word as your default e-mail editor offers another benefit—Smart Tags. This handy Word feature recognizes different data types (such as names) in your document and enables you to perform a number of actions using that data. See the section entitled "Using Smart Tags," later in this chapter.

Where you'll really notice the difference is in the menu commands available to you. Open a few of the menus and you'll see the difference.

COMMUNICATING WITH E-MAIL

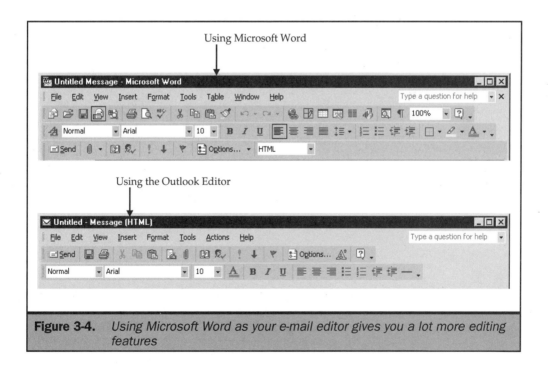

Figure 3-4. *Using Microsoft Word as your e-mail editor gives you a lot more editing features*

Creating a New Message

Composing e-mail messages is what this chapter is all about, so roll up your sleeves and get ready to go to work. The first order of business is to open a new e-mail message form and learn what makes it tick (see Figure 3-5).

Regardless of whether you use the Outlook e-mail editor or Microsoft Word, the basic elements of the message form remain the same:

■ **Menu and toolbars**   The menu and toolbars in a message form contain commands for formatting, viewing, adding attachments, sending, and otherwise manipulating the message.

■ **To**   The one thing every message must have is a recipient in the To field, which makes perfectly good sense, since it's impossible to deliver a message (or anything else, for that matter) if you don't know where it's going. A message can have multiple recipients. Clicking the To button displays the Select Names dialog box containing the listing from the default address book. Select as many recipients as you need.

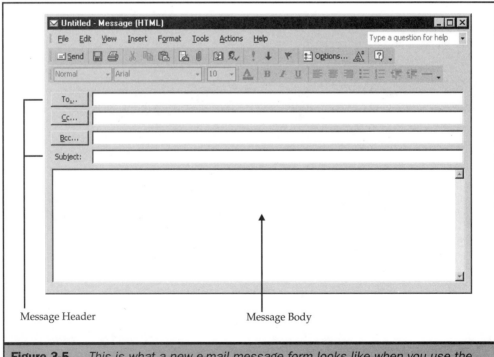

Figure 3-5.   *This is what a new e-mail message form looks like when you use the Outlook e-mail editor*

- **Cc**   The Cc field is used for sending copies to recipients other than the primary recipient(s) named in the To field. Cc is a holdover from the preelectronic memo days when you would send a carbon copy. If you're sending a note to the leader of a project, you might want to keep all the team members in the loop by including them in the Cc field. Clicking the Cc button displays the Select Names dialog box.

- **Bcc**   For those times when you want to send a copy of a message to someone other than the primary recipient, but don't want the primary recipient to know about it, use the Bcc field (blind carbon copy). You might use it to send a message to a team member who has a lot on his plate and occasionally forgets things, and a blind copy to the project leader to ensure your note doesn't get lost in the shuffle. Clicking the Bcc field brings up the well-known (if you read the last two items) Select Names dialog box. Since the Bcc field is hidden by default, you'll have to select View | Bcc Field to display it.

- **Subject**   This all-important field should not be taken lightly. Its main purpose in life is to induce the recipient to open and read your message. Since priority flags are often misused or overused, people who receive a lot of mail frequently decide which messages to open first, based on the Subject line. Therefore, you should make yours brief, informative, and accurate.

- **Message body**   The message body window in which you type your message is actually a text editor. As soon as you begin typing your message here, all the text editing functions of your selected editor (Outlook or Microsoft Word) become available.

> **Tip**   *One of the drawbacks of sending e-mail to multiple recipients is that when you use the To or Cc fields, you expose all addresses to everyone who receives a copy of the message. To keep all e-mail addresses confidential, address the message to yourself and include all your recipients in the Bcc field. This way yours is the only address visible.*

Once you understand the components of an e-mail message, you're ready to create one of your own.

Composing the Message

Creating an e-mail message in Outlook is a simple task. The most complicated thing about composing a message is deciding which of the various methods you want to use to open a new message form. As you can see in Table 3-1, Outlook offers you a number of ways to start your new message.

There are actually a number of other ways to open a new e-mail message form, as you'll discover throughout this book. However, each of those methods utilizes an existing Outlook item and incorporates specific information from the item into the new e-mail message form. The methods presented in Table 3-1 simply open a blank e-mail message form.

From This Outlook Folder	Use This Action
Any folder	Press CTRL+SHIFT+M
Any folder	Click the down arrow to the right of the New button and select Mail Message
Any folder	Click File	New	Mail Message
Inbox, Outbox, Drafts, Sent items	Press CTRL+N
Inbox, Outbox, Drafts, Sent items	Click the New button on the Standard toolbar
Inbox, Outbox, Drafts, Sent items	Right-click a blank spot (not an e-mail message) in the Information viewer and select New Mail Message

Table 3-1.   *Methods Used to Open a New E-mail Message Form*

Now, on to actually creating an e-mail message:

Press CTRL+SHIFT+M (or use your preferred method) to open a new e-mail message form (as shown in Figure 3-5).

Tip   *One new feature in Outlook 2002 is the ability to change, on the fly, the e-mail account from which you send a message. So, if you have multiple e-mail accounts, be sure to select the account from which you want the current message sent. Click the Accounts button on the Standard toolbar in the message form and select the appropriate account.*

1. Enter the NAME(s) of the recipient(s) in the To, Cc, and Bcc fields using one of the following methods:

   ■ **Type the full e-mail address**   If you know the recipient's e-mail address (for example, bsmith@iquest.net), you can type it in directly. Be sure to type it correctly, since a single mistake will prevent the message from ever reaching its intended destination.

   ■ **Enter an address book name**   If you know (or think you know) the recipient's name as it's listed in one of your address books, type it in. To be sure it's accurate, you can use the Check Names feature by clicking the Check Names button on the message form's Standard toolbar. If you're using the Outlook e-mail editor you can also choose Tools | Check Names from the Menu bar in the mail message form.

   ■ **Open the Select Names dialog box**   Click the To button to display the Select Names dialog box. Double-click the name(s) of the individual(s) to whom you want to address the message to add them to the Message Recipients list on the right. When you close the Select Names dialog box, they appear in the To field. To display names from other address books, open the Show Names From The drop-down list and select the desired address book.

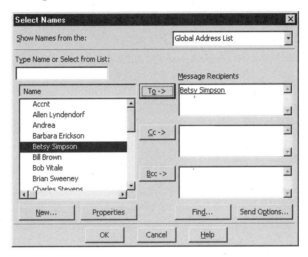

Tip   *Instead of opening and closing the Select Names dialog box for each of the recipient fields (To, Cc, and Bcc), you can select names from the list and click the appropriate button (To ->, Cc ->, or Bcc ->) to add all three in one operation.*

Tip   *You can select multiple nonadjacent names by holding down the* CTRL *key as you click each name. To select multiple adjacent names, hold down the* SHIFT *key, click the first name, then click the last name.*

2. If you used the Select Names dialog box to add recipients, click OK to close it and return to the e-mail message form, which should look something like this one if you've added the three different types of recipients.

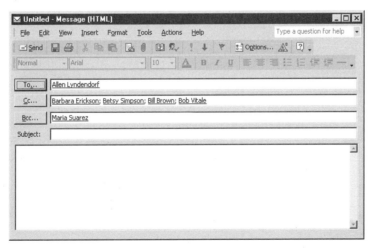

3. Fill in the Subject line with a concise, informative word or phrase that describes the message contents. In other words, don't write "Quick question" when you need directions to the meeting site. Enter "Need directions to the meeting" instead. The more information your Subject line imparts (without going overboard), the more likely you'll get a quick response.

4. Type your message in the message body window. Again, it's important to remember that most people receive a lot of e-mail. Try to be as concise and informative as possible when composing business-related messages. At this point, your message should resemble the following:

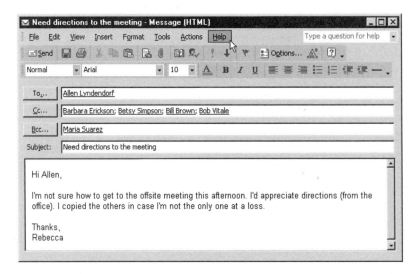

5. Click the Send button to transmit the message.

You can add a frequently used e-mail address to a toolbar by assigning the address to a command button as a hyperlink. See Chapter 24 for details.

MOUS EXAM PRACTICE:
In this section, you learned the basic elements that comprise an e-mail message, as well as the means to utilize those elements. Now might be a good time to write to all those friends and family members who've been wondering for years if you're still alive. Open a new message form and send them each a single message. Then select a group of them and send the message to one, and copy the others. Try addressing the messages by selecting names from your various address books. Then enter some addresses manually. By the time you're done, your friends and relatives will be longing for the good old days, and you'll be an expert at composing and addressing e-mail.

Formatting Messages

If you're exchanging e-mail with others who use an e-mail application that supports text formatting, you can add verve, flair, and emphasis to your messages by including formatting. If you're exchanging e-mail with another Outlook user whose default editor is Microsoft Word, you can even include things like tables and bullet lists. To use the formatting features of your Outlook editor, whether it's Microsoft Word or the standard Outlook editor, you first must create an e-mail message or open a message saved in the Drafts folder. Next, move to the body of the message. The formatting features do not work in any area of the message except the body. If you place your cursor in any of the recipient fields or the Subject field, you'll notice that the formatting commands on the toolbars and menus are grayed out, which means they're unavailable.

Selecting the Message Format

The first and most basic formatting option is the overall message format. Your choices include Plain Text, HTML, and Microsoft Outlook Rich Text (Rich Text). Each provides a different level of formatting:

- **Plain Text**   There's not much more to be said about this than it's plain text. No-frills, mono-spaced type with absolutely no formatting options is what you'll get when you select this format. As grim as that may sound, it's often the best choice, especially if the bulk of your e-mail is sent to recipients over the Internet. Not all e-mail software supports text formatting. Therefore, unless you know that your recipients are using e-mail software that supports text formatting, it's a good idea to stick with Plain Text.

- **HTML**   The HTML format, which provides a variety of formatting options, is available when you use the Outlook editor or Microsoft Word 2000 or 2002 as your e-mail editor, but not if you use Microsoft Word 97. The features you get with the HTML format include text formatting (font and paragraph), bullets, numbering, HTML styles, and Web pages, as well as the ability to use stationery and signatures.

- **Microsoft Outlook Rich Text**   The Microsoft Outlook Rich Text format provides basic text formatting features, such as font and paragraph formatting, bullets, and alignment, as well as the use of signatures.

Regardless of which e-mail editor you choose, Outlook is configured to use HTML as the default message format. You can change the default setting by selecting a different format from the Compose In This Message Format option on the Mail Format tab of the Options dialog box (Tools | Options). You can also change the message format on the fly by selecting a different format from the Format menu of the message form itself.

Keep one thing in mind when sending formatted messages: if you send HTML or Rich Text messages to people whose e-mail software doesn't support formatting, they may get the message, but lose the formatting. Even those recipients whose e-mail programs support these formats may receive something different from what you send, since other factors, including their installed fonts and option settings, may influence the way your message appears.

Font Formatting

When the word "formatting" pops up in cocktail chatter, as it tends to do from time to time, most peoples' minds turn to thoughts of font formatting. This makes sense since font formatting is the most visual and the most easily identified type of formatting. Font formatting is all about dressing up your text in a manner befitting the occasion. Using a wacky, slanted font when e-mailing jokes to your golfing buddies makes sense. However, using that same font when e-mailing the budget report to your CEO would probably not be a smart move. Then again, if your company makes practical joke novelties, it might be the perfect font to send the CEO.

Text that is red, bold, and underlined commands immediate attention. A script font presented in silver or gold implies pomp and sophistication, while a straight, sans serif (no frills), black font has a businesslike quality. The bottom line is that in addition to dressing up the appearance of your text, font formatting can also help convey your message.

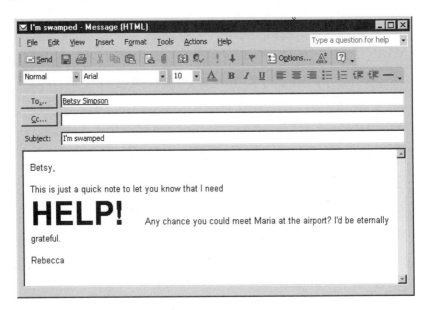

Applying font formatting to text is a simple and straightforward task, as you'll see if you follow these steps:

1. Press CTRL+SHIFT+M to open a new mail message form.

2. Since, by default, the message format is set to HTML you shouldn't have to do anything. However, if you've changed the default setting, choose either HTML or Rich Text from the Format menu on the Menu bar—both support font formatting.

Note

The choices available on the Format menu depend on the message format currently in use. So you may or may not see both HTML and Rich Text on the menu.

3. Enter the desired recipients in the To, Cc, and Bcc fields.

4. Enter an appropriate description of the message contents in the Subject field.

5. Type your message in the message body window.

6. Format the text by highlighting the characters, words, or blocks of text you want to dress up, then use the appropriate toolbar button (see Figure 3-6) to apply the formatting.

   ■ **Style**   Styles are groups of font settings that are applied all at once. A style can include one or more of the following: font type, font size, font style (bold or italic), font color, and font effects such as underlining. For example, when you apply the Heading 1 style to a block of text in an HTML message, it changes the font to Times New Roman, the font size to 24pt, and the font style to bold.

   ■ **Font**   Whether you wear formal attire or your favorite Hawaiian shirt and shorts, it's still you underneath it all. The same goes for your text. No matter how you dress it up, it's still the same combination of characters. It just looks different. That's where the font comes in—it's the basic attire for your text. Click the down arrow to the right of the Font field to display a drop-down list of available fonts.

   ■ **Font Size**   When composing an e-mail for the visually impaired, you might want to increase the size of the font to ensure they don't miss anything. If, on the other hand, you want to include some fine print in the hopes the

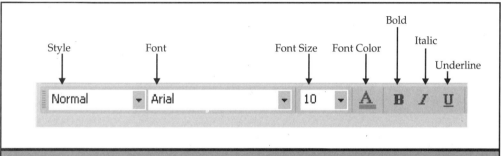

Figure 3-6.   *The Formatting toolbar contains all the font options you'll need*

recipients miss it, you can decrease the font size. Click the down arrow to the right of the Font Size field and choose a size from the drop-down list to apply to the selected text.

- **Font Color**   You can use color in your text to add emphasis or just to liven up the appearance of your e-mail. Click the Font Color button to display a color palette, then click the color of your choice to apply it to the selected text.

- **Bold**   There's not much more to say. Highlight the text and click the Bold button to make the selected text **bold**.

- **Italic**   Italic is the *slanted font style* used in this sentence. Highlight the text and click the Italic button to apply the italic style to the selected text.

- **Underline**   You're on your own with <u>this</u> one.

If you're using Word as your e-mail editor and you're working on a Plain Text message, clicking any of the formatting buttons prompts Word to ask if you want to switch to an HTML or Rich Text format.

7. Click Send to transmit the message.

If you want one-stop shopping for font formatting options, there's another way to apply font formatting to selected text. Highlight the text and choose Format | Font from the Menu bar to display the Font dialog box.

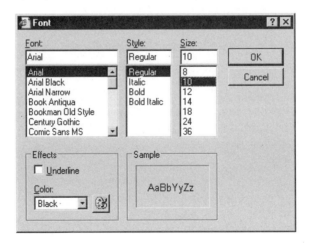

Select the font, font style, font size, font color, and even whether or not to underline the selected text. Then click OK to apply the formatting.

Remember, no matter how you apply the formatting, what your recipients see depends on their e-mail software, installed fonts, and so on.

Paragraph Formatting

Paragraph formatting is the less glamorous of the two main formatting features, but no less important. As with font formatting, paragraph formatting is restricted to HTML and Microsoft Outlook Rich Text messages. Before moving on to the techniques and features available for paragraph formatting, it's important to understand how Outlook defines a paragraph. A paragraph is everything that precedes a hard return. A hard return is an invisible formatting character that is embedded in the document every time you press the ENTER key while composing the message body. This means that as far as Outlook is concerned, a paragraph can be a blank line, a single character, a word, a sentence, or even an entire novel, as long as you don't press the ENTER key. Once you press the ENTER key, you've started a new paragraph.

HTML messages can take advantage of what is called a soft return. By holding down the SHIFT key when pressing the ENTER key, you can start a new line that is considered part of the same paragraph as the preceding line. As a matter of fact, both HTML and Microsoft Outlook Rich Text automatically add soft returns to the end of the line, and word wrap takes over and creates a new line. This is what makes it possible to have a paragraph as long as a novel.

Putting paragraph formatting to work is even easier than using font formatting. Try it for yourself and see (remember, formatting is only available in HTML and Rich Text messages):

1. Press CTRL+SHIFT+M to open a new e-mail message form.
2. Enter the desired recipients in the To, Cc, and Bcc fields.
3. Type a brief description of the message contents in the Subject field.
4. Type your message in the message body window.
5. Select the paragraph(s) you want to format. Don't forget that Outlook considers a paragraph anything that precedes a hard return.

Tip *You can select a single paragraph by placing your cursor anywhere in the paragraph. To select multiple paragraphs, highlight the text in the paragraphs you want to format. As long as you highlight some text from each paragraph, the formatting will apply to all the paragraphs selected.*

6. Click the appropriate button on the Formatting toolbar, seen in Figure 3-7, to apply the paragraph formatting.
   - ■ **Left**   This is the default paragraph alignment. It lines the paragraph flush against the left margin of the message body window.
   - ■ **Center**   If you want the paragraph contents centered in the middle of the message body window, use the Center command.
   - ■ **Right**   To line a paragraph flush against the right margin, use the Right command. This is frequently used to format a column of numbers to ensure they line up correctly.

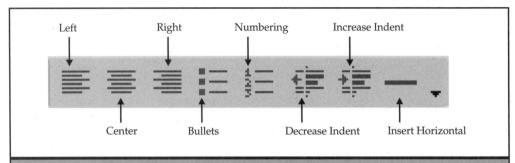

Figure 3-7.   *You'll find Paragraph formatting commands on the Outlook Formatting toolbar for quick access*

- **Bullets**   To create a list of bulleted items, use the Bullets command. It indents the line and places a bullet at the beginning of the line.

- **Numbering**   If you're creating an HTML message, you can create a numbered list with the Numbering command. It is similar to Bullets in that it indents the line and places the character (a number, in this case) at the beginning of the line. What's nice is that if you apply the numbering format to the first line before creating additional lines, every time you press the ENTER key a new line is created with the next number in the sequence. Unfortunately, numbering is not available in Rich Text messages.

- **Decrease Indent**   This command moves the selected paragraph to the left a predetermined number of spaces. One thing to note is that Decrease Indent will not move an aligned paragraph beyond the left margin determined by the alignment setting. In other words, a center-aligned paragraph will not move any further to the left than it is, even though it is far to the right of the left margin of the message body window. If, however, you move it to the right using the Increase Indent command, you can then return it to its original position using the Decrease Indent command.

- **Increase Indent**   This command moves the selected paragraph to the right a predetermined number of spaces.

- **Insert Horizontal Line**   The Insert Horizontal Line command is a handy device that does just what its name states: it inserts a horizontal line at the place in the message body where the cursor happens to be when you click the Insert Horizontal Line button. As with the Numbering command, the Insert Horizontal Line command is available only in HTML messages.

Note   *A new paragraph, created when you hit the ENTER key, inherits the paragraph formatting of the previous paragraph. This means that if you are typing a paragraph that is right-aligned and you press the ENTER key to start a new paragraph, the new paragraph will automatically be right-aligned as well.*

7. Click Send to transmit the message.

As with font formatting, what your recipient sees of the paragraph formatting you apply is dependent upon a number of things that are out of your control—the recipient's e-mail software, installed fonts, and so on.

In addition to using the toolbar buttons, there are two additional ways to apply paragraph formatting. You can select the paragraph(s) to format and choose Format | Paragraph to display the Paragraph dialog box.

However, as you can see, the paragraph formatting options are limited to Left, Center, or Right alignment, and Bullets.

If the message is in the HTML format, you can also apply paragraph formatting by selecting the paragraph(s) and right-clicking anywhere on the selected paragraph(s) to display a shortcut menu containing formatting commands.

MOUS EXAM PRACTICE

In this section, you learned how to customize the look of outgoing e-mail. Now try it yourself. Open the Outlook Options dialog box (choose Tools | Options), and switch to the Mail Format tab. See what your basic message format is set to, and change it to a different format. Then save the change and return to Outlook. Open a new message form and see how the form has changed. Take a look at the Format menu and see what menu items appear.

Flagging Outgoing Messages

Sometimes just sending a message isn't enough. For example, suppose you're sending a message requesting that a co-worker remain available for a conference call the following day. Wouldn't it be nice if the message would also tap her on the shoulder tomorrow and remind her about the call? If you use a flag on the message, it can. Flagging messages enables you to add an information bar to the top of the message that includes a comment indicating the type of flag and, if you set a reminder, the date and time it will go off.

To flag an outgoing message, follow these steps:

1. Press CTRL+SHIFT+M to open a new mail message form.

2. Enter the desired recipients in the To, Cc, and Bcc fields.

3. Type a brief description of the message contents in the Subject field.

4. Type your message in the message body window.

5. Click the Flag For Follow Up button on the Standard toolbar to display the Flag For Follow Up dialog box.

You can also access the Flag For Follow Up dialog box by pressing CTRL+SHIFT+G *or by choosing Actions | Follow Up from the message form menu bar.*

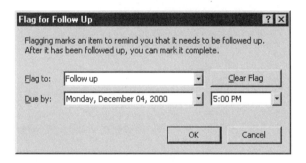

6. From the Flag To drop-down list, select the comment you want to include in the information bar added to the top of the message.

7. If you want to include a reminder, select the reminder date from the Due By drop-down calendar. When you select a date, the day, date, and time are included in the reminder.

When you include a reminder, the time is automatically set for the end of the selected workday (by default 5:00 P.M.). You can change the time by using the drop-down list in the time field, or by editing the time manually. In addition, you can change the default time setting by changing the end time for your workday in the Calendar options. See Chapter 10 for more information on setting Calendar options.

8. Click OK to save the flag and return to the mail message form. As you can see in Figure 3-8, the information bar appears at the top of the message and includes the comment and reminder (if you add one).

If you change your mind about flagging a message, you can reopen the Flag For Follow Up dialog box and click the Clear Flag button.

9. If your message is ready to go, press Send to send it on its way.

As with many Outlook features, flagging may appear differently to your recipients, depending on the e-mail software they use. Only other Outlook users will see the information bar with the comment and reminder information. In addition, only other Outlook users will have a reminder set to go off at the designated date and time.

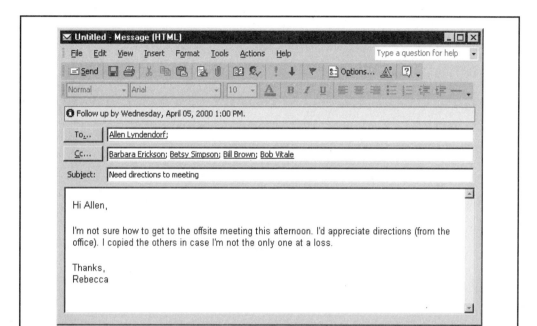

Figure 3-8.   *Flagging a message is a good way to let the recipient know of any subsequent action that needs to be taken*

Non-Outlook users will have two additional lines added to the header of the message they receive—one that includes the comment, and another that includes Reply-By followed by the date and time.

Setting Message Options

One thing you can't fault Outlook for is a lack of options. It seems no matter where you turn there are tons of settings you can adjust to make things work your way. This is certainly the case with outgoing e-mail messages. Outgoing message options include message settings, voting and tracking options, delivery options, and even the ability to assign specific messages to contacts and categories.

The Message Options dialog box includes a variety of options that enable you to set delivery, tracking, and voting options as well as some message settings. These options are especially handy if you exchange e-mail with other Outlook users on a Microsoft Exchange Server network.

Setting message options is easy if you follow these steps:

1. Press CTRL+SHIFT+M to open a new mail message form.
2. Add the desired recipients to the To, Cc, and Bcc fields.
3. Enter a brief description of the message contents in the Subject field.
4. Type the message in the message body window.
5. Click the Options button on the Standard toolbar to display the Message Options dialog box.
6. Set the desired options from among those available:

   ■ **Importance**   From the Importance drop-down list, select the importance setting to attach to this message. Recipients can use this setting to determine how urgent the message is, and how quickly they need to deal with it. However, use the High setting judiciously. If you overuse it, it will quickly lose its impact, and recipients may begin to ignore it, even when you send a message that really is important. You can relax now—I have no intention of making any reference to the boy who cried wolf.

   ■ **Sensitivity**   When you're sending sensitive or confidential information in a message, you may want to alert the recipient to that fact by selecting a sensitivity setting from the drop-down list. However, keep in mind that no e-mail is entirely secure unless you employ the security measures available by using digital signatures and encryption. See Chapter 19 for more information on security measures.

   ■ **Security Settings**   The options found here enable you to keep your message safe from prying eyes. See Chapter 19 for more information on using digital signatures and encryption.

   ■ **Use voting buttons**   If you're on a Microsoft Exchange Server network, you'll love the voting buttons feature. It enables you to send a message to other users on the network, asking a simple question (such as, "Do you want to go out for lunch today?") and enabling them to respond by clicking a Yes, No, or Maybe button in the message. You can determine the response buttons that appear by making your selection from the Use Voting Buttons drop-down list. Although voting buttons are available in non-Exchange Server environments, they do not function when used with Internet e-mail. The recipient of a message with voting buttons receives the message only.

   ■ **Request a delivery receipt for this message**   If you want to be notified when the recipient receives the message, enable this option.

   ■ **Request a read receipt for this message**   If you want to be notified when the recipient opens the message, enable this option. Obviously there's no way to know if the recipient actually reads the message, so opening the message is as close as you can get.

- **Have replies sent to** If you want someone else to receive replies to the message, enter the individual's e-mail address in the text box, or use the Select Names button to choose a name from your address book.

- **Save sent message to** By default, this option is enabled and set to the Sent Items folder. You can disable the option by removing the check mark. You can also choose a different folder by clicking the Browse button and selecting a folder from the Select Folder dialog box.

- **Do not deliver before** Enable this option to specify the earliest time at which you want the message delivered. Use the drop-down calendar to select a delivery date. To change the delivery time, edit it manually. When you hit the Send button, the message is deposited in your Outbox, where it remains until the specified time. One thing to note is that the delivery time is determined by the clock on the Microsoft Exchange server, not on your desktop computer. Therefore, if the clock on the server is five minutes slower than the clock on your desktop computer, the message will appear to be sitting in your Outbox an extra five minutes before being delivered.

- **Expires after** If your message is time-sensitive, enable the Expire After option and set the date and time after which the message becomes invalid. When the time passes, the message is automatically deleted from the user's Inbox unless it has been opened, in which case a line is drawn through the message information making it appear to be crossed out.

- **Attachment format** Since only ASCII files can be transported via e-mail, any attachment other than a plain text file must be ASCII encoded before it can be sent with an e-mail message. The three most popular encoding methods are MIME (Multipurpose Internet Mail Extensions), UUENCODE (UNIX-to-UNIX encoding), and BINHEX (binary to hexadecimal). However, unless you're sending an attachment to someone who requires a specific format, leave this option set to Default.

- **Encoding** Outlook contains multilingual support, allowing users to view and edit documents in as many as 80 languages. Use this drop-down list to select the character set for the e-mail message.

- **Contacts** To assign the message to one or more contacts, click the Contacts button and select the names. You might use this feature to link a message concerning a project update to all team members working on the project. It's like tossing a hard copy in each person's file folder.

- **Categories** To enable quick and easy organizing of sent messages, you can assign them to categories (such as Business, Personal, and so on). Click the Categories button and make your selection from the Categories dialog box that appears.

7. Click Close to apply the message options to the message.

8. Click Send to transmit the message.

If you are sending the message to another user on the Exchange Server network, all the options will work as advertised. If you are sending the message to someone over the Internet, the results will vary depending on the e-mail software used by the recipient(s).

MOUS EXAM PRACTICE
In this section, you learned to set options for individual e-mail messages. To effectively utilize the message options, it's important to understand the implications of each setting. Begin by reviewing the option descriptions. Then send a few messages to yourself using the various options. Change only one setting at a time to ensure you understand how each option affects the message.

Using Smart Tags

A new Word feature, called Smart Tags, is now available in Outlook whenever you use Word from within Outlook. Therefore, if you use Word as your default e-mail editor, Smart Tags are available in e-mail messages, regardless of the message format (HTML, Rich Text, or Plain). Smart Tags are also available if you use the New Letter To Contact command in the Contacts folder.

The premise behind Smart Tags is that certain types of data, such as names, dates, times, phone numbers, and others are easily recognizable, and therefore, easily manipulated. For example, anything that starts with Mr., Mrs., or Dr. is probably a name. Also, Word's dictionary contains a large selection of common names. Consequently, Word can recognize names with fairly good accuracy. When it does, it adds a Smart Tag to the text. As soon as a Smart Tag is added, a dotted line appears under the text. Any time you pass your mouse pointer over the text, the Smart Tag icon appears. If you look closely at Figure 3-9, you'll see that all three names in the body of the message are underlined, and the one on which the cursor rests is displaying a Smart Tag icon.

Note   *If a name appears in the last sentence of your document, a Smart Tag is not attached. A new sentence must be started or a hard return must be entered before a Smart Tag is added.*

To utilize a Smart Tag, move your mouse pointer over the icon to display the down arrow. Now, click the down arrow to open the drop down menu, which contains a variety of commands including the following (for names):

■ **Send Mail**   Choose this command to open a new e-mail form with the name already entered into the To field. This is only useful if the individual is in one of your address books.

■ **Schedule a Meeting**   Clicking this command opens a new meeting request form addressed to the person.

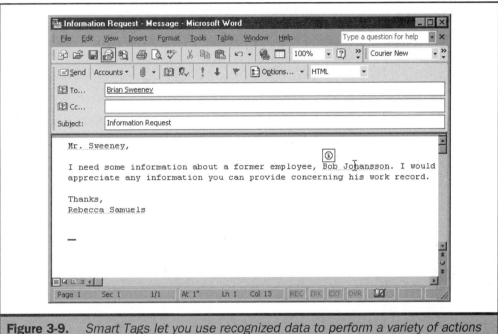

Figure 3-9. *Smart Tags let you use recognized data to perform a variety of actions*

- **Open Contact**   If the name appears in your Contacts folder, this command opens the associated contact record.

- **Add to Contacts**   If the name does not appear in your Contacts folder, but you'd like it to, use this command. It opens a new contact record and adds the name to the Full Name field.

- **Insert Address**   If the name appears in one of your address books, this command inserts a hard return after the name, and pastes the address into the message. Of course, you must have an address entered in the contact record for this to be of any value.

- **Remove this Smart Tag**   If you find the underlining or the icon annoying, you can remove the Smart Tag by using this command. However, by making a change in the document (adding a hard return after, or modifying the first letter of the first word of the sentence following the sentence containing the tagged name) you can reattach the Smart Tag.

- **Smart Tag Options**   Use this command to display the AutoCorrect in E-mail dialog box, which contains options for customizing Smart Tags.

Smart tags associated with dates, times, and other data types, will have different options available.

You can remove the underlining of Smart Tags, without removing the smart tags, by opening the Options dialog box (click Tools | Options on the message form Menu bar). Click View to display the view options tab and deselect the Smart tags option in the Show section. You can selectively enable and disable the various Smart Tag data types by choosing Tools | AutoCorrect Options from the message Menu bar and clicking the Smart Tags tab.

Spell Checking Messages

No matter how great your spelling skills may be, you're bound to make mistakes sooner or later. They may only be typographical errors, but the party who receives your e-mail won't know that. Therefore, you'll probably want to take advantage of the Outlook spell checker, especially on your business correspondence. The spell checker is so good, it will make everyone you exchange e-mail with think you actually stayed awake during your high school English classes.

Using the spell checker is a breeze:

1. Press CTRL+SHIFT+M to create a new mail message.

2. Enter the desired recipients in the To, Cc, and Bcc fields.

3. Enter a brief description of the message contents in the Subject field.

4. Type your message in the message body window.

5. With the cursor still in the message body, press F7 or choose Tools | Spelling to start the spell checker. When it encounters a misspelled word, it displays the Spelling dialog box. The Spelling dialog box indicates the word it thinks is misspelled and generally offers one or more suggestions.

Note *The spell checker considers any word not found in its dictionary a misspelled word. Therefore, you'll probably encounter a number of correctly spelled words coming up as misspelled. When that happens, just add them to the dictionary. However, be careful not to add misspellings or they'll never be caught again.*

6. Select the way you want Outlook to deal with the misspelled word. Your choices include:

   ■ **Ignore**   Click this button to move on to the next misspelled word without making any change to the current misspelled word.

   ■ **Ignore All**   This command is similar to the Ignore command except it automatically ignores every instance of the misspelled word, not just the current instance.

   ■ **Change**   After you've selected the correct word from the Suggestions list or typed your own in the Change To field, click this button to replace the misspelled word with the selected word.

- ■ **Change All**   Use this command to replace every instance of the misspelled word with the selected word.

- ■ **Add**   The Outlook dictionary is by no means complete. Therefore, you're bound to encounter correctly spelled words that the spell checker thinks are misspelled simply because they are not in the dictionary. When you run across such words, add them to the dictionary. The next time the spell checker encounters them it will recognize them as properly spelled words. You can also use this command to add proper names, abbreviations, or other shorthand you use regularly.

If you accidentally add a misspelled word to the dictionary, you can remove it by opening the Custom.dic file found in C:\Windows\Application Data\Microsoft\Proof folder. Use Notepad or some other text editor to open the file, then delete the misspelled word. Save and close the Custom.dic file and return to Outlook. The next time you run the spell checker, it will catch the misspelling. You can also use this method to add a list of special terms, names, or other words you want the spellchecker to ignore. It will save you the aggravation of having to deal with them one at a time as you use them.

- ■ **Suggest**   If you type a word in the Change To field, the Suggest button becomes available. When you click the button, a list of suggested spellings for the word you typed appears in the Suggestions window.

- ■ **Options**   Click this button to display the Spelling tab of the Options dialog box. Here you can set general options as well as add custom and international dictionaries.

- ■ **Undo Last**   After you've made a correction, you can undo it by clicking Undo Last.

7. Repeat the process for each misspelled word. After you deal with the last misspelled word, an information box appears and informs you that the spell check is complete.

8. Click OK to return to the e-mail message.

9. Click Send to close and send the message on its way.

If you move too fast and sometimes forget to spell check your messages, you can have Outlook do it automatically before sending messages. All you have to is enable the Always Check Spelling Before Sending option located on the Spelling tab of the Options dialog box (Tools | Options).

Adding Attachments

The e-mail revolution did for 20th century communication what the telephone did for 19th century communication: reduce the time and cost of communicating with others no matter where on the planet they might be, while at the same time increasing the ease with which it's done. However, unlike the telephone, e-mail also enables users to send more than just words. By taking advantage of the attachments feature of e-mail, you can send not only messages, but also documents, spreadsheets, artwork, software programs, and anything else that comes in the form of a computer file.

Outlook users have one advantage over other e-mail software users, in that in addition to regular computer files, they can also attach Outlook items to e-mail messages. You can attach tasks, appointments, notes, and so on. This, of course, is only useful when exchanging such information with another Outlook user who can then utilize the item within Outlook.

Inserting Files

Since so much modern work is done on computers, the ability to transmit computer files, along with e-mail messages, is a phenomenal time- and money-saver. Authors can send completed manuscripts to publishers, programmers can send computer programs, financial analysts can send entire spreadsheets. The uses are seemingly endless. What used to require a special courier or an hour-long fax call can now be accomplished with the click of the Send button.

Adding file attachments to Outlook e-mail messages is quite easy:

1. Create a new e-mail message using the method described earlier in this chapter.

2. Click the Insert File button on the Standard toolbar to open the Insert File dialog box shown in Figure 3-10. Your Insert File dialog box may look different depending on the version of Windows you're using. However, it works the same in all versions.

3. Click the down arrow to the right of the Look In field to display the drop-down tree view of your computer system.

4. Use the tree view to locate the file you want to attach.

5. Double-click the file to attach it to your e-mail message (see Figure 3-11). You can also click the down arrow next to Insert and choose Insert As Attachment.

New (and welcomed) in this latest version of Outlook, is the Attach field, which appears when you add an attachment to a Plain Text or HTML message. However, if you add an attachment to a Rich Text message the field is not present, and the attachment appears in the message body.

Note   *You can also insert the contents of a text file in an e-mail message rather than attaching the text file itself. In other words, all the text from the document is simply tagged on to the message you've already typed in the message body window. This is useful when sending to a recipient who is having difficulty receiving your attachments. Follow the previous procedure and click the down arrow to the right of the Insert button and select Insert As Text.*

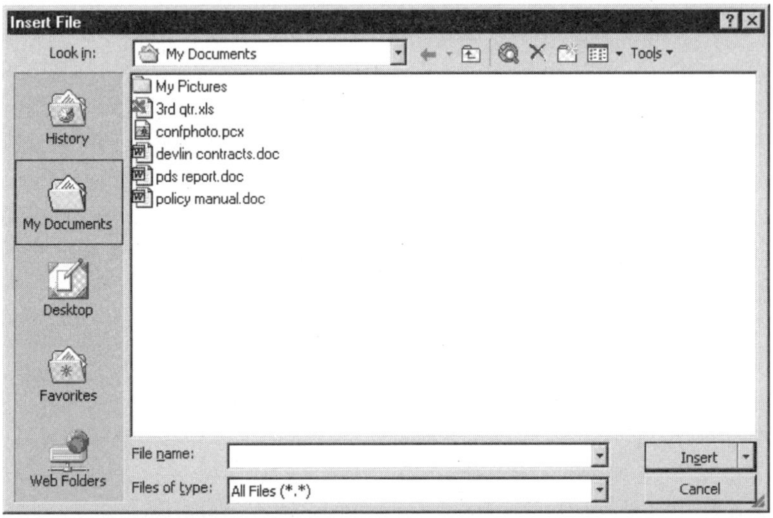

Figure 3-10. *The Insert File dialog box enables you to search your hard disk(s) to locate the file you want to attach*

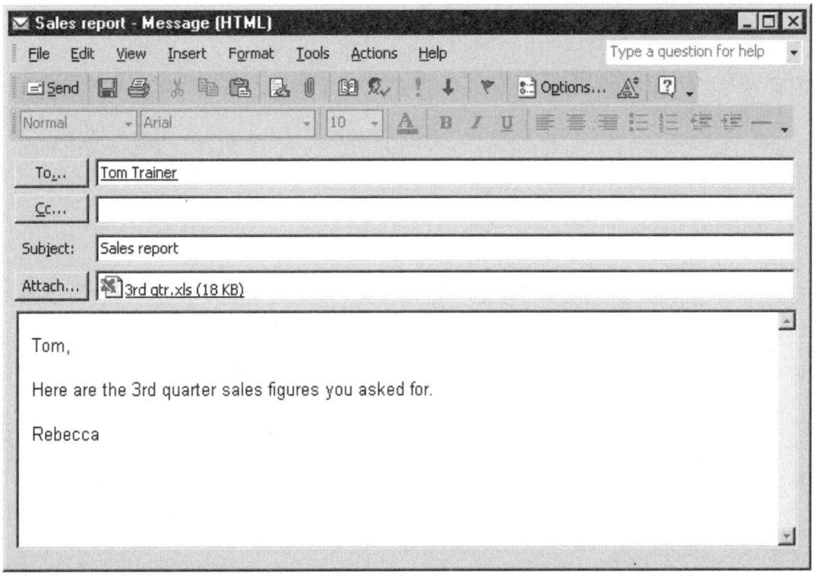

Figure 3-11. *The attachment icon, file name, and file size appear in the Attach field in Plain Text and HTML messages*

6. Repeat the process to add all the attachments you want to include with the e-mail.

You can select multiple files (from the same folder) and add them all at once.

7. Click Send to transmit the message.

As powerful as the file attachment feature is, it does have some limitations. Network administrators and Internet service providers (ISPs) frequently put a size limit on the messages that are allowed to pass through their servers. Consequently, some messages with extremely large attachments may not make it. Check with your administrator to find out if there's a limit on the size of messages you can send and receive.

One way to reduce the size of file attachments is through the use of file compression software such as WinZip. Depending on the file type, compression software can reduce the size of a file by 50 percent or more. You can find file compression shareware and trialware on many of the download sites on the Internet, such as ZDNet and CNET. However, be sure that the recipients also have file compression software to restore the file to its original state, or they will be unable to access the file.

Including Outlook Items

The ability to exchange Outlook items such as contacts, meetings, notes, and other files comes in quite handy at times. If you have contact information in your Contacts folder you want to share with a number of other Outlook users, all you have to do is insert the contact(s) in an e-mail message and send it to everyone with whom you want to share the data. When they receive the message, they simply drag the attached contacts to their respective Contacts folders and drop them. The contacts are automatically added to each user's Contacts database.

Fortunately, one of the changes in Outlook 2002 includes the ability to exchange Outlook items as attachments with other Outlook users via Internet e-mail. However, anyone using an Internet e-mail client other than Outlook will not be able to utilize Outlook items received as attachments.

Although you can't exchange Outlook items with users of non-Outlook clients, you can include the information from an item by inserting it as text only. See the steps that follow for more information.

To attach an Outlook item to an e-mail message, follow these steps:

1. Create an e-mail message using the method described earlier in this chapter.

2. Click the down arrow on the Insert File button and select Item to attach an Outlook item to your message. If you're using the Outlook e-mail editor choose

Insert | Item from the message form Menu bar. In either case, the Insert Item dialog box seen in Figure 3-12 appears.

3. From the Look In pane, choose the folder containing the item(s) you want to insert. The folder's contents are displayed in the Items list below the Look In pane.

4. Select the appropriate Insert As option:

   ■ **Text Only**   To include the information only from the Outlook item, choose this option. This adds the data from the selected item to your message as text. Therefore, it becomes part of the message itself and has no trouble traveling over the Internet (see Figure 3-13).

   ■ **Attachment**   Select this option to include the Outlook item itself. Remember, this only works if you're sending the e-mail to someone connected to your network.

   ■ **Shortcut**   Rather than send any of the information, you can choose to send a shortcut or pointer to the information. However, to be of any use, the recipient must have permission to access your folders.

Tip   *You can insert multiple Outlook items from the same folder by holding down the* CTRL *key and selecting adjacent or non-adjacent items. To select a series of adjacent items, select the first item, hold down the* SHIFT *key and then select the last item.*

COMMUNICATING WITH E-MAIL

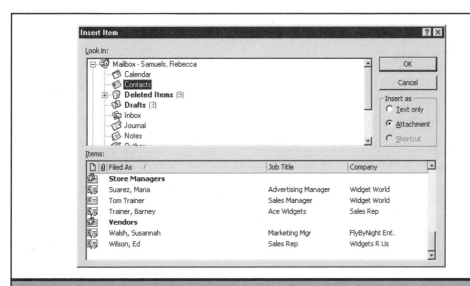

Figure 3-12.   *The Insert Item dialog box provides access to all your Outlook folders and items*

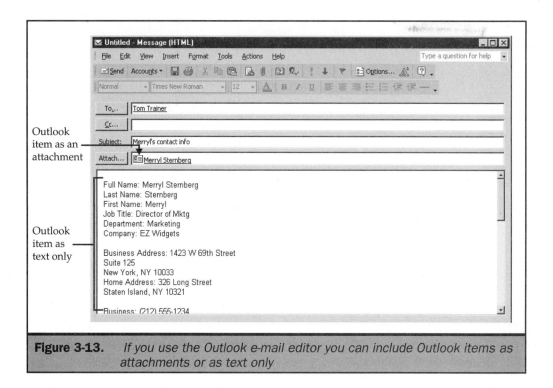

Figure 3-13.   *If you use the Outlook e-mail editor you can include Outlook items as attachments or as text only*

5. Click OK to insert the item(s) in the e-mail message.

    If you're using Word as your e-mail editor, you can only include an Outlook item as an attachment.

6. Click Send to transmit the message.

Once the recipients receive your message, they can either drag the Outlook item to the appropriate folder and drop it (Outlook users only), or cut and paste the text information into another PIM.

Attaching Objects to Messages

If you select Microsoft Outlook Rich Text as your message format, you can also include objects in your messages. Objects can be documents, charts, worksheets, graphics, controls or just about any other type of file. You can either embed or link the objects you include in messages. Embedded objects become part of the message and retain no connection with the original file from which they were taken. Linked objects, on the other hand, remain connected (as long as the connection is open).

For example, if you insert a linked Excel spreadsheet in a message, double-clicking the spreadsheet launches Excel and opens the original document. In addition, when the original spreadsheet is modified, the linked spreadsheet is also modified. An embedded spreadsheet does not change no matter what happens to the original.

Note *In order for a linked object to work properly, the original file must be accessible either by virtue of residing on an available drive (local or network), or over an open Intranet or Internet connection.*

To insert an object, follow these steps:

1. Create an e-mail message using the method described earlier in this chapter.
2. Choose Format | Rich Text to change the message format to Microsoft Outlook Rich Text. If Rich Text is not an option, change the message format to Plain Text, then return to the Format menu and select Rich Text.
3. Place the cursor in the message body window and choose Insert | Object from the Menu bar to open the Insert Object dialog box.
4. To create a new object, select Create New and then the kind of object you want to create from the Object Type list. The program associated with the object type opens and you can create the new object.

Note *Objects you create are embedded in the message, since there is no existing file with which to link them.*

5. To embed an existing object or create a link to an existing object, select Create From File to display the Create From File text box, the Browse button, and the Link option.
6. Click the Browse button to locate the file you want to insert in the message.
7. To link the file rather than embed it, click the Link option. This links the entire file.

Tip *To link or embed only part of the file in your message, open it in the associated program and copy the portion you want to link or embed. Next, move to the Outlook message form and place the cursor in the message body window. Then choose Edit | Paste Special from the Menu bar. To embed the information, select Paste. To link the information, select Paste Link.*

8. Click Send to transmit the message.

Linking and embedding objects works as advertised when the e-mail is sent to recipients on the network or via the Internet to other Outlook users. However, both linked and embedded objects are converted to unusable attachments when transmitted to Internet mail recipients using non–Rich Text compliant e-mail programs. If you're not sure, send the information as a file attachment.

MOUS EXAM PRACTICE
In this section, you learned to attach everything but the kitchen sink to an Outlook e-mail message. Now try your hand at creating messages and attaching various files, items, and objects to them. Begin by inserting a computer file from your hard disk into an e-mail. Next, create a message and include an Outlook item. Try using both methods—inserting the item as an attachment and as text only. Send both items to someone with an Internet e-mail account and ask them what they actually receive. Finally, create a message and use embedding and linking of objects to include additional information in your e-mail.

Sending E-mail Messages

Whether you're using your Exchange Server account or an Internet account, sending e-mail is pretty much the same. If you've left the default setting to send immediately unchanged, you don't have to do anything to send your messages as long as you're online (connected). Exchange messages are automatically sent to the Outbox, where they remain until the next server sweep picks them up and distributes them. Internet e-mail is sent to the Outbox to wait while the transfer is completed. If you're offline (not connected either to the network or your Internet account), all messages remain in the Outbox until the next time you connect. They are then retrieved by the next server sweep.

You can manually send e-mail messages by utilizing one of the commands found on the Send/Receive submenu. Choose Tools | Send/Receive from the Menu bar to display the Send/Receive submenu. As you'll discover when you open the menu, you have several choices, which include the following:

- **Send All** This command enables you to send, without receiving, e-mail messages on all your accounts. If you're not connected, using the Send command causes Outlook to attempt to establish a connection.

- **Send and Receive All** Similar to the Send command, this not only sends, but also checks for and downloads all incoming mail as well.

- **Specific Accounts** There is no "Specific Accounts" command, but rather a numerical listing of all your existing e-mail accounts. Select a particular account to send and receive e-mail for only that account.

- **All Accounts** Like the Send and Receive All command, this command transmits outgoing e-mail and picks up incoming e-mail from all your existing accounts.

- **Work With Headers** Select this command to display another submenu containing commands for downloading, marking, and processing headers from existing e-mail accounts. Headers include basic information about the e-mail such as From, Subject, and so on.

- **Download Address Book** If you plan to work offline, you'll want to download the Microsoft Exchange Server address book. This command displays the Download Offline Address Book dialog box with options for determining the extent of information included in the download.

- **Free/Busy Information**   If you've elected to publish your free/busy information, use this command to perform a manual publish. See Chapter 10 for details on free/busy information.

In addition to the Send/Receive submenu, you'll note there's also a Send/Receive Settings submenu on the Tools menu, containing several commands that enable you to further define the manner in which the Send/Receive commands work:

- **Define Send/Receive Groups**   This is just another way to access the Send/Receive Groups dialog box. See Chapter 19 for more information on Send/Receive Groups.

- **Disable Scheduled Send/Receive**   If you've established an automatic schedule for sending and receiving e-mail, you can temporarily (or permanently, if you never toggle this option again) nullify the Send/Receive schedule by checking this option.

- **Show Progress**   If you want to see exactly what's transpiring during a Send/Receive operation, check this option and Outlook will display the Outlook Send/Receive Progress dialog box, which provides a listing of tasks being performed, and any errors encountered.

MOUS

MOUS EXAM PRACTICE
In this section, you learned to send e-mail messages using various methods. To try your hand at sending messages, first disable automatic sending by choosing Tools | Options to open the Options dialog box. Then click the Mail Setup tab and remove the check mark from the Send Immediately When Connected option. All messages will be stored in the Outbox until you send them using one of the Outlook send commands. Now, send yourself a couple of messages, and try using the different send commands covered in this section. When you're finished, don't forget to return to the Mail Setup tab of the Options dialog box and reenable the Send Immediately When Connected option.

Saving Drafts of Messages

During a busy workday, it's not uncommon for a number of things to interrupt you while you're in the process of composing an e-mail message—a co-worker knocking on your door, the phone ringing, an urgent e-mail requiring an immediate response, or a hundred other distractions. While you're distracted, your unfinished message is hanging out in RAM limbo. Therefore, it's a good idea to save your message to ensure it doesn't get lost in the event of a computer crash, a power surge, or some other minor calamity.

Outlook provides a separate folder just for this purpose: the Drafts folder. As a matter of fact, by default, Outlook saves unsent messages to the Drafts folder every three minutes. However, to be on the safe side you should probably save unfinished messages yourself by pressing CTRL+S. When you're ready to finish the e-mail, pick up where you left off. If you've closed the message since you saved it, you can reopen it by opening the Drafts folder and double-clicking the message.

Recalling Sent Messages

Did you ever dash off one of those e-mails you know you shouldn't send, but in the heat of the moment you lose the ability to think rationally and send it anyway? Usually what happens next is that about three nanoseconds after it disappears your brain returns and you realize that you just did something you wish you hadn't. Well, if you're on a Microsoft Exchange Server network, there may be hope. Under certain circumstances, you can actually recall the message after you send it.

Before you get too excited, however, be advised that for it to work, the stars, moon, and planets have to be properly aligned, and you must have a little bit of good karma stored up. Okay, that may be a slight exaggeration, but there are a number of factors that influence the effectiveness of the Recall Message feature:

- **Recipient's e-mail system**   The recipient must be using Outlook and be on the Microsoft Exchange Server network for the feature to work properly. Do yourself a favor, and do *not* try to recall a message sent to an Internet mail recipient. You'll only make matters worse. All that happens is the original message stays intact and the recipient receives a follow-up message that says you would like to recall the original message.

- **Message status**   Only unread messages can be recalled. If the recipient has opened the message, you're out of luck. Of course, if the recipient has read the message, it no longer matters whether you can recall the message.

- **Message location**   The message must still be in the recipient's Inbox. If the message has been moved, the message recall fails. This is true even if the moved message is still unread. If your recipient employs the Rules Wizard to automatically sort incoming mail, your message may never see the Inbox.

- **Network status**   The user must be logged on to the Microsoft Exchange Server network for a recall to work. If you attempt to recall a message and the user is not logged on, the recall will not be attempted until the next time the user logs on. At that time, all the other factors come into play.

To recall a sent message, follow these steps:

1. Open your Sent Items folder and locate the message you want to recall.
2. Open the message.

3. Choose Actions | Recall This Message from the Menu bar to display the Recall This Message dialog box.

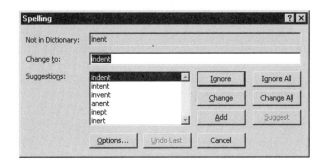

4. Select the appropriate options for the recall.

   ■ **Delete unread copies of this message**   To simply remove the unread message from the recipient's Inbox, select this option.

   ■ **Delete unread copies and replace with a new message**   If you want to send a new message to replace the original, use this option. It creates a new message that is an exact duplicate of the original, which you can edit and send.

   ■ **Tell me if recall succeeds or fails for each recipient**   Unless you check this option, you'll never know whether the recall has succeeded. With this option enabled, you receive an e-mail response informing you of the success or failure of your recall attempt.

5. Click OK to recall the original message. If you selected Delete Unread Copies And Replace With A New Message, the new message form opens with all the original message information included. Modify it and send it on its way.

If the recipient is logged on to the network, you'll get an e-mail response informing you of the success or failure of your recall attempt within a short while. That's assuming, of course, you enabled the Tell Me If Recall Succeeds Or Fails For Each Recipient option. However, if the recipient is not logged on to the network, you'll hear nothing until the next time the user logs on.

Unfortunately, even when a recall works, the recall notification process almost entirely defeats the purpose of the operation. A second message appears in the recipient's mailbox, indicating that you want to recall the message. If the recipient opens the recall notification message before opening the original message, both disappear, and your recall has truly worked (although, of course, leaving the recipient wondering what was in the message that made you want to recall it). However, should the notification merely pique the recipient's curiosity and he or she decides to read the original message, all is lost. Not only has the message been seen, but the recall fails because the message is no longer unread.

Resending Sent Messages

Occasionally e-mail messages never arrive at their intended destination, perhaps because of happenstance, foul play, or a blip in the electronic ether. If the lost message required no response from the recipient, you may never know. However, if you're expecting a response and don't get one, or someone asks you to send information and it never arrives, you'll probably want to send the message again. When you encounter a situation involving an errant e-mail message, you can use the Resend This Message command.

Here's all you have to do to resend a previously sent message:

1. Open the Sent Items folder and locate the message you want to resend.
2. Double-click the message to open it.
3. Choose Actions | Resend This Message to create a new message containing all the information of the original, including the recipients, subject line, contents, and attachments.
4. Make any changes to the new e-mail you feel are necessary.
5. Click Send to send it on its way.

From this point forward, the resent message behaves like every other sent message, and a copy is saved in your Sent Items folder (unless you've changed the default settings).

MOUS Exam Core Objectives Explored in Chapter 3

Objective	Activity	Heading
OL10-1-2	Compose and send messages to	"Creating a New Message"
		"Sending E-mail Messages"
OL10-1-3	Insert signatures and attachments	"Adding Attachments"
OL10-3-5	Set message options	"Setting Message Options"

MOUS Exam Expert Objectives Explored in Chapter 3

Objective	Activity	Heading
OL10E-2-1	Modify message formats	"Selecting the Message Format"

Chapter 4

Reading and Replying
to Messages

As important as writing and sending e-mail is, the flip side of the coin—reading and replying to incoming e-mail—is equally important. So much of today's communication, both personal and business, is conducted via e-mail that dealing with incoming e-mail is a skill everyone must master.

While it's true that receiving e-mail requires no effort if you're on a Microsoft Exchange Server network, and very little if you use an Internet e-mail account, there are quite a few things you can do with incoming e-mail after it lands in your Inbox. You can open it, read it, discard it, reply to it, store it, flag it, or even ignore it if you choose. That's what this chapter is all about: providing you with the skills to dispatch your incoming e-mail quickly and effectively.

Configuring the Inbox

The first thing you'll want to do is set up the Inbox to suit your work habits and needs. Fortunately, Outlook provides a number of options that enable you to customize the Inbox so that managing your incoming e-mail will be a breeze.

AutoPreview

For a sneak peek at the contents of each incoming message, you can turn on AutoPreview. It's a handy feature that displays, in the Information viewer, the first line or two of each message in addition to the usual header information.

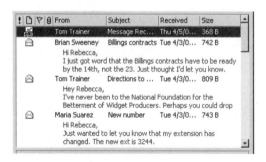

It's especially helpful if you're pressed for time and receive a lot of e-mail every day. You can take a quick look and decide for yourself the importance of the message, without even opening it.

To activate the AutoPreview feature, follow these steps:

1. Click the Inbox shortcut on the Outlook Bar to open the Inbox folder.

2. Choose View | AutoPreview from the Menu bar to enable AutoPreview.

You can also activate AutoPreview by right-clicking a blank spot (below the last message) in the Inbox Information viewer and selecting AutoPreview from the shortcut menu that appears.

3. Scroll through the Information viewer to scan the messages in the Inbox. The message contents appear with a blue background.

4. Choose View | AutoPreview a second time to turn off the AutoPreview feature.

The only downside to AutoPreview is that it utilizes a lot of Information viewer real estate. If you have a large number of incoming messages, you may find it easier to turn AutoPreview off and rely on the Subject line to determine the importance of each message.

You can instruct Outlook to AutoPreview only those items that are marked as unread. Choose View | Current View | Customize Current View to open the View Summary dialog box. Then click Other Settings and check the Preview Unread Items option in the Other Settings dialog box.

Preview Pane

The Preview Pane offers another means of viewing the message contents without actually opening the message. Unlike AutoPreview, the Preview Pane displays the entire message, not just the first line or two. However, Preview Pane actually splits the Information viewer into two panes. The top pane retains the standard header information, while the bottom pane displays the message contents (see Figure 4-1).

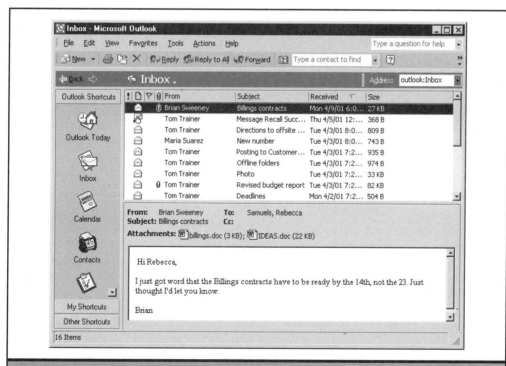

Figure 4-1.   *The Preview Pane enables you to read a message without opening it*

Activating the Preview Pane is as simple as choosing View | Preview Pane from the Menu bar. This immediately splits the Inbox Information viewer into two panes, with the Preview Pane inhabiting the bottom pane. After the Preview Pane is activated, select a message in the top pane of the Inbox Information viewer to display it in the Preview Pane. Scroll through the message to read the entire contents. If the message has one or more attachments, and the message is in HTML or Plain Text format, the icon, filename, and file size appear on the header (see Figure 4-1). Double-click an attachment to open or save it. Of course, you must have the program associated with the file type installed to open the attached file.

If the received message is a Rich Text message, attachments appear in the body of the message. To open or save the attachment, you can double-click the attachment in the Preview Pane or right-click it and select Open or Save As. You can also open the message and perform either action.

The Preview Pane is no different from other Outlook features in that it has several options you can set to customize the way it works. To change the Preview Pane settings, right-click the divider between the Information viewer and the Preview Pane, and choose Preview Pane Options from the shortcut menu.

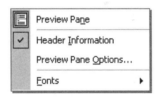

The available choices include hiding the Preview Pane itself, hiding the Preview Pane header information and setting Preview Pane options.

Selecting Preview Pane Options displays the Preview Pane dialog box shown in Figure 4-2. The available options include the following:

- **Mark messages as read in preview window** This option works in conjunction with the next option to give you a chance to preview messages or move quickly through them without necessarily marking them as read. Once you select this option you have the amount of time specified in the next option to display the message in the Preview Pane before it is automatically marked as read.

- **Wait ___ seconds before marking item as read** Only available if the preceding option is checked, this option indicates the amount of time a message can be viewed in the Preview Pane before it is marked as read. This is handy if you want to search for a particular message by skimming the contents of the Inbox, without marking each message as read. When you return to view your unread e-mail at a later time you won't mistakenly think you've read everything you skimmed.

- **Mark item as read when selection changes**   The default setting for the Preview Pane, this option causes a viewed message to be marked when the next message is selected.

- **Single key reading using SPACEBAR**   With this option enabled, you can move through the messages (sequentially) by pressing the SPACEBAR. To move forward, press the SPACEBAR. To move backward, hold the SHIFT key down while pressing the SPACEBAR. If a message has more information than fits in the Preview Pane, pressing the SPACEBAR scrolls through the message until the end is reached, at which time the next message is displayed.

One last thing. If you like the Preview Pane but don't like the amount of space it takes, you can resize it by dragging its top border up or down to increase or decrease its height. You can also change its width by dragging the left border left or right. Just be aware that this resizes the Information viewer at the same time.

Receiving E-mail

If you're on a Microsoft Exchange Server network, all you have to do is log on to the Microsoft Exchange Server and sit back and wait for mail to come to you. It's that easy. The server handles the receipt and distribution of all incoming as well as outgoing mail. This means that the Microsoft Exchange Server intercepts all messages addressed to you, whether from other users on the network or from the Internet (except those addressed to any Internet mail accounts you have added to your profile), and places them in your mailbox.

When you "receive" mail, you're not actually receiving the messages on your computer, but rather being notified that mail has been placed in your mailbox on the server. When you

Figure 4-2.   *The Preview Pane options let you change the way the Preview Pane looks and works*

open, read, delete, or otherwise perform an action on individual pieces of e-mail, it is all taking place on the Microsoft Exchange Server, not on your computer.

You can have your mail delivered to and stored on your computer rather than on the server. You do this by adding personal folders to your profile and changing the delivery location in the Deliver New E-Mail To The Following Location option found on the E-mail Accounts dialog box (Tools | E-mail Accounts | View Or Change Existing E-mail Accounts). However, be advised that most network administrators make daily backups of everything on the server, including e-mail. Once you change the delivery location to your personal folders, your e-mail will no longer be stored on the server, and consequently will not be backed up regularly unless you do it yourself.

So, if the only mail service you have installed is Microsoft Exchange Server, there's little you need to do to receive mail except log on to the server. One thing to remember is that when the server goes down, so does your mail service. Until it comes back up, you won't be able to receive (or send) mail unless you have an Internet mail account with an outside connection.

No matter which mail services you use, all your incoming e-mail is, by default, deposited in your Inbox. When new messages arrive, you may or may not receive notification, depending on how your set up your mail receipt options.

Receiving Notification of New Mail

There are several ways you can tell when new mail arrives in your Inbox. The first telltale sign is the melodious sound emanating from your speakers (of course, you must have a sound card installed and speakers attached). By default, Outlook is programmed to emit the Windows New Mail Notification sound, which you can change by opening the Sounds applet in the Control Panel and selecting a different sound file (see Figure 4-3).

If you're running Windows Me or Windows 2000 the applet is called Sounds and Multimedia, and the dialog box will appear somewhat different than the one pictured in Figure 4-3. Use the Sounds tab to achieve the same results.

Adding Visual Notification

Ah, but what if you don't have sound on your system, or you want double insurance that you don't miss new mail? No problem. You can also instruct Outlook to display a message informing you of the fact that new mail has arrived. To add a visual notification, follow these steps:

1. Choose Tools | Options to display the Options dialog box.

2. Click the E-mail Options button on the Preferences tab to open the E-mail Options dialog box, shown in Figure 4-4.

3. Check the Display A Notification Message When New Mail Arrives option.

4. Click OK to save the change and return to the Options dialog box.

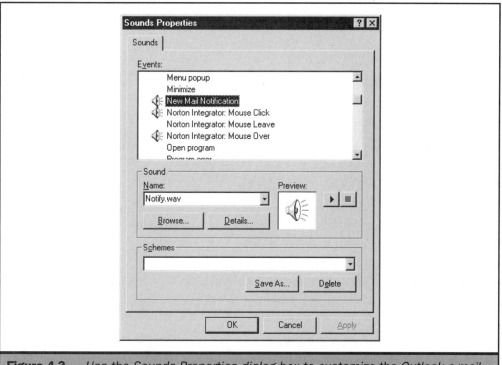

Figure 4-3.   *Use the Sounds Properties dialog box to customize the Outlook e-mail notification sound*

5. Click OK to return to the active Outlook window.

Now each time a new message arrives, Outlook interrupts whatever you're doing and presents you with a notification dialog box. Of course, Outlook must be running and you must be connected to the Microsoft Exchange Server or your Internet connection to receive notification.

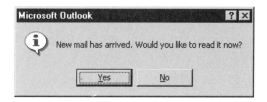

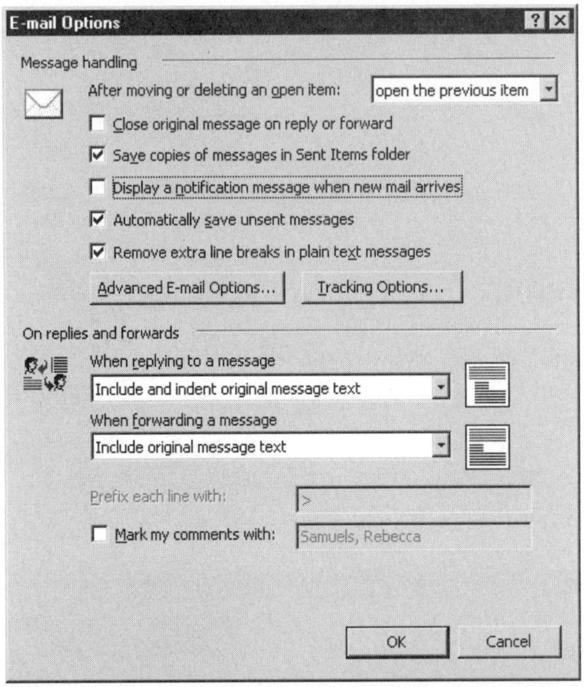

Figure 4-4.   *You can customize the way Outlook handles e-mail by taking advantage of the large selection of e-mail options*

Click Yes to open the new message immediately. Click No to return to the task at hand. You can then return to Outlook at a later time and open the message at your convenience. If you elect to click Yes and open the message immediately, the Previous Item and Next Item buttons do not work. You'll have to close the message and return to the Inbox to open your other messages. According to Microsoft, this is not a bug, but rather a design feature. In spite of this declaration, most users have a difficult time grasping the benefit derived from disabling the buttons.

In theory, there's another default setting that alerts you to the fact that new mail has arrived. Your mouse pointer momentarily changes shape, resembling a small envelope. However, unless you spend an inordinate amount of time staring at your mouse pointer, you'll probably miss this one.

Tip

There is another way that Outlook indicates the presence of new mail. The Inbox shortcut on the Outlook Bar sports a number in parentheses next to the word Inbox, indicating how many unread messages are in your Inbox. Each time a new piece of e-mail arrives, the number is increased by one until you open the e-mail, which then decreases the number by one. The same is true of the Folder List. If you generally read all your messages when they come in, or if you have an idea of how many unread messages are in your Inbox, you can generally tell by the number in parentheses whether or not you have new mail.

Creating Customized Notifications

Perhaps you're not concerned about getting e-mail from the majority of the folks with whom you correspond, but there are probably a few, such as your boss, her boss, and the CEO, that you don't want to keep waiting for a reply. If this is the case, don't bother setting a general notification alert. Instead, set an alert to go off each time you receive e-mail from any of those three individuals.

In order to do it, all you have to do is fire up the Rules Wizard and create a special notification rule. Here's how:

1. Choose Tools | Rules Wizard from the Menu bar to open the Rules Wizard dialog box, shown in Figure 4-5.

2. Click the New button to begin creating a new rule.

3. Select the Start From A Blank Rule option.

Note

Although there is a notification template you can use, it restricts notification to messages with a particular Importance setting—something which you can't possibly anticipate.

4. Select Check Messages When They Arrive, and click the Next button to display the conditions screen.

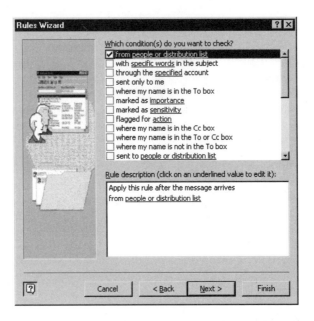

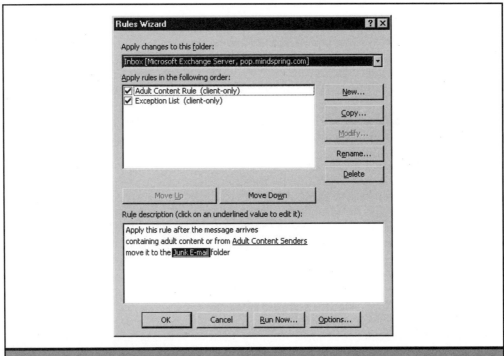

Figure 4-5.   *You can use the Rules Wizard to customize the way Outlook handles both incoming and outgoing messages*

If you want to create a custom message that notifies you of any new mail, regardless of the sender, click Next without checking any conditions. Then answer Yes when you're informed the rule will be applied to every message you receive.

5. Check the From People Or Distribution List option.

6. Move to the Rule description pane at the bottom of the Rules Wizard and click the blue, underlined "people or distribution list" link to open the Rule Address dialog box seen in Figure 4-6.

7. Select the names of those individuals to whom this rule will apply. In other words, choose those people whose e-mail is important enough to trigger a special notification when it arrives.

8. Click OK to close the Rule Address dialog box and return to the Rules Wizard. The Rule description window now contains the names you selected.

9. Click Next to move to the action screen, scroll down the list of possible actions to take, and check Notify Me Using A Specific Message.

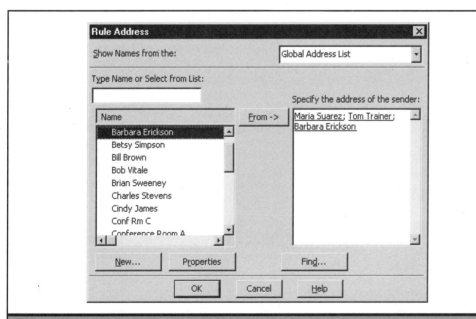

Figure 4-6.   *The Rule Address dialog box provides access to all your address books*

COMMUNICATING WITH E-MAIL

10. Click the "a specific message" link in the Rule description box to display the Notification Message dialog box.

11. Enter the text for the notification message that will appear when you receive mail from any of the individuals selected in Step 7.

12. Click OK to save the message and return to the Rules Wizard. Once again, the new information you entered now appears in the Rule Description pane.

13. Click Next to view the exceptions screen. If there are any circumstances under which you don't want to be notified of incoming mail from any of the selected individuals, check that option here. For example, you may not care unless you're the only recipient.

14. Click Next to view the final screen. Give the new rule an appropriate name and set the final option. If you want to apply the new rule to messages already received, check Run This Rule Now On Messages Already In "Inbox". Leave Turn On This Rule checked to ensure the rule actually works. If you remove the check mark, the rule will not run.

15. Click Finish to activate the rule. An information dialog box appears, informing you this rule is client-only and will not work unless Outlook is running.

16. Keep that in mind, and click OK to return to the opening screen of the Rules Wizard, where your new rule now appears in the Apply Rules In The Following Order list.

17. Click OK to save the new rule and return to the active Outlook window.

The next time you receive an e-mail message from any of the individuals named in the new rule, the custom message you created appears. As you can see, not only is your custom message included, but also the sender's name and the message subject.

COMMUNICATING
WITH E-MAIL

If you think you're seeing double when an e-mail arrives that meets the rule criteria, don't worry—it's not your failing eyesight or the fact that you've had one too many. It's the result of what appears to be a bug that causes Outlook 2002 to list each message twice in the notification dialog box.

By the way, if you have created a custom notification rule *and* you have the Display A Notification Message When New Mail Arrives option enabled, you'll get a standard notification message and a custom message each time new mail arrives from one of the individuals named in the custom notification rule.

Checking Internet Mail Manually

If you have a network connection to the Internet that remains open all the time, using automatic checking is probably a good idea. However, if you have to dial out to get your Internet e-mail each time, you may prefer to check it manually. Having a dial-up connection launch itself and start dialing unexpectedly, especially if you're in the middle of another task, can be rather annoying, to say the least.

To check your Internet e-mail manually, open the Inbox (or any folder that holds mail items) and choose Tools | Send/Receive. From the submenu, select Send and Receive All, or select the specific account for which you want to download messages. In addition to checking for incoming mail, this also sends any messages sitting in the Outbox. If you take a look at the Send/Receive submenu, you'll notice that your only choices are Send All, and Send and Receive All. There is no Receive-only command. If you want to be able to receive mail without sending at the same time, there is a way: use Remote Mail. For information on setting up and using Remote Mail, see Chapter 17.

You can also automate the sending and receiving of e-mail by using Send/Receive Groups, which are covered in detail in Chapter 19.

Opening and Reading E-mail

For the most part, you'll probably open and read (or at least scan) most e-mail you receive. The process is simple: double-click the message you want to open, and just like magic, it appears in its own message window, as shown in Figure 4-7.

Just for the record, there are a couple of other ways you can open a message:

- Right-click the message and choose Open from the shortcut menu that appears.
- Highlight the message and press CTRL+O.
- Highlight the message and choose File | Open | Selected Items.

Once you're done reading the message, you can close it, delete it, reply to it, forward it, move it, or just pretend it's not there. Oh yes, there's one more thing you can do: read other messages without closing the current message. Simply click the appropriate button on the Standard toolbar in the message window. The Previous Item button (up arrow)

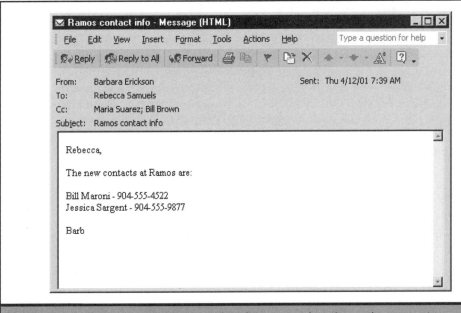

Figure 4-7.   *Opening a message makes it easy to view the entire contents at a glance*

opens the previous message, the Next Item button (down arrow) opens the next message. This version of Outlook has a greatly improved system of navigating through messages using the Previous and Next buttons. Now each button includes a drop-down list that enables you to move to the next or previous message that is: unread; part of the same conversation thread; from the same sender; of High importance; flagged; or is the first or last message in the folder. Using this method you can cycle through all your messages without opening and closing each one individually.

Don't forget, if you prefer not to open any messages, you can always use one of the two methods described earlier in this chapter for previewing messages—AutoPreview or the Preview Pane.

Changing the Formatting of Received Messages

Occasionally you may receive messages that are difficult to read, either because the type is too small or the formatting is too extravagant. Or perhaps someone has gone overboard with colors and the whole thing is giving you flashbacks to the psychedelic Sixties. Whatever the reason, you can modify the contents of received messages. Rich Text messages are editable as they arrive. All you have to do is highlight the offending text and choose Tools | Font to change the font formatting, or Tools | Paragraph to change the paragraph formatting. You can even add or delete text from the message.

You can also change HTML messages, but you must choose Edit | Edit Message from the message form Standard toolbar before Outlook lets you do any editing. Plain Text messages are a little trickier. First, you must choose Edit | Edit Message to make the message editable. However, since Plain Text accepts no formatting, the only thing you can do at this point is add or delete text. To apply formatting to a Plain Text message, you have to next change it to a different format. Choose Format and select either Rich Text or HTML. The message text immediately assumes the default font of the selected format. You can now apply font and paragraph formatting.

If you make any changes to the message, Outlook asks if you want to save those changes when you close the message. Click Yes to save the changes or No to return it to its original state.

If you find reading Plain Text messages difficult due to the 10-point Courier font Outlook uses by default, you can change the settings so all Plain Text messages you receive are automatically displayed with a different font. See Chapter 6 for details on changing default fonts in e-mail messages.

Viewing Message Headers

You can view or hide the header information on mail you receive from other users on the Microsoft Exchange Server, including the To, Cc, and Subject information. Although the header also contains the From information (the sender), it remains visible even when you hide the header information. To hide or display the header information, open the message and choose View | Message Header. If the header information is already visible, this command hides it. If, however, the header information is hidden, this command displays it.

Right about now, you're probably yawning and thinking "What's the big deal about headers?" Truthfully, hiding the message header is no big deal with Microsoft Exchange Server mail except that it may give you a little extra room to read the message itself. Where header information does become important is when it comes to Internet e-mail. Here, the message header provides a host of information, including the exact path the message took in getting to you. While you may not care, your network administrator will want that information to track down any bulk mailers that are sending you junk e-mail (also known as spam).

The Internet header information is not displayed in the message header above the actual message, but rather in the Internet Headers pane in the Message Options dialog box (see Figure 4-8). While in the Message window, choose View | Options to open the Message Options dialog box.

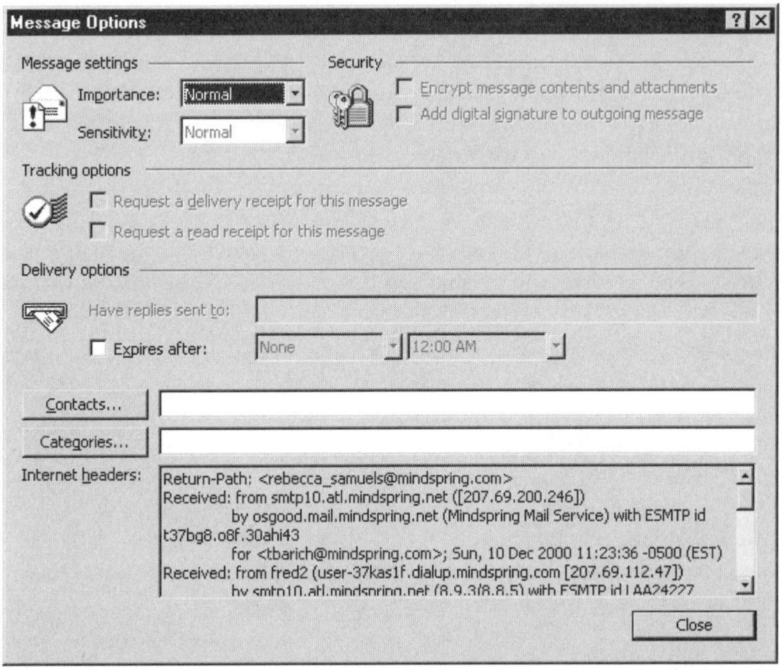

Figure 4-8. *The Internet headers information lets you track the e-mail to its source*

MOUS

MOUS EXAM PRACTICE

In this section, we covered opening and reading e-mail messages, the most basic of Outlook tasks. Now try the various methods available for opening and viewing messages to see which works best for you. In addition, try changing the formatting on some of your incoming messages so you're ready if you ever need to edit a piece of e-mail you receive. It's also a good idea to familiarize yourself with the way headers work on both Microsoft Exchange Server mail and Internet mail. Practice hiding and displaying the message headers, and locating the Internet header information on messages you receive over the Internet.

Responding to and Forwarding Messages

While many messages you receive may be informational only, there will probably be a large percentage that require something more than simply reading and storing (or deleting). When you run into one of these messages, you'll have a choice of actions to take. The most common action taken is responding to the sender. If the message was sent to multiple recipients, including yourself, you may elect to respond not only to the sender, but to all your fellow recipients as well. In some cases, you may not want to respond to the message, but rather send it on to someone else to read. This is called forwarding. No matter which action you choose, the ability to do more than read and store e-mail makes it a powerful form of communication.

Before you jump into replying and forwarding messages, there is one thing you should be aware of that applies to all three features (Reply, Reply to All, and Forward). When you send the message, Outlook adds a banner to the original message indicating the action taken (replied to or forwarded), and the date and time the action was taken.

ⓘ You replied on 4/12/00 11:40 AM. Click here to find all related messages.	
From: Cindy James	Sent: Thu 4/12/01 8:34 AM
To: Samuels, Rebecca	
Cc: Maria Suarez; Brian Sweeney	
Subject: New deadlines	

The same thing happens when you save the reply or forwarded message to the Drafts folder to finish it later, or when you delay the delivery of the message by choosing the Do Not Deliver Before option in the Message Options dialog box. This is all well and good, except for two potential problems. First, the banner in the original message remains even if you change your mind and decide not to send the reply or forward. Second, the date and time in the banner reflect the date and time the action was taken, not the date and time the message was actually sent. If you set the message to be sent some time in the future, this may cause confusion when, from your end, it appears your reply or forward was sent much sooner than the recipient received it.

Replying to E-mail Messages

Frequently, incoming e-mail either asks a direct question, or by virtue of the contents, deserves or perhaps begs a response. When you encounter such a message, the natural thing to do is respond. It's actually quite simple. All you do is click the Reply button on the message form Standard toolbar while the message is open.

You can also select the message in the Inbox Information viewer and press CTRL+R, *or click the Reply button on the Inbox Standard toolbar, or right-click the message and select Reply from the shortcut menu that appears.*

This opens a new mail message form addressed to the sender which, by default, contains the contents of the original message, including the header information (see Figure 4-9).

Although the entire text of the original message is, by default, included in a reply, it's not always necessary or desirable to leave it in the reply. By keeping the original text, you are increasing the size of your reply, which requires more bandwidth when sending it and more hard disk space when storing it. This is especially true as a message thread or conversation develops, in which the sender responds to your reply with a message that requires a response, which in turn requires a response, which requires a response—you get the picture. By the third or fourth response, the message may be several pages long. Therefore, you should retain the original message or relevant parts of it only when their omission might lead the recipient to misunderstand your reply.

You can change the default setting that causes Outlook to retain the original message in a reply. Choose Tools | Options and click the E-mail Options button on the Preferences tab to open the E-mail Options dialog box. Select a different setting from the When Replying To A Message drop-down list. See Chapter 8 for more information.

As you can see in Figure 4-9, the Subject line is already filled in as well. But now the Subject line from the original message is preceded by RE, meaning "in reference to." You'll also note that the cursor is in the message body window, ready for you to type your response. Enter your reply, apply any formatting you want, add any desired

COMMUNICATING
WITH E-MAIL

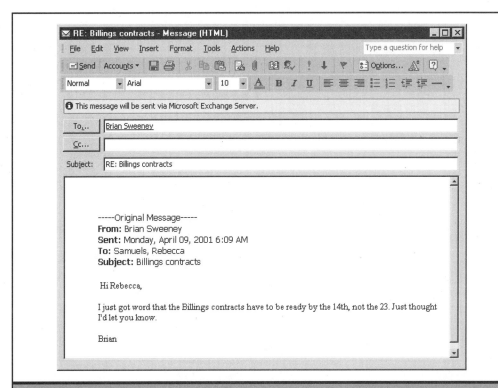

Figure 4-9. *Using the Reply button offers a quick way to respond to the sender*

attachments, and you're ready to send your reply back to the sender. The final step is to click the Send button and transmit the message.

Replying to All

When you receive a message with multiple recipients, you can respond to all the other recipients as well as the sender by using the Reply to All command. It is identical to the Reply command except that the new message created is automatically addressed to the sender and any recipients in the To and Cc fields of the original message. Anyone who was sent a blind copy (Bcc) of the original message does *not* receive a copy of the response when Reply to All is used.

Forwarding Messages to Others

Some messages contain information you want or need to share with others who did not receive the message. While you could certainly cut and paste the information into a new message and send it to the person you have in mind, there's a much simpler way: forward the original message. The most direct method is to click the Forward button on the message form Standard toolbar while the message is open. As you can see in Figure 4-10, this opens a new message form that looks strikingly similar to a reply message form.

When you look closely, you'll see the differences include the fact that there are no recipients added, and the Subject line contains the Subject line from the original message preceded by FW rather than RE. The FW, as you've probably already deduced, designates it as a forwarded message.

Now enter the recipient(s) to whom you want to pass this message, and add your own note (such as, "Thought you might find this interesting"). Apply any formatting you want, and click Send to transmit the forwarded message.

As is the case with both the Reply and the Reply to All features, you can forward a message without opening it. Select it and press CTRL+F, click the Forward button on the Inbox Standard toolbar, or right-click the message and select Forward from the shortcut menu.

Automating Message Replies and Forwarding

As easy as replying and forwarding is, Outlook provides a way for you to reply to and forward messages without ever lifting a finger. This little bit of digital wizardry is the domain of none other than the Outlook Rules Wizard. It enables you to create special rules that automatically craft and send a predetermined response, or that forward an incoming message to others without clicking a single mouse button (except while you're creating the rules, of course).

Creating a reply or forwarding rule is easy with the Rules Wizard. Since the possibilities are endless, the following exercise walks you through creating a rule that forwards all messages from your former team members to the new team leader who has just taken over for you (since your promotion, of course):

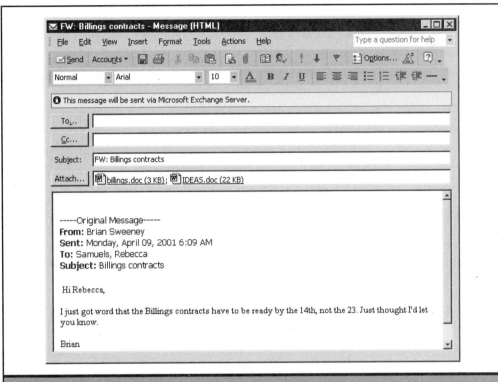

Figure 4-10.   *A forwarded message is indicated by the FW: in the Subject field*

1. Choose Tools | Rules Wizard from the Menu bar to display the Rules Wizard dialog box. As you can see in Figure 4-11, the opening screen of the Rules Wizard displays any existing rules you may have.

2. Click New to move to the next screen and begin creating your rule.

3. Select the Start From A Blank Rule option, choose Check Messages When They Arrive, and click Next to move to the conditions screen.

4. Check From People Or Distribution List, then click the "people or distribution list" link in the Rule Description pane to open the Rule Address dialog box (see Figure 4-12).

5. Double-click the names of the people whose mail you want forwarded by this rule to add them to the Specify The Address Of The Sender list, and click OK to add them to the rule.

6. Click Next to move to the actions screen, and select Forward It To People Or Distribution List.

7. In the Rule Description pane, click the "people or distribution list" link to open the Rules Address dialog box again.

8. Select the name of the individual to whom you want the messages forwarded, and click OK to return to the Rules Wizard.

9. Click Next to proceed to the exceptions screen, and select any appropriate exceptions to the rule. Then click Next to proceed to the final screen.

10. Give the new rule a name and check the desired options, then click Finish to save the new rule and return to the opening Rules Wizard screen.

11. Click OK to close the Rules Wizard and return to the active Outlook window.

The next time mail arrives in your mailbox from any of the individuals you named in the new rule, it will be forwarded to the new team leader automatically. A banner is added to any messages forwarded by the rule indicating that the message was AutoForwarded.

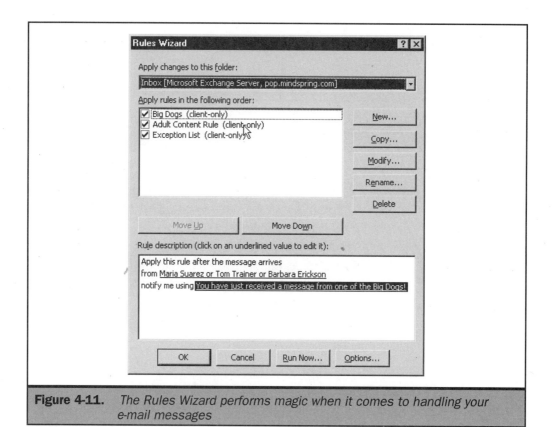

Figure 4-11. *The Rules Wizard performs magic when it comes to handling your e-mail messages*

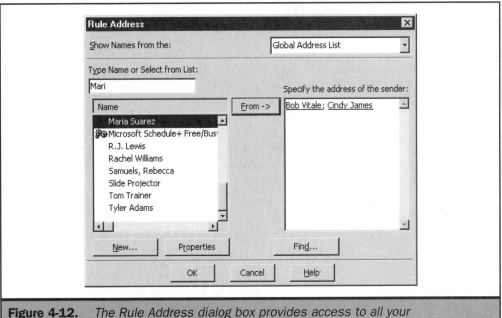

Figure 4-12. *The Rule Address dialog box provides access to all your address books*

There are a few things to be aware of when using automatic reply and forwarding rules. The first is that, under certain circumstances, the mail forwarding rule may not work. When this happens, it's probably the result of one of two things (assuming the rule is valid). Either the message is marked as private, in which case it will not be forwarded in order to ensure the sender's privacy, or your Microsoft Exchange Server version is 5.5 (or higher), which by default, does not allow Internet e-mail forwarding. If the problem is the latter, ask your network administrator to enable Internet e-mail forwarding.

The last thing to note is that mail forwarding rules are executed on the server, and as a result, do not place a copy of the forwarded message in your Sent Items folder. To add to the confusion, no banner is added to the original message indicating that a copy was forwarded to the new team leader. Unfortunately, you have to accept it on faith that Outlook is actually forwarding the messages. However, if you're from Missouri (the Show Me state) or just plain skeptical, you might want to check with the new recipient and see if forwarded messages from the indicated senders are making their way to his or her Inbox.

You can also use the Out of Office Assistant to automate replies and forwarding. For more information, see Chapter 20.

Using Voting Buttons to Respond

A handy feature available to Outlook C/W users on a Microsoft Exchange Server is the ability to add voting buttons to an outgoing e-mail. A sender can pose a direct question in a message and provide voting buttons the recipient(s) can use to reply. Should you receive such a message, replying is almost too easy. As you can see in Figure 4-13, there's no need to type a response unless you want to.

Simply click the appropriate voting button, and a dialog box appears asking if you want to send the response immediately or edit the message first. Make your selection and click OK. If you choose to edit the message, a new message form appears with your response as the Subject line. Enter whatever text you want and click Send.

Handling Attachments

Ask any writer what his or her favorite e-mail feature is and chances are, the response you'll get will be "file attachments." Thanks to the ability to send and receive fully formatted documents as e-mail attachments, deadlines are sometimes met with only seconds to spare. Sure, you can fax documents and have them arrive almost instantaneously. Ever tried faxing a 50-page chapter? Or looked at the phone bill after you've done it? Then there's overnight delivery. It's fast, but still costs an extra day, not to mention a rather substantial amount of money (especially when compared to the cost of e-mail attachments). When it comes to delivering most files, documents, spreadsheets, artwork, and so on, there's no comparison in time, work, and financial savings—e-mail beats the other methods hands down.

If you're thinking that receiving attachments is a breeze, since they arrive automatically with the messages to which they're attached, you're only partially right. To receive attachments, just sit back and wait for someone to send them. However, if you want to put those attachments to good use when they arrive, you'll need to learn to save them, open them, and in some cases, even put them to work.

Saving Attachments

Getting junk e-mail has, unfortunately, become all too common. Getting junk attachments, fortunately, is not at all common. Therefore, if you receive an attachment, chances are it's something you want. If it has more than a momentary value, you'll probably want to store it on your hard disk for future use. Saving an attachment you receive is easy if you follow these steps:

1. Open the e-mail message containing the attachment. You can also save an attachment from the Preview Pane, if the attachment appears in the Preview Pane.

2. Right-click the attachment and select Save As from the shortcut menu to open the Save Attachment dialog box, seen in Figure 4-14.

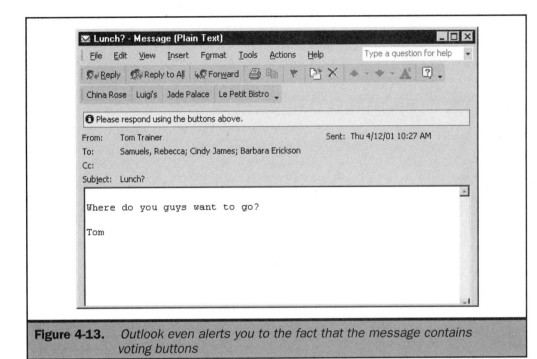

Figure 4-13.   *Outlook even alerts you to the fact that the message contains voting buttons*

3. From the Save In drop-down list, choose the folder in which to save the attachment.

4. Click Save to place a copy of the attachment in the selected folder, and return to Outlook.

5. Close the open message and you're all finished.

Now, whenever you need the attachment, simply return to the folder in which you stored it and retrieve it. If you have a number of attachments you plan to save in different folders, you can open Windows Explorer and drag attachments from messages to the desired folders. You can also drop attachments on the My Documents or Favorites shortcuts in the Other Shortcuts group.

Opening Attachments

If the program with which the attachment is associated is installed on your computer, you can open the attachment by double-clicking it. In other words, if you have Microsoft Word installed on your computer, you can open a Word document you receive as an attachment by double-clicking the file. As soon as you double-click an attachment, the associated program launches and opens the file.

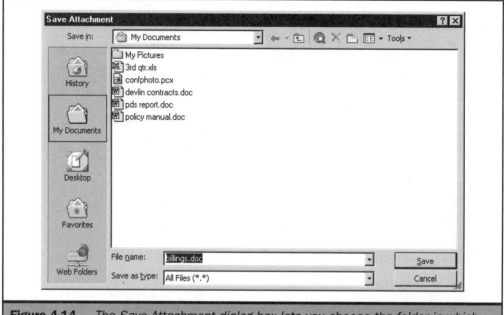

Figure 4-14.   *The Save Attachment dialog box lets you choose the folder in which to save the file*

By default, Outlook warns you that attachments can contain viruses and scripts that may have adverse affects on your computer. If you're aware of the risks and don't want the alert to appear each time you open an attachment, check the Always Ask Before Opening This Type Of File option.

Note   *Microsoft has taken it upon itself to automatically block a whole class of file types from incoming mail, that have the potential to do harm to your computer. This makes it impossible to exchange files of these types when using Outlook. Included among the blocked file types are executables such as .exe and .com files, help files including Windows help files (.hlp) and HTML help files (.chm), as well as a lengthy list of about 34 more file types (check the help files for a complete listing). See your administrator to unblock file types as necessary. One last thing, even though you can't receive the blocked file types, you can still send them.*

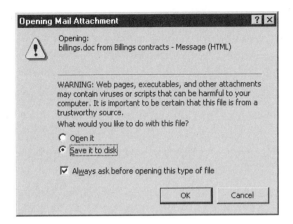

Another method you can use to view or save attachments is to right-click the message with the attachment and select View Attachments from the shortcut menu. You can also open attachments by right-clicking the attachment and selecting Open from the shortcut menu that appears. If Quick View appears on the menu as one of the choices, this means there is a file viewer available to display the file without launching the associated program. However, in order to edit the file, you'll have to have the associated program installed.

Using Outlook Items Received as Attachments

One of the nice things about using Outlook is the fact that you can share all kinds of information with other Outlook users. The ability to add Outlook items such as contacts, appointments, tasks, and notes to e-mail messages makes exchanging data almost fun, and most certainly a snap. When you receive an Outlook item as an attachment, all you have to do is drag it to the appropriate folder or Outlook Bar shortcut and drop it. The item becomes part of that folder.

For example, suppose a co-worker sends you a contact record from her Contacts database. To add it to your Contacts database, simply drag it to the Contacts shortcut icon on the Outlook Bar or the Contacts folder in the Folder List and drop it. It's added to your Contacts database automatically.

You can also drag Outlook item attachments to folders of a different type (for example, a Contact record to the Calendar folder) to create a new item using the information contained in the attached item.

Creating Address Book Entries from Received Mail

Adding a sender's or fellow recipient's e-mail address to your Contacts folder is not really a major chore, but why waste your time entering it manually when you can have

Outlook do the work for you? Save your energy and time for something more productive.

To add an address from an e-mail message into your Contacts folder, open the message, right-click the address you want to enter, and select Add to Contacts. Immediately, a new Contact form opens with the user's name and e-mail address already entered. You can add other information now or at some time in the future. Click Save and Close to save the new Contact and return to the active Outlook window.

Printing Messages

When you receive a great compliment via e-mail, or one of the kids sends you a great poem or letter, you might want to print a hard copy you can carry around and show everyone. Since there's only one print style (Memo) for received e-mail messages, nothing could be simpler.

All you have to do to print an e-mail message is highlight the message in the Inbox and click the print button, or if the message is open, click the Print button on the message form Standard toolbar. Next thing you know, you've got a hard copy. You can also use the Print command on the File menu, or right-click a message and choose Print from the shortcut menu.

If you're connected to more than one printer, or if you want to change the printer properties, you can open the Print dialog box shown in Figure 4-15 by choosing File | Print from the message form Standard toolbar.

Note   *If you're printing an HTML message, the Print dialog box that appears is a little different from the one pictured in Figure 4-15.*

If you're connected to multiple printers, select the printer from the Printer Name drop-down list. Click the Properties button to modify the settings for the printer you select. What you see in this dialog box depends entirely on the make and model of the printer you select. The other options include the number of pages to print of a multiple-page document, as well as the number of copies you want to print. In the Print dialog box displayed from Plain Text and Rich Text messages (see Figure 4-15), you can also modify the page setup and even define your own print styles.

MOUS EXAM PRACTICE
In this section, you learned to produce printouts of your e-mail messages. Since printing is fairly straightforward, you should begin by printing messages without opening them. Next, try opening some messages and then printing them. Use all three methods for activating the Print command: Click the toolbar Print button, right-click the message and choose Print from the shortcut menu, or choose File | Print from the Menu bar. Once you're comfortable with printing basics, modify some of the print options to see how they change the resulting printouts.

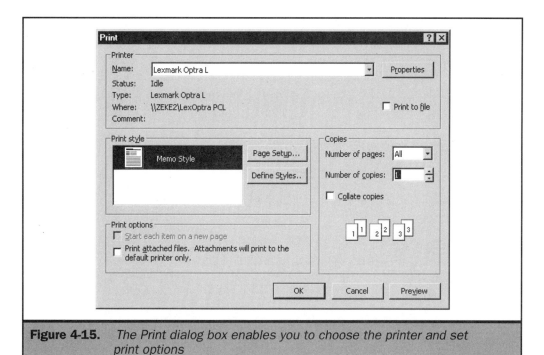

Figure 4-15. *The Print dialog box enables you to choose the printer and set print options*

MOUS Core Exam Objectives Explored in Chapter 4

Objective	Activity	Heading
OL10-1-1	Display messages	"Opening and Reading E-mail"
OL10-1-1	Print messages	"Printing Messages"

The
Complete
Reference

Chapter 5

Tracking and Managing Mail

If the only service Outlook e-mail provided was the sending and receiving of messages and attachments, it would still be an exceptional communication tool. However, it doesn't stop there. In addition to sending and receiving mail, Outlook also offers a powerful set of e-mail management and tracking features, which is what this chapter is all about. Here you'll discover ways to store, view, and manipulate e-mail messages you send and receive. You'll even learn to automate e-mail handling by using the Rules Wizard.

Viewing E-mail

One of the things frequently taken for granted is the way information appears on the screen. When you open an Outlook mail folder, whether it's the Inbox, Outbox, or Sent Items folder, the message data appears in the Information viewer, giving you a quick glimpse of the folder contents. This is usually the first place you look when searching for a stray piece of e-mail. Using the Advanced Find feature is great if it's a complex search, but when you know the message you're searching for is there, and you know who sent it and approximately when it arrived, it's much easier to just take a quick peek in the folder.

Now, take a closer look at the Messages view, the default view of the Inbox, and see what makes it tick. The first thing to do is pick it apart and examine each of its elements. You'll soon see that each part, taken separately, doesn't amount to much, but put them altogether and you've got a powerful tool for displaying and manipulating your Inbox information (see Figure 5-1).

Note   *All of the Inbox views, with the exception of the Message Timeline, incorporate the same basic elements.*

The Messages view is practically the same in all the mail folders. The only difference is that the Inbox folder includes From and Received information, whereas the other mail folders display To and Sent data. This, of course, makes sense because the Inbox holds incoming mail and the Outbox, Drafts, and Sent Items folders contain outgoing mail.

If you understand the various pieces of information that make up the Messages view, a single glance can tell you a lot about the messages in your Inbox:

■ **Header Status**   When you download headers, this column indicates that the item is a header only, and whether or not it's been marked for downloading.

■ **Importance**   The Importance column indicates whether the message is (according to the sender) of high, normal, or low importance. High and low importance are indicated by symbols (see Table 5-1), while normal importance is indicated by the lack of a symbol.

■ **Icon**   The Icon column indicates whether a message has been opened or not, what type of message it is, and any action that has been taken. See Table 5-1 for an explanation of the symbols used.

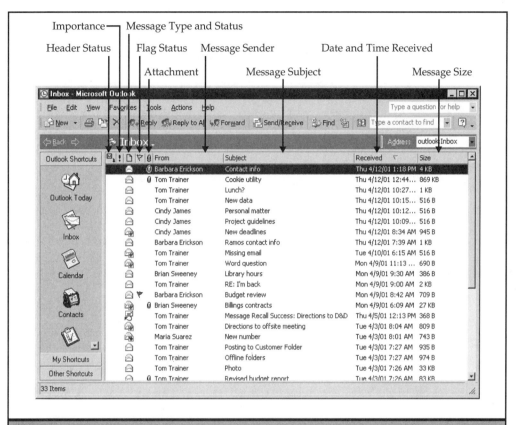

Figure 5-1. *The Messages view offers a wealth of information about the contents of your Inbox*

- **Flag Status** A red flag in this column indicates the message has been flagged for follow-up either by the sender or by you. A gray flag in this column indicates the follow-up has been performed and marked completed.

- **Attachment** If the message has one or more attachments, a paperclip icon appears in this column.

- **From** Here you'll find the sender's name. This does not include the sender's e-mail address, but rather the display name on the mailbox or Internet mail account the sender uses.

- **Subject** The message's Subject line text appears in this column.

- **Received** This column includes the date and time the message was received. One thing to note about this information is that it's determined not by your computer, but rather by the Microsoft Exchange server. Since your mailbox is on the server, the date and time in the Received column reflect the date and time set on the Microsoft Exchange server. In other words, if the server is an hour faster than your computer, you'll appear to be receiving messages from the future.

As you can see, each of the columns provides a small piece of information. Put them altogether and you have a comprehensive view of your Inbox contents. For an explanation of the symbols that appear in each column, see Table 5-1 and Table 5-2. These symbols are used in all Inbox views, including the Message Timeline view.

This Symbol	In this Column	Means
	Header Status	The header is unmarked.
	Header Status	The header is marked to download the message. No copy is left on the server.
	Header Status	The header is marked to download a copy of the message. This leaves a copy on the server.
	Header Status	The header is marked to delete the message from the server.
!	Importance	The message has a high importance or priority (according to the sender).
↓	Importance	The message has a low importance or priority (according to the sender).
	Icon	The message has been read.
	Icon	The message is unread.
	Icon	The message has been forwarded.

Table 5-1.   *Standard Symbols Used in Mail Folders*

This Symbol	In this Column	Means
	Icon	The message has been replied to.
	Icon	The message is unsent, saved, or both.
	Icon	The message is encrypted.
	Icon	The message contains a digital signature.
	Icon	The message contains an invalid digital signature.
	Icon	The message is a Microsoft Mail 3.x form.
	Icon	The message is a meeting request.
	Icon	The message is a meeting request that has been accepted.
	Icon	The message is a meeting request that has been tentatively accepted.
	Icon	The message is a meeting request that has been declined.
	Icon	The message is a cancelled meeting notice.
	Icon	The message is a task request.
	Icon	The message is a task request that has been accepted.
	Icon	The message is a task request that has been declined.

Table 5-1.   *Standard Symbols Used in Mail Folders* (continued)

COMMUNICATING WITH E-MAIL

This Symbol	In this Column	Means
🖼	Icon	The item is a downloaded header only. The message is still on the server.
⚑	Flag Status	The message has been flagged for follow-up.
⚐	Flag Status	The message is flagged as complete.
📎	Attachment	The message has an attachment.

Table 5-1.   *Standard Symbols Used in Mail Folders* (continued)

For those users on a Microsoft Exchange Server network, the additional symbols shown in Table 5-2 may appear as well.

This Symbol	In this Column	Means
🗒	Icon	The message has been posted to a folder.
✉	Icon	An attempt to recall the message was made.
🗐	Icon	The message was successfully recalled.
🗐	Icon	The message recall failed.
🖂	Icon	The message is a delivery receipt for a message successfully delivered.

Table 5-2.   *Microsoft Exchange Server Symbols Used in Mail Folders*

This Symbol	In this Column	Means
✔	Icon	The message is a read receipt for a message that has been read.
↻	Icon	The message is a delivery receipt for a message that was not delivered.
✖	Icon	The message is a read receipt for a message that has not been read.
⚔	Icon	The message is a conflict notification for an offline folder item.

Table 5-2.   *Microsoft Exchange Server Symbols Used in Mail Folders* (continued)

If you find the symbols confusing, you can change three of the five columns (Importance, Flag Status, and Attachment) that display symbols to display text instead. Right-click the desired column header and select Format Columns to open the Format columns dialog box.

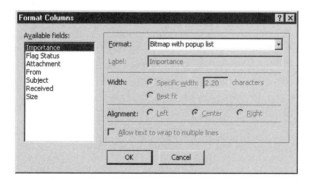

From the Format drop-down list, select Text With Popup List for the Importance or Flag Status column. The Attachment column has several choices for text. After you make your choice, click OK to save the change and return to the Inbox. Since the columns don't automatically resize themselves (at least not by default), you'll have to widen the column to see the text. Move the mouse pointer to the vertical line separating the column header from the next column until the mouse pointer turns into a crosshair with a pair of double-sided arrows pointing left and right.

Hold down the left mouse button and drag to the right to widen the column and display the text that now replaces the symbol.

You can also use the Best Fit command to resize the column to accommodate either the column name, or the longest field entry in the column, whichever is longer. Right-click the column header and select Best Fit from the shortcut menu.

If you change your mind and decide you'd rather have the symbol, return to the Format Columns dialog box and choose Bitmap With Popup List from the Format drop-down list. The column returns to its original width.

Sorting E-mail

Before jumping into sorting, you should familiarize yourself with the concepts and terms used. The first thing to understand is that the Inbox, like the other Outlook folders, is primarily a database. A database is a storage container for information. It is composed of individual records, which in turn are composed of fields. Databases are all around you. Take a cookbook, for example. The cookbook (the database) is a collection of recipes (the records), which contain ingredients and steps (the fields).

The Inbox database contains messages, which are the records. Each message is composed of fields such as From, To, Cc, Subject, Received, and so on. The fields displayed in the Messages view are Header Status, Importance, Icon, Flag Status, Attachment, From, Subject, and Received. These fields are used to perform a sort. Sorting involves rearranging the order in which the records (messages in this case) appear, based on the information contained in one or more fields. Understanding the following terms will make sorting a breeze.

- **Sort order** The order in which the messages (records) are arranged in the Inbox. The sort order, which is determined by the field(s) selected for the sort, can either be ascending or descending.

- **Ascending** Records are arranged from first to last as determined by the first character of the sort field. An ascending alphabetical listing is sorted from A to Z, with A appearing at the top of the list and Z appearing at the bottom. A numerical listing with an ascending sort order displays the lowest numbers at the top and the highest at the bottom. For example, if you use the From field to do an ascending sort, Athena appears at the top of the Message viewer, while Zeus appears at the bottom. If you use the Received field, and have messages ranging from May 1st to May 31st, May 1st appears at the top of the view, and May 31st at the bottom.

- **Descending** This one's easy—it's the opposite of ascending. Z appears at the top of the list and A drops to last place.

The hierarchy of internal data fields such as Header Status, Importance, Icon, Flag Status, and Attachment is predetermined, and has nothing to do with alphabetical or numeric considerations.

By default, the Messages view displays your e-mail messages in the order of their Received date/time information. The default sort order is descending, which means the most recent messages appear at the top of the list. As handy as this may be, there will undoubtedly be times when you want to see the order reversed, or when you want to use a different sort criterion altogether, such as sender, subject, or message type. Fortunately, changing the sort order in Outlook is as easy as it is flexible.

To begin with, you can change the sort order or criterion with a single mouse click. In the default view, Messages, you can change the sort order from descending to ascending (earliest messages first) simply by clicking the header on the Received column. As you can see in the following illustration, the recessed triangle (arrow) in the header changes from pointing downward to pointing upward, indicating the sort order is now ascending.

In addition to changing the sort order, you can also change the sort criterion with a click of your mouse. Click any of the column headers to sort the Inbox by that particular piece of information. For example, if you want the messages sorted by sender, click the From column header. The Inbox is immediately sorted by sender in ascending order. The default sort order for all Inbox columns except Received is ascending. If you want to change the sort order to descending, click the header again, and the triangle now points in the opposite direction.

Tip	*The Header Status, Importance, Icon, Flag Status, and Attachment column headers do not display the recessed triangle indicating sort order, which means you may have difficulty determining whether the order is ascending or descending. Right-click the column header and select Sort Ascending or Sort Descending to be sure you've got the sort order you want.*

What makes the sort feature even handier is the fact that you're not limited to sorting by a single field. You can sort by as many as four fields at one time. This means if you have a lot of messages of varying types and importance from each of your senders, you can perform an ascending sort by Importance to ensure the high priority messages appear at the top of the Inbox. Then do an ascending subsort by From to see all high priority (from the Importance sort) messages by Angela first, followed by all high priority messages from Bill next, and so on. If you're so inclined, you can then do an additional descending subsort by Received to see all the high priority messages from Angela, starting with the most recent, followed by all the high priority messages from Bill, starting with the most recent, and so on.

When performing multiple sorts, Outlook applies additional subsorts to the existing sorts. The way you perform a sort using multiple fields is almost as easy as sorting by a single field. All you have to do to include a column in the sort is hold the SHIFT key down while clicking column headers. In the previous example, you would start by right-clicking the Importance column header and selecting Sort Ascending. Next, hold down the SHIFT key and click the From column header. Still holding the SHIFT key down, click the Received column header. Your Inbox should now be sorted first by Importance, next by From, and finally by Received. As you've by now surmised, holding down the SHIFT key retains the existing sort criteria, and adds additional field(s) as subsort criteria.

COMMUNICATING WITH E-MAIL

To change the order (ascending or descending) of a secondary sort field, you can click the column header while holding the SHIFT *key.*

In addition to using simple sorts, there is another Outlook feature called grouping. It allows you to add messages to specific groups for easier sorting and viewing. For more information on grouping and sorting, see Chapter 23.

One last thing to keep in mind: you can sort any mail folder, including Drafts, Outbox, Sent Items, or a custom folder you create to hold mail, using the techniques described here. As a matter of fact, these sorting methods work on any table view (a view with columns and rows) in Outlook.

Locating E-mail Messages

The most direct method for locating messages is to use the Outlook Find feature, which comes in two flavors, Find and Advanced Find. Find is a simple, one-criterion text search that is quick and dirty. However, it's not terribly robust.

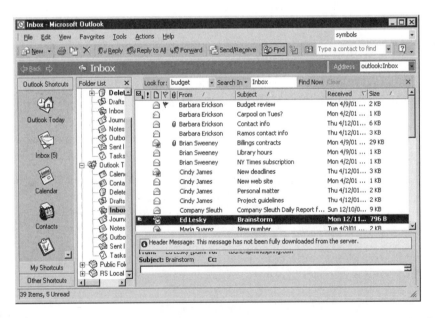

To use the Find feature, press CTRL+E or click the Find button on the Standard toolbar. This opens the Find window shown in the preceding illustration. Now all you have to do is enter the text you want to search for and click Find Now. Outlook searches all text fields for the text. The results of the search are displayed in the Information viewer below the Find window. If you happen to be in the wrong folder you can select the folder of your choice from the Search In drop-down list.

If your search was successful, you can close the Find window and go about your business. However, if the message(s) you were looking for did not appear, you can click Clear and try again, or, if you're ready to bring out the big guns, you can use the Advanced Find (see Figure 5-2).

The advantage of using the Advanced Find is primarily the fact that you can use multiple criteria to narrow your search quickly and efficiently. Since the results may come from multiple folders, the found messages are displayed in a separate window at the bottom of the Advanced Find dialog box (see Figure 5-2).

Note *When adding search criteria to the Advanced Find dialog box, be advised there is an implied AND between every condition you add. In other words, a search with more than one criterion finds only those messages that meet all the search criteria.*

To use the Advanced Find feature to locate messages, follow these steps:

1. Press CTRL+SHIFT+F, or right-click the Folder banner and choose Advanced Find to display the Advanced Find dialog box.

Tip *You can also right-click a shortcut in the Outlook Bar and choose Advanced Find from the shortcut menu, or choose Tools | Advanced Find.*

2. Select Messages from the Look For drop-down list. Note that you can select files as well as a variety of Outlook items.

3. To change the folder in which the search is conducted or to include additional folders, click the Browse button to display the Select Folder(s) dialog box, seen in Figure 5-3.

4. Check each folder you want to include in the search.

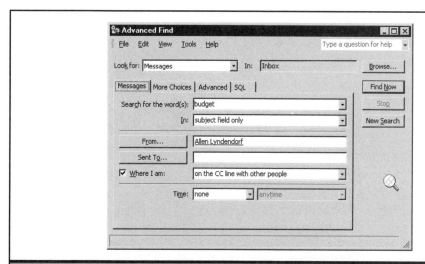

Figure 5-2. *Use the Advanced Find when the Find feature just isn't enough*

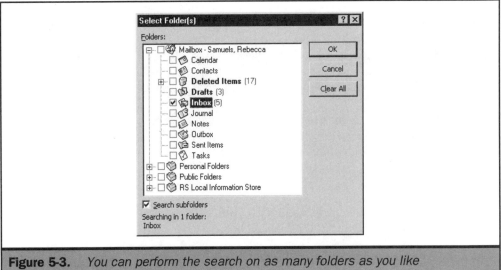

Figure 5-3. *You can perform the search on as many folders as you like*

5. Enter the search criteria in the remaining options on the Messages tab. Your choices include

■ **Search for the word(s)**   Type the words, characters, or phrases you want to search for. One nice thing about this field is that it retains previously entered data for use at a later time. Open the drop-down list to see a selection of previously used words or phrases.

■ **In**   Indicate which text fields you want to include in the search for the designated text. Like The Search For The Word(s) field, the In field also retains previously entered search data that can be accessed from its drop-down list.

■ **From**   If you want to find messages from specific senders, enter their display names or e-mail addresses here. You can also add senders by clicking the From button to display the Select Names dialog box, which provides access to all your address books. However, be careful not to use any display names that contain additional text beyond the actual name. For example, (E-mail) is automatically added to the name of each individual in the Contacts list who has an e-mail address. Consequently, when the search is performed, Outlook looks for only those messages that contain the name *and* the appended text.

■ **Sent To**   This field works the same as the From field, including the caveat about using the Contacts list to select names. The only difference between the two is that the names entered here are searched for in the To, Cc, or Bcc fields in outgoing messages.

- **Where I am**   Indicate whether you're the only recipient, one of multiple recipients in the To field, or one of multiple recipients in the Cc field.

- **Time**   Use this field to search on the basis of a date field, such as Received, Sent, or Due. Select the date field from the first drop-down list, and the time frame from the second drop-down list.

6. Click the More Choices tab to view additional search options (see Figure 5-4).

7. Set the More Choices search criteria. Your options include

- **Categories**   If you assign messages to categories, enter the category or categories to which the messages you're looking for are assigned. There is one thing to note about this field. If you perform a search that includes multiple categories, it will not only locate messages assigned to both but also messages assigned to one or the other. This is because Outlook sticks an implied OR between multiple selections in this field. Unfortunately, there's no way around it.

- **Only items that are**   You can choose to search for messages that have been read or messages that remain unread. Use the drop-down list to make your selection.

- **Only items with**   This option lets you include or exclude items that contain attachments.

- **Whose importance is**   If you know the Importance status of the message(s), put that knowledge to good use by making your selection from this drop-down list.

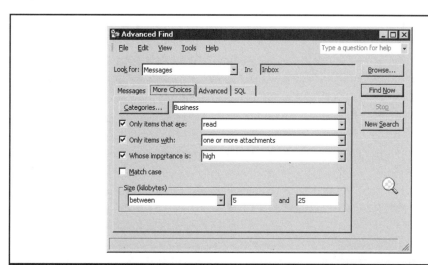

Figure 5-4.   *The More Choices tab provides just that—more choices for narrowing your search*

■ **Match case** If you've entered text in the Search For Word(s) field on the Messages tab, you can use this option to search only for those instances of the word(s) that match the exact case of the text you entered. Check the option to enable it.

■ **Size (kilobytes)** This option can be helpful if you remember receiving a large attachment with your message. Indicate an operator (equals, between, less than, or greater than) and the size.

8. Set the options on the Advanced tab. For more information on setting Advanced options, see Chapter 23.

9. Click Find Now to perform the search. As you can see in Figure 5-5, the results are displayed in a window appended to the Advanced Find dialog box.

Okay, now that you've found the messages you're looking for, what are you going to do with them? Fortunately, you've got quite a few options. You can open them, print them, even move, delete, or reply to them. Right-click one of the messages to display the shortcut menu with available commands.

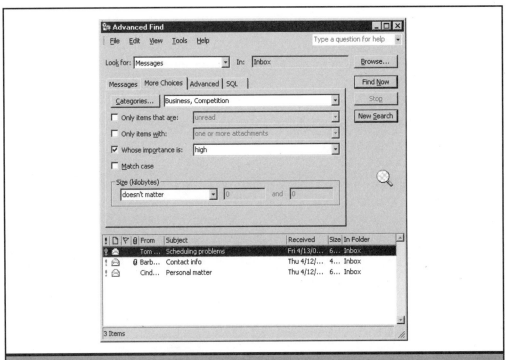

Figure 5-5. *Advanced Find displays header information for all messages meeting your search criteria*

Note

If you receive a task request, a meeting request, or an e-mail message using voting buttons, you'll also find the related options on the shortcut menu. For example, the shortcut menu that appears when you right-click a task request includes Accept and Decline. A meeting request shortcut menu includes Accept, Tentative, and Decline. A voting button message might contain Yes, No, and Maybe, or whatever other choices the sender included. One more thing. If you get a message from the System Administrator, the Reply and Reply to All commands are missing since these messages are automatically generated and no reply is allowed.

In addition to the shortcut menu of commands, the menu bar in the Advanced Find dialog box provides a large selection of commands. While it's not as extensive as the commands available in the Inbox, there's still quite a bit you can accomplish using the Advanced Find menu bar. One last thing. If you want to start over, click the New Search button to clear the existing search criteria and start from scratch.

MOUS

MOUS EXAM PRACTICE
In this section, you learned how to use the Find and Advanced Find features. Now try your hand at searching for messages. Begin by performing a simple text search using the Find feature. Try locating messages with certain data in the various message text fields (Subject, To, Cc, the message body). When you're comfortable with the Find feature, move on to Advanced Find. Search for messages containing a single criterion. Try all the different options. If you don't have mail that meets different criteria, send yourself some. Add attachments, categories, importance levels, or whatever you need. After you find the messages you searched for, perform actions on them using the shortcut menu. Finally, try using some of the commands located on the Advanced Find menu bar.

Applying Filters

The Filter feature provides a means for displaying only selected messages in a folder, while hiding the rest. Filtering is basically an Advanced Find performed on a single folder. Messages that meet the filter (search) conditions appear. Those that fail to meet the conditions are hidden.

As you can see in Figure 5-6, the Filter dialog box is a stripped-down version of the Advanced Find dialog box. Missing are the Look For and (first) In options, as well as the Browse, Find Now, Stop, and New Search buttons, along with the menu bar of commands.

To filter messages, follow these steps:

1. Right-click a blank spot on the Inbox Information viewer below the last message and select Filter to open the Filter dialog box, shown in Figure 5-6. You can also open the Filter dialog box by right-clicking a column header, selecting Customize Current View, and clicking the Filter button on the View Summary dialog box that appears.

Tip   *If you frequently use filters, you might want to add the Filter command to a toolbar or menu for easier access. Open the Customize dialog box, click the Commands tab, and drag the Filter command (which you'll find in the View category) to the toolbar or menu of your choice, and drop it. For more information on customizing menus and toolbars, see Chapter 24.*

2. Enter the filter conditions in the Messages tab. See the earlier section, entitled Locating E-mail Messages, for a detailed explanation of each option.

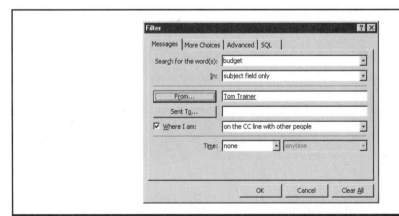

Figure 5-6.   *With the Filter dialog box, you can create filtering rules as simple or as complex as you need*

Don't add any names that have additional text appended to them, such as Contacts list entries that include (E-mail) or (Business Fax). If you do, Outlook will search for the appended text and, when it doesn't find it, exclude the messages even though they may be from the correct party.

3. Set the filter conditions on the More Choices tab. Again, see the earlier section, entitled Locating E-mail Messages, for detailed explanations of these options.

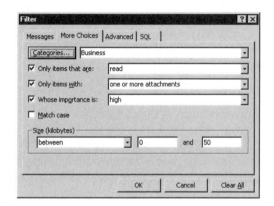

4. Set the options on the Advanced tab to suit your needs. For details on Advanced options, see Chapter 23.

5. Click OK to filter out all messages that do not meet the criteria you established in the Filter dialog box.

When you return to the Inbox or other folder to which you've applied the filter, you'll notice the words (Filter Applied) next to the Folder name on the banner. This comes in handy when you have one of those days and open your Inbox only to find most of your messages missing. Before you panic, check the Folder banner and see if you forgot to remove your last filter.

If the filter doesn't work as anticipated, open the Filter dialog box and carefully examine the conditions you've set. Remember, if your filter contains multiple conditions, the message must meet all conditions or it is excluded. Another common problem encountered by everyone, including the experts, is the ever-popular typo. A single misspelling or transposed number can ruin an otherwise perfect filter.

To remove a filter, reopen the Filter dialog box and click Clear All. Then click OK to return to the active Outlook folder. The filter is removed, all your records reappear, and the (Filter Applied) disappears from the Folder banner.

COMMUNICATING WITH E-MAIL

MOUS EXAM PRACTICE
In this section, you learned to work with filters, a powerful tool for finding and viewing messages based on the particular criteria you define. Now, practice applying all sorts of conditions to your messages to get a feel for exactly how conditions are met and applied. Try creating a filter with a single condition first. Then add a second condition, followed by a third, and so on, until you understand how filtering works.

Switching Views

The Inbox and other mail folders come with a selection of predesigned views. The Message view is the default view for all Outlook mail folders. However, you may find that one of the other views provides a more useful display of your folder contents. To switch between views, choose View | Current View to display the submenu of available views.

Actually, all but the last view, Message Timeline, are variations on the original view: Messages. In most cases, the variation is the application of a filter or a grouping. Occasionally, additional fields are added, as in the case of the By Follow-Up Flag view. The Message Timeline view provides an actual timeline on which the individual messages are plotted chronologically, using the dates in the Received field. Another way to change views is by displaying the Advanced toolbar (right-click anywhere on the Standard toolbar and choose Advanced from the shortcut menu) and using the Current View drop-down list, which contains all the views available in the active folder. You can even add the Current View drop-down list to the Standard toolbar, or others, if you want. See Chapter 24 for details on adding commands to toolbars.

Following Message Threads or Conversations

If you spend any time on newsgroups, you're probably familiar with message threads. They are series of messages all spawned by a single message. Threads include the original message, responses to the original message, responses to the responses, and so on. Message threads, or conversations—as Microsoft likes to call them—are now a feature of Outlook.

Here's the way it works. Every original message contains a hidden field called Conversation, which holds a duplicate of the text entered in the Subject field. When you forward or reply to a message, the text in the Conversation field of the original message is automatically assigned to the Conversation field of the response or forward. The same Conversation field data is passed on to each subsequent reply or forward for as long as the responses/forwards continue. Since the information is contained in a separate Conversation field, you can change the Subject field and still retain the link to the conversation.

As handy as this feature is, there are a couple of things that can throw a monkey wrench into the works. The first is two original messages with identical Subject lines, and therefore, identical Conversation fields. In that case, all messages relating to either will show up in the same message thread or conversation. There's no way around it.

The second thing that can bollix up the works is mail responses or forwards you receive from the Internet. You're fine as long as the responder doesn't change the Subject line. When Outlook receives a reply or forward from an Internet mail account, it strips the RE or FW from the Subject line and enters the remaining text in the Conversation field. If there's no RE or FW it merely inserts the Subject line in the Conversation field.

Now that you understand what message threads are, the next step is to utilize them. Suppose you run into a complex problem and send out a message requesting help from several coworkers, who either respond or forward your note to someone else who might have an answer. By the time you're done, you may have a large number of responses, many of which could possibly contain helpful information. Rather than attempting to sort or apply filters, you can easily gather all the messages together by locating the conversation.

It's actually rather simple. Right-click any message and select Find All | Related Messages to open the Advanced Find dialog box with the search conditions automatically entered on the Advanced tab (see Figure 5-7). The search is conducted automatically, so there's no need for you to do anything except sit back and wait for the results.

You can also locate all messages in a conversation by selecting one message from the thread and choosing Actions | Find All | Related Messages from the Menu bar to open the Advanced Find dialog box and start the search.

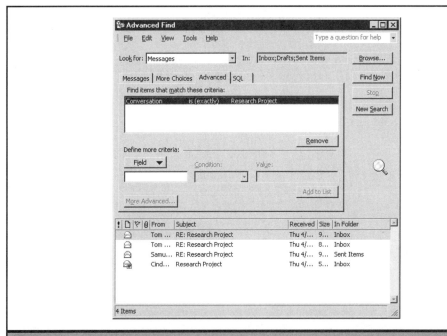

Figure 5-7. *The Advanced Find searches for all messages with matching data in the Conversation field*

Storing E-mail Messages

One reason for e-mail's tremendous popularity is that it provides an electronic "paper trail" of all your important communications. What's especially nice is that, unlike actual paper communications, you can store a vast quantity of e-mail information in a thimbleful of space. As your collection of important e-mail grows, it will lose its value if it's not readily available when you need it. Therefore, you should devise and execute a plan for storing your e-mail so you have ready access to it.

Note *If you're wondering why it's necessary to organize your e-mail at all since Outlook provides such powerful sorting, searching, and filtering tools, the answer is simple. If you can't remember the sender, subject, or other important piece of information that will enable you to find the message(s), those powerful tools will be about as useful as an electric blanket on a wilderness trek. The other thing to consider is efficiency. The larger the number of messages that have to be searched, the longer the search takes, and the greater the chance you'll turn up messages you don't want.*

The storage system provided by Outlook is not unlike the typical filing cabinet storage system used for paper documents. It's just cleaner, quicker, completely searchable, and takes up no floor space at all. Outlook, as you already know, is a folder-based program. Everything in Outlook is stored in folders. By default, the only folders that exist are Calendar, Contacts, Deleted Items, Drafts, Inbox, Journal, Notes, Outbox, Sent Items, and Tasks. Fortunately, you are by no means limited to just those ten folders. As a matter of fact, the number of folders you can have is theoretically unlimited. However, folders stored on the Microsoft Exchange server are limited by three factors: the version of Microsoft Exchange running on the server, the hard disk space available on the server, and any restrictions placed on mailbox folder size by the administrator. If you use Personal Folders to store information, you are limited by the amount of disk space on your computer.

To effectively store your important e-mail, you should create a system of Outlook folders that separates mail either by sender, subject, or some other criterion that suits your purpose. For example, you might create one folder called Vendors and another called Customers. You could then create a series of subfolders under Vendors for each vendor you buy from, and a series of subfolders under Customers for each customer you sell to. Regardless of the system you devise, the process for creating and managing the folders is the same.

Creating Mail Folders

Creating mail folders in Outlook is so easy even your boss could do it. Here's all you have to do:

1. Press CTRL+SHIFT+E, or right-click the Folder banner, or a folder in the Folder List, and select New Folder, to open the Create New Folder dialog box, shown in Figure 5-8.

2. Choose the type of items the folder will hold by clicking the appropriate icon. Since each Outlook folder is a discrete database, it can hold only one type of information. For a mail folder, use the Mail and Post type, which is selected by default.

3. Enter a name for the new folder. Make the name brief and descriptive so you don't have trouble recognizing it in the future. This may sound silly when you only have a few folders in your mailbox or Personal Folders, but as the number of folders grows, so does the potential for confusion. From the Location drop-down list, choose the folder to which you want to add the new folder. You can also click the search button to the right of the list to open the Select a Folder dialog box, which displays all available folders. If you want to create a new folder at the same level as the existing folders, select Mailbox.

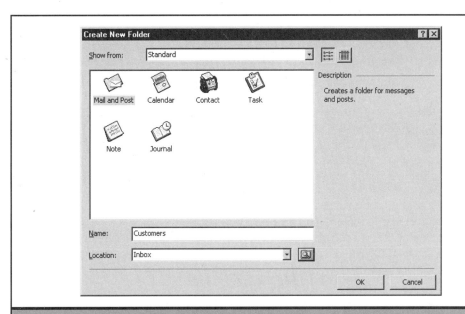

Figure 5-8.   *Use the Create New Folder dialog box to indicate the name, content type, and location of the new folder*

4. Click OK to create the new folder. The first time (and every time, unless you disable the feature), the Add Shortcut To Outlook Bar? dialog box appears.

5. Click Yes if you want a shortcut to the folder added to the Outlook Bar.

To stop Outlook from displaying this dialog box each time you create a new folder, check the Don't Prompt Me About This Again option.

If you already have an existing mail folder you've customized with permissions, rules, forms, and views, you can create a new folder that contains the same customizations by right-clicking the folder you want to copy and selecting Copy [folder name] from the shortcut menu. If you only want to copy certain customizations from the original folder, choose File | Folder | Copy Folder Design to open the Copy Design From dialog box.

Moving and Copying Messages

The next step in organizing your e-mail messages is to move the messages you want to keep into your new storage system. The two main commands you'll need to master for manipulating your messages are Move To Folder and Copy To Folder. You might also brush up on Cut, Copy, and Paste, as well as your drag-and-drop skills since you can also use them to move and copy messages.

The first thing to do is select the messages you want to cut or copy. To select a single message, click the message to highlight it. To select multiple adjacent messages, click the first message in the series, hold down the SHIFT key, and select the last message in the series. Outlook automatically selects everything in-between. You can select multiple non-adjacent messages by selecting the first message, then holding down the CTRL key while selecting additional messages.

To move messages with the Move To Folder command, highlight and press CTRL+SHIFT+V to open the Move Items dialog box.

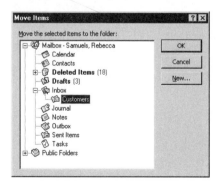

You can also right-click the highlighted message(s) and select Move To Folder from the shortcut menu that appears, or you can choose Edit | Move To Folder.

In the Move Items dialog box, select the folder to which you want to move the highlighted messages, then click OK to complete the move and return to the active Outlook window. If you don't see an appropriate folder to move the messages into, you can create a new folder on the fly. Click the New button to open the Create New Folder dialog box. Enter a name for the new folder, leave the folder type as Mail and Post, and select the location for the new folder. Finally, click OK to create the new folder and return to the Move Items dialog box, where the new folder now appears in the list. If this is the first folder you've created, you'll be prompted to add a shortcut to the Outlook Bar for the new folder. Make your choice and proceed.

The Copy to Folder option works in a similar fashion. Highlight the messages to copy, then choose Edit | Copy To Folder to display the Copy Items dialog box.

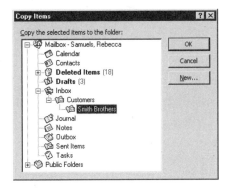

As you can see, the Copy Items dialog box appears identical to the Move To Folder dialog box, except for its name. Choose the folder in which you want to place a copy of the selected messages and click OK to complete the copy.

Although Outlook has specific commands for moving and copying messages from one folder to another, many users find drag and drop is the quickest and easiest way to get the job done. Display the Folder List, open the folder from which you want to move messages, highlight the messages you want to move, drag them to the Folder List, and drop them on the folder you want to move them to. You can also use drag and drop to copy folders. This method, however, requires you use the right mouse button to drag them to the new folder. When you release the right mouse button to drop the messages, choose Copy from the shortcut menu that appears.

Now, if you're experienced with word processors, you'll be happy to know you can use Cut, Copy, and Paste to move and copy messages as well. Highlight the messages you want to move, press CTRL+X to cut or CTRL+C to copy, move to the target folder, and press CTRL+V to paste the messages. You can also invoke the Cut, Copy, and Paste commands from the Edit menu if you prefer.

MOUS

MOUS EXAM PRACTICE

There are a variety of ways to move messages, so you'll want to make sure you familiarize yourself with all of them. Since drag and drop is a technique used for many other Outlook operations, let's begin there. Select one or more messages and drag them to a different mail folder. For practice, drag messages from the Inbox to the Drafts folder, and back again. Next, use the Move To Folder command to accomplish the same results. Finally, try moving messages between folders using copy and paste commands.

Deleting Messages

If storing messages is not in the plans, you may want to do a little housekeeping and get rid of all the unwanted messages hanging around taking up space. Remember, there's probably a size limit on your mailbox, imposed by your system administrator. Therefore, you should limit the amount of unnecessary e-mail you retain. Deleting messages is as simple as highlighting them and pressing the DELETE key. Of course, like most other tasks in Outlook, there are a number of different ways to delete messages. You can highlight the messages and

- Press CTRL+D
- Right-click and select DELETE from the shortcut menu
- Click the Delete button on the Standard toolbar
- Choose Edit | Delete from the Menu bar
- Drag them to the Deleted Items folder

Take your choice—they all accomplish the job of tossing your unwanted messages in the Deleted Items folder. However, before proceeding, there are a couple of things you should know about the Deleted Items folder. First of all, it's actually a way station for messages en route to the electronic ether. The messages (or other Outlook items) are not really deleted, they're just transferred here to await your final decision. Should you change your mind about eliminating a message, you can open the Deleted Items folder and retrieve it. That's the good news.

Note *The Deleted Items folder is like any other Outlook folder. You can set its properties, add subfolders to it, and do practically anything with it you can do to other Outlook folders.*

The bad news is that, in effect, all you've done by deleting a message is move it from one Outlook folder to another. You haven't really cleaned up your mailbox at all. It's kind of like straightening up by throwing everything in the closet and slamming the door shut. So, if you're trying to reduce the size of your mailbox, you'll have to go one step further and empty the Deleted Items folder. Fortunately, this is a simple matter of right-clicking the Deleted Items folder or the Deleted Items shortcut on the Outlook Bar and selecting Empty "Deleted Items" Folder from the shortcut menu. You'll also find the same command on the Tools menu. To ensure you really want to delete the contents of the Deleted Items folder, Outlook asks you to confirm your decision.

Outlook provides one additional safety net in case you're having a really bad day and empty your Deleted Items folder while dazed and confused. It's the Recover Deleted Items command. Highlight the Deleted Items folder and choose Tools | Recover Deleted Items to open the Recover Deleted Items From – Deleted Items dialog box (as shown in Figure 5-9).

Note   *Recover Deleted Items only works on items stored on a Microsoft Exchange server. The version and settings on the Exchange server may affect the ability to retrieve deleted items.*

Select the items you want to recover and click the Recover Selected Items button. Voilà! Your messages are restored to your Deleted Items folder.

Note   *If the Recover Deleted Items From – Deleted Items dialog box doesn't contain the messages you're looking for, the reason is probably that the time limit for retaining deleted items on the server has expired. Check with your system administrator about the length of time deleted items remain on the server, and ask if the missing messages can be recovered from a server backup.*

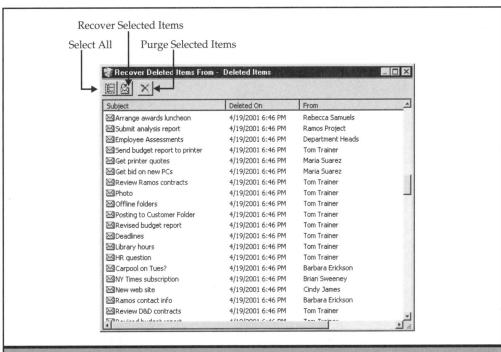

Figure 5-9.   *The Recover Deleted Items command can be a lifesaver when you change your mind about deleting an Outlook item*

The Recover Deleted Items From – Deleted Items dialog box has an additional feature that enables you to permanently delete sensitive messages so they can never be recovered. It's called Purge. Select the message(s) you want to send into electronic oblivion and click the Purge Selected Items button.

Using the Save As Command

In addition to storing messages by moving them to other Outlook folders or by archiving them (discussed later in this chapter), you can also use the Save As command. This not only enables you to save the messages anywhere on your hard disk but also gives you the opportunity to choose the file format of the saved message.

To begin, select a message in one of your mail folders and choose File | Save As to open the Save As dialog box. From the Save In drop-down list, select a drive and folder in which to save the message. By default, the message subject is used for the new message filename. You can change it by entering your own name in the File Name field. Finally, select the file type you want to use for the saved message.

Your choices include

- **Text Only (*.txt)**   Select this format if you want to save the message as a text file. This is ideal if you intend to distribute the message to a variety of users, since all operating systems provide a rudimentary text editor in which the file can be opened.

- **Outlook Template**   Use this format to create an Outlook template, which can then be opened in the Forms Designer and used as the basis for a custom mail form.

- **Message Format (*.msg)**   The message format provides an easy way to save individual messages outside the Outlook environment, while retaining the Outlook format.

- **HTML (*.htm; *.html)**   Since HTML is becoming a universal standard, it should come as no surprise that the default format for saving messages is HTML. This enables anyone with a web browser to open the message.

After you've made your selection, click Save to store a copy of the message on your hard disk.

MOUS EXAM PRACTICE

Using the Save As command is pretty simple, so you shouldn't need a lot of practice. However, since saving them is only half the job, you may want to save a message in all four different formats and practice opening and using each format. You might also use a message saved in the Template format to create a custom form. (See Chapter 25 for more information on designing custom forms.)

Modifying Incoming Message Options

Contrary to what many users think, message options are not just for outgoing messages. There are several ways you can organize your incoming messages by changing their options. These include changing the Importance level, adding or removing flags, changing the expiration date, and assigning messages to contacts and categories.

Reprioritizing Messages

If you've received any mail marked with a high Importance level, you've probably realized that not everyone has the same priorities. What seems extremely important to one person may be of little or no consequence to another. Therefore, when you receive e-mail messages whose Importance setting is inappropriate according to your standards, you can change it.

All you have to do is right-click the message, select Options from the shortcut menu, and choose a different Importance level from the Importance drop-down list. Then click Close to effect the change. Before returning you to the active window, Outlook asks if you want to save the changes. Click Yes to save the new Importance level. When you return to the active window, you'll see that the Importance column now reflects the new Importance level.

Flagging Received E-mail for Future Action (or Inaction)

Follow-up flags serve the purpose of adding comments and reminders to a message, thereby notifying the recipient of any additional action that should be taken concerning the message. There are any number of reasons for changing the flagged status of incoming messages. You may want to add a flag to remind yourself to follow up on the message, or you may want to change the comment or reminder time on a message with an existing flag. Of course, when you've completed the follow-up action, you'll want to either mark the flag as completed or perhaps remove the flag altogether.

To modify an existing flag, select the message and press CTRL+SHIFT+G, or open the message and click the Flag button on the Standard toolbar in the message form. This opens the Flag For Follow Up dialog box containing the flag information.

To change the comment, select a different flag from the Flag To drop-down list. To change the reminder manually, edit the Due By field or select a different date from the drop-down calendar available in the field. You can also change the time manually or make a selection from the drop-down list. Click the Clear Flag button to remove the flag or check the Completed option to mark the flag completed.

To add a flag to a flagless message, right-click the message and select Flag for Follow Up from the shortcut menu. The Flag for Follow Up dialog box appears. Select the desired comment from the Flag To drop-down list, and set the reminder in the Due By field. Then click OK to add the flag. When you return to the mail folder, you'll see a flag icon in the Flagged Status column.

To mark a flag completed, right-click the message and select Flag Complete from the shortcut menu. Using this command changes the comment in the message to indicate the date and time the flag was completed and changes the flag icon from red to gray.

To remove a flag altogether, right-click the message and select Clear Flag from the shortcut menu. The flag icon disappears from the mail folder and the comment line is removed from the message. There is no evidence remaining that the flag ever existed.

Assigning Messages to Contacts and Categories

One of the handiest things about having your e-mail management and your personal information management handled by the same program is the ability to link your messages to other components. One way in which Outlook provides this service is by letting you assign e-mail messages (and other items) to individual contacts. In other words, if you get an e-mail message that comes from or relates to a particular contact, you can assign the message to that contact. The message then appears in the Activities tab of the individual's contact form when you search for All Items or for E-mail Items.

What's nice about this is that you don't actually move the message from its original location; you merely link it to the contact. It can remain in its designated storage folder and still be accessible from the contact's record.

Using categories is another means of organizing your messages that transcends all methods of physically—electronically speaking—arranging your messages. By assigning messages to categories, you can create organizational collections of related messages regardless of which folders they reside in.

To assign an incoming message to a category, right-click the message and choose Categories from the shortcut menu. You can also select the message and choose Edit | Categories to open the Categories dialog box.

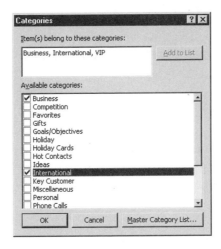

Check the category or categories to which you want to assign the message. Checking a category adds the category name to the Item(s) Belong To These Categories list. Click OK to make the assignment and return to the active Outlook window. You can also assign messages to categories by using the Categories field in the Message Options dialog box. Right-click the desired message and select Options from the shortcut menu to open the Message Options dialog box. Then click the Categories button to display the Categories dialog box.

To view messages by category, right-click any of the column headers in the Information viewer and choose Customize Current View to display the View Summary dialog box.

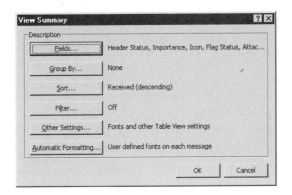

Now, click the Group By button to display the Group By dialog box. From the Group Items By drop-down list, select Categories, and click OK to return to the View Summary dialog box. Click OK to return to the mail folder, which should look something like Figure 5-10.

The easiest way to open the Group By dialog box is to right-click the Information viewer column header and select Group By Box from the shortcut menu. This displays the Group By Box directly above the column headers. It's just a wide, dark gray band the width of the Information viewer that holds field names when a group view is enabled. Double-click anywhere in the Group By Box and the Group By dialog box opens. To hide the Group By Box, right-click a column header and select Group By Box again.

If you're reading the previous tip and thinking it's easier to right-click a blank spot in the Information viewer and select Group By from the shortcut menu, you're only partially right. First of all, if your Inbox is loaded, you have to scroll to the bottom of the Information viewer. Second, if you don't keep your Outlook window maximized you may not be able to find a blank spot at the bottom of the Information viewer, which makes this method entirely useless. The preceding tip works every time, without having to scroll to the bottom of your Information viewer or look for a blank spot.

To view your messages, click the plus sign to the left of the group header to expand the group and display the messages. You can also expand and contract groups by double-clicking anywhere on the header (except the plus sign).

Figure 5-10. *The Group By command organizes your e-mail messages by the categories to which they're assigned*

Note *The Group By feature only works in table and timeline views.*

To remove the category groups, return to the Group By dialog box and select None from the Group Items By drop-down list. Then click OK to return to the active Outlook view.

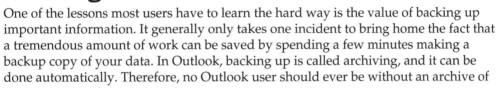

Archiving E-mail

MOUS One of the lessons most users have to learn the hard way is the value of backing up important information. It generally only takes one incident to bring home the fact that a tremendous amount of work can be saved by spending a few minutes making a backup copy of your data. In Outlook, backing up is called archiving, and it can be done automatically. Therefore, no Outlook user should ever be without an archive of important e-mail messages.

Archiving moves messages that meet the archive criteria into a personal folder (.pst) on your hard drive. The directory structure of your mailbox is retained as messages are archived. For example, if you archive a subfolder, the parent folder is created in the archive file to maintain the directory structure, even though the parent folder's contents are not archived.

Using AutoArchive

By default, certain Outlook folders are scheduled for regular AutoArchiving, as the automatic archiving process is called. Unfortunately, the mail folders are not among those set to AutoArchive by default. However, you can schedule AutoArchive to periodically back up your mail folders, and you can perform a manual archive whenever you want.

The first thing you may want to do is set the general AutoArchive options, which include the length of time between archives, whether you want to be prompted before AutoArchiving begins, and the name and location of the default archive file.

To change the basic AutoArchive options, follow these steps:

1. Choose Tools | Options and click the Other tab.

2. Click the AutoArchive button to display the AutoArchive dialog box (seen in Figure 5-11).

3. Set the AutoArchive options to suit your needs. Your choices include

   ■ **Run AutoArchive Every __ Days** Check this option to enable AutoArchiving. Then select the desired number of days you want to pass between AutoArchive sessions. Unless this option is checked, none of the other options is available.

   ■ **Prompt Before AutoArchive Runs** If you want Outlook to warn you before it performs an AutoArchive, check this option.

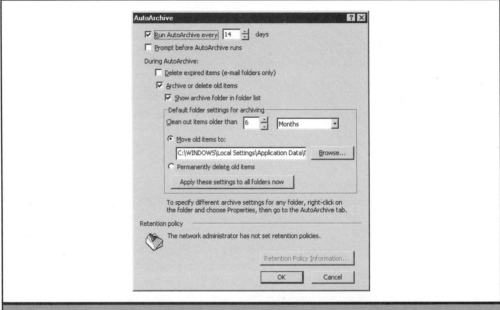

Figure 5-11.   *Use the AutoArchive dialog box to automate your Outlook archiving operations*

- **Delete Expired Items When AutoArchiving (E-Mail Folders Only)**   Only mail items with expiration dates are affected by this option. During an AutoArchive, messages with expiration dates that have passed are moved to the Deleted Items folder if you check this option.

- **Archive Or Delete Old Items**   Check this option if you want to AutoArchive more than just expired e-mail messages. The remaining options become available when this option is enabled.

- **Clean Out Items Older Than**   Indicate the aging criteria you want to use for archiving Outlook items.

- **Move Old Items To**   The location and name of the default archive (.lis) files are shown in this box. To change either one, click the Browse button to open the Find Personal Folders dialog box, where you can select a different archive file or create a new one. The first time you set the AutoArchive options, it's a good idea to change the default archive file to one with a unique name, especially if you share your computer with other Outlook users. The default file is named archive.lis and will end up being used by everyone on the computer, which means multiple users' archive data will all be tossed into one archive file.

- **Permanently Delete Old Items**   If you don't want to retain copies of your Outlook items, you can have AutoArchive simply dump all items meeting the aging criteria in the Deleted Items folder.

- **Apply These Settings To All Folders Now**   The name of this button is somewhat misleading. Rather than actually applying the selected settings to all folders, clicking the button merely forces folders with custom settings to use the default settings. Folders that have AutoArchiving turned off are not affected at all.

- **Retention Policy Information**   Click this button to see the settings for the length of time deleted items are retained, as well as other storage retention policies the system administrator has implemented on the Exchange server.

4. Click OK to close the AutoArchive dialog box and return to the Options dialog box.

5. Click OK to return to the active Outlook window.

Once you have the basic options taken care of, it's time to move on to setting the AutoArchive schedule for the Inbox. Start by right-clicking the Inbox shortcut in the Outlook Bar or the Inbox folder in the Folder List, and selecting Properties from the shortcut menu. Next, click the AutoArchive tab to view the AutoArchive options. As you can see in Figure 5-12, several of the options here are duplicates of those found in the general AutoArchive settings.

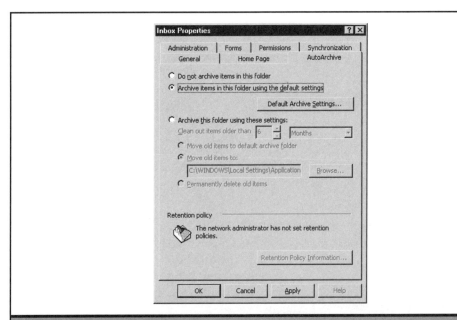

Figure 5-12.   *The folder AutoArchive options lets you set a schedule for archiving each Outlook folder individually*

COMMUNICATING WITH E-MAIL

Select and set the appropriate options from the following:

- **Do Not Archive Items In This Folder**   To turn off AutoArchiving altogether for the folder, select this option.
- **Archive Items In This Folder Using The Default Settings**   Use this option to accept the default options set for AutoArchiving in the Outlook Options dialog box. Click the Default Archive Settings button to see the current defaults.
- **Archive This Folder Using These Settings**   Select this option to customize the AutoArchive settings for this folder. In the Clean Out Items Older Than option, enter the number of days, weeks, or months you want to use to determine the age limit of items retained in your Inbox. Select the action you want applied to those messages that meet the criteria:
- **Move Old Items To**   Check this option to save archived items to the archive folder listed in the textbox below the option. To change the archive folder, click Browse and select a different .pst file.
- **Permanently Delete Old Items**   The operative word here is "permanently." Check this option only if you want to delete messages meeting the age criteria, never to see them again. They do not go to the Deleted Items folder, and they are not available for recovery using the Recover Deleted Items command.
- **Retention Policy Information**   Click this button to see any restrictions imposed on your mailbox by the system administrator.

When an AutoArchive is performed, any messages that meet the age requirement are moved from the Inbox to the archive file or permanently deleted depending on your selection. That's all there is to it. Now click OK to save the settings and return to the active Outlook window.

An AutoArchive will be performed the next time you start Outlook after the appropriate time period indicated in the AutoArchive dialog box has passed.

When Outlook performs an AutoArchive, it indicates the AutoArchive progress on the right side of the status bar at the bottom of the Outlook window. If you decide you want to stop the archive for any reason, click the down arrow to the right of the archive indicator and choose Cancel Archiving from the shortcut menu that appears.

Archiving Manually

As good as AutoArchive is, it can't handle every possible situation. Suppose you've just received a ton of important e-mail or created a new folder that contains valuable data, and your next AutoArchive session isn't scheduled for a few days. You could wait for the upcoming AutoArchive and hope nothing happens to your data, or you could archive it manually. The smart money is on archiving it manually.

To perform a manual archive, follow these steps:

1. Choose File | Archive from the Menu bar to open the Archive dialog box.

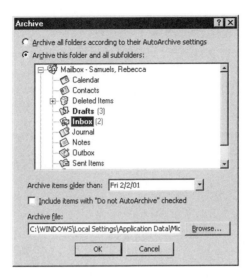

2. Select the type of archive to perform by choosing one of the first two options:

- **Archive all folders according to their AutoArchive settings**   Instead of waiting for the next scheduled AutoArchive, you can accelerate the schedule by selecting this option. Everything is done automatically using the existing AutoArchive settings for each folder.

- **Archive this folder and all subfolders**   If you want to archive individual folders or folders not scheduled for AutoArchive, or you want to change the age criteria, use this option.

3. If you selected **Archive All Folders According To Their AutoArchive Settings**, skip to Step 5. Otherwise, select the folder(s) you want to include in this manual archive.

4. Set the remaining archive options:

- **Archive Items Older Than**   Enter a date or select one from the drop-down calendar to determine the items you want included in this archive.

- **Include Items With "Do Not AutoArchive" Checked**   Select this option to archive items marked Do Not AutoArchive. To see if a message is marked Do Not AutoArchive, open the message and choose File | Properties from the message form menu bar.

- **Archive File**   Select the archive file into which you want the selected folders archived. Click the Browse button to select a different archive file.

5. Click OK to start the archive.

As is the case with an AutoArchive, you can watch the progress of the archive in the Outlook window status bar. To cancel the archive, click the down arrow to the right of the archive indicator and choose Cancel Archiving from the shortcut menu that appears.

COMMUNICATING WITH E-MAIL

Troubleshooting Archive Problems

As simple and straightforward as archiving and AutoArchiving seem to be, there are a few problems that can turn an archiving session into a nightmare. When you perform an archive, whether it's an AutoArchive or a manual archive, and nothing seems to happen, or not all the messages that should be archived are archived, don't panic. There's probably a simple solution.

The most common reason for messages not being archived is because they don't meet the criteria necessary for inclusion. Unfortunately, the criteria used by the Outlook archiving feature (manual or AutoArchive) to determine the age of messages is not, as you might think, the date of the message, whether it's the Received or Sent date. The date Outlook uses to determine the age of items is the Modified date, a hidden field that changes when you perform one of the following actions on the item:

- Forward the item
- Reply to the item
- Reply to All
- Edit and Save the item
- Move or Copy the item

The last set of actions, Move and Copy, changes the Modified date of items in the mailbox folders, but not in Personal Folders. If you move or copy items within Personal Folders or from mailbox folders to Personal Folders, the Modified date does not change. However, if you move or copy an item from a Personal Folder to a mailbox item, the Modified date does change.

To view the Modified date of messages, follow these steps:

1. Open the mail folder containing the messages you want to archive.

2. Right-click one of the column headers in the Information viewer and choose Field Chooser to display the Field Chooser.

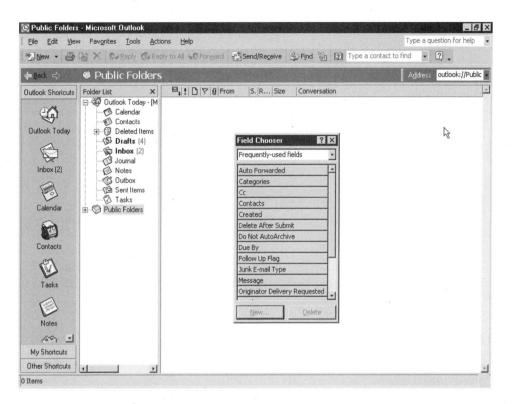

3. From the drop-down list of field sets (Frequently-Used Fields appears by default), select All Mail Fields.

4. Scroll down the list of fields and locate Modified.

5. Drag the Modified field to the Information viewer header and drop it when a pair of red arrows appears above and below the header row. The arrows indicate the point at which the new field header will be inserted.

When you drop the field on the header row, a new header for the field appears at the insertion point indicated by the red arrows. Now the Modified date for messages in the folder appears in the column below the header. If your messages have not been archiving as you expected, this date is probably the reason.

Although the Modified date is the most likely culprit, there is another problem that can cause an archive to malfunction—the simple fact that you've exceeded your mailbox limits. Creating an archive requires messages to be copied on the server first. If you're at or near your mailbox limit, there won't be enough room to make the necessary copies. Check with your administrator to see if this is the problem.

Retrieving Archived Messages

Now that you've got your messages safely tucked away in an archive file, there remains one last thing to consider: how to access them should the need arise. The answer is quite simple since Outlook automatically adds a set of Archive folders to your profile when you perform an archive operation. If you haven't designated a custom .pst archive file, Outlook uses the default file C:\Windows\Local Settings\ Application Data\Microsoft\Outlook\archive.pst. To access the archived items, open the Folder List and use the Archive folders the way you use all other Outlook folders.

Caution   *At the time of this writing, Outlook did not automatically create a set of archive folders the first time you archive. Instead, it attempted to use your existing Personal Folders file, if you already created one. Be sure to create a separate archive file (name it Archive.pst for easy identification) to ensure your personal folder data and your archived data don't end up in the same file. With any luck, the bug will be fixed by the time you read this.*

To remove an archive file from your Folder List, right-click the archive folder and select Close "[file name]" from the shortcut menu. To open an existing Personal Folder file, choose File | Open | Outlook Data File to display the Create or Open Outlook Data File dialog box. Locate the existing file, or enter a name for a new file, and click OK. If you have an old (or new) Personal Folders archive file, you can also import the archived data and return it to its original folder rather than open it in a separate set of archive folders. To import messages from your archive file, use the Import and Export Wizard:

1. Choose File | Import And Export from the Menu bar to start the Import and Export Wizard, shown in Figure 5-13.

2. Select Import From Another Program Or File, and click Next.

3. Scroll down the list of file types and select Personal Folder File (.pst). Then click Next to display the File To Import options in the Import Personal Folders dialog box.

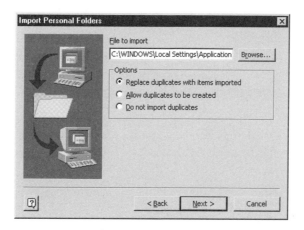

4. Click the Browse button to display the Open Personal Folders dialog box, from which you can locate the archive file.

5. Set the remaining options, which include

   ■ **Replace Duplicates With Items Imported**   If the imported data includes items identical to those already contained in the folder into which you're importing the data, the existing items will be replaced with ones being imported.

   ■ **Allow Duplicates To Be Created**   Select this option to create a duplicate item rather than replace an existing item with an identical imported item.

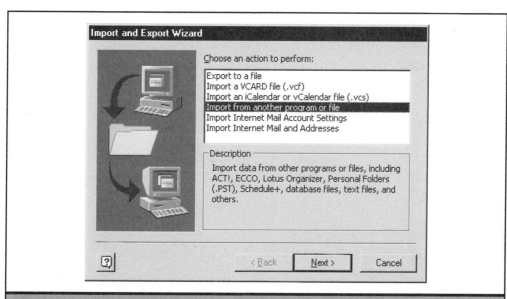

Figure 5-13.   *Retrieving your archived messages is a breeze with the Import and Export Wizard*

■ **Do Not Import Duplicates** This option prevents duplicate items from being imported at all.

6. Click Next to display options for the source folder(s) and the target folder(s).

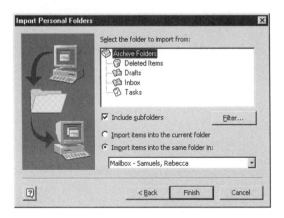

7. Select the top-level folder (Archive Folders in the previous illustration) to import items from all folders, or select a single folder to limit the import to that folder.

8. Set the remaining options:

   ■ **Include Subfolders** Check this option to import the contents of any subfolders of the folder selected in Step 7.

   ■ **Import Items Into The Current Folder** Enable this option to use the folder you were in when you launched the Import and Export Wizard as the target folder for imported items.

   ■ **Import Items Into The Same Folder In** Choose this option and make a selection from the drop-down list to import the items into a mailbox or set of personal or public folders.

   ■ **Filter** To apply filtering conditions to the imported items, click this button, which opens the Filter dialog box. For more information on using filters, see the section entitled Applying Filters, earlier in this chapter.

9. Click Finish to start the import.

After the import finishes, the imported items should appear in the appropriate folder(s). The import process does not move archived items but rather places copies of the archived items into the target folders. Therefore, the archived file remains unchanged by the import process.

COMMUNICATING WITH E-MAIL

MOUS EXAM PRACTICE

In this section, you learned about archiving, one of the most important tasks you can perform in Outlook. Now, begin your practice by setting the general AutoArchive options found on the Other tab of the Options dialog box. Next, open the properties dialog boxes for each of your mail folders and set the AutoArchive options for each folder. Then try your hand at performing a manual archive. After you feel comfortable getting your important data into an archive file, practice getting it back out. Next, use the Import and Export Wizard to retrieve archived items into your existing folders. As you're working with the archive feature, whether automatic or manual, remember that Outlook uses the hidden Modified date field to determine which messages meet the age criteria.

Printing E-mail Messages

No matter how much you love electronic communication and storage technology, there are bound to be times when nothing short of a printed copy (hard copy) of your messages will do. Some messages are important enough to save a copy in every medium available to you, including hard copy. Perhaps you're on your way to a meeting and will need a copy to reference during the meeting. There are any number of reasons for printing messages you receive in Outlook. Fortunately, the process is simple, as long as you're connected to a printer.

Printing Basics

To make a quick printed copy of a message, select the message in the Inbox (or other mail folder) Information viewer and click the Print button located on the Standard toolbar. Outlook immediately sends the message to the installed printer designated as the default printer.

If you want to print multiple messages all at the same time, highlight the messages you want to print and click the Print button. Unless you change the default print options, multiple messages print continuously without a page break between messages. If you want each message on its own page, you must enable the Start Each Item On A New Page option in the Print dialog box. Be advised that if your default mail format is HTML, you cannot print multiple messages on the same page. It's the result of a bug that automatically checks, and then disables, the option when you have multiple messages selected. If you want more than just a quick hard copy of your messages, or if you want a report that lists your messages and includes basic header information, you may want to customize the Outlook print options.

If you want a hard copy of an e-mail message, but want to keep the sender (or recipients) confidential, you can prevent some or all of the header information from appearing on the printout. Open the message and choose Tool | Forms | Design This Form to open the message in the Design mode. Then right-click the header field you want to hide in the printout and choose Properties from the shortcut menu. Click the Validation tab and remove the check mark from the Include This Field For Printing And Save As option. Click OK to save the change, then press ALT+F4 to close the message form. Answer Yes when asked if you want to save changes. The next time you print the message, the header information you deselected does not appear on the printout.

Setting Print Options

Like most other Outlook features, printing offers a number of customization options, enabling you to control the way Outlook prints your messages and reports. You can determine how many copies to print, which pages of a multipage message print, whether you want each message printed on a separate page, and more.

To set the Outlook print options, follow these steps:

1. Choose File | Print or press CTRL+P to open the Print dialog box, seen in Figure 5-14.

Another Outlook printing bug disables most of the printing options when you select a single HTML message from the Information viewer and open the Print dialog box (the problem does not appear if you select multiple messages). To regain the lost print options, open the message first, then choose File | Print from the message form menu bar. This opens the print dialog box used by Internet Explorer, which contains most of the same print options.

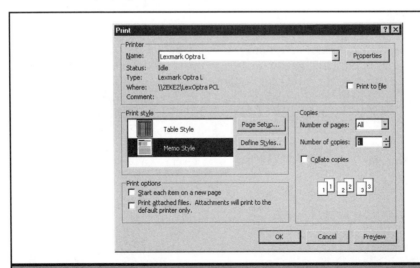

Figure 5-14.   *The Print dialog box is your print options control center*

2. Set the printer options, which include

- **Name**   From the Name drop-down list, select the printer you want to use.

- **Properties**   Click this button to display the properties dialog box for the selected printer. What you see here depends entirely on the printer you select from the Name drop-down list.

- **Print to file**   If you want to create a print file rather than a hard copy, check this option. The message is then sent to a file, which you can later use to print a hard copy.

3. Choose the print style and set the print style options:

- **Table Style**   Select this style to print your message information as it appears in the Information viewer.

- **Memo Style**   This is the default style, which prints both the header information and contents of each message selected.

- **Page Setup**   Click Page Setup to display the Page Setup dialog box for the selected print style. Here you can modify the font used, as well as the type and size of paper. You can also set margins and orientation, and even add headers and footers to the style.

- **Define Styles**   If you want to create your own custom style, click this button and select the style you want to use as the foundation for the new style. You can then customize all the Page Setup properties for the new style.

4. Configure the print options:

- **Start each item on a new page**   If you select multiple items for printing, check this option to ensure each message prints on a separate page. If this option is not checked, multiple messages print continuously, squeezing as many messages as will fit on each page.

- **Print attached files. Attachments will print to the default printer only.** If the message you're printing has an attachment that is printable, select this option to print it at the same time the message prints. If the attachment is an Outlook item, it prints on a separate page. However, for other files, you must have a program installed that can open the attachment for printing. Depending on the document type, you may see the Opening Mail Attachment dialog box, which asks if you want to open the message or save it to disk. If you know the source of the file and want to print it, choose to open the message. If you have a program installed that is associated with this file type, it will print; otherwise, Outlook informs you there is no program associated and it cannot print the attachment.

COMMUNICATING WITH E-MAIL

5. Set the Copies options next:

- **Number of pages** If the message is a multipage message, select the pages you want to print. Your choices include All, Even, and Odd.

- **Number of copies** Indicate the number of copies of the selected message(s) you want to print.

- **Collate copies** This feature comes in handy when printing multiple copies of multipage messages. It prints out a full copy of the message before starting on copy two. Without this option selected, all copies of page one are printed, followed by all copies of page two, and so on. You then have to collate (arrange in sequence) the message pages when you're finished printing. The only reason not to select this option is that it can be rather time-consuming if you're printing large messages, large quantities, or both. Normally, a print job is sent to the printer once, and multiple copies are printed from the same information. However, with Collate Copies enabled, the print job is re-sent each time a new copy is started.

6. Click OK to start the print job.

If you want to see what the printout will look like before actually printing it, click the Preview button. This gives you a fair representation of how the printed document will appear.

MOUS

MOUS EXAM PRACTICE
Start your practice by printing a single message from the Inbox. Then open the message and print it. Now, in the Information viewer, hold down the CTRL key and select a number of different messages to print. Next, set the print options. Select a couple of messages in the Inbox and open the Print dialog box. Print the messages continuously, and then set the appropriate option to print each message separately. Then try printing two copies of a message. You might also print the Information viewer contents using the Table Style. If you have any messages with attachments, try printing them and note what happens to the different attachment types.

◼ MOUS Exam Core Objectives Explored in Chapter 5

Objective	Activity	Heading
OL10-1-1	Print messages	"Printing E-mail Messages"
OL10-3-1	Move messages between folders	"Moving and Copying Messages"
OL10-3-2	Searching for messages	"Locating E-mail Messages"
OL10-3-3	Save messages in alternate file formats	"Using the Save As Command"
OL10-3-5	Set message options	"Archiving E-mail"

◼ MOUS Exam Expert Objectives Explored in Chapter 5

Objective	Activity	Heading
OL10E-2-2	Filter and organize messages	"Applying Filters"

COMMUNICATING WITH E-MAIL

Chapter 6

Setting E-mail Options

If there's one thing Outlook has plenty of, it's options. The e-mail client, being one of the most important components of Outlook, has more than its share. The e-mail options include everything from setting the default message format to selecting the punctuation character used for separating addresses in outgoing messages. By judiciously enabling and disabling the desired options, you can ensure that Outlook e-mail functions precisely the way you want it to.

Setting E-mail Options

The first and primary set of options is aptly named E-mail Options. These settings let you decide how Outlook handles messages as well as replies and forwards. To access the E-mail Options, choose Tools | Options from the Menu bar, then click the E-mail Options button on the Preferences tab to open the E-mail Options dialog box shown in Figure 6-1.

As you can see, the first set of options is the Message Handling group, which includes the following:

■ **After moving or deleting an open item**   From this drop-down list, select the action you want Outlook to take after you move or delete an open message. You can have Outlook open either the next or the previous message, or simply

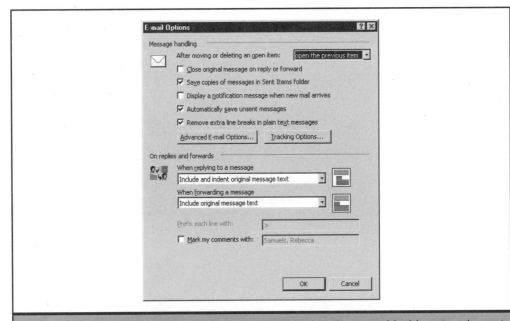

Figure 6-1.   *Customizing the Outlook e-mail client is a breeze with this extensive set of options*

close the Message window and return to the Inbox Information viewer where you can select your own message to open.

■ **Close original message on reply or forward**   Unless you check this option, the original message remains open, even after you click Reply or Forward. Once you respond to a message in such a manner, you can have Outlook close the original message by checking this option.

■ **Save copies of messages in Sent Items folder**   If you want to maintain a record of e-mail you send to others, this option is a must! When you enable this option, a copy of every message you send is automatically saved in the Sent Items folder.

■ **Display a notification message when new mail arrives**   Turned off by default, this option, when enabled, results in a small notification message displaying each time a new message arrives in your Inbox. This includes messages that are moved to other folders by any rules you create, since all messages are deposited in the Inbox before rules are applied. However, it's interesting to note that you do not receive a notification if you happen to be in the folder to which a message is sent when the message arrives. So keep your eyes open.

■ **Automatically save unsent messages**   If you get a lot of phone calls or other interruptions, you'll probably want to enable this option. Every three minutes, it saves a copy of any open messages you're working on to the Drafts folder. In the event your system crashes or you close the unfinished message, you can return to the Drafts folder and pick up where you left off.

■ **Remove extra line breaks in plain text messages**   Since not all e-mail programs are created equal, the inclusion of line breaks in plain text messages varies from program to program. Enable this option to clean up extra line breaks in incoming e-mail messages.

■ **Advanced E-mail Options**   Click this button to display the Advanced E-mail Options dialog box, described in detail later in this chapter in the section entitled "Configuring Advanced E-mail Settings."

■ **Tracking Options**   This button opens the Tracking Options dialog box, which is covered later in this chapter in the section entitled "Selecting E-mail Tracking Options."

The next set of options available in the E-mail Options dialog box is the On Replies And Forwards options. These options give you the opportunity to determine how the contents of the original message are handled, as well as any comments you add to the reply or forward. Frequently, when replying to a message, you want to include all or part of the original message to ensure there's no confusion about your reply. When forwarding a message, there's no doubt about including the original message, but Outlook lets you decide how you want the original message included.

Unfortunately, Outlook does not provide a simple way to include only part of the original message in your reply. Therefore, you have two choices. You can leave the original message out of your reply and copy and paste those parts of the original message you want included, or you can include the original message and use the Mark My Comments With option. You can then insert your comments in the original message and delete those parts that don't require responses.

 The small display boxes to the right of the first two options provide a crude preview of the way your reply or forward will look with the options you select.

The options for replies and forwards include

- **When replying to a message**   From this drop-down list, choose the manner in which you want the original message handled when replying. You can choose to leave it out of your reply, include it as an attachment, include the text, include but indent the text, or include the text and precede each line with a special character separating it from your comment. One minor fly in the ointment: If you use the Outlook e-mail editor rather than Word, the Include And Indent Original Message Text option fails to indent the original text when replying to a Plain Text message.

- **When forwarding a message**   Your options for forwarding a message are identical to those for replying, with one exception. There is no option to *not* include the original message, which makes sense since the object of forwarding is to pass the original message on to someone else.

- **Prefix each line with**   If you elect to prefix the lines of the original message when including it with a reply or forward, this option becomes available. Enter the character(s) you want to use to set the original message apart from your reply or note. Regardless of the e-mail editor you use, the prefix character only appears in Plain Text messages. If you use Word as your e-mail editor, HTML and Rich Text messages are indented, but no prefix is used. If, on the other hand, you use the Outlook e-mail editor, the HTML messages are offset by a vertical blue line running down the left margin, while Rich Text messages are simply indented.

- **Mark my comments with**   If you want to leave the original message intact, and insert comments where needed, use this option to insert your name, initials, or some other appropriate text, in brackets, preceding your comments. This option does not work when replying to Plain Text messages if you're using the Outlook e-mail editor.

Any changes you make in the E-mail Options dialog box take effect as soon as you click OK twice (once to close the E-mail Options dialog box, and again to close the Options dialog box), and return to the active Outlook window.

Configuring Advanced E-mail Settings

While the basic e-mail options cover basic message handling, and reply and forward handling, the Advanced E-mail Options dialog box deals with saving and sending messages, as well as enabling e-mail notification. Here you'll discover options to change the time between AutoSaves of unsent messages, to set the default sensitivity and importance of outgoing messages, and more.

To change the advanced settings, follow these steps:

1. Choose Tools | Options to open the Options dialog box.

2. Click the E-mail Options to display the E-mail Options dialog box.

3. Click the Advanced E-mail Options button to open the Advanced E-mail Options dialog box shown in Figure 6-2.

4. Set the Save Messages options, which include:

   ■ **Save unsent items in**   From this drop-down list, select the mail folder into which you want unsent items saved. Your choices are limited to the four standard mail folders: Drafts, Inbox, Sent Items (incorrectly listed as Sent Mail), and Outbox. Unless you have a good reason for changing this option, it's best left at Drafts. Storing unsent messages anywhere else will be confusing at best.

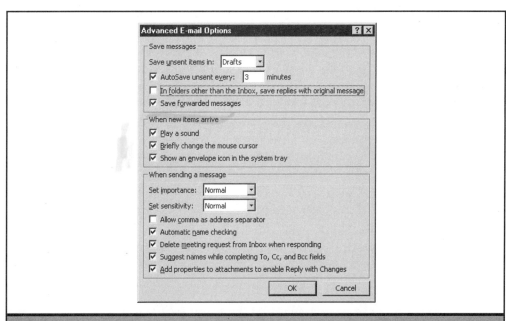

Figure 6-2.   *Fine tuning Outlook e-mail is easy when you use advanced options*

COMMUNICATING WITH E-MAIL

■ **AutoSave unsent every __ minutes**   Check this option to automatically save unsent messages to the folder indicated in the previous option. Set the number of minutes between saves. The maximum time between saves is 99 minutes. If you type a long message without stopping, the AutoSave feature does not kick in until about 15 to 20 seconds after you stop typing, regardless of the number of minutes you set.

■ **In folders other than the Inbox, save replies with original message**   If you save and reply to messages in a folder other than the Inbox, you can check this option to have copies of replies or forwards saved in the same folder as the original message. When the option is disabled, replies and forwards are saved (along with other sent mail) in the Sent Items folder regardless of the location of the original message. This option works in conjunction with two other options: the Save Copies Of Messages In Sent Items Folder option in E-mail Options, and Save Forwarded Messages In Advanced E-mail Options.

■ **Save forwarded messages**   If you want copies of forwards saved in your Sent Items folder or other designated folder (see previous option), check this option.

5. Next, set the arrival notification options.

■ **Play a sound**   With this option checked, Outlook plays the Windows New Mail Notification sound every time a new message arrives in your Inbox. To change the sound, open the Sounds applet in the Windows Control Panel (Start | Settings | Control Panel | Sounds or Start | Settings | Control Panel | Sounds and Multimedia in Windows 2000 or Windows Me) and select the Windows New Mail Notification event. Then click the Browse button to select another sound file with which to replace it.

■ **Briefly change the mouse cursor**   Check this option and your mouse pointer briefly changes to a mail symbol each time a new piece of e-mail arrives.

■ **Show an envelope icon in the system tray**   When this option is enabled, a small envelope appears in the system tray on your Windows taskbar when new mail arrives. Double-click the icon to bring Outlook to the foreground so you can open your new mail. Once you've opened all the new mail, the icon disappears.

6. Set the When Sending A Message options.

■ **Set importance**   Make your selection from the drop-down list to set the default importance level for outgoing messages. All messages you send, including replies, are sent with the importance level you set here. Forwards are not affected by this option, and retain their default importance level of Normal. Of course, you can still change the importance level of individual messages as you see fit, regardless of the setting in this option.

- **Set sensitivity** Similar to Set Importance, this option enables you to set the default sensitivity level for outgoing messages. However, this option only applies to new outgoing messages and not to replies or forwards.

- **Allow comma as address separator** By default, Outlook uses a semicolon as the separator between addresses in a message with multiple recipients in the To, Cc, or Bcc fields. With this option checked, you can use either a semicolon or a comma as the separator when you enter addresses manually. Note, however, that Outlook automatically replaces commas you enter with semicolons.

- **Automatic name checking** If you enter addresses manually, it's a good idea to leave this option enabled. It double-checks the address you entered to ensure it is either in one of your address books or is a valid Internet address. If the address is valid, it's underlined. However, when it comes to Internet addresses, Outlook is only interested in the format. In other words, any Internet address that conforms to the Internet address format (username@domainname) is considered valid, regardless of whether or not the address appears in your address books. If multiple addresses are found, the address you entered is underlined with a red wavy line. Right-click to view the other available addresses. If multiple addresses are found, but one has previously been used, the name is underlined with a green, broken line to remind you there are other addresses. If you type a partial name or address, and only one matching entry is found, Outlook automatically enters the matching entry in the address field as soon as you move to another field.

- **Delete meeting request from Inbox when responding** If you want Outlook to do a little housecleaning on its own check this option. When it's enabled, any meeting request to which you respond is automatically removed from your Inbox.

- **Suggest names while completing To, Cc, and Bcc fields** This is a new option that adds autocompletion to e-mail forms. With this option checked, Outlook checks the text you entered in the To, Cc, and Bcc fields and compares it with entries in your address books. As it finds matches, it offers to complete the name for you. If it finds the right one you can press the ENTER key to accept it. If you're unhappy with the suggestion, keep typing.

- **Add properties to attachments to enable Reply with Changes** Check this option if you would like to be able to modify an attachment and reply to the original sender.

7. Click OK to save the new settings and return to the E-mail Options dialog box. Then click OK again to return to the Options dialog box, and finally click OK a third time to return to the active Outlook window.

The new settings take effect immediately.

COMMUNICATING WITH E-MAIL

Selecting E-mail Tracking Options

E-mail tracking options provide you with a means of controlling the way in which Outlook handles requests (meeting and task), read receipts, and voting responses. You can determine when and how requests and responses are processed, how to handle Internet e-mail requests for read receipts, and more.

For tracking options to work as expected, you must be exchanging e-mail with Outlook users who are on a Microsoft Exchange Server–compatible mail system. Delivery and read receipts returned as plain text messages are not recognized by Outlook as true receipts, and as a result are not tracked.

Follow these instructions to set Outlook tracking options:

1. Choose Tools | Options and click the E-mail Options button to display the E-mail Options dialog box.

2. Click the Tracking Options button to open the Tracking Options dialog box seen in Figure 6-3.

Processing responses and receipts can be performed manually or automatically. When a response or receipt notification is opened or deleted, it is manually logged. When you set automatic processing options, the responses and receipt notifications are logged automatically, regardless of whether or not you open or delete the notifications. However, for automatic logging to occur, certain conditions must be met. The receipt must remain in the Inbox folder, the original message you sent with the request must remain in the Sent Items folder, and a period of approximately one minute must pass with no mouse or keyboard activity.

3. Set the desired options from the following:

   ■ **Process requests and responses on arrival**   This option automatically logs voting button responses, as well as meeting and task request responses. For voting button responses, you can see the results on the tracking tab of the original message you sent. Task request responses are indicated on the information bar of the original sent message. Meeting request responses are logged in the meeting request form itself, not in the e-mail message sent.

   ■ **Process receipts on arrival**   This option automates the processing of incoming receipts. If you receive a delivery or read receipt notification from a message you've sent that included requests for either, the receipt(s) will be logged on the Tracking tab of the sent message even if you don't open the receipt notification. If this option is disabled, the receipts are not logged until you manually process them (open or delete them). By the way, the Help files tell you this option automatically deletes delivery and receipt notifications. Unfortunately, the Help files are wrong.

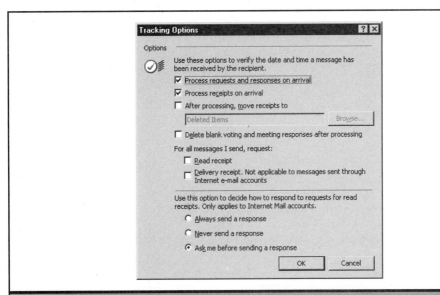

Figure 6-3. *The Tracking Options dialog box contains a multitude of options for automating the processing of requests, responses, and receipts*

- **After processing, move receipts to**   Use this option to move notification receipts to another folder after they've been processed either manually or automatically. Of course, the target folder must be a mail folder.

- **Delete blank voting and meeting responses after processing**   Voting button and meeting request responses in which the recipient only selects the desired button (and does *not* edit the response) are automatically sent to the Deleted Items folder after the response has been processed. Task responses, which are not affected by this option, are always deleted after they are processed.

- **Request a read receipt for all messages I send**   Select this option to automatically include a request for a read receipt on all your outgoing messages, including meeting and task requests. You can override this setting on individual messages by changing the option in the message Options (regular e-mail) or Properties (task and meeting requests) dialog box.

- **Request a delivery receipt for all messages I send**   If you want to make sure all your outgoing messages make it to their destinations, check this option. All outgoing messages, including task and meeting requests, are automatically sent with a delivery receipt requested. You can also override this setting for individual messages. (C/W configuration only.)

- **Always send a response**   This and the next two options apply only to Internet e-mail accounts. Use these options to handle read and delivery receipt requests from Internet e-mail senders. Check Always Send A Response if you want Outlook to automatically generate and send the appropriate notification in response to a request.

- **Never send a response**   With this option checked, Outlook always ignores requests for receipts from Internet mail messages.

- **Ask Me Before Sending A Response**   Check this option to instruct Outlook to prompt you for approval before sending a response.

4. Click OK until you return to the active Outlook window.

As soon as you return to Outlook, the new options take effect. Some options are retroactive, while others only work on new responses or receipts. The processing options (the first two) only work on new items. The move option (third) works on existing items that meet the conditions.

Changing the Default Message Format

Outlook gives you three options for the default format for outgoing messages. To ensure that any recipient can receive and read your message, there is Plain Text. For fancier-looking e-mail, you can use HTML or Rich Text, both of which permit font and paragraph formatting. However, when selecting either of the last two formats you run the risk of a recipient receiving a message that appears differently from what you sent. They may not be able to read the message at all. When exchanging e-mail with other Outlook users, you can use any of the formats without worry. However, when exchanging e-mail with users who employ a different e-mail client, it's always a good idea to try a sample message to be sure their software is compatible with Outlook when it comes to message formatting in anything other than Plain Text.

To change the default message format, choose Tools | Options to open the Options dialog box. Then click the Mail Format tab to set format, signature, and stationery and font options for outgoing messages as shown in Figure 6-4. See Chapter 19 for more on signatures and stationery.

From the Compose In This Message Format drop-down list, choose the default format for outgoing messages. You can always change the message format for individual messages before sending them.

In addition to setting the default format for messages, you can also elect to use Microsoft Word as your default e-mail editor by selecting Use Microsoft Word To Edit E-mail Messages. Since Word automatically converts Rich Text files, you may want to use Word to read incoming RTF messages. Check the Use Microsoft Word To Read Rich Text E-mail Messages option. This will ensure that all formatting in the message is retained.

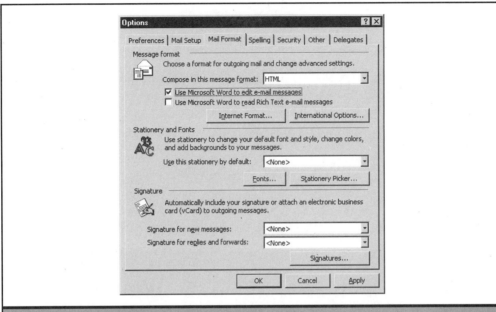

Figure 6-4. *Mail Format options provide plenty of control over how your messages appear*

Setting Format Options for Internet E-mail

Outlook now contains a set of e-mail format options that apply exclusively to Internet e-mail. To access these options, choose Tools I Options I Mail Format and click the Internet Format button to display the Internet Format dialog box seen in Figure 6-5.

For outgoing HTML messages containing references to images on the Internet, you can check the first option. This adds a copy of the Internet image(s) rather than simply pointers to the location of the picture(s) on the Internet.

Since there's no guarantee that recipients of your Internet e-mail will have a Rich Text–compliant e-mail program, you can instruct Outlook to automatically convert Rich Text messages to HTML or Plain Text messages. This comes in handy when sending a message to multiple recipients, some of whom are on your Exchange server network, and others who are Internet recipients.

The final set of options pertains to Plain Text messages. The first sets the number of characters at which text wraps automatically. Since many e-mail clients use shorter text wrapping settings, you might want to reduce this number to improve the appearance of your messages when people reply to them.

The last Plain Text option instructs Outlook to use the UUENCODE format for attachments you include with plain text messages. Select this format when exchanging e-mail with UNIX e-mail clients or other non-MIME-compatible e-mail programs.

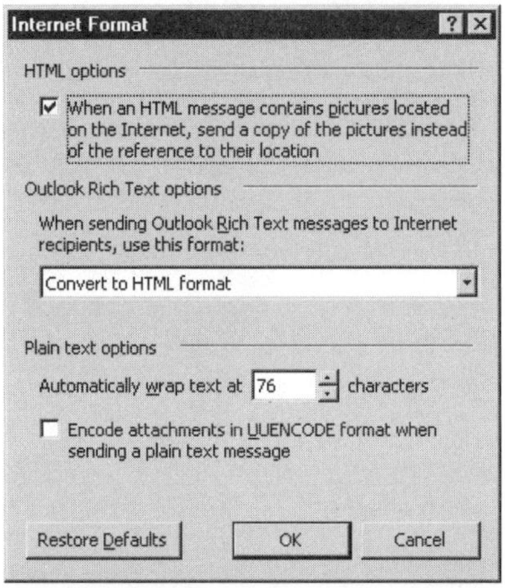

Figure 6-5. *Internet e-mail now has its own set of format options*

If, after fiddling around with the Internet Format options, you find that things are not working as expected, you can return everything to normal by clicking the Restore Defaults button, which resets all the options.

Setting International Options

For those users of non-English versions of Outlook, there are some options that may be of interest. To access the international options, choose Tools | Options and click the Mail Format tab. Then click the International Options button to display the International Options dialog box.

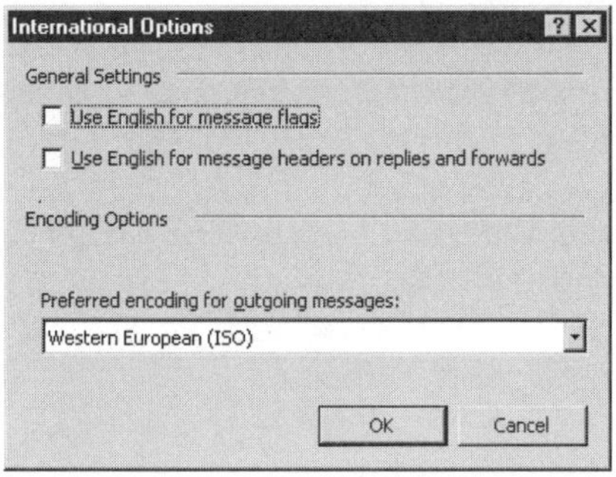

The International Options include the following:

- **Use English for message flags**   When this option is checked, Outlook uses the English version for message flags regardless of what your default language is.

- **Use English for message headers on replies and forwards**   This option is similar to the previous option in that it utilizes English for message header information such as To, From, Sent, and Subject, regardless of your default language.

- **Preferred encoding for outgoing messages**   From the drop-down list, select the default language to use for outgoing messages. You must, of course, have the selected language installed to use this option.

If you receive any volume of e-mail in languages other than your default language, you should not use the Preview Pane for reviewing incoming messages. When you respond to messages viewed in the Preview Pane, your default language is used in the reply rather than the language specified in the original message. By opening the message before replying, the language in the original message is used in the response rather than your default outgoing language.

MOUS

MOUS EXAM PRACTICE
In this chapter, you learned to set mail options, of which Outlook provides a large number. Begin by setting basic e-mail options and working your way up. Modify options individually and check to see if the results are what you expect. Continue setting mail options until you have Outlook working the way you prefer.

MOUS Exam Expert Objectives Explored in Chapter 6

Objective	Activity	Heading
OL10E-7-2	Modify Mail Services	All headings

Chapter 7

Working with Address Books and Directory Services

Since the Outlook e-mail component is one of the most important elements of the program, the ability to store and locate e-mail addresses easily is critical. Fortunately, Outlook provides the means to do both. By using directory services to locate e-mail addresses from all around the globe, and employing the Address Book to store and retrieve them, you can make light work of managing your e-mail addresses. This chapter takes you on a tour of the Address Book, walks you through installing and using address books, and helps you understand and work with directory services.

 Understanding the Address Book

The Address Book is actually not a single address book, but rather a collection of all your installed address books. The Address Book provides an interface that enables you to access any of your address books from within the same dialog box. Depending on your Outlook configuration and the information services installed, you may have one or more of the following address books:

- **Global Address List (GAL)**   This is the primary address list for your organization's e-mail system. Maintained by the system administrator, the Global Address List contains all company user, group, and distribution list e-mail addresses. To ensure its integrity, only the system administrator can add, delete, or modify entries in the Global Address List. This address book is always stored on the Microsoft Exchange Server. If you're running a stand-alone version of Outlook, you will not see the Global Address List.

- **Outlook Address Book**   This is an address book automatically generated from data in your Contacts folder. The Outlook Address Book is directly linked to your Contacts folder. This means that changes made to individual contacts in the Contacts folder are automatically reflected in the Outlook Address Book. Since the information in the Outlook Address Book is taken directly from the Contacts folder, attempting to edit an Outlook Address Book entry opens the corresponding contact form in the Contacts folder. Depending on the Contacts folder used to create the Outlook Address Book, this address book can be stored either on the Microsoft Exchange Server or on your local hard disk.

- **Personal Address Book**   For those e-mail addresses you want to keep private and store on your own computer, you can use the Personal Address Book (PAB). This address book is not connected to either the Global Address List or the Outlook Address Book.

Address books are added to individual profiles. The Outlook Address Book is automatically added when you install Outlook. If you're connected to a Microsoft Exchange Server network, both the Global Address List and the Outlook Address Book are added by default.

Installing Address Books

If the address book you want to use is not available in your profile, you can add it quite easily. To add an address book to your profile, follow these steps:

1. Choose Tools | E-mail Accounts to open the E-mail Accounts dialog box shown in Figure 7-1 for your profile.

2. Select Add A New Directory Or Address Book and click Next to display the Directory Or Address Book Type screen.

3. Select Additional Address Books and click Next to proceed to the Other Address Book Types screen shown in Figure 7-2.

Note *You can only add one instance of either the Outlook Address Book or a Personal Address Book. Attempting to add a second instance results in an error message informing you the address book is already installed and cannot be installed again.*

4. Choose the type of address book to add and click Next. If you're adding the Outlook Address Book, skip to Step 7. If you're adding a Personal Address Book, the Personal Address Book dialog box shown in Figure 7-3 opens.

5. Complete the necessary information for the Personal Address Book:

   ■ **Name**   Since you can have multiple Personal Address Books, you may want to give each one a unique name (Friends, Family, and so on). If you use a distinctive name, it will appear on the list in parentheses next to Personal Address Book—for example, Personal Address Book (Family).

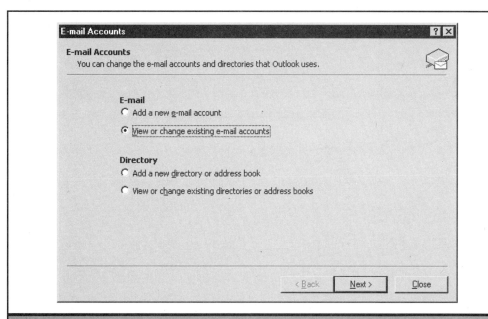

Figure 7-1.   *The E-mail Accounts dialog box offers access not only to e-mail accounts, but also to address books and directories*

COMMUNICATING WITH E-MAIL

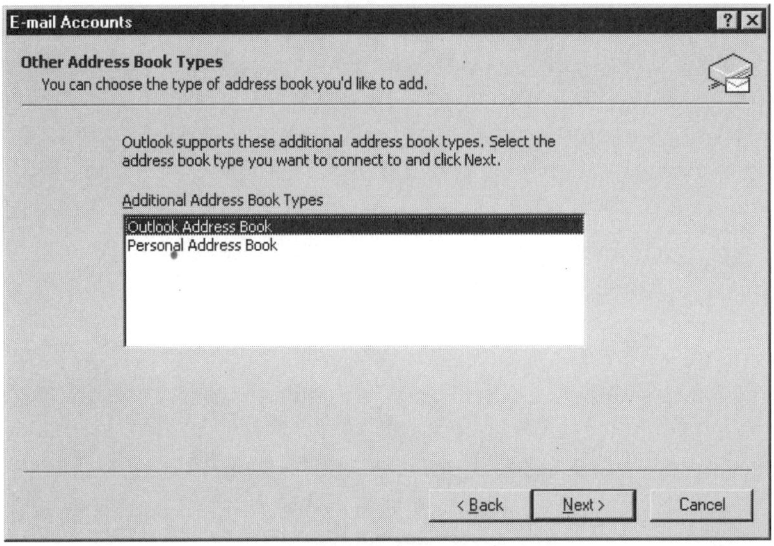

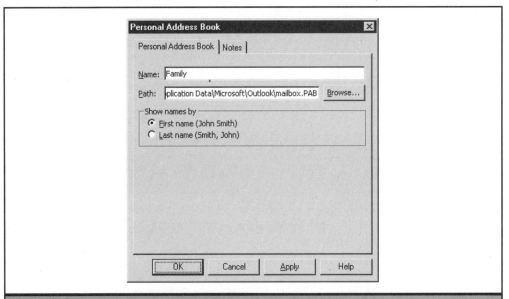

Figure 7-2. *Choose the type of address book to add*

Figure 7-3. *Use the Personal Address Book dialog box to specify the name and path of the new address book*

■ **Path** If you want to store your Personal Address Book in a different location than the one selected by default, enter the new path here. If you're not sure of the location you want to use, click the Browse button to display the User Personal Address Book dialog box. You can then select an existing Personal Address Book or specify a location for a new Personal Address Book.

■ **Show Names By** Set this option to determine the default sort order for names listed in the new Personal Address Book.

■ **Notes** Click the Notes tab and enter a description or any miscellaneous information related to the new Personal Address Book in the Notes text box.

6. Click OK to save the settings and create the address book.

Note *No matter which address book you add, a message informs you that the new service will not become available for use until you exit and then restart Outlook.*

7. Choose File | Exit to close Outlook.

8. Restart Outlook using the same profile to which you added the new address book(s).

As soon as you restart Outlook, the new address books are available for use. By default, Outlook uses your Contacts folder as the Outlook Address Book. If you have folders in addition to the Contacts folder that contain contact items, you can designate them as Outlook Address Books. Open the Folder Properties dialog box (right-click the desired contact folder in the Folder List and select Properties), and check the Show This Folder As An E-Mail Address Book option on the Outlook Address Book tab.

Note *If the Show This Folder As An E-Mail Address Book option on the Outlook Address Book tab is grayed out, it means one of three things: the Outlook Address Book is not added to the current profile; you've added the service but forgotten to exit and log off and then restart Outlook; or your profile is damaged and doesn't recognize the Outlook Address Book.*

Using the Address Book

Although there are numerous Outlook components that access the Address Book information, there is only one Address Book dialog box that gives you access to all the Address Book features. Therefore, the first order of business is to open the Address Book. From any folder, click the Address Book button on the Standard toolbar, press CTRL+SHIFT+B, or choose Tools | Address Book from the Menu bar to open the Address Book dialog box (see Figure 7-4).

As you can see in Figure 7-4, upon opening, the Address Book dialog box displays names from the default address list. On a Microsoft Exchange Server mail system, the default address list is usually the Global Address List. See "Setting Address Book Options," later in this chapter, for details on changing the default address book.

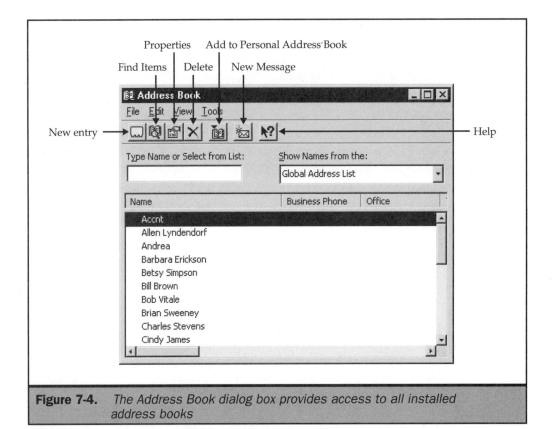

Figure 7-4. *The Address Book dialog box provides access to all installed address books*

Regardless of which address book you designate as the default address list, you can access all the installed address books from the Address Book dialog box by making the appropriate selection from the Show Names From The drop-down list.

Addressing E-mail

Addressing e-mail from within the Address Book is simple and straightforward. Select the address book of your choice, and highlight the names you want to include in the To field of a new e-mail message. Then click the New Message button on the toolbar to create a new mail message with the selected names entered as recipients in the To field.

Due to the increase in e-mail viruses attaching themselves to Outlook, Microsoft has taken the precaution of alerting you each time address book entries are accessed. Therefore, you'll see a warning dialog box asking if you want to allow the address book entries to be used. Select an access time and click Yes to continue.

If you want to include recipients in other fields or from other address lists, click the To, Cc, or Bcc button to display the Select Names dialog box. Then select the desired address book from the Show Names From The drop-down list. Now select the names and click the appropriate button.

Adding, Modifying, and Deleting Address Book Entries

Any address book is only as good as the information it contains. Therefore, you'll want to make sure you keep yours up to date by adding new entries as needed, modifying existing entries that change, and deleting old entries you no longer need.

To add a new entry to the address book, follow these steps:

1. Click the Address Book button on the Standard toolbar to open the Address Book. You can also press CTRL+SHIFT+B, or choose Tools | Address Book from the Menu bar to open the Address Book.

2. Click the New Entry button or choose File | New Entry from the Menu bar to open the New Entry dialog box.

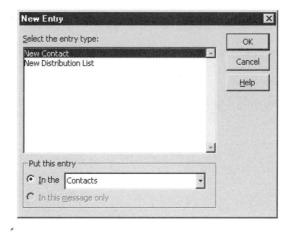

3. Although you would expect to begin by selecting the entry type from the Select The Entry Type list, you're actually better off starting with the Put This Entry option first since your entry-type choices change depending on where you plan to add the new entry:

   ■ **In The __** From the drop-down list, select the address book in which you want to place the new entry. The address book designated as the default address book for personal addresses is displayed. You'll notice that the only address books in which you can create new entries are the Personal Address Book (if you've added one) and any contacts folders you've designated to be used as address books. The latter appear under the Outlook Address Book item.

   ■ **In This Message Only** This option is only available if you open the Address Book from within an e-mail message form and create a new entry.

Of course, when you open the Address Book from within an e-mail message, it appears as the Select Names dialog box.

4. Choose the type of entry you want to create. Your choices depend on the type of address book you select in the Put This Entry option:

■ **Contacts** When you select Contacts or any other contacts folder designated as an address book, you can create a new contact or a new distribution list. In each case, the corresponding Outlook form opens, enabling you to create the desired item on-the-fly.

■ **Personal Address Book** If you select a Personal Address Book, you're presented with a selection of different mail system address types. Select the appropriate mail system type for the new entry. A Personal Address Book form opens with the mail address tab displayed.

5. Fill in the necessary information. The fields you see depend entirely on the entry type you select.

6. After you've entered the appropriate information, click OK to save the new entry.

The new entry now appears in the designated address book. To use it, simply select the appropriate address book from the Show Names From The drop-down list, and click the New Message button on the Address Book toolbar.

If you find that you need to make a change to an entry, choose the address book in which it resides, and double-click the name to open its form. Make the necessary changes and click OK to return to the Address Book.

Deleting an address book entry is even easier. Select the address book containing the entry, highlight the entry, and press the DEL key or click the Delete button on the Address Book toolbar. Since entries you delete cannot be recovered, Outlook asks if you're sure you want to delete the entry. If you're sure, click Yes, otherwise click No. You can also right-click an entry and select Delete from the shortcut menu that appears.

To change the default address book for new entries, choose Tools | Options to open the Addressing dialog box. Then select a different address book from the Keep Personal Addresses In drop-down list.

In addition to the New Entry command, there are a couple of other ways to add information to the Address Book. Since only the administrator can add Global Address List entries, these methods only work for the Outlook Address Book and the Personal Address Book:

■ **From an e-mail message** Open the e-mail message and right-click the name in the message header. Then choose Add To Personal Address Book or Add To Contacts. If you don't see Add To Personal Address Book, it's probably because you've selected an Outlook Address Book contacts folder as the folder in which to store personal addresses. When you select an Outlook Address Book contacts folder, you only have the choice of saving as a contact. When you select a Personal Address Book, your choices include both.

■ **Add an existing entry to the Personal Address Book**   Before jumping into
the mechanics of this method, there is one thing you must understand. For this
method, Outlook redefines the term *Personal Address Book.* Here, *Personal
Address Book* refers to the address book selected in the Keep Personal Addresses
In option in the Addressing dialog box. Therefore, if you have an Outlook
Address Book contact folder selected in this option, adding an entry to the
Personal Address Book means creating a new contact. If, on the other hand, you
have a "real" Personal Address Book selected in the Keep Personal Addresses
In option, adding an address to the Personal Address Book means just that. To
add an existing address list entry to the (newly defined) Personal Address
Book, open the Address Book, right-click the entry, and select Add To Personal
Address Book from the shortcut menu. One more thing to note: you can add
entries from the Global Address List or from any address book except the one
that appears in the Keep Personal Addresses In option.

Note   *When you add an entry from the Global Address List to the Personal Address Book, the
display name may change due to the fact that the Personal Address Book uses the first
name and last name fields to create the display name. If the display name in the Global
Address List is not a combination of the two, the display names will not match up.*

If your designated Personal Address Book is a real Personal Address Book (not a
contacts folder), and you attempt to add entries from the same Personal Address Book,
the Add To Personal Address Book command disappears from the shortcut menu and
is grayed out on the File menu. Since the source and target address books are the same,
it's like trying to lift yourself by your own bootstraps. No matter how hard you try, it
won't work.

Note   *When an Outlook Address Book contacts folder is the designated Personal Address Book
and you attempt to save a Global Address List entry to your Personal Address Book, you
cannot use the Save And New command on the new contact form to save the new entry.
You receive an error message informing you that a dialog box is open and you must close
it. This is a bug. Simply use the Save And Close command instead.*

Sorting the Address Book

Sorting your Address Book will enable you to find addresses quickly. The sort order
of the Global Address List, like everything else about the Global Address List, is
determined by the administrator and cannot be changed by users. However, the
Outlook Address Book and the Personal Address Book can be sorted according to
your preferences. To sort both (assuming you have a Personal Address Book added
to your profile), requires two similar, but separate procedures.

To change the sort order of an Outlook Address Book, choose Tools | E-mail
Accounts from the Outlook Menu bar to open the E-mail Accounts dialog box. Select
the View Or Change Existing Directories Or Address Books option and click Next.

Double-click Outlook Address Book to display the Microsoft Outlook Address Book dialog box.

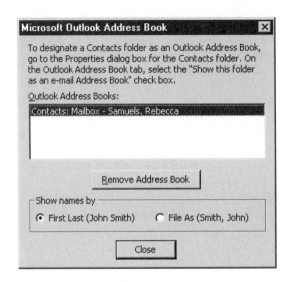

By default, the sort order is first name, last name. To reverse it, select File As (Smith, John) in the Show Names By options. Click Close when you're finished. For the change to take effect, you must exit and log off Outlook and then restart it.

Changing the sort order of a Personal Address Book is similar. Start by opening the E-mail Accounts dialog box (Tools | E-mail Accounts), and selecting the View Or Change Existing Directories Or Address Books option. Click Next to open the Directories And Address Books screen. Then double-click the Personal Address Book for which you want to modify the sort order. This opens the Personal Address Book dialog box.

Like the Outlook Address Book, the Personal Address Book default sort order is first name, last name. Make your selection in the Show Names By options to change the setting.

If you change the sort order of a Personal Address Book and the Address Book listing remains the same, it may be the result of having both the first and last names entered in the First Name field. This is a common problem with names entered manually in the Personal Address Book. When you create a new entry and place both first and last names in the Display Name field, they are both automatically entered in the First Name field. Since the sort is based on first and last names, it will not work without data in both fields. If both names are in the First Name field, the sort order remains the same no matter what your sort order selection. To remedy the situation, edit the entry so the first and last names are in the appropriate fields.

Searching the Address Book

There are two methods for searching the Address Book after you open it. For a simple search, start typing the name you're searching for in the Type Name Or Select From List search box. For a more sophisticated search, use the Find feature.

To use the Find feature, click the Find Items button on the toolbar or press CTRL+SHIFT+F to open the Find dialog box. Depending on the address book selected in the Show Names From The drop-down list, you'll see either the Find dialog box shown in Figure 7-5 or the one shown in Figure 7-6.

Enter the search criteria in the appropriate field(s) and click OK to search the selected address book. The Find feature filters out all address book entries that do not meet the search criteria and displays only those entries that do match the criteria.

Importing Address Books

Whether you want to use an existing address book that belongs to another Outlook user or you want to use an address book from your old e-mail software, you'll appreciate the ability to import address books into Outlook. The Outlook import feature enables you to convert address book information from a variety of programs, including Outlook, Outlook Express, ACT!, Ecco, Eudora, and more.

Importing an Outlook Personal Address Book

Outlook has a powerful import feature that enables you to import Outlook Personal Address Books as well as information from other programs. How the importing of a Personal Address Book works depends on the services in your profile. If you've already installed Personal Address Book as an information service, the import works differently than if you have no Personal Address Book installed.

With the service already added to your profile, you can only import your existing Personal Address Book into a contacts folder. If you haven't installed Personal Address Book as an information service, you can import any Outlook Personal Address Book from any source into a contacts folder.

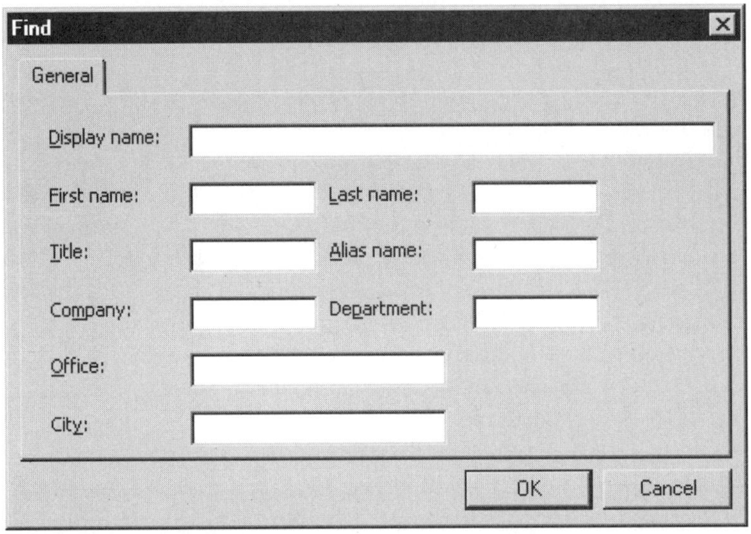

Figure 7-5. *The Find dialog box displayed when searching the Global Address List*

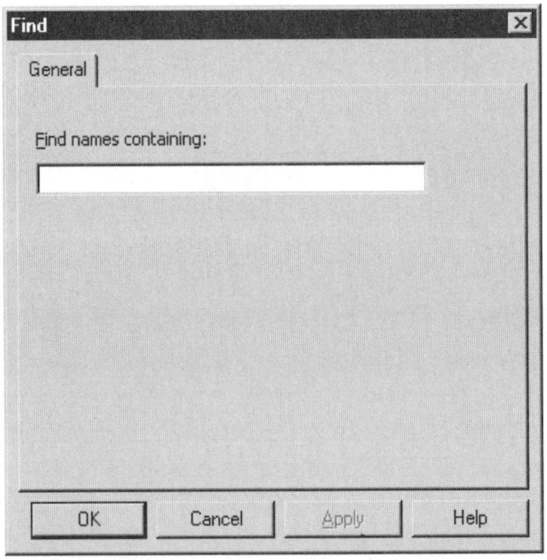

Figure 7-6. *The Find dialog box used when searching the Outlook Address Book or the Personal Address Book*

To import a Personal Address Book, follow these steps:

1. Choose File | Import And Export to launch the Import and Export Wizard.

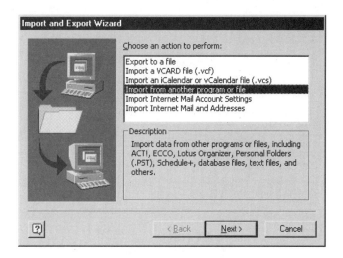

2. Select Import From Another Program Or File, and click Next to display the Import A File screen.

You can double-click your selection in most of the Import and Export Wizard screens to make your selection and move to the next screen without having to click the Next button.

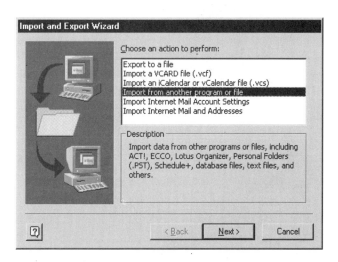

3. Scroll down, select Personal Address Book, and click Next. If you have a Personal Address Book added to your profile, you'll see the dialog box shown in Figure 7-7; otherwise you'll see the dialog box shown in Figure 7-8.

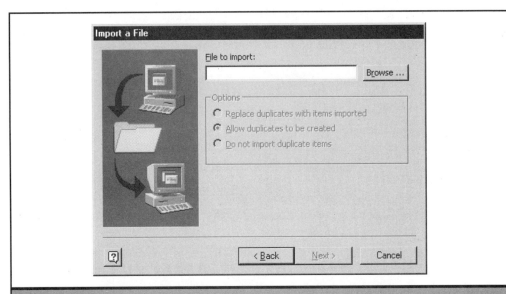

Figure 7-7.   *If this dialog box appears, you already have a Personal Address Book added to your profile*

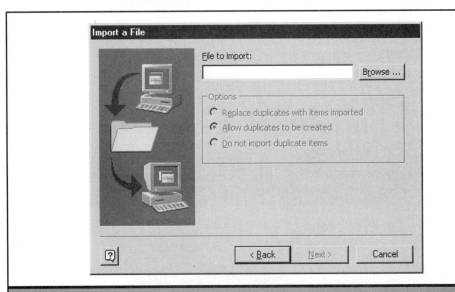

Figure 7-8.   *You'll see this dialog box only if you don't already have a Personal Address Book added to your profile*

4. Select the destination folder if you see the dialog box shown in Figure 7-7. Enter the path and name of the Personal Address Book file to import if you see the dialog box shown in Figure 7-8.

5. Click Next to display the summary screen, which indicates the action to be performed and gives you a chance to map custom fields and change the target folder.

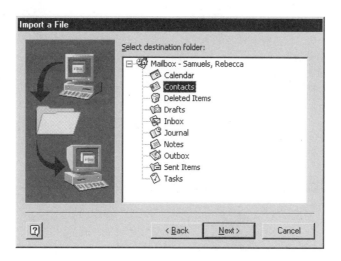

COMMUNICATING WITH E-MAIL

Note   *The Map Custom Fields button enables you to indicate which fields in the destination folder will hold information from custom fields you created in the Personal Address Book you're importing.*

6. Click Finish to complete the import.

When you open the Contacts folder into which you imported the Personal Address Book, you'll now see a contact record for each individual in the original Personal Address Book.

Note   *If you import a Personal Address Book that contains a Personal Distribution List, you may end up with duplicate contacts. This is due to the fact that a separate contact is created for each entry in the Personal Distribution List. If the Personal Address Book also contains a separate listing for the individuals included in the Personal Distribution List, duplicate records result. You'll have to weed them out manually.*

Importing from Other Files

Importing e-mail and contact information from other files and programs is similar to importing Outlook Personal Address Books. Choose File | Import And Export from the Menu bar to launch the Import and Export Wizard. Select Import From Another Program Or File to import address information from contact managers such as ACT! or Ecco, or choose Import Internet Mail And Addresses to import address information from other e-mail software such as Eudora or Netscape Mail.

To import files from contact managers and text-delimited files, you must first install a special import/export engine called a translator for the file type. If it's not installed and you select a file type other than .mmf, .pab, or .pst, an error message appears asking if you want to install a translator. You'll need your Outlook 2002 or Office 2002 CD to complete the install.

If you select Import From Another Program Or File and the import/export engine is installed, the Import A File dialog box appears.

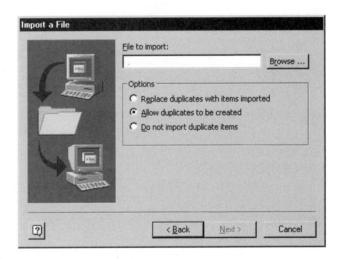

If your program is not listed on the Import A File screen, try exporting the address information from your program into a delimited (separated) text file, and then import the resulting text file into Outlook using the appropriate Comma Separated Values or Tab Separated Values file type.

Selecting Import Internet Mail And Addresses, which requires no additional import/export engine, opens the Outlook Import Tool dialog box.

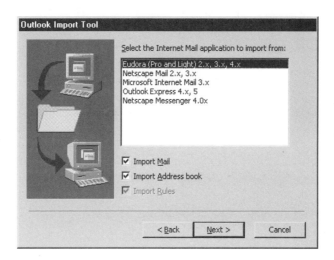

Whichever option you choose, follow the instructions on each screen to finish importing the address information into Outlook.

   Outlook will not directly import address information from Netscape 4.5x and higher. The solution is a little complicated, but works nevertheless. Export the address information from Netscape as LDIF. Next, import the information into Outlook Express. That's right, Outlook Express, not Outlook. Finally, import the Outlook Express data into Outlook using the Import Internet Mail And Addresses action.

   When you import Outlook Express address information into Outlook, Digital IDs are left behind. You'll have to export them manually and import each one into the appropriate Outlook contact record.

Making the Address Book Work Your Way

While less complex than some Outlook components, the Address Book still has its share of customizing options. To get the most out of your Address Book, you might want to spend a little time whipping it into shape.

Setting Address Book Options

The Address Book options enable you to designate the default address list, the location for storing personal addresses, and the order of address books used for name checking.

To set the address book options, choose Tools | Options from the Address Book Menu bar to display the Addressing dialog box.

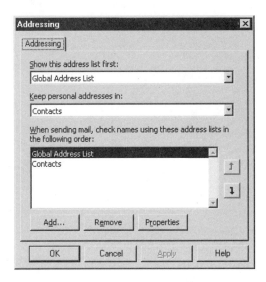

From the Show This Address List First drop-down list, choose the address book you want automatically displayed each time the Address Book or a Select Names dialog box opens. All your installed address books appear on the drop-down list.

Use the Keep Personal Addresses In drop-down list to designate the Personal Address Book or contacts folder to use for personal addresses. Your selection here determines which address book Outlook uses to store addresses when you employ the Add To Personal Address Book command. The drop-down list includes Personal Address Book (if you have Personal Address Book added to your profile) and all contacts folders whose properties are set to show as an e-mail address book.

The final option lets you decide which address books are used and the order in which they're used to perform name checking. You can add, remove, and reorder the address books used. Click the Add button to include an installed address book not listed. To keep an address book from being used in name checking, highlight it and click Remove. This does not affect the address book itself. It simply removes it from the name checking list. Finally, you can change the order in which the address books are used in name checking by selecting an address book in the list and clicking the up or down arrow button to the right to change its position.

Modifying the Appearance of the Address Book

The way the Address Book looks is almost etched in stone. However, there are a couple of changes you can make to its appearance. The first thing you can do is hide the toolbar by choosing Tools | View | Toolbar (use the same command to make it reappear). When the toolbar is visible, the Toolbar command has a check mark next to it. When it's hidden, the check mark disappears.

The other thing you can do to change the Address Book appearance is adjust the width of columns in the display list. Move your mouse pointer over one of the vertical separators between the column headers, and drag it to the left or right. Moving the pointer to the right expands the column, while moving it to the left narrows the column.

Working with Distribution Lists

Distribution lists are handy devices for speeding up addressing of e-mail by creating groups of frequently used recipients. For example, suppose you're a project leader and it's your job to keep all team members informed of progress and changes involving the project. You could, of course, create an e-mail message, open the Select Names dialog box, and add each team member to the recipients list. However, why bother, when all you have to do is create a distribution list containing the names of each team member? The next time you send a message to the team, you only have to select the distribution list from the Address Book, and the e-mail is automatically addressed to everyone on the team. Distribution lists can be used for e-mail messages, task requests, meeting requests, and can even be included in other distribution lists. Although distribution lists can only be created in one of the contacts folders of the Outlook Address Book, you can include recipients from any of your installed address books.

Creating Distribution Lists

Building a distribution list is a snap. You can create one from existing entries in your Address Book, or you can enter new addresses on-the-fly. Or you can use a combination of both.

Follow these steps and see for yourself how easy it is:

1. Press CTRL+SHIFT+L or choose File | New | Distribution List to open a blank Distribution List form (see Figure 7-9).

Note   *If you happen to be typing an e-mail message when you decide to create a new distribution list, use the menu method. Pressing CTRL+SHIFT+L in the body of a message will not open a new distribution list form. Instead, it will either do nothing (Plain Text message) or insert a bullet in the text (Rich Text or HTML message). Although this is a bug, you can use it as a shortcut key to add bullets to your messages. In the unlikely event that Microsoft fixes the bug, you'll be out of luck.*

2. Enter a brief and descriptive name for the new distribution list.

COMMUNICATING WITH E-MAIL

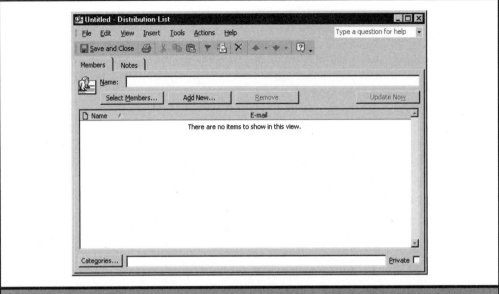

Figure 7-9. *You can create a new distribution list by adding existing Address Book entries or creating new ones*

3. Click the Select Members button to display the Select Members dialog box.

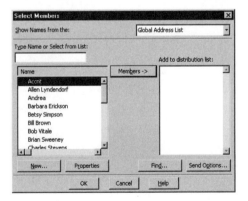

4. Select the desired address book from the Show Names From The drop-down list to display its entries.

5. Select the names you want to include in the new distribution list and click Members.

If you're creating a distribution list in a Microsoft Exchange Server personal mailbox or public folder, the number of entries you can include is limited to 165 contacts or 141 address book items.

6. If necessary, repeat the process for each address book installed.

7. Click OK to close the Select Members dialog box and return to the distribution list form.

8. If you want to add any names not found in your address book, click Add New to display the Add New Member dialog box.

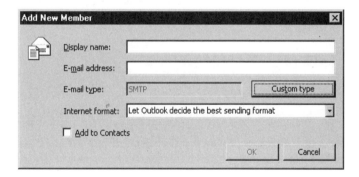

9. Fill in the appropriate information and click OK to add the entry to the new distribution list form.

10. Use the Notes tab to record notes or miscellaneous information (project date, purpose, team member responsibilities, and so on) about the new distribution list.

11. To assign the new distribution list to a category, click the Categories button on the Members tab and select the appropriate category.

   If you want to mark the new list as private, check the Private box in the bottom-right corner. Marking a distribution list Private hides it from others who may have access to your address book.

12. Click Save And Close to add the distribution list to the Contacts folder.

The new distribution list appears in the Contacts address book and in the Contacts folder. To add or remove names, open the Contacts folder and double-click the distribution list. Select names and click Remove to eliminate them from the list. Add new names by clicking Select Members or Add New. When you make changes to an original contact or Personal Address Book entry, the change is not reflected in the distribution list until you click the Update Now button. So if you add a contact whose e-mail address later changes, changing the e-mail address in the contact form will not change the contact's e-mail address in the distribution list until you open the list and click the Update button.

Using Distribution Lists

Using a distribution list is no different than using a single e-mail address. Only the results are different. To address an e-mail using a distribution list, create the e-mail; click the To, Cc, or Bcc button; select Contacts from the Show Names From The drop-down list; and add the distribution list of your choice.

Distribution lists are great for meeting and task requests as well. If you already have a distribution list in place to exchange information with team members, calling a meeting or assigning a task is a snap. For a task request, it's simply a matter of opening a new task request form and entering the distribution list name in the To field. The task request is then sent to the individuals on the distribution list.

 Outlook cannot track tasks sent to multiple recipients. Therefore, your copy of the task will not be updated as the recipients make changes to the original task.

To use a distribution list in a meeting request, press CTRL+SHIFT+Q to open a new meeting request form. Type the distribution list name in the To field, or click the To button, open the Contacts address book, and select the desired distribution list. When you open the Scheduling tab, you'll see that the distribution list appears as a required attendee. You can expand the list to add the individual names to the attendees list by clicking the plus sign (+) to the left of the distribution list.

 You can also open a new Meeting Request form by clicking the down arrow on the New button and selecting Meeting Request, or by choosing File | New | Meeting Request.

It's a good idea to expand the list for two reasons. First, if you don't expand it, any recipients who respond will be listed as Optional rather than required, since Outlook checks the names against the attendees list. If it finds only an unexpanded distribution list, it assumes the respondent(s) to be optional. The second reason for expanding the list is to ensure that all recipients receive the correct updates. If a meeting request is sent to an unexpanded distribution list that is later expanded and changed, attendees may receive the wrong update messages.

 After you expand a distribution list on the attendees list, you cannot contract it again. It's like letting the genie out of the bottle—it's easy to let him out, but impossible to get him back in.

Viewing Distribution Lists

By default, the only way to view distribution lists is by scrolling through your Address Book or picking through the Contacts folder. This is fine if you only use a handful of distribution lists. However, if you create and use a large number of distribution lists, you may want to consider creating a custom view to display all your distribution lists at a glance.

Here's how:

1. Click the Contacts icon in the Outlook Bar to open the Contacts folder.

2. Choose View | Current View | Define Views to open the Define Views For "Contacts" dialog box, shown in Figure 7-10.

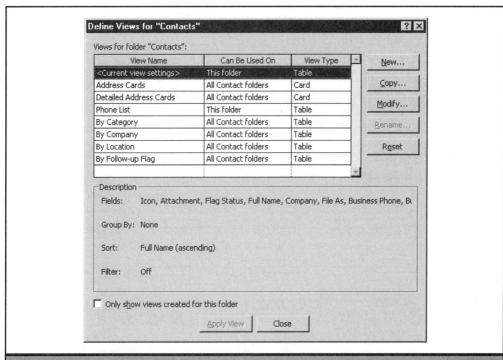

View Name	Can Be Used On	View Type
<Current view settings>	This folder	Table
Address Cards	All Contact folders	Card
Detailed Address Cards	All Contact folders	Card
Phone List	This folder	Table
By Category	All Contact folders	Table
By Company	All Contact folders	Table
By Location	All Contact folders	Table
By Follow-up Flag	All Contact folders	Table

Description

Fields: Icon, Attachment, Flag Status, Full Name, Company, File As, Business Phone, Bι

Group By: None

Sort: Full Name (ascending)

Filter: Off

Figure 7-10.   *You can modify existing views or create new views to suit your needs*

3. Click New to open the Create A New View dialog box.

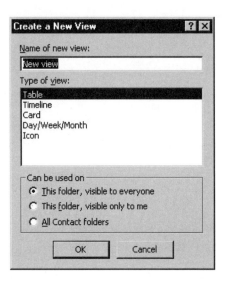

4. Replace "New View" with **Distribution List** in the Name Of New View field.

5. Select Table from the Type Of View list, and click OK to display the View Summary dialog box.

6. Click the Filter button and select the Advanced tab to display the advanced filter options.

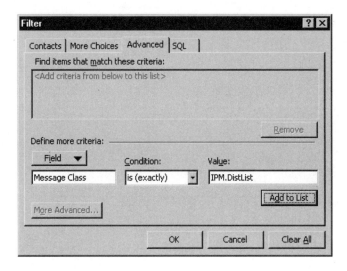

7. Click the Field button and choose All Distribution List Fields | Message Class from the menu that appears.

8. From the Condition drop-down list, select Is (Exactly).

9. Enter **IPM.DistList** in the Value field and click Add To List.

10. Click OK to close the Filter dialog box, and click OK again to close the View Summary dialog box.

11. Click Close to finish creating the new view and return to the Contacts folder.

12. Choose View | Current View Distribution List to display all your distribution lists.

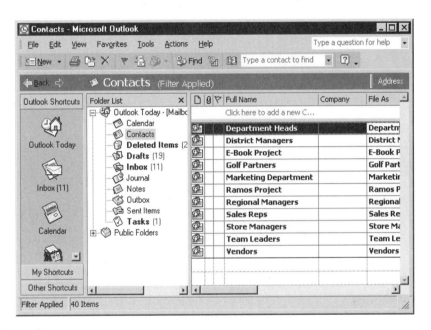

If you prefer a card view to a table view, you can select Card as the type of view in the Create A New View dialog box. Each distribution list will appear as an address card.

Understanding Directory Services

Outlook 2002 supports Lightweight Directory Access Protocol (LDAP) directory services. LDAP provides access to online databases of searchable information. In this context, directories are databases of information that are used primarily for data lookup and are usually updated at regular intervals. At their most basic level, directory services could be compared with the hard copy telephone books that everyone has at home. They contain named entries, which in turn consist of a series of attributes of varying types and values. Using the phone book example, the individual's name is the named entry, "phone number" is an attribute type, and the actual digits that make up the number are the attribute's value. LDAP services are mainly used in Outlook to perform lookups and name checking on large Internet directories.

Adding LDAP Directory Services

The Lightweight Directory Access Protocol should be installed when you install Outlook. However, individual LDAP directories are not. Therefore, before you begin using LDAP services, you must first add each LDAP directory service you want to use to your profile.

If the Lightweight Directory Access Protocol is not installed, you'll need your Outlook or Office 2000 CDs to install it. You'll be asked to insert the appropriate CD if necessary.

The following steps will walk you through the process:

1. Choose Tools | E-mail Accounts to open the E-mail Accounts dialog box.
2. Select Add A New Directory Or Address Book and click Next to display the Directory Or Address Book Type screen.
3. Select Internet Directory Service (LDAP) and click Next to display the Directory Service (LDAP) Settings screen shown in Figure 7-11.

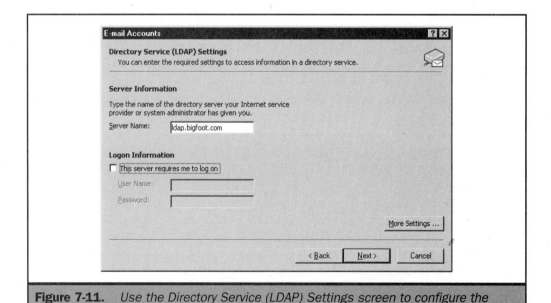

Figure 7-11. *Use the Directory Service (LDAP) Settings screen to configure the directory service of your choice*

4. In the Server Name field enter the name of the server on which the LDAP directory is running. You can enter the host name or the IP address of the LDAP server.

5. Most Internet directories do not require a username and password. However, if you're using one that does, check the This Server Requires Me To Log On option and enter the appropriate information:

   ■ **User Name**   Enter your distinguished name here. A *distinguished name* is a collection of information that uniquely identifies you throughout the world. It's similar to the way your full name and physical address (Jane Doe, 123 Appleview Drive, Philadelphia, PA 19118, USA) uniquely identifies you. The format of the distinguished name (dn) is common name (cn), organization (o), country (c)—for example, cn=Jane Doe, o=McGraw-Hill, c=US. If the directory service requires a username, check with your administrator for the precise distinguished name to use.

   ■ **Password**   If a password is required, enter it here. If you don't know your password, check with your administrator.

6. Click the More Settings button to display the Microsoft LDAP Directory dialog box.

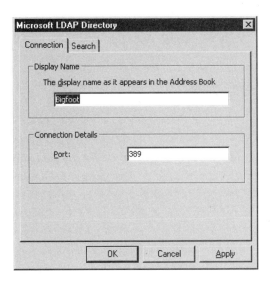

7. Complete the information on the Connection tab:

   ■ **Display Name**   Enter the name of the directory as you want it to appear in your Address Book.

   ■ **Port**   By default, the port number is 389. If you access the Internet through a local area network (LAN), you may need to use a different port number. Check with your system administrator.

8. Click the Search tab and enter the necessary information:

- **Search Timeout In Seconds**   Set the amount of time you want Outlook to search for the directory service before giving up. It's best to leave this setting at 60 seconds unless you are encountering regular time-out problems.

- **Specify The Maximum Number...**   For more efficient searching you can limit the number of matches that are returned for a successful search. You can enter a setting from 1 to 999.

- **Search Base**   This field lets you narrow your search by indicating the topmost level of the directory to include in the search. LDAP directories are hierarchical in nature, starting with country at the top, organization next, and distinguished names next. Therefore, if you want to restrict the search to Microsoft employees in the United States, enter o=Microsoft, c=US.

9. Click OK to save the settings and return to the Directory Service (LDAP) Settings screen.

10. Click Next to display the Congratulations screen.

11. To add the new directory service, click Finish.

12. Exit Outlook and restart it to complete the directory service setup.

After you restart Outlook, the new LDAP directory service will be available for use. Keep in mind that you're not limited to only one LDAP directory service. You can install as many as you wish.

Using Directory Services

Using an LDAP directory service is almost as easy as using any other Outlook address book. To search an Internet LDAP directory, make sure you have an open connection to the Internet established. Then press CTRL+SHIFT+B or click the Address Book button on the Standard toolbar to open the Address Book. Select the desired LDAP directory and press CTRL+SHIFT+F or click the Find Items toolbar button to display the Find dialog box.

Enter the name or text string you want to search for, and click OK to perform the search. If matching entries are found, they appear in the Address Book display window.

Part III

Working with Contacts

The
Complete
Reference

2002
Outlook

Chapter 8

Understanding and Using Contacts

If you've ever used an address book, collected business cards, or written a phone number on a cocktail napkin, you've already performed basic contact management chores. Outlook takes each of those methods of managing contacts to new heights by simplifying and automating the storing, organizing, retrieving, and utilizing of contact information. In this chapter, you'll learn to enter contact information in the Outlook Contacts folder, organize and display it in a variety of ways, and even use it to create e-mail messages and appointments automatically.

Adding Contacts

MOUS

As you'll no doubt agree, there's not much point in having a Contacts folder without contacts. Therefore, the first order of business is to enter your contact information into the Outlook Contacts folder. You actually have a couple of ways to accomplish that task. You can either enter the information manually or import it from another address book, a contact manager, or a delimited text file.

Adding Contacts Manually

Even if you have an existing address book or file to import into Outlook, you'll eventually have to enter some contact information manually. The process is as simple and quick as you want or need it to be. You begin by opening a new contact form and adding at least a name. After that, it's up to you just how much information you include. Of course, since the purpose of maintaining contact information is to be able to get in touch with the individuals you're keeping track of, it only makes sense to add a phone number, mailing address, or some other tidbit of actual contact data.

To add a contact to your Contacts folder, follow these steps:

1. Press CTRL+SHIFT+C to open a new contact form (see Figure 8-1).

   There are a number of ways to open a blank contact form. From any Outlook folder, you can press CTRL+SHIFT+C, choose File | New | Contact from the Menu bar, or click the down arrow on the New button and choose Contact. From within the Contacts folder, you can press CTRL+N, click the New button, or right-click a blank spot in the Information viewer and select New Contact.

   As you can see in Figure 8-1, the contact form contains five tabs, each of which contains different information relating to the contact:

   - **General**   The General tab contains fields for basic contact information such as name, address, phone number, and so on.

   - **Details**   The Details tab provides fields for maintaining additional contact information such as birthday, spouse's name, and more.

   - **Activities**   Here you'll find all Outlook items linked to the contact. E-mail messages, other contacts, journal entries, notes, and tasks that are connected to the contact are listed here.

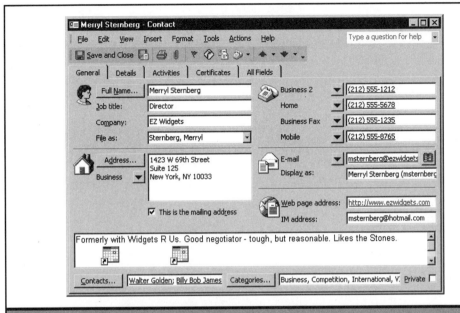

Figure 8-1.   *Use the contact form to enter as little or as much contact information as you wish*

- **Certificates**   The Certificates tab displays any digital certificates you use to encrypt mail sent to this contact.

- **All Fields**   Use this tab to display fields and their contents as related to the selected contact.

2. Enter the desired information on the General tab. Although filling out the form is mostly common sense, there are a couple of things to be aware of:

- **Full Name**   You can enter the contact's complete name in the Full Name field, and Outlook will separate it into first and last. If there is any question about the way Outlook separates the name, click the Full Name button to display the Check Full Name dialog box. Here you can adjust the name so it's recorded properly.

- **File as**   By default Outlook assumes you want to file contact names by last name first, then by first name. However, you can change the order by making the appropriate selection from the drop-down list. Since this is merely a matter of preference, make the choice you feel the most comfortable with. However, no matter what your choice is, maintain it for all contacts to avoid confusion when sorting and searching.

- **Address**   This field is similar to the Full Name field in that you can enter the address and Outlook automatically separates it into the various components. Click the Address button to verify that Outlook has done so correctly.

- **Phone numbers** Outlook provides multiple fields for most phone numbers. Click the down arrow button to select a different phone number field.

- **E-mail** As with the phone number fields, Outlook provides multiple e-mail fields that can be selected by using the drop-down menu that appears when you click the down arrow. You can also add an e-mail address from the Address Book by clicking the Address Book button to open the Select Name dialog box.

- **Web page address** If the contact's company has a web site, you enter the URL, or web address, here. A valid URL entered here is automatically converted to a hyperlink.

- **IM address** Use this field to enter the contact's Internet Mail (IM) address. Currently Hotmail is the most popular Internet Mail service in use. This is also the address used for Instant Messaging. See Chapter 22 for more information on using Instant Messaging with Outlook 2002.

- **Notes** While you won't find a label that says Notes field, that's just what the blank display area above the last row of fields is. Not surprisingly, it's a text field in which you can jot notes, ideas, and even insert items, documents, and files (as attachments).

- **Contacts** You can link the current contact with other contacts to create contact groups. This is a great way to organize contacts from the same company or co-workers on the same project.

- **Categories** By assigning contacts to categories, you can break your contacts down into broad, related groups such as business contacts and personal contacts.

- **Private** You can mark individual contacts Private to prevent them from being visible to others with whom you share your Contacts folder.

3. Enter additional information about the contact on the Details tab (see Figure 8-2).

As with the General tab, there are a couple of fields you might want to pay extra attention to:

- **Directory server** If you have NetMeeting installed and use a particular Internet Locator Service (ILS) server for conducting online meetings, enter the server name or IP address here. For more information on NetMeeting, see Chapter 22.

- **E-mail alias** This is generally the contact's e-mail address.

- **Internet Free-Busy Address** Outlook enables you to share your free/busy information with others by publishing it to a web site, FTP site, or network server. This is handy for providing access to your free/busy information to others who are not on your Exchange Server network. Use this field to enter the location of the file in which your free/busy information is stored. This can be a URL (http://...), an FTP site (ftp://...), or a network server (file://...).

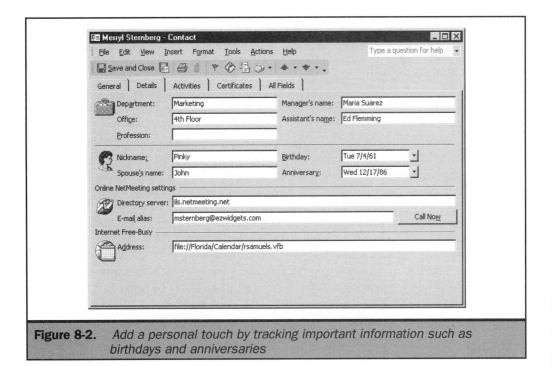

Figure 8-2.   *Add a personal touch by tracking important information such as birthdays and anniversaries*

4. If you want to use digital certificates to encrypt e-mail you send to this contact, click the Certificates tab and use the Import button to locate and import the desired certificate.

5. Click Save And Close to save the new contact and return to the active Outlook window.

The new contact is immediately added to your Contacts folder. If you open the Contacts folder to the default view, Address Cards, you'll find a new address card for the contact you just created.

Automating Contact Entry

Outlook is a productivity tool, so it should come as no surprise that it gives you the opportunity to create new contacts with a minimum of time and effort. Since Outlook can't read your mind (at least not yet), you will, of course, have to supply some of the contact data. However, Outlook lets you take advantage of its storage and retrieval features to create new contacts by using existing contacts to provide some of the information.

Using the New Contact From Same Company Command

If you want to create a new contact based on an existing contact, you can simplify matters by selecting the original contact and choosing Actions | New Contact From

Same Company from the Menu bar. This opens a new contact form with the company, address, business phone, business fax, and web page already entered. Outlook copies the data from these fields from the original contact and enters it automatically in the new form. Fill out the remaining information, and click Save And Close to save the new contact. You can also use the New Contact From Same Company command from within an open contact by selecting Action | New Contact From Same Company from the menu of the contact form.

Adding Multiple Contacts with Save And New

When you're creating more than one contact in a single session, you might want to use the Save And New command found on the File menu. This command enables you to save the contact you're working on and open a blank contact form, all in one fell swoop. Open a new contact form, enter the appropriate information, and click the Save And New button (or choose File | Save And New) to save the contact and open a blank contact form.

Even handier than Save And New is a command that not only saves the existing contact, but also opens a new contact form and fills in some of the contact information using the newly saved contact as the source. This command, Save And New In Company, is not available on any of the standard contact form toolbars or menus. However, you can easily add it to any toolbar or menu on the contact form.

Here's how to add it to the contact form Standard toolbar:

1. Open a new contact form.

2. Double-click a blank spot to the right of the Standard toolbar in the form to open the Customize dialog box.

3. Click the Commands tab to view the available commands.

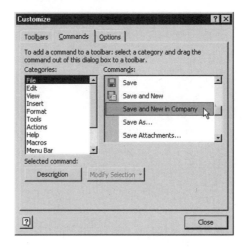

4. Select File in the Categories list, and locate Save And New In Company in the Commands list.

5. Drag the Save And New In Company command to the contact form Standard toolbar, and drop it between the Save And Close button and the Save And New button. You can drop the command as soon as your mouse pointer turns into a vertical I-bar.

6. Right-click the new button and select Begin A Group to insert a vertical separator between the Save And Close button and the Save And New In Company button.

7. Click Close to exit the Customize dialog box and return to the contact form, where you'll now see the Save And New In Company button on the toolbar.

The next time you want to create multiple contacts from the same organization, create the first contact and fill in all the appropriate information. When you're finished, click Save And New In Company to save the contact. Outlook immediately opens a new contact form containing the following information from the saved contact:

- Company
- Business phone
- Business fax
- Address
- Web page address

You'll also notice that the File As field is filled in using the company name. However, since this is generally used for the contact name, it will change unless you're recording a contact with no name.

For more information on customizing toolbars and menus, see Chapter 24.

Using Copy to Create Similar Records

Another method you can use to speed up contact entry is the Copy command. It makes an exact copy of the selected contact. To use the Copy command, open the Contacts folder, select the contact you want to duplicate, and press CTRL+C. Now press CTRL+V to paste a copy of the selected contact in the Contacts folder.

You can also make a copy of a contact by holding down the CTRL key, then dragging the contact you want to copy and dropping it on the Contacts shortcut on the Outlook Bar or on the Contacts folder in the Folder List.

Open the copy, change the name and other appropriate information, and save the new contact. Make sure you change all pertinent information such as linked contacts, birthdays, and so on.

WORKING WITH CONTACTS

Although Outlook 2002 duplicate checking is turned on by default, it does not warn you when you create or save a duplicate created using the Copy command. Therefore, any copy you create and fail to change will remain in your Contacts folder as a duplicate until you weed it out manually.

Adding Contacts from Other Outlook Components

In addition to the straightforward methods of creating a contact by opening a new contact form and entering or modifying the contact data, you can also create new contacts from existing Outlook items such as e-mail messages and appointments.

Creating a Contact from an E-mail Message

One of the most common ways to create a contact from an Outlook item is to use an incoming e-mail message. Since the message already contains the sender's display name and e-mail address, it gives you a head start on entering the contact data.

To create a contact from an e-mail message, follow these steps:

1. Click the Inbox icon to open the Inbox.

2. Double-click to open the incoming message you want to use to create a new contact.

3. Right-click a display name or e-mail address in the From, To, or Cc field in the header and choose Add To Contacts. A new contact form opens with the display name entered in the Full Name field and the e-mail address in the E-mail field.

 If you want to add multiple contacts from the same e-mail message, you'll have to do it one at a time since you cannot select multiple display names or addresses.

4. Fill in the remaining contact information as desired, and click Save And Close.

That's all there is to it. The contact is immediately added to your Contacts folder.

Creating Contacts from Other Outlook Items

Another handy but often-overlooked method of creating contacts is the use of drag-and-drop. You can drag other Outlook items such as notes, tasks, and e-mail messages to the Contacts folder icon and drop them to create new contacts. You can drop the items on the Contacts shortcut on the Outlook Bar or on the Contacts folder in the Folder List. When you drop the item, a new contact form containing information from the dropped item opens. The information that appears depends on the item type you drop.

- ■ **E-mail messages**   The sender's display name and e-mail address are entered automatically in the new contact form. In addition, the message header, contents, importance, and categories are included in the Note field of the contact form.

■ **Appointments and meetings**   The name and e-mail address of the originator of the appointment or meeting are entered in the new contact form. The appointment or meeting contents are included in the Note field of the new contact form.

■ **Tasks**   Regular tasks as well as incoming task requests generate a new contact using the display name and e-mail of the originator of the task (you) or the task request (the sender). Tasks you assign to others generate contacts using the task request recipient. If a task request contains multiple recipients, only the first recipient is used. The content of the task or task request is included in the contact form Note field.

■ **Notes and journal entries** •The contents of the note or journal entry are included in the contact form Note field.

■ **Files**   If you drag a computer file to the Contacts icon, a new contact form opens and a shortcut to the file is added to the Note field of the form.

You can also right-drag (hold down your right mouse button instead of your left, and drag the item) Outlook items to the Contacts icon and drop them with somewhat different results. As soon as you drop the item, a shortcut menu appears providing you with several choices.

> Copy Here as Contact with <u>T</u>ext
>
> Copy Here as Contact with <u>S</u>hortcut
>
> <u>C</u>opy Here as Contact with Attachment
>
> <u>M</u>ove Here as Contact with Attachment
>
> <u>C</u>ancel

■ **Copy Here as Contact with Text**   This copies the item following the earlier rules and adds the item contents as text in the contact form Note field. This is the default command for a regular drag-and-drop action.

■ **Copy Here as Contact with Shortcut**   This enters name and e-mail address information following the earlier rules and adds a shortcut to the item in the contact form Note field.

■ **Copy Here as Contact with Attachment**   This enters name and e-mail address information following the earlier rules and inserts the item as an attachment in the contact form Note field.

■ **Move Here as Contact with Attachment**   This enters name and e-mail address information following the earlier rules, adds the item to the new contact as an attachment, and deletes the original item.

When you use the Move Here As Contact With Attachment option and change your mind before saving the new contact, the original item is deleted anyway. Fortunately, Outlook stores it in the Deleted Items folder, so you can retrieve it if need be.

Receiving Contacts in E-mail

Since e-mail provides a quick and easy method of sharing all types of information, it only makes sense that you can exchange contact information with others via e-mail. The two most common forms of contact information you're likely to receive are Outlook contact records from other Outlook users and vCards from Outlook and non-Outlook users.

Both Outlook contact records and vCards are sent as e-mail attachments. When you receive either one, the easiest way to add the information to your Contacts folder is to drag the attachment(s) to the Contacts shortcut on the Outlook Bar or to the Contacts folder in the Folder List. Dropping a contact item on the shortcut adds the contact to your folder with no muss or fuss. The only time you'll have to do anything is if you already have a contact by the same name or with the same e-mail address in your Contacts folder.

When you drag a vCard to the Contacts shortcut or to the Contacts folder, a new contact form opens with all the information in the vCard entered in the appropriate field(s). Modify the information as needed and click Save And Close.

Importing Contacts from Other Sources

In addition to using Outlook contacts from other users and vCards from vCard-compatible contact managers, you can also utilize contact information from a wide range of compatible and incompatible sources, including contact managers, databases, and spreadsheets. You can accomplish this by importing the data from the original source into Outlook, which has converters for the following popular contact managers, databases, and spreadsheets, among others:

- ACT! 2.0, 3.*x*, 4.0
- dBase
- ECCO 2.0, 3.0, 4.0
- Lotus Organizer 4.*x*, 5.*x*
- Lotus Organizer 97
- Microsoft Access
- Microsoft Excel
- Microsoft FoxPro
- Schedule+

If you don't find your program on the list, don't panic, there's still hope. In addition to importing specific file formats, Outlook also imports delimited text files. *Delimited* text files are ones in which information contained in individual fields is separated (delimited) by a special character, and individual records (groups of related fields) are separated by a hard return or other special character. This enables other programs to recognize both fields and records, and therefore to import the information with a minimum amount of fuss. Any contact manager, database, or spreadsheet program worth its salt can export information to a delimited text file.

To import contact data, begin by launching the Import and Export Wizard. Choose File | Import And Export from the Menu bar.

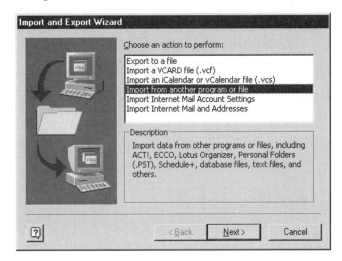

After the Import and Export Wizard opens, select Import From Another Program Or File and click Next. This opens the Import A File screen. Select the file format of the information you want to import and click Next.

 Depending on the format you choose, you may have to insert your Office CD. Not all converters are added when you install Outlook. If the converter you want to use isn't installed, insert your CD and follow the onscreen instructions.

From this point forward, the file type selected dictates the remaining screens. Follow the instructions, entering information and setting options as needed. One thing you should be aware of is the mapping of custom fields. This is especially helpful if you're importing a non–contact manager file, such as a database, spreadsheet, or delimited text file. The manner in which you name your fields (Name, Address, Phone, and so on), may be confusing to Outlook, and it may require that you specify which imported fields match up with which Outlook fields. This is called *field mapping*.

The Map Custom Fields dialog box presents you with a list of fields from the file you're importing, on the left, and a list of Outlook fields on the right.

To match (map) the fields, drag them from the list on the left to the corresponding fields on the right. This enables Outlook to enter the correct contact data in the new contact records that are created when you complete the import process.

For more information on importing data into Outlook, see Chapter 21.

Dealing with Duplicate Contact Records

If you maintain a large Contacts database, you'll find that duplicate records are a fact of life. Whether your memory is slipping and you forget someone's already in your Contacts folder, or you receive contacts as attachments from others, you're bound to end up with duplicate contacts. Fortunately, Outlook 2002 incorporates automatic duplicate checking, which keeps an eye out for contacts with identical names or e-mail addresses. When you attempt to add a duplicate record, Outlook warns you and offers a couple of options.

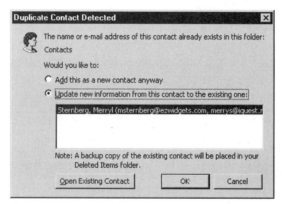

If you want to proceed, you can either add the duplicate and have two records containing the same name or same e-mail address, or you can elect to have the existing record updated using the new record you're adding. If you update the contact, a copy of the original contact is placed in the Deleted Items file where you can later retrieve it if necessary.

When you elect to update the existing contact, all information from the new contact is copied to the existing contact and replaces the original information. There are some exceptions. Categories, text in the Note field, and attachments are not copied. You'll have to manually copy these yourself. Certificates as well as links on the Activities tab are copied, but do not replace the original data. They are added to any existing certificates or links.

Remember, using the Copy and Paste or the Cut and Paste commands to create new contacts from existing contacts does not trigger duplicate detection by Outlook.

So, what do you do if you accidentally or intentionally create duplicate records? Obviously, you cull the unwanted duplicates. However, there's one small problem. How do you decide which one to keep and which to delete? While there's no perfect solution other than opening each record and comparing it field for field, there are a couple of indicators you may find helpful in weeding out duplicates.

The best way to spot duplicates is to change the Contacts folder view to a table view such as the Phone List view. Then click the Full Name header to sort the list by name. This will enable you to readily see those contacts with duplicate names.

Now, how do you decide which of the duplicates to keep? While you could open each duplicate and see which one has the most current information, there's an easier way—add the Modified field to the view. The Modified field contains the date the record was created or last changed. To add the Modified field, right-click any column header and select Field Chooser to open the Field Chooser dialog box seen in Figure 8-3.

From the field type drop-down list, choose All Contact Fields. Scroll down and locate the Modified field. Drag it to the Information viewer, and drop it between the Full Name header and the Company header. Expand the column width so you can see the date and time the contact records were last modified. Next, return to the Field Chooser and locate the Size field. Drag it to the Information viewer and drop it between the Modified header and the Company header. This field indicates the size of the record. Now you can compare duplicates to see which is the most recent and which contains the most data. This should help you make the decision.

MOUS EXAM PRACTICE

In this section, you learned about creating contacts using different sources. Now you can practice the various techniques. Begin by opening a new contact form and filling out the information. Try using each of the different methods available for opening blank contact forms. Use the Save And New command, and take advantage of the Copy and Paste commands as well. Next, create contacts from incoming e-mail messages. Finally, try your hand at dragging and dropping to create contacts from other Outlook items.

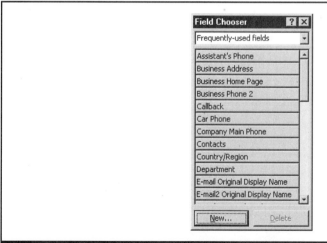

Figure 8-3. *Adding fields to a view is easy with the Field Chooser*

Modifying and Deleting Contacts

Adding contacts to your Contacts folder is only half the battle. As with most things in life, your contacts' information is bound to change from time to time, and in some cases, become totally obsolete. When that happens, you'll need to change those records that need modifying and delete those records that no longer serve a useful purpose.

Editing Existing Contacts

Modifying existing contacts is actually pretty straightforward. It's a simple matter of double-clicking the contact record to open it, making the necessary changes, and then saving the record to retain the changes. If you're fortunate enough to have a co-worker who is maintaining the same contact information and who has updated records for some of your contacts, it's even easier. In that case, you can ask your co-worker to send you the updated contacts, which you can then add to your Contacts folder. When asked if you want to update existing contacts, answer yes, and the latest information replaces the old, outdated information.

If you find yourself in a situation in which the same information has changed in a number of contacts, such as the company name or address, you can make the changes without opening and closing each contact record by using a table view.

Open the Contacts folder and choose View | Current View | Phone List to display your contacts in the Phone List view. Sort the list by the field you want to modify by clicking the field header (see Figure 8-4).

If the field you want to sort by doesn't appear in the list, right-click one of the field headers and select Field Chooser from the shortcut menu. From the Field Chooser, drag the field you want to modify and drop it between the Full Name header and the Company header. Repeat for all the fields you want to change. If the field doesn't appear in the Frequently-Used Fields group, use the drop-down list to select All Contact Fields.

Move to the first record you want to change, and click the field you want to edit. This places the field in edit mode. Replace or modify the information as needed, and then press ENTER to save the change. Highlight the new information and press CTRL+C to copy it. Move to the next record, highlight the old field entry, and press CTRL+V to replace it with the new (copied) information. Press ENTER to save the record. Repeat the process for each record you want to change.

In addition to changing the contents of a contact record, you can also change a couple of its basic properties. Open the contact record and choose File | Properties to display the contact's Properties dialog box (see Figure 8-5).

As you can see, the Properties dialog box tells you a lot about the contact record. It indicates the record's location, its size, when it was sent, received, and last modified, and it offers you the opportunity to change two contact record options: Importance and whether to AutoArchive the item. To change the Importance level, make a new selection from the Importance drop-down list. If you want the Outlook AutoArchive

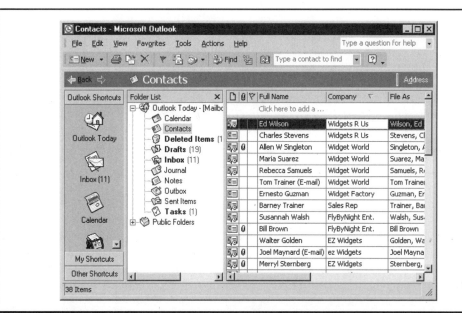

Figure 8-4. *Line up all the records by the field you want to change*

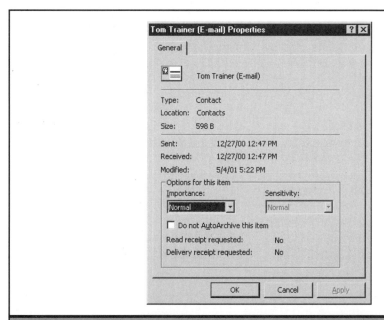

Figure 8-5. *The contact's Properties dialog box provides a wealth of information about the contact record*

feature to skip this record when performing a scheduled AutoArchive operation, check the Do Not AutoArchive This Item check box. Click OK when you're finished.

By default, the remaining options are determined by other Outlook settings and are therefore read-only options. In other words, you can't change them. However, there's a way to circumvent the read-only restriction. Choose Edit | Revise Contents from the contact form Menu bar before opening the contact's Properties dialog box.

Eliminating Unwanted Contacts

When business associates change jobs and friends lose touch, you may find yourself with contact records that are no longer of use to you. In that case, you'll want to do a little housecleaning and get rid of the unwanted contacts. Not only do they unnecessarily clutter up your Contacts folder, but they also take up valuable hard disk space, and slow down your search and sort operations.

If you find yourself with unwanted contacts, the solution is simple: delete them. How you delete them is up to you, and you have a number of methods from which to choose. You can delete them individually, or you can delete them en masse.

To eliminate a single contact record, open the Contacts folder, select the record, and press DEL or click the Delete button on the Standard toolbar. You can also press CTRL+D or right-click the contact and select Delete from the shortcut menu. In addition, you can select the record and choose Edit | Delete from the Menu bar.

In either an Address Cards view or a table view, you can select multiple contacts by holding down the CTRL key and clicking the contacts you want to select. Then use any of the available methods to delete all the selected contacts in one operation. You can also select a series of sequential contacts by clicking the first contact, holding down the SHIFT key, and clicking the last contact in the series. The first, last, and all contacts between are selected.

MOUS EXAM PRACTICE
In this section, you began to familiarize yourself with the techniques necessary to edit and delete contacts. Now practice by creating a few "dummy" contacts you can modify and delete without fear of losing important information. Then make some simple changes to a single contact. Next, open a table view and try editing a series of contacts. When you've got the hang of modifying contacts, delete the "dummy" contacts using the methods described earlier.

Working with Contacts

Creating contacts is just the beginning. To use your Contacts database effectively, you should also take advantage of some of the more advanced contact features available in Outlook, such as adding attachments, flagging contacts for follow-up, linking items and files to contacts, and more.

Attaching Items to a Contact Record

Attaching items to a contact record is very similar to the procedure used for attaching items to e-mail messages. Open the contact record and choose Insert from the Menu bar to view the menu of items you can insert in a contact.

 If you want to insert an object and the choice is grayed out on the menu, close the menu and return to the contact form. Place the cursor in the Note field of the contact form, and open the Insert menu again. Now all three choices, including Object, are available.

Select the type of item to insert and follow the onscreen instructions. Your choices include

- **File** If you want to attach a computer file, this is the selection to use. It displays the Insert File dialog box, which enables you to locate and select the desired file from anywhere on your computer system.

- **Item** To attach an Outlook item, choose Item. This opens the Insert Item dialog box, which provides you with a tree-like view of your folders, from which you can choose one or more items to attach.

- **Object** You can embed a data object, such as a picture or spreadsheet, into the contact record. Choosing this command opens the Insert Object dialog box from which you can select the object to attach.

Tip *If you want to attach a file, you can click the Insert File button on the contact form Standard toolbar.*

As you can see in Figure 8-6, the attachments are inserted into the Note field of the contact form.

File and item attachments are represented by their respective icons. In Figure 8-6, the 1Qtr Summary.doc file is a Microsoft Word document, and Modem Settings is an Outlook note. Objects are embedded in their entirety—therefore, you see the entire object, not merely a representation, as in the case of the embedded spreadsheet in Figure 8-6.

To open a file or item attachment, double-click the icon. In the case of a file attachment, the program associated with the file launches and opens the file. This, of course, means you must have either the associated program or a file viewer that supports the file format installed on your computer.

You can modify an embedded object by double-clicking it and making changes directly to the object. If, instead of embedding the object, you chose to link the object, double-clicking it opens the associated program. From there you can make any necessary changes. As with a file attachment, you must have the associated program installed on your computer to modify a linked object.

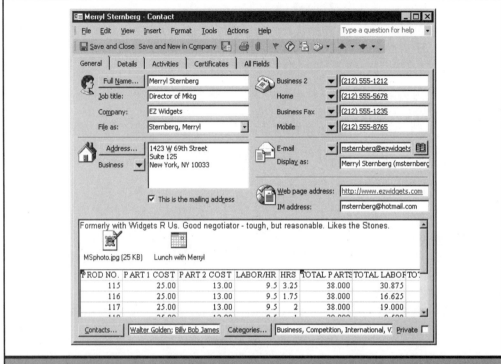

Figure 8-6. *Use attachments to keep information related to the contact at your fingertips*

Flagging Contacts

Flagging is not merely reserved for e-mail messages. Anytime you want to remind yourself—or someone else to whom you send or forward a contact—to follow up on a contact, you can set a follow-up flag to ensure you don't forget. For example, suppose you know the contact is moving to a new office and will have a different address and phone number in two weeks. Rather than make the change now and create confusion if you need to get in touch before the two weeks is up, why not flag the contact for follow-up on the date the change becomes effective?

To flag a contact, open the contact and click the Flag For Follow Up button on the contact form Standard toolbar to open the Flag For Follow Up dialog box.

Flag for Follow Up	? X

Flagging marks an item to remind you that it needs to be followed up. After it has been followed up, you can mark it complete.

Flag to: [Follow up ▾]   [Clear Flag]

Due by: [Friday, May 18, 2001 ▾]   [5:00 PM ▾]

☐ Completed

[OK]   [Cancel]

From the Flag To drop-down list, select the type of flag and create your own custom flag by entering text manually. Using the earlier example, you might type "Change phone number" in the Flag To field. If you want to set a reminder for the flag, enter a date and time in the Due By field, or select a date from the drop-down calendar that appears when you click the down arrow at the end of the field. By default, Outlook uses the end of workday time as the reminder time. You can change it by using the time drop-down list or by placing your cursor in the field and editing it manually. Click OK to save the flag and return to the contact. An information bar appears at the top of the General tab indicating the flag type and reminder date and time.

When viewing flagged contacts in an Address Cards view, the first line of the card indicates the flag type. In a table view, a red flag appears in the flag column indicating the contact has been flagged.

Linking Activities to a Contact Record

As handy as attachments are, they have one drawback: they increase the size of the contact record to which they're attached. Since the attached file, item, or object is actually stored in the contact record, the size of the record is increased by the size of the attachment. This can be a problem depending on the number of contacts and attachments, as well as any size limitations imposed by the administrator on your mailbox space on the server.

Fortunately, there's a way to have your cake and eat it too! Rather than attach the items, you can create a link from the contact record to the item. This enables you to keep the item immediately accessible without having to store the item and utilize valuable hard disk space. As always, Outlook provides a couple of different ways for you to achieve your goal. The first is the Link command. The second method is through the use of hyperlinks.

WORKING WITH
CONTACTS

Using the Link Command

For linking most items and files, you'll find the Link command to be the quickest and easiest method to use. It provides a dialog box from which you select the item or file and does not require you to know the names of items or the proper syntax to use when creating the link. To see just how easy it is, try the following steps to link an item to a contact:

1. Open the contact in which you want to create the links.

2. Choose Actions | Link | Items to display the Link Items To Contact dialog box.

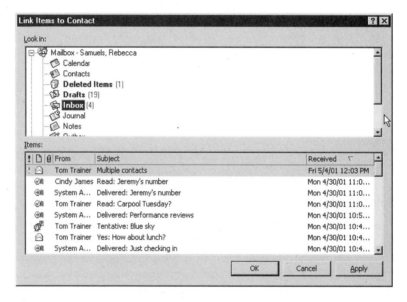

3. From the Look In list, select the folder containing the item(s) you want to link.

4. Select the item(s) from the Items list.

5. Click OK to create the link and return to the contact.

Linking files is a little different. Rather than creating a direct link to the file, Outlook creates a journal entry that includes a shortcut to the linked file.

Begin by choosing Actions | Link | Files to open the Choose A File dialog box. Next, locate and double-click the desired file to open the Journal Entry dialog box.

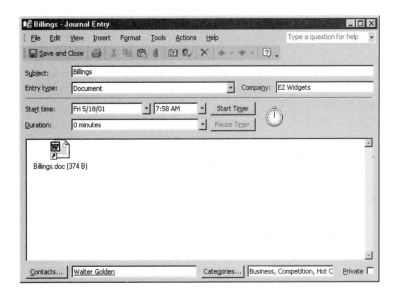

Make any necessary changes to the journal entry and click Save And Close.

Whether you've linked an item or a file, nothing appears to have changed when you return to the contact record. To see the new link(s), click the Activities tab. At first glance, nothing may appear. This is because Outlook has to search for the linked activities. If there is a delay, you'll notice the blue magnifying glass to the left of the Stop button going around and around. This indicates the search is in progress. When the search is complete, the magnifying glass stops and the linked activities are listed.

By default, Outlook displays all linked items. However, you can narrow the search by selecting a different activities view from the Show drop-down list. To view a linked item in the Activities tab, double-click it. If it's an Outlook item, it opens immediately. If it's a file, the journal entry opens. Double-click the file attachment in the journal entry to open the file in the program associated with the file type.

When you delete an item from the Activities tab, you are actually deleting the listed item, not merely the link to the item. In the case of a linked file, you're deleting the journal entry containing the file shortcut. Fortunately, anything you delete from the Activities tab is immediately sent to the Deleted Items folder, from which you can retrieve it if necessary.

You can't use the Link command to link objects to a contact form. However, you can elect to link an object when inserting it as an attachment. Although it saves some (not all) disk space, it does not add the linked object to the Activities tab. Your best bet is to link the object as a file, using the Actions | Link | File command.

Using Hyperlinks

While the Link command is quick and easy, it is also limited. The only things you can link to a contact with it are files and Outlook items. Hyperlinks expand the types of things you can link to include Outlook folders, personal and public folders, items, files, web sites, and FTP sites. To create a hyperlink, you must know the name and location of the folder or item you want to link to. You must also know the proper syntax to use.

Start by opening the contact in which you want to create the link. Then move your cursor to the Note field. Type the link using the syntax in Table 8-1.

To Open	Use This Syntax	Example
Outlook folder on the server	\<Outlook:*Foldername*>	\<Outlook:Inbox>
Personal or private folder	\<Outlook://*Foldername*>	\<Outlook://Personal Folders/Customers>
Outlook item	\<Outlook:*Foldername*/ ~*Itemname*>	\<Outlook:Contacts/ ~Bob Smith>
Outlook item in a subfolder	\<Outlook:*Foldername*/ *Subfoldername*/~*Itemname*>	\<Outlook:Contacts/Vendors/ ~Pete Brannigan>
Item in a public folder	\<Outlook://Public Folders/*Public Foldername*/*Foldername*/~*Itemname*>	\<Outlook://Public Folders/All Public Folders/Authors/ ~Stephen King>
File in a public folder	\<Outlook://Public Folders/*Public Foldername*/*Foldername*/ ~*filename.ext*>	\<Outlook://Public Folders/All Public Folders/Reports/ ~1QtrSales.doc>
Folder on your computer	\<file://*computername*/*driveletter*/ *foldername*>	\<file://Florida/c/ My Documents>
File on your computer	\<file://*computername*/*driveletter*/ *foldername*/*filename.ext*>	\<file://Florida/c/ My Documents/1QtrSales.xls>
Web site	\<http://www.*domain name*>	\<http://www.ezwidgets.com>
FTP site	\<ftp://*domain name*>	\<ftp://ezwidgets.com>

Table 8-1.   *Syntax Used When Creating Outlook Hyperlinks*

If the text string you're entering for the link contains no spaces, you can leave the less than (<) and greater than (>) signs off the beginning and end, respectively, of the link.

One last thing to be aware of. Links cannot contain items that include the following four characters in the item name: \ / " >. Outlook also has a bit of trouble when using hyperlinks to link to messages that have been replied to or forwarded. If you leave the RE: or FW: off and use the rest of the subject as the item name, Outlook finds the first message containing the specified text in the subject field.

Calling Contacts

Next to e-mail, the phone is probably your most frequently used means of communicating with business associates, friends, and co-workers. Since the Contacts folder is the logical place to store the phone numbers for those folks with whom you stay in touch via telephone, it's also the logical place from which to initiate phone calls. Fortunately, nothing could be simpler.

Obviously, the first thing to do is look up the contact. The next step depends on whether you have a modem hooked up to your phone line. If you have a modem, you may be able to let Outlook do the dialing for you. However, if you're in a corporate environment, chances are, even with a modem hookup, you're not going to be able to take advantage of the AutoDial feature. Most modem hookups in a corporate environment are separate from the company phone system and are therefore not able to work or play together.

However, if you have a phone line that's attached to both your modem and your phone, you can take advantage of the AutoDial feature. Open the Contacts folder, right-click the contact you want to call, and select Call Contact from the shortcut menu to open the New Call dialog box.

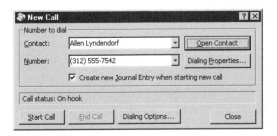

By default, Outlook lists the Business phone first. To use a different number, select one from the Number drop-down list or enter a new one manually. If you have the contact record already open, all you have to do is click the AutoDialer button.

If you haven't already set up your dialing properties, click the Dialing Properties button and do so now. The required information is pretty much common sense. When you're finished setting up the dialing properties, click Close to return to the New Call dialog box. You're now ready to let Outlook do the dialing for you. If you want to track

WORKING WITH CONTACTS

the call with a journal entry, check the Create New Journal Entry When Starting New Call option. Click Start Call to place the call. Outlook dials the selected number and displays the Call Status dialog box.

When the party answers, click Talk. If no one answers, click Hang Up to end the call. When you're through with the call, hang up and click End Call. That's all there is to it.

Mapping a Contact Address

A handy feature that first appeared in Outlook 2000 is the ability to display a map showing the contact's address. To use this feature, you must have an Internet connection. First, establish your connection to the Internet. Then open the contact whose address you want to map. Click the Display Map Of Address button on the contact form Standard toolbar. This launches your web browser and takes you to the Expedia.com web site. See Figure 8-7.

The initial view is an overview of the area. To see more detail, click the magnifying glass with the plus (+) sign or select a wider line in the Zoom Level box. You can use the Map Mover arrows to pan the map. You can even get driving directions to the location by clicking the Get Driving Directions link. When you're finished, return to Outlook and close the contact.

 If you're planning to visit the client, you might want to click the Get Driving Directions link and copy the directions into the Note field of the contact form.

Printing Contact Information

As convenient as an electronic address book is, there are times when nothing short of a hard copy will do. It's a little difficult standing at an airport phone cubicle and trying to fire up your laptop just to get a phone number. Or suppose you're in a meeting and you need a phone number to get some quick information from a colleague or business associate. Again, using a laptop is not only cumbersome, but also unnecessary. When the need arises, having a printed copy of your contacts can be a lifesaver.

To make life even easier, Outlook accommodates a variety of paper sizes and different address book types, such as Day-Timers, Day Runners, and Franklin Day Planners, as well as customized formats.

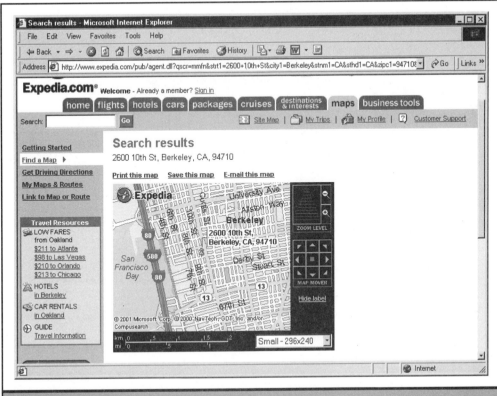

Figure 8-7.   *Pinpoint your contact's address in a flash*

To print your contact information, follow these steps:

1. Open the Contacts folder and click the Print button to display the Print dialog box shown in Figure 8-8.

2. From the Name drop-down list, select the printer you want to use.

3. Click the Properties button to set options for the selected printer. The options that appear depend entirely on the printer you've selected. Each printer has its own unique set of options.

4. Choose a style for the hard copy from the Print Style list. Your options depend on the current view selected in the Contacts folder. If the current view is an Address Cards view, your choices include

   ■ **Card Style**   Each contact appears on the printout displaying the same information and in the same format as it appears in the Address Cards view. The page setup calls for printing on a full 8.5×11-inch sheet of paper.

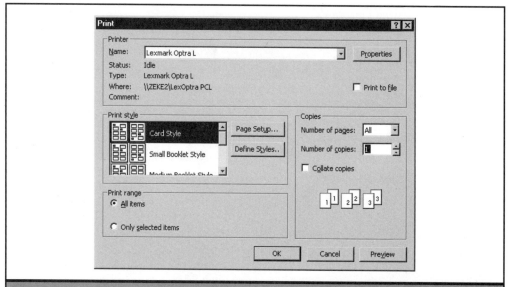

Figure 8-8. *The Print dialog box lets you decide how and what to print*

■ **Small Booklet Style** This is the Card Style with a page setup calling for an 8.5×11-inch sheet using the 1/8 sheet booklet size setting. In other words, it divides the full page into eight smaller pages, which can later be folded to form a small booklet.

■ **Medium Booklet Style** The Medium Booklet Style is also the Card Style with a different page setup. It uses an 8.5×11-inch sheet and divides it into four sections employing the 1/4 sheet booklet size setting.

■ **Memo Style** Use the Memo Style when you want to print more complete information for each contact. In addition to the fields from the General tab of the contact record, a number of fields from the Details tab are included. You can even include notes and attachments.

■ **Phone Directory Style** This is a great style to use when you want a phone list that is broken down alphabetically. Each contact is listed with all available phone numbers.

5. Click Page Setup to open the Page Setup dialog box and to change the settings for the selected style. The Page Setup dialog box may appear different from the one in Figure 8-9 depending on the print style selected.

6. Change the Format options to suit your needs. Different print styles offer a different range of options. Figure 8-9 shows the Format options for the Card Style, as well as for the Small and Medium Booklet Styles. The other print styles have more limited Format options.

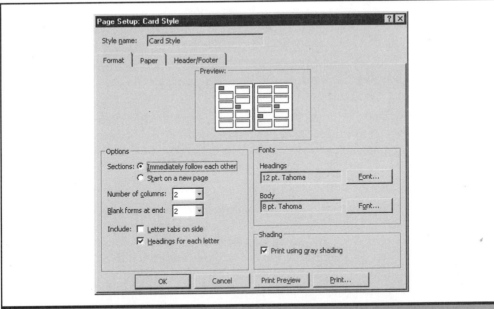

Figure 8-9.   *Customizing your hard copy is easy with the Page Setup dialog box options*

- **Preview**   Keep an eye on this small display area. It provides a rough estimation of the appearance of your printout, depending on the options you choose.

- **Sections**   Your selection here determines whether each alphabetical section (A, B, C, and so on) begins where the last section leaves off, or if it starts on a new page regardless of where the last section ends. Choose Immediately Follow Each Other for a continuous printout with each section starting where the last one ends. Choose Start On A New Page to start each section on its own page.

- **Number of columns**   Select the number of columns you want to appear on each page of the printout.

- **Blank forms at end**   This option enables you to designate the number of blank address book forms you want added to the printout. The pages are not actually blank, but contain field names and lines that make it easy to enter contact information. In theory it sounds good. However, it rarely gets used and is generally nothing more than a waste of paper. Therefore, you should set it to zero unless you find you actually use the "blank" pages.

- **Include**   If you have a large number of contacts to print, adding headings and letter tabs can prove helpful when searching for specific contacts. Check Letter Tabs On Side to include a vertical letter bar similar to the one that appears on address card views in the Contacts folder. The letters represented on each page appear in black. To add a letter heading to the beginning of each alphabetical section, check Headings For Each Letter.

■ **Fonts**   You can change the fonts used to print both headings and the body of the printout. Click the appropriate Font button and select the font, the font style, font size, and language.

■ **Shading**   While it may seem like a minor option, this can make all the difference in the appearance of your printout. With Shading checked, each contact name is offset in a shaded box, enabling you to quickly discern names at a glance. It also adds shading to letter tabs if you include them.

7. Click the Paper tab and adjust the settings as needed. Here's what you'll find:

■ **Type**   This selection indicates the actual type of paper you're using. It includes most standard paper types as well as a number of address book papers from Avery and one from FiloFax. In addition, you can specify a custom paper if your paper type doesn't appear on the list.

■ **Dimensions**   The width and height of the paper type selected are displayed here. If you're using a standard paper type, leave these dimensions as they are. If you select a custom paper, enter your own dimensions.

■ **Paper source**   Let Outlook know where to find the paper by making your selection from the Paper Source drop-down list. Unless your printer has multiple trays or unless you plan to feed the paper manually, you can leave this at the default setting.

■ **Margins**   Indicate the distance from the top, left side, right side, and bottom of the page you want the printing to appear. Inches are automatically assumed; therefore, you can just enter the distance and Outlook will add inch marks (").

■ **Size**   At first glance you might think that paper type and page size are the same. Be assured, they are not. The paper type indicates the exact size of the sheet used for printing. The page size refers to the page layout that gets printed on each sheet. For example, a small booklet may have as many as eight pages printed on a single sheet.

■ **Orientation**   Select Portrait to print the page vertically, or Landscape to print the page horizontally. The height and width of the page automatically adjust to the selected orientation. The preview box to the left of the orientation choices displays a rough estimation of the way the sheet will print depending on the options you've selected.

8. Click the Header/Footer tab to add headers and/or footers to the printout. Header information appears at the top of each page, while footer information appears at the bottom of each page. Text or data entered in the left text box appears on the left side of the page, text entered in the middle text box appears

in the middle of the page, and so on. You can use the Header/Footer toolbar
to add such things as page number, total number of pages, and more.

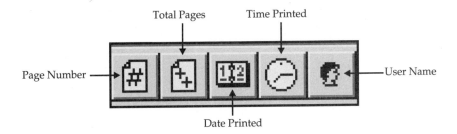

Total Pages   Time Printed

Page Number

User Name

Date Printed

9. Click OK to save your settings and return to the Print dialog box.

10. Select the range of items you want to print. Your choices include All Items
    and Only Selected Items. If you highlighted certain contacts before opening
    the Print dialog box, choosing Only Selected Items prints only those items;
    otherwise choose All Items to print all contacts in the current view.

*If you want to print a selection of contacts without selecting each one individually,
apply a filter to the view before clicking the Print button. When you go to print,
choose All Items to print everything in the filtered view.*

11. Set the Copies options, which include the following:

    ■ **Number of pages** You can elect to print all pages, odd-numbered, or
      even-numbered pages. This is especially handy if you want to use both sides
      of the paper. Print only the even-numbered pages; then reinsert the printed
      copies in the printer and print the odd-numbered pages. Of course, you'll
      have to be careful to reinsert them in the correct order and facing the right
      direction, or you'll end up with a mess. Try printing a couple of test pages
      before printing your entire Contacts folder.

    ■ **Number of copies** The name pretty much says it all.

    ■ **Collate copies** This potentially handy option automates the collating of
      multiple copies of multipage printouts. Normally, Outlook sends the print
      data for each page to the printer, which then prints the specified number of
      copies before moving on to the next page. Therefore, if you print ten copies
      of a five-page contact list, you'll end up with ten copies of Page 1, followed
      by ten copies of Page 2, and so on. You then have to separate them and put
      each five-page copy together manually. If you select Collate Copies, Outlook
      instructs the printer to print a single copy of each of the five pages, and then
      to start over until all ten copies are complete.

WORKING WITH
CONTACTS

> **Note** *While the Collate Copies option sounds great, it can be time-consuming since Outlook is forced to keep resending the same page information to the printer each time it starts a new copy. In the earlier example, with collating turned off, Outlook would send the page information only five times. However, with collating turned on, it is forced to send the page information 50 times. Depending on the size of the print job and how quickly your printer assimilates the data, this could result in an extremely lengthy print process. If you have a large print job, do a small test run before letting Outlook collate the whole thing.*

12. Click OK to print the contact information.

If you want to see what your printout is going to look like before printing it, click the Print Preview button in the Print dialog box.

Creating Other Items from Contacts

Earlier in this chapter, you discovered how to create contacts from other Outlook items. Now, taking advantage of the close integration of the various Outlook components, you're going to learn how to generate an assortment of Outlook items from contacts.

E-mailing Contacts

If you've got e-mail and you've got contacts, it's only natural that the two should converge. Clearly, one of the most common ways of communicating with a contact is by e-mail. And what better way to share contact information than via e-mail?

Sending E-mail to Contacts

If you're working in the Contacts folder and decide to send e-mail to a contact, there's no need to head back to the Inbox to do it. Simply right-click the contact you want to e-mail and select New Message To Contact from the shortcut menu that appears. Next thing you know, a new mail message form opens addressed to the selected contact. If you're so inclined, you can even select multiple contacts. Then choose Actions | New Message To Contact to open a new mail message addressed to all the selected contacts.

Another method you can use to create an e-mail message from a contact is the drag-and-drop method. Drag the contact to whom you want the message addressed and drop it on any mail folder (Inbox, Outbox, Drafts, Sent Items) shortcut in the Outlook Bar or on the desired mail folder in the Folder List. A new message form addressed to the contact(s) opens immediately.

Sending Contact Information via E-mail

In addition to sending e-mail to contacts, you can also send contacts to e-mail recipients. It's a great way to share contact information with co-workers, business associates, and friends. For sharing with other Outlook users, you can simply attach Outlook contacts to your e-mail message. To send contact information to non-Outlook users, you can attach contact information in the form of vCards (electronic business cards). Either way, the recipients can access and use the contact information.

To send Outlook contacts to other Outlook users, follow these steps:

1. Open the Contacts folder.

2. Select the contact(s) to send, and press CTRL+F or choose Actions | Forward to open a new mail message form. Outlook attaches the contact(s) to the message. If you select a single contact, the subject line includes the contact name preceded by *FW:*, indicating a forward. If you select multiple contacts, the subject line is blank, and all the shortcuts appear in the message as attachments.

 You can also right-click the selected contact(s) and choose Forward Items. However, if you select a distribution list, the Forward command is not available on the shortcut menu. You'll have to press CTRL+F or choose Actions | Forward from the Menu bar.

3. Add the desired recipients to the To, Cc, and Bcc fields.

4. Type your message in the message body.

5. Click Send to transmit the message and its attached contact item.

If you're a drag-and-drop fan, you can right-drag a contact and drop it on a mail folder shortcut on the Outlook Bar or in the Folder List. From the shortcut menu that appears, select Copy Here As Message With Attachment. This opens a new mail message form with the contact name as the subject line and the contact item inserted as an attachment. If you select multiple contacts, the subject line is left blank and the contacts are inserted as attachments.

 Using the Move Here As Message With Attachment produces the same results with one difference: the contact is removed from the Contacts folder.

To share information with non-Outlook users, you can send contact information in the vCard format. Most popular contact managers and personal information managers (PIMs) support the vCard format. To send a contact as a vCard, select the contact(s)

you want to send and choose Actions | Forward As vCard. This opens a new mail message form with the contact(s) included as .vcf attachment(s).

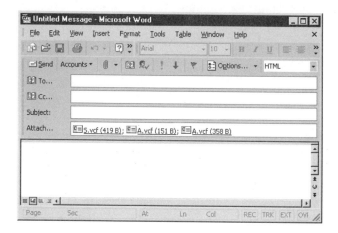

If you forward a single vCard, the subject line includes *FW:* followed by the contact name; otherwise the subject line is blank.

 You cannot forward distribution lists as vCards. If you select a distribution list or multiple contacts, one or more of which is a distribution list, the Forward As vCard command is unavailable.

You can also create vCards from contacts, and store them on your computer for later use. This is especially helpful if you want to create a vCard of your own contact information to attach to an e-mail signature.

To create a vCard from a contact, open the contact and choose File | Export To vCard File to display the VCARD File dialog box, which automatically opens to the Signatures folder. You can save the vCard file as is by clicking Save, or you can change the name and location before clicking Save. A new file using the contact name and the .vcf extension is created in the designated folder.

Creating Tasks, Meeting Requests, Notes, Journal Entries, and Appointments

Creating tasks, meeting requests, and appointments from contacts is as easy as selecting the contacts and choosing the appropriate command from the Actions menu. If you're using a single contact to create these items, you can right-click the contact and select the appropriate command from the shortcut menu.

The Advanced toolbar contains buttons for the New Meeting Request To Contact and the New Task For Contact commands. Right-click the Standard toolbar and select Advanced from the shortcut menu.

The available commands are

- **New Appointment with Contact**   This opens a new appointment form with the selected contact(s) entered in the Contacts field.

- **New Meeting Request to Contact**   This opens a new meeting request form addressed to the selected contact(s), and including the selected contact(s) in the Contacts field.

- **New Task for Contact**   This opens a new task form and enters the selected contact(s) in the Contacts field. If you click the Assign Task button, the task form is converted to a task request addressed to the selected contact(s).

- **New Journal Entry for Contact**   Opens a new journal entry form with the contact name as the subject, the company name in the Company field, and the contact added to the Contact field. If you select multiple contacts, only the first contact is used in creating the journal entry.

You can also create these Outlook items by dragging contacts to the appropriate Outlook Bar shortcut or Folder List folder. Dragging and dropping a contact on the Calendar shortcut or folder creates a new meeting request addressed to the contact. However, if you right-drag (click the right mouse button and hold while dragging) the contact to the Calendar shortcut or folder, you can choose to create a new appointment or a new meeting request.

Dragging a contact to the Tasks shortcut or folder produces similar results. A simple drag-and-drop operation results in a new task request addressed to the contact. Right-dragging the contact, however, displays a shortcut menu that offers you the opportunity to create a task request or a task.

Dragging a contact to the Journal shortcut or folder creates a new journal entry with the contact as the subject, in the Contacts field, and added to the Note field as a shortcut. Right-dragging provides the additional choice of adding the contact as an attachment. Dragging or right-dragging multiple contacts leaves the Subject and Contacts fields blank, but includes the selected contacts as shortcuts or attachments, depending on your method and choice.

To create an Outlook note from a contact, you have but one choice: drag the contact to the Notes shortcut or folder and drop it. If you right-drag the contact, the shortcut menu offers a single choice for creating a note: Copy Here As Note With Text. It produces exactly the same results as a simple drag-and-drop. If you try to drag multiple items, only one note is created, using the first contact item.

Writing Letters to Contacts

If you have Microsoft Word 97 or later installed on your computer, you can even use your contacts to automate the process of letter writing. Select the contact to whom you want to write a letter, and choose Actions | New Letter To Contact from the Menu bar. This opens Microsoft Word and launches the Letter Wizard that walks you through the steps of creating the letter. See Figure 8-10.

Set the appropriate options on the Letter Format tab, and click Next to view the Recipient Info tab. Here you'll find that the name, company, and address information from the selected contact has already been entered. Make any necessary changes and click Next to move to the Other Elements tab. Set the additional options found here, and click Next to display the Sender Info tab. Enter your name, return address, and closing information. Click Finish to create the new letter to the selected contact.

If you have Automatic Journaling turned on for the selected contact and for Microsoft Word, a journal entry is created for the letter. However, the entry is not associated with the contact to whom the letter is written. Consequently, it does not appear in the Activities tab of the contact's form. If you want the letter associated with the contact, you have to open the journal entry and enter the contact's name in the Contact field.

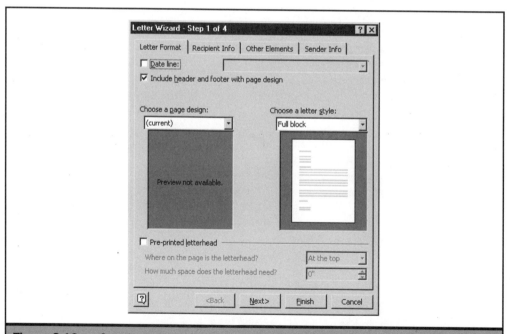

Figure 8-10.   *Creating a letter is a walk in the park when you use the Letter Wizard*

MOUS Exam Core Objectives Explored in Chapter 8

Objective	Activity	Heading
OL10-4-1	Create contacts	"Adding Contacts"
OL10-4-1	Edit contacts	"Modifying and Deleting Contacts"

WORKING WITH
CONTACTS

The
Complete
Reference

2002
Outlook

Chapter 9

Managing Contacts

Using contact information effectively requires the ability to view, locate, sort, and organize contacts quickly. Outlook provides all the tools you need to make sure your contact information is readily available when you need it. All you have to do is learn to put each of these tools to work for you. In this chapter, you'll learn to switch between the various standard views, as well as to use and create your own custom views. In addition, you'll discover a number of different methods for finding contacts as well as for sorting and organizing contacts.

Viewing Contacts

Whether you want to merely inspect the contents of your Contacts folder or search for a particular piece of information, Outlook offers a variety of ways to view your contact information. The Contacts folder offers two types of views: *address card* views and *table* views. The address card views, of which there are two by default, display primary contact information in a manner similar to what you might find on a Rolodex card display (see Figure 9-1). Table views, on the other hand, provide a column and row listing of contact information, in which the rows represent individual contacts and the columns contain specific pieces of information about the contact (see Figure 9-2).

Figure 9-1.   *The Address Cards view provides a quick view of basic information for each contact*

Figure 9-2.   *The Table List view is a frequently used table view that offers a simple listing of contacts.*

The Address Cards view displays a limited number of fields in each "card." Therefore, contacts with information in none or only some of those fields appear smaller and less complete.

Changing Views

To facilitate viewing your contact information, Outlook offers a number of standard views you can use. As noted earlier, they come in two flavors: address card views and table views. Switching between views is simple. Open the Contacts folder and choose View | Current View to display a submenu of available views.

The Advanced toolbar contains a Current View drop-down list that makes switching views a lot easier. Right-click anywhere on the Standard toolbar and select Advanced from the shortcut menu to display the Advanced toolbar.

The address card views include

- **Address Cards**   This view provides a separate card for each contact and displays the mailing address, all four primary phone numbers, and all e-mail addresses for the contact.

■ **Detailed Address Cards**   As the name implies, this view is the same as the Address Cards view with more data. The additional information displayed includes full name, company, job title, home address, alternate phone numbers, web page, categories to which the contact is assigned, and any notes you've entered.

The table views available in the Contacts folder include

■ **Phone List**   Here you'll find each contact listed along with the company name, the File As designation, the four primary phone numbers (business phone, business fax, home phone, and mobile phone), the AutoJournal setting, and categories to which the contact is assigned.

■ **By Category**   Contacts are grouped by categories and display full name, company, File As, categories, business phone, business fax, home phone, and mobile phone information.

■ **By Company**   This view groups contacts by company and displays full name, job title, company, File As, department, business phone, business fax, home phone, mobile phone, and categories information.

■ **By Location**   Contacts in this view are grouped by the Country/Region field and display full name, company, File As, state, country/region, business phone, business fax, home phone, mobile phone, and categories information.

■ **By Follow-up Flag**   This view groups contacts by flag status and displays icon, attachments, follow-up flag, full name, company, File As, business phone, business fax, home phone, mobile phone, and categories information.

One thing to note about both types of views is that by default you can edit most of the information in the view without opening the contact record. However, certain fields, such as Icon, Attachments, and Notes, cannot be edited unless you open the contact record.

If you want to ensure that you or someone else doesn't accidentally change the contents of a field while in a contacts view, you can disable in-cell editing. Choose View | Current View | Customize Current View and click Other to open the Other Settings dialog box. Remove the check mark in the Allow In-Cell Editing option.

Customizing Contact Views

Contact views, like other Outlook views, are highly customizable. You can add and remove fields, change fonts, column widths, in-cell editing, and more. To customize the currently displayed view, choose View | Current View | Customize Current View to open the View Summary dialog box.

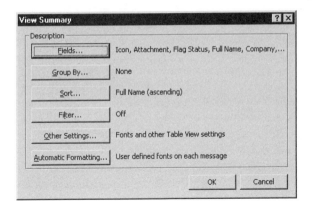

Click the appropriate button to customize the view settings. For details on customizing Outlook views, see Chapter 23.

Sorting Contacts

Without the ability to sort your information, the contact views would lose a great deal of their usefulness. Seeing your information may be nice, but manipulating it to suit your needs is where the real value lies. Fortunately, Outlook provides a variety of ways in which you can manipulate your contact information. *Sorting,* as you're probably aware, is the arranging of information in a specific order based on criteria you select. For example, if you want a listing of all contacts arranged by their location, you would perform a sort using the Country/Region field as the sort criterion. If you wanted to sort on multiple fields, you might set a secondary sort for State, and a third for Last Name.

The other important thing to understand about sorting is whether the sort is ascending or descending. *Ascending* sorts are arranged from first to last, and *descending* sorts are just the opposite—from last to first. Using the earlier example of a sort based on Country/Region, Albania would appear before Zimbabwe in an ascending sort, and after Zimbabwe in a descending sort.

Using a Quick Sort in Table Views

To make life easier, Outlook affords you the opportunity to perform a quick sort within a table view simply by clicking the column header of the field you want to use for the sort. In other words, if you're in the Phone List view and you want to sort the list by company, click the Company header. Like magic, the Phone List rearranges itself and displays contacts by company. The first time you click a header, the sort is ascending. Click the header a second time and the order is descending. Each time you click the header the sort order is reversed.

You can also right-click a field header and select Sort Ascending or Sort Descending from the shortcut menu.

In the event you want to sort a view by more than a single field, you can do so with the use of the SHIFT key. Set the sort order for the first field, and then hold down the SHIFT key and click the header of the field you want to use for the secondary sort. If need be, while still holding down the SHIFT key, click the header a second time to change the order (ascending or descending). You can continue to hold the SHIFT key and select up to four fields for the sort order. If you try to exceed four sort fields, Outlook informs you that you're attempting to use too many sort levels.

> **Note** *If you change your mind about including a field in a multifield sort, you'll have to start over. There's no way to remove a field from the sort except to release the SHIFT key and click the first field in the new sort. Of course, you can always return to the Sort dialog box and click Clear All, but that still removes the sort from all fields, not just the one you want to delete.*

An example of a multilevel sort would be the Phone List view sorted first by Company, then by Last Name, and finally by First Name. Assuming the sort order for each field is ascending, all contacts from company A would appear first, followed by all contacts from company B, and so on. Within each company group, contacts whose last names start with *A* would appear first, followed by contacts with last names starting with *B*, and continuing until the end of the alphabet is reached. In the event that two or more contacts within any company have the same last name, the one whose first name begins with *A* appears first, followed by the one whose first name begins with *B*, and so on.

A salesperson who travels a regular route might add a ZIP Code field to the Phone List and then sort the view first by ZIP Code, then by Company, and finally by Last Name. When it comes time to make the rounds, it would be easy to set up appointments in a logical fashion based on the route traveled.

Using the Sort Dialog Box

For sorting card views or for sorting table or card views using fields that don't appear in the view, you can use the Sort dialog box. It allows you to select any field available in the contact form and use it to perform a sort, regardless of whether the field appears in the view you want to sort.

To use the Sort dialog box, follow these steps:

1. Open the Contacts folder.

2. Open the view you want to sort.

3. Choose View | Current View | Customize Current View to display the View Summary dialog box.

You can also right-click a blank spot in the view and select Sort from the shortcut menu to display the Sort dialog box. In a table view, you can right-click any column header and select Customize Current View to display the View Summary dialog box.

4. Click the Sort button to open the Sort dialog box.

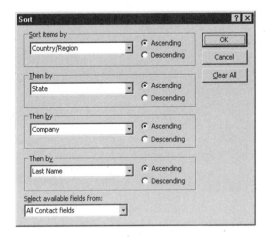

5. From the Select Available Fields From drop-down list choose All Contact Fields. This ensures that all the fields used in the contact form are available for use as sort criteria.

6. Select the field to use as the primary sort field from the Sort Items By drop-down list.

7. Select the Ascending or Descending option, as appropriate.

8. If you want to perform a multilevel sort, repeat the field and sort order selections using the three Then By options as needed.

9. Click OK to close the Sort dialog box.

If any of the fields you've selected do not appear in the view by default, Outlook asks if you want them added when the view is sorted. Click Yes to add the field to the view or No to sort by the field without adding it to the view. If you elect to add the field, it appears as the very last column. Also, the field remains in the view until you remove it.

10. Click OK to perform the sort and close the View Summary dialog box.

Although you can sort on most contact fields, there are a few that cannot be used. These include Categories, Notes, Children, and Send Plain Text Only. Consequently, they do not appear in the Sort dialog box drop-down lists. Now, if you're thinking you'll get around this by using the Field Chooser to add these fields to the current view and then perform a quick sort, think again. While it sounds like a good idea, the only thing you'll receive for your trouble is a curt message informing you that "You cannot sort by this field."

MOUS

MOUS EXAM PRACTICE

In this section, you learned to sort contact records. Begin your practice now by applying a quick sort using a single field. Start with a table view, and click the field header to sort the view by that field. Note the type of sort that's applied. Is it ascending or descending? Now reverse the sort by clicking the header again. Right-click a header and use one of the sort commands. Next, try sorting using multiple fields by holding down the SHIFT key and clicking each header. Finally, switch to an address card view, right-click a blank spot in the Information viewer, and select Sort to display the Sort dialog box. Choose a single field and sort order first, and then try multiple fields.

Applying Filters to Contacts

In addition to sorting your contact views, you can also modify them by filtering out certain records and displaying only those that meet the criteria you determine. Filters enable you to temporarily hide those contacts that do not meet your criteria. To apply a filter to your contacts, open the Contacts folder and select the view of your choice. Right-click a column header in the Information viewer and select Customize Current View to display the View Summary dialog box. Now click Filter to display the Filter dialog box.

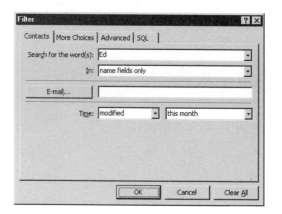

You can directly access the Filter dialog box by right-clicking a blank spot on the Information viewer and selecting Filter from the shortcut menu.

Use the Contacts tab to apply a simple filter based on keywords found in a particular field, an e-mail address, or the time a contact was created or modified. Enter the keyword(s) in the Search For The Word(s) field, and select the field type in which to search for the keyword(s). You can type an e-mail address directly into the E-mail field, or click the E-mail button and select an existing e-mail address from one of your address books.

To locate groups of contacts based on similar e-mail addresses, you can enter a partial address. For example, to find all contacts from educational institutions, you could enter .edu.

To filter contacts based on their creation or modification dates, make the appropriate selection from the Time drop-down lists. The first list lets you determine whether to use the Created or Modified date. From the second Time drop-down list, select the timeframe to use. Click OK to save the filter settings and return to the View Summary dialog box. Click OK again to apply the filter and return to the Contacts folder.

In a Microsoft Exchange Server environment, the Created and Modified dates are determined by the Microsoft Exchange Server's clock, not your desktop's clock. However, the Outlook Filter feature uses your desktop's clock when searching for date criteria. In other words, if your desktop clock indicates today's date is the 15th of the month, but the Microsoft Exchange Server's clock says it's the 14th, all contacts you modify today will bear a Modified date of the 14th. However, when you apply a filter using Today as the Modified date, Outlook searches for contacts bearing a Modified date of the 15th.

If you want to apply a more sophisticated filter, return to the Filter dialog box and click the More Choices tab. Here you'll find additional criteria on which to base the filter.

The More Choices tab offers the following filter criteria:

- **Categories**   Enter the category, or click the Categories button and choose the category from the dialog box that appears. To use multiple categories, separate each one with a comma. However, be aware that there is an implied *Or* between each category you enter. Therefore, a filter that includes both Business and Competition in the Categories field will search for any contacts that are assigned to either the Business or the Competition category, or both. Unfortunately, there's no way to force it to search for only those records containing both categories. Fortunately, there is a way to get around this problem using the Advanced tab. Take the earlier example of Business and Competition categories. Enter filter criteria that say "Categories contains Business and Competition."

- **Only items that are**   Since the only choices here are Read and Unread, this option is of little use in filtering contacts.

- **Only items with**   If you want to filter out contacts on the basis of attachments (with or without), check this option and make the appropriate selection from the drop-down list.

- **Whose importance is**   In spite of the fact that you can actually set the Importance level for a contact in the contact Properties dialog box, this option is grayed out. The apparent reason is that Importance is not a standard contact field.

- **Match case**   Check this option to force Outlook to search for the exact combination of upper- and lowercase letters entered in the Search For The Word(s) option on the Contacts tab.

- **Size (kilobytes)**   Select the appropriate conditional operator from the drop-down list and enter the value in kilobytes.

The third tab in the Filter dialog box is the Advanced tab, which enables you to add sophisticated filtering criteria based on multiple fields.

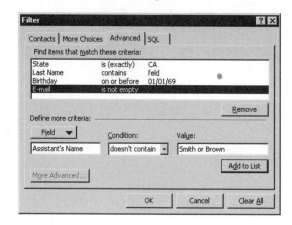

In addition, it offers the full range of contact fields to choose from. To create an advanced filter, click the Field button and move your mouse pointer to All Contact Fields. A large menu containing all the contact fields appears. Select the field you want to use for the first set of conditions. From the Condition drop-down list, select the appropriate conditional operator. In the Value field, enter the data corresponding to the field on which the condition is based. In other words, if you select a name or other text field, the information you enter should be text. If you select a date field, such as Birthday, the information should be in a date format (mm/dd/yy).

 You can use And between multiple values to search for only those records containing all values entered. You can also use Or between values to search for any of the values entered.

When you've entered all necessary information, click the Add To List button to add the new condition to the Find Items That Match These Criteria list. Repeat the process for each filter condition you want to use. Then click OK to apply the filter. All records matching the filter criteria you entered appear, while the remaining records are temporarily hidden.

The fourth and final tab, SQL provides additional filtering capabilities enabling you to use SQL language commands to create the filter criteria. When you use the SQL tab, all other tabs are disabled.

When you're finished using the filtered view, it's always a good idea to remove the filter. Opening your Contacts folder at some later date only to find that half your contacts seem to have disappeared can be rather disconcerting. Fortunately, Outlook provides a reminder by adding a (Filter Applied) notice to the Folder banner, and another to the status bar. Whenever you decide to remove the filter, it's quite simple. Open the Filter dialog box and click Clear All.

Finding Contacts

Being able to locate contact information when you need it is one of the primary benefits to using the Outlook Contacts folder. While you can certainly apply a filter when necessary, there are much simpler ways to find individual contacts or groups of related contacts. As with most tasks, Outlook provides a variety of ways to locate contact data:

- **Keyboard** Search by the first letter(s) of a contact name.
- **Letter tabs** Use this feature for an alphanumeric search.
- **Find A Contact** This feature provides a simple search in several sources.
- **Find** For a more sophisticated search, use the Find button located on the Standard toolbar or choose Tools | Find. This displays the Find Items In Contacts pane, which enables you to search for any text string in the Name, Company, Addresses, and Category fields.

■ **Advanced Find**   The Advanced Find feature provides the ability to extend
your search to every field and to use multiple search criteria. It will help you
achieve the equivalent of finding a needle in a haystack.

Using the Keyboard

If you open an address card view in the Contacts folder and type the first letter or first
few letters of a contact name, Outlook takes you to the first contact whose name begins
with the letter(s). If you enter multiple letters, they must be quickly typed in succession
for the procedure to work properly. Pausing too long between letters causes Outlook to
consider them separate searches, and results in locating the contact whose File As name
begins with the second letter typed.

Using the Letter Tabs

Both the Address Cards view and the Detailed Address Cards view contain letter tabs
that run down the right side of the Information viewer (see Figure 9-3).

*Since the letter tabs are only useful for an alphanumeric search, sorting an address
card view by a non-text field, such as Anniversary or Birthday, causes the letter tabs
to disappear. When you re-sort the view using a text field, the letter tabs reappear.*

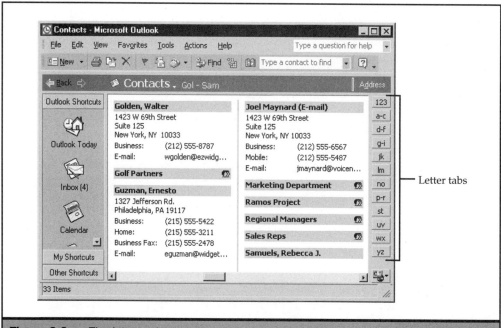

Figure 9-3.   *The letter tabs provide one-click navigating through the Contacts folder*

The vertical bar contains buttons with letters of the alphabet (and one button with numbers). Click a button to view contacts beginning with the letter(s) appearing on the button.

 Right-clicking anywhere on a letter tab displays the same shortcut menu that appears when you right-click a blank spot on the Information viewer.

Using Find A Contact

Use this option, located on the Standard toolbar, to conduct a simple search for contact information.

Find a Contact

Enter a contact name in the Find A Contact text box, or select a previously used name from the drop-down list. Then press ENTER to locate the contact record. Outlook begins by searching both First Name and Last Name fields in the Contacts folder and its subfolders, and then moves on to other address books. It displays the first contact or addressee it encounters. If multiple matches are found, the Choose Contact dialog box appears.

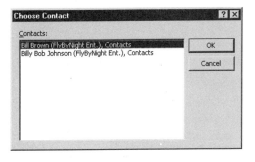

 If you encounter a problem searching on a last name, it may be the result of a contact whose entire name is entered in the First Name field of the Contact form. This frequently happens when Personal Address Book entries are imported into the Contacts folders. Find A Contact will not locate a last name when it is part of the First Name field. Find the contact by searching on the first name, and edit the record to reflect the correct entries in the First Name and Last Name fields.

One handy feature of the Find A Contact option is that it retains previous entries you've searched for. Therefore, you can repeat a search at a later time simply by selecting one of your past searches from the drop-down list.

If Outlook hangs and you receive an application error or page fault error while using the Find A Contact feature, it may be the result of a corrupt QuickFindMRU Registry key. To resolve the problem, close all programs, open the Windows Registry and delete the HKEY_CURRENT_USER\Software\Microsoft\Office\10.0\Outlook\Contact\ QuickFindMRU key. Restart Windows and a new QuickFindMRU key will be regenerated automatically when you open Outlook. Warning! Only experienced users should modify the Windows Registry. Always back up your Registry before making any changes.

The drop-down list retains the last 12 names you've used as the search criterion. Once you reach 12, the last item on the list is removed to make room for your latest search name.

Using the Find Feature

If the Find A Contact feature is too limited for your needs, try the Find feature, which enables you to search on more than just the First Name and Last Name fields. Click the Find button on the Standard toolbar to display the Find pane in the Information viewer, as shown in Figure 9-4.

Enter the keyword(s) for which you want to search, select the folder in which to search, and click Find Now. If you want to search on multiple keywords, separate them with commas. Any contacts containing the keyword(s) are displayed in the Information

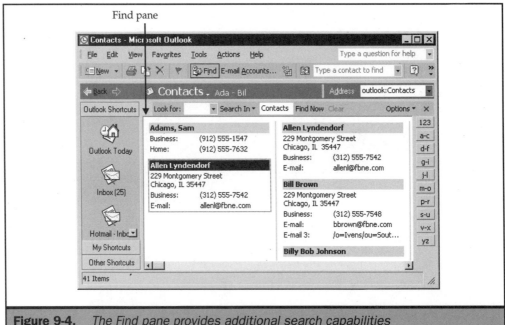

Figure 9-4. *The Find pane provides additional search capabilities*

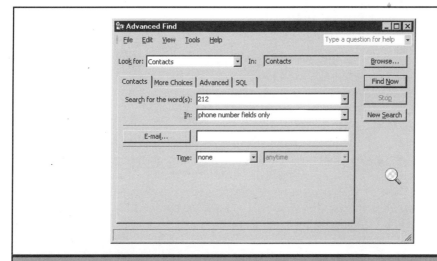

Figure 9-5.   *Use the Advanced Find dialog box for complex searches*

viewer. Be advised, however, that only Name, Company, Addresses, Category, E-mail, and Notes fields are included in the search.

If the search is unsuccessful, you can click the Clear button and try a new search, or you can press CTRL+SHIFT+F to open the Advanced Find Dialog box, seen in Figure 9-5.

The Advanced Find feature is almost identical to the Filter feature discussed earlier in this chapter. The only difference is in the ability to select the type of item to search for and the folder in which to conduct the search. Also, the results are displayed in a pane at the bottom of the Advanced Find dialog box. For details on using the Advanced Find feature, see the earlier section entitled "Applying Filters to Contacts."

Organizing Contacts

Keeping your contacts organized ensures the most efficient use of your time by providing ready access to data when you need it. Outlook offers a variety of ways to impose order on your contact information. You can utilize the flexible folder system upon which Outlook is based to create a hierarchy of contact folders and to maintain separate contact databases. If you have an extremely large database of customers, vendors, and employees, you might create a subfolder for each, thereby eliminating the need to sift through the entire database when searching for any one of the three. If you have a small- to medium-sized database of contacts that includes customers, vendors, and employees, you can keep them all in the same folder, but assign them to different categories. This enables you to filter out one group or the other when the need arises. You can even use custom formatting to make sure specific contacts or groups of contacts stand out when you view the Contacts folder. For more information on custom formatting, see Chapter 23.

Using the Organize Feature

The Outlook Organize feature offers one-stop shopping for tools to whip your Contacts folder into shape. It lets you utilize folders, categories, and views to organize your contact information. Open your Contacts folder and click the Organize button on the Standard toolbar to display the Organize pane, shown in Figure 9-6.

Assigning Contacts to Categories

By default, the Organize pane opens to the Using Categories options (shown in Figure 9-6). To assign one or more contacts to a category, select the contacts in the Information viewer (to select multiple contacts, hold the CTRL key down and click the desired contacts). Then choose the category from the Add Contacts Selected Below To drop-down list, and click the Add button. All the selected contacts are assigned to the designated category. If you open any of the contacts, you'll see the category assignment in the Categories field of the contact form.

There's no way to assign contacts to more than one category at a time. However, the selection of contacts remains intact until you change it. Therefore, you can repeat the assignment process for as many categories as you want without having to reselect the same group of contacts each time.

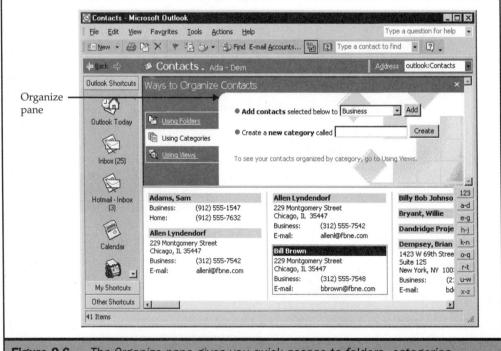

Figure 9-6.   *The Organize pane gives you quick access to folders, categories, and views*

You can even create a new category if the existing categories don't meet your needs. Simply type the category name in the Create A New Category Called field and click the Create button. The new category is created and added to the Add Contacts Selected Below To drop-down list. You can assign contacts to the new categories as you would assign them to any category.

MOUS EXAM PRACTICE
This one's so easy it doesn't require a lot of practice. However, to use categories effectively, you'll have to learn to choose the right category and also to create and modify categories. So, plan your category needs, create new ones and modify existing ones as needed, and then start assigning your Outlook items to the appropriate categories.

Using Folders

Another feature of the Organize pane is the Using Folders feature. It enables you to move contacts from one folder to another and even create new folders on-the-fly. Click the Using Folders link in the Organize pane to display the folder options.

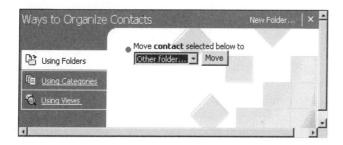

In the current view, select the contact(s) you want to move to another folder. From the Move Contact Selected Below To drop-down list, choose the folder into which you want to move the selected contact(s). Remember, you can only move contact items to a folder designated to hold contact items. Select Other Folder to display the Select Folders dialog box, where you can choose from all available folders. Select the desired folder and click OK to move the contact(s), or create a new folder by clicking the New button. Any new folders you create here are added to the drop-down list in the Organize pane.

Moving contact items to a non-contact folder creates items of the type the folder holds, using the information from the contact records you're attempting to move. You can take advantage of this to create e-mail messages addressed to selected contacts, as well as appointments, tasks, or notes for the selected contacts, by moving them to the appropriate folder.

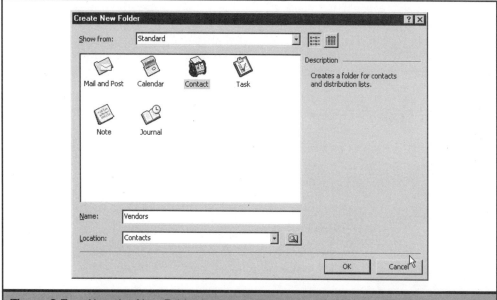

Figure 9-7. *Use the New Folder button to create new folders on-the-fly*

If you want to create a new contacts folder, click the New Folder button located in the upper-right corner of the Organize pane to open the Create New Folder dialog box shown in Figure 9-7.

By default, the folder type is Contact. To change it, click the appropriate icon or select Other Folder to view a folder tree of all existing folders. To use an existing folder, select it and click OK. It immediately appears in the Move Contact Selected Below To drop-down list. Click the Move button to send the selected contacts to the new folder.

You can even create a new folder by clicking the New button, which displays the Create New Folder dialog box. In the Name field, enter a name for the new folder. From the Location drop-down list, select the existing folder to which you want the new folder added as a subfolder, and click OK to create the new folder.

Using Views

The third feature found in the Organize pane lets you change and customize views. Click the Using Views link to display the view options.

The current view is highlighted in the Change Your View list. To change the view, scroll down the list and select the desired view. The Information viewer immediately reflects your choice. To modify the view, click Customize Current View in the top-right corner of the Organize pane. This displays the View Summary dialog box, from which you can add and remove fields, apply sort and filter conditions, and more. See Chapter 24 for more information on customizing views.

When you're finished using the Organize pane, you can close it by clicking the Organize button on the Standard toolbar or the small X located in the top-right corner of the Organize pane.

Using the Move To Folder Command

The Organize pane, while useful, also takes up quite a bit of the Information viewer space. Therefore, if your goal is to move contacts, you may prefer to use the Move To Folder command. Select the contact(s) you want to move and press CTRL+SHIFT+V to display the Move Items dialog box.

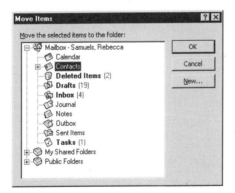

Select the folder to which you want the items moved, and click OK to effect the move. That's all there is to it. You can even create a new folder by clicking the New button and providing a name and location for the new folder.

In addition to using the Move To Folder command, you can also drag selected contacts to the target folder in the Folder List or to an Outlook Bar shortcut icon.

Using Categories to Organize Contacts

Categories provide a simple and effective way to create groups of related contacts without having to physically segregate them. While extremely large contact databases may see a significant reduction in search times by separating related groups of contacts and placing them in separate folders, the benefit for small databases will be negligible. As a matter of fact, separating small databases into a series of folders will probably cost more time spent in hopping from folder to folder when searching for information. The easiest and most efficient way to create groups of related contacts in a small- to medium-sized contacts database is with the use of categories.

Using the Categories Command

The quickest and easiest way to assign a contact to a category is by using the Category button on the contact form during the creation or modification of the contact. Located at the bottom of the contact form, the Categories button, when clicked, displays a list of all existing categories, as shown in Figure 9-8.

You can assign the contact to as many categories as you want by checking each category. To create a new category, enter a name for the category in the Item(s) Belong To These Categories list and click the Add To List button.

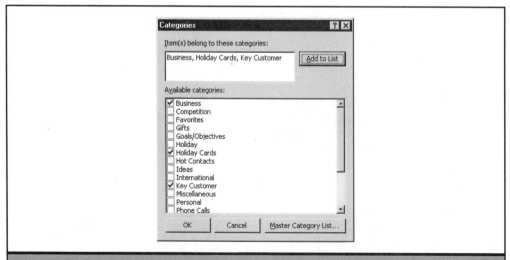

Figure 9-8.   *Check all the categories to which you want the selected contact assigned*

You can also assign multiple contacts to one or more categories at the same time by using the Categories command:

1. Open the Contacts folder.
2. Select the contacts you want to assign to one or more categories.
3. Choose Edit | Categories from the Menu bar to open the Categories dialog box. You can also right-click one of the selected contacts and select Categories from the shortcut menu.

Note *If any of the selected contacts are already assigned to categories, those categories appear with a check mark in a gray box.*

4. Check the category or categories to which you want to assign the selected contacts.

Tip *You can use categories that are already assigned (check mark in a gray box) to some of the selected contacts by removing the check mark and adding it again. This does not add a second assignment to the contacts already assigned, merely a single assignment to all selected contacts.*

5. Click OK to make the category assignments and return to the Contacts folder.

To remove category assignments, follow the preceding steps and remove the check marks in gray boxes from the categories whose assignments you want eliminated.

You can also add a new category while making the assignments. Enter a name for the new category in the Item(s) Belong To These Categories box, and click the Add To List button.

Using the Outlook Organize Feature

As discussed in an earlier section, you can use the Organize feature to assign contacts to categories. Click the Organize button to display the Organize pane, which opens, by default, with the Using Categories options visible. In the Information viewer, select the contact(s) you want to assign to a category. From the Add Contacts Selected Below To drop-down list, choose the category to which you want the contact(s) assigned, and click Add. To create a new category, enter a name in the Create A New Category Called field and click Create.

Using the By Category View

Realizing the importance of using categories to organize contacts, the Outlook programmers thoughtfully provided a standard view for displaying contacts by category assignments. The view, called By Category, creates a contact group for each category used. Choose View | Current View | By Category to switch to the view. As you can see in Figure 9-9, the groups are arranged alphabetically by category name.

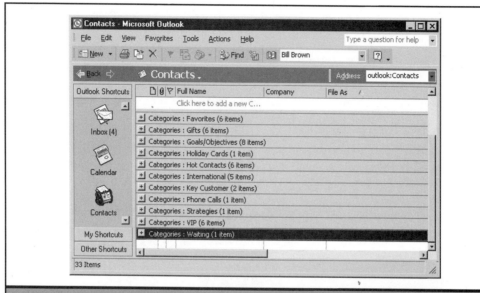

Figure 9-9.   The By Category view lets you organize your contacts according to their category assignments

Contacts assigned to multiple categories appear in all category groups to which they're assigned. To display the contacts in a category group, click the plus (+) sign to the left of the category name. To hide the contacts, click the minus (-) sign.

MOUS EXAM PRACTICE
In this section, you saw how categorizing your contacts can make searching and sorting your Contacts folder a lot easier. Start your practice by opening an existing contact and using the Category button to assign the contact to a category. Next, select multiple contacts in the Contacts folder and use the Categories command to assign them to one or more categories. Add a couple of new categories, and use the Organize feature to categorize some of your contacts. After you've assigned your contacts to categories, see how they appear when you display them in the By Category view.

Using Custom Colors to Classify Contacts

There's a handy feature in Outlook 2002 called Automatic Formatting that enables you to classify contacts by using custom colors and fonts. While it doesn't create groups of contacts, it does enable you to visually identify contacts of different types without having to resort to additional actions such as sorting and filtering. As a matter of fact, if you've added any distribution lists to your Contacts folder, you've already seen the results of Automatic Formatting. All distribution list items are automatically bolded as a result of a default rule created using Automatic Formatting.

To create your own Automatic Formatting rules, follow these steps:

1. Open the Contacts folder.
2. Choose View | Current View | Customize Current View to display the View Summary dialog box.
3. Click the Automatic Formatting button to open the Automatic Formatting dialog box.

4. Click the Add button to create a new rule.
5. Enter a name for the rule in the Name field.
6. Click the Font button and select the font, font style, font size, and font color from the font dialog box that appears. Click OK to return to the Automatic Formatting dialog box.

Be sure not to duplicate the formatting used in an existing rule, or you won't be able to tell the items apart by visual clues. You can check existing rules by highlighting the rule and examining the contents of the Font field.

7. Click the Condition button to display the Filter dialog box. This is the identical Filter dialog box used to create filters. See the section earlier in this chapter entitled "Applying Filters to Contacts" for details on using the Filter Dialog box.

8. After you set the condition(s) for the new rule, click OK to return to the Automatic Formatting dialog box.

 An example would be creating a rule called Department Heads based on a filter condition that states the Job Title field contains the words Department Head.

9. Click OK to save the new rule and return to the View Summary dialog box.

10. Click OK to return to the Contacts folder and apply the new formatting.

You can disable a rule without deleting it by opening the Automatic Formatting dialog box and removing the check mark next to the rule. Should you decide to remove a rule altogether, you can do so by selecting the rule and clicking the Delete button.

Setting Contact Options

Although Outlook can hardly be considered stingy when it comes to options, the Contacts folder is more limited than some of the other folders in customizable features. There are two sets of options you can customize for the Contacts folder: the Contact Options found on the Preferences tab of the Options dialog box, and the options located in the Contacts Properties dialog box.

Contact Options

The Contact Options enable you to set the default order for the Full Name and File As fields found in the contact form and to select the contacts for which AutoJournaling is turned on. To set these options, choose Tools | Options to open the Options dialog box with the Preferences tab displayed. Click the Contact Options button to display the Contact Options dialog box.

From the Default "Full Name" Order drop-down list, select the order in which you want the name information displayed in the Full Name field of each contact record.

Move to the next option and select the information and order of appearance for the File As field. You can elect to use the contact name, the company name, or both.

The next option, Check For Duplicate Contacts, is checked by default. It ensures that anytime you enter a new contact with the same name or same e-mail address as an existing contact, Outlook alerts you to the fact. Be advised, however, that it does not consider contacts created using the Copy command as duplicates. Therefore, if you make a copy of an existing contact, Outlook will not warn you that you've just created a duplicate contact.

The final option enables you to create a second Contacts Index (the vertical letter tab used for navigating the address card views) in a different language. Check the option and select the desired language. The next time you return to an address card view in the Contacts folder, you'll see both the original and new letter tabs, side by side.

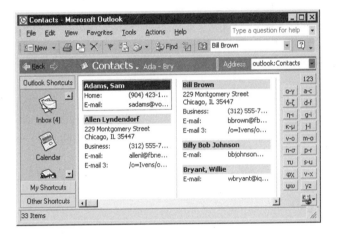

Click OK when you're done, and return to the Options dialog box.

You can now set AutoJournaling options for your contacts by clicking the Journal Options button to display the Journal Options dialog box.

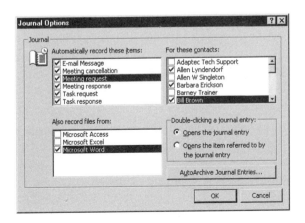

From the Automatically Record These Items list, select the Outlook items you want automatically recorded in the journal. Then move to the For These Contacts list, and choose for which contact you want the selected Outlook items recorded. If you want to include items from other Microsoft Office applications, make the appropriate selection(s) in the Also Record Files From list. Only compatible, installed programs appear on this list. Click the AutoArchive Journal Entries button to display the AutoArchive tab of the Journal folder Properties dialog box. Here you set the AutoArchive options for the Journal folder. See Chapter 18 for more information on AutoArchiving. Click OK to return to the Options dialog box.

Setting Contacts Folder Properties

The Contacts folder, like all Outlook folders, has a variety of properties that you can set to change the way the folder appears and behaves. These properties include everything from the form used to post items to the folder, to designating a home page for the folder. To access the Contacts Properties dialog box (shown in Figure 9-10), right-click the Contacts shortcut on the Outlook Bar (or the Contacts folder in the Folder List) and select Properties.

 The Folder List must be locked into place before right-clicking works. If you click the folder name to display the Folder List, then try right-clicking, you'll find that nothing happens. Click the yellow pushpin in the top-right corner of the Folder List to keep it open.

As you can see, the Contacts Properties dialog box contains eight tabs, which in turn contain a variety of options that affect the way the folder looks and works. Here's a quick rundown of what each tab contains:

- **General**   The General tab contains the name, description, and default form used for the folder. In addition, you can view the folder size, which includes the size of all subfolders as well.

- **Home Page**   This tab contains options enabling you to assign a home page to the folder, and to make it the default view when the folder is opened. You can designate a web page, image, or a document as the Home Page. To have Outlook display the designated home page as the default view every time you open the folder, check the Show Home Page By Default For This Folder option.

- **Outlook Address Book**   Use this tab to set options to display the contents of the folder as an Outlook address book, and add it to the Show Names From The drop-down list in the Address Book.

- **Activities**   Use this tab to designate those Outlook items associated with a contact that you want to keep track of for each contact in the folder.

- **Administration**   Here you'll find options for administering the folder. However, these options are available only to users with administrator rights. The only

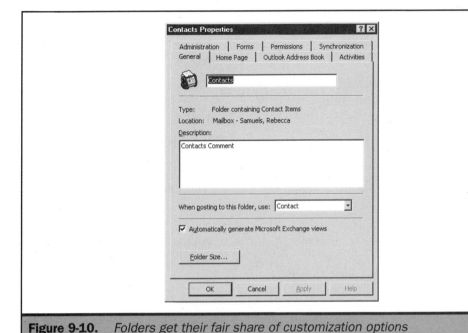

Figure 9-10.   *Folders get their fair share of customization options*

folders for which Outlook users generally have administrator rights, and therefore access to Administration options, are public folders they've created.

■ **Forms**   This tab provides options to determine which forms can be used to post information to the folder.

■ **Permissions**   Use this form to give others access to the folder by granting permissions. The Permissions tab options are available only to the folder owner. Other users can see the tab if they have access to the folder, but they cannot change the permissions.

■ **Synchronization**   This tab contains a single option for setting filters that determine how the folder is synchronized.

Of the preceding Contacts Properties dialog box tabs, only the Outlook Address Book and Activities tabs are pertinent to this section. The remaining tabs are common to various other Outlook folders, and are therefore covered in detail in Chapter 18.

Setting Outlook Address Book Tab Options

The Outlook Address Book tab enables you to designate a contact folder as an Outlook Address Book, and to give the address book a unique name distinct from the folder name. This means the folder appears as a selection in all address book lists in Outlook (Address Book, Select Names dialog box, and so on). The Outlook Address Book tab itself is simple and straightforward, containing only two options.

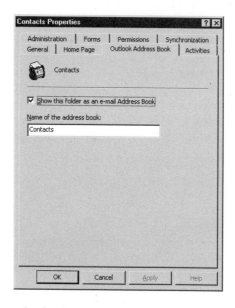

To use the folder as an Outlook Address Book, check the Show This Folder As An E-Mail Address Book option. By default, the folder name is automatically inserted as the name for the Outlook Address Book. You can change it by entering the name of your choice in the Name Of The Address Book option.

If you don't want to use the folder as an Outlook Address Book, remove the check mark. When you're through, click OK to save the settings and return to the active Outlook window. If you want to make further changes, click Apply to activate the changes and keep the dialog box open.

Using the Activities Tab Options

The Activities tab of the contact folder Properties dialog box displays the existing folder groups, which are selections of one or more Outlook folders from which activities linked to contacts in the folder are displayed. Folder groups are used to create custom views in the Activities tab of the contact record form. When you open a contact record, click the Activities tab, and display the contents of the Show drop-down list, you are looking at all the existing folder groups found in the Activities tab of the contact folder Properties dialog box.

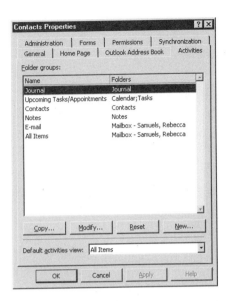

The Folder Groups pane displays the existing folder groups and indicates which folders are included in each group. The options below the display pane enable you to modify existing folder groups, add new ones, and set the default view for the Activities tab of the contact record form. Your options include

- **Copy**   Click this button to create a copy of an existing folder group. This is useful if you want to use the existing folder group as the basis for a new folder group. Make the desired changes and give the group a new name.

- **Modify**   To change an existing folder group, select the group and click Modify. The View Title And Folders dialog box opens. You can then add or remove individual folders from the group, and change the folder group name.

- **Reset/Delete**   The name of this button changes depending on the type of folder group selected. When a default folder group (Journal, Upcoming Tasks/Appointments, Contacts, Notes, E-mail, and All Items) is selected, the button name is Reset. Clicking the Reset button removes any changes made to the selected folder and returns it to its original state. When you select a non-default folder group, the button name changes to Delete, and as you might surmise, the selected folder group is eliminated.

- **New**   Use this button to create a new folder group.

- **Default activities view**   Select the folder group you want to set as the default view for the Activities tab of the contact record form. The folder group you select here appears in the Show field of the contact form Activities tab, and the related activities are displayed.

WORKING WITH CONTACTS

While the Reset/Delete button performs its action directly, the Copy, Modify, and New buttons open the View Title And Folders dialog box, from which you can make your own selections.

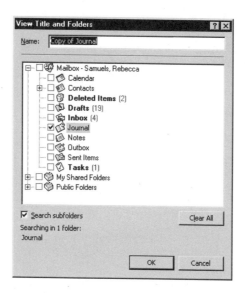

The tree-like display of folders is the same no matter which button you click. The only differences are the text displayed in the Name field, and the folders checked in the display window. Using the View Titles And Folders dialog box is easy. Check the folders you want to include in the folder group, indicate whether to search subfolders (this option appears even if no subfolders exist, but will apply in the event you later create subfolders), modify the name if necessary, and click OK to save the folder group.

There are a couple of things you should know about folder groups to make using them a little easier:

- You can change the folders included in a default folder group, but you cannot delete or rename the group.

- Different folder groups display different fields in the Activities tab of the contact record form. A folder group created with the New button retains the display format of the All Items folder group. A new folder group created using the Copy button retains the display format of the original folder group.

- Each time you restart Outlook, folder groups containing public folders do not automatically restore activities links. If you try to use such a folder group, it may appear that the activities have disappeared. To resolve this, simply open the public folder containing the linked items. This happens by design to prevent a prolonged Outlook startup while the links are being re-created.

After you finish modifying and creating folder groups, click the OK button to save your changes and return to the active Outlook window.

MOUS Exam Core Objectives Explored in Chapter 9

Objective	Activity	Heading
OL10-4-2	Organize and sort contacts	"Sorting Contacts"
		"Using Categories to Organize Contacts"
OL10-4-3	Link contacts to activities and journal entries	"Assigning Contacts to Categories"

The
Complete
Reference

Outlook 2002

Part IV

Managing Time and Details

The Complete Reference

Outlook 2002

Chapter 10

Working with the Calendar

The Outlook Calendar is a powerful scheduling tool, which when used effectively and consistently can create order out of chaos. As a matter of fact, you may become so efficient that instead of needing more hours in the day, you'll find yourself heading home early. However, to get to that point, you must develop the necessary skills to master the Calendar. That's what this chapter is all about: helping you become proficient in Calendar basics. You'll learn to get around the Calendar folder, switch and customize Calendar views, and more.

Navigating the Calendar Window

The first thing to do in any software component, including the Outlook Calendar, is to familiarize yourself with the working environment or user interface. You've got to learn what each of the elements on the screen is, what it does, and how it operates. It's like checking out a new power tool and figuring out where all the buttons and switches are and what they do.

Touring the Calendar Window Components

The best place to start learning about what makes the Calendar tick is with the default view, Day/Week/Month. As you can see in Figure 10-1, the Day/Week/Month window consists of three distinct elements: the Appointment area, the Date Navigator, and the TaskPad.

These three primary elements provide you with everything you need to regain control of your schedule and your time.

- **Appointment area** This is where you record your appointments, meetings, and events. The Appointment area, like any good appointment book, provides time blocks in which you can insert your appointment information. Unlike a typical appointment book, the Outlook Calendar Appointment area is flexible enough to handle even the most unpredictable schedule.

- **Date Navigator** This pair of mini-calendars offers a view of the current month and the next month. In addition to providing you with a handy view of two months' worth of dates, the Date Navigator also lets you switch dates quickly, change appointment dates, and even display multiple days in the Appointment area.

- **TaskPad** The TaskPad is a mini-version of the Tasks folder. It lets you create tasks and to-do lists on the fly without having to leave the Calendar folder. Items entered in the TaskPad become part of the Tasks folder, and items entered in the Tasks folder are added to the TaskPad. Changes in one are reflected in the other.

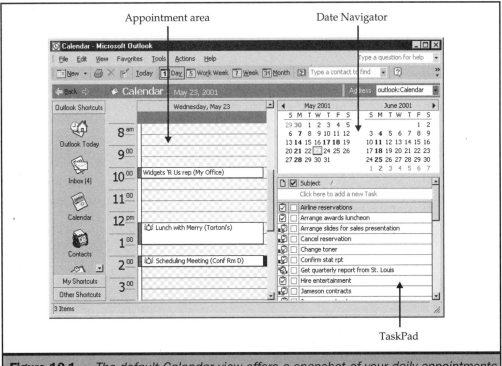

Figure 10-1.   *The default Calendar view offers a snapshot of your daily appointments and to-do items*

Using Shortcut Keys to Get Around

If you're into shortcuts, hate your mouse, or just like to have alternate ways of doing things, you may be interested in the shortcut keys available for navigating the Day/Week/Month view. See Table 10-1 for a listing.

Press	To Go To
LEFT ARROW	Previous day
RIGHT ARROW	Next day

Table 10-1.   *Shortcut Keys for Navigating the Day/Week/Month View*

MANAGING TIME
AND DETAILS

Press	To Go To
TAB	Next appointment
SHIFT+TAB	Previous appointment
ALT+HOME	First day of the current week
ALT+END	Last day of the current week
ALT+UP ARROW	Same day of the previous week
ALT+DOWN ARROW	Same day of the next week
ALT+PAGE UP	First day of the month
ALT+PAGE DOWN	Last day of the month
CTRL+TAB or F6	Move between Appointment area, TaskPad, and Folder List (when open)

Table 10-1.   *Shortcut Keys for Navigating the Day/Week/Month View* (continued)

Using a two-key shortcut requires holding the first key down while pressing the second key. If the shortcut includes three keys, hold the first two down and press the third.

Switching Dates

By far the easiest way to switch to dates in the recent past or immediate future is by using the Date Navigator. Click a date on one of the visible Date Navigator calendars to display the desired day in the Appointment area. To switch to another month, use the arrows on either side of the Date Navigator calendars. The left arrow moves you back one month at a time, and the right arrow moves you forward one month at a time. You can also click (and hold) the month name and year to display a pop-up list of the previous three months and the next three months.

If you want to switch a date in the distant past or future, it's easier to use the Go To Date command. Press CTRL+G or right-click a blank slot in the Appointment area, and select Go To Date. You can also choose View | Go To Date. All three methods open the Go To Date dialog box.

The dialog box opens with the currently selected date in the Date field. Enter the date you want to switch to. You can use one of the following methods to enter the date:

- **Type the date**   Type the date you want to move to. Use the date format designated in the Regional Settings applet of the Control Panel.

- **Use the Date pop-up calendar**   Click the down arrow at the right end of the Date field to display the pop-up calendar. Select the date from the calendar. The pop-up calendar works the same as the Date Navigator calendars. The right and left arrows move you forward and back through subsequent months, and clicking the month name and year displays the previous and next three months in a pop-up list. You can also click the Today button to return to the date indicated by the clock on your local computer as today.

- **Use plain English**   If you don't want to mess around with dates and calendars, you can also use plain English. If you want to go to next Tuesday, just say so. Type **next Tuesday** and Outlook understands, taking you to the first upcoming date that falls on a Tuesday. The variety of words, phrases, and abbreviations you can use is extensive. Try things like **a week from next Wednesday** or **30 days from the 1st of next month**. You can abbreviate the names of months and days (such as Feb, Jan, Tues, Wed, and so on). You can even use holiday names such as **Christmas 2001** for December 25, 2001, or **Independence Day 2003** for July 4, 2003.

From the Show In drop-down list, choose the calendar in which to display the selected date. Your choices include the Day Calendar, Week Calendar, Month Calendar, and Work Week Calendar. Click OK to display the selected date in the appropriate calendar view.

Exploring Calendar Views

Outlook provides a number of different views for displaying your Calendar information. The default view, Day/Week/Month, offers an ideal environment for managing your daily schedule and to-do items. However, when you need a quick look at everything that's on your plate, you may want to take advantage of one of the available table views.

Switching Views

The Calendar folder comes with seven different standard views—ten if you count the four variations on the Day/Week/Month view. Here's a quick look at those standard views and what they do:

- **Day/Week/Month**   The default view, which contains the Appointment area, the Date Navigator, and the TaskPad.

- **Day/Week/Month View with AutoPreview**   True to its name, this view turns on the AutoPreview in the Day/Week/Month view. Notes from Calendar items appearing in the Appointment area are displayed when you use this view.

- **Active Appointments**   Use this view to display Calendar items that have not yet occurred. All appointments in the past are excluded from this view.

- **Events**   If you've scheduled any events (appointments or activities that last more than 24 hours), you can use this view to display them all at once.

- **Annual Events**   This view is handy for separating out those events that occur only once a year, such as birthdays and anniversaries.

- **Recurring Appointments**   You know what these are: the boss's Monday morning pep talks, the monthly visits to see your parole officer, your weekly excursions to the canine therapist because your dog thinks he's a cat, and so on. The Recurring Appointments view excludes all Calendar items except those that are recurring items.

- **By Category**   If you assign Calendar items to categories, you can use this view to display all items grouped by category.

To switch between standard Calendar folder views, choose View | Current View to display the submenu of available views. You can also display the Advanced toolbar, which contains a Current View drop-down list from which you can select the view to use. Right-click anywhere on the Standard toolbar and select Advanced from the shortcut menu to display the Advanced toolbar.

The Day/Week/Month view has its own selection of subviews, each of which is accessible from the Standard toolbar. These views include:

- **Day**   This is the default view in which a single day's worth of appointments appears in the Appointment area.

- **Work Week**   When you select this view, the Appointment area displays the days designated as your workweek in the Calendar options.

- **Week**   The Week view changes the Appointment area to display the current week as a group of seven boxes, one for each day of the week. The appointments for each day appear in the box.

- **Month**   The Month view is similar to the Week view in that each day of the month is displayed as a separate box. However, by default, the Month view takes up the entire Information viewer, hiding the Date Navigator and TaskPad.

Tip   *You can display the Date Navigator and TaskPad in the Month view by dragging the right border of the Information viewer to the left. The border moves left in increments large enough to display one or more Date Navigator calendars. Since Outlook fails to remember this setting, you'll have to resize the Month view each time you switch to another view and back to the Month view.*

Switching between the Day/Week/Month variations is a snap since there's a button for each on the Standard toolbar. Click the appropriate button to display the view. If you happen to be a shortcut lover, there's even better news. Outlook provides a number of keyboard shortcuts that enable you to both switch between and modify the Day/Week/Month views. See Table 10-2 for a list of available shortcuts.

Press	To Display
ALT+1 **or** ALT+Y	Day view
ALT+5 **or** ALT+R	Work Week view (regardless of the number of days in your Work Week)
ALT+- (ALT + minus sign) or ALT+W	Week view
ALT+= (ALT + equal sign) or ALT+M	Month view
ALT+2 through ALT+4	Day view displaying 2 to 4 days (ALT+2 displays 2 days, ALT+3, 3 days, and so on)
ALT+6 through ALT+0	Day view displaying 6 to 10 days

Table 10-2. *Shortcut Keys for Switching Between Day/Week/Month Views*

Although you can use the number pad for the minus sign in the shortcuts in Table 10-2, you cannot use it to enter numbers. The shortcuts only work if you use the row of number keys above the letters on the keyboard.

Using the Date Navigator

The Date Navigator is a handy device that not only lets you switch between dates quickly with a mouse-click or two but also provides an easy means of customizing the information displayed in the Appointment area. The Date Navigator is the pair (by default) of mini-calendars that appears in the top-right corner of the Calendar window.

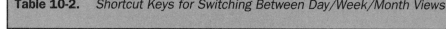

To switch dates using the Date Navigator, simply click the desired date or click the month name and year to display a pop-up menu containing the currently selected month, the three previous months, and the next three months. Select the month you want to view and then select the date.

While it's a great time-saver for switching dates, the real value of the Date Navigator is its ability to customize the Appointment area of the Day view. You can display multiple dates in the Appointment area by highlighting the desired dates in the Date Navigator using one of the following methods:

■ **Select consecutive days**   You can select any number of days in a given week by dragging your mouse pointer over the desired days. However, once you pass either end of the week, the entire week and the next (or previous) week are selected. To select multiple consecutive days spanning, but not including, two weeks, hold the SHIFT key down while dragging your mouse pointer.

■ **Select nonconsecutive days**   You can select up to 14 nonconsecutive days by holding down the CTRL key and selecting each date. However, regardless of the order in which you select them, they are displayed in ascending date order in the Appointment area.

■ **Select weeks**   To select a week at a time, move the mouse pointer to the left of the week row and click as soon as the pointer shifts from left to right. You can display up to six weeks' worth of dates in the Appointment area using this method.

■ **Select months**   If you want to display an entire month's worth of dates in the Appointment area, click anywhere on the top row displaying the letters representing the days of the week. This is a great way to display the Month view without hiding the Date Navigator and the TaskPad.

You can also use the Date Navigator to change the week displayed in the Work Week view. Click the Work Week button on the Standard toolbar. Then click a date in the Date Navigator, and the workweek in which the date falls displays in the Work Week view. However, if you use a nonstandard workweek (such as Tuesday through Saturday), clicking some dates may display the next or previous workweek instead.

If you find the Date Navigator in need of a little sprucing up, you can change its font by opening the Other tab on the Options dialog box (Tools | Options) and clicking the Advanced Options buttons. There you'll find the Date Navigator Font button, which enables you to select a different font, as well as its size, style, and color.

Working with Calendar Views

Each of the Calendar views offers a different look at your scheduling information. Managing your schedule effectively often requires using different views to accomplish different scheduling tasks.

Using the Day View

The Day view, which is the default Day/Week/Month view, displays a single day in the Appointment area. As you can see in Figure 10-2, each appointment appears in the appropriate time slot.

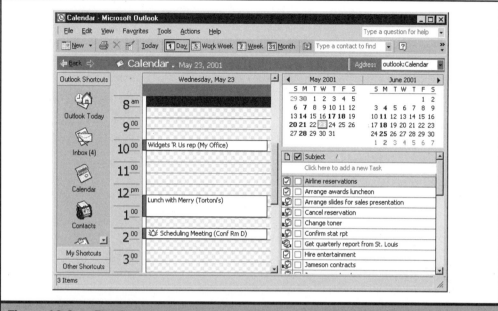

Figure 10-2.   *The Day view provides a quick look at a single day's worth of appointments*

If the Day view is not visible, you can display it by clicking the Day button on the Standard toolbar or pressing the shortcut key ALT+1. Once you have the Day view open, you can change the dates using either the Date Navigator or the Go To Date command, both of which are discussed earlier in this chapter. Using the Date Navigator, you can even display multiple dates in the Appointment area of the Day view.

To utilize the Day view effectively, there are a couple of things you should know:

- The Appointment area scroll bar enables you to move through the time slots for the selected day.

- Double-clicking an appointment opens the appointment form.

- Right-clicking an appointment displays a shortcut menu with commands that affect the selected appointment.

- Right-clicking the date header or a blank spot in the Appointment area displays a shortcut menu with general Calendar folder commands.

- Double-clicking the date header opens a blank Event form using the current date for the Start and End times.

- Double-clicking an open time slot in the Appointment area opens a blank appointment form using the current date and the selected time slot as the date and time for the appointment.

■ Double-clicking the time bar (the vertical bar containing the time of day) opens a blank appointment form using the current date and selected time as the date and time for the appointment.

■ Right-clicking the time bar displays a shortcut menu containing commands for creating new calendar items and for customizing the time bar.

■ A small yellow box with an up or down arrow appears at the top and/or bottom of the time bar when additional appointments are scheduled but not visible.

Using the Work Week View

The Work Week view, which opens when you click the Work Week button or when you use the shortcut key ALT+5, is the Day view with multiple dates displayed. The dates displayed are those days of the current week that are designated as the days of your workweek. By default, the workweek days include Monday through Friday (see Figure 10-3).

Since the Work Week view is a variation of the Day view, all commands and features used in the Day view also apply to the Work Week view. See the previous section on the Day view for details.

Using the Week View

The Week view, shown in Figure 10-4, displays the days of the current week in the Appointment area. As you can see, the time bar and time slots are replaced by date boxes which hold information about scheduled items.

To open the Week view, click the Week button on the Standard toolbar or use the ALT+- (ALT + the minus key) or ALT+W shortcut. The Week view provides a number of options for getting things done quickly:

■ Use the scroll bar to move through the weeks of the year. Although the scroll bar appears to have a limit of one year if you drag it from top to bottom, you can continue to scroll in either direction by clicking the arrow buttons at either end of the scroll bar.

■ Double-click an appointment to open the appointment form.

■ Right-click an appointment to display a shortcut menu containing commands that affect the appointment.

■ Right-click the date or a blank spot on the Appointment area to display a shortcut menu of general Calendar folder commands.

■ Double-click the date or a blank spot to open a new event form scheduled for the date selected. Since time slots are not available in the Week view, you cannot double-click to open a new appointment form. However, you can right-click the date and select New Appointment to open a blank appointment form for the selected date.

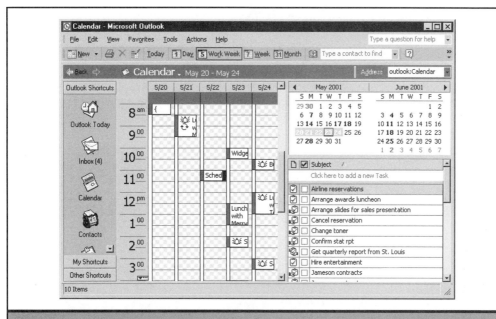

Figure 10-3. *Use the Work Week view for a quick glance at your appointments for the current workweek*

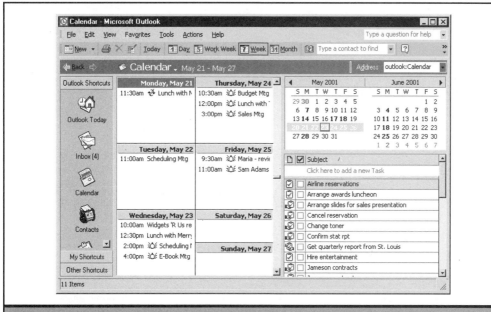

Figure 10-4. *The Week view provides a compact view of your weekly calendar*

■ To create an event spanning several days, highlight multiple dates by dragging your mouse pointer over them. Then right-click any of the selected dates and choose one of the commands for creating a new appointment, event, or meeting request.

■ A small yellow box with an up or down arrow appears at the top and/or bottom of the time bar when additional appointments are scheduled but not visible. To view the additional appointments, click the yellow box to open the Day view.

■ To change the date of a scheduled item, drag it to the appropriate date box.

Using the Month View

The last variation of the Day/Week/Month view is, appropriately, the Month view, which displays an entire month's worth of dates in the Information viewer. As Figure 10-5 shows, the Month view hides the Date Navigator and TaskPad to make room for the large number of days it must display.

If you prefer to restrict the Month view to the Appointment area and keep the Date Navigator and TaskPad onscreen, you can drag the right border of the Information viewer to the left until both components reappear.

Displaying the Month view is as easy as clicking the Month button on the Standard toolbar or using the ALT+= (ALT + the equals sign) or ALT+M shortcut key.

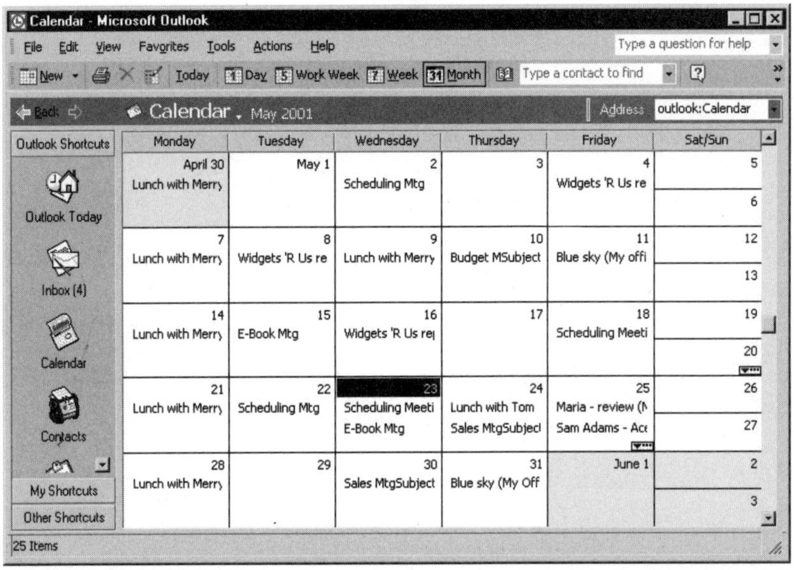

Figure 10-5.   *Use the Month view to see how your schedule for the entire month is shaping up*

There's another way to display the Month view that automatically confines it to the Appointment area without having to drag the Information viewer border. Move to the Date Navigator and click anywhere in the row of letters representing the days of the week. This immediately opens the Month view in the Appointment area only, leaving the Date Navigator and TaskPad as they are.

Since the Month view is an expanded version of the Week view, it functions in the same manner. For details on manipulating the Month view, see the previous section on the Week view.

Depending on the size of your Outlook window, the start times of appointments may or may not display in the Month view.

Using Table Views

The remaining Calendar folder views are table views that display your Calendar information using the column and row format. You can switch to the table views by choosing View | Current View and selecting one of the table views from the submenu that appears. They include Active Appointments, Events, Annual Events, Recurring Appointments, and By Category. Their names aptly describe the content they display. You can also select these views from the Current View drop-down list found on the Advanced toolbar. To display the Advanced toolbar, right-click anywhere on the Standard toolbar and select Advanced from the shortcut menu.

For more information on using and customizing table views, see Chapter 23.

Using AutoPreview and the Preview Pane

As with most Outlook folders, the AutoPreview and Preview Pane features are offered in the Calendar folder. The AutoPreview feature is only available in table views and a special Day/Week/Month view, appropriately named the Day/Week/Month View With AutoPreview. As you can see in Figure 10-6, with AutoPreview enabled, the first few lines of notes from the appointment, event, or meeting form are displayed.

To enable AutoPreview, switch to a table view and choose View | AutoPreview. Return to the View menu and click AutoPreview a second time to turn AutoPreview off.

You can also turn AutoPreview on and off by right-clicking a blank spot in the Information viewer and selecting AutoPreview from the shortcut menu.

The Preview Pane available in both the table and Day/Week/Month views splits the Information viewer into two panes. Choose View | Preview Pane to activate the Preview Pane. The Preview Pane appears on the bottom and contains the Calendar item form. Unfortunately, you cannot scroll through the form, so only that portion of the form that fits in the available space is accessible. If you have the Folder List open and the Outlook window resized to less than maximum, you may not be able to see the

MANAGING TIME AND DETAILS

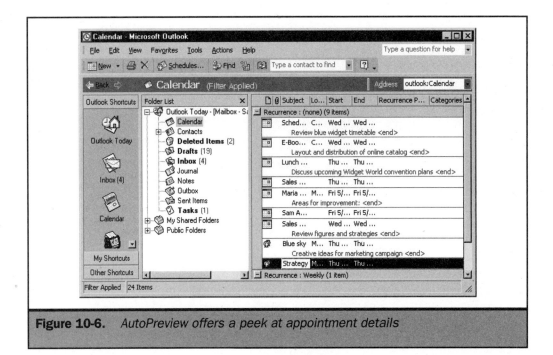

Figure 10-6.   *AutoPreview offers a peek at appointment details*

entire form. In that case, close the Folder List and maximize the Outlook window to view the form in the Preview Pane.

To hide the Preview Pane, right-click the Preview Pane header and select Preview Pane. You can also return to the View menu and click Preview Pane to turn the Preview Pane off.

For information about customizing the Preview Pane, see Chapter 23.

Customizing the Calendar

As powerful and easy to use as the Calendar is, you may want to do some fine tuning to make it work just the way you like. Fortunately, Outlook provides a number of features and options you can use to customize the Calendar folder.

Setting Basic Calendar Options

The first thing you'll want to do is check the Calendar options to ensure the default settings are optimized for your needs. To access the options, choose Tools | Options to display the Options dialog box.

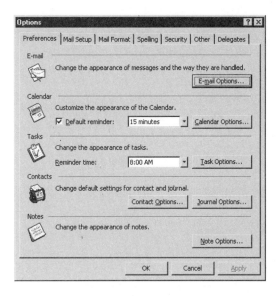

The first Calendar option appears on the Preferences tab in the Calendar section. It enables you to set the reminder default. Place a check mark in the Default Reminder box to include a reminder in each new appointment, event, or meeting request form. Use the drop-down list to designate how soon before the appointment you want the reminder activated.

Click the Calendar Options button to display the Calendar Options dialog box.

The Calendar Options dialog box contains a variety of options for customizing your workweek, changing the Date Navigator appearance, and more. Your options include the following:

■ **Calendar workweek**   Begin setting the workweek by checking the days that comprise your workweek. Since most jobs are Monday through Friday, those days are selected by default. Next, use the First Day Of Week drop-down list to designate the starting day for your week. This day determines the order that days appear in the Week view, Month view, and Date Navigator. From the First Week Of Year drop-down list, select the start date for your year. Next, enter the start time for your day. This is the first time slot that appears in the Day view. The default is 8:00 A.M. However, if you work the third shift and start at eleven at night, enter **11:00** P.M. Finally, enter the time your workday normally ends. See the notes following this list for additional information about setting Work Week options.

■ **Show week numbers in the Date Navigator**   Check this option to display a week number next to each week in the Date Navigator. The numbers range from 1 to 52, indicating the position of the week in the currently selected year.

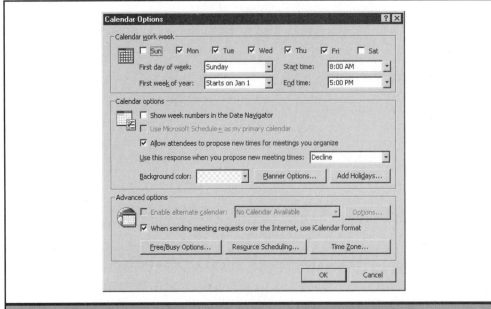

Figure 10-7. *Calendar Options offer a variety of ways to customize the Outlook Calendar folder*

- **Use Microsoft Schedule+ as my primary calendar** This option is only available if Schedule+ was running on your computer before Outlook was installed. It is used mainly in mixed environments (some Outlook users and some Schedule+ users) to make sure everyone can view shared calendar information. See your administrator for more information.

- **Allow attendees to propose new times for meetings you organize** This new feature adds an additional button to meeting request forms, allowing attendees to suggest new times when they would be available for the proposed meeting. Check this option to enable the button in meeting request forms you send.

- **Use this response when you propose new meeting times** When responding to meeting requests you receive from people who have activated the previous option in their Calendar options, the selection here is used as the default response when you suggest a new time for the meeting.

- **Background color** The color you select from this drop-down list appears as the background for the Appointment area in both the Day and Work Week views.

- **Planner Options** See the Setting Planner Options section later in this chapter.

- **Add Holidays** See the Adding Holidays section later in this chapter.

■ **Enable alternate calendar**   This handy option lets you view a calendar other than the Roman calendar if you use a language different from English. Unless an alternate calendar is available, this option is disabled. The Options button, when enabled, allows you to change the settings for the alternate calendar selected.

■ **Send meeting requests using iCalendar by default**   If you send a lot of meeting requests to non-Outlook users (they must have iCalendar-compliant software) or Outlook users using Internet mail, you may want to check this option. It sends each meeting request in iCalendar format. The option is only available if you've added an Internet e-mail account to your profile.

■ **Free/Busy Options**   See Understanding Free/Busy Time later in this chapter.

■ **Resource Scheduling**   See Setting Resource Scheduling Options later in this chapter.

■ **Time Zone**   See Modifying and Adding Time Zones later in this chapter.

Before moving on, there are a couple of things you should be aware of when setting your Work Week options:

■ You cannot set working hours that span midnight. For example, if you work the third shift, your workday may start at 11:00 P.M. and end at 7:30 A.M. the next morning. Setting those times as the Start and End times results in an error message informing you that "The end date you entered occurs before the start date." Unfortunately, this is a bug and there's no way around it.

■ Setting Sunday as the First Day Of Week displays Monday, not Sunday, as the first day in the Week view and the Month view. This is due to the fact that Outlook considers Saturday and Sunday a single entity, which it displays using Saturday as the placement criterion. If you change the First Day Of Week option to Saturday, the Sat/Sun block appears as the first day in both the Week and Month views.

Setting Planner Options

When it comes to planning and scheduling meetings, the Meeting Planner comes in quite handy. To make it even more useful, Outlook provides several options for customizing the way it works. To set these options, choose Tools | Options and click the Calendar Options button on the Preferences tab to open the Calendar options dialog box. Then click the Planner Options button to display the Planner Options dialog box shown in Figure 10-8.

As you can see, the Planner Options come in two flavors: Meeting Planner options and Group Schedule options.

The Meeting Planner options include:

■ **Show popup calendar details**   Check this option to enable (or disable) the popup calendar box used to show the meeting schedule details.

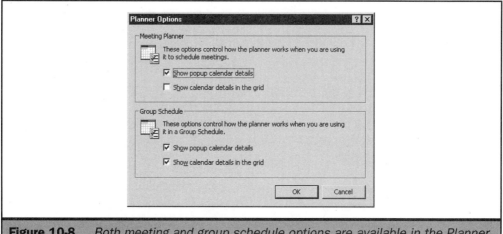

Figure 10-8.   *Both meeting and group schedule options are available in the Planner Options dialog box*

- ■ **Show calendar details in the grid**   Use this option to set the default state for the Show Calendar Detail setting found in the drop-down menu displayed when you click the Options button on the Meeting Planner.

The Group Schedule options are identical to the Meeting Planner options. However, they affect the manner in which the Meeting Planner functions when performing group scheduling.

Adding Holidays

Having your Outlook Calendar display upcoming holidays can be a great help. However, since holidays are not automatically included with the typical Outlook installation, you'll have to add them yourself if you want them to appear on your Calendar. Fortunately, this is easy enough for even the most inexperienced user to accomplish with little effort.

Follow these steps to add holidays to the Outlook Calendar:

1. Choose Tools | Options to open the Options dialog box.
2. Click Calendar Options on the Preferences tab to display the Calendar Options dialog box.
3. Click the Add Holidays button to display the Add Holidays To Calendar dialog box.

4. Select the regional holidays you want to include on the Calendar. You can select multiple sets of holidays if you want. This is great if you have a mix of ethnic contacts whose holidays you want to remember.

5. Click OK to add the holidays and return to the Calendar Options dialog box.

6. Click OK to close the Calendar Options dialog box, and OK again to close the Options dialog box.

Although you can add multiple Calendar subfolders to the original Calendar folder, you cannot add holidays to any Calendar folder except the original. Attempting to add holidays to a subfolder results in the holidays being added to the main Calendar folder. If the Calendar folder already contains the holiday set selected, duplicate holidays will appear. This is by design.

The next time you open your Calendar, the holidays you've added will appear in the appropriate date slot as all-day events.

Understanding Free/Busy Time

When you schedule an item in your Calendar, Outlook marks that block of time with a free/busy designation. This enables others on the Exchange Server network to tell at a glance when you are available and when you're not. It comes in quite handy for preventing those endless quests to find a mutually acceptable meeting time. If you're tired of playing the "No, that's no good for me, how about . . .?" game, you'll love having everyone's free/busy time available on the network.

You can see the free/busy times when you click the Scheduling tab of a meeting request or use the Meeting Planner. The time designations are described in Table 10-3.

By default, free/busy time is stored in your mailbox on the server. However, if you work offline, or interact with people who are not connected to your Microsoft Exchange server, you can provide access to your free/busy time by publishing it in a separate file (.vfb) to another site. You can publish free/busy time to a Web site, intranet, FTP site, another computer on the network, or the Microsoft Web site.

MANAGING TIME
AND DETAILS

Free/Busy Designation	Indicates	Color Used in Free/Busy Table
Free	Time slot is available for scheduling	White or clear
Busy	Time slot is already spoken for	Blue
Out of office	User will be unavailable	Gray
Tentative	User has tentatively filled this time slot (but may be open to a better offer)	Blue w/diagonal lines
Unknown	The user's free/busy information is unavailable	White w/diagonal lines

Table 10-3.   *Free/Busy Time Designations*

Note   *Outlook searches for free/busy information in one of three places. It first checks the location specified in the Global Address List entry, then in the contact record Internet Free-Busy Address field, and finally, in the Internet Free/Busy section of the Free/Busy options.*

Whether you use the Microsoft Exchange server to store your free/busy information or a separate .vfb file at another location, or both, you can use the Free/Busy Options dialog box to configure the way Outlook manages your free/busy information. Follow these steps to set the Free/Busy options:

1. Choose Tools | Options to open the Options dialog box.
2. Click the Calendar Options button to display the Calendar Options dialog box.
3. Click the Free/Busy Options button to open the Free/Busy Options dialog box (shown in Figure 10-9).
4. Set the Free/Busy options. Your choices include

   - **Publish __ month(s) of Calendar free/busy information on the server**   Indicate the number of months' worth of free/busy time to publish on the server.

   - **Update free/busy information on the server every __ minutes**   As you schedule and accept appointments and meetings, your free/busy time changes. Use this option to determine how often you want your free/busy time updated on the Microsoft Exchange server. Since frequent updating may cause a strain on the server, you should check with your administrator before reducing the time between automatic updates.

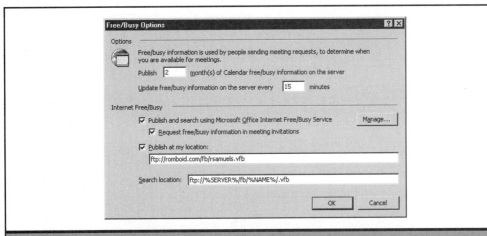

Figure 10-9. *The Free/Busy Options lets you determine how, when, and where to publish your free/busy information*

- **Publish and search using Office Internet Free/Busy Service**   Microsoft now provides a [free] Free/Busy service that stores your free/busy information on the Internet using Microsoft servers. You'll need a Microsoft Passport (easy, free, and part of the Internet Free/Busy setup), Internet Explorer 5 or higher, and, of course, an Internet connection. Check this option and click the Manage button to connect to the Internet Free/Busy service Web site. An easy to follow wizard walks you through the entire setup. The advantage to such a service is the ability to access free/busy information from any location. The disadvantage is that you are dependent upon Microsoft's servers being available at all times, and you're entrusting your information to a third party.

- **Request free/busy information in meeting invitations**   Use this option to request authorization to view free/busy information from attendees you're inviting who have not yet granted you permission to view their free/busy information.

- **Publish at my location**   If you want to publish your free/busy time to a location other than the Microsoft Exchange server or with the Microsoft Office Internet Free/Busy Service, check this option. Indicate the URL or path (location and name) of the .vfb file in which you want free/busy information stored. It's a good idea to make sure all users employ the same folder name, such as fb, when storing their free/busy time, no matter which location they choose. The folder must be shared if it's on a local computer or server on the network. In addition, correct syntax is critical for proper publishing.

■ **Search location**   This option lets Outlook know where to look for other users' free/busy information if it doesn't find it on the Microsoft Exchange server. Enter the server on which the free/busy (.vfb) file is stored. You can use %SERVER% and %NAME% parameters when entering the URL. For example, if you use an FTP site, you might enter **ftp://%SERVER%/fb/%NAME%.vfb**. Outlook substitutes the server and user's name when searching. When sending meeting requests via Internet e-mail, Outlook uses the SMTP address to search for the free/busy file. Outlook replaces %SERVER% with the e-mail address server information (everything after the @ sign), and replaces %NAME% with the e-mail address name (everything before the @ sign).

> **Note**   *Publishing your free/busy time requires the Web Publishing Wizard. Therefore, if it was not installed during the Windows installation, you will be asked to install it before you're allowed to publish your free/busy information.*

5. Click OK three times to close the dialog boxes and return to the active Outlook window.

> **Tip**   *If you plan to use an FTP site, make sure it allows anonymous logins and make sure the permissions for the fb folder allow users to read and write to the folder.*

The Microsoft Exchange server will now update your free/busy information on the server in accordance with the settings in the first two options.

> **Note**   *Outlook applies the Free/Busy options on a per user, not per profile basis. Therefore, changing the options in one profile changes them for all profiles created by the user currently logged on.*

If you checked the Publish My Free/Busy Information option and filled in the appropriate target URL, you can manually publish your information as long as you're connected to the server via a LAN or the Internet. To publish your free/busy information, choose Tools | Send/Receive | Free/Busy Information.

> **Tip**   *If you rely on published free/busy information, you should empty your Internet Explorer cache on a regular basis since Outlook uses Internet Explorer to retrieve free/busy information. If you're lax in this minor housekeeping chore, you may end up viewing old, cached free/busy data. To clear the cache, open the Internet Options dialog box (from Internet Explorer or the Control Panel) and click Delete Files. Check Delete All Offline Content and click OK. Click OK again to close the Internet Options dialog box.*

Setting Resource Scheduling Options

This set of options is generally used for automating the scheduling of resources such as conference rooms, equipment, and so on. Therefore, you should not change the settings unless you are the administrator of such resources, and the delegate of the resource mailbox. For details on scheduling resources and setting Resource Scheduling options, see Chapter 12.

Modifying and Adding Time Zones

If you travel a lot, or if you regularly do business with contacts in another time zone, you'll find that the Time Zone options come in quite handy. When you're on the road, you can change the Calendar folder time zone to match the time zone in which you're traveling. If you do business with individuals in a different time zone, you can even add their time zone to your Day/Week/Month view to make scheduling decisions based on both time zones.

Choose Tools | Options to open the Options dialog box. Then click the Calendar Options button to display the Calendar Options dialog box. Finally, click the Time Zone button to open the Time Zone dialog box.

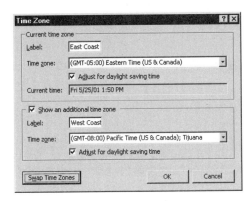

 You can also access the Time Zone options by right-clicking the time bar in the Day or Work Week view and selecting Change Time Zone.

Set the Time Zone options to suit your needs.

- **Label**   Use this field to give the default time zone a name. The name appears at the top of the time bar in the Day and Work Week views.

- **Time zone**   Set or change the default time zone used in the Calendar and other Outlook folders. Be advised, however, that this also resets the Windows Regional Settings time zone, which controls the clock on your local computer. Changing this time zone affects all other applications that use the clock.

- **Adjust for daylight saving time**   Check this option if you want the time adjusted for daylight saving time. Again, this option resets the Regional Settings applet option and affects all Windows applications.

- **Current time**   This field, which is for informational purposes only, displays the current time for the selected time zone. It cannot be edited from within Outlook. Double-click the time display in the Windows taskbar system tray to reset the system time.

- **Show an additional time zone**   Check this option to display a second time zone in the Day and Work Week views. Checking the option enables additional Label, Time Zone, and daylight saving fields. Enter a name, select a time zone, and set the daylight saving option for the second time zone. This time zone is for convenience and does not affect Outlook or any other Windows applications *unless* you use the Swap Time Zones button.

- **Swap Time Zones**   If you've added a second time zone, click this button to reverse the order in which the time zones appear and the way they are used. Switching time zones changes the Windows clock settings and therefore affects all Outlook folders and any Windows applications that use the clock. This option is especially handy if you divide your time between two time zones. It continues to work even if you choose not to display the second time zone.

With a secondary time zone selected, the time bar in the Day and Work Week views displays hours for both time zones. The secondary time zone hours appear to the left of the default time zone hours.

Tip   *If the Time Zone options aren't enough to take care of your needs, you can always make adjustments using the Regional Settings applet in the Windows Control Panel. However, it's important to remember that the settings here affect all Windows applications, including Outlook. In addition to changing the default time zone and daylight saving settings, you can also change the time format, date style, and date separator. To modify these settings, choose Start | Settings | Control Panel from the Windows taskbar to open the Control Panel dialog box. Then double-click the Regional Settings applet to display the Regional Settings Properties dialog box.*

Integrating Calendar with Other Outlook Components

The integration of its various components is one of Outlook's most attractive features. In addition to the integration found in the other components, the Calendar folder has the added advantage of having a direct pipeline to the Tasks folder. It's called the TaskPad, and it enables you to add, remove, edit, and view tasks without leaving the Calendar folder.

Creating To-Do Lists with TaskPad

The TaskPad is a handy device that appears in the Calendar folder default view. As you can see in Figure 10-10, the TaskPad resembles a small lined pad used for jotting down to-do list items.

The first thing to understand about the TaskPad is that it's an extension of the Tasks folder. Items added to or changes made in the TaskPad appear in the Tasks folder and vice versa. The major functional difference between the two is in the available views. The TaskPad views are fewer and more limited than the Tasks folder views. In addition, any changes made to a view in one do not affect the view by the same name in the other.

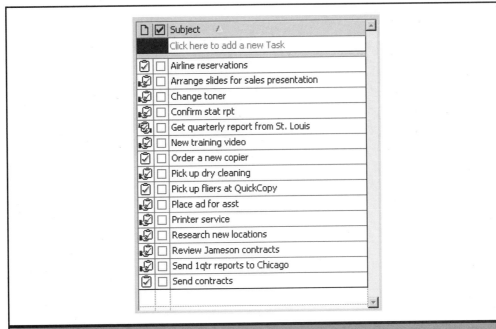

Figure 10-10.   *Use the TaskPad to add tasks and to-do items on the fly when you're in the Calendar*

MANAGING TIME AND DETAILS

Using the TaskPad is as simple or complex as you need it to be. For adding quick to-do items, just click the Click Here To Add A New Task field and start typing. Press the ENTER key when you're finished. If you want to add a task with dates, times, reminders, or details, double-click the Click Here To Add A New Task field or a blank line in the TaskPad to open a new task form (see Figure 10-11).

Enter the appropriate information in the new task form and click Save And Close to add the task to the TaskPad and the Tasks folder. For detailed information on creating tasks, see Chapter 13.

To edit a TaskPad item subject, single-click the item and make the change. To edit an item's details, double-click the item to open the form and make the necessary change(s).

Viewing TaskPad Items

Although not as versatile as the Tasks folder, the TaskPad is no slouch when it comes to views. It comes with six standard views and an option to show or hide items without due dates. You can even customize TaskPad views. The one thing you can't do is create new views for the TaskPad. If you don't like the standard views, you'll have to switch over to the Tasks folder and create your custom view there.

To change views in the TaskPad, choose View | TaskPad View to display a submenu of available views. You can also right-click the Click Here To Add A New

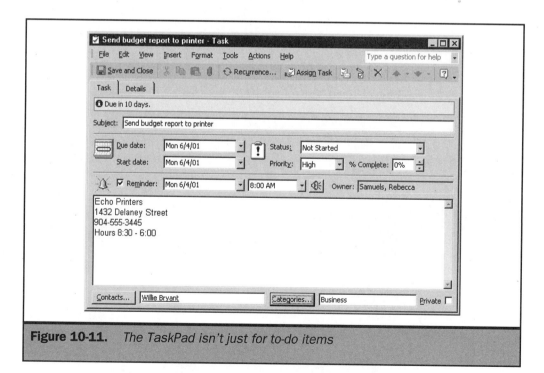

Figure 10-11.   *The TaskPad isn't just for to-do items*

Task field or a blank line on the TaskPad and select TaskPad View from the shortcut menu. The available TaskPad views include

- **All Tasks**   This one's pretty straightforward—it includes all tasks. One thing to note: this view ignores the Include Tasks With No Due Date option, showing tasks regardless of whether they have due dates.

- **Today's Tasks**   Use this view to see all tasks with no start date or with a start date equal or prior to today's date.

- **Active Tasks for Selected Days**   This view works in conjunction with the Date Navigator. It displays tasks with no due dates or with due dates that fall on or after the date(s) selected.

- **Task for Next Seven Days**   This view utilizes the start date, showing only those tasks with no start date or with start dates within seven days of today's date.

- **Overdue Tasks**   Any task whose due date has passed is included in this view.

- **Tasks Completed on Selected Days**   Use this view with the Date Navigator to display only those dates marked complete on selected dates.

- **Include Tasks with No Due Date**   This option, which instructs Outlook to display tasks without due dates in all reports, is enabled by default. Click it to disable it.

You can customize the TaskPad views, just as you can customize all Outlook views. However, the amount of space allocated for the TaskPad severely limits the usefulness of customizing TaskPad views. You're probably better off moving to the Tasks folder if you want to see customized views of your task and to-do items. See Chapter 23 for details on customizing Outlook views.

In addition to customized views, the TaskPad also offers the AutoPreview feature. To turn it on, right-click the Click Here To Add A New Task field or a blank line on the TaskPad and select AutoPreview.

Sorting and Filtering TaskPad Items

Sorting and filtering the TaskPad is identical to sorting and filtering any other table view. Click a field header to sort by that field. Click the field header a second time to reverse the sort order. To sort by multiple fields, hold down the SHIFT key and click the desired field headers. You can also right-click any of the field headers and select Sort Ascending or Sort Descending from the shortcut menu. For more sophisticated sorts, you can open the View Summary dialog box by right-clicking a field header and selecting Customize Current View. Click the Sort button and create your custom sort in the Sort dialog box.

You can rearrange your TaskPad items manually by dragging them up and down the list. However, once the list has been sorted or grouped, dragging no longer works. To remove Sort or Group By attributes, right-click one of the TaskPad column headers, select Customize Current View, open the appropriate dialog box (Sort or Group By), and click Clear All.

Applying filters to the TaskPad is accomplished using the View Summary dialog box. Click the Filter button to open the Filter dialog box. Enter your filter criteria and click OK to apply the filter. See Chapter 23 for more information on sorting and filtering Outlook views.

Using Drag and Drop to Create Outlook Items in the Calendar

Outlook offers tight integration between all components. The Calendar folder, with its embedded TaskPad, offers even tighter integration than the other primary Outlook folders. The ability to create tasks and to-do items from within the Calendar folder is only part of the story. It also offers the ability to create other Outlook items from both Calendar items and task/to-do items.

The most direct method is to use drag and drop. For example, in the Day/Week/Month view, you can drag a to-do item to the Appointment area or the Date Navigator and create a new appointment item scheduled for the selected date, and include the to-do item information in the notes field.

 No matter where you drop the to-do item, the default time set for the new appointment is the time designated as the start of your workday. This is true even if you drop the to-do item on a specific time slot in the Day view or the Work Week view.

You can also create a task item by dragging an appointment from the Appointment area and dropping it on the TaskPad. This opens a new task form that includes the appointment subject, date, and details.

Using either appointments or tasks, you can employ the drag-and-drop method to create other Outlook items as well. Simply drag the appointment or task, and drop it on the appropriate shortcut on the Outlook Bar or on a folder in the Folder List. If you want to include the appointment or task as an attachment, right-drag it and make the appropriate selection from the shortcut menu that appears when you drop the item.

Using iCalendar and vCalendar

Outlook supports both iCalendar and vCalendar, the two leading file formats used for exchanging calendaring and scheduling data across a variety of platforms and software applications. Both formats are transportable over the Internet. Outlook users can take advantage of either format for exchanging calendar and free/busy information with other Outlook users and non-Outlook users, employing vCalendar- or iCalendar-compliant e-mail or PIM software, such as Lotus Notes, ACT!, or Lotus Organizer.

Outlook provides a number of ways you can exchange calendar information using one format or the other:

- **Forward as iCalendar**   Select the Calendar item(s) to forward and choose Actions | Forward As iCalendar to create a new e-mail message with the item(s) inserted as attachments. You can perform the same action from within an open Calendar item form.

- **Send as iCalendar**   This command is available only from within an open meeting request form. Create a new meeting request and choose Tools | Send As iCalendar to enable the iCalendar format. Then click Send to dispatch the meeting request. You can also use the command if you make changes to an existing meeting request and want to send updates. In that case, enable Send As iCalendar and click Save And Close.

- **Save as iCalendar or vCalendar**   To save a Calendar item as an iCalendar or vCalendar file you can later attach to an e-mail, select the Calendar item and choose File | Save As to open the Save As dialog box. From the Save In drop-down list, choose a location in which to store the file. Select the appropriate file type from the Save As Type drop-down list, change the filename if necessary, and click Save.

- **Open an iCalendar or vCalendar attachment**   If you receive an iCalendar or vCalendar attachment in e-mail, double-click the attachment to open the item in Outlook. Click Save And Close to add it to your Calendar.

- **Import an iCalendar or vCalendar file**   You can also use the Import and Export Wizard to import an iCalendar or vCalendar file you receive on disk. See Chapter 21 for more information on importing and exporting.

MANAGING TIME AND DETAILS

Publishing Your Calendar as a Web Page

The ability to publish your Calendar as a web page lets you share your Calendar information across platforms and around the globe. You can publish your Calendar as an HTML document on a local computer, an intranet, or a server on the Internet. Anyone with a browser and access to the host computer can view your Calendar information.

The actual publication of your Calendar is relatively simple. From the Calendar folder, choose File | Save as Web Page to display the Save As Web Page dialog box.

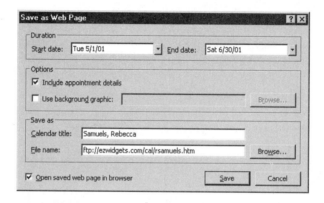

By default, Outlook assumes you want to publish the current and next months' Calendar information. To modify the range of information, change the Start Date and End Date by entering the desired dates. You can select the desired dates from the pop-up calendar available in each field or enter it manually. If you want the Notes information for each Calendar item published as well, check the Include Appointment Details option. You can gussy up the published calendar by including a graphic as the background. Check the Use Background Graphic option, and enter the path and name of the image file to use.

The next step is to give the published calendar a title and indicate the location and filename to which you want it saved. In the Calendar Title field, enter a name to appear as the title in the published document. Enter the path and filename for the published calendar in the File Name field. Use the appropriate protocol (file:// for a file on a network server, http:// for the Internet, ftp:// for an FTP site). If you want to save the calendar to your computer or another computer on the network, click the Browse button, select the location, and enter a filename. Select the final option, Open Saved Web Page In Browser, if you want to immediately open the saved calendar using your default browser. It's a good idea to leave this checked so you can verify that the calendar has been properly published.

Now you're ready to begin publishing. If you're publishing via a LAN or Internet connection, make sure the connection is established. Click the Save button. What happens next depends on the location to which you're publishing. If you selected a local or network computer as the target, the calendar is published immediately and opens in your browser (if you checked the Open Saved Web Page In Browser option). That's all there is to it.

Archiving the Calendar Folder

As your Calendar information grows, you'll find that doing a little housekeeping on a regular basis helps keep your Calendar uncluttered, and makes your Microsoft Exchange Server administrator happy by reducing the load on the server. However, you may not be prepared to permanently delete old, expired Calendar items that often prove useful when trying to piece together events from the past. Fortunately, Outlook offers a compromise: move the obsolete information to an archive file for storage and easy retrieval at a later date.

You can perform archiving operations automatically, using the AutoArchive feature, or manually by using the Archive command. The Calendar folder is one of the primary folders for which AutoArchiving is turned on by default. Whichever method you use, archiving the Calendar folder is the same as archiving other Outlook folders. For more information on archiving automatically and manually, see Chapter 18.

Although the process is the same no matter which Outlook folder you archive, there are a couple of things you should be aware of when archiving the Calendar folder:

- Past occurrences of recurring appointments are not archived if any future occurrences are still due. Outlook needs all occurrences in the series to keep track of future occurrences.

- If you archive an item after "snoozing" its reminder, the reminder is still active. Therefore, the reminder will reappear at the scheduled time, but you will not be able to open the item unless you retrieve it from the archive file.

Using the Calendar Folder Print Features

Although you'll probably spend the majority of your time working on the electronic version of your Calendar, there are times when a hard copy comes in handy. When you find you need one to take on the road, or you want a printout for a colleague, Outlook provides a number of options for printing your Calendar information.

Printing the Calendar

You can print from the Day/Week/Month view and any of the table views. However, depending on where you are when you decide to print your Calendar, you'll find you have significantly different choices.

MANAGING TIME AND DETAILS

Printing from the Day/Week/Month View

If you decide to print your calendar from the Day/Week/Month view, you'll discover you have a wide variety of styles to choose from. No matter which Day/Week/Month view you're in (Day, Work Week, Week, Month), the choices remain the same.

To print your Calendar from the Day/Week/Month view, follow these steps:

1. Click the Print button on the Standard toolbar or press CTRL+P to open the Print dialog box, shown in Figure 10-12.

2. Select the printer to use from the Name drop-down list. The Properties button displays options unique to the specific printer you select. See the printer manual for information on setting printer properties.

3. Choose a style from the Print Style list. Your choices include

   ■ **Daily Style**   Use the Daily Style to print a single day's worth of appointments per page. The date and Date Navigator calendars for the current and next month appear at the top of each page. In addition, the TaskPad and a blank notes area are included as well. The notes area in the lower-right corner is for you to jot your own notes, not for notes from Calendar items. A separate page is printed for each date in the print range.

   ■ **Weekly Style**   The Weekly Style prints the Week view on a single page, which is headed by the date and the Date Navigator calendars for the current and next month. Each week in the print range prints on a separate page. Neither the TaskPad nor the notes area are included in the Weekly Style by default.

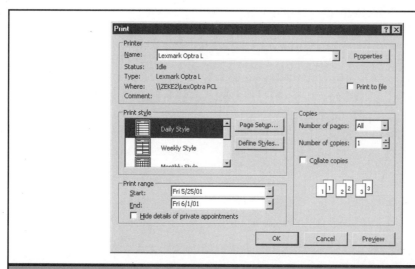

Figure 10-12.   *Set the Print options to suit your needs*

- **Monthly Style**   If you've been paying attention, you'll have already figured out that the Monthly style prints the Month view for the date(s) in the Print Range field. As with the other styles, the date and Date Navigator calendars for the current and next appear at the top of each page. Each month prints on a separate page. Once again, the TaskPad and notes area do not appear in this style by default.

- **Tri-fold Style**   This style is handy for creating three-fold booklets from your Calendar. By default, the left pane contains the daily calendar, the middle pane contains the TaskPad, and the right pane contains the weekly calendar. Sorry, no Date Navigator calendars in this one.

- **Calendar Details Style**   If you just need a quick listing of your Calendar items by date and time, this is the style for you. Dates are separated by date headers, and Calendar items are listed by appointment times. Detail information is included for each Calendar item.

- **Memo Style**   The Memo Style, which is available only if you've selected a calendar item, prints the selected Calendar item and all its details. The Print Range field disappears and only the one selected appointment prints.

> **Note**   *The Memo Style options include Start Each Item On A New Page and Print Attached Files. Their names clearly describe their functions.*

4. If you selected any style *except* Memo Style, set the range of dates to include by entering a start date and an end date. You can enter the dates manually or by selecting them from the pop-up calendar available in each field.

> **Note**   *If the start date is in the first week of the current month and the week contains days from the previous month, the Date Navigator calendars at the top of each printed page will be the current month and previous month. Otherwise, they will be the current month and the next month.*

5. If you want to print the appointment without any specific information other than the date and time, check the Hide Details Of Private Appointments option. The item appears on the printout as Private Appointment.

6. From the Number Of Pages drop-down list, select the pages you want to print. To print on both sides of the paper without having a duplex printer, first print the even pages, then reinsert the paper in the printer and print the odd pages.

7. Enter the number of copies you want to print.

8. Check the Collate Copies option if you're printing multiple copies of multipage calendars, and you want each copy assembled individually. In other words, a single copy of each page is printed until one complete copy of the calendar is finished. This process is repeated until all copies of the calendar are printed.

Without the Collate Copies option selected, all copies of page 1 are printed, followed by all copies of page 2, and so on. You then have to assemble each copy yourself.

> **Tip** *Although it sounds like a great time saver, Collate Copies can actually take longer depending on the size of the job and your printer. Without automatic collating enabled, the data for each page is sent to the printer only once, and multiple copies of that page are printed. When the Collate Copies option is enabled, the data must be resent to the printer for every page printed. Therefore, with Collate Copies checked, printing 20 copies of a 5-page calendar requires that data for 100 pages be sent to, and assimilated by, the printer. Whereas, with Collate Copies disabled, only 5 pages of data are transmitted to and processed by the printer.*

9. Click OK to print your Calendar.

You can also click the Preview button to see what the printout will look like before actually committing yourself to the print job.

Printing from a Table View

Since table views are less complex than Day/Week/Month views, the choices and options for printing from table views are more limited. The process, however, is the same. With a Calendar table view open, click the Print button or press CTRL+P to open the Print dialog box (seen in Figure 10-13).

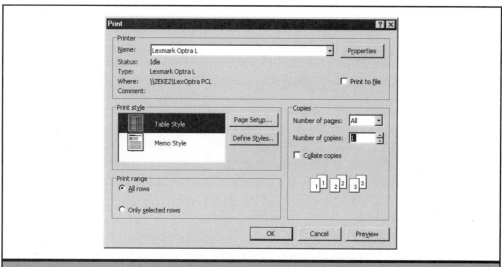

Figure 10-13. *Printing from table views offers a limited selection of styles and options*

From the Name drop-down list, select the printer to use. Set the properties for your printer by clicking the Properties button. Consult your printer manual for information on setting printer properties. Next, move to the Print Styles list and choose the style for this printout. The standard styles include

- **Table Style** This is a straightforward recreation of the table view on your screen in hard copy.
- **Memo Style** Use the Memo Style to print selected Calendar items with all their detail information.

If you're using the Table Style, check the appropriate option to determine whether to print all items (All Rows) or only selected items (Only Selected Rows). Next, select the pages to print. To print using both sides of the paper without a duplex printer, choose Odd, then reinsert the paper upside down and print again, choosing Even. Finally, select the number of copies to print and decide whether you want Outlook to collate the copies for you or if you want to do it yourself.

For the Memo Style, your options include Start Each Item On A New Page and Print Attached Files, plus the standard Number Of Pages, Number Of Copies, and Collate Copies options.

Due to an Outlook 2002 bug, when your default Mail Format is set to HMTL, the Start Each Item On A New Page option is only available if you select a single item, in which case it's unnecessary. If you select multiple items, the option is grayed out, and each item prints on a separate page by default.

To print the job, click the OK button. If you want to see what the finished job will look like, click the Preview button.

MOUS EXAM PRACTICE

In this section, you learned to select printers and print styles, set print options, and print a hard copy of your Calendar. Rather than wasting paper, ink, and your administrator's patience, practice printing by selecting various print styles and option settings and using the Preview button to see how your selections will look. Try printing (previewing really) from different Calendar views and see how they affect your print options.

Customizing Print Styles

In addition to setting general print options for each style, you can also modify their Page Setup options. Outlook provides three sets of Page Setup options for each print style.

MANAGING TIME AND DETAILS

Formatting Options

The formatting options, found on the Format tab of the Page Setup dialog box, enable you to modify the basic design of each printed page. To set the Page Setup formatting options, choose File | Page Setup to display a submenu of print styles. Select the print style to display the associated Page Setup dialog box (see Figure 10-14).

 Depending on the view you're in, and the style you choose, the settings may be different from those shown in Figure 10-14.

By default, the Page Setup dialog box opens to the Format tab, which contains three groups of settings:

- **Options**   The Options settings vary from print style to print style. They generally consist of options for including such things as the TaskPad, a notes area (not to be confused with a Calendar item Notes field), page layout information, and a print range. All styles with the exception of the Memo Style, which has no Options settings, include some or all of these Options settings.

- **Fonts**   In all print styles except the Memo Style, you can use the Font options to change the font used in the date headings that appear at the top of the report and the Calendar item listings. Click the appropriate font button to display the

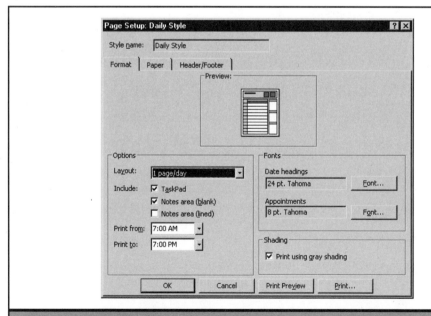

Figure 10-14.   *Each Page Setup dialog box carries the name of the print style selected*

Font dialog box, in which you can select a different font, font style, and/or font size. The Memo Style also has font options. However, they only affect the title (the calendar owner's name) and the field names (Subject, Locations, and so on).

- **Shading**   Most of the styles use gray shading to offset title and date headers. You can elect to add or remove the shading using the Print Using Gray Shading option.

Note   *When you turn on gray shading and use the Print Preview button to see what the final printout will look like, it appears that the gray shading option isn't working. This is a bug. In spite of the fact that you can't see it, the printout will contain the gray shading. For a rough idea of where gray shading is used, check the small Preview pane above the options on the Format tab. It always displays the page with shading enabled.*

Paper Options

The Paper tab of the Page Setup dialog box, shown in Figure 10-15, contains options for designating the type, size, and source of the paper you're going to use, and more. The Paper options are identical for all print styles:

- **Paper**   The paper options let you select from a list of standard paper types and sizes. You can even select a custom size and indicate the dimensions manually.

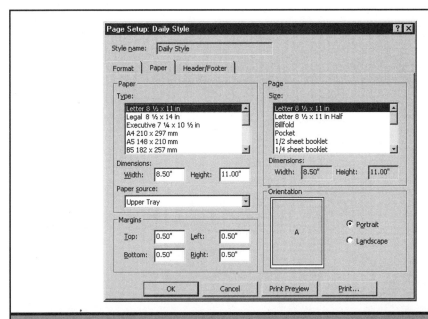

Figure 10-15.   *Use the Paper tab to select your paper and finalize the page layout design*

MANAGING TIME AND DETAILS

If your printer has multiple paper trays, or if you plan to feed the paper manually, you can designate the source for the paper as well.

■ **Page** The Page options determine how the individual page layouts designed on the Format tab are arranged on the individual sheets of paper of the type and size selected in the Paper options. You can select standard page sizes, for which the dimensions are set, or you can designate a custom size and enter the dimensions yourself. Use this option to squeeze more data on a single sheet of paper or to create small booklets.

■ **Margins** The margins are the spaces between the edge of the paper and the beginning of the print. Adjust them according to your needs. Since most printers need a minimum amount of margin space to grip the paper as it passes through the printer, you probably won't be able to set the left or right margins too close to zero. If the margins are too small, Windows will alert you to the fact.

■ **Orientation** Although orientation is normally a simple and straightforward decision between Portrait and Landscape, the introduction of Page options complicates it a little. The definitions of Portrait and Landscape don't change, just the way they're applied. Portrait prints the page vertically and Landscape prints the page horizontally. In most print jobs, the paper and the page are one and the same. In the Outlook Calendar, however, that's not always the case. Therefore, check the preview display in the Orientation section to verify that your choice is the correct one.

Header/Footer Options

The final set of Page Setup options can be found on the Header/Footer tab of the Page Setup dialog box (see Figure 10-16).

As you can see in Figure 10-16, the options consist mainly of text boxes in which you can enter any information you want, which is then added to the top or bottom of each printed page. The Header/Footer options are pretty straightforward. They contain a text

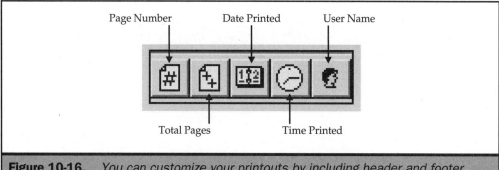

Figure 10-16. *You can customize your printouts by including header and footer information*

box for the left, middle, and right portion of the page for both headers (which appear at the top of the page) and footers (which appear at the bottom of the page).

You can enter the text you want to display, or you can use the Header/Footer toolbar located beneath the middle pane of the Footer option.

To use the toolbar, place the cursor in the desired header or footer text box and click the appropriate button on the toolbar.

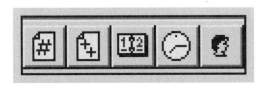

If you so desire, you can even include multiple items in a header or footer section. For example, you might want the Date Printed and the Time Printed to appear one after the other in the top-right corner of the page. Place your cursor in the right Header text box and click the Date Printed button. Then press the SPACEBAR to add a space, and click the Time Printed button.

The last option on the Header/Footer tab lets you reverse the position of the right and left panes of both the headers and footers. This comes in handy when you're printing booklets and you want certain information to always appear either on the outside or inside edge of the page. To reverse the left and right pane positions, check the Reverse On Even Pages option.

MOUS Exam Core Objectives Explored in Chapter 10

Objective	Activity	Heading
OL10-2-5	Print calendars	"Printing Calendars"

Chapter 11

Scheduling
Appointments
and Events

If there's one Outlook component that can increase your productivity and help you organize your time effectively, it's the Calendar. Not only does it let you keep track of your appointments and events (appointments that last 24 hours or more), it also provides reminders to ensure you don't forget your appointments. In addition, you can insert attachments, link contacts to appointments, and even create recurring appointments and events. In this chapter, you'll learn to add, modify, customize, and delete appointments and events.

Calendar Item Basics

Before jumping into the details of scheduling and tracking, there are some basics you should learn that apply to all Calendar items, including appointments, events, and meetings. These basic features include

- **Locations**   For each scheduled item, you can include the site at which the activity takes place. Although there are no default locations, each time you enter a new location it becomes part of the Location drop-down list.

- **Reminders**   To ensure you don't forget a scheduled item, you can have Outlook tap you on the shoulder and alert you when it's due. Just set a reminder.

- **Attachments**   You can keep track of files, documents, and Outlook items related to a scheduled item by inserting them in the scheduled item as attachments.

- **Editing and deleting techniques**   Opening, closing, modifying, and deleting Calendar items are the same no matter which type of Calendar item you're working with.

A good understanding of these features will make your scheduling chores a lot easier.

Designating Locations

A location is exactly what the name implies: a place where the scheduled appointment, event, or meeting occurs. The Appointment tab of the new Calendar item form contains a Location field into which you can enter the appropriate location for the item. The nice thing about the Location field is that it retains, in a drop-down list, the last ten locations you entered. The next time you create a new scheduled item, you can select the location from the list. However, after the tenth location, each new entry you make replaces the oldest location on the list.

While there's no way to selectively edit the Location drop-down list, you can delete the entire list and start over. This comes in handy if you move to a new location in which none of the old Location descriptions apply. Be advised, however, that this procedure involves editing the Windows registry, which should be done by experienced users only. Be sure to make a backup of your registry before making any changes. To erase the contents of the Location drop-down list, find the HKEY_CURRENT_USER\Software\ Microsoft\Office\10.0\Outlook\Preferences key and delete the LocationMRU value.

Close the registry and return to Outlook. You'll see that the Location drop-down list is now blank. The next time you make an entry in the list, the LocationMRU value is recreated in the registry.

Staying on Schedule with Reminders

When it comes to getting your Calendar organized, scheduling appointments, events, and meetings is only half the battle. The most important part of getting organized is remembering to attend all your scheduled activities. Fortunately, Outlook not only provides you with the precise tools you need to get organized but also gives you handy little devices called reminders that make sure you stay on schedule. Reminders are notices that alert you with both visual and sound cues when scheduled items are due. Using reminders is quick and easy once you understand the way they work.

Setting Reminders

When you create any scheduled item, whether it's an appointment, event, or meeting request, you fill out the Appointment tab of the Calendar item form. Although there are some minor differences between the Appointment tabs of the three different Calendar item types, each one contains identical Reminder features (see Figure 11-1).

The first thing you have to do is place a check mark in the Reminder box to turn the reminder on. Next, select the amount of time prior to the scheduled item that you want the reminder to go off. For this, you have two choices. You can either select a predefined time from the Reminder drop-down list, or you can enter the time manually. To enter times manually, you must include the number and the time unit. For example, you can type in **13 minutes**, **3 hours**, or **2 days**. You cannot, however, enter a combination of time units. So, if you want a reminder that goes off 1 day, 3 hours, and 15 minutes before a scheduled item, you'll have to convert everything to a single time unit such as 1635 minutes or 27.25 hours.

 *You can use **m** for minutes, **h** for hours, or **d** for days rather than type the entire word. Outlook will finish it for you.*

The next reminder option you can set changes the sound produced when the reminder activates. Click the sound button located next to the Reminder time drop-down list to display the Reminder Sound dialog box.

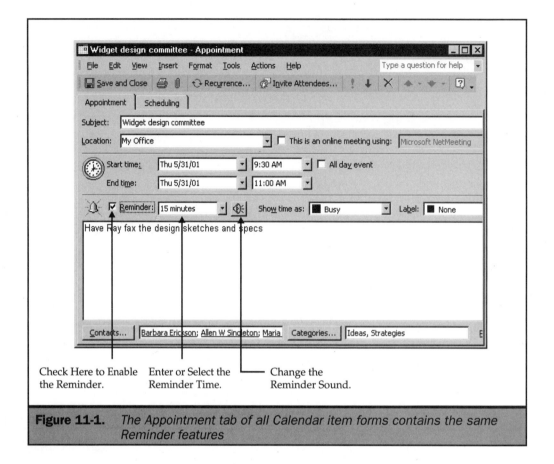

Check Here to Enable   Enter or Select the   Change the
the Reminder.   Reminder Time.   Reminder Sound.

Figure 11-1. *The Appointment tab of all Calendar item forms contains the same Reminder features*

If you want to prevent a sound from playing when a reminder displays, remove the check from the Play This Sound option. To change the sound played, click Browse to display the Reminder Sound File dialog box, from which you can choose any sound file located on your local or network drives. When you're finished changing the options in the Reminder Sound dialog box, click OK to save the changes and return to the Appointment tab of the form.

Using Reminders

After you set reminders, you can forget about your appointment or other scheduled item until it's time for the reminder to go off. As long as you set the reminder properly, and your system clock is set with the correct date and time, the reminder will pop up at the designated time to let you know the appointment is due.

When a reminder appears, you have several ways to deal with it. You can toss it away, reset it to go off at a later time, or open the item to which it refers. To eliminate the reminder altogether, click the Dismiss button. This deletes the reminder and leaves you on your own to remember the scheduled item. If you want Outlook to remind you again as the appointment gets closer, select a time from the Click Snooze To Be Reminded Again In drop-down list, then click the Snooze button. This works like the snooze button on your alarm clock, only here you have the option to select the amount of time before the reminder reappears. If you don't like the selections in the drop-down list, you can enter your own reminder time manually.

If you want to view or edit the scheduled item before doing anything with the reminder, click the Open Item button to display the item itself. When you close the item, the reminder is still displayed and awaiting your command. Either Dismiss it or Snooze it.

Setting Reminder Options

The changes you make to reminder options in individual Calendar items affect only the forms in which you make the changes. In the event that you want to turn off reminders or change the sound file used for all reminders, you can change the reminder default settings.

Choose Tools | Options to display the Options dialog box. The first reminder option, Default Reminder, is actually considered a Calendar option, and is found in the Calendar section of the Preferences tab. To enable reminders by default, place a check mark in the Default Reminder option and select (or enter) a reminder time. With this option checked, all new appointments automatically contain an active reminder set for the designated time.

To view the rest of the Reminder options, click the Other tab, then click Advanced Options to open the Advanced Options dialog box. Finally, click the Reminder Options button to display the Reminder Options dialog box.

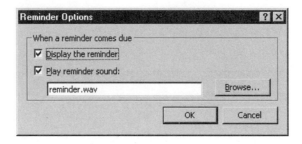

As you can see, the options are similar to those available on an individual Calendar item form. However, unlike those in the item forms, the settings here apply to all new forms you create. To turn reminders off for all new forms, clear the check mark from Display The Reminder. If you want to eliminate sounds for all new forms, remove the check mark from Play Reminder Sound. You can also change the default sound file used for all reminders by clicking Browse and selecting the sound file of your choice. When you're finished, click OK three times to save the new settings and return to the active Outlook window.

Including Attachments

Attachments are useful not only for transmitting information with e-mail messages but also for keeping track of information related to scheduled items. Inserting attachments in scheduled items lets you include files, documents, and Outlook items associated with the scheduled item. For example, you might want to include all the contact records for attendees of a meeting, or budget reports in Excel or Word for an appointment with the budget director.

Including attachments with Calendar items is very much the same as inserting attachments in e-mail messages or other Outlook items. Begin by opening the scheduled item into which you want to insert the attachment. Then select the type of attachment you want to add from the Insert menu.

   If you want to include an object such as a graph, worksheet, or image, click the Notes field first. Otherwise, the Object command is grayed out (unavailable).

Depending on the type of attachment you select, an appropriate dialog box appears. The following types of attachments can be inserted in a scheduled item:

- **File**   Select File to include a computer file in the scheduled item. The Insert File dialog box opens, from which you can select any file on your available local or network drives.

- **Item**   Use this command to insert an Outlook item as an attachment. The Insert Item dialog box appears, providing you with a view of all your Outlook folders and their contents.

- **Object**   This command adds the actual object (as opposed to the file) as an attachment. For example, if you include an Excel worksheet using the Object command, the entire worksheet appears in the Notes field of the scheduled item, not just an icon representing the worksheet file. When you select Object, the Insert Object dialog box displays. Here you can create a new object from scratch or use an existing file to create the object.

If you want to include a file as an attachment, you can avoid the extra step required when using the Insert menu by clicking the Insert File button (the one with a paper clip icon) to open the Insert File dialog box.

You can insert files and Outlook items using the drag-and-drop method. Tile Outlook and the scheduled item side by side. Open the Outlook folder of your choice (including My Computer) and drag items (or files) into the Notes field of the scheduled item. You can include objects by using the Copy and Paste commands.

Unfortunately, attachments do not travel well in Calendar items sent via e-mail in the iCalendar format. Therefore, if you plan to send Calendar items with attachments to others through your local e-mail system or through Internet e-mail, do not use the Forward As iCalendar command on the Actions menu. If you have an Internet e-mail service added to your profile, you might also want to make sure the When Sending Meeting Requests Over The Internet, Use iCalendar Format option found in the Calendar Options dialog box (Tools | Options | Calendar Options) is disabled. By the way, you'll get a warning even if the option doesn't exist (no Internet e-mail service installed) or if it's disabled. In either of those cases, you can safely ignore it and your attachment will get through just fine.

Modifying and Deleting Calendar Items

Although there are a number of differences between appointments, events, and meetings, the methods used to edit and delete all three are the same. To edit a scheduled item, simply open the item and make the necessary change(s). You can open an item by double-clicking it in any view, or by selecting it and pressing the ENTER key or CTRL+O. You can also right-click the item in any view and select Open from the shortcut menu. If you select multiple items, they will open using any of these techniques. Regardless of how you open the item, make sure you click Save And Close to save any changes you make while it's open.

You can select multiple items in a table view by moving the mouse pointer to the left edge of the table. When the cursor turns into a right-pointing arrow, hold down the left mouse button and drag up or down to select adjacent items.

Deleting scheduled items is even easier. Select the item(s) you want to remove and press the DELETE key or CTRL+D. You can also use the Delete button found on the Standard toolbar, or you can right-click selected items and choose Delete from the shortcut menu. All scheduled items you delete are placed in the Deleted Items folder from which they can be recovered until the folder is emptied.

If you're running out of storage space on the server and want to minimize the amount of stuff that collects in the Deleted Items folder, you can bypass the folder altogether by holding down the SHIFT key when you delete Calendar items.

Adding Appointments and Events

Appointments and events are similar creatures with some small differences. Both are scheduled items that do not include any outside attendees or resources. That's not to say you can't add an appointment or event for which you plan to meet with other people. It simply means that no invitations, either for people or resources, will be dispatched when you create the scheduled item. The main difference between an appointment and an event is the duration of the activity. Events are appointments that last a full day (24 hours) or more. Conventions, business trips, vacations, and marathon negotiating sessions are examples of activities that would likely fall into the category of events.

Although appointments and events do not include inviting outside attendees and resources, they can be converted to Calendar items that do. An appointment to which attendees and resources are invited is a meeting. Events to which you invite people and resources are called invited events. Both are covered in the section entitled "Scheduling Events" later in this chapter.

Adding Appointments

You can create an appointment from anywhere within Outlook. If you happen to be in the Calendar folder, press CTRL+N or click the New button to open a new appointment form (see Figure 11-2). You can also double-click a blank time slot in the Day view or a blank spot in any other view in the Calendar folder.

If you're in an Outlook folder other than the Calendar folder, press CTRL+SHIFT+A to open a new Appointment form.

In the Subject field of the open form, enter a brief description of the appointment. This is the data that shows in all the Calendar views, so make it clear and concise. If the appointment is going to take place in a special location, enter it in the Location field. If it's a location you've used before, select it from the Location drop-down list (see the "Designating Locations" section earlier in this chapter for more on locations). Since this is a regular appointment, ignore the This Is An Online Meeting Using option. If this activity is going to last 24 hours or more, check the All Day Event option to convert the form to an event form.

Select the date and time the appointment begins from the Start Time drop-down lists. You can also enter the dates and times manually if you prefer. When entering dates manually, you can use plain English phrases such as **next Tuesday** or **a week from Friday**. Although you don't have quite as much latitude when entering times,

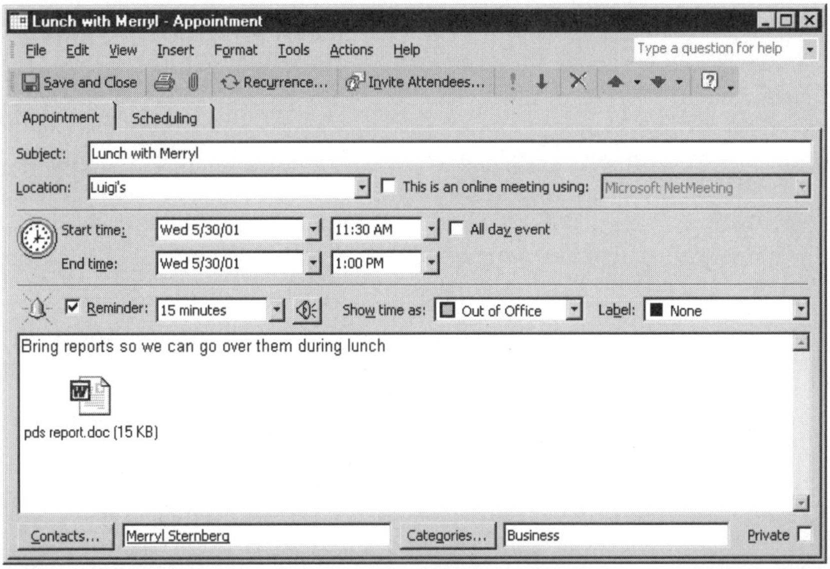

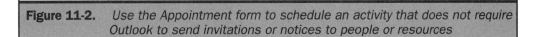

Figure 11-2.   *Use the Appointment form to schedule an activity that does not require Outlook to send invitations or notices to people or resources*

you can eliminate the colons and the AM or PM. For example, if you want to set the start time to 3:12 in the afternoon, you can enter 312p, which Outlook immediately converts to 3:12 PM. If you're using an event form, the time fields do not exist.

You can also cycle through the start and end times by placing the cursor in either field and using the UP and DOWN ARROW keys. Pressing the DOWN ARROW key increases the time by the designated interval (30 minutes by default), while pressing the UP ARROW key decreases it by the same amount.

By default, Outlook assumes you want each appointment to last 30 minutes. Therefore, the date and time in the End Time fields are adjusted to be 30 minutes (or the current default time interval) after the Start Time. You can manually change the end time, which leaves the Start Time as is.

To change the default appointment duration, open the Day or Work Week view and right-click the time bar. From the bottom of the shortcut menu, select the time interval to use. This changes not only the time slots in the view but also the default time interval used in all appointment, event, and meeting forms.

MANAGING TIME
AND DETAILS

If you want Outlook to remind you about the appointment, check the Reminder option and set the time and sound options. See the section entitled "Staying on Schedule with Reminders" earlier in this chapter for more information on setting and using reminders. To the right of the Reminder options, you'll find the Show Time As option. Use this option to designate the manner in which the time slot for this appointment is displayed when others view your free/busy information. Make the appropriate selection from the drop-down list. The next field, Label, provides a color coding system that enables you to easily distinguish different types of appointments. From the label drop-down, list select a "label." As soon as you make your selection, a border of the associated color is applied to the appointment, and the same color is used for the text in the appointment.

Use the Notes field (the large text box below the Reminder options) to enter any pertinent information relating to the appointment. It's great for jotting down notes and ideas that occur to you prior to the meeting. When the meeting comes due, you can print the item, including all notes and even the attachments. When you attend the meeting, you'll have your agenda and necessary materials at your fingertips with little or no last-minute effort.

If the appointment is with, or concerns, one or more individuals in your Contacts folder, you can link those contacts to the appointment by clicking the Contacts button to display the Select Contacts dialog box. Choose the appropriate Contacts folder and select all the contacts associated with the appointment. Click OK to close the dialog box and return to the appointment form. If you're using categories to track Calendar items, click the Categories button and select the categories to which you want the item assigned. The final option on the appointment form is the Private option. Check this option if you want the appointment hidden from others with whom you share your Calendar folder.

The Scheduling tab is only for meetings and invited events, so you can ignore it when scheduling an appointment. When you're through, click Save And Close to save the new appointment or event.

MOUS EXAM PRACTICE
In this section, you learned to create appointments. Start your practice by opening an appointment form from within the Calendar folder. Enter the appropriate information and save the new appointment. Don't forget to utilize English phrases when entering dates, and shortcuts when entering times.

Scheduling Events

Events, as mentioned earlier, are appointments that last for 24 hours or more. This means you can create events that span a single day or multiple days. As you can see in Figure 11-3, the event form is comparable to the appointment form with some small differences.

- The form title bar says Event rather than Appointment.
- The All Day Event option, which is unchecked for an appointment, is checked for an event.

- The times of day for the Start Time and End Time fields are hidden in the event form.

- The Show Time As option, which is set to Busy for an appointment, is set to Free by default for an event.

As you can see in Table 11-1, Outlook offers a variety of ways to create an event. The procedure for filling out an event form is almost identical to that used in completing an appointment form. Therefore, you should refer to the previous section "Adding Appointments" for details and tips on filling in the event form fields. The only differences are in checking the All Day Event option, and not setting any start and end times (dates, yes; times, no). Although the default value for Show Time As is different, setting the option is the same in either form.

MOUS EXAM PRACTICE

This section covered the methods used for creating events. Start by opening an appointment form and use it to create an event. Then use one of the methods described earlier in this section to open an event form. Finally, use the Work Week, Week, or Month view to create multiday events.

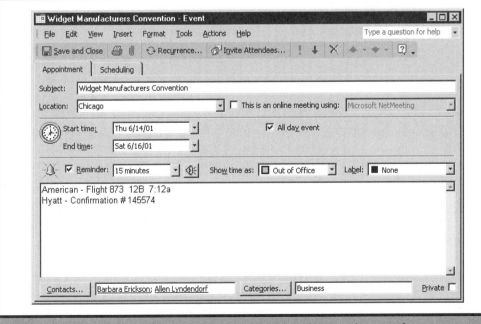

Figure 11-3. *The event form is almost identical to the appointment form*

MANAGING TIME
AND DETAILS

To Create an Event From	Do This
Any Outlook folder	Press CTRL+SHIFT+A and check the All Day Event option
Calendar folder	Press CTRL+N or click the New button and check the All Day Event option
Calendar folder	Choose Actions | New All Day Event
Day/Week/Month view	Double-click the date header
Week or Month view	Double-click a blank spot in a date box
Work Week, Week, or Month view	Select multiple dates and press CTRL+N or click the New button on the Standard toolbar
An appointment form	Check the All Day Event option

Table 11-1. *Methods for Creating an Event*

Creating Recurring Calendar Items

If you have appointments, events, or meetings that occur at regular intervals, you can save yourself a lot of time and work by creating a single recurring item rather than individual items for each occurrence. For example, if you have an employee meeting every Monday morning, a lunch date every Tuesday, a sales meeting the last Thursday of each month, or even a weekend retreat every quarter, you've got ideal candidates for recurring Calendar items.

Begin by creating a regular appointment, event, or meeting. Then, with the item form open, click the Recurrence button on the Standard toolbar in the form. The Appointment Recurrence dialog box seen in Figure 11-4 opens, providing you with the necessary options for establishing a recurrence pattern for the item.

As you can see in Figure 11-4, the Appointment Recurrence dialog box uses information from the Appointment tab of the Calendar item form to make certain assumptions about the recurring item. The Start, End, and Duration fields are filled using information from the Start Time and End Time fields in the form. You can change any of the three fields by making selections from the drop-down lists or entering your own data. As you modify data in one field, the other field affected by the change is recalculated automatically. For example, if you change the Start time, the End time adjusts itself to accommodate the information in the Duration field. Changing the End time results in the Duration field being updated to reflect the difference between the Start and End times. If you decide to change the Duration data, the End time is adjusted to ensure the appropriate difference between Start and End times.

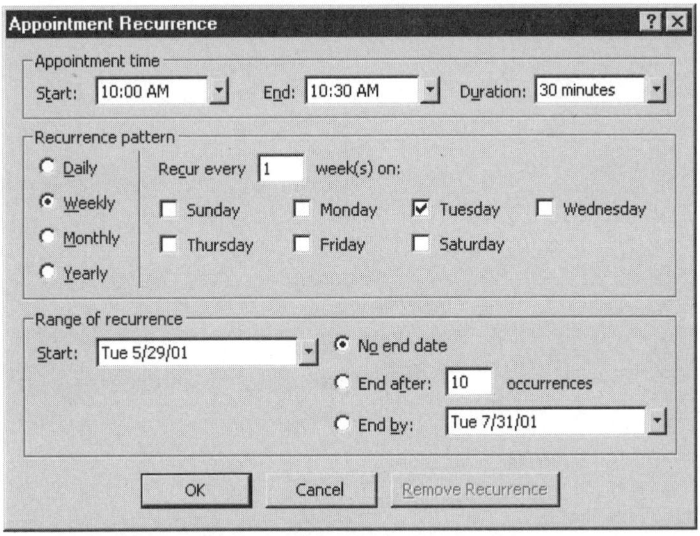

Figure 11-4.   *The Appointment Recurrence dialog box opens with a weekly recurrence pattern by default*

Outlook assumes the recurrence for all items is going to be weekly, beginning on the Start date, and recurring every week on the same day of the week, using the Start day. You have a multitude of options here. As a matter of fact, by combining the three different sets of options, the possibilities are limitless. Start by selecting the type of recurrence. Your choices include Daily, Weekly, Monthly, and Yearly. Depending on the recurrence type you select, the dialog box changes to accommodate the related options.

Figure 11-4 shows the default recurrence type, Weekly. The Weekly type lets you indicate the number of weeks between recurrences, and the day or days on which you want the item to recur. For your Monday morning pep talk to your employees, you could leave the settings as they are. However, for a production meeting that occurs on Tuesday and Friday of every other week, you would change the Recur Every __ Week(s) On option to 2, and check off Tuesday and Friday.

For a Daily recurrence pattern, your choices are more limited (see Figure 11-5). You can select the number of days between recurrences by adjusting the Every __ Days option. If the item occurs every Monday through Friday, select Every Weekday.

The next recurrence type is Monthly, the options for which are shown in Figure 11-6.

There are two options for items recurring monthly. You can set the items to repeat based on the date of the month or on the day of the week. The first set of options is for using the date of the month. In the example shown in Figure 11-6, the item is scheduled for May 29, 2001. Therefore, Outlook assumes you want to repeat the item on the 29th of each month. With this option selected, you can change the date and the number of months between recurrences.

MANAGING TIME
AND DETAILS

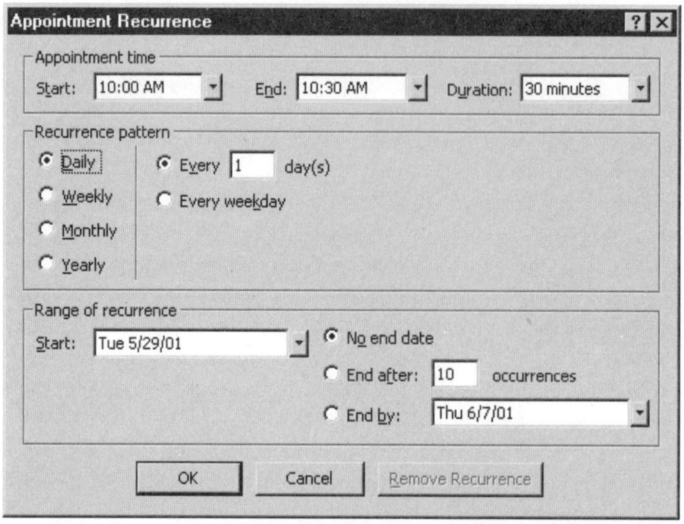

Figure 11-5. *Set intervals between daily occurrences or choose weekdays only*

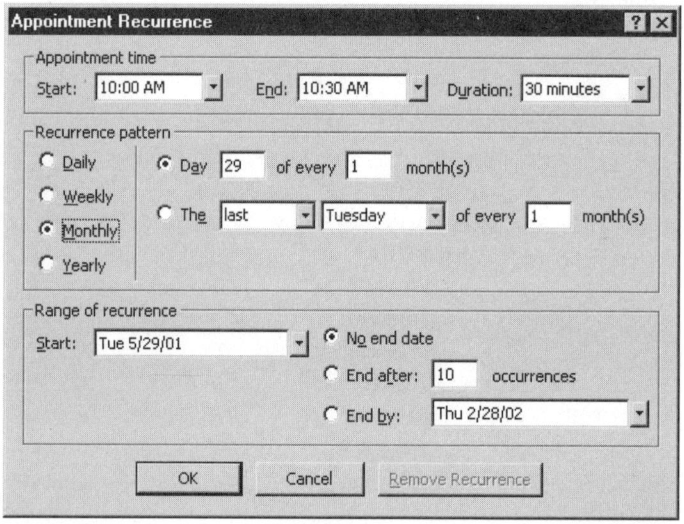

Figure 11-6. *You can set monthly recurrences by date or by day*

However, May 29, 2001, is also the last Tuesday in the month. Therefore, you can elect to have the item repeat the last Tuesday of each month, regardless of the date on which it falls. Use this option for your monthly sales meeting, for example. With the option enabled, you can select the week of the month (first, second, third, fourth, or last), the day of the week, and the number of months between recurrences. The day of the week drop-down list offers a variety of choices in addition to the specific days of the week. Other choices include day, weekday, and weekend day.

The final recurrence type, Yearly, offers options similar to those found in the Monthly type. As you can see in Figure 11-7, the first option lets you select the month and date for the annual occurrence. Using the second option, you can elect to have the item repeat on a specific day of the month each year.

As far as Outlook is concerned, the recurring item is going to last forever, unless you indicate otherwise in the Range Of Recurrence options. The Start date is the date from the Start Time field in the original item. You can change it by entering another date in the future or by selecting a future date from the pop-up calendar. As with other Outlook date fields, you can use plain English when entering the Start date.

The options for ending the recurring item include the following:

- **No end date**   If you want the recurring item to repeat for an indefinite time, select this option. The recurring item will continue to repeat using the current settings until you change the option or delete the item

- **End after __ occurrences**   If the recurring item has a limited number of recurrences, such as a class or seminar, use this option. Indicate the number of times you want the item to repeat. Changes you make here are reflected in the End By date as well.

- **End by**   If the recurring item has a specific end date, enter it here. You'll notice that changing the End By date also changes the End After __ Occurrences number to reflect the number of occurrences between the Start date and the End By date.

After setting the Appointment Recurrence options, click OK to return to the Calendar item form. If any occurrences of the item conflict with existing scheduled items, a banner appears informing you of the fact (see Figure 11-8). Unfortunately, Outlook doesn't provide you with details other than the number of conflicts, so you'll have to track the conflict(s) down yourself.

While the basics are the same for regular Calendar items and recurring Calendar items, there are differences when it comes to editing and deleting them. Recurring items are not single items—they are series of identical single items. Therefore, when it comes to editing and deleting, you have to tell Outlook whether it's the series or an individual item you're changing or deleting.

To edit a recurring item, use the method you normally use to edit any other Calendar item (double-click the item, select the item and press ENTER, and so on). Before the item opens, the Open Recurring Item dialog box appears.

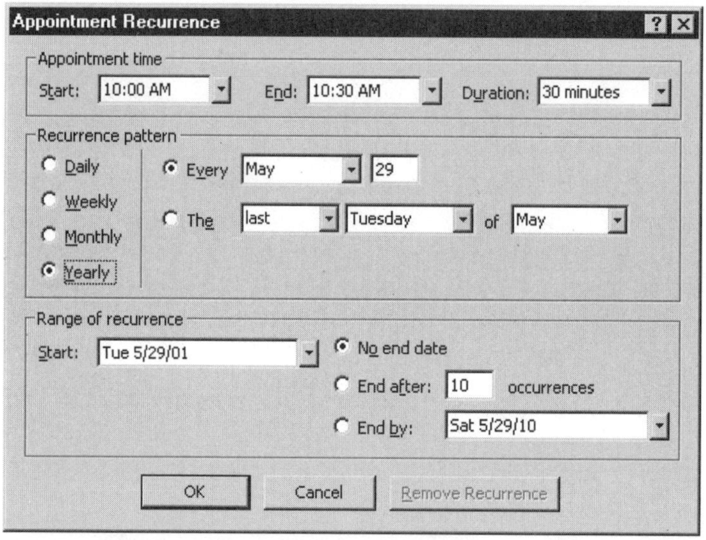

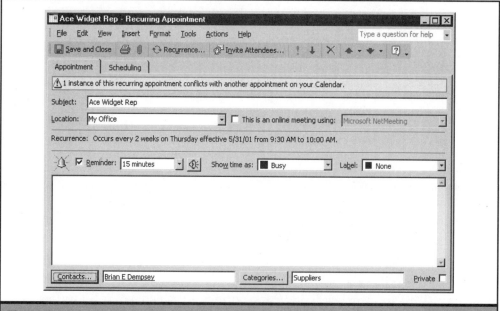

Figure 11-7.   *Use the Yearly recurrence pattern for birthdays, anniversaries, and other annually recurring events*

Figure 11-8.   *The Start Time and End Time fields in a recurring item form are replaced with the recurrence pattern information*

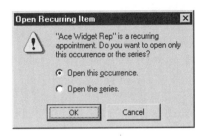

Indicate whether it's the individual occurrence or the entire series you want to open. If you select Open This Occurrence, a regular form opens for the item. You can then make the necessary changes and click Save And Close to apply them. Use this method to reschedule occurrences that conflict with other scheduled items. If, however, you want to change every instance of the recurring item, select Open The Series. This opens the recurring item form in which you can change everything except the start and end dates, start and end times, and recurrence patterns. To change those items, click the Recurrence button to open the Appointment Recurrence dialog box. Use this method if your Monday morning pep talk is being permanently changed to a Tuesday morning pep talk.

Deleting a recurring item offers basically the same options. The Confirm Delete dialog box appears, offering you a choice between deleting the selected instance of the recurring item or the entire series.

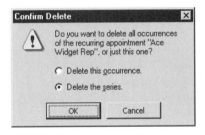

Tip   *Opening a recurring item in Outlook Today opens the entire series. Therefore, if you decide to delete the item, you are actually deleting the entire series, not just a single instance. Unfortunately, Outlook doesn't bother to ask you to confirm the series deletion, it just does it. On the plus side, however, Outlook does drop the deleted recurring item into the Deleted Items folder. To recover the recurring item, move it back to the Calendar folder.*

MANAGING TIME
AND DETAILS

MOUS Exam Core Objectives Explored in Chapter 11

Objective	Activity	Heading
OL10-2-1	Add appointments and events to the Outlook calendar	"Adding Appointments"
		"Scheduling Events"

MOUS Exam Expert Objectives Explored in Chapter 11

Objective	Activity	Heading
OL10E-3-2	Set private appointments	"Adding Appointments"

Chapter 12

Scheduling Meetings
and Invited Events

M eetings and invited events are two Calendar items that involve other people and resources. You're probably all too familiar with meetings, so there's no need to explain what they are. Invited event, on the other hand, is a term not frequently encountered beyond Outlook. Events, as discussed in Chapter 11, are activities that last 24 hours or longer. An invited event is simply an event to which you formally invite people and/or resources. A weekend retreat, a two-day seminar, or a trade show you want others to attend all fall into the category of invited events. Resources are things such as conference rooms, audio/video equipment, and other similar items that may be required for meetings.

Using the Meeting Planner

The Meeting Planner, also known as the Plan A Meeting dialog box, provides you with all the tools you need to plan and organize a meeting of any size. Using the Meeting Planner enables you to quickly and easily determine the best time for yourself, the proposed meeting attendees, and the resources you require. Planning a large meeting without the Meeting Planner often results in endless "No, that's not good for me. How about....?" conversations or e-mail messages with each attendee. Think about doing that with five, ten, or fifty attendees! Using the Meeting Planner eliminates the need to have even a single discussion about attendees' schedules. You can access the Meeting Planner (shown in Figure 12-1) by choosing Actions | Plan A Meeting from the Calendar folder Standard toolbar.

Adding and Removing Attendees

Begin by adding the desired participants to the All Attendees list. You can either enter the attendees' names manually or click the Add Others button to choose names from the Address Book or add a public folder. To select attendees, click Add From Address Book to display the Select Attendees and Resources dialog box, shown in Figure 12-2.

Using the Select Attendees and Resources dialog box is much the same as adding recipients to e-mail messages. The process is the same: select the address book, then choose the attendee or resource from the listing on the left, and click the appropriate button to add it to the "invited" list on the right. The difference is in the buttons, which include:

- **Required** Use this button to select attendees whose presence is required at the meeting. The meeting request lists required and optional attendees separately. In addition, if no other item is scheduled, Outlook automatically marks the time slot on required attendees' calendars as Tentative until they respond. Their free/busy time is updated accordingly when they respond to the meeting request.

- **Optional** For attendees whose presence at the meeting is not critical, use the Optional button. These attendees will be listed on the meeting request as Optional, and the meeting is added to their calendars with the free/busy time marked as Tentative.

■ **Resources**   Use this button to include conference rooms, equipment, furniture and other items that have been set up as resources. In order for a resource to be available for a meeting request, it must have its own mailbox on the server and appear on the Global Address List.

Outlook permits you to select distribution lists as attendees. However, regardless of which designation (Required or Optional) you give them, the individual members of the list appear as optional attendees when they accept your invitation. That's because Outlook compares the meeting request responses with the All Attendees list and assumes anyone not specifically listed is an optional attendee. Unless you expand the distribution list on the All Attendees list, only the distribution list name appears. To make sure all distribution list members are treated as required attendees, expand the distribution list before sending the invitations. Expanding the distribution list before sending invitations also ensures that updates to the meeting reach the correct attendees.

Note   *Attendees who are part of the distribution list and who are already on the All Attendees list will be added a second time. To avoid confusion, make sure you eliminate duplicates before sending invitations.*

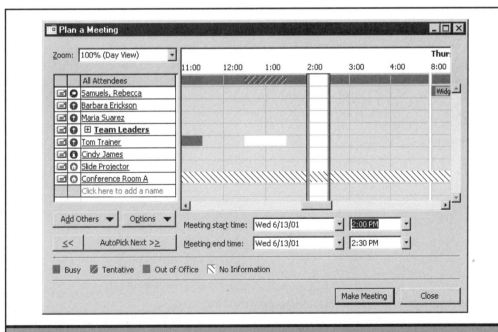

Figure 12-1.   *Organizing a meeting is a snap with the Meeting Planner*

MANAGING TIME
AND DETAILS

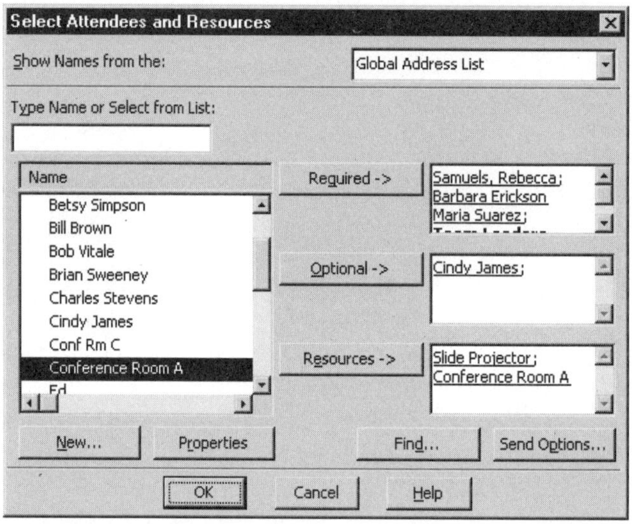

Figure 12-2.   *You can invite attendees and resources from any of your address books*

After you select the attendees and resources, click OK to add them to the All Attendees list. If you decide you want to eliminate an attendee or resource from the list, you have a couple of options. You can highlight the name in the All Attendees list and press the DEL key. When you Tab to the next name, the deleted entry disappears altogether. You can right-click the name and select Clear from the shortcut menu. A third option is to return to the Select Attendees and Resources dialog box and delete the name from the list of invitees.

One thing to be aware of when entering a large number of attendees is that the All Attendees list can hold more names than it displays. As you add more names, it may appear that earlier names have disappeared from the list. This usually happens when you use the TAB key to scroll through the list. Don't worry, the attendees are still there. You can see them by enlarging the Meeting Planner window.

Next, check the availability of attendees and resources to make sure there are no conflicts. The Meeting Planner displays the free/busy time for all invited attendees. Of course, free/busy information is available only for those attendees who are either on the Microsoft Exchange Server network or who publish their free/busy time to a server for which you've designated the appropriate search path in your Free/Busy Options (see Chapter 10 for more information on free/busy data).

Tip   *To make sure you have the latest available free/busy information, you may want to click the Options button and select Refresh Free/Busy from the menu that appears.*

If there's a conflict with anyone's (or anything's) schedule, you can use the AutoPick button to locate a time at which everyone is available according to their published free/busy data. The AutoPick feature searches for the first time slot for which all of the attendees and resources are free.

Note

The AutoPick feature treats those schedules for which no free/busy time is available as if the time were marked Free.

The Meeting Planner uses the currently selected date and time for the meeting. If you want to change either, edit the Meeting Start Time and Meeting End Time fields.

MOUS

MOUS EXAM PRACTICE
Since this section deals with adding and deleting attendees and resources, you should begin your practice by entering some names in the All Attendees list. Then use the Invite Others button to display the Select Attendees and Resources dialog box. Add some required attendees, some optional, and at least one resource. While you're in the dialog box, remove some of the attendees after you add them. After you close the Select Attendees and Resources dialog box, try removing a couple of attendees directly from the All Attendees list.

Working with the All Attendees List

The Meeting Planner also offers a few other options for manipulating the All Attendees list. If you want to leave an attendee or resource on the list without sending an invitation, click the envelope icon to the left of the name and select Don't Send Meeting To This Attendee. You can also display a shortcut menu of commands that apply to the attendees by right-clicking an attendee name. The available commands include some or all of the following:

- **Properties**   This command displays the properties dialog box or contact record for the attendee, depending on the Select Attendees and Resources dialog box source from which the attendee was selected. For example, an attendee who is listed in both the Global Address List and the Outlook Address Book will display the properties dialog box if added to the meeting request form from the Global Address List, and the contact record if added from the Outlook Address Book.

- **Send Options**   Unfortunately, this command will probably net you nothing more than an error message indicating that the command "is not valid for this recipient." The Outlook address books do not currently provide these send options.

- **Add to Contacts**   Use this command, which is unavailable for attendees added to the list from the Contacts folder, to create a record in the Contacts folder for the selected attendee. However, if you add an attendee from the Global Address List who also has a contact record, the option is available in spite of the fact that a contact record already exists. If you attempt to add the attendee, Outlook warns you (when you save the new contact record) that you're about to create a duplicate contact record.

- **Look up Contact** Use this command to search for the attendee in the Contacts folder. This command is available only for those attendees not selected from the Contacts folder to begin with. Since clicking the Properties command for an attendee selected from the Contacts folder displays the contact record, there's no reason to have to go searching for the record.

- **Open Calendar** If the attendee has a mailbox on the server, *and* you have the proper permissions, you can view his, her, or its (a resource) calendar for the meeting date by using this command.

- **Editing options** The remaining commands are common text editing options that work as anticipated.

 Double-clicking an attendee name in the All Attendees list opens the attendee's properties dialog box or contact record (depending on the source from which the attendee was selected).

This ends the Meeting Planner phase of scheduling a meeting. The next stage involves using the meeting request form to send the invitations.

 MOUS EXAM PRACTICE
In this section, you learned to use the Meeting Planner to take the hassle out of scheduling meetings. For this practice session, open the Meeting Planner and add attendees and resources from all your address books. If you have distribution lists, add one of those also. Check the schedules for those attendees whose free/busy time is available. Schedule the meeting for a time when others have conflicting appointments. Then use the AutoPick feature to find a time slot when everyone is free. Next, use the options and commands associated with the All Attendees list to view attendees' properties and calendars.

Using the Meeting Request Form

When all the attendees and resources have been added and the schedule is set, it's time to get the ball rolling and send out the invitations. Click the Make Meeting button to create a meeting request (see Figure 12-3) utilizing the information you've entered into the Meeting Planner.

If you'd prefer to bypass the Meeting Planner, you can start with a meeting request form by pressing CTRL+SHIFT+Q, or choosing Actions | New Meeting Request.

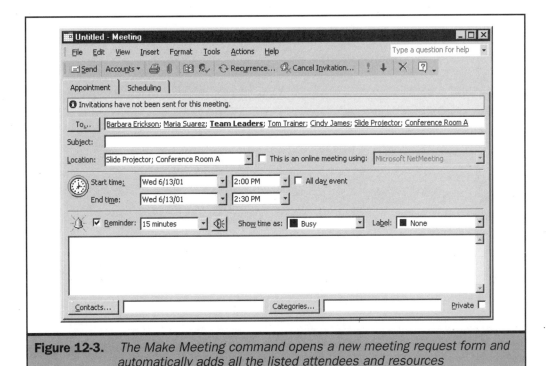

Figure 12-3. *The Make Meeting command opens a new meeting request form and automatically adds all the listed attendees and resources*

Enter a brief description of the meeting purpose in the Subject field. This is also your opportunity to turn the meeting into an invited event if it's going to last 24 hours or longer. Check the All Day Event option to remove the time fields and change the form title to Invited Event.

In the Notes field, add your comments, any additional information, or attachments pertinent to the meeting. If there are any individuals in your Contacts folder who are associated with the meeting, you may want to link them to the meeting request by clicking the Contacts button and selecting them from the Select Contacts dialog box. If you use categories to organize your folders, click the Categories button to assign the meeting request to one or more categories.

To make changes to the attendees or review their schedules, click the Scheduling tab, which, as you can see in Figure 12-4, is a near replica of the Meeting Planner attached to the meeting request form.

 If some of your attendees seem to have disappeared from the All Attendees list, maximize and restore the meeting request form to force a redraw. The lost attendees should reappear.

Making changes here is the same as making changes on the Meeting Planner. When you're ready to send the invitations, click the Send button on the form's Standard toolbar.

MANAGING TIME
AND DETAILS

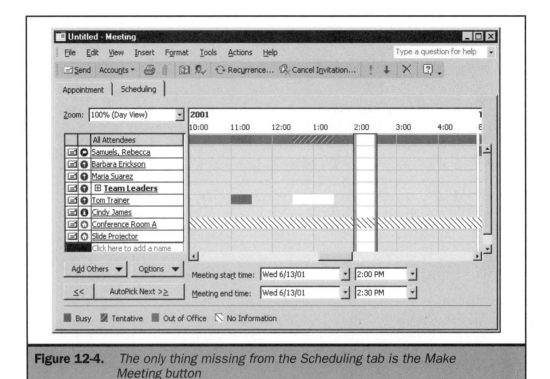

Figure 12-4.   *The only thing missing from the Scheduling tab is the Make Meeting button*

All you have to do now is sit back and wait for the responses to start rolling in. One more thing: the first time you book resources that are available (and for which you have the appropriate permissions), a Resources Booked dialog box appears informing you that the resources were successfully booked. If, on the other hand, the resource is unavailable or you don't have proper permissions, a dialog box appears notifying you that your request was declined, and the reason why. There are actually a number of reasons why resource requests may be turned down. See the section entitled "Scheduling Meeting Resources" for more information.

After you send the meeting invitations, Outlook converts the Meeting Request form to a Meeting form and adds a third tab, called Tracking (see Figure 12-5).

The Tracking tab displays the response status of each invitee. You can tell, at a glance, who has responded, how they've responded, and whether they're a required, optional, or resource invitee. If you're having second thoughts about the Required/Optional status of a particular attendee, you can change it by clicking the Attendance field and selecting a different status from the drop-down list that appears. You can also add or change an attendee's Response information by clicking the Response field and making the appropriate selection from the drop-down list. This is useful if the individual responds by phone or some means other than e-mail (which Outlook tracks automatically).

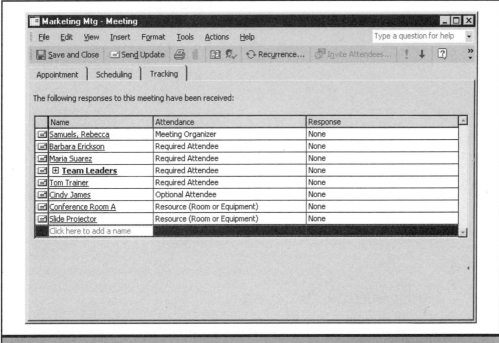

Figure 12-5.   *Keeping track of attendee status and responses is a breeze*

> **Tip**   *If you've gotten verbal commitments from all your attendees, or you're the boss and no one dares to refuse your meeting requests, you can eliminate all responses by choosing Actions | Request Responses from the meeting request form Standard toolbar. Removing the check mark suppresses both automatic and manual responses from attendees. However, since it does the same with resources, you will not be notified of any problems that render the resource unavailable.*

If the meeting time is etched in stone and you don't want to be bothered by attendees proposing alternate meeting times, choose Actions | Allow New Time Proposals to remove the check mark and disable the option.

Converting Existing Appointments and Events

As you're no doubt aware, all Calendar item forms contain a Scheduling tab. The easiest way to convert an appointment to a meeting request is to click the Scheduling tab and add one or more attendees. Outlook immediately converts the appointment form to a meeting request form. You'll note that, as soon as you add an attendee, the Invite Attendees button located on the Standard toolbar changes to Cancel Invitation. This enables you to switch the meeting request form back to an appointment form, and cancel any invitations that were about to be sent.

See the section entitled "Using the Meeting Request Form" earlier in this chapter for more information on using meeting request forms.

Scheduling Meeting Resources

The ability to treat meeting resources like meeting participants makes scheduling meeting and invited events even easier. No more telephone tag with the resource administrator, trying to determine if and when the resource is available. A simple meeting request and an almost instantaneous response let you know whether the resource is available and if you can reserve it. However, as with other meeting invitees, there are some requirements that must be met before resources can be scheduled. A resource account must be established and options set.

Setting Up a Resource Account

To take advantage of resource booking, you must first set up an account for each resource you want to make available for scheduling. This requires a mailbox on the Microsoft Exchange Server for each resource. Ask your system administrator to add the mailbox if one doesn't already exist. Generally, the resource mailbox will be assigned to one owner, who then controls the manner in which the resource behaves. There may be a resource coordinator or other individual in your organization who handles all resources, or the responsibility may fall to someone on the administrative staff. Whoever that person is, he or she alone will have the ability to determine how the resource account is configured.

The first thing the owner must decide is who will be permitted to book the resource. For example, a small conference room on the second floor will probably have different permission settings than the big, luxurious conference room on the top floor, used by the big brass. By setting the permissions and other resource options, you can regulate and automate much of the resource scheduling process. For the resource owner, this eliminates the hassle of checking each reservation to ensure there are no problems with improper bookings or conflicting schedules.

After the resource mailbox is set up on the Microsoft Exchange Server, you (the owner) must create a profile for the resource. See Chapter 2 for detailed information on adding and removing profiles. It's only after the profile has been created that you can configure the resource account.

If Outlook is open, close it. Log back on to Outlook using the resource profile. Once you're logged on as the resource, all options you set apply to the resource account. Choose Tools | Options to open the Options dialog box, and click the Calendar Options button on the Preferences tab to display the Calendar Options dialog box. Now click the Resource Scheduling button to open the Resource Scheduling dialog box.

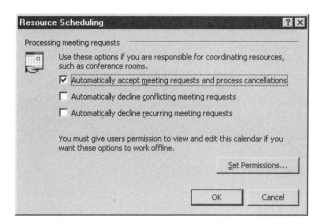

As you can see, the Resource Scheduling dialog box contains three options and a Set Permissions button. These four items provide the tools for you to control the resource and automate its response to meeting requests:

- **Automatically accept meeting requests and process cancellations**   Check this option to enable automatic scheduling and responding on behalf of the resource. Any meeting requests and cancellations that do not conflict with any other resource settings will be accepted and processed automatically. In addition, turning this option on makes the next two options available for setting.

- **Automatically decline conflicting meeting requests**   Along with its own profile, the resource now also has its own calendar. As meeting requests arrive, the resource account checks its calendar against the incoming requests. Check this option to have the resource automatically decline any requests that conflict with its schedule.

- **Automatically decline recurring meeting requests**   To ensure the resource does not get tied up for extended periods of time without your direct knowledge, you can check this option to prevent anyone from booking the resource on a recurring basis.

- **Set Permissions**   The Set Permissions button provides quick access to the Calendar Properties dialog box. Using the options on the Permissions tab, you can control which users are allowed to reserve the resource.

If you want everyone in the organization to have the ability to book the resource, you can bypass the Set Permissions button and head right for the OK button. The first time you set the Resource Scheduling options and click OK to save them, Outlook displays the Set Permissions for Offline Use dialog box.

MANAGING TIME
AND DETAILS

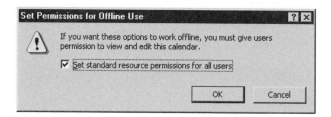

As you can see, the Set Standard Resource Permissions For All Users option is checked. This automatically sets the default permissions for the Calendar folder to Author, which means everyone on the Microsoft Exchange Server network can book the resource. To accept these permissions settings, click OK.

Setting Resource Permissions

Until you set the Calendar folder permissions, either through the Set Permissions for Offline Use dialog box or through the Permissions tab of the Calendar Properties dialog box, no one can book the resource except you (the owner). You can set or change permissions using the Permissions tab of the Calendar Properties dialog box, shown in Figure 12-6.

To schedule a resource, the user must have permissions to both read and create items.

For detailed information on setting permissions for both resources and folders, see Chapter 18.

Managing Resources

Although setting up a resource account requires creating a profile and logging on as the resource, managing it is a lot easier. While you can log on using the resource profile each time, there's a way to manage the resource from within your own profile. However, to do this the resource mailbox must be assigned to your user account on the server.

The first thing to do is add the resource mailbox to your Microsoft Exchange Server E-mail account. Choose Tools | E-mail Accounts to display the E-mail Accounts dialog box. Select View Or Change Existing E-mail Accounts and click Next. Select Microsoft Exchange Server and click Change to open the Exchange Server Settings dialog box. Click More Settings to open the Microsoft Exchange Server dialog box. Next, click the Advanced tab to display the Advanced options. Finally, click the Add button to open the Add Mailbox dialog box.

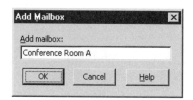

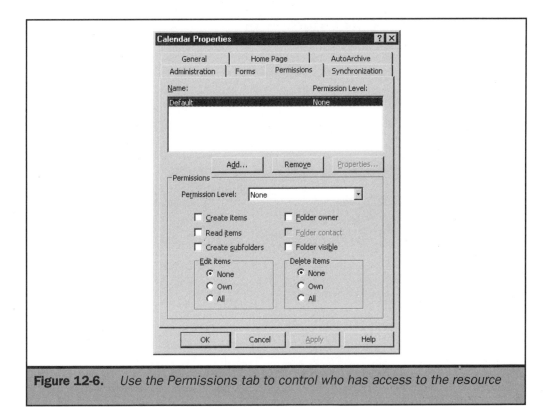

Figure 12-6.   *Use the Permissions tab to control who has access to the resource*

Enter the mailbox name in the Add Mailbox field. While you don't have to enter the entire name, what you do enter must be accurate since Outlook attempts to resolve the name based on the text you type.

If you don't know the exact name of the resource mailbox, cancel out of all the dialog boxes and open your Address Book. In the Global Address List, right-click the resource listing and click Properties. Use either the Display name or the Alias, both of which appear on the General tab of the properties dialog box.

Click OK to add the mailbox. If the name resolves correctly, the mailbox is added and you return to the Microsoft Exchange Server dialog box. If the name doesn't resolve, Outlook tells you to try again. If Outlook finds multiple names containing the text you entered, the Check Name dialog box appears with all possible candidates. Select the correct one. Click OK, Next, and Finish until you return to the active Outlook window. You'll find that the resource mailbox has been added to your Folder List as another set of folders.

MANAGING TIME
AND DETAILS

By right-clicking the Calendar folder in the resource mailbox folders, you can access the folder's Permissions tab and set and modify permissions for all users. In addition, you have complete access to all the resource mailbox folders including the Inbox and Sent Items folders. Here you'll find messages sent to the resource, and automatic responses sent from the resource to users who made requests.

If you don't like cluttering your Folder List with an additional set of folders, you can also access the resource mailbox folders by choosing File | Open | Other User's Folder to display the Open Other User's Folder dialog box.

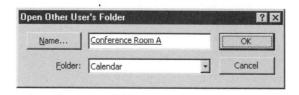

Click the Name button to display the Select Name dialog box. Choose the Global Address List and select the resource from the listing. Click OK to return to the Open Other User's Folder dialog box. Now select the desired folder from the Folder drop-down list. To set permissions for booking the resource, select the Calendar folder. Click OK to open the resource Calendar folder in a separate window (see Figure 12-7).

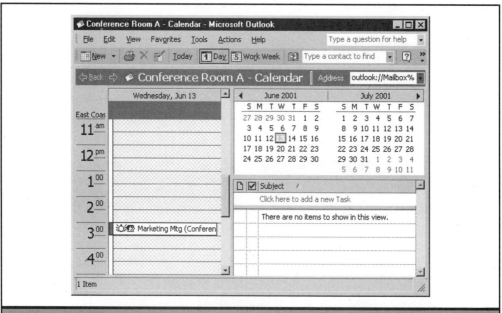

Figure 12-7.   *The resource Calendar folder opens in its own window*

You can now view the Calendar, and add, remove, and modify Calendar items. You can also change permissions for the resource. In the resource folder window, choose File | Folder | Properties for [folder name] to open the resource folder properties dialog box. Click the Permissions tab and set user permissions following the methods outlined in the earlier section "Setting Resource Permissions." When you're finished with the Calendar folder, press ALT+F4 to close it.

MOUS EXAM PRACTICE

In this section, you learned to establish resource accounts, set user permissions, and manage resources. Depending on your needs, you may or may not be able to get the administrator to set up the mailboxes needed to create resource accounts. Create a user profile for the resource, then log on to Outlook using the resource profile. Next, set permissions for different users and follow up with them to see the differences in their experiences depending on the permissions they've been assigned. Finally, add the resource mailbox to your Microsoft Exchange Server e-mail account in Outlook, and manage it by logging on with your own profile.

Changing a Scheduled Meeting

Editing a scheduled meeting or invited event is simply a matter of opening the meeting or invited event form and making and saving the appropriate changes. Start by opening the Calendar folder and locating the item you want to change. When you find the item, double-click it to open it. Make the necessary changes and click Save and Close. If you make changes to the dates, times, or location, Outlook kindly offers to send all attendees an e-mail notifying them of the changes. If you click Yes, Outlook e-mails each attendee an updated version of the meeting request. If you add or delete attendees, Outlook displays the Send Update To Attendees dialog box.

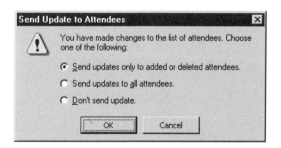

Here you can elect to send updates to all attendees, only those who have been added or removed, or to no attendees at all. Make your selection and click OK to continue.

If you decide to cancel a meeting, the process is equally simple. Locate the meeting on your Calendar and open it. Choose Actions | Cancel Meeting from the meeting form's menu bar. A Microsoft Outlook dialog box appears, asking if you want to delete the meeting and send cancellation notices to all attendees, or just delete the meeting without notifying anyone. Make your selection and click OK.

If you elected to cancel the meeting without sending notification, the meeting is removed from your Calendar and dumped into the Deleted Items folder. If, however, you choose to send notifications, you're returned to the meeting form where the information banner indicates that the meeting has been canceled. Click Send to cancel the meeting and send the cancellation notices to attendees.

Note   *Unlike meeting requests, which automatically add the meeting to the attendees' calendars, cancellations only send an e-mail notifying the attendee of the cancellation. However, the e-mail contains a Remove From Calendar button that makes deleting the meeting effortless.*

MOUS   *MOUS EXAM PRACTICE*
In this section you learned to modify scheduled meetings by changing meeting details or by canceling the meeting altogether. Begin by creating some practice meetings using the skills you learned in earlier sections of this chapter. Then, open an existing meeting and change the date and/or time. Save the modified meeting and see what happens. Repeat the process and try changing some of the other meeting details. When you've got modifying down pat, start canceling the practice meetings. This will not only provide you with some practice, but also clear the bogus meetings from your calendar.

Tracking Meeting Request Responses

As you receive responses to your meeting requests or invited event requests, you don't have to do anything to process them. Outlook automatically records both positive and negative responses, as well as the lack of a response. When you open the meeting form, the information banner gives you a brief rundown of the responses received thus far. To see how each attendee responded, click the Tracking tab. This may be all the tracking you require. However, if you arrange a large number of meetings, you will probably want something a little more comprehensive.

At first glance, creating a meeting response folder and then using the Rules Wizard to automatically move responses into it sounds like a great idea. Unfortunately, Outlook can only process meeting request responses from within the Inbox. If you create a rule to move them to a new folder, the move takes place almost instantaneously, which means the responses don't remain in the Inbox long enough for Outlook to process them. If you open the message in the new folder, Outlook can't find the meeting, and again fails in its attempt to process the response.

A better idea is to create a custom Inbox view that groups messages by the Message Class field. Use the following steps to create your own custom view:

1. Open the Inbox folder and choose View | Current View | Define Views to open the Define Views For "Inbox" dialog box, shown here.

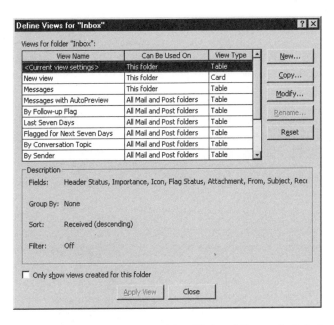

2. Select Messages in the Views For Folder "Inbox" list and click the Copy button to open the Copy View dialog box.

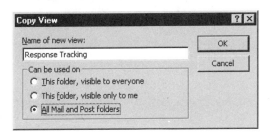

3. Enter a name for the new view. Use something like "Response Tracking."

4. Select the All Mail And Post Folders option, and click OK to open the View Summary dialog box.

5. Click Fields to display the Show Fields dialog box. From the Select Available Fields From drop-down list, select All Mail Fields.

6. Scroll down the Available Fields list and select Message Class. Then click the Add button to add the Message Class field to the pane on the right.

7. Click OK to return to the View Summary dialog box.

8. Click Group By to open the Group By dialog box.

9. From the Select Available Fields From drop-down list, select All Mail Fields.

10. From the Group Items By drop-down list, select Message Class, then click OK to return to the View Summary dialog box.

11. Click OK to return to the Define Views For "Inbox" dialog box.

12. Click Apply View to return to the Inbox, which now displays your new view (see Figure 12-8).

As you can see in Figure 12-8, the new view does more than just separate out meeting responses. It also shows regular messages, meeting requests you've received, and other different types of messages. Therefore, you can also use it to track other things, such as incoming meeting or task requests. The next time you display your list of Current Views, you'll see the new view has been added to the bottom of the list.

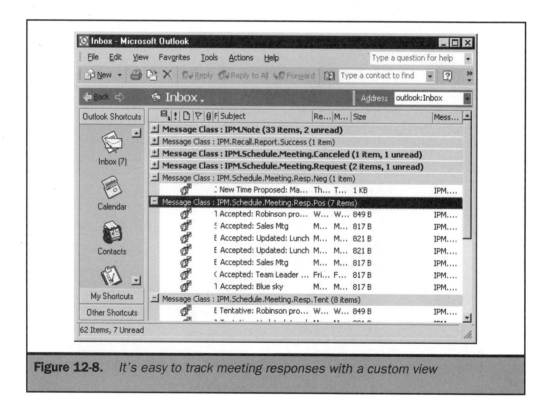

Figure 12-8. *It's easy to track meeting responses with a custom view*

Replying to Meeting Requests You Receive

When you're on the receiving end of a meeting request, your options for handling the request are somewhat limited. You can open the request and respond to it, or you can ignore it. The latter method, which tends to make your boss and co-workers unnecessarily cranky, is not recommended unless you're seriously thinking about a career change. Therefore, the first method is probably your best bet.

> *There is a third alternative for dealing with meeting requests, but it's not recommended. You can use the Resource Scheduling Options, found in the Calendar Options dialog box (and discussed in the section entitled "Setting Up a Resource Account" earlier in this chapter) to automate the process. These options apply to any mailbox, regardless of whether the mailbox owner is a person, place, or thing. However, no reminders are set, and you receive no notification when requests are accepted or declined automatically. As a result, you'll have no control over your schedule and may be totally ignorant of meetings you've agreed to attend.*

To reply directly to a meeting response, open it and click the appropriate response button. As you can see in Figure 12-9, the meeting request form contains four active (three, if the sender has turned off the Allow New Time Proposals option) response buttons and a Calendar button.

The response buttons are straightforward. You can answer yes (Accept), no (Decline), maybe (Tentative), or suggest a new time that better suits you.

If you want to check your schedule before replying, click the Calendar button to display your Calendar for the proposed meeting date. When you click Accept, Tentative, or Decline, a Microsoft Outlook dialog box appears asking if you want to send the response immediately, edit the response first, or simply not send a response at all. Make your selection and click OK.

> *After you send a response, the meeting request may disappear from your Inbox. If this occurs, it's because the Delete Meeting Request From Inbox When Responding option in the Advanced E-mail Options is turned on (the default). To turn it off, choose Tools | Options, click the E-mail Options button on the Preferences tab, and then click the Advanced E-mail Options button. Remove the check mark from the Delete Meeting Request From Inbox When Responding option.*

If you decline, the meeting is eliminated from your Calendar and moved to the Deleted Items folder. If you reply with Accept or Tentative, the response is recorded in the meeting form, which you can view by opening your Calendar to the scheduled date and double-clicking the scheduled meeting.

MANAGING TIME
AND DETAILS

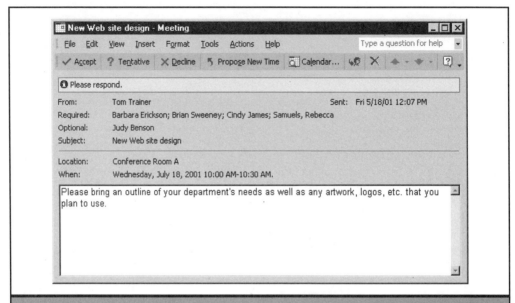

Figure 12-9.   *Use the meeting response buttons to notify the meeting originator of your intentions*

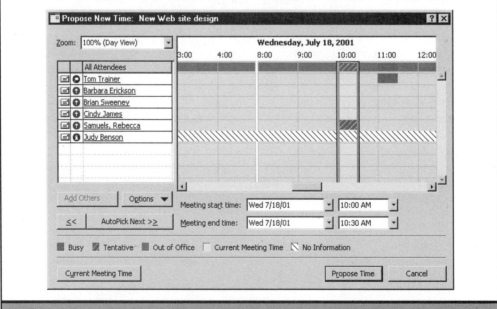

Figure 12-10.   *The Propose New Time dialog box lets you view everyone's free/busy time to make selecting an available time slot easy*

New to Outlook 2002 is the Propose New Time command. Clicking the Propose New Time button opens the Propose New Time dialog box, which, as you can see in Figure 12-10, is almost identical to the Meeting Planner.

Use the Meeting Start Time and Meeting End Time fields to select a new time for the meeting. Once you've found a desirable time slot, click the Propose Time button to create a response message to the meeting originator similar to the one shown in Figure 12-11.

Enter a brief message and click Send. The meeting remains on your calendar, marked as tentative for the original (not the new proposed) time.

MOUS EXAM PRACTICE

In this section, you learned to respond to meeting requests using the response buttons available in the meeting request form. Since the meeting organizer cannot respond to meeting requests you'll have to ask a colleague to send you some fictitious meeting requests. Respond using all four buttons, and monitor the effect it has on your calendar.

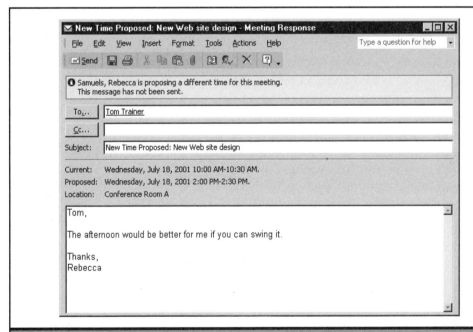

Figure 12-11.   *The Propose New Time response sends an e-mail message to the meeting originator, informing him or her of your desire to change the meeting time*

MANAGING TIME
AND DETAILS

MOUS Exam Core Objectives Explored in Chapter 12

Objective	Activity	Heading
OL10-2-1	Add meetings to the Outlook calendar	"Using the Meeting Planner"
OL10-2-1	Scheduling resources for meetings	"Scheduling Meeting Resources"
OL10-2-3	Respond to meeting requests	"Replying to Meeting Request"

MOUS Exam Expert Objectives Explored in Chapter 12

Objective	Activity	Heading
OL10E-3-3	Cancel meetings	"Changing a Scheduled Meeting"
OL10E-3-4	Update meetings	"Changing a Scheduled Meeting"

The Complete Reference

2002 Outlook

Chapter 13

Managing Tasks

In case you're thinking the reason the last three chapters focused on the Calendar and scheduling was to make sure you don't miss your appointments and meetings, you're only partially right. The most important reason for getting your schedule organized is to make sure you can find the time to do all the tasks on your seemingly endless to-do list. Fortunately, Outlook makes keeping track of your tasks easy and even helps you find more time, by enabling you to assign some of your tasks to others. In this chapter, you'll discover how to create, organize, track, and delegate tasks. By the time you're through, you may even find time to add a round of golf to your list of to-do items.

Creating Tasks

Keeping track of your tasks starts with adding them to the task list. Not surprisingly, the way to get something on the task list is to create a task. Creating tasks, like creating most other Outlook items, involves opening the appropriate form (the task form in this case) and entering all pertinent information about the item (task).

Begin by pressing CTRL+SHIFT+K to open a new task form (see Figure 13-1).

The first field to fill out is the Subject field. Since this becomes the name of the task, enter something brief and descriptive. There's nothing worse than trying to find a particular task that's buried in a sea of cryptic names. The Due Date and Start Date

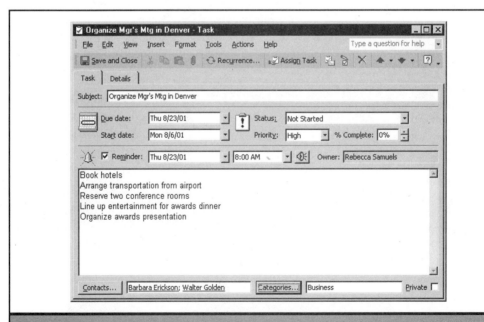

Figure 13-1.   *You can use the task form to enter a lot of information about the task at hand*

fields are next. They're self-explanatory and easy to fill in using either plain English commands (next Tuesday, a week from Friday, 27 days from Independence Day, and so on) or the pop-up calendar that appears when you click the drop-down arrow in each field.

> **Note** *You can enter a due date without entering a start date. However, you cannot enter a start date without a due date. If you enter a start date without a due date, Outlook automatically enters the same date in the Due Date field.*

Depending on the due date you enter, a yellow information bar may or may not appear above the Subject field. If the task is due in 14 days or fewer (or if it's *overdue* by 14 days or fewer) from today's date, the yellow bar appears and indicates the number of days in which the task is due (or overdue). If the due date is 15 days or more from today's date (in either direction), no information bar appears.

The Status field provides a drop-down list from which you can select several different status indicators. Select the one that suits your level of progress at this stage. To make life a little easier for you, this field automatically adjusts the % Complete field (and vice versa) depending on your selection. If you select Not Started, the % Complete field is set to 0%; if you select Completed, the % Complete field changes to 100%.

Use the Priority drop-down list to indicate just how important this task is. If the task is going to be completed in stages, you can indicate how much progress you've made by entering a percentage in the % Complete field, indicating how much of the job is done. As noted earlier, the % Complete field is associated with the Status field. Entering 0 here causes the Status field to be set as Not Started. When you enter 100 in the % Complete field, the Status field changes to Completed.

The next step is to adjust the reminder to ensure you're notified when the due date arrives. The reminder is automatically set for the default Reminder time of the Due Date day. To change the reminder date, enter a new date or select one from the pop-up calendar. Do the same for the time. If you want to change the sound associated with the reminder, or disable it, click the sound button and make the desired change.

> **Note** *You'll find the Reminder time option on the Preferences tab of the Options dialog box. Choose Tools | Options from the Outlook Menu bar (not the task form Menu bar) to display the Options dialog box.*

As you can see in Figure 13-1, the name of the task's owner also appears. However, since it reflects the original creator, or the person to whom the task has been assigned, it cannot be edited. This is true even in a table view, where it appears you can edit it. If you create a custom view and add the Owner field, it appears at first glance that Outlook will allow you to edit the data. However, as soon as you try to save your change, a dialog box appears, informing you that you must be in a public folder to change this field and that as a result, your change will not be saved.

MANAGING TIME AND DETAILS

The next field available for your use is the Notes field. It's handy for jotting notes about the task, associated things that need doing, phone numbers and addresses needed to complete the task, and anything else you can think of.

The remaining fields, Contacts, Categories, and Private, are located along the bottom of the form. Use the Contacts field to link the task to individuals in your Contacts folder. Either enter the contact's name, or click the Contacts button and choose the contact(s) from the Select Contacts dialog box that appears. Assigning tasks to categories is a great way to organize them. Click the Categories button and check one or more categories to which you want the task assigned. Finally, check the Private option to prevent others who have access to your Tasks folder from seeing the task. This is excellent if you share folders with a coworker whose birthday is coming up, for example. It would be a shame if he or she spotted a task to pick up a birthday present or organize a surprise lunch.

After you enter all the pertinent data about the task, click Save And Close to save the task and return to the active Outlook window.

Adding Attachments to Tasks

If you have other Outlook items that are related to the task, such as e-mail messages, appointments, or notes, you can insert them in the task form as attachments. You can also add files, documents, and objects to a task. The method used in the task form is the same as that used in e-mail messages and other Outlook items.

Open the task in which you want to include an attachment. Choose Insert from the Menu bar and select the attachment type from the Insert menu that appears. Your choices include File, Item, and Object.

Objects can only be added directly to the Notes field. Therefore, unless the cursor is in the Notes field, the Object command is unavailable on the Insert menu. Click anywhere in the Notes field to position the cursor. Since the object will be inserted wherever the cursor appears, it's a good idea to place the cursor where you want the object to rest.

After you select one of the Insert commands, the associated dialog box appears. Make the appropriate selections and entries necessary to add the desired attachment. You can also drag other Outlook items and drop them in the task Notes field to insert them as attachments.

Filling in Task Details

The Details tab, shown in Figure 13-2, provides another set of fields you can use for entering additional information about the task.

The information you can track using the Details tab includes the following:

- **Date completed** Once the task is completed, enter the completion date here. As with other Outlook date fields, you can enter the date in date format, with

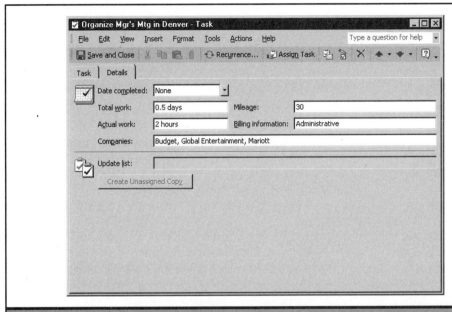

Figure 13-2.   *The Details tab offers some simple project management tracking fields*

English words and phrases, or by displaying and using the pop-up calendar. Entering a date in this field automatically updates two fields on the Task tab: Status and % Complete. The Status field is changed to Completed and the % Complete field to 100%. Conversely, marking those fields as Completed and 100% automatically enters the current date in the Date Completed field.

■ **Total work**   Use this field to enter the estimated number of minutes, days, weeks, months, or years you expect this task to take. You can enter time using abbreviations such as *2m* for 2 minutes, *2h* for 2 hours, or *2w* for 2 weeks. However, you must use only numerals to indicate numbers, and you are limited to a single time unit. One other thing to be aware of: Outlook recalculates time based on the length of your working day. For example, with the default workday set to 8 hours, Outlook changes 12h to 1.5 days. Using that same algorithm, 3000m becomes 6.25 days, and 80h becomes 2 weeks.

■ **Actual work**   This is where you enter the time it really took you to complete the task, not the fanciful number you entered in the previous field. It too calculates using the same algorithm.

■ **Companies**   Enter the names of any organizations associated with the task. If there are none, feel free to improvise and use it to hold other data you may want to record. You can enter up to 255 characters.

- **Mileage** If you do any traveling to accomplish the task, enter the mileage you rack up here.
- **Billing information** If the task is a billable activity and you're using the Details tab to track billing information, use this field to enter rates, policies, and other billing-related information.

When you glanced at Figure 13-2, you probably noticed there are a couple more items on the Details tab. They are the Update List field and the Create Unassigned Copy button. These features are only available for a task that has been assigned to another user. Until then, they remain grayed out. For an explanation of what they do, see the next section, "Assigning Tasks."

MOUS EXAM PRACTICE
This section focused on creating tasks in your task folder. To hone your task management skills, practice creating tasks by opening and completing task forms. Next, try your hand at assigning some of your fictitious tasks to coworkers. Of course, check with them before doing so, and let them know you're just practicing. Ask them to respond in a variety of ways. Add attachments to some tasks and fill in the Details tabs on others.

Assigning Tasks

If you're in a position to delegate tasks to others, or have the good fortune to work with colleagues willing to share the workload, you may find it necessary or desirable to assign some of your tasks to others on occasion. When the time comes, you can create a task request to assign a brand-new task, or you can transform an existing task into a task request. The resulting task request form, seen in Figure 13-3, is identical regardless of which method you use.

Creating a New Task Request

To create a task request, press CTRL+SHIFT+U from any folder, or choose Actions | New Task Request from within the Tasks folder. You can also click the New button from within the Tasks folder. Or, from any folder, click the New down arrow and choose New Request from the menu. When the form opens (see Figure 13-3), use the To field to enter the name of the individual to whom you want to assign the task.

You can also create a preaddressed task request form by dragging a contact from the Contacts folder and dropping it on the Tasks icon on the Outlook Bar.

You can type the name, or click the To button and select the name from the Select Task Recipient dialog box that appears.

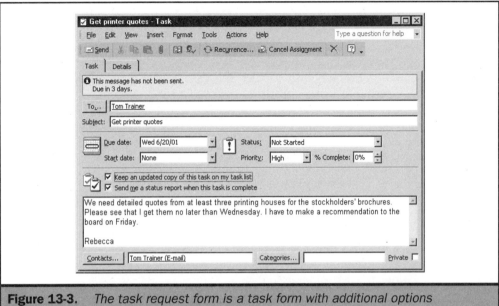

Figure 13-3. *The task request form is a task form with additional options*

Note
You can assign a single task to multiple users or even to distribution lists. However, the original owner will not receive updates even if the update option is checked on the task request form. Nor will the original owner receive any status reports—unless the task is reassigned by one of the original assignees and accepted by the new assignee. At that point, the original owner receives status reports, and each assignee who reassigned the task receives updates and status reports.

The next step is to fill in the task request form using the steps outlined in the earlier section on creating tasks. Although the task request form is almost identical to the task form, there are a couple of new options.

- **Keep an updated copy of this task on my task list** This option retains a copy of the assigned task on your task list. In addition, any changes made to the task by its new owner generate an e-mail, including update information, that is sent to you automatically. However, if you assign the task to multiple recipients, including a distribution list, the task will still be included on your task list, but it will not be updated.

- **Send me a status report when this task is complete** When the new owner(s) mark the task as complete, a special status report e-mail message is automatically generated and sent to you. Unlike the previous option, this option works even with multiple assignees.

Assigning a task with a reminder causes the reminder to be removed so the new owner can set his or her own reminder. In the event the task is declined and you elect to handle the task yourself, you'll have to set a new reminder.

When all the information is complete, click Send to transmit the request. Now, before you sit back, put your feet on the desk, and start to relax, keep one thing in mind: the recipient(s) may decline your gracious offer, in which case the task drops back into your lap.

Assigning an Existing Task

If you have an existing task you would like to assign to a coworker, there's no need to reinvent the wheel by creating a new task request form. All you have to do is convert the existing task to a task request form. It's as easy as opening the task and clicking the Assign Task button on the form's Standard toolbar. The task immediately turns into a task request form, sporting a To field and the two options for keeping a copy of the task on your list and sending a status report. See the earlier section "Creating a New Task Request" for details on using the To field and the new options.

Reassigning Tasks

Not only can you assign tasks, you can also reassign them. Assuming that you're not at the bottom of the food chain in your organization, you can take a task assigned to you and reassign it to someone else. There are two ways to accomplish this: accept the task and reassign it, or simply pass the task along by reassigning it upon receipt.

To use the accept and reassign method, open the task request and click Accept to add the task to your task list.

 You can accept (or decline) a task request without opening it by right-clicking the request in the Inbox and selecting Accept (or Decline) from the shortcut menu.

Next, open the task and convert it to a new task request by clicking the Assign Task button. When you accept the task, a Task Accepted message is sent to the previous owner. As soon as you assign the task, a Task Update message is sent to all previous owners. Depending on where you are in the chain of assignments, the ownership of the task may appear differently.

 You can assign a task that appears on your task list (not to be confused with a task request in your Inbox) without opening it, by right-clicking the task and selecting Assign Task from the shortcut menu.

To reassign a task without accepting it, simply open the task request and click the Assign Task button to create a new task request. Enter the new assignee's name and click Send. When the new task request is sent, Task Update messages are also sent to all previous assignors or owners.

Creating Unassigned Copies of an Assigned Task

When tasks are assigned and reassigned, there's one additional feature available to everyone *except* the current task owner. It's the ability to create an unassigned copy of the task. You can use the Create Unassigned Copy button found on the Details tab of the task form in your task list (see Figure 13-4).

Clicking the Create Unassigned Copy button converts the existing copy (if you're not the current owner, you only have a copy of the task) of the task into a full-fledged task of which you're the proud new owner. This feature comes in handy if the user to whom you assigned the task is unable to make any progress and you want to reassign it to someone else. You cannot assign the copy of the task retained in your task list since it is an assigned copy. Converting it to an unassigned copy gives you all the rights of an original owner.

Note   *The warning that appears when you click the Create Unassigned Copy button is somewhat misleading. It informs you that converting your copy of the task to an unassigned copy will result in your no longer receiving updates. That's not entirely true. You will receive update notices. What is true, however, is that since the assigned task copy no longer exists, the updates cannot be processed. Therefore, you will continue to remain in the loop, but no longer have a task on your task list reflecting changes made by the current owner. In addition to update notices, you will also continue to receive all status reports sent by the current owner.*

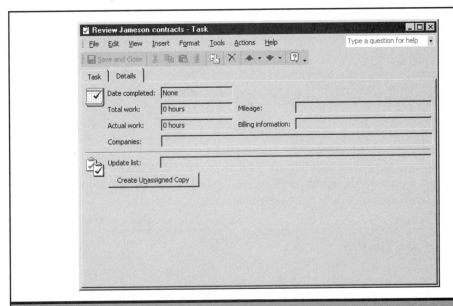

Figure 13-4.   *Converting a copy of an assigned task is easy when you use the Create Unassigned Copy feature*

No one else in the chain of assignment is affected by the creation of an unassigned task. All other previous owners/assignors retain their copies of the original task and continue to receive updates, which can be processed.

MOUS

MOUS EXAM PRACTICE
This section covered all aspects of assigning tasks. Since all task assignments use a task request form, practice by creating a task request form from scratch. Next, try assigning an existing task by using the Assign Task button to convert the task to a task request form. Ask some of your coworkers to assist in reassigning tasks. Have someone send you a couple of tasks, and reassign them using the methods described in this section. Finally, create an unassigned copy of an assigned task you retained on your task list.

Modifying and Updating Tasks

You can edit any task you own. You cannot modify tasks you've assigned to others, even if you retained a copy on your task list by checking the Keep An Updated Copy Of This Task On My Task List option on the task request form. Only the new owner of that task can edit it.

To make changes to a task, switch to the Tasks folder and double-click the task to open it. You can also right-click the task and select Open from the shortcut menu.

Make the necessary changes and click Save And Close to save your changes. If you're the original owner of the task, nothing further occurs. If, however, you inherited the task from someone else, all users appearing in the Update List on the Details tab of the task form will receive a Task Update message indicating the changes you've made.

Note

Task Update messages are also sent to members of the task's Update List each time the task is assigned or reassigned. Unfortunately, these update notices, unlike those generated by editing a task, do not indicate the specific action (assigning the task) taken.

When a task is marked done by changing its Status to Completed or its % Complete to 100%, the task is literally crossed off your task list. It still appears on the list, but has a horizontal line drawn through it. If it happens to be an assigned task, all previous owners who elected to receive updates are automatically sent a Task Update message and a Task Completed status report. As soon as the Task Update message is processed, the task is also crossed off each of their task lists.

Deleting Tasks

Deleting a task is quite easy. Open the Tasks folder, highlight the offending task, and use one of the following methods to eliminate it:

■ Click the Delete button on the Standard toolbar.
■ Press CTRL+D.

- Press DEL.
- Choose Edit | Delete from the Menu bar.
- Right-click the task and select Delete from the shortcut menu.

When you delete a task you own, it disappears from your task list, never to be seen or heard from again unless you resurrect it from the Deleted Items folder.

If you delete a task you assigned to someone else (and chose to retain an updated copy), you remove it from your Tasks folder. However, you will continue to receive updates and status reports (assuming you requested both when you assigned the task). The information bar of Task Update messages informs you that the task was not found on your task list. Obviously a nonexistent task can't be updated, but you will at least continue to be kept apprised of its progress.

Creating Tasks from Other Outlook Folders

The beauty of Outlook is the tight integration of its various components. This is especially true of the Tasks folder. In addition to the usual ability to create folder items from other types of Outlook items, the Tasks folder also provides almost seamless integration with the TaskPad found in the Calendar folder.

Using the Calendar TaskPad

As you can see in Figure 13-5, the TaskPad, which is located in the Calendar folder, is a mini-version of the task list. In addition, it remains in constant communication with its parent, the Tasks folder. This means that changes made in one are immediately reflected in the other.

For detailed instructions on using the TaskPad, see Chapter 10.

Using Drag-and-Drop to Create Tasks

By now you should be an old hand at using drag-and-drop to create one type of Outlook item from another. If you're not, this may be the time to learn and to take advantage of the technique, which is quick and easy. Using drag-and-drop enables you to create a task from an appointment, a note, an e-mail message, or any other Outlook item, with just a couple of mouse clicks. Outlook uses the original item to complete fields in the new task. The resulting task will, of course, vary depending on the type of original item and its contents.

Begin by opening the folder containing the original item you want to use as the basis for the new task. Next, locate the item, drag it to the Outlook Bar, and drop it on the Tasks shortcut. You can also drag it to the Folder List and drop it on the Tasks folder. Either way, a new task form opens with the appropriate information from the original item already entered in the new task form. Make any necessary changes and click Save And Close to add the new task to your task list.

MANAGING TIME AND DETAILS

Figure 13-5. *You can add tasks to your Tasks folder without leaving the Calendar folder*

You can also use right-dragging to create a task from another Outlook item. This time when you drop the item on the Outlook Bar icon, a shortcut menu appears, offering you several choices. They include

■ **Copy Here as Task with Text**   This command creates a new task and uses the original information to fill in the Subject field and Date field (if the original item has a date field). It also includes all basic information from the original item in the task's Notes field.

■ **Copy Here as Task with Shortcut**   This command is the same as the previous command, except the basic information from the original item is not entered in the task's Notes field. Instead, a shortcut to the original item appears in the Notes field.

■ **Copy Here as Task with Attachment**   The only difference between this command and the Copy Here As Task With Shortcut command is that the shortcut in the task's Notes field is replaced with the original item as an attachment.

■ **Move Here as Task with Attachment**   If you want to eliminate the original item from its folder, you can use this command, which is identical to the Copy Here As Task With Attachment, except that the original item is deleted from its folder.

If you right-drag a contact to the Outlook Bar Tasks icon or the Tasks folder in the Folder List, you'll find an additional command, Address New Task, on the shortcut menu that appears. Its action is a little different from the rest of the commands. Rather than creating a new task, this command creates a new task request form, addressed to the contact.

MOUS EXAM PRACTICE
This section showed you how to create tasks by using the TaskPad in the Calendar folder and by employing the drag-and-drop method. Open the Calendar view and create simple to-do list items first; then create detailed tasks using the TaskPad. Next, try creating tasks by dragging different Outlook items and dropping them on either the Tasks icon in the Outlook Bar or the Tasks folder in the Folder List. Try right-dragging to accomplish the same thing.

Creating Recurring Tasks

Recurring tasks are those delightful jobs that just won't go away. Until you can find some way to eliminate or delegate them, you might as well make life easy and create a single recurring task, rather than an individual task for each occurrence.

The first thing to do is open a task form and create the task as you would any other task (see the "Creating Tasks" section earlier in this chapter). After you enter all the pertinent information about the task, click the Recurrence button on the Standard toolbar of the task form. This opens the Task Recurrence dialog box, shown in Figure 13-6.

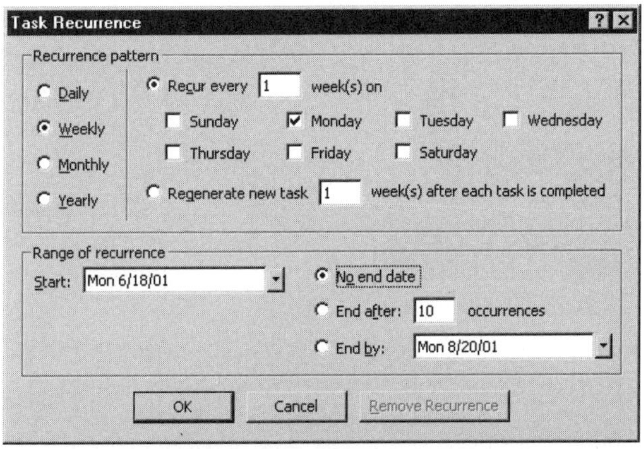

Figure 13-6. *Your recurrence options are almost limitless*

MANAGING TIME AND DETAILS

By default, the recurrence pattern selected is Weekly. As you can see in Figure 13-6, the Weekly pattern enables you to set several options that affect the frequency and duration of the recurrence. The Task Recurrence dialog box offers several options that enable you to customize recurring tasks. The first three sets of options included in the following list are all incorporated into the Task Recurrence dialog box under the heading Recurrence Pattern:

- **Recurrence type**   Your choices for the recurrence type are Daily, Weekly, Monthly, and Yearly, all of which are self-explanatory.

- **Recurrence interval**   This option, which varies according to the recurrence type you select, lets you set the frequency and specific date or day on which the task recurs.

- **Regenerate new task**   The Regenerate New Task option appears on all Task Recurrence dialog boxes, regardless of which recurrence type you choose. Since tasks, unlike appointments and meetings, do not disappear if you ignore them, you may want to utilize this option to make sure new instances are scheduled only when the last instance has been completed. As soon as you mark the task completed, it's crossed off your task list and a new identical task is added, with the due date set according to the other recurrence options you set.

- **Range of recurrence**   Regardless of which recurrence type you choose, the Range Of Recurrence options are the same. The only thing that alters them is selecting the Regenerate New Task option. It disables the End By option and grays it out. The Range Of Recurrence options let you designate when the recurring task starts and when it stops. These options are self-explanatory as well.

If you want more information on these options, see Chapter 11, which describes in greater detail recurring appointment options, many of which are identical to recurring task options.

Editing Recurring Tasks

You can edit a recurring task just as you would edit a non-recurring task. If you change anything but the start and end dates, clicking Save And Close saves the changes and applies them to all future occurrences. However, changing the start date or end date causes Outlook to warn you that you're about to change the date for the current instance of the recurring task. If you click OK, a new non-recurring task is added to your task list and the next regularly recurring task is also added. For example, if you have a weekly task that starts every Tuesday and you change the start date to Wednesday, Outlook creates (with your OK) a one-time task for this Wednesday and a recurring task starting next Tuesday.

Although the Help file fails to mention it, changing the due date in either a daily or a yearly recurring task does not trigger the creation of a separate task. However, changing the start date in either does prompt Outlook to warn you that you're about to change the date of the current occurrence.

If the task becomes obsolete before it expires as a result of the Range Of Recurrence options you set in the Task Recurrence dialog box, you can remove it with a minimum amount of fuss. Select the task and press DEL, or right-click the task and choose Delete from the shortcut menu. A dialog box appears, asking if you want to delete the upcoming occurrence of the task or the entire series. If you just want to remove the current instance of the task, select Delete This One. If you want to remove the recurring task permanently, select Delete All.

Assigning Recurring Tasks

You can assign recurring tasks the same way you assign non-recurring tasks. However, since there is no command to create a recurring task request form, you must first create a recurring task, or receive a task request for a recurring task, and then assign it. Clicking the Assign Task button turns a recurring task into a (recurring) task request form. The assignment process is the same for recurring tasks and non-recurring tasks alike. There's only one difference. In the (recurring) task request form, the Keep An Updated Copy Of This Task On My Task List option is grayed out and completely unavailable. There are no exceptions with a recurring task. No one gets a task update no matter what actions are taken. However, the status report option remains functional, and when checked, previous owners receive all status reports sent by the current owner.

Working with Recurring Tasks

Since recurring tasks are series of tasks rather than individual tasks, there are some differences you should be aware of when working with them. The first thing to remember is that certain actions taken on a recurring task can be applied to either the current task in the series or to the entire series. For example, editing start dates and end dates can affect only the current instance or the entire series, depending on how you effect the change. To change only the current instance, open the task, make the change, and click Save And Close. A new, non-recurring task is created.

To change the start date or due date for the entire series, open the task and click the Recurrence button to open the Task Recurrence dialog box. Change the entry in the Start field to the new date on which you want the first occurrence to begin. The start date depends on the recurrence pattern. Therefore, if you enter a start date that is incompatible with the selected recurrence pattern, Outlook changes the date to agree with the recurrence pattern. For example, if your recurrence pattern is set for weekly and every Thursday, entering Monday's date as the start date will not work, since the task must start on a Thursday. Therefore, Outlook changes the start date to the date of the upcoming Thursday.

To change the due date, you must change the recurrence pattern. Using the example of a weekly recurrence due every Thursday, changing the day to Friday changes the due date from Thursday's date to Friday's date.

Outlook also offers a feature called Skip Occurrence, which applies only to recurring tasks. As you might guess, the Skip Occurrence command (Action | Skip Occurrence) allows you to eliminate the current instance of the recurring task, while leaving the series intact and unchanged. Unlike marking a recurring task Complete, which leaves a crossed-out copy of the task on your task list, using the Skip Occurrence command zaps the current instance, removing it from your task list permanently.

Since the function of the Skip Occurrence command is to eliminate the current instance of the task and make the next occurrence in line the current task, it cannot work if the Regenerate New Task option is selected in the Task Recurrence dialog box. The Regenerate New Task option determines the date of the next occurrence based on the date on which you mark the current instance Complete. Therefore, Skip Occurrence has no means by which to determine what the next occurrence may be and to "skip" to it. As a result, the Skip Occurrence option is grayed out and unavailable for a recurring task on which the Regenerate New Task option is enabled.

Responding to Task Assignments

Unless you're the CEO of the company, you're bound to receive a task request now and again. When you do, you'll want to be prepared to respond. Knowing the consequences of your actions will help you make an informed decision. To begin with, you have five choices for dealing with a task request:

- **Accept the task**   Accepting a task request changes your role from temporary owner to owner.

- **Decline the task**   When you decline a task, your temporary ownership ends and the task reverts to the individual who sent you the task request.

- **Reassign the task**   You can pass the buck by assigning the task to someone else, thereby transferring temporary ownership.

- **Delete the task request**   While this may sound irresponsible, there are some good reasons (discussed shortly) for deleting a task request.

- **Ignore the task request**   This action (inaction?), on the other hand, is not recommended. Not only is it impolite, but it also tends to make the sender cranky.

When you receive a task request and open it, you'll find that the Standard toolbar contains buttons to accommodate four of the five actions you can take to respond to the task request.

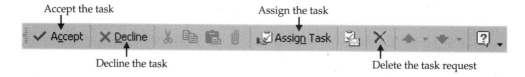

Accepting a Task

If you decide to assume ownership of the task, all you have to do is click the Accept button. This adds the task to your task list and sends a Task Accepted e-mail message to the individual who assigned the task to you. However, before the message is sent, Outlook gives you the opportunity to edit the response to the previous owner.

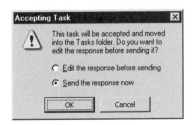

If you elect to edit the response, you can change any field in the task form except the To field. This comes in handy if you are willing to take the task, but must change the start or due date. You may also need to edit the response if you've already started the task and want to let the previous owner know how much has been done thus far. You can add a message in the Notes field explaining the reasons for the change(s). If you choose not to edit the Task Accepted response, the message is sent immediately.

If, after clicking Accept and choosing to edit the response, you change your mind about accepting the task, you can still back out. At first glance it appears that you're stuck since there's no Cancel button. However, clicking the close button (the X in the top right corner of the form) or pressing ALT+F4 *gives you the opportunity to close the form without saving the changes. This drops the task request right back in your In box without retaining the changes or sending any responses.*

If the sender was not the original owner, a Task Update message will also be dispatched to all previous owners who elected to keep an updated copy of the task in their Tasks folder.

Task Update messages will not be generated if you were one of multiple assignees to whom the task was sent or if the task is a recurring task. See earlier sections in this chapter on assigning tasks and recurring tasks for more information.

Declining a Task

When you are unable or unwilling to accept a task request, you can click the Decline button. Like accepting a task, declining a task prompts Outlook to ask if you want to edit the response before sending it. However, in this case the only fields you can change are the Notes, Contacts, Categories, and Private fields. You'll probably want to use the Notes field to let the sender know why you can't accept the task or perhaps the conditions under which you could accept the task. For example, if you're going to be out of town when the task is due, you might suggest you'd be willing to take it on if the task could be postponed.

If you're declining the task, there's really no reason to change the Contacts and Categories fields. However, the Private field is another matter. By marking the Task Declined response Private, you prevent other users listed as alternate recipients on the previous owner's mailbox from receiving copies of your Task Declined response. Alternate recipients, who are generally assistants or coworkers sharing responsibilities for projects, can be assigned to a mailbox on the Exchange Server by the administrator. By the way, you'll know if any alternates exist if you receive an "Undeliverable" message from the system administrator. Don't worry about the fact that the "Undeliverable" message states that the response could not be delivered to the sender. The reason the sender is listed instead of the alternates, who are the real undeliverables, is that the mailbox is in the sender's name and Exchange is protecting the identity of the alternates.

Declining a task removes it from your task list (as soon as you receive a task request, Outlook automatically adds it to your task list), and permanent ownership reverts to the sender, even if the sender was merely a temporary owner passing the task request along. In addition, any previous owners receive a Task Update message. However, this is the last update notice they'll receive. When a task is declined, the Update List on the Details tab of the task form is reset, cutting all previous owners out of the loop concerning any future actions taken on the task.

Reassigning a Task

If you don't want to accept or decline the task, you can always pass it along to some other unsuspecting soul. To do this, open the task request and click the Assign Task button. The task request e-mail message immediately becomes a task request form. Enter the address of the new assignee in the To field and click Send. This immediately sends a task request to the addressee, and a Task Update message to all previous owners. The Task Update messages do not indicate that the task has been reassigned, merely that you've taken some action on the task request.

Note *As good as Outlook is, it cannot track tasks sent to multiple users or distribution lists. Therefore, if you assign the task to multiple users or a distribution list, you receive a warning that the task will no longer be updated on previous owners' task lists.*

Reassigning a task, of course, has risks. Since the original assignor expects you to handle the task, you'll have to rely on your assignee to complete the job properly. If he or she fails to deliver, you're the one who will have to answer for that failure. Another thing to keep in mind is that if your assignee declines the task, you (regardless of whether you are the original owner or an assignee) become the permanent owner of the task.

Deleting a Task Request

At first blush, the thought of deleting a task request seems rude at best, and suicidal (careerwise) at worst. However, you may be perfectly justified if you already know the task is obsolete and the request just made its way to you. Or you may have gotten it by mistake. If you're the CEO and you receive a task request from the new kid in the mailroom, it's probably safe to delete it without worrying too much.

Deleting a task request is easy. Click the Delete button on the Standard toolbar of the task request. A dialog box with several options appears.

The dialog box, which is aptly named Delete Incomplete Task, contains three options:

- **Decline and delete**   Use this option to remove the task from your task list and decline the request in one fell swoop.
- **Mark complete and delete**   If you've already done the task, you can remove it from your task list and notify the sender that it's done by using this option. Depending on the options selected in the original task request, this may generate both a Task Update message and a status report (completed).
- **Delete**   This is the last-resort option that simply deletes the task from your task list without notifying the sender or anyone else in the loop.

As soon as you click OK, the task is deleted from your calendar, and any updates or reports generated by your selection are sent.

Ignoring a Task Request

While this is not really an option, there's nothing to prevent you from not acting on the task request. This can even happen unintentionally if you decide to close it and give it some thought before deciding what to do. Whatever the reason, the results are the same. The task is added to your task list and remains there until you take action on it. The sender receives no notification, and you are presumed to be the owner. In the event the task due date passes, the task is marked overdue on your task list. Once again, neither you nor any previous owners receive any notification.

While you're deciding what to do about the task, you might want to send all previous owners a status report letting them know that you're not ignoring them, merely giving the matter consideration. Open the task request, which should still be in your Inbox, or the actual task on your tasks list, and choose Actions | Send Status Report. This creates an e-mail message, addressed to everyone on the Update List, containing the basic information from the task request. Add a message explaining the reason for the delay and click Send.

MOUS EXAM PRACTICE

To make sure you understand the implication and results of each of the ways you can deal with a task request, ask your coworkers to send you a bunch of task requests (fictitious, of course), to which you can respond. Use a different response for each. Edit some responses and just send others. Ask your coworkers to report back on the results of your responses.

Exchanging Task Information with Others

For those times when you merely want to share task information, rather than assign tasks, you have two choices—you can simply send the data, or you can give the other user(s) access to your Tasks folder.

Sharing Tasks Folders

The Tasks folder, like all other Outlook folders, can be shared with other Outlook users. Of course, the one required ingredient to the sharing formula is appropriate permissions. Whether you want to view other users' task information or you want others to view yours, the necessary folder permissions must first be granted. Once the permissions are in place, viewing other users' task information is a simple matter of using the Other User's Folder command.

Choose File | Open | Other User's Folder to display the Open Other User's Folder dialog box.

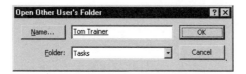

Click the Name button to open the Select Name dialog box, from which you can choose the user whose task information you wish to view. If you accessed the Other User's Folder command from within the Tasks folder, Tasks will appear in the Folder field. If you've accessed the command from another folder, select Tasks from the Folder drop-down list. Click OK to open the other user's Tasks folder in a new window.

If you have the proper permissions, the Tasks folder opens; otherwise Outlook informs you that the folder is unavailable. Depending on the permissions you've been assigned, you may be able only to view the folder or to make some additions, changes, and deletions.

Another way to share your Tasks folder with another user is to assign the user delegate access. For additional information on delegate access and user permissions, see Chapter 16.

Sending Task Data

The best method for sending task information depends on the type of e-mail account your recipient has. Unfortunately, Outlook items do not travel well as attachments to Internet e-mail messages. Therefore, when sending to a recipient with an Internet e-mail account, there's only one way to ensure your task information gets through intact—send it in the body of an e-mail message as text. For a recipient on your Exchange Server you can either send a task item as an attachment (as long as the recipient uses Outlook), or send it as text in the message.

To incorporate the task information in an e-mail message, simply drag the task to the Outlook Bar and drop it on the Inbox icon. A new e-mail message appears with all the task information included in the message body, and the task name in Subject field.

Attaching a task to an e-mail message is almost as easy. Right-click the task you want to send, and select Forward from the shortcut menu. This opens a new e-mail message form with the task name in the Subject line, and the task item inserted in the message as an attachment. Complete the necessary information and click Send to transmit the task.

Viewing and Tracking Tasks

If you have a lot on your plate and you depend on Outlook to manage your tasks, you'll find there are a number of ways to keep track of what you've accomplished, what's still ahead, and how tasks you've delegated are progressing. You can achieve this by using the viewing and tracking features available in Outlook. The Tasks folder, like other Outlook folders, provides a variety of views for organizing and manipulating task information. In addition, updating and tracking delegated (assigned) tasks is simple with the automatic updating and notification system built into the Tasks folder.

Using Tasks Views

The Tasks folder offers ten standard views that let you arrange and rearrange your task information so you can find what you need when you need it. The Tasks folder views consist of nine table views and one timeline view. They include everything from a simple task list to a couple of views used specifically for tracking assigned tasks. Of course, as with other folder views, you can customize the existing views and create your own as the need arises.

MANAGING TIME
AND DETAILS

By default, the Tasks folder opens with the Simple List view. True to its name, the Simple List view contains only four fields (columns): Icon, Complete, Subject, and Due Date (see Figure 13-7).

To switch views, choose View | Current View to display a menu of available views. Select a view from the list, or choose Customize Current View to make changes to the view presently on display. Since the views in the Tasks folder are consistent with other folder views, there's no need to go into detail on the basics. For basic information on using Outlook views, see Chapter 23. The remainder of this chapter focuses on special features and troubleshooting for the Tasks folder views.

The best place to start is with a couple of useful features found only in the Tasks folder that work hand in hand with each other. The first is the ability to manually rearrange the task items in table views by dragging them up and down the list. The second feature, called Save Task Order, enables you to save a manually arranged sort order as the default sort order for all views in the Tasks folder. There is one catch, however. Both features require that you first remove any Group By and Filter options that may be currently applied to the view. The manual sort feature requires that all Sort options be removed as well.

Sorting Tasks Folder Views Manually

As the previous section indicates, the first thing you must do to sort any task view (of the table type) manually is to remove all Group By, Sort, and Filter options. Right-click

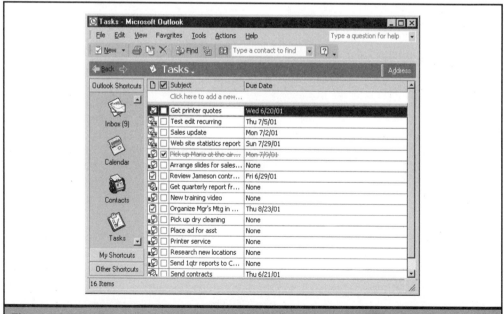

Figure 13-7.   *The Simple List view provides a quick overview of your tasks*

any field header in the current view and select Customize Current View from the shortcut menu to open the View Summary dialog box.

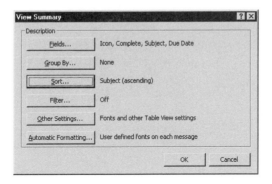

If options are set for Group By, Sort, or Filter, click the corresponding button to open the associated dialog box. Then click the Clear All button to remove any settings, and click OK to return to the View Summary dialog box. When all three are cleared, click OK to return to the Tasks folder. Now you're set to start rearranging the view manually by dragging and dropping tasks. As soon as you move a task above or below the adjacent tasks, a red line with a pair of inward-pointing arrows appears between tasks. This indicates where the task will land if you choose to drop it.

 You can also right-drag the task and have the choice of moving it or copying it when you reach your destination. As soon as you drop the task, a shortcut menu appears, offering you both options as well as Cancel.

Drop the task to relocate it. Continue the process until the list is sorted exactly the way you want it. When you've got it arranged to your satisfaction, it's time to take advantage of the second feature, Save Task Order.

Using the Save Task Order Command

The Save Task Order command is a handy feature that sets the default sort order for all Tasks folder views to match the order in effect at the time you apply the Save Task Order command. In other words, if you've sorted the current view by Due Date, all other views will be sorted (by default) by Due Date as well. However, the application of Filter, Group By, or new Sort conditions will override the saved sort order in all views.

Unless all Group By and Filter settings are disabled, the Save Task Order command is grayed out on the Actions menu. When used in conjunction with a manual sort, this is no problem, since manual sorting requires Group By, Filter, and Sort options all to be turned off. However, if you want to use a sort on one or more fields rather than a manual sort, just make sure the Group By and Filter options have been removed. To check, right-click a column header in the task view and choose Customize Current View to display the View Summary dialog box. If Group By or Filter is enabled, click its button to open the associated dialog box and click Clear All. Click OK twice to return to the Tasks folder.

When you have the task view in the order you want, choose Actions | Save Task Order from the Menu bar. From this point forward, all views will utilize the sort order applied when you used the Save Task Order command as the default sort order. However, any Group By, Sort, or Filter options applied will take precedence. Therefore, to return to the default sort order, you must clear those options.

Troubleshooting Tasks Folder Views

While using views in the Tasks folder, you may encounter some problems not found in most other Outlook folders. The standard Tasks folder views are all table views with the exception of one timeline view. The problems you may experience are, for the most part, found in the table views.

Sorting Problems   If you create custom views by modifying existing views or by creating your own from scratch, you'll find you cannot sort by certain fields, including Company, Categories, Contact (as opposed to Contacts), Notes, or Read. There appears to be no clear reasoning behind most of these exclusions. In any event, attempting to sort by one of these fields results in an error message informing you that "You cannot sort by this field."

The way to work around this problem is to use the Group By feature instead of the Sort feature. Right-click a field header and select Customize Current View to display the View Summary dialog box. Click the Group By button to display the Group By dialog box.

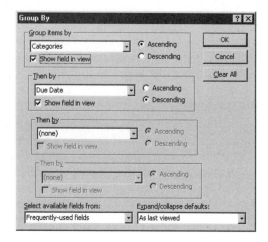

From the Group Items By drop-down list, select the non-sorting field of your choice. If you want to display the field in the current view, check the Show Field In View option.

You cannot use more than one non-sorting field in the Group By dialog box. Outlook permits you to select more than one, but as soon as you exit the Group By dialog box and try to close the View Summary dialog box, Outlook informs you the operation is too complex.

Select either Ascending or Descending for the order, and click OK twice to return to the active view. The view will now be grouped by the field chosen, enabling you to view your tasks in the order you desire.

Locating the Missing Private Field   Another problem you may encounter when customizing Tasks folder views is how to include the Private field in the view. While the Private field appears on both the task form and the task request form, the one place it does not appear is on the list of available task fields you can use for customizing a Tasks folder view. Fortunately, there's a simple work-around for this problem. In either the Field Chooser or the Show Fields dialog box, select the Private field from the All Contact Fields list. The Private field doesn't appear in the All Task Fields list. However, both the Tasks folder and the Contacts folder use the same field for storing the Private status of records. You can access the Field Chooser by right-clicking a column header and selecting Field Chooser from the shortcut menu.

Printing a Timeline View   One thing the Tasks folder has in common with the Journal folder is the inability to print the timeline view. Actually, any folder containing a timeline view will exhibit the same behavior. The reason for this lack of printing support is easy to understand since it would require printing a banner. However, there is a way to improvise and get a printout of the information in the timeline. Export the data to an Excel file, and use the Excel Chart Wizard to create a Gantt chart, which you can print.

MOUS EXAM PRACTICE
This section covered some basic features and some not-so-basic features of the Tasks folder views. Switch between the different views to see what each view consists of. Then try sorting a table view manually. Once you've got the table view sorted manually, set the new sort order as the default, using the Save Task Order command.

Organizing Tasks

Since the Tasks folder provides the same basic sorting, filtering, and grouping features as the other Outlook folders, there's no need to cover them in depth here. You'll find detailed information on all three features in Chapter 23.

There are, however, a couple of differences of which you should be aware. The opening tab of the Filter dialog box is always named for the folder from which it's invoked. Therefore, when setting filter conditions for a Tasks folder view, the opening tab is called Tasks.

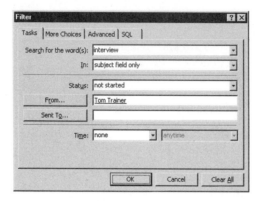

In addition, some of the options on the Tasks tab are unique to the Tasks folder. As you can see, the Status field, which appears in no other folder, appears as a filter criterion. Since task requests and notices are sent via e-mail, the Tasks tab also contains From and Sent To fields. The remaining filter criteria are standard for all Outlook folders.

Another difference you'll find is in the Tasks folder Group By feature. Here you'll find that certain fields cannot be used together in building a grouping. When you attempt to use more than one non-sorting field to create a grouping, Outlook balks and lets you know in no uncertain terms you can't do it. See the "Troubleshooting Tasks Folder Views" section earlier in this chapter for more information on this problem.

Keeping Track of Tasks with Categories

Although Outlook makes no claim to being a project management tool, you can perform some rudimentary project management tasks by taking advantage of several Tasks folder features, including Categories, Group By, and the Task Timeline view.

Using the Tasks folder for simple project management starts with assigning tasks to categories. For each task that has multiple components, you'll want to create a new category with a unique name—most likely the name of the primary task. For example, if you're in charge of organizing the next annual managers meeting, you'll have a number of subtasks that must be undertaken to achieve your goal. Therefore, you might create a new category called Managers Meeting, to which all related tasks, such as reserving rooms, booking flights, renting cars, and so on, are assigned.

While you can create a category from any folder using the same steps, the following instructions assume you are in the Tasks folder. To create a new category, choose Edit | Categories to open the Categories dialog box, as shown in Figure 13-8.

In the Item(s) Belong To These Categories text box, type the name of the new category you want to create. Next, click the Add To List button to add the new category to the Available Categories list. The new category is added to the list and is automatically checked. The check mark indicates that the currently selected task will be assigned to the

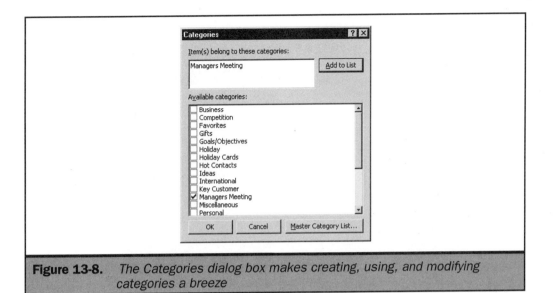

Figure 13-8. *The Categories dialog box makes creating, using, and modifying categories a breeze*

category. Therefore, unless you selected a related task before creating the category, you'll want to remove the check mark to ensure only tasks related to the primary task are assigned. Click OK to save the new category and return to the active view.

The next step is to assign all related tasks to the category. Open (or create) each related task, and move to the bottom of the task (or task request) form. Click the Categories button and check the new category. Click OK to assign the task to the new category and return to the task form. Change or add any other necessary information and close the task form. Repeat the process for each related task. You can assign a task to more than one category.

You now have an easy method for sorting, grouping, and filtering all related tasks. The final step is to combine two existing view types and create a custom view that groups tasks by category, but displays them on a timeline. To create a custom timeline view grouped by category, choose View | Current View | Define Views to open the Define Views For "Tasks" dialog box seen in Figure 13-9.

Click New to display the Create A New View dialog box shown in Figure 13-10.

Enter a name for the new view. Then select Timeline from the Type Of View list. Click OK to save the settings and display the View Summary dialog box. Click the Group By button to display the Group By dialog box. From the Group Items By drop-down list, select Categories. Click OK twice to save the Group By settings and return to the Define Views For "Tasks" dialog box. Click Apply View to return to the Tasks folder, where the new view is displayed (see Figure 13-11).

Another thing you might want to do is create a task item for the primary item and attach each of the individual projects to it. In the example used for this section, you would create a task called Meeting Manager and set the due date for the last date on which everything has to be completed. Minimize all windows except Outlook and the Meeting

MANAGING TIME
AND DETAILS

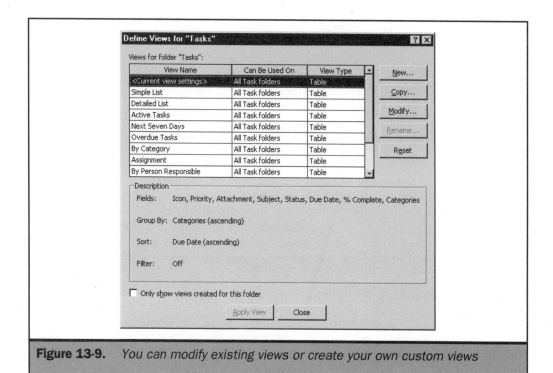

Figure 13-9.   *You can modify existing views or create your own custom views*

Manager task. Right-click a blank spot on the Windows taskbar and select Tile Windows Vertically. This places the Outlook window and the task form side by side. Next, drag the

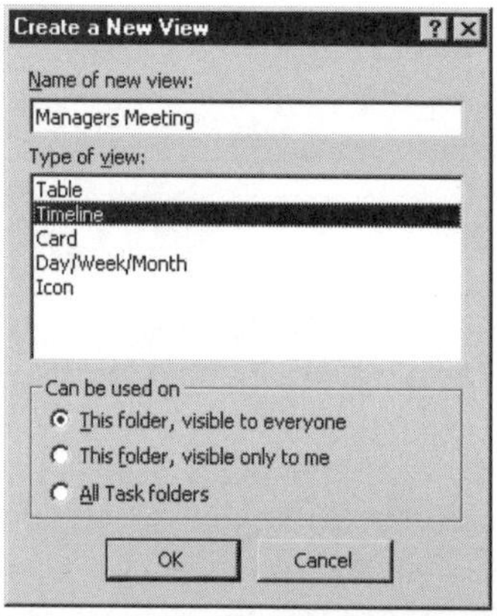

Figure 13-10.   *View basics are pretty straightforward*

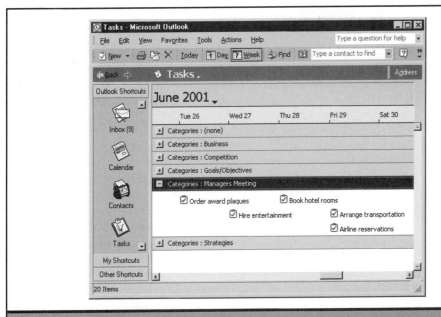

Figure 13-11.   *The new view gives you a good overview of your projects*

related tasks from the Tasks folder, and drop them in the Notes field of the Meeting Manager task. Now, anytime you open the Meeting Manager task you can also open any of the related tasks by double-clicking the appropriate icon in the Notes field.

MOUS EXAM PRACTICE
As you discovered in this section, you can perform simple project management tasks by assigning your Outlook tasks to categories. Begin by creating several new categories. Then create a series of related tasks, and assign each one to a category. Next, create a new timeline view grouped by categories. You might also create a table view grouped by categories.

Understanding Task Request Responses

Whether you're the original owner of a task request or the fourth assignee/owner in a chain of reassignments, tracking the progress and whereabouts of the task can be somewhat confusing—unless you understand the task request notification process.

There are two types of notifications:

■ **Task responses**   Responses, which include Task Accepted messages and Task Declined messages, are direct replies to the last sender of the task request from

MANAGING TIME
AND DETAILS

the new assignee, indicating either an agreement or a refusal to accept ownership of the task.

■ **Task updates**   Task Update messages are sent to all users whose names appear on the Update List of the task Details tab. Updates are sent when a task is reassigned or when the task owner makes a change to the task, such as changing the date(s) or modifying the status of the task. Updates are also sent to all previous assignors, except the last assignor (who gets a Task Response), when a task request is accepted or declined.

Updates generated by changes to a task that has been accepted are straightforward, reflecting the owner and the changes made. So far, so good. However, the confusing part comes when updates are generated by assignments and reassignments. The contents of these task updates are different depending on who sends them and who receives them. It's the task ownership that's in question. For example, if Joe assigns the task to Mary, who assigns it to Bill, who in turn assigns it to Ted, the updates will appear as follows: Joe's updates will indicate Mary is the owner, Mary's updates will indicate Bill is the owner, and Bill's update will indicate Ted is the owner. You can see how confusing this can get.

Note   *Reassigning tasks is a little like playing musical chairs. If someone declines the task, ownership reverts back to the last assignor. At this point, the assignor becomes the de facto owner of the task, and the Update List on the Details tab of the task is automatically cleared. All previous assignors disappear from the Update List, and the current owner is now stuck with only two choices: add the task to his or her Tasks folder, or assign it to someone else. Declining the request from the previous assignor is no longer an option.*

Another thing to be aware of concerning task requests and updates is the manner in which they're processed. When a task request or update is opened and acted upon (regardless of the action taken), the task is modified accordingly in the Tasks folder, and the Task Request message or Task Update message is permanently deleted from the Inbox. It does not even stop at the Deleted Items folder—it just disappears. By default, Outlook tracking options are set to process task updates automatically. Therefore, a task update you receive will be processed and deleted within a very short time (depending on server traffic) if you don't spot it and open it first. This means you may not even be aware that an update has occurred. Since the task itself is updated with the same information included in the update message, this is not really a problem. However, it means the only way you'll be aware of a change in the task is if you open the task and check.

Tip

*If you want to be able to access those deleted updates and requests (and any other permanently deleted Outlook items), you can do so by adding a new DWORD value to an existing key in the Windows Registry. Warning! Editing the Registry can have unexpected results and should only be done by experienced users. Always make a backup of your Registry before making any changes. Add the DWORD value **DumpsterAlwaysOn** to the* `HKEY_LOCAL_MACHINE\Software\Microsoft\Exchange\Client\` `Options` *key, and set its Value data to 1. Log off of Outlook and log back on. Now, no matter what folder you're in, the Recover Deleted Items command appears on the Tools menu. Since the notices are e-mail messages, you'll have to open the Inbox and use the Recover Deleted Items command from there to view deleted updates. See Chapter 5 for information on using the Recover Deleted Items command.*

To disable this automatic processing of task updates, choose Tools | Options from the Menu bar. On the Preferences tab of the Options dialog box, click the E-mail Options button to display the E-mail Options dialog box. Then click the Tracking Options button to open the Tracking Options dialog box. Remove the check mark next to the Process Requests And Responses On Arrival option. Be advised, however, that this option also controls the automatic processing of meeting requests (not task requests); therefore you will be turning that feature off as well.

Setting Task Options

The Tasks folder has several options you can set to customize the way the folder looks and operates. To modify the default Tasks folder options, choose Tools | Options from the Menu bar to display the Options dialog box, shown in Figure 13-12.

As you can see in Figure 13-12, the Preferences tab of the Options dialog box contains a section entitled Tasks, which includes a Reminder Time drop-down list and a Task Options button. From the Reminder Time drop-down list, select the default time for all new tasks. Click the Task Options button to display the Task Options dialog box.

Task Options ? X

Task options

☑ Overdue task color:

Completed task color:

☑ Keep updated copies of assigned tasks on my task list
☑ Send status reports when assigned tasks are completed
☑ Set reminders on tasks with due dates

OK   Cancel

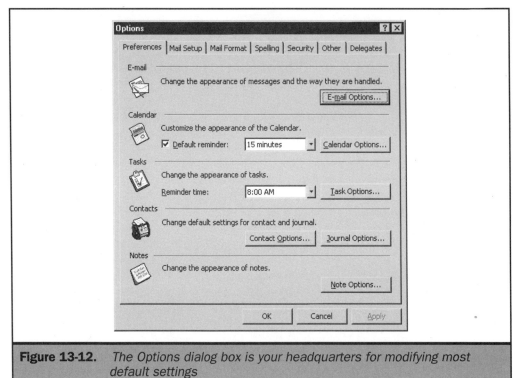

Figure 13-12. *The Options dialog box is your headquarters for modifying most default settings*

Here you can designate the text color for displaying overdue and completed tasks in Tasks folder views. From each drop-down list, select the desired color.

The Task Options dialog box also includes the following options:

- **Keep updated copies of assigned tasks on my task list**   This option appears on all task requests. Checking it here automatically checks the option on all new task request forms. Since it's likely you'll want to remain informed about a task you assign, it's a good idea to leave this option checked.

- **Send status reports when assigned tasks are completed**   If you want to receive notification in the form of a status report when an assigned task is marked complete, check this option. Again, all this does is ensure that the option of the same name on the task request form is automatically checked.

- **Set reminders on tasks with due dates**   Check this option to automatically set reminders for all new tasks that include due dates. The reminder is automatically set using the default setting from the Reminder Time option located on the Preferences tab of the Options dialog box.

Once you've made all the necessary changes to task options, close all the dialog boxes and return to the active Outlook window. The changes should take effect immediately.

The next set of task options is buried a little deeper. Click the Other tab and then click the Advanced Options button to open the Advanced Options dialog box (see Figure 13-13).

In the Appearance Options section, you'll find two task-related options for setting working hours. In the Task Working Hours Per Day field, enter the number of hours you consider a workday. Although many people work more than eight hours a day, eight is still considered a standard workday and is therefore the default setting. The same goes for the next option, Task Working Hours Per Week. This is the number of hours your workweek generally consists of. Both fields are used by Outlook when calculating the Total Work and Actual Work fields found on the Details tab of the task form. For example, if you leave the default settings for Task Working Hours Per Day at 8 and enter 4 hours in the Total Work field in the task form, Outlook converts it to 0.5 days.

Once you've made all the necessary changes to task options, close all the dialog boxes and return to the active Outlook window. The changes should take effect immediately.

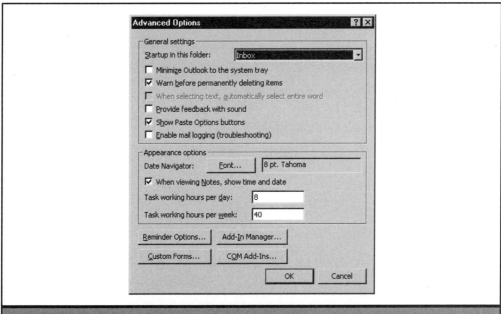

Figure 13-13. *The Advanced Options settings cover a variety of Outlook features, including tasks*

MOUS Exam Core Objectives Explored in Chapter 13

Objective	Activity	Heading
OL10-5-1	Create tasks, update tasks, and update one-time tasks	"Creating Tasks"
OL10-5-2	Modify task organization and task view (assigning tasks to one or more contacts)	"Assigning Tasks"
OL10-5-3	Accept, decline, or delegate tasks	"Responding to Task Assignments"
OL10-5-5	Use categories to manage tasks	"Keeping Track of Tasks with Categories"

MOUS Exam Expert Objectives Explored in Chapter 13

Objective	Activity	Heading
OL10E-5-1	Assign tasks	"Assigning Tasks"
OL10E-5-2	Manage assigned tasks	"Creating a New Task Request"
OL10E-5-3	Change task settings	"Filling in Task Details"
OL10E-5-4	Create and manage task lists	"Creating Tasks"
		"Setting Task Options"
OL10E-5-5	View task lists of other users	"Exchanging Task Information with Others"
OL10E-5-6	Send task information to other users	"Exchanging Task Information with Others"

The Complete Reference

Chapter 14

Using the Journal

The Outlook Journal offers a means of keeping track of your Outlook activities and Office documents with little or no effort. Items you can record in the Journal folder include e-mail messages, meeting requests, task requests, Word and Excel documents, and more. To make journaling even easier, Outlook provides an AutoJournal feature that takes over and does most of the work for you.

Adding Journal Entries

You can add Journal entries either by enabling the AutoJournal feature or by creating entries manually. As good as AutoJournaling is, it doesn't fully automate the Journal entry process. There are some items not included in AutoJournaling. Therefore, you may have to create some Journal entries manually even if you turn AutoJournaling on.

> **Note**   *The first time you open the Journal folder by clicking the Outlook Bar shortcut in the My Shortcuts group or the Journal folder in the Folder List, a dialog box displays informing you that you can also use the Activities tab on each contact item for tracking e-mail and other activities. This is a handy feature that may negate the need for using the Journal altogether. Review the features of both and decide for yourself.*

Configuring Automatic Journaling

If you decide to open the Journal folder, Outlook immediately displays the Journal Options dialog box.

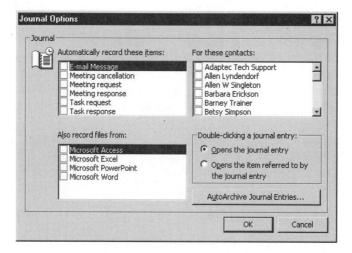

If you plan to use the Journal to record items and documents for some or all of your contacts, you'll want to set the options and save yourself the time and effort of recording Journal entries manually.

Indicate the items and documents you want recorded by checking the appropriate selections in both the Automatically Record These Items list and the Also Record Files From list. Then move to the For These Contacts list, and choose the contacts for whom the selected items and documents will be recorded.

Tip *Although selecting some of the Microsoft Office documents for AutoJournaling might sound like a good idea, it can often be more trouble than it's worth. Every Office document of the type selected is recorded in the Journal, regardless of whether it relates to any other information in Outlook. As a result, your Journal can quickly become cluttered with everything from a letter to Mom to your first chapter of the great American novel.*

The next set of options enables you to determine what happens when you double-click a Journal entry. By default, double-clicking a Journal entry opens the entry itself. However, you can change that by selecting Opens The Item Referred To By The Journal Entry. The next time you double-click a Journal entry, the item or document referred to in the entry will open instead. For example, by default, double-clicking a Microsoft Word Journal entry opens the Journal entry containing a shortcut to the associated Word document. Changing the default double-click option results in the Microsoft Word document itself opening when you double-click the Journal entry.

The last option, the AutoArchive Journal Entries button, provides access to the AutoArchive tab of the Journal Properties dialog box. Here you can set the AutoArchiving options for the Journal folder. For more information on AutoArchiving, see "Configuring AutoArchive Settings" in Chapter 18.

Tip *Warning! This tip involves editing the Windows Registry, which should be performed by experienced users only. Modifying the Registry can have unexpected results that may adversely affect the operation of your installed hardware and software. You can change a number of Journal settings by modifying the values for HKEY_CURRENT_USER\ Software\Microsoft\SharedTools\Outlook\Journaling subkeys. The numeric values AutoJournaled, Enabled, and JournalByContact can be set to off (0) or on (1). Some keys, such as Letters and Notes, are included only to ensure that they appear on the Entry Type list; therefore, setting their options has no effect on them. They cannot be AutoJournaled regardless of their settings.*

The beauty of AutoJournaling is that you don't have to do anything after you set the AutoJournal options. As long as the items, documents, and contacts have been selected in the Journal Options dialog box, anytime you create a selected item or document for an indicated contact, the Journal entry is recorded automatically.

Creating Journal Entries Manually

 Unfortunately, not all Outlook items are eligible for AutoJournaling. Phone calls, notes, letters, faxes, tasks, and appointments are among the Outlook items that cannot be journaled automatically. Consequently, if you want these items entered in the Journal folder, you'll have to create the Journal entries manually.

If you use the Journal a lot, you may want to move its shortcut from the My Shortcuts group on the Outlook Bar to the Outlook Shortcuts group. Open the My Shortcuts group, and drag the Journal icon to the Outlook Shortcuts group. When the Outlook Shortcuts group opens, drop the Journal shortcut above or below an existing shortcut.

The process is not difficult; therefore, creating manual Journal entries is more of a nuisance than an onerous task. Press CTRL+SHIFT+J from any folder to open a new Journal entry form (see Figure 14-1). From within the Journal folder click the New button on the Standard toolbar or press CTRL+N.

You can also create a new Journal entry by right-clicking a blank spot in the Journal folder Information viewer and selecting New Journal Entry from the shortcut menu.

Enter a brief description of the Journal entry in the Subject field. Make it short and to the point, so you can easily identify it later. Next, select the type of entry you're making from the Entry Type drop-down list.

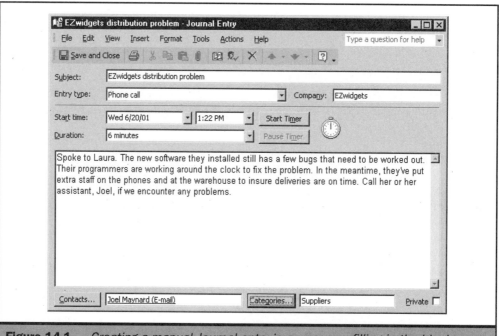

Figure 14-1. *Creating a manual Journal entry is as easy as filling in the blanks*

*Warning! This tip involves editing the Windows Registry, which should only be done by experienced users. You can create custom entry types by adding them to the Windows Registry. Locate the HKEY_CURRENT_USER\Software\Microsoft\SharedTools\ Outlook\Journaling key and add a subkey for each new entry type. Give the new key an appropriate name (for example, Life Event, Equipment Service, Promotion, and so on). Next, add a string value named **Description**. For the string's Value Data, enter the text you want to appear in the Entry Type drop-down list. Close the Registry and return to the Journal. The next time you open a Journal entry and display the Entry Type drop-down list, you'll find the new entry type listed.*

If the Journal entry is associated with a specific company, enter its name in the Company field. By default, the Start Time field contains today's date and the current time (according to your computer's clock). If you're recording an event that happened earlier, you can enter a different date and time, or use the pop-up calendar and drop-down time list in the Start Time field.

For keeping track of the amount of time you spend on an activity, you can activate the timer by clicking the Start Timer button. When you're finished with the call, meeting, or other activity, you can click Pause Timer to stop the timer. Time is recorded in one-minute increments in the Duration field. If you're making a record of an event that took place earlier, you can manually enter the time in the Duration field. Use the Notes field to keep track of phone calls, meeting notes, and miscellaneous information related to the entry.

To associate the Journal entry with one or more contacts, click the Contacts button and choose the contacts from the Select Contacts dialog box. If you're using categories to organize your Journal entries, you may want to assign the entry to a category by clicking the Categories button and selecting the appropriate category from the Categories dialog box. The final option on the Journal entry form is the Private option. If you share your Journal folder and want to prevent others from seeing this entry, check the Private option.

MOUS EXAM PRACTICE
In this section you learned to create Journal entries manually. Begin by trying the various methods for opening a new journal entry form, including the shortcut key CTRL+SHIFT+J, the New button drop-down list, and the CTRL+N shortcut from within the Journal folder. Next, fill out the form with the appropriate information. Finally, use the timer feature to track the duration of the activity.

Adding Attachments to Journal Entries

Journal entries, like most Outlook items, can contain attachments as well as information. For example, suppose you're recording notes to send to coworkers who were unable to attend an important meeting. You might want to include appointment items, contact records, Word documents, Excel spreadsheets, and e-mail messages related to the

MANAGING TIME
AND DETAILS

topics discussed at the meeting. It's easy if you create a Journal entry for the meeting and insert the necessary items as attachments.

While Outlook 2000 limited you to inserting objects only, Outlook 2002 allows you to include items, files, and objects as attachments to a journal entry. Adding attachments to Journal entries is identical to adding attachments to other Outlook items.

To insert an Outlook item, choose Insert | Item from the Menu bar. The Insert Item dialog box seen in Figure 14-2 opens.

Locate the folder containing the item(s), select the item(s), and click OK. The item(s) are automatically inserted as attachments. To insert the item text or to insert a shortcut to the item, select the appropriate Insert As option in the Insert Item dialog box.

Tip	*You can also add Outlook items to a Journal entry by using the drag-and-drop method.*

In addition to items, you can also attach computer files to a journal entry. The process is similar to inserting items, except this time you locate the folder on your hard drive and select an item contained in the folder. Choose Insert | File from the Menu bar, or click the Insert File button on the Standard toolbar to display the Insert File dialog box. From the Look In drop-down list, locate the folder containing the file(s) you want to attach. Then select the file(s) and click Insert to add them to the journal entry. You can elect to insert the file as text or as a shortcut, by clicking the down arrow on the Insert button and making the appropriate choice from the drop-down menu that appears.

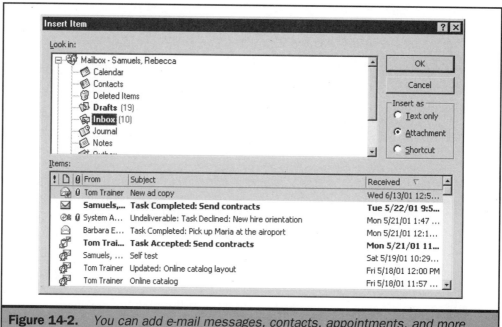

Figure 14-2.   *You can add e-mail messages, contacts, appointments, and more from the Insert Item dialog box*

If you're so inclined, you can also open the Windows Explorer and use the drag-and-drop method to insert files from your hard disk.

The third type of attachment is an Object. *Objects* include such things as images, documents, spreadsheets, charts, ActiveX controls, and so on. To include an object in a document, place your cursor in the Notes field of the Journal entry form and choose Insert | Object to display the Insert Object dialog box.

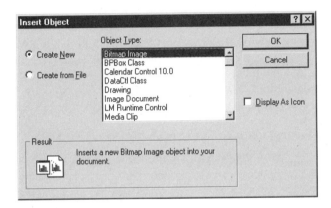

To create a new object, select the type of object you want to create from the Object Type list and click OK. This opens the program associated with the object type so you can create the object. To insert an existing object, select Create From File and click the Browse button to locate the desired file. By default, Outlook embeds the object in the Journal entries. This means that the object is included in the entry form and can be edited in the form as long as the program associated with the object is installed on your computer. Changes made to an embedded object are not reflected in the original object. To retain the relationship between the inserted object and the original object, check the Link option.

There's one important thing to keep in mind when inserting attachments—you're attaching the actual item, file, or object, not merely creating a link (unless you insert a shortcut). Therefore, the size of the Journal entry is increased by the size of the item you're attaching.

Using Outlook Items to Create Journal Entries

Creating Journal entries from other Outlook items is accomplished by dragging the item to the Outlook Bar or Folder List and dropping it on the Journal shortcut or folder. A new Journal entry opens using the item's subject as the Journal entry subject and selecting an appropriate entry type based on the item type. In addition, a shortcut to the original item is included in the Notes field of the Journal entry.

If you right-drag the item and drop it on the Journal shortcut or Journal folder, a shortcut menu appears offering you several options. You can create a new Journal entry and include the dragged item as a shortcut or as an attachment.

Viewing Journal Entries

By default, Journal entries are displayed in the By Type timeline view. *Timeline* views, of which the Journal has several, display information along a horizontal time scale, letting you view Journal entries in relation to their start times. The timeline views go one step further and organize Journal entries by groups within the time scale (see Figure 14-3).

To fine-tune a timeline view, you can take advantage of one of the three variations offered for each timeline view: Day, Week, or Month. The Day view breaks each day on the timeline into 24 one-hour sections. This enables you to view the activities for any given day on an hour-by-hour basis. The Week view, which is the default, divides the timeline by days. The final variation, Month, also breaks the timeline up into days.

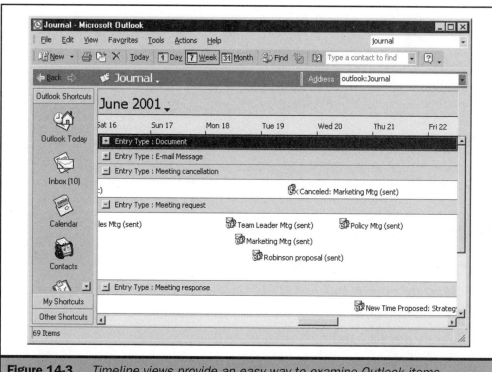

Figure 14-3. *Timeline views provide an easy way to examine Outlook items chronologically*

However, each section is much smaller, permitting a larger number of days to be displayed at once. As a result, only the Journal entry icons appear in this view. To see the subject, you must open the Journal entry. To switch between the timeline view variations, click the appropriate button on the Standard toolbar, as shown in Figure 14-3.

To use a timeline view effectively, you should familiarize yourself with its features. You can navigate a timeline view by scrolling left and right through dates, and up and down through groups of Journal entries. You can also change dates by clicking the day or month header and selecting a new date from the pop-up calendar that appears.

Another handy feature is the ability to select all entries in a group by right-clicking the group header. A shortcut menu appears, providing you with a number of commands that affect the selected Journal entries.

In addition to timeline views, the Journal contains several table views you can use. Table views display the Journal entry information in the rows and columns format similar to a spreadsheet layout.

You can't sort the table views by Contact or Category. However, you can still organize a table view using those fields. Right-click the Contact (or Category) field header, and choose Group By This Field from the shortcut menu.

Both timeline and table views have many features in common with other Outlook views. Right-clicking the headers (whether field or date) displays a shortcut menu with commands that affect the view. Double-clicking a blank spot on the Information viewer opens a new Journal entry form. For more information on working with Outlook views, see Chapter 23.

Using Timeline Shortcuts

The timeline view offers a unique environment and a number of helpful keyboard shortcuts for getting around the view quickly and easily without using the mouse. There are three groups of shortcuts you can use, depending on the focus of your actions. The first group affects the time scale itself. The next group of shortcuts works on items you've selected, and the third group applies to item groups that are selected.

To move around on the time scale, use the following shortcuts:

- **TAB key**   Press TAB to move from the top date header to the smaller date header, and then to the first item group header. Press SHIFT+TAB to cycle through them in the opposite order.

- **Arrow keys**   The RIGHT ARROW and DOWN ARROW keys move you forward through the time increments on the selected date header. Press LEFT ARROW or UP ARROW to move backward through the time increments on the selected header.

When you select one or more items in an item group, the following shortcuts apply:

- **Arrow keys**   When you highlight a group header, the RIGHT ARROW and LEFT ARROW keys move you forward and backward, respectively, through the displayed items and the group header. To select multiple adjacent items, hold the SHIFT key and press RIGHT ARROW or LEFT ARROW. You can even select multiple non-adjacent items by holding the CTRL key down and pressing RIGHT ARROW or LEFT ARROW to move through the items. When you reach an item you want to select, press the spacebar. Continue holding the SHIFT key to move to the next item you want to select.

- **ENTER key**   Press ENTER to open the selected item.

- **ESC key**   Press ESC to close an open item.

- **HOME key**   Pressing HOME selects the first item in the group. To move to the first item without selecting it, hold down the CTRL key and press HOME.

- **END key**   To select the last item in the group, press END. To move to the last key without selecting it, hold the CTRL key while pressing the END key.

The final collection of shortcut keys is for working with item groups:

- **Arrow keys**   Press UP ARROW or DOWN ARROW to move from group to group either up or down. The RIGHT ARROW and LEFT ARROW keys expand (right) and collapse (left) the groups.

- **ENTER key**   When an item group is selected, pressing the ENTER key will either expand or collapse it, depending on its current state.

- **Plus and minus keys on the number pad**   The plus (+) key on the number pad expands the selected group, and the minus (–) key collapses it.

If you're not a fan of keyboard shortcuts, you can rely on your mouse to get you around.

Using the Preview Pane

To preview Journal entries without opening them, you can activate the Preview Pane. Choose View | Preview Pane to split either a timeline or table view into two panes. The top pane retains the Journal items and groups, while the bottom pane contains the Preview Pane. Select an item in the top pane to display the journal entry form in the Preview Pane. To hide the Preview Pane, choose View | Preview Pane from the Menu bar again. To display Preview Pane options, right-click the thin blue line separating both panes, and select Preview Pane Options from the shortcut menu. For detailed information on setting Preview Pane options, see Chapter 23.

Turning on AutoPreview

Another useful viewing feature is AutoPreview, available in table views only. The AutoPreview feature displays the first few lines of each Journal entry's Notes field in the view. Choose View | AutoPreview to turn on the AutoPreview feature. To turn it off, repeat the process.

Printing Journal Entries

Printing Journal entries is easy. As a matter of fact, since your choices are rather limited, you'd have to work at making it difficult. The first thing to note is that you can't print a timeline view. Therefore, printing in the Journal folder is restricted to printing items and printing table views.

Tip *Although you can't print a timeline view from Outlook, you can export the data to an Excel file using the Import and Export Wizard. You can open the file in Excel and create a Gantt chart, which you can then print from Excel. Like timeline views, Gantt charts are graphical representations of data displayed chronologically on a horizontal timeline.*

To print a journal item in either type of view, right-click the item and select Print from the shortcut menu. You can also open the item and click the Print button on the Standard toolbar.

To print a table view, press CTRL+P, click the Print button on the Standard toolbar, or choose File | Print to display the Print dialog box, shown in Figure 14-4.

Select the printer to use from the Name drop-down list. Click the Properties button to set options for the selected printer. Check your printer manual for information on setting printer options. Move to the Print Style list and choose Table Style.

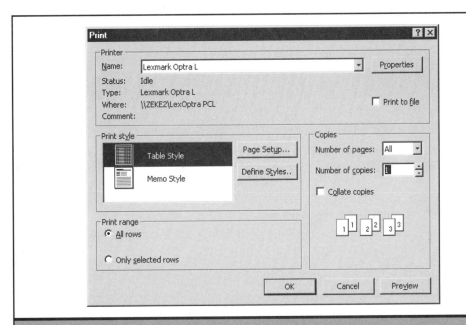

Figure 14-4. *Use the Print dialog box to set your print options*

MANAGING TIME
AND DETAILS

Tip *You can use the Memo Style to print one or more selected items from either a table or timeline view. Each item prints on its own page and includes all fields that contain data.*

If you want to include only selected rows in the printout, click Only Selected Rows; otherwise leave All Rows selected. To use the Only Selected Rows option, you must have first selected one or more rows in the view, before opening the Print dialog box. Next, select the pages you want to print and the number of copies. If you're printing more than one copy of a multipage job, you can elect to have Outlook collate the copies for you by checking the Collate Copies option. When all the options are set, click OK to commence printing.

MOUS Exam Expert Objectives Explored in Chapter 14

Objective	Activity	Heading
OL10E-4-5	Create and modify Journal entries	"Creating Journal Entries Manually"

The Complete Reference

Chapter 15

Using Notes

O utlook notes items have gained the reputation for being the electronic equivalent of paper sticky notes. This description of the notes items is based on two things: their appearance, which faithfully mimics that of a yellow sticky pad note, and the ability to "stick" them on other Outlook items. What these electronic scraps are especially handy for is jotting down temporary information you use once and discard, or quick notes you can later transfer to a permanent residence in a contact or appointment item.

Creating Notes

As with so many other tasks in Outlook, there is a variety of ways to create a new note. You can press CTRL+SHIFT+N, or choose File | New | Note from any Outlook folder. If you're in the Notes folder, you can click the New button on the Standard toolbar, press CTRL+N, or right-click a blank spot on the Information viewer and select New Note. Whichever method you choose, you end up with a small yellow square like the one in Figure 15-1.

You can also create notes by dragging other Outlook items to the Notes shortcut on the Outlook Bar or to the Notes folder in the Folder List. The information from the dragged items appears in the body of the newly created notes.

As soon as you open a new note form, you can start typing. Begin by entering a title for the note. Make it brief and descriptive. Press the ENTER key to separate the title line from the body text of the note. Anything appearing on the first line (before the first hard return—an invisible formatting character created when you press the ENTER key) appears in the Information viewer as the note title when the note is selected.

The title banner does not physically display the note title. However, pausing your mouse pointer over the title banner causes the note title to appear in a small pop-up box similar to a ToolTip.

After you enter the note title and press the ENTER key, begin typing the body of your note. Type as much information as needed. The note form is a simple text editor, which means it word-wraps, employs Cut, Copy, and Paste commands, and continues to add new lines as you type. The only thing that is somewhat disconcerting about it is the lack of a scroll bar. As your text exceeds the visible space in the note, new lines are added and the existing text scrolls up. However, no scroll bar appears to alert you to the fact that you can scroll through the text. Fortunately, you can scroll up and down by using the arrow keys to move the cursor through the text. In addition, the PAGE UP and PAGE DOWN keys function as expected in a text editor.

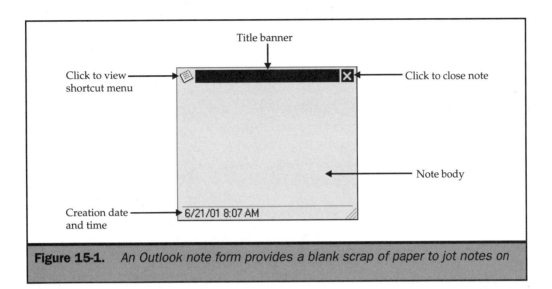

Title banner

Click to view
shortcut menu

Click to close note

Note body

Creation date
and time

6/21/01 8:07 AM

Figure 15-1.   *An Outlook note form provides a blank scrap of paper to jot notes on*

Note   *Only the first 255 characters of a note title appear in the Icon view when the note is selected. Anything beyond 255 characters is cut off in the title. It still appears in the note itself, but not in the note title. Remember, the title is all the text on the first line preceding the first hard return.*

To edit an existing note, double-click the note in the Notes folder Information viewer and make the necessary changes. When you're finished editing, click the X in the upper-right corner to close the note. There's no need to save the note since closing a note also saves it.

Note   *Although notes are generally used for jotting short bits of information, they can hold quite a bit of data. An individual note can contain up to 29,919 characters.*

If you decide a note is no longer serving any useful purpose, you can eliminate it by selecting it and pressing DELETE, or by clicking the Delete button on the Standard toolbar. You can also right-click the note and select Delete from the shortcut menu.

MOUS   ***MOUS EXAM PRACTICE***
In this section, you learned how to create and modify notes. Now create a couple of notes items from other Outlook folders using the CTRL+SHIFT+N method. From within the Notes folder, use each of the various methods available for creating new notes. You might also try dragging different Outlook items to the Notes folder to see how the information is added to a new note. After you've created a number of notes items, try your hand at editing them. Open them, modify their contents, and close them.

MANAGING TIME
AND DETAILS

Managing Notes

Outlook notes are straightforward and uncomplicated, which makes managing them relatively simple. However, they are Outlook items, and as such, inherit many of the features of their more sophisticated siblings. Therefore, you still have a variety of options when it comes to organizing and viewing notes.

Organizing Notes

Outlook is an information manager, which means that organizing every piece of information, including notes, is a priority. Like other items, notes begin to lose their effectiveness if they are allowed to proliferate with wild abandon. To ensure that notes retain their usefulness, Outlook provides a number of ways you can organize them as they accumulate.

Assigning Notes to Categories and Contacts

Using category and contact assignments can make sorting, filtering, and viewing notes a snap. Category assignments provide a quick and easy way to separate notes into related groups. The process of assigning notes to categories is similar to that of assigning other Outlook items to categories, as you'll see if you follow these steps:

1. Open the Notes folder.

2. Select the note(s) you want to assign to one or more categories.

3. Right-click any one of the selected notes and choose Categories from the shortcut menu to display the Categories dialog box.

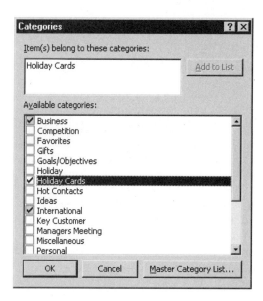

You can also choose Edit | Categories from the Menu bar to display the Categories dialog box.

4. Check the categories to which you want the selected notes assigned.

 If any of the selected notes already have category assignments, they appear as check marks in gray boxes. This does not mean all selected notes (unless only one note is selected) are assigned to the checked category. For example, one or more notes in the preceding illustration are already assigned to the Business and International categories. To assign all selected notes to the category, remove the check mark and add it again. The gray box turns white indicating the assignment affects all selected notes.

5. Click OK to save the category assignments and return to the Notes folder.

You can also categorize individual notes during creation or editing. While the note is open, click the note icon in the upper-left corner of the note and choose Categories from the shortcut menu. This displays the Categories dialog box. Follow the steps outlined earlier to make category assignments.

Linking contacts to notes is great for quick notes you plan to add to a contact record at a later time. If you forget to transfer the information, having a link to the contact makes it very easy to match the note with the contact and update the contact record, regardless of how much time has elapsed.

Linking a contact to a note is even easier than assigning a note to a category; however, you can only link one note at a time. Open the note you want to link and click the note icon in the upper-left corner. From the shortcut menu, select Contacts to open the Contacts For Note dialog box.

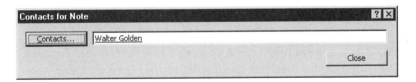

Click the Contacts button to display the Select Contacts dialog box. Choose the contact(s) you want to link to the note and click OK to return to the Contacts For Note dialog box. Click Close to add the link(s) and return to the note.

If you decide to add the note information to the contact record, open the note and copy the text. Then click the note icon and select Contacts from the shortcut menu. Double-click the contact name to open the contact record. Paste the note text into the note field of the contact record.

Using Organize to Manage Notes

The Organize feature is available throughout Outlook, and the Notes folder is no exception. You can use Organize to move notes to other folders and to switch views. To move notes, click the Organize button on the Standard toolbar to display the Organize pane in the Information viewer.

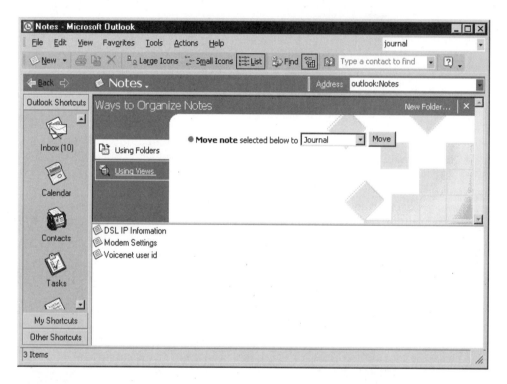

Select the notes you want to move and choose a target folder from the Move Note Selected Below To drop-down list in the Organize pane. Then click the Move button to complete the move.

To create a new folder, click the New Folder button in the top-right corner of the Organize pane. To close the Organize pane, click the X located to the right of the New Folder button.

Sorting and Filtering Notes

Notes, like other Outlook items, can be sorted and filtered using the sort and filter features. Applying a filter to notes enables you to establish certain criteria which a note must meet to remain visible. All notes not meeting the criteria you set are hidden while the filter is applied. The process is very similar to that used for sorting and filtering other Outlook items. There are, however, a couple of minor differences that will be covered here.

To filter your notes, right-click a blank spot in the Information viewer and select Filter to open the Filter dialog box.

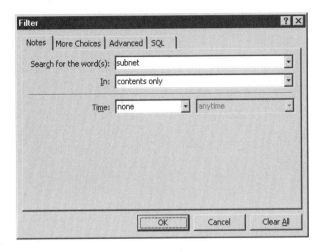

As you can see, the opening tab is called Notes. This is due to the fact that the first tab of the Filter dialog box is automatically customized for each folder where it's used. Enter the text you want to use as the search criterion in the Search For The Word(s) field. From the In drop-down list, select the field in which to search for the text. You'll find the selection is rather limited. You can choose Contents Only or Subject Field Only. The Contents Only selection applies to the body of the note, while the Subject Field Only applies to the note title. Since the title is also considered part of the contents, any text included in the title will be found regardless of which selection you make.

The last option on the Notes tab is Time. Use this option to filter notes based on the date they were created or modified. Select Created or Modified from the Time drop-down list. From the second Time drop-down list, select the timeframe to use.

The created and modified dates and times for non–Personal Folder items are determined by the Microsoft Exchange server, not the local user's computer. However, the Time option uses the local computer's clock. Therefore, if the clock on the server is different from the clock on the user's computer, the Time option may not work as anticipated.

Click OK to apply the filter. All records not matching the filter criteria are hidden. Filters are applied only to the views in which they are created. Since Large Icons, Small Icons, and List are simply variations on the Icon view, the same filter applies to each of them. However, if you switch to another view, all your notes will be visible (unless the view has its own filter). It's a good idea to remove a filter when you're finished using it to ensure you don't return to the view at a later time and think half your notes are gone.

When you apply a filter in a table view, (Filter Applied) appears in the Folder banner, alerting you to the fact that a filter has, indeed, been applied. However, when you apply a filter to an icon view, the (Filter Applied) notice on the banner does not appear. If you seem to be missing notes, check the left side of the status bar, where you'll find a Filter Applied notice (if a filter has actually been applied).

To remove a filter, return to the Filter dialog box and click the Clear All button. See Chapter 23 for complete details on using the other Filter dialog box tabs.

Sorting the Notes folder is even easier. The first thing to understand is that sorting applies to the entire folder, not just the current view of the folder contents. Therefore, when you sort your notes, the same sort order is carried over when you change views.

In an icon view, you must use the Sort dialog box, which can be accessed by right-clicking a blank spot in the Information viewer and selecting Sort from the shortcut menu. You can then select up to four fields on which to base the sort order. For details on using the Sort dialog box, see Chapter 23. You can also open the Sort dialog box by choosing View | Current View | Customize Current View and clicking the Sort button on the View Summary dialog box.

A table view in the Notes folder can be sorted quickly and easily by clicking the field headers at the top of the Information viewer. Click the header of the field you want to use to sort the view by. The first time you click a header, the sort order is ascending (from A to Z). Click the header a second time to reverse the sort order. A small recessed triangle indicates whether the order is ascending (upward triangle) or descending (downward triangle). You can sort using multiple fields by holding down the SHIFT key while clicking the field headers.

You can also sort a table view by right-clicking a column header and selecting Sort Ascending or Sort Descending from the shortcut menu.

Since some sort order is necessary, you cannot remove a sort order, merely change it.

MOUS EXAM PRACTICE
In this section, you learned a variety of techniques for organizing your notes. Begin your practice by assigning notes to categories. Then use the Contacts command to link some of the notes to different contacts. Use the Organize feature to move notes between folders. Remember, only notes folders can accept notes items. Next, apply one or more filters to different Notes folder views. After you master the Outlook Filter feature, sort the Notes folder on a single field. Then try multiple fields. In each case, change the sort order from ascending to descending to see how the notes are affected.

Viewing Notes

As your inventory of notes grows, you may find you need to change the way you view your notes. With only a handful of notes to manage, the default view (the Icon view with large icons) is probably sufficient. However, if you amass a large number of notes, you'll soon discover the limitations of the default view. By customizing the Icon view and taking advantage of the other standard views, you'll quickly overcome those limitations.

Customizing Icon Views

As you can see in Figure 15-2, the default Icons view displays each note in the Information viewer with a large icon and the first 25 characters of the note title.

The sort order of the Icons view is by creation date and time, with the most recently created note appearing in the top-left corner of the Information viewer. If the note title is longer than 25 characters, highlighting the note displays up to 230 additional characters of the title. To see the note body, or anything beyond the total of 255 title characters, you'll have to open the note by double-clicking it.

Figure 15-2. *The Icon view becomes a little chaotic as your notes multiply*

The Icons view is fine until you start to add a substantial number of notes, after which it becomes rather cluttered and hard to use. To restore some order, you can take advantage of the following customization options available only to the Icons view:

- **Large Icons**   This is the default option applied to the Icons view. It displays a large icon for each note in the Information viewer.

- **Small Icons**   This option replicates the default view, but replaces the large icons with small icons. The notes are still ordered (by Created date) from left to right.

- **List**   The List option does two things. It uses small icons and displays notes from top to bottom (by Created date), using multiple columns when necessary.

You can apply any of the preceding options to the Icons view by clicking the appropriate button on the Standard toolbar or right-clicking a blank spot in the Information viewer and making your selection from the shortcut menu. The same commands are also available on the View menu.

Switching Views

Even with the customization options, the Icons view may not be suitable for your needs. Therefore, Outlook provides a number of standard views in addition to the Icons view. To switch views, choose View | Current View and select the desired view from the submenu that appears. Outlook offers the following views for your viewing pleasure:

- **Icons**   This is the default view, in which notes are displayed with large icons and titles. The default sort order is by the Created date field, and notes are arranged from left to right.

- **Notes List**   This table view presents notes in a straight list format with Icon, Subject, Created, and Categories fields displayed.

- **Last Seven Days**   This table view is identical to the Notes List view, but displays only those items created or modified within the last seven days. Keep in mind that in a Microsoft Exchange Server network, the Created and Modified dates are assigned by the server, not the local computer, for all non–Personal Folders items. If there's a difference between the server's clock and your local computer's clock, this view may not produce the results you expect.

- **By Category**   If you assign notes to categories, use this view to group all notes by category assignments. Category groups appear alphabetically.

- **By Color**   If you use color to distinguish notes from one another, use this view to group them by the color applied.

In addition to using the View menu to switch views, you can also use the Organize feature. Click the Organize button on the Standard toolbar to display the Organize pane. Then click the Using Views link to display the views options.

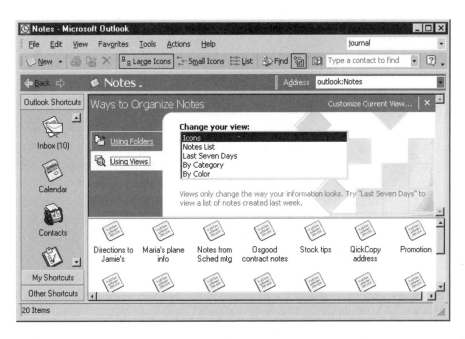

From the Change Your View list, select the view you want to use. You can even modify the currently selected view by clicking Customize Current View to display the View Summary dialog box. To close the Organize pane, click the Organize button again. For more information on customizing Outlook views, see Chapter 23.

 Just as easy to use and requiring less space than the Organize pane is the Current View drop-down list, found in the Advanced toolbar. Right-click anywhere on the Standard toolbar and click Advanced to display the Advanced toolbar.

Using the Preview Pane

A handy device you can use to enhance the current view is the Preview Pane, shown in Figure 15-3.

To access the Preview Pane, choose View | Preview Pane from the Menu bar. The Information viewer is split horizontally into two panes. The top displays the current view, and the bottom displays the contents of the selected note. To close the Preview Pane, choose View | Preview Pane again. You can also right-click the thin blue line separating the Preview Pane from the top viewer and select Preview Pane from the shortcut menu. While you're there, you'll also notice additional Preview Pane options. See Chapter 23 for details on setting these options.

Using AutoPreview

The AutoPreview feature, which is available only in table views, reveals the first few lines of the note in addition to the other information normally displayed in the view.

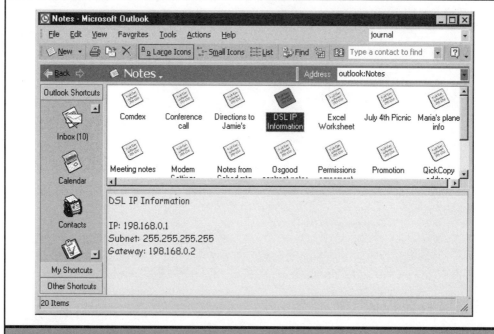

Figure 15-3. *Use the Preview Pane for a quick glimpse of the note's contents*

It provides a quick and easy way to scan your notes to find a tidbit of information or to determine the note's usefulness. See Figure 15-4.

To activate the AutoPreview feature, open a table view and choose View | AutoPreview from the Menu bar. The first few lines of the notes are displayed in blue. To turn off AutoPreview, choose View | AutoPreview a second time.

Customizing Notes

As simple and uncomplicated as notes are, there are still a number of things you can do to customize the way they look and behave. You can change both their color and their size to make them easier to distinguish and use. In addition, you can choose from several options that set defaults for the Notes folder.

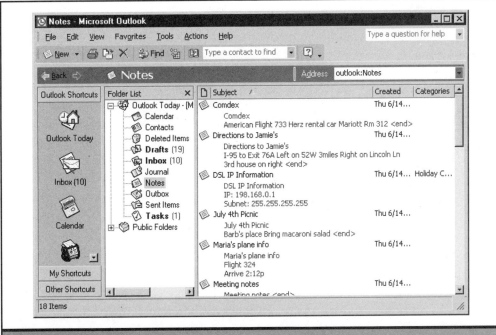

Figure 15-4.   *Using AutoPreview gives you a quick glimpse of each note's contents*

Colorizing Notes

Colorizing can be very helpful in separating notes into easily distinguishable groups, especially if you use the Icons view. Changing a note's color changes not only the color of the icon but the background of the note as well. To change the color, right-click a note and choose Color to display a submenu of color choices. Select the color you want to use for the chosen note. Immediately, the note icon changes to the selected color. If you open any of the affected notes, you'll see the note background is also changed. You can also change a note's color by opening the note, clicking the note icon in the top left corner of the note, and selecting Color from the shortcut menu.

Resizing Notes

Although notes accept a large amount of text without resizing, you may find that you want to view more of the note's content by enlarging the note. Or, conversely, you may have a small note that requires less room and can therefore be reduced in size. Whichever you choose, the process is the same. Use your mouse pointer to grab any one of the sides or corners and drag in the appropriate direction. You can begin dragging when the mouse pointer turns into a double-pointed arrow.

Dragging away from the note center enlarges the note. Dragging toward the note center reduces the note. To expand the width and height at once, drag one of the corners.

You can also modify the size of a note by double-clicking its title banner to maximize and restore it. When you maximize a note, it fills your screen. Restoring it returns it to its original size.

Setting Notes Options

There are several options you can utilize to set some of the default values for your Outlook notes. The first set of options controls the default appearance of new notes; the second determines whether the creation/modification date and time are displayed in notes. Setting these options is a breeze if you use the following steps:

1. Choose Tools | Options from the Menu bar to display the Options dialog box.

2. Click the Notes Options button on the Preferences tab to display the Notes Options dialog box.

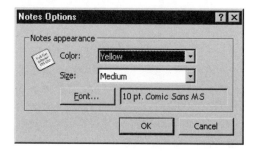

3. Set the desired options. Your choices include

- **Color**   As you saw the moment you created your first note, the default color for new notes is yellow (in keeping with the sticky note tradition). However, if you prefer something a little more (or less) exciting, select a different color from this drop-down list. Existing notes are not affected. However, any new notes you create will be the color chosen here.

- **Size**   If you find the size of new notes to be inadequate, change it to something smaller or larger by changing this option.

- **Font**   In a fit of lightheartedness, the Outlook programmers decided to use the 10-pt. Comic Sans MS font as the default. If you prefer something different, or you'd like to change the size or color of the font, click the Font button to display the Font dialog box. Select the font, font style, font size, and color you want displayed in your notes. Click OK to return to the Notes Options dialog box.

4. Click OK to save the new settings and return to the Options dialog box.

5. Click the Other tab on the Options dialog box to access additional options.

6. Click the Advanced Options button to view the Advanced Options dialog box.

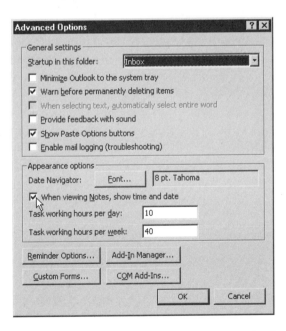

7. Check When Viewing Notes, Show Time And Date to display the creation/ modification date and time in notes. Remove the check mark to hide the date and time in notes.

8. Click OK to return to the Options dialog box.

9. Click OK to close the Options dialog box and return to the active Outlook window.

Upon opening the Notes folder, you will not immediately see any evidence of change, since the first set of options only affects notes created after the options are set, and the date and time option only affects notes' contents.

Using Notes

By now, you've probably gotten an idea of what you can use Outlook notes for, but this section will take you through some of the specific features that make putting notes to work for you even easier.

Creating Other Outlook Items from Notes

The first thing to remember is that drag and drop is alive and well in the Notes folder. You can drag a note to any other Outlook folder and drop it to create a new item of that folder type. In addition, the contents of the note are included in the newly created item. For example, if you drag a note to the Contacts folder, a new contact form opens, with the note contents entered in the contact form note field. Not only is the body of the note added but also category and contact assignments, as well as creation/modification date and time.

You can drag the note to either an Outlook Bar shortcut or to the appropriate folder in the Folder List. If you right-click and drag a note to a different folder, you get a shortcut menu with a number of options when you drop the note. Your choices include creating a new item with a copy of the note as text, as an attachment, or as a shortcut—or you can move the note and include it as an attachment.

Saving Notes as Text or RTF Files

If you want to exchange information contained in an Outlook note with a non-Outlook user, you can use the Save As command to save the note as a text (.txt) file or as a Rich Text Format (.rtf) file. Text files are almost universally readable, and Rich Text Format files are readable by users of most popular word processors. To save a note in either format, select the note and choose File | Save As from the Menu bar to open the Save As dialog box, shown in Figure 15-5.

From the Save In drop-down list, select the location for the saved file. Move to the Save As Type drop-down list and select Text Only (*.txt) or Rich Text Format (*.rtf) depending on your preference. Ignore the other choices as they're unsuitable for notes. Click the Save button. You can now transfer the files to disk or send them via e-mail to non-Outlook users, who can open and view their contents in a compatible text editor or word processor.

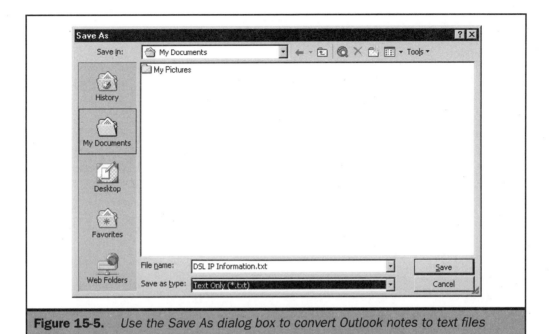

Figure 15-5.   *Use the Save As dialog box to convert Outlook notes to text files*

Forwarding Notes

Another handy feature the Notes folder offers is the ability to instantly create a new e-mail message with the selected note included as an attachment. The feature is called Forward and can be accessed a number of ways.

Select one or more notes from the Information viewer. Then right-click any of the selected notes and choose Forward from the shortcut menu. A new e-mail message form appears with the notes added as attachments. If multiple notes are selected, nothing appears in the Subject line of the message. If only a single note is selected, the Subject line includes FW:, followed by the note title.

You can also select the notes to forward and press CTRL+F or choose Actions | Forward from the Menu bar. You can forward an open note by clicking the note icon in the upper-right corner and selecting Forward from the shortcut menu.

Printing Notes

Printing notes is one of the easiest tasks you'll ever perform in Outlook. All you have to do is select a note in any view, right-click, and select Print from the shortcut menu. Outlook immediately prints the note in the memo style using your default printer.

Selecting multiple copies and using the Print command on the shortcut menu causes the Print dialog box to open. From this dialog box, you can select the desired print style, Table or Memo.

If you want to have more control over your print job, select one or more contacts and click the Print button on the Standard toolbar to display the Print dialog box. Here you can designate the printer to use, modify the print style, determine the number of copies printed, and more.

You can print open notes by clicking the note icon in the upper-left corner and selecting Print from the shortcut menu. The Print dialog box appears, enabling you to set the options for the print job.

MOUS Exam Core Objectives Explored in Chapter 15

Objective	Activity	Heading
OL10-5-4	Create and modify notes	"Creating Notes"
OL10-5-5	Use categories to manage tasks and notes	"Assigning Notes to Categories and Contacts"

The
Complete
Reference

Outlook 2002

Part V

The Microsoft Exchange Server Advantage

Chapter 16

Sharing Information

In addition to being able to exchange Outlook items with other users via e-mail, and to share free/busy information with ease, Outlook users on an Exchange Server have a couple of additional features at their fingertips that allow for even more extensive data sharing. Since Outlook information is folder based, these methods involve sharing one type of Outlook folder or another. The two basic types of folders available in Outlook are

- **Private folders** Although there are several types of private folders in Outlook, only your server-based mailbox folders can be shared directly with other users. Since personal folders and all offline folders are stored on your local hard drive rather than on the server, they cannot be shared directly. Private mailbox folders can be shared either by giving another user delegate privileges or by assigning permissions.

- **Public folders** Public folders exist for the express purpose of sharing information between Outlook users. They can be created by users with the necessary permissions, who then decide which users get access to the folders.

Sharing Private Folders

All users on an Exchange Server network have the option to allow other users to access their mailbox folders. If you're asking why anyone would want to open himself or herself to such an invasion of privacy, there are a couple of things to consider. To begin with, sharing your private folders doesn't mean opening the doors and letting everyone on the network rummage around in your mailbox. You, and you alone, determine who has access and precisely how much access each user receives. The second thing to consider is the convenience it affords you. By giving other users limited access, you can allow them to view information you would normally have to either send them or relay to them in some other manner. For example, if you have a custom journal folder in which you're tracking a particular project, you can give everyone on the team permission to view that folder. Or if you're busy enough to have a trusted assistant, you might want to give him or her the ability to schedule appointments, respond to meeting requests, and handle tasks for you. Remember, you can create new folders for the special projects and share them, rather than your primary mailbox folders.

Outlook offers two methods for giving other Outlook users access to your mailbox folders. You can either use the Delegate Access feature, or assign users permissions to individual folders. The methods are similar in that they give an individual user specific permissions to a single folder. However, which method you use depends on your needs. The primary differences between delegate access and folder permissions are the folders on which each works, the ease of applying one over the other, and the level of permissions granted.

- **Delegate access** You can give any user delegate access to six primary Outlook folders: Calendar, Tasks, Inbox, Contacts, Notes, and Journal. This is handy for granting access to multiple folders in a single operation. Unfortunately, delegate access is limited to those six folders. In addition, the permissions you provide are more limited than those available when you assign permissions to individual folders, with one exception. No matter which level of permission (except None) you assign a delegate, it always includes the ability to send items on your behalf (the From field reads "From: [delegate's name] on behalf of [your name]").

■ **Folder permissions** Folder permissions are not as easy to apply, since you must apply them one folder at a time. However, by assigning permissions to individual folders, you have the ability to control more precisely which permissions each user is assigned. In addition, your choice of permissions is greater.

Delegating Access to Your Data

When the need arises, you'll find that assigning delegate access privileges is easy. Simply choose Tools | Options to open the Options dialog box. Then click the Delegates tab to display the available options as seen in Figure 16-1.

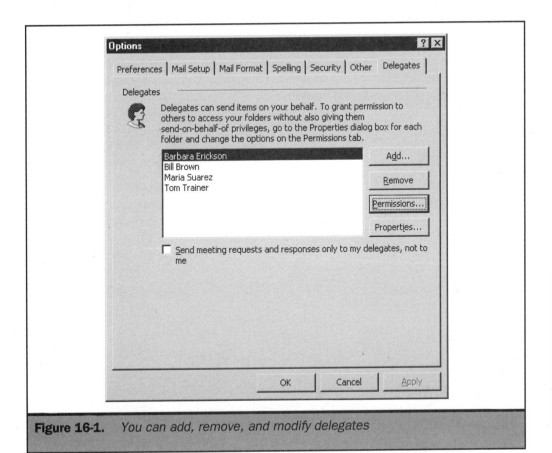

Figure 16-1.   *You can add, remove, and modify delegates*

If you don't see a Delegates tab in the Options dialog box, it's because you don't have the Delegate Access add-in installed. To install the add-in, have your original CD handy, choose Tools | Options, select the Other tab, click the Advanced Options button, click Add-In Manager, check Delegate Access, and click OK.

To give a user permission to act as a delegate on your behalf, click the Add button to open the Add Users dialog box, which displays all the users in the Global Address List. Select the user(s) you want to assign delegate permissions to, and click the Add button. Click OK to open the Delegate Permissions: [user name] dialog box shown in Figure 16-2.

If the Delegate Permissions dialog box does not appear and the user is simply added to the Delegates list on the Delegates tab, it means you've designated personal folders as your default delivery location. To assign delegate permissions, your default delivery location must be your server-based mailbox. To change the default delivery location, choose Tools | E-mail Accounts, select View Or Change Existing E-mail Accounts, and then click Next to view your existing e-mail accounts. From the Deliver New E-mail To The Following Location drop-down list, select your server-based mailbox. Click Finish to return to the active Outlook window. Although delegate access goes into effect immediately, you'll probably want to exit Outlook and restart it to re-create the Outlook Bar shortcuts, ensuring that they point to the server-based folders, rather than to the personal folders.

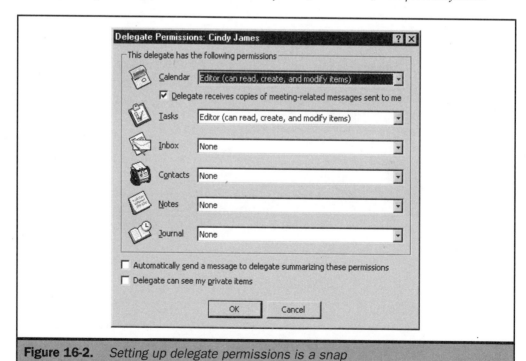

Figure 16-2.   *Setting up delegate permissions is a snap*

As you can see in Figure 16-2, six primary folders appear, each with its own drop-down list of permissions. By default, the Calendar and Tasks folders have Editor permissions already applied. The reason that both folders are delegated is that without permission to access the Tasks folder, a delegate who opens your Calendar folder will see his or her own TaskPad in the Day/Week/Month view, not yours. You can reset these or any other folder permissions by making the appropriate selection from the drop-down list. Your choices for permissions include the following:

- **None**   With the delegate permissions set to None, the user has absolutely no access whatsoever to the indicated folder.

- **Reviewer**   Assign Reviewer permissions to a delegate you want to authorize to read folder items and to respond to them on your behalf. A user with Reviewer permissions can open items in the folder, but cannot create new items or modify existing items.

- **Author**   A user with Author permissions can both read and create items in the designated folder. As with all permissions except None, an Author can also send and respond to items on your behalf. What a user with Author privileges cannot do is modify or delete existing items.

- **Editor**   An Editor is at the top of the delegate food chain, with permissions to read, create, modify, and delete items in the folder.

Tip   *Make sure the folder to which you're assigning delegates doesn't have Show Home Page By Default For This Folder checked on the Home Page tab of the folder's Properties dialog box. None of the delegate permissions allows a delegate to show, hide, or disable the folder home page, which means the delegate won't be able to view the contents of the folder.*

In addition to permissions, there are a few additional options on the Delegate Permissions dialog box:

- **Delegate receives copies of meeting-related messages sent to me**   This option is related to and dependent on the Calendar permissions. If you assign Editor permissions to a delegate, this option becomes available. When checked, it creates and sends the delegate a copy of any meeting-related e-mail you receive.

- **Automatically send a message to delegate summarizing these permissions**   Check this option to automatically notify a new delegate, via e-mail, of the permissions you've assigned.

- **Delegate can see my private items**   By default, delegates can see all items in a folder for which they have permissions, except items marked private. Check this option if you want the selected delegate to view all your items, including those marked private.

Once you're finished setting permissions and options, click OK to save the settings and return to the Delegates tab of the Options dialog box. Continue to add or modify delegates as needed. When you're done, click OK to close the Options dialog box and return to the active Outlook window.

Although the Delegate Permissions dialog box offers a limited set of permissions, you can customize them after you add a delegate by opening the Properties dialog box for the appropriate folder and modifying the delegate's permissions. You'll find the delegate has been added to the Permissions tab of the folder's Properties dialog box. After you modify the permissions and return to the Delegate Permissions dialog box, note that the user's permissions now read "Custom."

Setting Folder Permissions

While assigning delegate access is convenient, and provides other users with the ability to send e-mail on your behalf, it's not nearly as powerful as setting individual folder permissions. Setting folder permissions enables you to tailor the permissions for each user much more precisely. In addition, you can assign owner permissions that allow the user to do everything with the folder that you yourself can do. However, unless you assign owner permissions to a user, he or she will not be able to send e-mail on your behalf.

To set folder permissions, right-click the folder and select Properties from the shortcut menu to open the folder's Properties dialog box. Then click the Permissions tab to view the permissions options. See Chapter 18 for detailed information on setting folder permissions.

Accessing Another User's Calendar

 Of course, if you can give others access to your Calendar folder, the opposite is also true—they can give you access to theirs. Since you've already learned that anyone other than the owner of a folder must be granted permissions to access the folder, it should come as no surprise that the first thing you'll need is permissions set by the owner. Once that's taken care of, you're ready to access that user's Calendar.

Once you have the proper permissions, viewing another user's Calendar is easy. Choose File | Open | Other User's Folder to display the Open Other User's Folder dialog box. Enter the user's name, or click the Name button to display the Select Name dialog box from which you can select an existing user. Now, from the Folder drop-down list, choose Calendar (if you started in your Calendar folder, Calendar is already selected). Click OK and the user's Calendar folder appears in a new window. What you can do while viewing another user's calendar depends entirely upon the permissions you've been granted.

 MOUS EXAM PRACTICE

In this section you learned to access another user's Calendar folder. Start by asking a co-worker to provide you with the proper permissions to access his Calendar folder. Then open his Calendar with the Open Other User's Folder command. This would also be a good opportunity to see firsthand how different permissions affect your ability to perform certain actions in another user's folder. Ask your co-worker to assign you different permissions at various times, and try to access or edit information. Of course, be sure not to make any permanent changes to important information. Perhaps have the co-worker add a couple of fictitious appointments for you to work with.

Creating and Using Public Folders

Public folders are similar in many ways to private folders. They are containers used to store Outlook items or files, they possess most of the same properties and options, and they can be created, deleted, and modified by anyone with the proper permissions. Public folders are unlike private folders in that they are not part of the owner's mailbox, they reside on a public folder server (which may or may not be the same server the owner's mailbox is on), and their main purpose in life is to store information for public viewing and consumption.

Public folders are great for providing users with a forum in which to exchange ideas and opinions by posting messages on a given topic. If you want to disseminate company-wide information without actually passing it around, you can create public folders and post notices, policies, and other related information. You can even create public folders to share files and Outlook items and information.

Creating Public Folders

By default, creating public folders is a privilege assigned to every user on the Exchange Server network. However, most administrators will quickly put an end to that to prevent the chaos that usually ensues. Therefore, you will only be able to create public folders if you have been assigned that right by your system administrator.

If you have the necessary rights, start by pressing CTRL+SHIFT+E or by choosing File | New | Folder to open the Create New Folder dialog box, shown in Figure 16-3.

 You can also right-click All Public Folders in the Folder List and choose New Folder to display the Create New Folder dialog box with All Public Folders automatically selected as the location for the new folder.

Give the folder a unique, descriptive name by entering it in the Name field. Then, from the Folder Contains drop-down list, select the item type you want the folder to store.

Like private folders, public folders can store only one type of Outlook item. The next step is to select a location for the new folder. Since this is to be a public folder, you must select All Public Folders or one of its subfolders. You cannot select Public Folders or Favorites. If you do, Outlook politely informs you, when you click OK to create the folder, that you can't do it.

Note *Favorites is a special folder that holds copies of the existing folders you use most frequently. You can add any existing public folder to Public Folders\Favorites by dragging the existing folder and dropping it on Favorites.*

After you've made your selections, click OK and the new folder is created. That's all there is to it. One more thing: unless you've turned it off, the Add Shortcut To Outlook Bar? dialog box appears, asking if you want to add a shortcut for the new folder to the Outlook Bar.

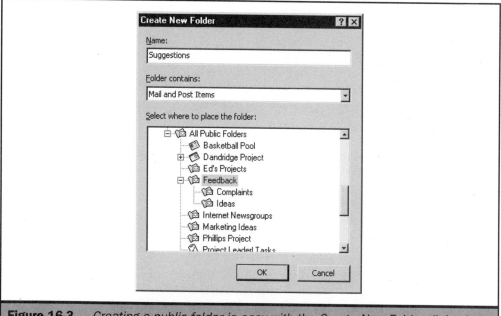

Figure 16-3. *Creating a public folder is easy with the Create New Folder dialog box*

Setting Public Folder Properties

Public folders, like private folders, have a number of options you can set to customize the way the folder looks and works. Accessing these options is the same for both public folders and private folders. Open the Folder List and right-click the public folder to open its Properties dialog box.

What you see depends not only on your permissions (owners see all available tabs), but also on the location of the public folder. Only folders located in the Public Folders\Favorites folder have Favorites and Synchronization tabs.

The similarity between public and private folder properties does not end with the method of accessing them. It also extends to who is permitted to modify folder settings. To edit a public folder's properties, you must have owner permissions. If you're not an owner, you'll only be able to view the General, Home Page, and Summary tabs, none of which you can change. The Summary tab indicates the owner and displays your permissions for the folder.

Most public folder properties are identical to those found in private folders. The major differences lie in the fact that you cannot AutoArchive public folders, and you can only designate public folders located in the Public Folders\Favorites folder as offline folders. The remainder of this section discusses the settings unique to public folders. For detailed information on private folder properties and permissions, see Chapter 18.

Setting Administrative Options

As you can see in Figure 16-4, the Administration tab of a public folder contains a number of options; all but one are available only in public folders. The first option, Initial View On Folder, is the only one available in both public and private folders. The remaining options are grayed out in private folders.

The Administration options include the following:

■ **Initial view on folder**   This option sets the default view that displays the very first time the user opens the folder. If the user never switches views, the designated view appears every time the folder opens. However, once the user switches to another view, this option no longer applies to the folder for that particular user. It still applies to other users who haven't yet opened the folder and switched to another view.

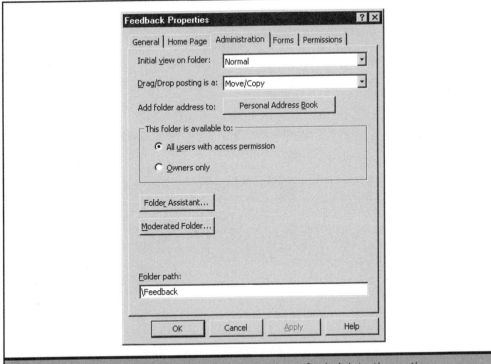

Figure 16-4.   *Public folder owners have a variety of administrative options at their disposal*

- **Drag/Drop posting is a** Use this option to change the default action resulting when you drag a mail item to the public folder and drop it. If you select Move/Copy, the item is simply moved or copied, depending on your choice. However, if you select Forward, the item is posted to the folder as a forwarded item. The original subject line is preceded by *FW*, indicating that it is a forward, and the From field contains your name, as the forwarder. This field has no effect on item types other than mail.

- **Add folder address to** This option enables you to add the selected folder to your Personal Address Book by clicking the Personal Address Book button. While you can add any folder type to the Personal Address Book, posting an e-mail message to a folder other than a mail folder doesn't make much sense. Therefore, you'll probably only use this option for public folders that contain mail items.

- **This folder is available to** You can use this option to block access to the folder by everyone except those with owner permissions. Although you can do the same thing by resetting default and individual permissions, this gives you a means of shutting off access quickly and temporarily. It comes in handy when you're performing basic maintenance on the folder, such as editing the folder design. All posts to the folder are bounced back to the sender(s) until you change the option.

- **Folder Assistant** Click this button to display the Folder Assistant dialog box, which lets you establish rules for handling items posted to the folder. You can create rules to return posted items to senders, automatically delete the items, forward them, or even respond to them with automatic replies. The rule criteria include From, Sent To, Subject, Message Body, Attachments, Size, Received Date, Importance, and Sensitivity.

- **Moderated Folder** If you use a public folder as a forum for a particular subject, you may want to control the messages that are posted to the folder. To ensure that only those messages that are truly on topic get posted, you can designate the folder a moderated folder and have all messages sent to a moderator who reviews the messages before posting them. Click the Moderated Folder button to open the Moderated Folder dialog box, which contains options for enabling the moderated folder option and assigning moderators. You can even choose to generate an automatic response as new items are received by the moderator.

- **Folder path** This field, which indicates the location of the folder on the server, is informational only.

When you're finished setting Administration options, click OK to save the changes and return to the active Outlook window.

Setting Favorite Options

When you add a public folder to the Public Folders\Favorites folder, Outlook makes a copy of the original folder. The Favorite tab, which is found only in the Properties dialog boxes of those copies located in the Public Folders\Favorites folder, lets you automate the process of adding copies of newly created subfolders (of the original folder) to the Public Folders\Favorites folder. For example, suppose you create a

Feedback folder in All Public Folders and add a copy to Public Folders\Favorites. When you add subfolders (i.e. Suggestions, Complaints, and so on) to the original Feedback folder, you can also have Outlook automatically add those subfolders to the copy of Feedback located in the Favorites folder.

As you can see in Figure 16-5, the Favorite tab contains only a single option.

By default, the option is deselected, which means no copies of subfolders you create in the original folder will be added to the copy in Public Folders\Favorites. If you want new subfolders of the original folder to be automatically copied to the Public Folders\Favorites folder, check the Add New Subfolders Of The Public Folder To This Folder option. You then have two choices for this option's settings:

- **Add immediate subfolders only**   Select this option if you only want the first level of subfolders to be copied. In other words, if you create a series of subfolders, Feedback\Suggestions\Manufacturing, only the subfolder immediately under the original folder—Suggestions, in this case—will be copied. Manufacturing will not be copied.

- **Add all subfolders**   With this option selected, every level will be copied, no matter how deep you go.

One thing to keep in mind about folders located in Public Folders\Favorites is that, while they are copies of an existing folder, there are some changes you can make

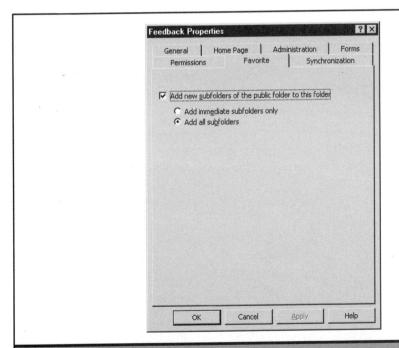

Figure 16-5.   *Adding copies of subfolders to the Public Folders\Favorites folder couldn't be any simpler*

to the copy that will affect the original, and others that will not. For instance, changing permissions in the copy, changes permission in the original. However, deleting the copy leaves the original intact.

Using Public Folders

Using public folders isn't much different from using private folders. For all folders except mail folders, select the folder in the Folder List and press CTRL+N to open a new form of the type appropriate for the selected folder. Fill out the form, and click Save And Close to save the new item in the selected folder. If you're in a public mail folder, pressing CTRL+N simply opens a standard e-mail message form. Sending an e-mail message from a public folder does nothing more than send the message to the recipient. Nothing is retained or stored in the public folder.

The most common use of public mail folders is for the purpose of posting messages related to a common topic, much like an Internet newsgroup. Posting simply adds the message to the folder. To post a message, open the public mail folder and press CTRL+SHIFT+S. A blank default post form appears. This is the form designated as the default form on the General tab of the folder's Properties dialog box. To use the standard post form shown in Figure 16-6, fill in the Subject line, type your message, and click Post to save it to the folder.

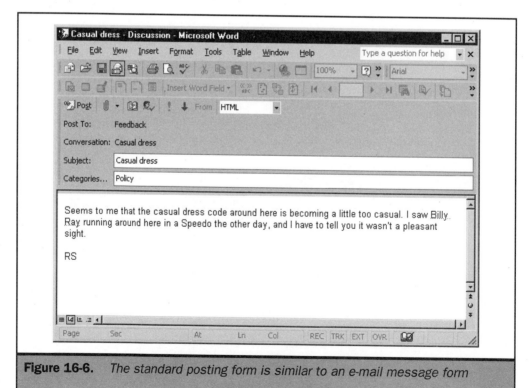

Figure 16-6. *The standard posting form is similar to an e-mail message form*

If the folder is unmoderated and you have permissions that allow you to both read and create items, you'll see your posted item almost immediately. If the folder is moderated, you may receive a reply informing you that each item must first be reviewed. Your post won't appear in the folder until after the moderator reviews and approves your message.

If you're already in the public folder to which you want to post, you can click the New button on the Standard toolbar to open a blank post form. If the folder has custom forms attached to it, you can also post by opening the Actions menu and selecting one of the forms at the bottom of the menu.

To read a message posted to a public folder, open the folder and double-click the message. As with a regular message, you have several options for dealing with a post. The Standard toolbar on the post form contains buttons that enable you to reply to or forward the post.

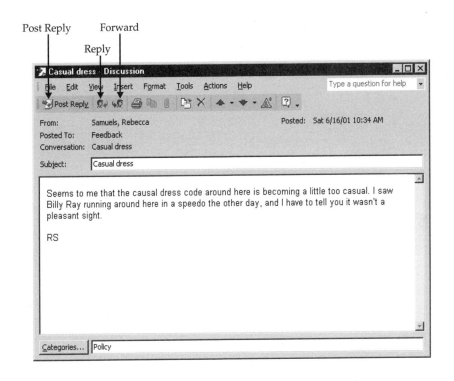

To post a response to the message, click the Post Reply button to open a reply form identical to the original post form. Enter a subject and include your response. Click Post to post it to the public folder. If you want to respond directly to the poster of the message, click the Reply button. This opens a standard e-mail message form with the poster's address entered in the To field, and *RE* added to the Subject line. Add your response and send the message. You can also forward a posted message to others.

Click the Forward button, enter the recipient(s), type a message if you wish, and send it on its way. Forwards and direct replies to senders have no effect on the posted messages or the public folder.

Users with the proper permissions can also delete posted items from a public folder. Right-click the item and select Delete from the shortcut menu. You can also select the posted item(s) and press DEL or click the Delete button on the Standard toolbar. You'll notice when you delete a posted item that the confirmation dialog box indicates the deletion is permanent. Posted items that are deleted are not transferred to the Deleted Items folder as are other deleted items.

One last thing about deleting posted items. The Tools menu contains a Recover Deleted Items command. Unfortunately, due to a bug in the program, the command doesn't work. Therefore, you cannot recover posted items you delete. Once you click Yes when asked if you're sure, they're gone for good.

MOUS Exam Expert Objectives Explored in Chapter 16

Objective	Activity	Heading
OL10E-3-1	View the calendar of another user	"Accessing Another User's Calendar"

The
Complete
Reference

Chapter 17

Working Offline
or on the Road

The advantages of using Outlook while being connected to an Exchange Server are numerous. The ability to send and receive mail, share folders and files, and have access to public folders are just a few of the benefits. However, what happens when you can't connect to the Exchange Server? Suppose you take a business trip or just want to work at home. And there's always the possibility that the Exchange Server will be down and you won't be able to log on. Fortunately, there are ways to have your cake and eat it too when you use Outlook with Microsoft Exchange Server. Outlook provides two features that enable you to continue working even when you're not directly connected to the Exchange Server. They are offline folders and Remote Mail.

Offline folders permit you to maintain exact duplicates of your mailbox folders on your hard disk. Unlike personal folders, offline folders are bi-directional. In other words, when you update offline folders, information is replicated in both sets of folders to ensure that offline folders and mailbox folders are the same. All you have to do is dial in to the Exchange Server and synchronize your offline folders with your mailbox folders. Any changes that have been made to your mailbox folder, such as newly arrived e-mail and changes made by a delegate, are downloaded to your offline folders. At the same time, any changes you've made to the offline folders are uploaded to the mailbox on the server.

Remote mail, on the other hand, lets you dial in to the Exchange Server (or Internet e-mail account) and send and retrieve e-mail while on the road. Remote mail has the added advantage of letting you download message headers only, thereby permitting you to pick and choose the messages you want to retrieve.

Using either of these features enables you to continue to reap the benefits of the Microsoft Exchange Server even when you're not able to maintain a constant connection.

Using Offline Folders

Offline folders are the key to working when a connection to the Exchange Server is unavailable. Offline folders are, as stated earlier, exact replicas of mailbox folders, whose identicalness is maintained by performing periodic synchronizations with the server-based mailbox folders.

When you enable offline folders, a special offline folder file with an .ost extension is created. By default, the primary folders Calendar, Contacts, Deleted Items, Inbox, Notes, Outbox, Sent Items, and Tasks are included. Outlook 2002, for the first time, enables you to selectively choose which primary folders to include as offline folders. As with previous versions, you can also select individual custom folders you create, as well as public folders for which you have permissions.

The size of your offline folder file reflects the combined size of your primary mailbox folders and any other folders you choose to include. Offline folders, like personal folders, have a size limit. As a matter of fact, both have the same size limitations, which are actually quite generous. An offline folder file (.ost) can contain a maximum of 16,384 folders, each of which can contain a maximum of 16,384 items. In addition, the total size of the file cannot exceed two gigabytes (2GB).

Enabling Offline Folders

Before you can use offline folders, you must first set them up. If you're not sure whether offline folders have been configured, press CTRL+ALT+S to open the Send/ Receive Groups dialog box. Select any of the existing groups, and click Edit to display the group's settings. Now, click the Inbox folder. If offline folders have not been configured, a dialog box appears, informing you of the fact and giving you the opportunity to configure them now. Click Yes to open the Offline Folder File Settings dialog box shown in Figure 17-1.

The first thing to do is change the name of the .ost file. By default, the offline folder file is named outlook.ost. If you have more than one profile, or if you share the computer with other users, you'll end up with a series of .ost files named outlook.ost, outlook1.ost, outlook2.ost, and so on. To avoid confusion, give the file a more easily identifiable name. Make life simple and use your profile name (i.e. rsamuels.ost or rebeccas.ost).

Finally, select the encryption setting. Your choices include

- **No Encryption**   Select this and the file is saved without encryption. The file size and compression ratio are almost identical to a compressible encryption file.
- **Compressible Encryption**   This is the default setting, which provides a certain amount of security while also offering the ability to significantly reduce the size of the file using file compression software such as WinZip. In a quick test, a 5622KB .ost file was reduced to 1132KB using WinZip 8.0.
- **Best Encryption**   If security is your first concern, select this setting. It provides a higher degree of encryption. The price you pay is a less compressible file. Using WinZip 8.0 to compress a 5648KB file resulted in a zipped file of 4075KB.
- **Compact Now**   This option is not available until after you've enabled offline folders and created the .ost file. When you return to the Offline Folder File Settings dialog box, you can use this button to compress your offline folder file

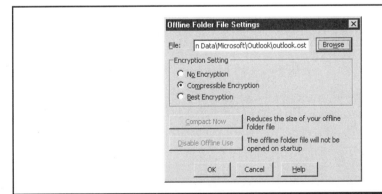

Figure 17-1. *Setting up offline folders is as easy as naming your offline folder file and selecting an encryption type*

manually. Although the file is compressed as you work, this button comes in handy by letting you compact the file immediately after deleting a large number of items.

- **Disable Offline Use**   Like the previous option, this one is only available after offline folders have been enabled. You can use it to entirely disable offline folders, or you can use it to change the folder name or the encryption settings. When you click this button, Outlook warns you that you won't be able to work offline. If you click Yes, offline folders are disabled.

When you're done, click OK to create the new file. A dialog box appears, asking if you want to create the file. Answer affirmatively, and you're ready to roll.

MOUS EXAM PRACTICE

In this section you learned to enable and configure offline folders. Since you're allowed only one set of offline folders per profile, you'll have to create multiple profiles to get any practice beyond the initial setup of offline folders for your primary profile. Therefore, you might want to create a series of profiles by making several copies of a profile without offline folders already configured (see Chapter 2 for more information). Then log on using the "clean" profiles, and open the Send/Receive Groups dialog box, edit one of the groups, and click the Inbox folder. Go through the entire setup process, and then exit Outlook and log back on using a different profile. Repeat the process until you're comfortable with configuring offline folders.

Setting Folders Options

By default, certain primary Outlook folders are automatically included in offline folders. However, some primary folders are not included, nor are public or custom folders you create. To add these folders or exclude folders included by default, you'll have to adjust the Send/Receive Groups settings.

Choose Tools | Send/Receive Settings | Define Send/Receive Groups or press CTRL+ALT+S to access the Send/Receive Groups dialog box seen in Figure 17-2.

If you check out the bottom of the dialog box, you'll find a section called When Outlook Is Offline. It provides two options for events that take place while you're working offline:

- **Include this group in send/receive (F9)**   First select a group in the display list at the top of the dialog box. Until you create new send/receive groups, All Accounts, which is the only one available, is selected by default. After you make your selection, check this option to include the account(s) in the group when you use the Send/Receive All (F9) command.

- **Schedule an automatic send/receive every ___minutes**   To keep your offline folders current without having to worry about manually synchronizing them, check this option and select a time interval between automatic synchronizations.

This comes in handy if you're working offline and want to automatically keep track of e-mail or updates to public folders, but can't maintain a constant connection to the network.

Remember, these settings take effect when you're offline. Therefore, for them to work, you must have an available connection to the network, either via a local area network (LAN) or a dial-up connection.

The next step is to customize the offline folder settings to properly reflect your needs. Double-click the All Accounts group to open the Send/Receive Settings - All Accounts dialog box shown in Figure 17-3.

If it's not selected, click the Microsoft Exchange Server icon to display the settings for your Microsoft Exchange Server account. The first thing you'll probably want to do is make sure all the folders you need (or want) offline are included. Add a check mark to folders you want included, and remove the check mark from those you want excluded. Next, make sure both the Send Mail Items and Receive Mail Items options are checked. This ensures that synchronization works both ways (from the server mailbox to your local .ost file or vice versa). Select the folder and click the Filter Selected Folder button to display the Filter dialog box. See Chapter 22 for more information on creating filters.

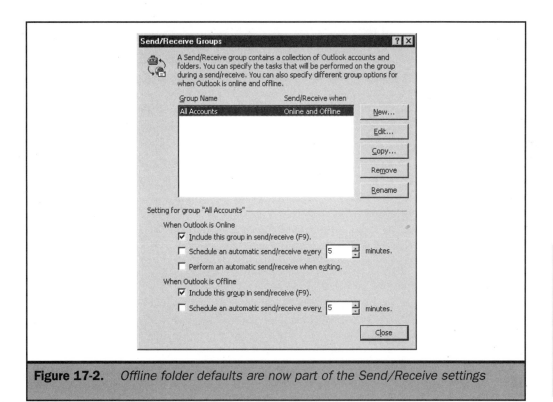

Figure 17-2.   *Offline folder defaults are now part of the Send/Receive settings*

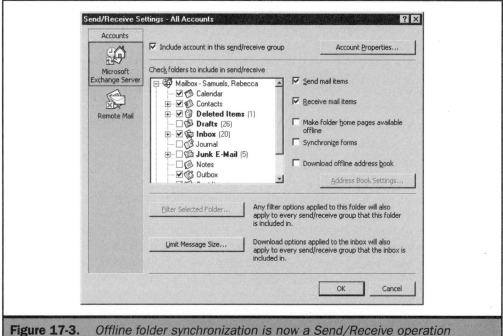

Figure 17-3.   *Offline folder synchronization is now a Send/Receive operation*

The dialog box also contains a number of options you can use to extend the usefulness of offline folders:

- **Make folder home pages available offline**   If you've assigned home pages to any of your folders, you can include them in the offline folder file by checking this option.

- **Synchronize forms**   If you use custom forms with Outlook, check this option to include those forms in the offline folder file.

- **Download offline address book**   If you want to keep a copy of the offline address book in your offline folders, check this option. By default, the Exchange Server uses the entire Global Address List (GAL) as the offline address book. However, starting with Microsoft Exchange Server 5.5, administrators were given the ability to create subsets of the Global Address List to use as offline address books. This can be a great help, especially to mobile users who have neither the need nor the space for the entire Global Address List.

- **Address Book Settings**   Click the Settings button to display the Offline Address Book dialog box. Here you'll find the following options for customizing the offline address book:

  - **Download changes since last Send/Receive**   Unless there have been a large number of deletions in the offline address book, you'll probably want to leave this setting enabled. When it's checked, only new and changed entries are downloaded during a synchronization. Since downloading an entire Global Address List can be quite time-consuming, it's best to do so only when it's absolutely necessary.

  - **Information to download**   Decide how much information you want to download. You'll probably want to select Full Details, unless a lot of detailed information is maintained in the Global Address List, in which case downloading may take quite a while.

  - **Choose address book**   If your administrator has created subsets of the Global Address List, they'll be listed here. Select the one you want to use. If the administrator has not created any subsets, or if the server is running Exchange 4.0 or 5.0, neither of which allows the creation of subsets, you'll have one choice only—the entire Global Address List.

Setting Connection Options

If you plan to work offline, you'll want to set the Connection Options to ensure that the choice to work offline or online is yours to make. By default, Outlook assumes you want to log on to the Exchange Server. Therefore, if you want Outlook to give you the option to work online or offline, you'll have to modify the connection settings. To access the settings, choose Tools | E-mail Accounts, select View Or Change Existing E-Mail Accounts, and double-click Microsoft Exchange Server to display the Exchange Server Settings. Click the More Settings button to open the Microsoft Exchange Server dialog box shown in Figure 17-4.

Select Manually Control Connection State, and check the Choose The Connection Type When Starting option. With this option checked, each time you start the program, Outlook asks if you want to connect to the network or work offline. Once you check the Connection Type When Starting option, you can ignore the next one, Default Connection State. The selection you make in the Default Connection State determines how Outlook starts. However, it only applies if you choose not to have Outlook prompt you for a connection type by checking the previous option. The first choice automatically connects you to the network when you start Outlook; the second choice starts Outlook offline. The last option, Seconds Until Server Connection Timeout, lets you determine how long Outlook should attempt to make a connection before alerting you that it is unable to connect.

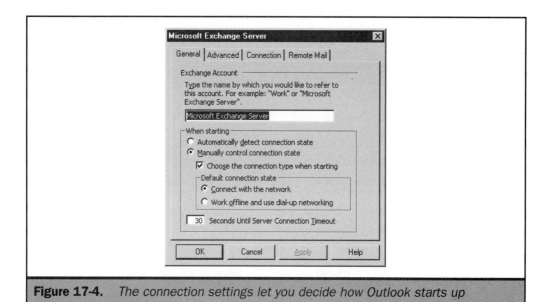

Figure 17-4.   *The connection settings let you decide how Outlook starts up*

Creating a Dial-Up Networking Connection

If you plan to work offline and synchronize (send/receive) from a remote location, you'll want to set up a Dial-Up Networking connection through which you can log on to the Exchange Server and synchronize your offline folders. You'll also need a Dial-Up Networking connection if you plan to use Remote Mail, which is discussed later in this chapter.

To create a Dial-Up Networking connection, choose Tools | E-mail Accounts, and select View Or Change Existing E-Mail Accounts. Then double-click an existing e-mail account to display the E-mail Accounts dialog box. Now click the More Settings button to open the [account name] dialog box. Don't give up on me yet, we're almost there. Click the Connection tab and you're ready to start.

Select Connect Using My Phone Line, which immediately enables the Modem options. If you have existing dial-up connections, they appear on the drop-down list. To create a new dial-up connection, click the Add button to launch the Make New Connection Wizard, which walks you through creating a new connection. Check with your network administrator for the correct phone number to use. To modify an existing connection, select it in the drop-down list and click the Properties button.

MOUS EXAM PRACTICE
Actually, this one's pretty easy and doesn't require a great deal of practice to master since the wizard does most of the work for you. The most difficult part of the whole process is getting to the wizard. Therefore, it's a good idea to run through the steps necessary to open the Connection tab of an e-mail account settings dialog box, until it's second nature.

THE MICROSOFT EXCHANGE SERVER ADVANTAGE

Synchronizing Offline Folders

Synchronizing offline folders is the process of connecting to the Exchange Server and making your mailbox folders and your offline folders exact replicas of one another. This is accomplished by copying any new items in either folder to the other. In addition, items deleted in one folder are deleted in the other. Finally, any modified items are copied from the folder with the most current version of the item, replacing the older version of the item in the other folder. For example, suppose you create a new contact on the server, delete an e-mail message on the server, and change the start time for an appointment in your offline folders. When you synchronize, the new contact is copied from the server to the offline folder file, the e-mail message is deleted in the offline folder, and the modified appointment is copied from the offline folder to the server, where it replaces the original. In Outlook 2002 synchronization has become part of the send/receive process.

You can connect to the Exchange Server either through your local area network (LAN) or through a Dial-Up Networking connection. However, be advised that synchronizing offline folders over a Dial-Up Networking connection may be much slower than connecting to the LAN. You may even experience timeouts. If that's the case, you might be better off using Remote Mail to download your e-mail messages and waiting until you can connect to the Exchange Server through the LAN before synchronizing.

Using Automatic Synchronization

The Send/Receive Groups dialog box (CTRL+ALT+S), seen again in Figure 17-5, contains several options to automate the synchronization (send/receive) process.

Begin by selecting the send/receive group for which you want to set the options. Now, move to the Setting For Group "Name Of Selected Group" section, where you'll find the following automatic synchronization (send/receive) options:

- **When Outlook Is Online** These options apply only when you're working in the online mode.

  - **Schedule an automatic send/receive every ___minutes** If you want to continuously update your offline folders while you're working online, check this option and enter the number of minutes between synchronizations. This comes in handy if your server is experiencing problems and going down frequently. If you get bounced off the network, you can keep working offline with up-to-date information.

  - **Perform an automatic send/receive when exiting** With this option checked, Outlook automatically synchronizes all folders you've selected as offline folders, each time you exit Outlook.

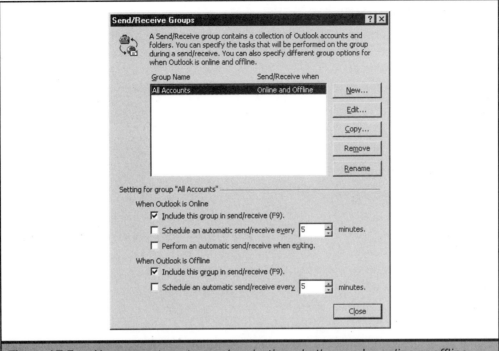

Figure 17-5. *You can automate synchronization whether you're online or offline*

■ **When Outlook is Offline**   These options only apply when you're working in the Offline mode.

■ **Schedule an automatic send/receive every ___ minutes**   If you get a lot of e-mail or share your folders with others who make frequent changes, you may want to check this option, and enter a time interval for the automatic synchronization. It ensures that you always have the most up-to-date information while you're working offline. Outlook automatically connects to the server using the designated Dial-Up Networking connection at the specified time interval and automatically synchronizes the selected folder group.

When you're finished configuring the synchronization options, click Close to save your changes and return to the active Outlook view.

Synchronizing Manually

If you're one of those folks who still prefers a standard transmission over an automatic so you have complete control over your car, you may prefer manual synchronization of your offline folders as well. Synchronizing manually gives you the option to synchronize all offline folders, a single folder, or a send/receive group. In addition, you can synchronize anytime you get the urge.

To synchronize manually, choose Tools | Send/Receive to display the submenu of Send/Receive commands.

Send All	
This Folder (Microsoft Exchange Server)	Shift+F9
Send and Receive All	F9
1 Microsoft Exchange Server	
2 All Accounts	
3 Inbox/Calendar only	
Work With Headers	▶
Download Address Book...	
Free/Busy Information	

Note   *Depending on the set of folders (server-based mailbox or personal folders), and the specific folder you're in, the commands will appear somewhat differently.*

The following commands can be used to perform a manual synchronization:

- ■ **This Folder**   If you're in an Exchange Server mailbox folder, the command is This Folder (Microsoft Exchange Server). To synchronize the currently open folder, use this command. If the folder you're in is not designated as an offline folder, this command is grayed out. You can also use the shortcut key, SHIFT+F9, to activate this command.

- ■ **Send and Receive All**   Use this command to synchronize all folders designated as offline folders in any of the send/receive groups for which you enabled (the default state) the Include This Group In Send/Receive (F9) option in the Send/Receive Groups dialog box. You'll also note that the command has a shortcut key assigned to it. By pressing F9, you can dispense with the menu, and perform a manual synchronization of all folders from anywhere in Outlook.

The next group of commands on the submenu lets you select specific send/receive groups to synchronize. If you have a Microsoft Exchange Server e-mail account, that appears first on the list. The next command is All Accounts. This command performs a send/receive operation for the default All Accounts send/receive group. Any additional send/receive groups you've created will also appear on the list. Selecting a specific send/receive group synchronizes that group only.

The last synchronization command is Download Address Book. This command opens the Offline Address Book dialog box, which provides options for downloading the offline address book. See "Setting Folder Options" earlier in this chapter for details.

Note

If you're connected to the Exchange Server, synchronization takes place as soon as you click the desired command. However, if you're working offline, Outlook must first connect to the Exchange Server using the Dial-Up Networking connection selected in the Dial-Up Networking tab of the Microsoft Exchange Server. Once the connection is established, synchronization proceeds.

As you can see, manual synchronization involves nothing more than selecting the appropriate command and letting Outlook do the rest. As the synchronization is occurring, you'll see its progress being reported in the Outlook window status bar.

MOUS

MOUS EXAM PRACTICE
In this section you learned how to synchronize your offline folders, both automatically and manually. Begin by opening the Send/Receive Groups dialog box and setting the automatic synchronizing (send/receive) options for the accounts in your All Accounts group. The first time around, set up a schedule to synchronize every one minute just so you can see how it works, without waiting around forever. Just be sure to go back and either disable the option or set it for a more reasonable send/receive schedule. Next, try your hand at manually synchronizing. Start by using the Send And Receive All command. At this point you'll have to go back and add (or copy) some new items into each of the folders you included when you set up offline folders so you have something to synchronize. Now, return to the Send/Receive submenu and synchronize individual folders.

Using Remote Mail

Remote Mail enables you to access your Microsoft Exchange Server mailbox while on the road, using a dial-up connection. Its advantages are easy to spot. You can send and receive your server-based e-mail while on the road, and by downloading headers only, you can decide which messages you want to retrieve. This can save time and money when using a Dial-Up Networking connection.

To use Remote Mail, you may need to create a Dial-Up Networking connection. For information on setting up a Dial-Up Networking connection, see "Creating a Dial-Up Networking Connection" earlier in this chapter.

Configuring Remote Mail

If you plan to use Remote Mail, you must have offline folders enabled. See the section entitled "Using Offline Folders" earlier in this chapter for information on configuring offline folders. Once offline folders are enabled, choose Tools | E-mail Accounts, select View Or Change Existing E-Mail Accounts, and click Next to display your existing e-mail accounts. Double-click Microsoft Exchange Server to view the account settings. Click the More Settings button, and then move to the Remote Mail tab to display the Remote Mail configuration options, shown in Figure 17-6.

Here's what you'll find:

- **Process marked items**   Choose this option if you plan to manually select individual e-mail messages for download.

- **Retrieve items that meet the following conditions**   If you want to automate the process by creating a filter that determines which messages are downloaded, choose this option.

- **Filter**   The Filter button only becomes available when you select the previous option. Click the button to display the Filter dialog box. Since it only applies to messages, it is less sophisticated than the Filter dialog box used to customize Outlook views. However, it still provides a variety of filtering criteria. If the simple options in the Filter dialog box aren't sufficient, click the Advanced button for more options. Be advised that the filter applies only to those messages whose headers you download first and then mark for retrieval. The filter overrides any selections you make in marking headers. Remote Mail filters do not apply when you use the Send and Receive commands.

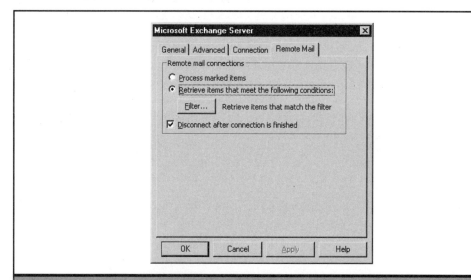

Figure 17-6.   *Remote Mail options let you decide how and when messages are transferred*

■ **Disconnect after connection is finished** To reduce the risk of keeping the connection open after you finish downloading your messages, you can check this option and Outlook will automatically close the connection after Remote Mail is finished.

You may want to ignore the Remote Mail filters since they are confusing and provide little benefit, and instead set up rules on your server-based mailbox. Have those rules channel into your Inbox only the mail you normally want while on the road. When you use Remote Mail on the road and retrieve your messages, the filters will already have been applied back at the server. In the event you decide you want to get those messages that have been filtered out, you can always perform a synchronization that includes the mail folders in which the filtered messages are stored.

When you're finished setting the Remote Mail options, click OK until you return to the Exchange Server Settings dialog box. Click Next, and then click Finish to return to the active Outlook window. You're now ready to begin using Remote Mail to send and receive e-mail.

MOUS EXAM PRACTICE
In this section you learned to set up remote mail. Like a number of features in Outlook 2002, the hardest part is getting to the configuration options. Run the steps outlined in this section until you can easily access the Remote Mail tab of the Microsoft Exchange Server dialog box. Then configure the remote mail options.

Sending and Receiving Remote E-mail

When it comes to retrieving your e-mail using Remote Mail, you have several options. You can manually download your remote mail, or you can automate the process. To manually download remote mail, establish your connection and choose Tools | Send/Receive | Work With Headers to display the submenu, which contains the following commands:

■ **Download Headers From** Selecting this command displays another submenu containing an All Accounts command as well as each of your existing e-mail accounts. It's important to understand that All Accounts means just that. This command does not refer to the All Accounts send/receive group, but to all of your existing e-mail accounts, regardless of what send/receive group they're enabled in. Downloading headers from any group means that the message itself will not be downloaded, only the header information, which includes Attachment icon, From, Received, Subject, and Size. Double-clicking on the header opens a dialog box offering choices on how to deal with the message, which is still residing on the e-mail server.

■ **Mark/Unmark Messages**   This command is useful only in dealing with message headers you've downloaded. Once the headers are in your mailbox, use this command to mark them for downloading or deletion. Begin by selecting the headers in your Inbox that you want to mark. Then access the appropriate command on the Mark/Unmark Messages submenu. The commands are pretty much self-explanatory. However, be aware that when you mark a message for download, the message is delivered to your Inbox, and the original message on the server is deleted. Therefore, if you wish to leave a copy on the server so you can retrieve it again at a later time, use the Mark To Download Message Copy command.

■ **Process Marked Headers From**   After you use the previous command to mark messages, use this command to process those that you've marked. Simply select the desired e-mail account, and the appropriate action is taken.

If you download headers from an Internet e-mail account, Outlook does not display the attachment icon in the headers of messages that contain attachments. One way to gauge if a message includes an attachment is to take a look at the Size field. Since most messages are relatively small, the size of a message can be a good indicator of the presence (or absence) of an attachment.

In addition to using the Mark/Unmark Messages commands, you can double-click a header in the Inbox and make a selection from the dialog box that pops up. Your choices include the ability to unmark a marked item, mark the item for download, mark the item to download a copy, or mark the item for deletion from the server. There's one last way you can mark messages for downloading. Right-click a header in the Inbox and select Mark To Download Message(s) or Mark To Download Message Copy, from the shortcut menu. As far as sending remote mail messages is concerned, simply compose them and send them as you normally would. They'll sit in the Outbox until you use one of the Send commands (Send, Send And Receive All, and so on).

MOUS EXAM PRACTICE

In this section you learned to send and receive remote mail. Since sending requires nothing more than the normal process, except perhaps, one extra step, you'll want to concentrate on the receiving of remote mail. Make sure there is mail on the servers from which you want to download remote mail (send yourself some to be on the safe side). Then establish your connection, and try downloading headers first. Next, mark the headers using the various marking commands. Finally, process the marked headers.

Working with Personal Folders

Personal folders are Outlook folders stored on your local computer rather than on the Microsoft Exchange Server. They're great for storing important Outlook items that you want to remove (or copy) from your server-based mailbox but don't want to archive. If you have personal folders added to your profile, you can move and copy Outlook items between your mailbox and your personal folders with ease.

Adding Personal Folders

Adding personal folders is easy. Choose File | Data File Management to open the Outlook Data Files (Figure 17-7).

If you haven't already added any personal folder, or a Hotmail account, which uses personal folders to store e-mail, the File | Data File Management option may not be available. In that case choose File | New | Outlook Data File to display the New Outlook Data File. Skip the next paragraph and follow the instructions for adding personal folders after the New Outlook Data File dialog box appears.

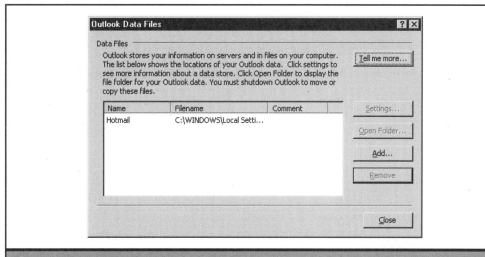

Figure 17-7.   *The Data Files dialog box displays all your existing services*

The dialog box displays any personal folders or archive files existing in the current profile. Neither exist by default. While personal folders can be added here, archive folders cannot. They are added the first time that you perform an archive. However, after that, they appear in the Outlook Data Files dialog box, and can be configured and even deleted.

To add personal folders, click the Add button, which displays the New Outlook Data File dialog box.

Select Personal Folders File and click OK to display the Create Or Open Data File dialog box. Enter a name for the file in the File Name field. Be sure to make it unique and easily identifiable. It's actually a good idea to give it the same name as your profile to avoid confusion. If you previously created a personal folder file that you wish to use in this profile, select it from the list or use the Look In drop-down list to locate it. Click Open to display the Create Microsoft Personal Folders dialog box, shown in Figure 17-8.

The text you enter in the Name field appears in the Outlook Folder List, as well as in the Outlook Data Files dialog box. The Encryption Setting option lets you decide just how much security you want applied to the file. For most users, Compressible Encryption is a good choice.

Adding a password is a good idea, especially if you share the computer with other users. Enter a password, and then enter it a second time to make sure you haven't made any typos. You can check the Save This Password In Your Password List to save yourself the trouble of having to enter it each time you want to access the personal folders. However, this means that anyone who logs on using your profile will also have complete access to your personal folders.

Setting Personal Folder Options

To change personal folder properties, open the Outlook Data Files dialog box (File | Data File Management) and double-click Personal to open the Personal Folders dialog box shown in Figure 17-9.

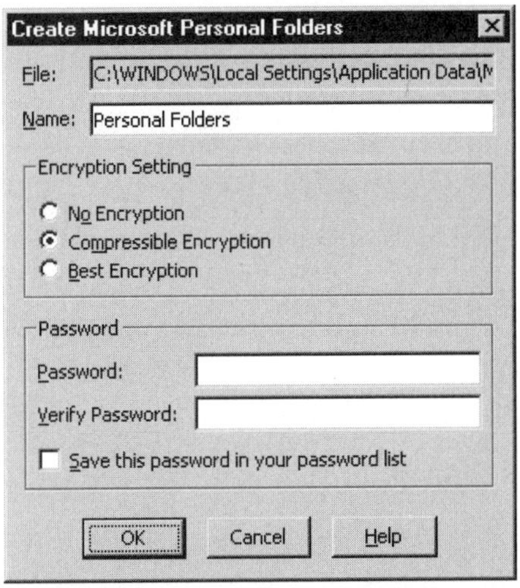

Figure 17-8.   *Set up your personal folders to suit your needs*

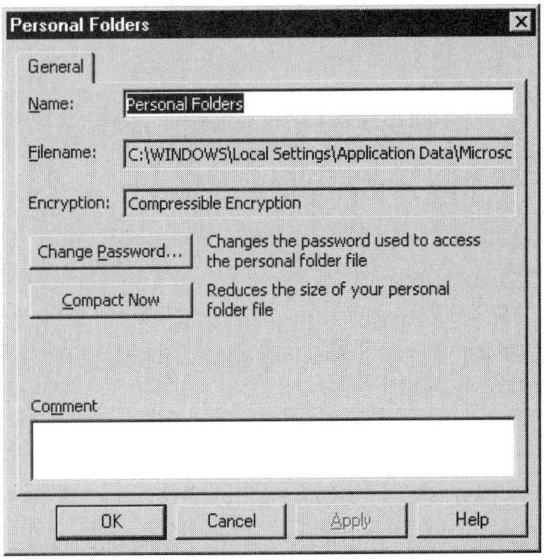

Figure 17-9.   *Customizing personal folders is easy*

You'll find the following options available in the Personal Folders dialog box:

- **Name**   Once again, you have the opportunity to change the name of this set of personal folders.

- **Filename**   This field is informational only and cannot be changed. It displays the path to the .pst file for this set of personal folders.

- **Encryption**   This field is also unchangeable and is here for informational purposes only. It displays the level of encryption selected when the file was created.

- **Change Password**   If you want to change your password (which you should, on a regular basis), this is the place to do it.

- **Compact Now**   Deleting Outlook items leaves a lot of empty space in a .pst file, but does not reduce the size of the file. Click the Compact Now button to recoup that empty space and shrink the size of the file.

- **Comment**   Use this text field to add any miscellaneous information you want.

Once you've configured your personal folder options, you're ready to use them. You can create, copy, move, and delete items in personal folders just as you can in your mailbox folders. However, remember, personal folder information is stored locally on your hard disk, not on the server. Therefore, unless you've designated your personal folders as the default delivery location, you'll probably want to do all your work in your mailbox folders and use the personal folders for storing important information you want safe and available anytime.

MOUS

MOUS EXAM PRACTICE
In this section you learned to create personal folders and configure them. Start by adding a set of personal folders to your profile. Since Outlook permits you to add multiple sets of personal folders, add a couple more to get some practice. However, be sure to give them names like Test1, Test2, and so on. This way you can use them to practice deleting personal folders later on. Next, try your hand at setting the personal folder options. Add a password and try opening your personal folders. Initially you might want to write it down until you've got it memorized. Next, change the password. Now try copying some of your existing items into your personal folders. When you feel comfortable working with personal folders, delete all except the ones you plan to use for yourself.

MOUS Exam Expert Objectives Explored in Chapter 17

Objective	Activity	Heading
OL10E-1-1	Configure offline folders	"Enabling Offline Folders"
OL10E-1-2	Synchronize folders	"Synchronizing Offline Folders"
OL10E-1-3	Set up remote mail	"Configuring Remote Mail"
OL10E-1-4	Download messages by remote access	"Sending and Receiving Remote E-mail"
OL10E-2-3	Create and use personal folders	"Working with Personal Folders"
OL10E-7-6	Configure a Dial-Up Networking connection	"Creating a Dial-Up Networking Connection"

The Complete Reference

Part VI

Getting More Out of Outlook

The
Complete
Reference

Chapter 18

Organizing and
Managing Folders

469

In case you hadn't noticed, everything in Outlook revolves around folders. Whether it's e-mail, scheduling, or contact management, each Outlook component is a folder. Folders are, in fact, nothing more than containers for holding related pieces of information. In addition to the information itself, Outlook folders contain two things: forms for entering information and views for displaying information. In this chapter, you'll learn to create, move, copy, delete, and modify folders.

Folders Overview

Each Outlook folder is unique in that it can only hold one type of Outlook item. For example, you cannot store appointment items in a mail folder or vice versa. When you create a folder, you must designate the type of item it will hold. Once you make that decision, you cannot change it.

When you attempt to move an item into a folder of a different type, the item you move is converted to the item type normally stored in the target folder. For instance, if you drop a task item in an e-mail folder, you end up with an e-mail message that includes the task information. Drop an e-mail message into a note folder and you end up with a new note that contains the e-mail message information.

The folder hierarchy begins with Outlook Today, which is simply an internal Web page presenting an overview of the server-based mailbox contents. The level below Outlook Today contains the primary folders: Calendar, Contacts, Deleted Items, Drafts, Inbox, Journal, Notes, Outbox, Sent Items, and Tasks. Personal and public folders, when added, are on a par with the mailbox.

To view the existing folder hierarchy, open the Folder List by choosing View | Folder List. If the Advanced toolbar is displayed, you can click the Folder List button to display the Folder List (see Figure 18-1).

> **Tip** *You can also click the current folder name on the Folder banner. Use this option to toggle the Folder List on and off for a quick peek. It drops the list on top of the Information viewer and obscures whatever you're working on. To keep the Folder List permanently in view, click the yellow pushpin in the top right corner. This also incorporates the Folder List into the Information viewer so all the folder information is visible.*

As you can see in Figure 18-1, subfolders are indicated by a plus or minus sign to the left of the parent folder. A plus sign indicates the subfolders are currently collapsed; a minus sign indicates they are expanded.

Working with Folders

The first order of business is to access the contents of the individual folders. Outlook provides a couple of different ways to do this. You can use the Outlook Bar or the Folder List to open an Outlook folder. By default, all primary Outlook folders are

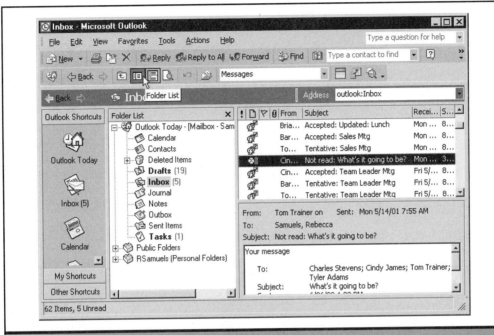

Figure 18-1. *The Folder List provides a tree-like view of the Outlook folder hierarchy*

represented on the Outlook Bar by a shortcut. However, not all folder shortcuts are in the Outlook Shortcuts group. Some are located in the My Shortcuts group, which means you may have to open that group to access shortcuts to some primary Outlook folders. The Folder List, on the other hand, contains all existing folders. The only problem here is that you have to display the Folder List to use it. Take your pick: both the Outlook Bar and the Folder List work equally well. It's just a matter of preference. In addition to clicking the shortcut or folder name, you can right-click either and select Open. It hardly seems worth the extra trouble. What does make the extra effort worthwhile is right-clicking and selecting Open In New Window when you want to display a folder in a separate window.

Before moving on, it's important to note that for many folder operations outlined in the upcoming sections, you must either be the owner of the folder or have permissions that enable you to create, edit, or delete items as needed.

Creating Folders

When you begin using Outlook, you start with a framework of primary folders that take care of your basic e-mail and information management needs. As you utilize more and more features, you may find that the initial handful of folders just isn't enough to organize all your data.

The first place you'll probably encounter a need for new folders is in organizing your e-mail. Just as with your paper correspondence, you'll want to retain copies of important e-mail messages. And, as with your hard copy correspondence, you'll find it much easier to track your e-mail messages if you file them in separate, clearly labeled folders with other related messages. When the time comes, simply create new folders for all the different categories of e-mail you save.

When you create new folders, save yourself time and aggravation by planning a logical hierarchy before you start. For example, if you're creating folders to hold e-mail, put them under the Inbox. If you're going to keep track of vendor e-mail, create a Vendor subfolder in the Inbox, then create a separate subfolder for each vendor.

While it would make sense to place new e-mail folders under the Inbox, there is no hard and fast rule that says you must. You can create new folders on the same level as the primary folders or under any existing folder you choose. You can even add subfolders that contain different items than the parent folder.

To create a new folder from anywhere within Outlook, press CTRL+SHIFT+E to display the Create New Folder dialog box, shown in Figure 18-2.

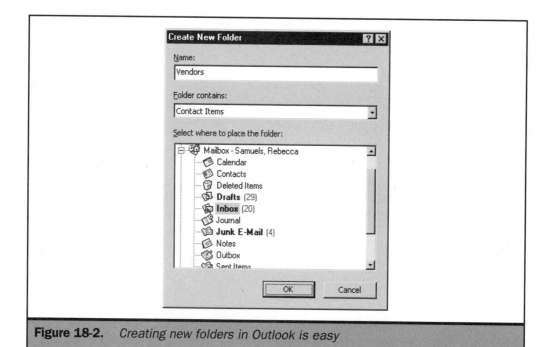

Figure 18-2. *Creating new folders in Outlook is easy*

Select the type of item the new folder will hold, then enter a name for the new folder in the Name field. To choose the parent folder for the new folder, enter the folder name in the Location field. You can also select a folder from the Location drop-down list, or click the Search button located to the right of the Location field, to display the Select Folder dialog box. You can place the new folder on any level except the first level. Only the mailbox, personal folders, and public folders can reside on the top level. Click OK to create the new folder.

Here are a few other ways to create a new folder:

- Choose File | New | Folder from the Menu bar.
- Click the down arrow to the right of the New button on the Standard toolbar, and select Folder from the drop-down menu.
- Right-click the Folder banner of the current folder and select New Folder from the shortcut menu.
- Right-click a folder in the Folder List and select New Folder from the shortcut menu.

If you happen to be a folder fanatic, you may want to add the Folder command (or New Folder command; they're the same) to one of your toolbars or menus. Right-click a visible toolbar and select Customize to open the Customize dialog box. Click the Commands tab and select File in the Categories list. Now drag the Folder (or New Folder) command and drop it on the toolbar or menu of your choice. For more on customizing toolbars and menus, see Chapter 24.

When you create a new folder, Outlook immediately asks if you want to add a shortcut for the new folder to the Outlook Bar.

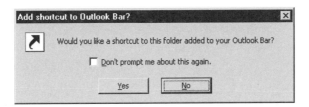

Unless this is a folder you plan to use regularly, you probably don't need a shortcut for it. As a matter of fact, most new folders will probably not require a shortcut on the Outlook Bar. Therefore, you might want to check the Don't Prompt Me About This Again option to avoid having to answer the question every time you create a new folder. Not only that, but adding a shortcut is easy. You can do it any time you want. Just open the Folder List, drag the folder to the Outlook Bar, and drop it between two existing folders. To remove a shortcut, right-click the shortcut and select Remove From Outlook Bar from the shortcut menu.

As soon as you create a new folder, it is added to the Folder List on the level you indicated when creating it. Outlook automatically sorts the Folder List alphabetically by folder name so the new folder appears accordingly. Unfortunately, you cannot set a different sort order nor can you sort the list manually.

Copying Existing Folders

You can also create a new folder by making a duplicate of an existing folder. This is an easy way to create a new folder that contains many of the same settings as an existing folder. The settings transferred depend to some extent on the folder type. For instance, contacts folders that are copied include general settings, home page settings, activities settings, permissions settings, forms settings, and administration settings—actually, everything but the synchronization and Outlook Address Book settings.

The only potential problem associated with using the Copy command is that you also duplicate the contents of the source folder. In some cases, this may be an advantage rather than a problem. Suppose, for example, you want to split your Contacts folder into a business contacts folder and a personal contacts folder. Using the Copy command enables you to create two new folders with most of the settings of the original folder as well as all the contacts. You can then filter out the non-business contacts from the business folder and delete them, and your business contacts folder is ready. Do the same for your personal contacts folder and you're finished.

The quickest way to copy a folder is to open the Folder List and right-drag (hold down the right mouse button instead of the left when dragging) the folder to a new location. Drop it on the target folder and select Copy from the shortcut menu.

If you prefer to use a method other than drag and drop, you can use the Copy command. Start by displaying the Folder List. Next, right-click the folder you want to copy, and select Copy "[folder name]" from the shortcut menu to open the Copy Folder dialog box.

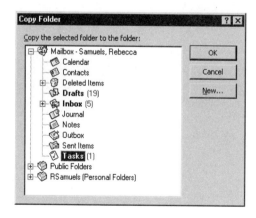

You can also copy a folder by clicking an Outlook Bar shortcut to open the desired source folder. Then choose File | Folders | Copy "[folder name]" from the Menu bar to display the Copy Folder dialog box.

From the Copy The Selected Folder To The Folder display list, choose the folder in which you want the copy placed. The folder you select here becomes the parent folder of the copied folder. If you want to create a new parent folder, click the New button and follow the instructions for creating a new folder. When you've selected the parent folder for your copy, click OK to create the copy and return to the active view. At this point, you can adjust the folder's contents and settings as necessary.

Using the Copy Folder Design Command

The Copy Folder Design command is a hybrid command that does not create a new folder, but rather, replaces some design elements of an existing folder with those of a different existing folder. You can use the command in conjunction with the New Folder command to create a customized folder. Unlike the Copy command, Copy Folder Design does not transfer the same group of customized settings to the target folder.

Note *To use the Copy Folder Design command, the Exchange Extensions Commands add-in (not to be confused with the Exchange Extensions Property Pages add-in) must be installed. To check or to install the Exchange Extensions Commands Add-in, choose Tools | Options | Other | Advanced Options | Add-In Manager.*

Begin by opening the Folder List and selecting your target folder. Next, choose File | Folder | Copy Folder Design to display the Copy Design From dialog box, shown in Figure 18-3.

Select the source folder from the Copy Design From This Folder list. As soon as you select a source folder, the Copy Design Of options become available. Check the appropriate option(s) from the following:

- **Permissions**   Any permissions setting you've configured in the source folder will be duplicated in the Permissions tab of the target folder's Properties dialog box.

- **Rules**   If the source and target folders are mail folders, any message handling rules in the source folder are applied to the target folder.

- **Description**   The only thing transferred when this option is checked is the text entered in the Description field on the General tab of the source folder's Properties dialog box.

- **Forms & Views**   Any custom forms and custom views associated with the source folder are transferred to the target folder.

Regardless of whether you check the Description option, the text entered in the Description field located on the General tab of the source folder's Properties dialog box

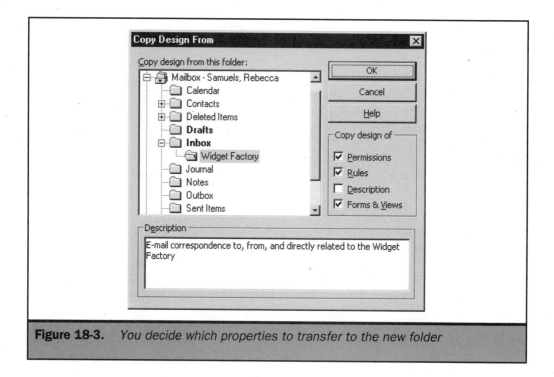

Figure 18-3.   *You decide which properties to transfer to the new folder*

appears in the Description window at the bottom of the Copy Design From dialog box. This is informational only and cannot be edited from within the Copy Design From dialog box. Click OK to complete the process.

Because the new settings transferred by the Copy Folder Design command replace any existing settings in the target folder, Outlook alerts you to the fact and asks for confirmation. Click Yes to complete the folder design transfer, or click No to return to the active view and start over.

Moving Folders

Once you begin taking advantage of the folder system used by Outlook, you'll find there are times when you want to move a folder from one location to another. For example, suppose you have separate Inbox subfolders for two companies you do business with and they merge. You'll probably want to create a new folder for the newly formed company and add the existing folders to it as subfolders.

By far the easiest method of moving a folder is a simple drag-and-drop procedure. Grab the folder you want to move, and drop it on the folder where you want it placed. That's all there is to it. One word of caution. Don't bother trying to move any of the primary Outlook folders (Calendar, Contacts, Deleted Items, Drafts, Inbox, Journal, Notes, Outbox, Sent Items, and Tasks). They cannot be moved under any circumstances.

If you right-drag a folder and drop it on a new location, a shortcut menu appears offering you the opportunity to move or copy the folder.

If you're not a drag-and-drop fan, there is another way to accomplish the task of moving a folder. Open the Folder List and right-click the folder you want to move. From the shortcut menu, select Move "[folder name]" to open the Move Folder dialog box.

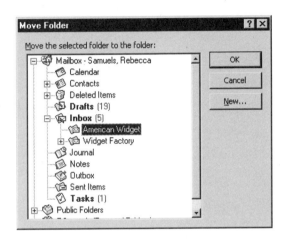

From the Move The Selected Folder To The Folder display list, choose the folder to which you want the selected folder moved. The folder you pick here becomes the parent folder of the folder you're moving. If you want to create a new folder into which to move the selected folder, click the New button and follow the instructions for creating a new folder. After you select the target folder, click OK to complete the move and return to the active view.

Tip *You can also select the folder and choose File | Folder | Move "[folder name]" to open the Move Folder dialog box.*

Regardless of which method you use to move the folder, nothing changes except the folder's location in the folder hierarchy. No contents, settings, or views are added or left behind. Everything is the same *after* the move as before the move.

Renaming Folders

Occasionally what seems like a good name for a folder turns out to be confusing or misleading and you find yourself wishing it had a different moniker. Fortunately, the solution for this dilemma is simple: rename the folder. Well, it's as simple as you choose to make it. Like most other tasks in Outlook, there are a couple of different ways to rename a folder.

The easiest method is to click the folder name in the Folder List and press F2 to turn on the edit mode for the folder name field. You can then edit the existing name or type a new name over the old name. To save the change, press the ENTER key when you're done. Right-clicking the folder name and selecting Rename "[folder name]" also turns the edit mode on. You could even highlight the folder name and choose Folder | Rename "[folder name]" from the Menu bar if you were so inclined.

Although you can also change the name of the shortcut in the Outlook Bar, don't confuse this with renaming the folder. The two procedures are distinct from one another. Changing the shortcut name has no effect on the folder name and vice versa.

If you insist upon using the most complicated method available, right-click the folder in the Folder List, select Properties from the shortcut menu, edit the name field on the General tab of the folder's Properties dialog box, and click OK to save the change. If you try any of these methods on the primary Outlook folders, you'll find they don't work. The reason is simple. You can't rename the primary folders.

Deleting Folders

When a folder outlives its usefulness, you can do a little housekeeping and remove it. Not only will this eliminate some unnecessary clutter in Outlook, it will also reduce your risk of exceeding any space limitations imposed by your administrator.

Deleting a folder is simple: open the Folder List, select the folder to delete, and press DEL. A confirmation dialog box appears asking if you really want to delete the folder, its contents, and any subfolders it may have hanging around. Unless you were just kidding when you hit the DEL key, click Yes.

There are a number of other methods you can use to delete a folder:

- Select the folder in the Folder List, and click the Delete button on the Standard toolbar.

- Drag the folder to the Deleted Items shortcut on the Outlook Bar, or to the Deleted Items folder in the Folder List.

- Right-click a folder in the Folder List and select Delete "[folder name]" from the shortcut menu.

- Select the folder in the Folder List, and choose File | Folder | Delete "[folder name]".

In most cases, you'll be asked to confirm your decision to delete the folder. As long as you're sure about the decision, answer affirmatively.

Deleting a folder deletes the entire contents of the folder as well as all subfolders and their contents. Therefore, it would behoove you to not take this action lightly.

Fortunately, even if you make a mistake or change your mind, you can save the deleted folder(s) from the clutches of oblivion by opening the Deleted Items folder and moving them back to their original location.

If you have a change of heart, but have already emptied your Deleted Items folder, don't despair. You may still be able to retrieve your deleted folders. Open the Deleted Items folder and choose Tools | Recover Deleted Items to open the Recover Deleted Items From dialog box. Select the folder(s) to recover and click the Recover Selected Items button. To permanently delete the items so they cannot be recovered using the Recover Deleted Items command, click the Purge Selected Items button.

Note *Your administrator determines the length of time deleted items remain on the server before being permanently deleted. Therefore, if the retention time has expired, the Recover Deleted Items command will not help. However, since any administrator worth his or her salt backs up the server regularly, you may still be able to recover your deleted folder(s) if you ask nicely (and infrequently).*

Archiving Folders

One of the advantages Outlook offers is the ease with which it enables you to store all your information. One of the disadvantages of Outlook is the ease with which it enables you to store all your information. Confused? Well, don't be. The problem is that most administrators limit the amount of space allocated to your mailbox. Chances are, you will eventually run up against that limit and have to do some serious housecleaning. Rather than waiting for that eventuality, you can take advantage of the Outlook archiving features to perform regular housekeeping chores on some or all of your folders.

The archiving feature, which uses rules you establish to move folder items into a special archive folder located on your local hard drive, comes in two flavors: automatic and manual. For a complete discussion of both methods, see the sections on archiving e-mail in Chapter 5.

Modifying Folder Properties

Folders are complex creatures and as such have quite a few settings you can apply to make them behave the way you want. These settings—also called properties—can be found in the folders' Properties dialog boxes. To access a folder's Properties dialog box, right-click the folder in the Folder List or the shortcut in the Outlook Bar, and select Properties from the shortcut menu.

With the exception of the contacts folders, the settings available in the folders' Properties dialog boxes are the same as those in the Properties dialog box shown in Figure 18-4.

See Chapter 9 for a complete discussion of the Activities and Outlook Address Book tabs, which are available only in contacts folders' Properties dialog boxes.

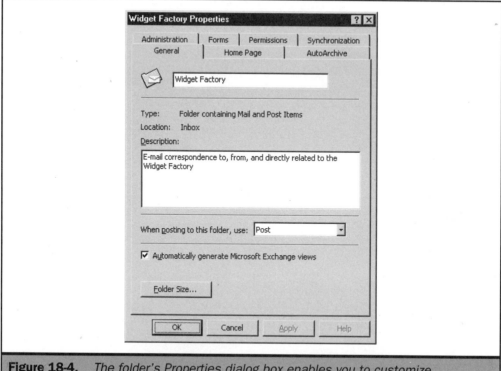

Figure 18-4.   *The folder's Properties dialog box enables you to customize
a multitude of settings*

Note   *Personal folder and public folder Properties dialog boxes contain some, but not all,
of the tabs described in this section.*

To open a folder's Properties dialog box, right-click the folder in the Folder List and
select Properties from the shortcut menu. As you can see in Figure 18-4, the properties
dialog box contains seven tabs, each of which contains related options. These options
enable you to set everything from folder permissions to AutoArchive rules to the
default form used to input data into the folder.

Setting General Options

The General Options tab is fairly simple and uncomplicated. It contains five basic
options that enable you to change the folder name, designate the default input form,
and more. The options you'll find here include:

- **Folder name**   Although there is no label for this field that says "Folder name,"
  that is precisely what the first field at the top of the tab is. You can change the

folder name of any folder you create, by editing or typing over the existing name. You cannot, however, change the folder name of any of the 11 (counting Outlook Today) primary Outlook folders.

■ **Description**   This field is a text box in which you can enter anything you want. If you create a series of subfolders with similar names, you might use this field to add some descriptive text that will help you easily identify each folder.

■ **When posting to this folder, use**   From this drop-down list, you can select a different form to use as the input form for the folder. If you leave the selection as is, Outlook automatically uses the default input form. The default forms are Post for mail folders, Appointment for calendar folders, Contact for contacts folders, Journal Entry for journal folders, and Note for notes folders. To use a custom form, select Forms from the drop-down list to open the Choose Form dialog box. There you can choose a form from either the Standard Forms Library, the Organizational Forms Library, or the Personal Forms Library. The custom forms must, of course, be compatible with the folder type.

■ **Automatically generate Microsoft Exchange views**   If you share folders with Microsoft Exchange users, you'll want to check this option to ensure that views you create for this folder are available to those users as well.

■ **Folder Size**   Click this button to display the Folder Size dialog box, which provides the folder name, the folder size, the combined size of the selected folder and its subfolders, and a listing of each subfolder and its size.

■ **Clear Offline Items**   This option appears only if you've enabled offline folders. Click the Clear Offline Items button to remove all items from the offline store for this folder.

After you set the General tab options, you can click the Apply button to put the options into effect without having to close the Properties dialog box. If you're finished setting options, you can click the OK button to apply the changes and close the Properties dialog box at the same time.

Adding a Folder Home Page

 An interesting feature that first appeared in Outlook 2000 is the ability to assign a home page to each folder. You can designate any Web page on the Internet, your company's intranet, or even an HTML document on your network or local hard drive. Whether you want to check the company intranet or just like to peruse the latest stock prices before you get started each day, you can make sure the Web page of your choice displays when you open a folder.

Assigning a Web page as the home page for one of your folders is easy. Open the folder's Properties dialog box and click the Home Page tab to display the Home Page options, shown in Figure 18-5.

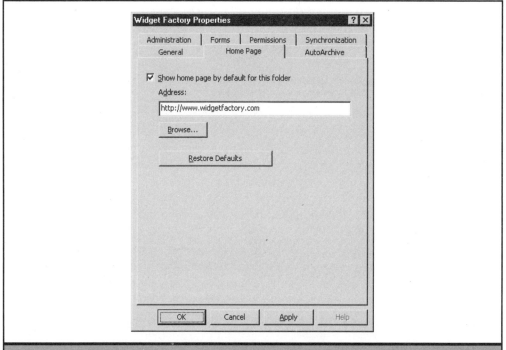

Figure 18-5. *Enter a URL or select a Web page from a local or network drive*

Note   *Since Outlook does not cache Web pages, you'll have to be connected to the network to view Web pages stored on the intranet or a network drive. The same goes for the Internet. You'll need to establish an Internet connection before Outlook will display a Web page.*

The fist thing you need to do is enter the URL or path of the Web page in the Address field. If you want to add an Internet address, type it in using the standard URL format: http://www.domainname (http://www.osborne.com). For a file on a local or network drive, use the file format: file:driveletter:\folder\filename (C:\My Documents\mydogsparky.htm). If you don't know the path, click the Browse button to open the Find Web Files dialog box. It's identical to other Windows Find or Open dialog boxes. Locate the file you want by using the Look In drop-down list. Once you find the file, select it and click OK to add it to the Address field on the Home Page tab.

As soon as you enter a URL or path in the Address field, the Show Home Page By Default For This Folder option becomes available. If you check this option, the Web page you assign in the Address field displays automatically every time you open the folder. If you leave the option unchecked, the folder displays normally.

Note *As of this writing, there is no means by which to toggle the Home Page on and off, as there was in Outlook 2000, which used the View | Show Folder Home Page command. Therefore, when you display the Home Page by default, you have no means by which to view the folder contents, other than to return to the folder's Properties dialog box and disable the Show Home Page By Default For This Folder option.*

The next button on the Home Page tab is the Restore Defaults button. If you decide you no longer want a home page to display or you simply want to start from scratch, click the Restore Defaults button to wipe the Home Page options clean.

If you've enabled offline folders, you'll find one more option on your Home Page tab. It's the Offline Web Page Settings button, which when clicked displays a Properties dialog box for the specific Web page entered in the Address field (see Figure 18-6).

As you can see in Figure 18-6, the Web page Properties dialog box has three tabs, each of which contains one or more options for synchronizing the Web page for offline use.

Note *If your home page is a file on a local or network drive, you'll only see a single tab, the Web Document tab.*

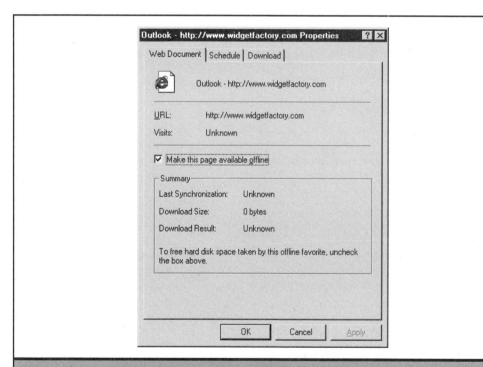

Figure 18-6. *Keep your home page up-to-date with offline Web page settings*

If your home page is a URL, you'll see the following three tabs:

- **Web Document** In addition to information about the Web page, you'll also find a single option here. By default, the option, Make This Page Available Offline, is checked. In theory, deselecting this option removes the Web page from your offline folders. However, in reality, the option appears to do nothing. The next time you return to the dialog box, the option has re-enabled itself and the Web page continues to appear whether you're working offline or online.

- **Schedule** The Schedule tab lets you decide whether to synchronize your home page manually or automatically using a schedule of your choosing. To create a new schedule, click Add and enter a name and simple schedule. To create a more sophisticated schedule, select a schedule and click the Edit button to display the dialog box of the same name as the schedule. This dialog box includes options enabling you to set extremely complex synchronization schedules for all offline Web pages.

- **Download** The Download tab offers options for determining the amount of content downloaded when offline Web pages are synchronized. You can indicate the level of linked pages to download as well as the type of content to download (or restrict). You can even have Outlook automatically send an e-mail message to a designated address each time the Web page changes.

When you're finished setting the Home Page options, click Apply and move on to another tab, or click OK to save the changes and return to the active view.

MOUS EXAM PRACTICE
In this section, you learned to add and display a Home Page to your Outlook folders. Begin your practice section by opening the Properties dialog box for one of your Outlook folders. Then add a Web page as the Home Page. Check the Show Home Page By Default For This Folder option to display the Home Page each time you open the folder. Now try adding a graphic file on your local computer.

Configuring AutoArchive Settings

If you have a hard time keeping up with your Outlook housekeeping chores, you might want to give AutoArchive a try. It moves aging Outlook items to a special archive folder at regularly scheduled intervals, thereby freeing up space in your mailbox. If you don't care about saving the items, you can instruct AutoArchive to delete them instead. You can create custom AutoArchive schedules and instructions for each folder by setting options on the AutoArchive tab shown in Figure 18-7.

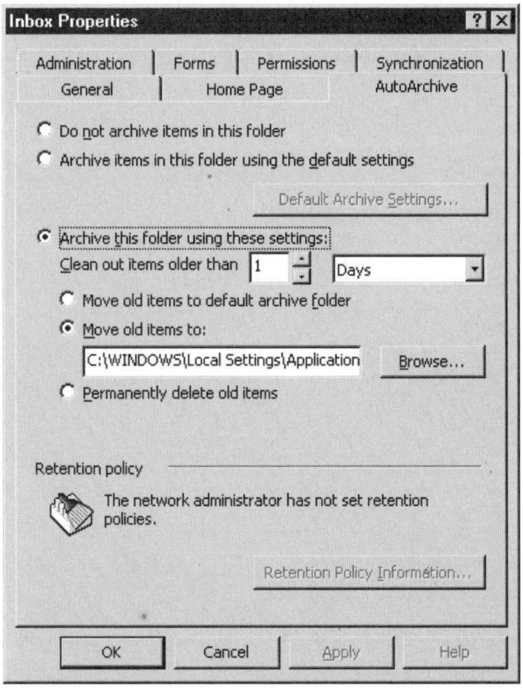

Figure 18-7. *You can specify detailed AutoArchiving settings for any folder*

Here's what you'll find:

- **Do not archive items in this folder**   Use this option to turn AutoArchiving off for this folder.

- **Archive items in this folder using the default settings**   If you want to AutoArchive the folder, but don't need customized settings, you can use the default AutoArchive settings by selecting this option.

- **Default Archive Settings**   If you're contemplating using the default settings for this folder, you can check them out by clicking the Default Archive Settings button to display the AutoArchive dialog box. See Chapter 5 for detailed information on changing default AutoArchive settings.

- **Archive this folder using these settings**   Check this option if you want to create custom AutoArchive settings just for this folder. As soon as you select this option, the remaining settings become available.

- **Clean out items older than**   Check this option to enable AutoArchiving for this folder. Then enter the aging criteria for AutoArchiving individual items.

- **Move old items to default archive folder**   If you select this option, all items meeting the age criteria will be moved to the folder designated in the default archive settings.

- **Move old items to**   To save items that meet the aging criteria to a folder different from the default archive folder, enter the path to the file here. To locate an existing archive file, click the Browse button.

- **Permanently delete old items**   If you don't want to save items that meet the age criteria, you can select this option and have AutoArchive delete them rather than move them to the archive file.

- **Retention Policy Information**   Click this button to view the limitations set by your system administrator on items stored in your server-based mailbox.

When you're finished setting the AutoArchive options, click Apply and move to the next tab, or click OK to return to the active view.

Setting Administration Options

The first thing to note about the Administration tab is that you won't see it unless the Exchange Extensions Property Pages add-in is installed. To install the add-in, choose Tools | Options to display the Options dialog box. Then click the Other tab and click the Advanced Options button to open the Advanced Options dialog box. Click the Add-In Manager button to display the Add-In Manager dialog box. Check the Exchange Extensions Property Pages option and click OK.

The next thing to note about the Administration tab is that unless you're in a public folder of which you're the owner, or to which you possess owner permissions, there's not much you can do with it. When you select the Administration tab in a private folder, the only option available to the folder owner or a user with owner permissions is the Initial View On Folder option. While you can use this option in a private folder as well as a public folder, there's really not much point unless you've given other users permission to view the private folder.

The Initial View On Folder option sets the default view that displays the very first time the user opens the folder. If the user never switches views, the designated view appears every time the folder opens. However, once the user switches to another view, this option no longer applies to the folder for that particular user. It does still apply to other users who haven't yet opened the folder and switched to another view.

By default, five selections appear on the drop-down list, regardless of the type of folder you're in. Four of the five default selections (Group By From, Group By Subject, Group By Conversation Topic, and Unread By Conversation) can be applied to mail folders only. So don't drive yourself crazy trying to apply them to a contacts folder or a calendar folder. The remaining selection, Normal, uses the standard form for the selected folder type.

The Initial View On Folder option is used mainly in conjunction with custom views to bring some facet of the folder information to the attention of all users on their initial visit to the folder. For example, you might create a custom view that groups items by the Modified date, thus ensuring every user sees the most recent additions to the folder upon his or her initial visit. Or you might just want to make all users aware you've created a new view so they can take advantage of it if they so desire.

The remaining options on the Administration tab apply to public folders only and are therefore covered in Chapter 16.

Associating Forms with Folders

You can associate custom forms with any folder for which you are the owner or for which you have owner permissions. All you have to do is use the Forms Manager, which can be accessed from the Forms tab of the folder's Properties dialog box, as seen in Figure 18-8.

Like the Administration tab, the Forms tab requires the Exchange Extensions Property Pages add-in and owner permissions. Without both, the tab does not appear on the folder's Properties dialog box.

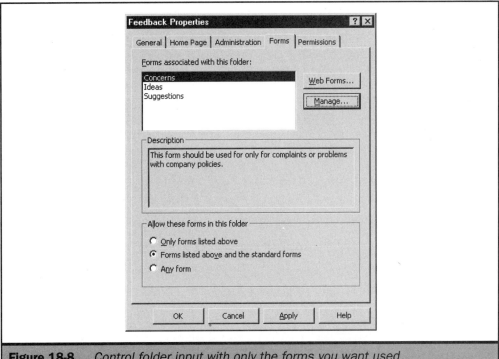

Figure 18-8. *Control folder input with only the forms you want used*

To find out whether the Exchange Extensions Property Pages add-in is installed, check the Add-In Manager dialog box. Start by choosing Tools | Options to display the Options dialog box. Then click the Other tab, and then the Advanced Options button to open the Advanced Options dialog box. Finally, click the Add-In Manager button to display the Add-In Manager dialog box. If the Exchange Extensions Property Pages option is checked, the add-in is installed. If it's not checked, click the check box to enable the option, and click OK. This will install the add-in.

If the problem is the lack of owner permissions, the only thing you can do is request that the folder owner provide you with the necessary permissions. One last thing. Even if you're the folder owner, or a user with owner permissions, the Allow These Forms In This Folder options are not available unless the folder is a public folder. In private folders, these options are grayed out.

Now, on to associating forms with the folder. The first order of business is to link custom forms to the folder. To start, click the Manage button to display the Forms Manager dialog box, shown in Figure 18-9.

You can also access the Forms Manager by choosing Tools | Options | Other | Advanced Options | Custom Forms | Manage Forms.

As you can see in Figure 18-9, the Forms Manager has two Set buttons and two display windows. The premise is simple: display existing forms in the left pane and move them to the right pane to associate them with the current folder (whose name appears next to the Set button above the right pane). When accessed from the Forms

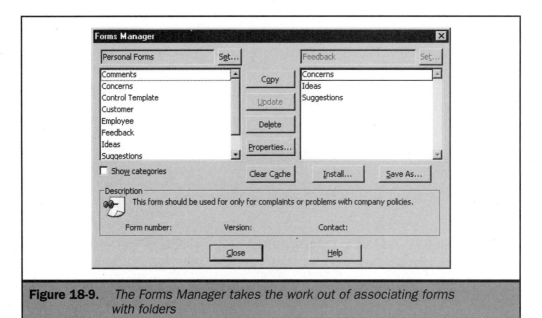

Figure 18-9.   *The Forms Manager takes the work out of associating forms with folders*

tab, only the left Set button is active. The right Set button is disabled to ensure you only associate forms with the currently selected folder. Click the left Set button to open the Set Library To dialog box (see Figure 18-10).

You can elect to use forms contained in a forms library or forms already associated with another folder. To use forms from a forms library, open the Forms Library drop-down list and select the desired library.

Note   *In reality, each folder contains its own forms library. When you associate a form with a particular folder, you are really placing a copy of the form in the folder's forms library.*

To use forms associated with a folder, select the particular folder from the Folder Forms Library display list. Click OK to return to the Forms Manager, where forms from the library or folder you selected now appear in the left pane. As you can see in Figure 18-9, the name of the selected library (or folder) appears to the left of the Set button, and all the associated forms are displayed beneath it.

Tip   *Outlook folders are limited to a single Outlook item type or message class. This means that forms associated with the folder must belong to a compatible message class. In spite of the fact that the Forms Manager allows you to add non-compatible forms to a folder's forms library, you will not be able to use them. To determine a form's message class, select the form and click the Properties button. The Message Class field indicates the selected form's message class.*

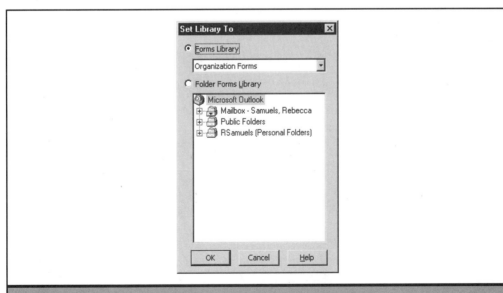

Figure 18-10.   *Select the library or folder containing the custom forms you want to use*

The next step is to choose the form(s) to link with the selected folder and make the association. From the left pane, select one or more forms, and click the Copy button to move them to the right pane. That's all there is to it. Once you click Close, the association is complete.

There are a number of other options in the Forms Manager, including the following:

- **Update** If changes have been made to forms since you first associated them with the folder, you can update the copies in the folder's forms library by selecting them and clicking the Update button. The forms originally associated with the folder are replaced by the most recent versions.

- **Delete** To remove a form from either list, select it and click the delete button. Use this one carefully. Deleting a form from the right list simply deletes the copy placed in the folder's forms library. However, deleting the form from the left pane actually deletes the original form. If you mistakenly delete the original form, you'll have to re-create it from scratch.

- **Properties** You can use this button to modify some of the form properties, such as name, category assignments, contacts, and comments. In addition, you can see non-editable information such as version, form number, the type of operating systems with which the form is compatible, and the message class to which the form belongs.

- **Show Categories** If the form has been assigned to categories and/or subcategories, checking this option changes forms lists to display available forms grouped by categories and subcategories.

- **Install** Use this button to add custom forms from a form setup file (.cfg) or a form message file (.fdm). This option is used in conjunction with the next option, Save As, which saves a selected form to one of the two form file formats. This enables you to share custom forms with other Outlook users.

- **Save As** Select the form to save, then click this button to display the Save As dialog box. Choose a target folder in which to save the form, enter a filename, select the file format (.fdm, or .cfg), and click Save. You can now send the file to any other Outlook user, who can add it to his or her forms library by using the Install command.

- **Clear Cache** To save time downloading forms from the server, Outlook maintains a forms cache on your local hard drive, where it stores copies of form definitions for those forms that have been used at least once. After an extended period of time, the cache may contain a collection of form definitions that are used infrequently. You can click the Clear Cache button to clean it out and start over.

You'll also notice in Figure 18-9 that the Forms Manager dialog box contains a section called Description. Here you'll see some of the properties of the selected form. This can be helpful in comparing copies in a folder's form library with the originals to determine if the folder contains the most current version of the form.

After you've associated forms with the folder and clicked Close, you return to the Forms tab, where the associated forms now appear in the Forms Associated With This Folder list. If you're in a public folder, the Allow These Forms In This Folder options are available. Select the appropriate option to determine which forms can be used in this folder. The options are self-explanatory.

Giving Others Permission to Access Folders

The Permissions tab of the folder's Properties dialog box is another of the tabs that requires the Exchange Extensions Property Pages add-in and owner permissions. Without them, the Permissions tab does not appear. See the previous section, "Associating Forms with Folders," for information on installing the Exchange Extensions Property Pages add-in.

If you have the Exchange Extensions Property Pages add-in installed, but do not have owner permissions to the folder, you'll see a Summary tab instead. This tab displays the current permissions settings for the folder, but does not permit you to make any changes to the settings.

Setting permissions for a folder determines the ability other users have to access and modify the folder and any items it contains. Only the original folder owner can grant permissions to other users, initially. However, by assigning owner permissions to another user, a folder owner can give others the same rights he has.

To access a folder's Permissions tab, right-click the folder shortcut in the Outlook Bar to open the folder's Properties dialog box. Then click the Permissions tab, which provides a variety of options that let you designate which users are allowed access to the folder (see Figure 18-11).

The first thing to decide is what the permissions setting is going to be for the bulk of users. As you can see in Figure 18-11, the only user listed is Default. This covers everyone with access to the folder except those users for whom you add customized permissions. You'll also notice that the role set for Default is None. This means that no one except the owner has permission to access the folder. You can change the role, or you can create your own custom role by setting the various options in the Permissions section. In addition to setting roles and permissions for the Default user, you can also add individual users for whom you want to provide special permissions.

Giving a specific user special permissions requires adding the user to the Permissions tab and assigning the desired role or setting custom permissions. To add a user, click the Add button to display the Add Users dialog box, shown in Figure 18-12.

Since users must be on the Microsoft Exchange Server network to book resources, you won't find users from your Outlook Address Book or Personal Address Book listed. The only selections available in the Show Names From The drop-down list are the Global Address List, which displays everyone in the organization, and address lists for individual sites in the organization.

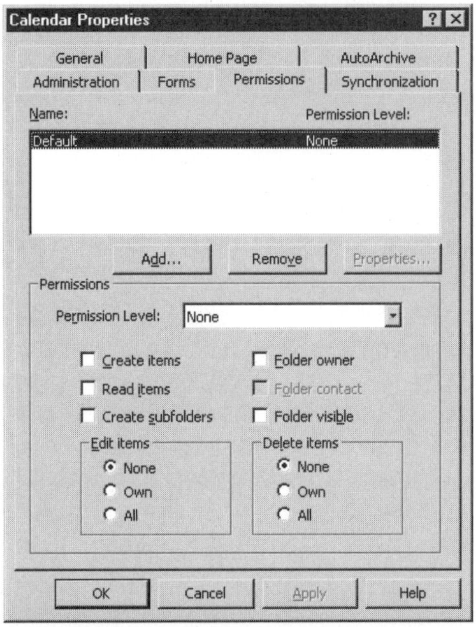

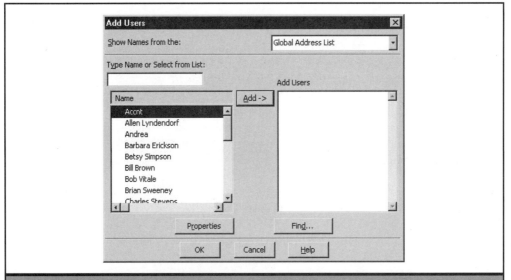

Figure 18-11. *Setting folder permissions is easy with all the options at your disposal*

Figure 18-12. *The Add Users dialog box displays users from your Global Address List*

Select the user(s) to whom you want to give special permission for accessing and using the folder, and click the Add button. Next, click OK to add them to the Permissions tab. Now you're ready to assign roles and set permissions.

Start with Default, then set the permissions for each user you added. For most of your users, the standard roles, which include the following, should suffice:

- **Owner**   If the folder is part of your mailbox or a folder you created, you will automatically have owner rights. The original owner can also give other users Owner rights. Owners can add and remove users, assign permissions, and do pretty much anything they want with the folder. Careful consideration should be used before assigning the Owner role to users.

- **Publishing Editor**   Assign this role to users to give them the ability to read, create, modify, and delete all folder items. In addition, Publishing Editors can create subfolders.

- **Editor**   An Editor can create, read, modify, and delete all items in the folder, but cannot create subfolders.

- **Publishing Author**   A Publishing Author has the same rights as the Publishing Editor with one exception. The ability to modify and delete items is limited to those items created by the Publishing Author.

- **Author**   This role gives the user rights similar to those of an Editor. The Author can create, read, modify, and delete items. However, modifying and deleting is limited to those items created by the Author.

- **Nonediting Author**   This role enables the user to read and create items. Deleting is limited to only those items created by the Nonediting Author, while editing is (as the name implies) completely forbidden regardless of who created the item.

- **Reviewer**   A reviewer gets to sit on the sidelines and watch the action without participating. Reviewers can view the folder and read items, but that's it. No creating, editing, or deleting is allowed.

- **Contributor**   The only permission granted to a Contributor is the right to create items. No reading, editing, or deleting is allowed.

- **None**   Not only can't you use the folder when assigned this role, you can't even see it. None means none—no reading, creating, editing, deleting, or even peeking is allowed!

Tip   *You can set roles and permissions for more than one user by selecting multiple users and making your choice from the Roles drop-down list, or by checking the desired permissions options. Of course, the selected users will all have identical permissions.*

In addition to the predefined roles found on the Roles drop-down list, you can create your own custom role known, appropriately, as Custom, by selecting the individual permissions you want to give a particular user. The permissions you can assign include:

- **Create items**   This gives the user permission to create folder items.
- **Read items**   With Read Items permission assigned, a user can view the folder and open any folder item.
- **Create subfolders**   Check this option to give the user permission to create subfolders of the folder.
- **Folder owner**   Contrary to what it might imply, checking this option alone does not automatically grant the selected user Owner permissions. What it does do, however, is enable the user to set his or her own permissions. There's one small catch, however. You must also provide Read Items permission so the user can open the folder to gain access to the Permissions tab of the folder properties.
- **Folder contact**   Check this option to designate the selected user as a folder contact. This means the selected user will receive copies of automatic notifications from the folder or of those sent to the folder.
- **Folder visible**   This misleadingly named option does not, by itself, make the folder visible. It requires that the Read Items option be checked as well. By itself, the Folder Visible option only makes a calendar folder's free/busy time available in the Scheduling tab of meeting and meeting request forms.
- **Edit items**   Fortunately, this permission is aptly named and enables the user to edit Calendar items according to the Edit Items option selected. The options are None, Own, and All. None speaks for itself. Own lets the user modify only those items he or she has created. All lets the user change any folder item regardless of its origin.
- **Delete items**   The Delete Items permission is identical to the Edit Items permission except that it enables the user to delete items from the folder. The options provide the same permission types as the Edit Items options.

In addition to adding users and setting permissions, you can also delete users. Highlight the user(s) you want to eliminate and click the Remove button. Outlook deletes the user without warning (or confirmation) as soon as you press the DEL key. Therefore, if you accidentally delete a user, you'll have to re-add him or her. If you happen to delete the Default user, don't worry. Just click the Apply button and the Default user is back with, you guessed it, the default setting of None.

MOUS

MOUS EXAM PRACTICE
In this section, you learned to assign permissions to your folder to enable others to access those folders. Begin by reviewing the different roles you can assign to ensure you understand the implications of the different permissions sets. First, create a new test folder (call it Test) to use for your practice. Then assign different permission levels to several co-workers and ask them to access the test folder. Have them report back on the things they are able to do while in your test folder. After some feedback, change the permissions level for each user and see what happens. Finally, before deleting the test folder, delete each of the users to whom you've assigned permissions.

Configuring Synchronization Settings

If you work offline, you'll undoubtedly find yourself setting the Synchronization tab options on occasion. However, before you can do that you must have offline folders enabled. See Chapter 17 for more information on enabling and using offline folders. Before proceeding, there are a couple of things you should understand about offline folders and synchronization. First, when you enable offline folders, all the primary Outlook folders (Calendar, Contacts, Deleted Items, Drafts, Inbox, Journal, Notes, Outbox, Sent Items, and Tasks) are included automatically. You cannot choose to make some available offline and others not available offline, as you can with folders you create yourself. Another thing to note is that public folders can only be used offline if they are in your Public Folders/Favorites folder. If you open the Properties dialog box for a public folder that is not in the Favorites folder, the Synchronization tab doesn't appear.

As you can see in Figure 18-13, the Synchronization tab contains a single option: Filter. In addition to the Filter button, the tab also contains statistics for the folder, indicating the date of the last synchronization, as well as the number of items in the folder and offline folder.

In the event you only want a portion of the file's contents while you're offline, you can use the Filter button to specify which folder items are synchronized. Sometimes you don't need or want the entire contents of a folder. For example, if you're going on the road and have a large Contacts folder, but limited storage space on your laptop, you can elect to synchronize only your business contacts and not your personal contacts (if you've assigned them to categories). Click the Filter button to display the Filter dialog box, and set the desired filter criteria. See the section entitled "Adding and Applying Filters" in Chapter 22 for more information on using filters.

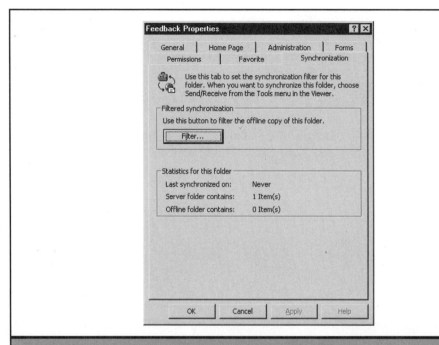

Figure 18-13. *Synchronize your offline folders so you can keep working when the server is down or while you're on the road*

MOUS Exam Expert Objectives Explored in Chapter 18

Objective	Activity	Heading
OL10E-4-6	Organize folders and set permissions	"Giving Others Permission to Access Folders"
OL10E-4-7	Organize information and Web addresses	"Adding a Folder Home Page"

The Complete Reference

Chapter 19

Advanced E-mail Techniques

O utlook has a host of clever automated procedures that provide a lot of additional power while, at the same time, eliminating a lot of the work. A simple one-time setup process creates permanent customized functions you can use over and over.

Using Send/Receive Groups

The first, and newest of these features is Send/Receive Groups. If you have multiple accounts, you may not find it necessary or even desirable to poll (the technical term for one program checking with another to see if it has any information to transmit—in this case, e-mail) every account each time you send and receive. To simplify the matter, Outlook 2002 now enables you to create different groups of accounts, called Send/Receive groups, that can be polled whenever you desire.

Creating and Modifying Send/Receive Groups

By default, every e-mail account you create is automatically assigned to a Send/Receive group called, aptly enough, All Accounts. To create other groups, press CTRL+ALT+S or choose Tools | Send/Receive Settings | Define Send/Receive Groups to display the Send/Receive Groups dialog box shown in Figure 19-1.

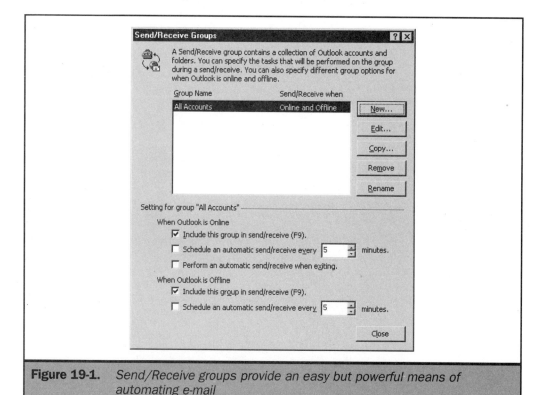

Figure 19-1. *Send/Receive groups provide an easy but powerful means of automating e-mail*

Begin by clicking the New button, which opens the Send/Receive Group Name dialog box.

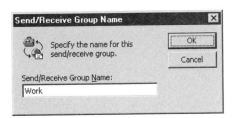

Enter a descriptive name for the new group and click OK to open the Send/Receive Settings - [group name] dialog box shown in Figure 19-2.

As you can see in Figure 19-2, all the settings are initially grayed out (disabled). You'll also note that each of the existing accounts has a red x attached to its icon. This indicates that the account is not yet part of the new group. Of course, since it's not part of the group, no group settings are available.

The first thing to do is add an account. From the Accounts list on the left, select the first account you want to include in the new group. Next, check the Include Account In

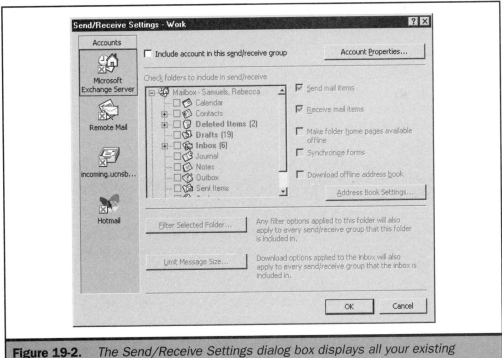

Figure 19-2. *The Send/Receive Settings dialog box displays all your existing e-mail accounts*

This Send/Receive Group option to add the account. As soon as you check the option, the remaining options become available, and the red x is replaced by a pair of blue arrows (see Figure 19-3).

The options you see depend entirely on the account type. The Exchange Server account has the most options, while Internet and remote mail accounts have fewer.

Setting Send/Receive Groups Options

As you can see in Figure 19-3, the Microsoft Exchange Server options are plentiful. They include everything from send and receive options to filters and size restrictions. Here's what you'll find:

- **Account Properties**   Click this button to open the Microsoft Exchange Server dialog box so you can review and modify the Microsoft Exchange Server account properties.

- **Send mail items**   If you want mail sent when the Send/Receive command is used, check this option.

- **Receive mail items**   Checking this option ensures mail will be retrieved each time the Send/Receive command is used.

- **Make folder home pages available offline**   To make your folder Home Pages available when working offline, check this option.

- **Synchronize forms**   In addition to synchronizing folder contents, you can also synchronize the forms used to create Outlook items. Check this option to ensure all changes made to forms are updated as well.

- **Download offline address book**   When working offline it's important to have the most current and up-to-date address book information. Therefore, you may want to check this option to download the address book to your local computer so it's available when you're offline.

- **Address Book Settings**   Click this button, which is enabled when you check the Download Offline Address Book option, to set options for the manner in which the address book is downloaded. It lets you select the address book(s) to download, and the amount of information from each to download.

- **Filter Selected Folder**   Select a folder from the display list and this button is enabled. Click the button to apply a filter to the folder that will restrict the data included in each Send/Receive operation.

- **Limit Message Size**   This option enables you to restrict messages included in Send/Receive operations based on the size of the messages. In order to ensure you don't miss important messages, you can add exceptions to the rule based on the sender, the message priority, and the flagged status.

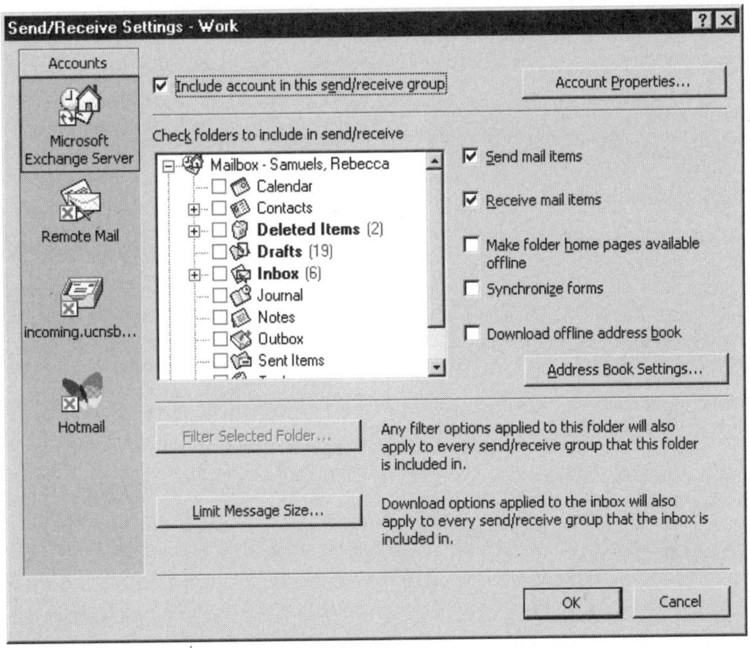

Figure 19-3.   *Adding an account activates its group options*

Other e-mail account types have fewer options. All include individual Send and Receive options. Internet and Remote Mail accounts also provide options for downloading headers.

Adding Signatures to E-mail

A signature is text you create and save so you can automatically add it to e-mail messages you compose. You can use an electronic signature very much the same way you use your written signature. The difference is that your electronic signature can contain a wealth of information in addition to your name. You can also provide your title, company name, address, phone number, and any other information you consider pertinent. While you could type that information at the end of each message you send, Outlook eliminates that need by providing boilerplates called signatures in which you can include all that data to use over and over. Some people use a signature to sign off with a joke, a bit of philosophical wisdom, or a blatant political rally cry. In fact, some people get carried away and create signatures longer than most of the messages they send. Your taste, and the sensibilities of the people who receive your mail, should determine your signature contents. You can create as many signatures as you wish, and append the appropriate one to each message you create.

Creating Signatures

Creating and saving signatures is a snap; coming up with the appropriate words is the hard part. When you've decided on the text for your signature, begin by choosing Tools | Options and moving to the Mail Format tab of the Options dialog box. Click the Signatures button, located at the bottom of the tab, to open the Create Signatures dialog box.

Check the default message format at the top of the dialog box before you begin designing your signature. Outlook uses the same format for your signature.

Selecting the Signature Design Options

When you're designing your first signature, there are no signatures to pick, of course, so click New to open the Create New Signature dialog box, shown in Figure 19-4.

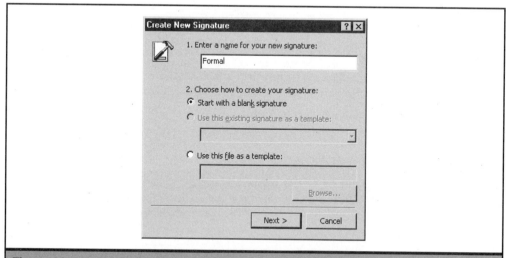

Figure 19-4.   *Start by giving your signature a name that reflects its contents*

Enter a name for this signature, then select one of the following options:

- **Start with a blank signature**   Select this option to create a signature from scratch. You can type the signature or cut and paste it from an existing document.

- **Use this existing signature as a template**   This choice becomes available only after you create your first signature. You can then use it to create variants of your signature, without having to start from scratch.

- **Use this file as a template**   This option allows you to use text previously saved as a Rich Text Format (RTF) file. Enter the path to the file or click Browse to locate the file on your hard drive. Most word processors (including Microsoft Word) provide an option for saving a file in RTF format.

Click Next to begin working on your signature in the Edit Signature dialog box.

Creating and Designing Signature Text

If you chose an existing signature or a template file, the text is already in the textbox. If you elected to start with a blank signature, you must type (or paste) the text for the signature (see Figure 19-5).

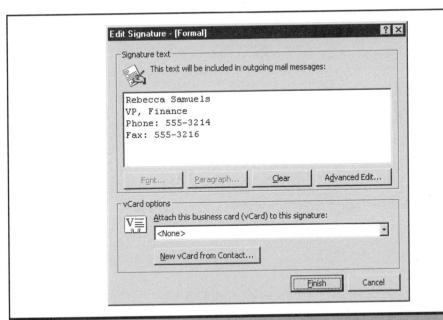

Figure 19-5.   *Plain text signatures have no formatting options, but they work for every type of message (plain text, RTF, or HTML)*

Once you've inserted the text, you can polish it up using one of the following options:

■ **Font** Click Font to open the Font dialog box, where you can change the font, font size, font style (bold, italic, and so on), color, and effects such as underline or strike-through.

■ **Paragraph** Click the Paragraph button to display the Paragraph dialog box, which gives you options to align the text to the left, center, or right. You can even add bullets if the text in your signature calls for it.

■ **Clear** Use the Clear button to delete the text and start again.

■ **Advanced Edit** The Advanced Edit button lets you use an editor other than the Outlook text editor to format your signature. As soon as you click it, Outlook launches the appropriate application. For plain text signatures, Notepad opens; for other signature types, Microsoft Word (RTF), or Front Page (HTML) opens. If your default message format (and therefore your signature) isn't plain text, Outlook offers plenty of formatting options (the Font and Paragraph buttons are accessible). Select some or all of the signature text and use the buttons on the dialog box to spiff up the formatting.

  Formatted signatures don't retain their formatting when you attach them to plain text messages.

Click Finish to save the signature and return to the Create Signature dialog box. If you don't want to create another signature (by clicking New) or attach a vCard (discussed next), choose OK twice to close all the dialog boxes.

Attaching a vCard

You can attach a vCard to your signature by choosing one from the drop-down list in the dialog box. If you don't have an appropriate vCard, click New vCard From Contact to create one. See Chapter 8 for more information on creating vCards.

Editing and Removing Signatures

When the need arises, you can return to the Mail format tab of the Options dialog box to edit or delete an existing signature. Click the Signatures button to open the Create Signature dialog box used to create the original signature. As you can see in Figure 19-6, all signatures you've created are displayed in the Signature list.

Select a signature (Outlook shows you its contents in the Preview box) to perform either of the following tasks:

■ Click Edit to open the Edit Signature dialog box (the same one you used to create the signature). All the edit and formatting options available when you created the signature are available again. Click OK when you finish making your changes.

■ Click Remove to delete the signature from your collection. Outlook asks you to confirm that you want to permanently remove the signature.

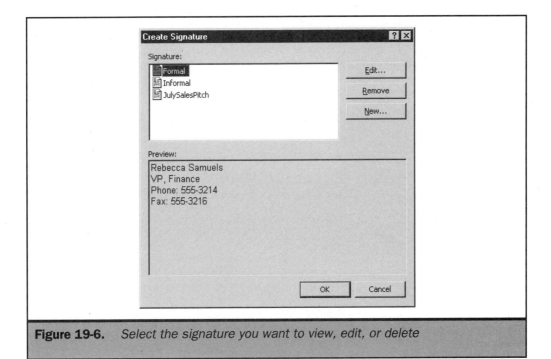

Figure 19-6.   *Select the signature you want to view, edit, or delete*

Choosing a Default Signature

When you leave the Create Signature dialog box, the last signature selected automatically becomes the default signature for new messages. If you want to change the default signature, you can make a different selection from the Signature For New Messages drop-down list. In addition, you can instruct Outlook which signature to use when you reply to or forward messages by making a selection from the Signature For Replies And Forwards drop-down list.

If you want to decide on a signature each time you create a message, select None from the drop-down list.

Each time you return to the Signature Picker dialog box to edit, remove, or create a signature, the signature that's selected when you leave the dialog box becomes the new default. Be sure to check the default signature on the Mail Format tab before clicking OK to close the Options dialog box.

If you opt to use signatures when you reply to or forward a message, you may find that a signature containing multiple fonts, or font attributes applied to text (such as bold or italic), appears as plain text in a reply. This happens when the format type of the original message is plain text. Outlook automatically forces the format of the reply to match the original message. The signature itself hasn't changed.

Using Signatures in Messages

After you create a signature, Outlook assumes you want to use it. If you selected anything but None as the default signature, your default signature appears automatically whenever you open a new message window.

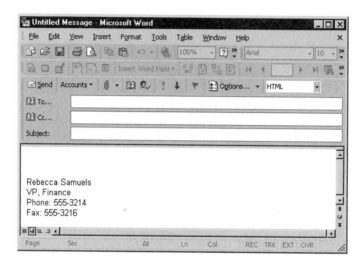

Create the message as usual. Be sure your insertion point is above the signature as you enter the text of your message. If you decide you don't want to use the signature in the current message, select the text of the signature and delete it.

 If you find you're deleting signatures more often than using them, save yourself some work by returning to the Mail Format tab of the Options dialog box and selecting None as the default signature. From then on, just insert a signature when you want to use one.

You can insert a signature manually if you selected None as the default signature, or if you have multiple signatures and want to choose a different (from the default) signature for the current message.

Position your insertion point where you want the signature to appear (usually at the end of the message). If you're using Word as your e-mail editor, click the down arrow to the right of the Options button on the Standard toolbar. Then select E-mail Signature from the drop-down menu to display the E-mail Options dialog box (shown in Figure 19-7).

If you're using the Outlook editor, click the Signatures button on the Standard toolbar and choose a signature from the drop-down menu. You can also choose Insert | Signature to display a submenu that lists all your signatures. Select the one you want to use.

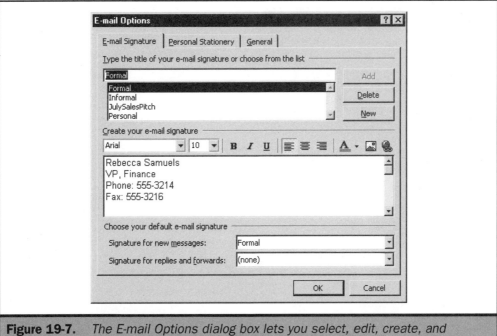

Figure 19-7.   *The E-mail Options dialog box lets you select, edit, create, and delete signatures*

Tip

The Signature submenu holds a maximum of ten signatures. If you've created more than ten signatures, and you don't see the signature you want to use, click More on the submenu to open the Select A Signature dialog box to see a complete list.

If you're replacing an existing signature, you might want to highlight it first so the new signature is inserted over the old one, thus eliminating the possibility of ending up with two signatures.

MOUS

MOUS EXAM PRACTICE

In this section, you learned to create, format, edit, and use signatures. Begin by creating several different signatures. Customize each one using the formatting features available for your default message format. Then set one of the signatures as your default signature. Next, compose an e-mail message to see how the default signature appears. Finally, manually change the signature from the default to one of the other signatures you created. Send yourself and your co-workers messages with the signatures to see how they appear when received.

Dealing with Junk Mail

Junk e-mail (more commonly known as *spam*) is an annoying problem that keeps growing. One serious problem with junk e-mail is that it usually costs the recipient more than it costs the sender (which is the opposite of the financials attached to junk mail that's delivered by the USPS). Whether you believe in the axiom that your time is worth money, or you actually pay by the minute for Internet access, the time spent waiting for junk mail to download to your Inbox and the time spent deleting it become significant as more and more junk mail arrives.

Outlook offers some assistance as you attempt to dodge the streams of junk mail that invade your mailbox.

Setting Filter Actions

You can have Outlook automatically filter junk mail as it arrives in your Inbox. In addition, you can configure automatic actions (such as delete, move to another folder, and so on) when the filter identifies junk mail. Outlook actually defines two types of undesirable e-mail: junk mail and adult content mail. To set up your junk mail filters, display your Inbox and click the Organize icon on the toolbar (or choose Tools | Organize). Then choose Junk E-Mail to see the window shown in Figure 19-8.

Outlook keeps a list of key words and phrases, and examines your incoming e-mail to see if those words exist in any message. If so, the message is deemed to be unsolicited junk mail, and the actions you specify are taken. If you wish, you can specify one action for junk messages and a different action for adult content messages.

Color Junk Mail Listings

By default, Outlook offers to change the color of the Inbox listing of any junk or adult content message. Select a color from the drop-down list; you can choose the same color for both types of filtered messages, or select a different color for each in order to identify the message type more easily. When you've selected the colors you want to use to identify these messages, click Turn On to save your configuration options.

The filtered messages remain in your Inbox, so you can decide whether you want to open a message (just to check), manually move the message to another folder, or manually delete the message.

Move Junk Mail

You can have Outlook automatically move your junk mail to another folder instead of sending it to your Inbox. To do so, select Move from the drop-down list next to the word "Automatically," and the drop-down list in the second box changes to a list of folders. Select the Junk E-Mail folder, the Deleted Items folder, or Other Folder (which opens a dialog box that displays all your Outlook folders so you can select one, or create one). Then click Turn On to save your configuration options.

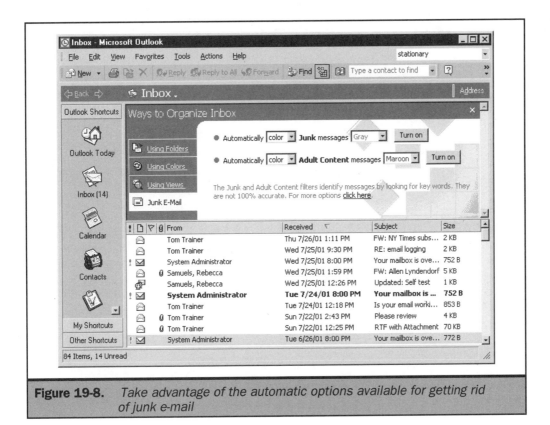

Figure 19-8.   *Take advantage of the automatic options available for getting rid of junk e-mail*

Unless you select Deleted Items as the dumping ground for both types of junk mail, Outlook does not permit you to use the same folder for both junk mail and adult content mail. If you choose the Junk E-Mail folder for both, you must create a second Junk E-Mail folder. You can give the second folder a different name or put it in another location (for example, put one folder named Junk E-Mail in your Exchange server mailbox and the other in your Personal folder).

If you select the Junk E-Mail folder, and that folder doesn't already exist, Outlook automatically opens the Create New Folder dialog box. Just like when you create a new folder, you're offered the opportunity to place a shortcut to the folder on your Outlook Bar.

Adding Senders to the List of Junk Purveyors

Outlook's filtering mechanism is helpful, but not foolproof. It's certainly possible to receive a great deal of junk mail that slips through the filters because the words and phrases that kick off the filters may not be contained in some junk mail.

To help filter junk, you can maintain a list of senders so mail from those senders is also filtered.

Add a Sender from a Message Listing

If you receive junk mail or adult content mail, right-click the message listing in your Inbox and choose Junk E-Mail from the shortcut menu. Then choose Add To Junk Senders List, or Add To Adult Content Senders List from the submenu. You can also choose Actions | Junk E-mail to display a submenu with the same choices.

 You cannot use this technique if the From field on the message is blank; Outlook issues the error message, "The operation failed. An object could not be found."

View and Update Your Junk Senders List

To view or edit the list of junk senders, display your Inbox and click the Organize icon on the toolbar (or choose Tools | Organize). Choose Junk E-Mail and scroll to the bottom of the Organize window and click the Click Here link. Then click Edit Junk Senders or Edit Adult Content Senders.

The Edit Junk Senders or Edit Adult Content dialog box opens, displaying the names of all the senders currently in the list.

Edit Junk Senders

EasyDough@moneybags.com
FreeFerAll@easyaspie.com
MakeMoreMoney@technodollars.co

OK
Cancel
Add...
Edit...
Delete

NOTE: You can also add names to the list by right-clicking a message in the view and selecting "Junk E-mail->Add to Junk Senders list"

To add a sender, click Add and enter the sender's name as it appears on e-mail messages. If you want to modify a name on the list select the listing and click Edit. To remove a sender from the list, select the listing and click Delete. When you're finished working with the Sender list, click OK to return to the active window.

 You can also have an Exception List, which means you can fine-tune the filters so they permit mail that meets your exception criteria to slip through the filter. This is useful if your mother sends you e-mail that contains phrases found on Outlook's "hit list." Creating and maintaining an Exception List is covered in the next section, "Using the Rules Wizard."

Using the Rules Wizard

The Rules Wizard is an automated organizer, helping you manage your e-mail so messages you send and receive are handled properly without the need for you to do any work. All you have to do is tell the wizard about a rule ("when my brother sends me a message, forward it to my sister if the subject line has the word loan in it"), and you can rest assured that the wizard will carry out the rule flawlessly and automatically.

 Rules created with the Rules Wizard do not work on messages received from an HTTP e-mail account such as Hotmail.

Understanding Server and Client Rules

Some rules you create can be implemented on the Exchange server, even when you're not logged in to the server. These are called server-based rules. In order to qualify as a server-based rule, all the elements of the rule must exist on the server. For example, if a rule involves moving messages to server-based folders, the rule is server-based since all mail is initially received at the server, and the destinations indicated in the rule are folders, which are also located on the server.

Other rules must wait for you to open Outlook and log on to the server before they're implemented, and these are called client-only rules. For example, if you instruct the wizard to move a message to a folder in your Personal Folders list, or to forward a message to a recipient in your Personal Address Book, the wizard can't complete its work until those entities are available as a result of your logon.

 When you create a rule, the wizard notifies you if the rule is a client-only procedure.

Creating a Rule

To create a rule, you must give the wizard some guidelines (it's a wizard, not a mind reader):

- When to apply the rule (when messages arrive, when you send a message, when a message contains certain words).
- What to look for in the message (a certain sender, certain recipients, a certain word in the subject field or message body).
- What to do when a message matches the criteria (move it, delete it, forward it, play a musical tone).

You can create a rule by stepping through the wizard windows, or by finding a message on which the wizard can base a rule.

 If you manage junk mail by filtering as described in the previous section, you've already begun using the Rules Wizard.

Creating a Rule with the Wizard

To create a rule by stepping through the wizard windows, choose Tools | Rules Wizard. When the Rules Wizard opens, all existing rules are listed. If you haven't yet created a rule, the list is blank.

If you're upgrading from Outlook 2000, you'll get the opportunity to upgrade your existing rules as well. Unless you're planning to revert back to the older version, it's a good idea to perform the upgrade.

To create a rule, click the New button in the Rules Wizard window. The first thing the wizard wants to know is whether you want to use a template or create a new rule from scratch. The templates, which are listed below the two options, provide an easy way to create the most commonly used rules. If you use a template, the next step is to let the Rules Wizard know the type of rule you want to create (see Figure 19-9).

Some types of rules require that you specify details, and the wizard provides an underlined link you can click to fill in the necessary data. For example, if you select the

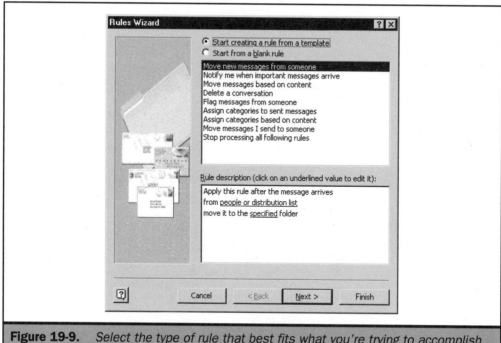

Figure 19-9.   *Select the type of rule that best fits what you're trying to accomplish*

rule type "Move new messages from someone," the bottom pane displays two underlined links:

- **People or distribution list**   Click this link to open a dialog box that has all the names in your address lists. You can select the sender(s) to whom this rule applies or enter a new sender.

- **Specified folder**   Click this to open a dialog box that displays all the folders in your Outlook system. Select the folder into which you want to move the messages that apply to your new rule.

After you select the type of rule and fill in the required information (if the rule requires information), click Next.

In the next wizard window, select the conditions that must exist to activate the rule. The list that appears in this window varies, depending upon the type of rule you selected in the first wizard window. For example, Figure 19-10 shows the conditions offered for the rule type "Move messages based on content."

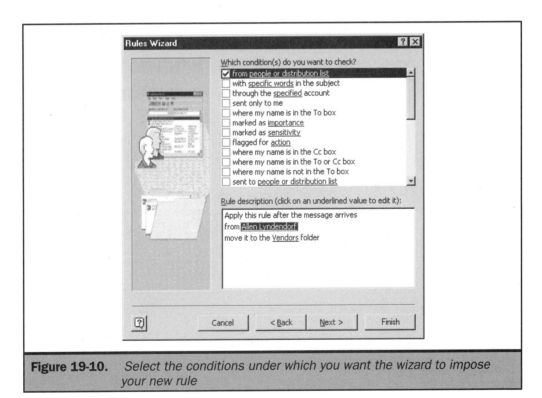

Figure 19-10.   *Select the conditions under which you want the wizard to impose your new rule*

Some of the conditions may require you to enter data. For example, if you're creating a rule based on words or phrases in the subject line or the message body (or both), click the appropriate link in the wizard window to enter the specifics. Some specifics can include multiple entries.

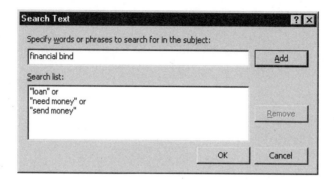

Continue to click Next to move through the wizard windows; the contents vary depending upon the type of rule you're creating, and the conditions you've set for the rule. You can also tell the wizard about exceptions to the rule (for example, you might want to ignore a rule based on the sender if a certain word appears in the subject line). The last wizard window asks you to name the rule (choose a name that's descriptive), and then asks if you want to turn the rule on now. Click Finish when you've completed this final wizard window.

The final wizard window may also ask if you want to run the rule against a folder, which means you can apply the rule to messages already in that folder.

Creating a Rule from a Message

If you receive a message from someone and decide that further messages from that person should be handled via a rule, you can create that rule by using the message as a template. Begin by right-clicking the message in your Inbox or any other folder, and choosing Create A Rule from the shortcut menu. This opens the Rules Wizard, which already has information filled in using data from the message you originally selected.

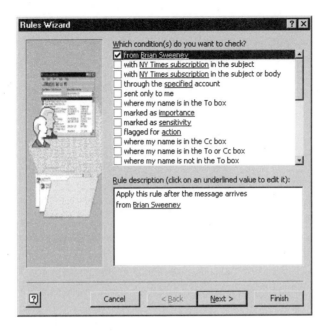

Finally, change details as desired, and click Next to add the action to be taken. Continue as outlined in the previous section on creating rules.

Managing Rules

After you create rules, you can edit, remove, and manage them from the Rules Wizard dialog box (see Figure 19-11). To open the Rules Wizard, choose Tools | Rules Wizard.

The opening window of the Rules Wizard provides an opportunity to fine-tune the way the wizard processes rules:

- To temporarily stop applying a rule, click the rule's check box to remove the check mark. When you want to re-apply the rule, click the blank check box to insert a check mark (it's a toggle).

- To permanently remove a rule, select its listing and choose Delete.

■ To change the specific data that kicks off the rule, select the rule's listing, then select the appropriate link in the bottom of the dialog box.

■ To change the name of a rule, select its listing and choose Rename.

■ To change the way the rule works, select its listing and choose Modify. The original wizard process runs again so you can make changes to the rule's configuration.

■ To change the order in which rules are applied, select a rule and use the Move Up and Move Down buttons to change its position in the list.

When you're through, click OK to save the changes and return to the active window.

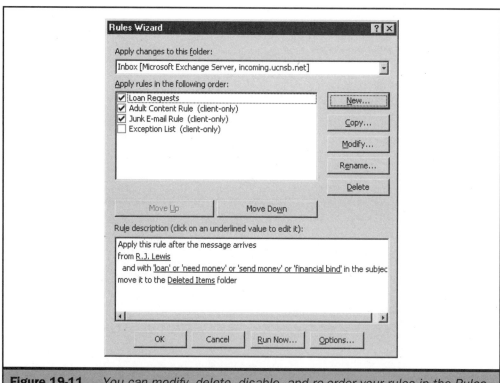

Figure 19-11.   *You can modify, delete, disable, and re-order your rules in the Rules Wizard dialog box*

Configuring the Order of Rules Processing

The fact that rules are processed in a certain order can lead to confusion and even problems. There are two sets of parameters the wizard uses when applying rules:

■ Rules are applied in the order in which they appear in the Rules Wizard list.

■ All server-based rules are applied (in order) before any client-based rules are applied (in order).

The server-based rules before client-based rules approach is in effect even if you're logged on. If you're not logged on, only the server-based rules are applied until you log on, at which point the client-based rules are applied.

You can face a real dilemma as a result of this ordered procedure, because it means that after the wizard applies a rule, it moves to the next rule and applies it, and that may mean that the second rule is applied to the messages that were already affected by the first rule. Sometimes that's okay, and sometimes it's not. For example, suppose you create the following two rules:

■ Messages in the Inbox that are from a sender named John Doe are forwarded to Jane Roe (who handles the John Doe account and must be kept informed), and the original message is deleted from your Inbox.

■ Any message with the word "advertisement" in the subject line is deleted.

If you receive a message from John Doe with the sentence "I like the advertisement you designed" in the subject line, and the rules are applied in the order indicated here, you have no problems. However, if the rules are applied in reverse order, Jane Roe never sees the message—it's deleted from the Inbox before the second rule is applied, and therefore isn't available for the actions included in the second rule.

If you have a lot of rules, especially if they're complicated (perform more than one action), you risk having rules applied improperly or not at all. There are a few guidelines to keep in mind as you manage rules:

■ Give careful thought to the order in which rules are applied, using the Rules Wizard window to change the order when necessary.

■ Take advantage of the action "stop processing more rules," which is available for every rule you create. Selecting this choice tells the Rules Wizard that all messages impacted by the current rule are not to undergo processing by any rules that follow this rule.

The "stop processing more rules" action isn't an absolute cure, because sometimes you may create rules that are specifically designed to work with each other, each rule enhancing (or further filtering) the work of the previous rule.

Rules for Meeting and Task Requests

The Rules Wizard is perfectly happy to apply rules against meeting requests and task requests (after all, they're messages), but you must configure the rule properly. You can only set up rules that affect incoming meeting and task requests; you cannot apply rules to task and meeting requests you send to others.

To set up a rule that's specific to such requests, choose the following options in the Rules Wizard:

1. Select Start From A Blank Rule.

2. Choose "Check messages when they arrive" as the type of rule and click Next.

3. Choose "uses the *form name* form" as a condition, and then click the form name link to choose the form.

4. In the Choose Forms dialog box that opens, select Application Forms from the drop-down list at the top of the dialog box.

5. Select Meeting Request or Task Request (or both) and click Add, then click Close to return to the Rules Wizard.

6. Click Next, and choose the actions you want to apply to these messages.

7. Complete the remaining Rules Wizard steps and click Finish.

Bear in mind a couple of things. One, the tracking features don't work if you move messages out of the Inbox into another folder with a rule. Two, moving a message to a special folder with a rule doesn't work the way it does when you manually move or drag a message. For instance, moving a meeting request to your Calendar folder with a rule doesn't automatically create an appointment.

Running Rules Manually

Usually you create a rule as a result of having performed a task manually many times. For example, you've manually been moving all the messages from your brother to a folder named Family Mail, or all the messages with the word "budget" in the subject line to a folder you created to store mail about the company budget.

While rules take care of the new, incoming mail, they aren't retroactive. In other words, rules take effect "from here on," processing actions against messages that arrive or are sent after the rule is created, but not affecting messages already contained in the folders to which the rules apply.

Fortunately, Outlook 2002, allows you to run a rule against existing messages, which provides a nifty way to clean up your Inbox or other folders automatically instead of manually. Here's how to run your rules manually:

1. Choose Tools | Rules Wizard.

2. Click Run Now to open the Run Rules Now dialog box shown in Figure 19-12.

3. Select the rules you want to run.

4. If necessary, change the folder you want to run the rules against by clicking Browse and selecting a new folder. Also, specify whether you want to run the rules against any subfolders.

5. Use the drop-down list at the bottom of the dialog box to select the messages for which you want to apply these rules: all messages, unread messages, or read messages.

6. Click Run Now, then click Close.

The rules are applied.

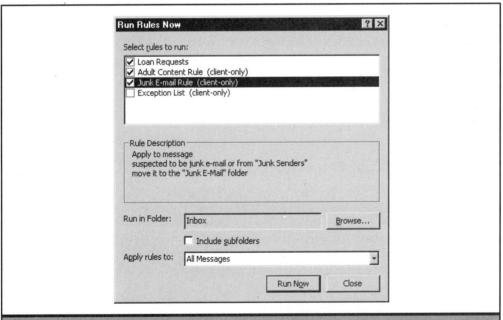

Figure 19-12.   *Catch up with old messages by applying rules against them*

Tricks and Tips for Rules

It's not possible to go over every possible criteria selection, and the resulting actions you might select as you create rules. As a remedy for this lack of ability to discuss every possible permutation and combination you could invent, it seems prudent to present some helpful information (based on problems that are frequently encountered).

Automatic Message Forwarding

One of the actions available to you when you create a rule is the ability to forward a message that meets certain criteria. However, unlike the sequence of events that occurs when you forward a message yourself, no copy of the forwarded message is sent to your Sent Items folder.

This means you have no way of determining whether the message was forwarded (except by calling the recipient). Unfortunately, this is one of those Outlook design issues that requires you to have blind faith that the Rules Wizard did what you commanded.

Bcc Is Not an Available Criterion

You cannot ask the wizard to filter incoming mail that has your name on the Bcc field. If you are creating a rule for outgoing mail, you cannot ask the wizard to select a message on the basis of a name in the Bcc field.

From E-Mail Address versus Reply To E-Mail Address

Some e-mail messages you receive may have both a From field and a Reply To field. If you reply manually, the message is sent to the Reply To address. However, if you create a rule that has Reply as an action, the message is sent to the name in the From field.

Moving Messages to Deleted Folders

If you create a rule that moves certain messages to another folder, and you delete the folder, the rule is supposed to stop functioning. However, you'll probably find that the rule continues to apply the action, moving messages into the deleted folder.

This occurs because a folder, like a message, is not permanently deleted until you delete it from the Deleted Items folder. When you delete a folder, it becomes a subfolder of the Deleted Items folder until you empty the Deleted Items folder. At that point, the rule will cease to function.

Creating Rules that Support OR as the Condition

Outlook does not offer any OR conditions in the Rules Wizard. This means you cannot create a rule that says "move a message to the Family Stuff folder if it is from Joe Blow OR has the word birthday in the subject field." If you select those two criteria in a rule, a message must meet both criteria in order to kick off the action of moving the message to the folder.

Sometimes the OR criterion is important, and you want to check for messages that have either of two criteria, but not both. The solution is to create two separate rules, and in each rule you must specify one criterion and specifically exclude the other. The Rules Wizard provides an opportunity to create exclusions in the next-to-last wizard window.

Assigning Categories Automatically

You can create a rule in which messages that meet your criteria are assigned to a category. This is handy if you use categories to track and sort messages. However, the Rules Wizard doesn't check up on you. If you haven't created the category, the wizard doesn't remind you to do so, it just ignores the problem and the rule.

Any rule that involves assigning a category is automatically a client-based rule.

MOUS EXAM PRACTICE
Create a rule that assigns messages from your boss to the VIP category. To see the results, add the Categories field to the Inbox and sort by clicking the Categories column header. Modify the rule to include your spouse and others whose messages you don't want to miss.

Using the Out of Office Assistant

The Out of Office Assistant is primarily designed to generate automatic replies to messages sent to you when you're not in your office and not checking e-mail. This is not the same as being out of the office and checking in from a remote location, because in that case you generally continue to check your e-mail. The automatic reply is usually worded to explain that you're out of the office.

In addition to generating an automatic reply, you can set rules to handle incoming messages automatically. This is useful if mail arrives that can't wait until your return to the office, and must be forwarded to someone else or otherwise managed automatically.

The automatic reply and the rules you establish don't work until you specifically notify the Out of Office Assistant that you're out of the office.

A bug in Microsoft Exchange Server 5.5 prevented the activation of the AutoReply when users created a rule that was configured as the last rule to process (a selection named "Do not process subsequent rules" is available when you create rules; it's discussed later in this chapter). The Out of Office AutoReply itself is a rule and is considered to be the last rule in the list of rules. If a user-created rule is configured to name itself the last rule, the AutoReply doesn't kick in. A fix is now available from Microsoft. You can get information about the problem and find a link to the fix in Knowledge Base Article Q248456.

One word of caution. When using the Out of Office Assistant (or any rules, for that matter) make sure you exclude any mailing lists you're on from automatic replies. It tends to make everyone on the list cranky.

Creating the AutoReply Message

The AutoReply message is created in the Out of Office Assistant dialog box, which you open by choosing Tools | Out of Office Assistant. Enter the message in the text box, as shown in Figure 19-13.

The AutoReply message isn't sent until you select the option I Am Currently Out Of The Office. This means you can create the AutoReply message at any time and implement it only when it's needed.

If an AutoReply is the only rule you want to set for the times you're away from the office, click OK; that's all you have to do. Remember to select the option that indicates you're out of the office when you want to implement this feature.

Here are a few things you should know about the way AutoReply works:

- AutoReply kicks in automatically when you tell the Out of Office Assistant you're out of the office, even if you don't enter text (senders receive a blank message).

- Each sender receives only one AutoReply. Outlook keeps track of the senders so that the first message from any sender kicks off an AutoReply. Subsequent messages from the same sender do not generate an automatic response.

- The list of senders who received the AutoReply message is cleared when you notify the Out of Office Assistant you are back in the office.

- The text in the Subject field of your AutoReply is: Out of Office AutoReply: *<original subject text>*.

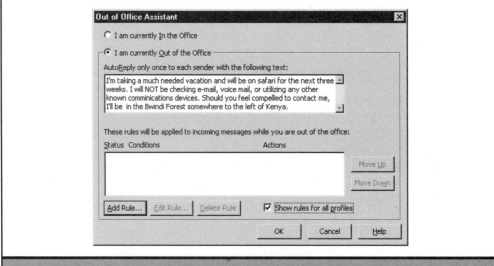

Figure 19-13. *Enter the text for your AutoReply message*

Creating Out of Office Rules

Suppose something's going on that can't wait until you return from your vacation. Perhaps there's a project you're running that can't stop just because you're absent. You'll want to forward messages concerning the project to another person in the company. Fortunately, in addition to creating an AutoReply (or instead of using an AutoReply), you can set rules to handle messages while you're out of the office.

To create a rule, choose Add Rule in the Out of Office Assistant dialog box. The Edit Rule dialog box opens (see Figure 19-14).

Use these guidelines as you create rules:

- Rules must be server-based; you cannot move a message to any folder that isn't in your server-based mailbox.

- You can have multiple conditions in a single rule.

- You can have multiple actions in a single rule.

- You can create multiple rules.

- Multiple rules are applied in the order in which they're listed.

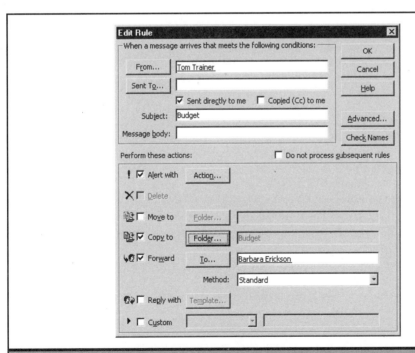

Figure 19-14. *The top half of the dialog box is for setting conditions; the bottom half is for designing actions that take place when those conditions are met*

Specifying Conditions for a Rule

The Out of Office Assistant provides several fields you can use to set the conditions for a message in order to qualify the message for this rule. Multiple entries are separated with a semicolon, and unlike the Rules Wizard, multiple entries indicate an OR condition for that field. A message doesn't have to match all the data you enter in any given field, it just needs to match one entry. However, if you enter data in more than one field, messages must match at least one entry in each field to qualify for the rule.

- ■ **From** Enter the names of senders, either by clicking the From button and selecting names from a list, or by typing the name directly in the From box. Separate multiple names with a semicolon, and click Check Names to make sure the name you typed has a match in your address lists.

- ■ **Sent To** Specify whether the message is sent directly to you, copied to you, or both. You can also further qualify the message by including additional names that must appear in the To field of the message. Click the Sent To button to select the name(s) from an address list, or enter the name(s) directly and check them against your list by clicking Check Names. Separate multiple names with a semicolon.

- ■ **Subject** Enter a word or phrase that must appear in the Subject field. Separate multiple words or phrases with a semicolon.

- ■ **Message body** Enter text that must appear in the body of the message. Separate multiple strings of text with a semicolon.

Setting Advanced Criteria

Click Advanced to use the additional qualifiers available in the Advanced dialog box, shown in Figure 19-15.

Most of the choices on the Advanced dialog box are self-explanatory, but a few bear some discussion.

Selecting the Only Items That Do Not Match These Conditions option provides a way to create a counterbalancing rule. For example, after you create a rule that specifies conditions based on certain senders and causes those messages to be forwarded to your boss, you may decide you want all other messages forwarded to your assistant. Create a rule in which the conditions are the same as the first rule, changing the person to whom the messages are forwarded. Finally, click the Advanced button and select the Only Items That Do Not Match These Conditions option.

Another clever use for the counterbalancing rule also provides a method of keeping your mailbox from becoming massively crowded while you're away. Create a rule that moves all messages with "urgent" in the Subject field to a folder you create in your server-based mailbox (name the folder Urgent or something similar). Then create a counterbalancing rule (messages that do not have "urgent" in the Subject field), and use the Reply With action and the Delete action (explained in the next section) to both send a message to the sender and delete the message from your mailbox. In the text of your Reply, explain what's going on. For instance, you might say, "If it's urgent that I

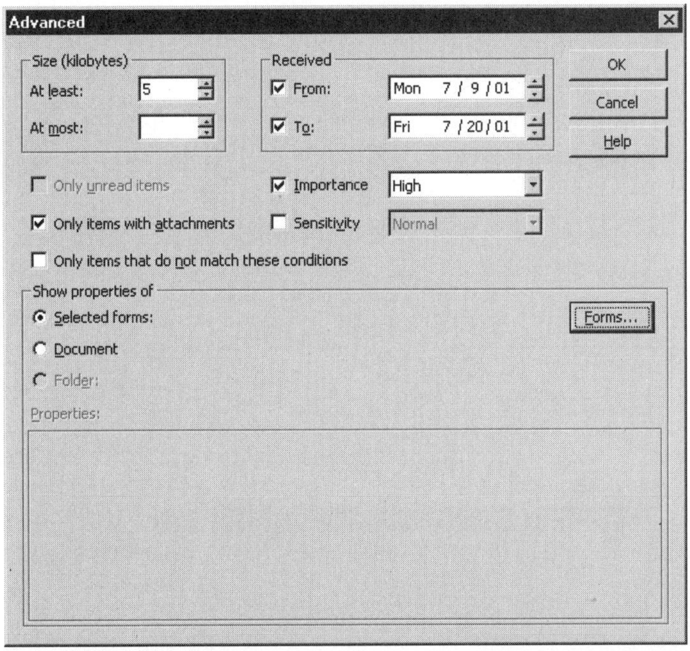

Figure 19-15. *You can narrow the criteria further with the choices in the Advanced dialog box*

see this message as soon as I return, please resend it with the word "urgent" in the Subject field. Otherwise, please send the message again after my return because the message you sent has been automatically deleted."

Configuring the Actions

When a message meets any of the criteria you set, an action results. You configure the action in the same Edit Rule dialog box in which you configured the conditions. Most of the actions are self-explanatory, but the following bear some discussion:

- **Reply with**   Select this option and click Template to open a standard message form. Enter text, insert an attachment if you wish, and add any additional recipients to the To or Cc fields. Then choose Save & Close. This reply is sent to the sender(s) named in your rule.

- **Custom**   This option initiates a third-party program you installed. Programs that perform special rule-based functions are available from several sources. Try http://www.slipstick.com for custom programs and links to other Web sites with custom programs.

- **Do not process subsequent rules** You can select this option to make this rule the last rule that's used, regardless of its position in the list of rules. However, it's best to select this option only for the last rule in a list of rules.

When you've finished configuring the rule, click OK to return to the Out of Office Assistant dialog box, where your rule is listed.

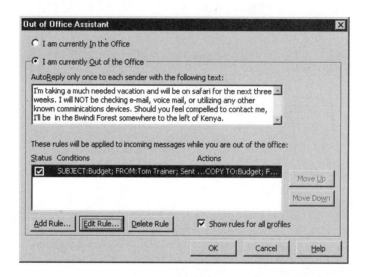

By default, the rule has a check mark, indicating that when you tell the Out of Office Assistant you're away, the rule runs. You can deselect the check mark for any rule you don't want to run while you're away.

If you have multiple profiles for logging on to Outlook, and you've created Out of Office Assistant rules on more than one profile, select the option Show Rules For All Profiles to have access to all the rules you've created.

You can edit or delete a rule by selecting its listing and clicking the appropriate button. You can even change the order of the list of rules by selecting a rule and using the Move Up and Move Down buttons.

Saving Time with Templates

Everyone who uses e-mail finds that he or she creates the same or similar messages frequently. For example, you may send a meeting request with basically the same contents to the same list of recipients whenever you need to meet about some department business, or you may send an e-mail message to the same person or group about a certain topic.

Any message that is essentially the same as a previous message can be turned into a template, which means you need only open the message form, change one or two items, and send the message. This is far easier than creating the message from scratch over and over. Templates work with all the Outlook message forms: e-mail messages, task requests, and meeting requests.

Creating a Template

To create a template, open a blank message form and enter the header information (recipients and subject). If this is an e-mail message form (rather than a task request or a meeting request), enter the message text. Figure 19-16 is an example of a message that's set up to be a template.

Instead of choosing Send, take these steps:

1. Choose File | Save As to open the Save As dialog box.

2. Select Outlook Template (.oft) from the drop-down list in the Save As Type field.

3. The folder in the Look In text box changes to the folder in which Office templates are located. The filename is the subject line of the message.

4. Choose Save.

5. Close the message window by clicking the X in the upper-right corner, or by choosing File | Close.

6. If Outlook asks if you want to save changes, click Yes.

7. If Outlook asks if you want to send the message now, choose Yes or No depending on the circumstances.

 If you're creating a template from an e-mail message form, you also have the opportunity to save the message in your Drafts folder. It's a good idea to do so because this gives you an additional (and easy to get to) copy of the template.

You can create as many templates as you need, using any of the Outlook message forms.

Using a Template

Sending a message from a template is as easy as opening the template, making any minor changes that might be necessary, and clicking the Send button. This is certainly faster and easier than selecting recipients and typing text in the message box.

Choose File | New | Choose Form to open the Choose Form dialog box. Select User Templates In File System (or the folder in which you saved the template) from the Look In drop-down list, and double-click the template you want to use. This opens the template. Make any necessary changes in the message and click Send to transmit the message.

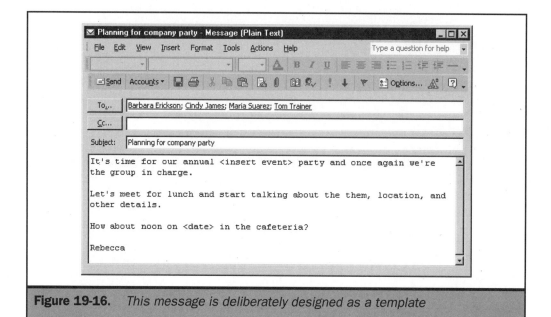

Figure 19-16. *This message is deliberately designed as a template*

The magic of all this is that when you selected the template, Outlook didn't open your template, it opened a blank message form based on your template. The changes you made were to the message, not the template. No matter what you do to a message based on a template, the template itself remains exactly the way it was when you originally saved it.

Unfortunately, this also has a small downside. You can't edit a template, so if you want to make changes you must start all over. If you want to delete a template, you must exit Outlook and use Windows Explorer or My Computer to find the file and delete it.

Configuring Secure E-mail

As electronic communications proliferate, so do security concerns. Unfortunately, the technology that makes electronic communication so easily available, also makes that communication susceptible to electronic snooping and other types of exploitation. To protect against such abuses, Outlook provides a number of security features to help you protect your e-mail communications.

Using Encryption and Digital IDs to Protect Your E-mail

One of the ways Outlook can help keep your e-mail messages confidential is with the use of encryption and digital certificates. Encryption is basically the scrambling of the message as it's sent, and the unscrambling of the message when it's received. Any spy movie buff can tell you that. However, today's forms of encryption are even more sophisticated thanks to computers. Digital certificates are electronic IDs that confirm you are who you claim to be. They include not only the information about you, but also encryption keys for scrambling and unscrambling messages.

To utilize encryption, you must obtain a digital certificate either from your network administrator (for sending messages via the network) or from a certification authority (messages over the Internet).

Once you've got your digital certificate(s) in place, the rest is easy. Begin by creating a new e-mail message. Then click the Options button on the Standard toolbar and the e-mail message form. Next, click the Security Setting button on the Message Options dialog box, to open the Security Properties dialog box seen in Figure 19-17.

To Encrypt the new message, check the Encrypt Message Contents And Attachments option. If you want to add a digital signature to the message, check the Add Digital Signature To This Message option. Digital signatures are electronic signatures that confirm the identity of the sender. Selecting the Add Digital Signature To This Message

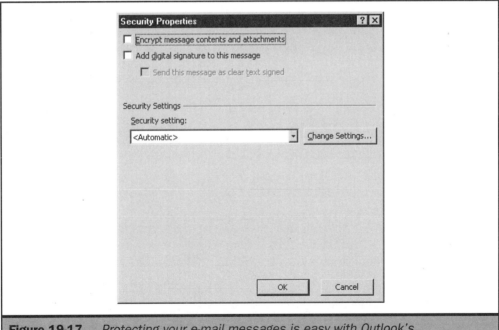

Figure 19-17.   *Protecting your e-mail messages is easy with Outlook's security settings*

option also enables the Send This Message As Clear Text Signed option, which allows recipients using e-mail programs that do not support S/MIME (Secure Multi-Purpose Internet Mail Extensions) to read the message. You can also change the settings used for the message by selecting a setting from the Security Settings drop-down list, or creating new settings by clicking the Change Settings button, which displays the Change Security Settings dialog box.

You can also set security defaults for messages by choosing Tools | Options and selecting the Security tab. At the top of the tab you find the same options described earlier, except those found here are for configuring default e-mail security settings, rather than settings for a single message.

Enabling Virus Protection

If you're not aware of e-mail viruses, especially those that take advantage of Microsoft Outlook, I suggest you run for a mirror and make sure you're still breathing. For the last couple of years viruses have been making headlines every few months. Unfortunately, Outlook is one of the prime targets for virus makers. While there are a number of things you can do to protect yourself against viruses, Microsoft has implemented a new feature in Outlook 2002 that helps prevent viruses from invading your system. The protection, however, is controlled by your Exchange administrator who can set varying levels of protection that may impact your ability to receive a variety of legitimate attachments in your e-mail. Since viruses are generally spread through file attachments that insinuate themselves in your system, the top-level virus protection Outlook uses blocks certain file types from being accessed or even appearing in your incoming messages. Check with your administrator to find out what level of virus protection is being used.

Some other things you can do to prevent virus infections include:

- If attachment files are allowed, do not open files from unrecognized sources.

- Keep your macro security level set to High or Medium to insure macro viruses in documents sent by others do not infect your copy of Word. On High, all unrecognized macros are automatically disabled. On Medium, you receive an alert, which enables you to make the choice for yourself. Choose Tools | Macro | Security to access the Security dialog box.

- With more and more people using HTML message formats, another problem has arisen—scripts and controls that contain viruses. To ensure you don't get bitten by this virus, leave your Secure content settings on Restricted sites, which prevents scripts and controls from running in HTML messages. You'll find the Secure content settings on the Security tab of the Options dialog box (Tools | Options).

Of course, there's one other thing you should do—get yourself a good antivirus program and run it frequently. Outlook is not the only source of viruses.

MOUS

MOUS EXAM PRACTICE
In this section, you learned to secure your e-mail utilizing a variety of Outlook features. Begin by checking with your administrator to find out what kind of digital certificates are available to you, and what level of virus protection has been enabled. Then create new messages, set their security options and send them to co-workers and friends. Check your other security settings to ensure your macro and HTML message protections are in place.

Performing Mailbox Cleanup Chores

While this is not strictly an e-mail chore since the Mailbox cleanup feature works on any of your Outlook folders, e-mail is certainly the one folder that tends to get filled to the brim quickly and frequently. Therefore, this seems like the best place to address the new Mailbox Cleanup feature.

This handy feature gives you a quick rundown on the size of your server-based mailbox folders, and provides access to some Outlook tools that will help you deal with the mounting volume of information you're amassing It's especially helpful if your administrator has imposed size restrictions on your mailbox. If you exceed those restrictions, your ability to send and receive e-mail may be suspended until you clean up your act. To utilize this feature, choose Tools | Mailbox Cleanup to open the Mailbox Cleanup dialog box shown in Figure 19-18.

To get a quick overview of the size of each folder, click the Click Here button to display the Folder Size dialog box. It contains a listing of each folder in your mailbox on the server, along with its current size. This dialog box is informational only.

Once you've determined which folders require cleaning up, you have your choice of three Outlook tools to help you with the task:

- **Find** This section enables you to locate messages of a certain size or age. This is helpful in quickly eliminating or relocating files that are taking up an unreasonable amount of space, or are no longer needed.

- **AutoArchive** Click the AutoArchive button to start archiving your folders according to the default AutoArchive settings for each folder. There are no confirmations needed. As soon as you click the AutoArchive button, the process begins.

- **Empty deleted items** Since you probably don't spend a lot of time in the Deleted Items folder, it's easy to forget about emptying it. It doesn't take long before it starts filling up with a large amount of useless and unneeded data that takes up valuable space on the server. Start by clicking the Click Here button to see just how much waste you've accumulated. Then click the Empty button to permanently dispose of it all. Outlook does ask you to confirm your decision before disposing of the folder's contents, however.

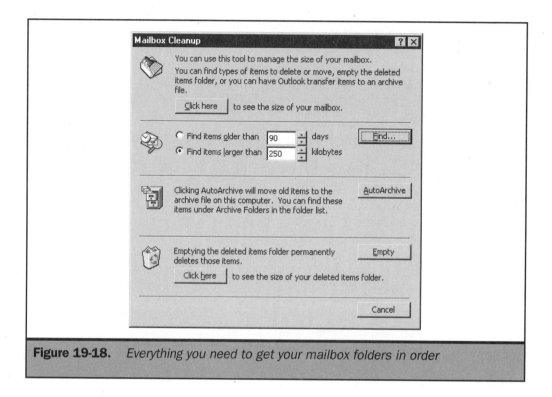

Figure 19-18. *Everything you need to get your mailbox folders in order*

As soon as you use any of the features (except the Click Here buttons), Outlook performs the operation and returns you to the active window.

MOUS Exam Core Objectives Explored in Chapter 19

Objective	Activity	Heading
OL10-1-3	Insert signatures	"Adding Signatures to E-mail"
OL10-3-4	Use categories to manage messages	"Assigning Categories Automatically"

MOUS Exam Expert Objectives Explored in Chapter 19

Objective	Activity	Heading
OL10E-7-5	Set security and encryption options	"Configuring Secure E-mail"

The Complete Reference

Outlook 2002

Chapter 20

Using the Outlook Speech and Handwriting Recognition Features

535

Outlook 2002 offers users the ability to control Outlook (and other Office applications) using voice commands. In addition it provides new technology that enables you to use handwriting to enter information into Outlook form text fields.

Installing Speech and Handwriting Modules

Unless you did a custom install when first installing Office/Outlook, Speech and Handwriting were not installed. Therefore, you'll have to dig out your Office XP disk and run the installation routine again.

System Requirements

Now, before you grab your Office XP disk and start installing, let's make sure your system can handle the software. You probably won't have too much trouble with the handwriting recognition feature, since its requirements are relatively modest. However, speech recognition takes a fair amount of computing power and may present a problem for some systems. Therefore, make sure you have the necessary requirements before proceeding with the installation. Keep in mind, these are minimum requirements. Using equipment that exceeds the requirements will improve the performance of both features.

You may be able to get away with equipment that doesn't quite meet the necessary requirements; however, you'll more than likely pay a price in speed and effectiveness.

Handwriting Recognition

In order to run the handwriting recognition software, your system must meet the following minimum requirements:

- A 75 megahertz (MHz) processor
- 24 megabytes (MB) of RAM (random access memory)
- Windows 98, Windows NT 4.0, or any later version of Windows

If you want to use handwriting to input text into an Outlook text field, you'll also want to have a handwriting input tool such as a digital pen and tablet. While you can use the mouse, it's rather awkward and time-consuming.

Speech Recognition

Speech recognition, by its very nature, requires quite a bit of processing power and memory to function effectively. Therefore, the requirements are much steeper than those for handwriting recognition. Here's what you'll need (at minimum) to use the Office speech recognition feature:

- A 400 megahertz (MHz) processor
- 128 megabytes (MB) of RAM (random access memory)
- Internet Explorer 5.0 or higher
- Windows 98, NT 4.0, or a later version of Windows
- A high-quality microphone attached to a sound card or USB port

While you might be tempted to go with an inexpensive, hand-held microphone, you should resist the temptation. Speech recognition software has a long way to go before it's perfected; therefore, you'll need every edge when it comes to having the software interpret your voice commands accurately. A good microphone is the first step toward that goal.

 For optimum results, use a headset microphone rather than a stationary, desktop unit.

Performing the Installation

This time, select Add Or Remove Features from the Microsoft Office Setup screen, then click Next to display the installation options. Click the plus sign (+) next to Office Shared Features to display the features shared by all the Office applications. Now click the Alternative User Input icon and select Run All From My Computer from the menu that appears. If you want to install only Speech or Handwriting, click the plus sign and select Run From My Computer for the feature you want to install. Click Update to begin the install.

 If you only want to install the Speech feature and you've got Microsoft Word 2002 installed, you can open Word and choose Tools | Speech from the Menu bar. An information dialog box appears asking if you want to install the Speech Recognition files. Click Yes, and the feature is automatically installed for you (as long as you've got the Office CD in the CD-ROM drive).

The next time you start Outlook, the Language bar appears on the Menu bar to the left of the Ask A Question textbox.

Installing the speech engine also adds a Speech command to the Outlook Tools menu. As you might suspect, this activates the speech module. After installation, the speech module runs by default, and the Language bar appears in the position you last left it.

The Language bar, unlike other Outlook toolbars, cannot be docked. It is always floating, which means you can place it anywhere you want, even inside an open form. No matter where you put it, it's always accessible.

As you can see, the Language bar initially contains four buttons, and a down arrow:

- **Microphone** The first time you click the Microphone button, the Welcome to Office Speech Recognition Wizard appears, informing you that you have to adjust the microphone and train Office for speech recognition before proceeding any further. Clicking Next walks you through the process.

- **Tools** Click the Tools button to display a menu of speech recognition commands.

- **Options** This command opens the Speech Properties dialog box in which you can set the language to use, create recognition profiles, adjust the microphone, and more.

- **Show Speech Messages** Check this command if you want vocal commands you issue to appear in the Voice Command textbox, which appears on the Language bar when this option is enabled.

- **Training** Due to the multitude of differences in individual speech patterns, speech recognition software must learn to recognize your particular speech idiosyncrasies. Click this command to start the Voice Training Wizard.

- **Add/Delete Word(s)** Use this command to display the Add/Delete Word(s) dialog box, with which you can add words not already contained in the speech recognition dictionary. This is handy for including special terminology and proper names. If you later change your mind you can return to the dialog box and remove added words as well.

- **Current User** In order to accommodate multiple users, the speech recognition software utilizes a separate speech profile for each user. The Current User command displays a submenu of existing profiles. Select the one you want to use for the current session.

- **Help** Click this button to access the Language bar-specific Help files.

- **Minimize** This is the small minus sign (-) above the down arrow, located on the right end of the Language bar. When you minimize the Language bar, a small icon containing the initials of the default language (EN for English) is placed in the system tray of the Windows taskbar. To restore the Language bar, click the icon and select Show The Language Bar.

- **Options** Click the down arrow beneath the Minimize button to display a drop-down menu of Language bar options.

The handwriting feature, by contrast, only appears when your cursor is placed in a form textbox. At that point, additional buttons and options appear on the Language bar.

The new buttons include the following:

- **Correction**   When you make a mistake in the Dictation mode or in the Handwriting mode, you can highlight the mistake and click this button to display a drop-down list of potential corrections.

- **Handwriting**   Clicking this button displays a drop-down menu of handwriting tools you can use to enter text by writing with a digital pen or your mouse.

- **Writing Pad**   This button displays the last handwriting tool you used. This way, you don't have to keep accessing the Handwriting menu if you frequently use the same tool.

After you finish the installation and familiarize yourself with the Language bar, you're ready to begin setting up the software.

Configuring Speech Recognition

The speech recognition feature in Outlook enables you to perform two basic operations using speech rather than inputting information with your mouse or keyboard. You can control the program by issuing voice commands rather than clicking toolbar buttons and making menu selections with your mouse, or pressing shortcut keys to activate commands. In addition, you can enter text in Outlook form textboxes by dictating the information rather than typing it. However, before you can take advantage of either of these benefits, you'll first have to take care of a couple of configuration chores.

Adjusting the Microphone

This simple exercise ensures that your microphone is working in top form—something very important when it comes to achieving accuracy with voice recognition technology. Begin by clicking the Microphone button on the Language bar. This launches the Welcome To Office Speech Recognition dialog box that starts the·configuration process.

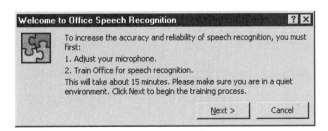

Click Next to open the Microphone Wizard, shown in Figure 20-1.

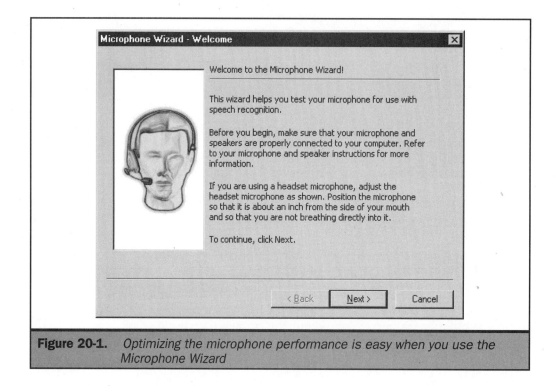

Figure 20-1.   *Optimizing the microphone performance is easy when you use the Microphone Wizard*

The first screen is informational only. Click Next to view the volume adjustment. Read the sentence in quotes and the program automatically adjusts the volume of your microphone. If the meter does not move at all, it means your microphone is not properly connected or enabled. Open the Control Panel and double-click the Speech applet. Click the Audio Input button and make sure your microphone is selected. Click OK to exit the Speech Properties dialog box. Don't forget to close Outlook and reopen it, otherwise the changes you've made will not take effect.

After adjusting the microphone volume, click Next to proceed to the final screen. Here you'll read another short sentence that will help you determine the best position for the microphone. When you're through, click the Finish button to close the Microphone Wizard.

Training the Software

As soon as you close the Microphone Wizard, the Voice Training Wizard appears (see Figure 20-2).

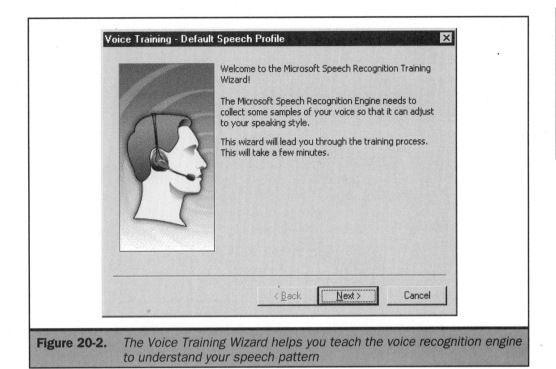

Figure 20-2. *The Voice Training Wizard helps you teach the voice recognition engine to understand your speech pattern*

As with the previous wizard, the opening screen is informational only. Click Next to get on with the work of training the voice recognition software. Select your gender and age group, then click Next until you wade through (and read) the next two informational screens that follow. Once you're past these, the actual training screen will appear, which provides a short paragraph for you to read aloud (see Figure 20-3).

As you read, the speech engine follows along, highlighting the words you speak. When you complete one text selection satisfactorily, another appears automatically. If the speech engine is unable to understand one of the words, it halts until you pronounce it clearly enough for the engine to recognize it.

Note   *Speech technology is still somewhat primitive and you'll find that the speech engine will mistakenly recognize words whose sound is close to those on the screen. Don't worry; you'll get a chance later on to work on troublesome and unrecognized words.*

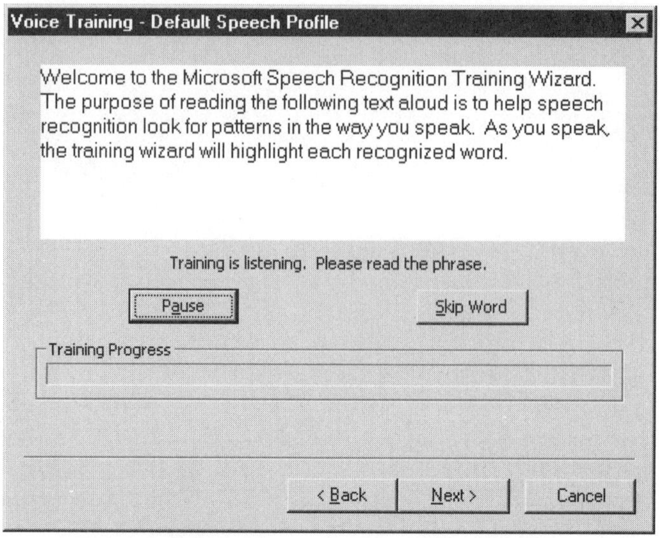
Voice Training - Default Speech Profile
Welcome to the Microsoft Speech Recognition Training Wizard. The purpose of reading the following text aloud is to help speech recognition look for patterns in the way you speak. As you speak, the training wizard will highlight each recognized word.
Training is listening. Please read the phrase.
Pause
Skip Word
Training Progress
< Back
Next >
Cancel

Figure 20-3. *Reading the text aloud enables the software engine to begin recognizing your speech style*

If you find that it simply refuses to recognize a particular word, click the Skip Word button and move on. You can work on that word later. Be sure to speak clearly, and at an even tone and pace. Speaking slowly or loudly will not improve the voice recognition. As a matter of fact, it may produce just the opposite result.

When you reach the end of the training session, your speech profile is updated with the data collected during the training. When the profile update is completed, click Finish to return to the active Outlook window. You'll now notice that the Language bar contains some additional buttons.

Microphone
Dictation
Voice Command
Tools

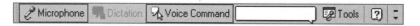

Now you're ready to begin using the speech recognition features.

Using Voice Commands in Outlook

One of the most powerful and practical uses of the voice recognition feature is the ability to control Outlook operations by using voice commands in place of mouse clicks and keystrokes. With voice commands you can speak a menu command, a toolbar or dialog box button, or a common keystroke. This is particularly handy for those users who, as a result of repetitive stress syndrome or some other physical disability, find it difficult to use the keyboard and/or mouse.

Using voice commands is simple. Be sure your microphone is on. You can tell if it's on by the buttons that appear in the Language bar. If the Voice Command button is not visible, the microphone is turned off. To turn it on, click the Microphone button on the Language bar. Then click the Voice Command button to enable the Voice Command mode. Now all you have to do is speak a command.

Note *Voice commands do not necessarily work in all windows that open within Outlook. For example, the Address Book menu and toolbar buttons do not respond to voice commands. The Print Preview screen is another example of this. It contains only buttons, none of which respond to voice commands. The Office Assistant is another area in which voice recognition does not work well.*

The trick is to enunciate clearly and use the precise wording that appears on the menu or button. For example, creating a new mail message entails saying "New" and then "Mail Message." You can either wait for the menu to open, or, if you know the exact command name, you can issue a single voice command, such as "New Mail Message."

Note *When you issue a voice command, the command appears in the text balloon to the right of the Voice Command button on the Language bar. If the action taken does not match the command given, check the text balloon to ensure that the speech recognition correctly interpreted your command.*

Interestingly, you can activate any of the Outlook Bar shortcuts by speaking their names, but you can't open the different shortcut groups by using theirs. In other words, you can open the Outbox (which, by default, resides in the My Shortcuts group) by saying "Outbox" even if the shortcut is not visible. However, you cannot display the shortcut by saying "My Shortcuts." You'll figure out as you go where you can use voice commands and where you can't.

You can also use voice commands to move through records in a folder. For example, to move to the first record, say "Home." To move down one record, say "Down." You get the idea. You can also move between fields in an Outlook form by saying "Tab." Try different navigation commands to see which ones work. Unfortunately, the voice recognition engine does not recognize keys such as SHIFT, ALT, and CTRL. Therefore, you can't move backwards through fields in a form by saying "Shift Tab." You can also use "Back" to return to previous folders, as well as web pages earlier displayed in the Information viewer. You cannot, however, use the word "Forward" since that command is reserved for forwarding e-mail messages.

As indicated by the use of the "Tab" command, some individual keys are recognized by their titles. TAB is one. ESCAPE is another. The latter comes in quite handy for backing out of everything from forms, to dialog boxes, to menus. Simply say "Escape" to close a drop-down menu, an open dialog box, or an open form. Of course, with forms, Outlook will ask if you want to save any changes you may have made. In this case, you can either say "Yes," "No," or "Cancel."

One thing to be careful of is leaving the microphone on during long periods of vocal inactivity or unrelated conversation. The microphone may pick up background noises or bits of conversation you may be engaged in, and execute totally inappropriate commands. If you don't plan to use the voice feature for a while, or you answer the phone, or start a conversation, you should turn the microphone off until you're ready to use it again. Turning the microphone off is easy, since while it's on the Language bar buttons all respond to voice commands. Therefore, you can simply say "microphone" to turn the microphone off. To turn it back on, you'll have to use the mouse.

I think you get the idea. Using voice commands can prove quite helpful once you get the hang of them. It's really a matter of trial and error. The more you use the feature, the more you'll discover exactly what you can and can't accomplish with voice commands.

Using Dictation in Outlook

In addition to issuing voice commands, the Outlook speech recognition feature also enables you to enter text into Outlook text fields by simply dictating. The dictation module, however, is somewhat less precise. This should come as no surprise since the number and variety of words it must recognize is significantly larger than the limited number used in voice commands. Unfortunately, in addition to being less precise, it's also more awkward to work with than much of the speech recognition software available today. If you (or the speech engine) make any mistakes (and believe me, one of you will) you'll have to use the mouse or keyboard to make corrections. A number of speech recognition packages permit you to utilize voice commands while dictating, which means you can correct your mistakes without the use of the mouse or keyboard. Having said that, the Office speech engine is already at your disposal and will be of great use to those whose manual skills are significantly limited.

Dictation is a text input method, which means you can only utilize it in those Outlook fields that accept text. As a matter of fact, unless you're in a text field, the Dictation button is disabled. So the first order of business is to position the cursor in an Outlook text field. It can be anything from the Find a Contact box to the body of an e-mail message form. The Dictation button immediately becomes available.

If you don't see a Dictation button on the Language bar, it means you forgot to turn the microphone on.

As you can see, in addition to activating the Dictation button, entering a text field also adds some new buttons to the Language bar. If you make a mistake, or if the speech engine misinterprets a word, you can use the Correction button to see a drop-down menu of alternatives. If you have the handwriting recognition feature installed, you'll also see the Handwriting and Writing Pad buttons when you enter a text field. Those will be discussed later in this chapter.

Once the microphone is on, click the Dictation button to enable the dictation mode.

Tip   *If you're in the voice command mode, you can say "dictation" to switch modes.*

As soon as you enable the Dictation mode, you can begin dictating the text you want to enter in the field. Begin speaking in a normal tone and at a normal pace, making sure to enunciate clearly. The blue bar that appears indicates that the computer is processing your voice. As soon as it recognizes the words, they appear in the text field. How quickly the computer processes your voice depends on the speed of your processor, the amount of memory installed, and the amount of time you spent training the voice recognition engine. Continue speaking while the computer is processing. It's not necessary to wait for words to appear before moving on.

In the event that you make a mistake, or the software fails to recognize a word you've spoken, you'll have to use your mouse or keyboard to back up and make the correction. You can either correct the mistake by retyping it, or you can place your cursor inside the word and click the Corrections button. This displays a list of alternate words or phrases from which you can select the appropriate one.

Optimizing the Speech Recognition Feature

Since speech recognition technology is far from perfect, it behooves you to put a little effort into tweaking it so it performs at its best. The most important thing you can do is train, train, and then train some more. In addition, you should occasionally adjust your microphone to make sure it's working properly. Finally, there are several options you can use to fine-tune the way the software operates.

Training the Speech Recognition Engine

If you think back to your childhood, you'll probably recall a catchphrase used by parents (probably everywhere in the universe) about practicing. That's right, "practice makes perfect." If you're a parent, you're probably using it on your kids. Well, now it's my turn. If you want to increase your productivity with the speech recognition feature, practice!

The best way to improve accuracy with speech recognition technology is to spend as much time as you have available in training the software. The more experience it has in comparing text it understands to your pronunciation of that text, the more frequently it's going to get it right, even when you don't enunciate perfectly. You can enter the training mode at any time. Click the Tools button on the Language bar and select training from the drop-down menu to open the Voice Training Wizard shown in Figure 20-4.

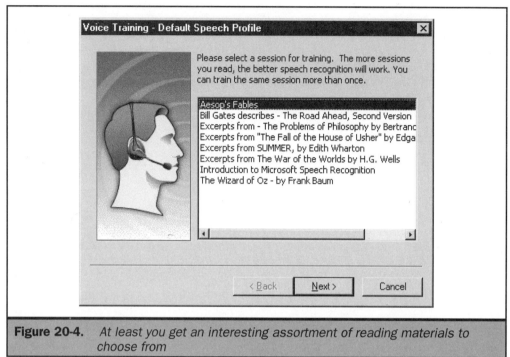

Figure 20-4. *At least you get an interesting assortment of reading materials to choose from*

Choose a reading selection and click Next. The Voice Training Wizard is the same wizard you used to train the software the first time you used it. Therefore, the training process is identical. You just have more interesting material to read for the exercises. As the wizard indicates: the more you train, the better. Try to set aside enough time to complete an entire session. Keep in mind that you can reuse the same reading material to train over and over. It will be just as effective in training no matter how many times you repeat the same session.

Setting Speech Properties

The speech recognition engine comes with a number of settings that you can adjust to improve its performance. Among those are the microphone adjustment and several other properties that provide you with the ability to fine-tune the software's performance.

To access these properties, click the Tools button on the Language bar and select Options from the drop-down menu to open the Speech Properties dialog box seen in Figure 20-5.

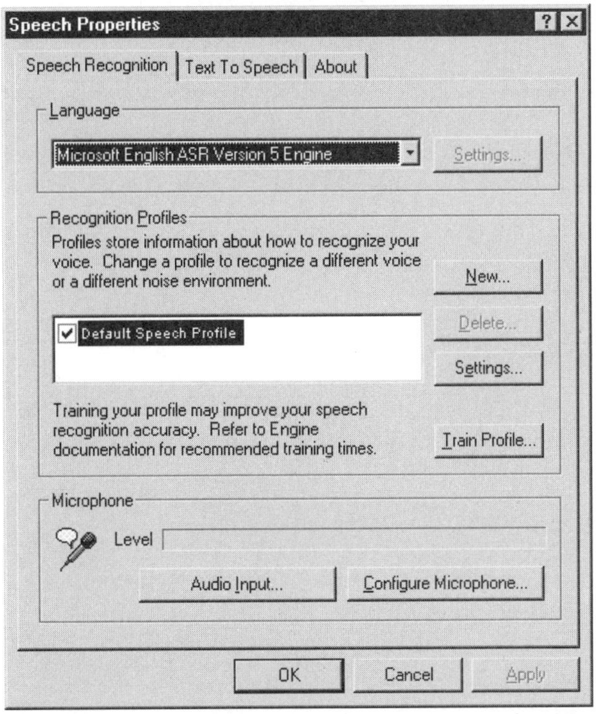

Figure 20-5. *The Speech Properties dialog box provides tools for optimizing the speech recognition engine*

As you can see, the Speech Recognition tab contains three sections, each with its own group of options.

- **Language** The Language options include a drop-down list of installed speech engines and a settings button to configure the selected speech engine. If you've installed the English language version of Office, the only speech engine available is the Microsoft English ASR Version 5 Engine, which has no user-modifiable settings.

- **Recognition Profiles** Speech profiles contain all the speech data gathered from training sections that enable the speech recognition engine to accurately interpret a particular user's speech style. If multiple users are logging on to the same computer, each should have his or her own profile. Click the New button to create a new profile. To Delete an existing profile, highlight the profile and click the Delete button. To adjust a profile's settings, click the Settings button to open the Recognition Profile Settings dialog box, which lets you change the engine's sensitivity to punctuation, denotes your preference regarding accuracy over response time, and tells you whether the software adapts to background speaking. The last button, Train Profile, puts the selected profile in the training mode, and launches the Voice Training Wizard.

■ **Microphone** Here you'll find three items, the Level indicator, and two buttons: Audio Input and Configure Microphone. If the microphone is turned on when you open the Speech Properties dialog box, the Level displays the sound level of the microphone as you speak into it. To change the microphone used with the speech engine, click the Audio Input button and select the input device you wish to use. To adjust the microphone settings, click the Configure Microphone button to launch the Microphone Wizard.

 You can also access the Speech Properties dialog box by opening the Windows Control Panel and double-clicking the Speech applet icon.

When you're through setting the speech engine properties, click OK to save any changes you made, and return to the active Outlook window.

Using the Handwriting Recognition Feature

I have to admit, I was quite skeptical about the handwriting feature before trying it. I figured, if anything, it would be less accurate than the voice recognition feature. Much to my surprise it almost flawlessly recognizes my worst scrawl made with my mouse. For the right user with the right equipment this feature may prove to be an extremely useful bit of technology. To really write with any ease, a digital pad with a digital pen is highly recommended. For a fairly good typist who has no physical disabilities preventing use of the keyboard, the feature has limited usefulness. However, for someone who cannot use his or her fingers but can grasp a pen, this will be a godsend.

This feature is not installed by default, so if you haven't yet installed it, return to the "Installing Speech and Handwriting Modules" section earlier in this chapter. Once it's installed, you can use handwriting recognition in any text field in Outlook. Begin by inserting your cursor in an Outlook text field. As soon as you do, you'll find that the Language bar has sprouted a couple of new buttons that can be used for handwriting: Corrections, Handwriting, and Writing Pad.

If you've used the handwriting feature before, the last handwriting tool you employed appears between the Handwriting and Help buttons.

The first time you use the feature you'll want to check out all the tools at your disposal for making the most of the handwriting recognition technology. Click the Handwriting button on the Language bar to display a drop-down menu containing a variety of handwriting tools.

One last thing. You can continue to use the Speech Recognition feature in either Voice Command mode or Dictation mode while using the Handwriting Recognition feature.

Working with the Writing Pad

The first selection you encounter on the Handwriting drop-down menu is the Writing Pad. When you select it, the Writing Pad opens. As you can see, the writing pad consists of a lined writing area, a pen-shaped cursor, and a number of buttons for enabling special characters and features.

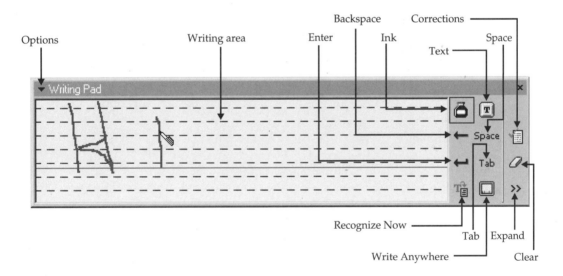

To enter text into the Outlook text field, all you have to do is start inscribing the text inside the lined area of the Writing Pad. For normal-sized text, draw your letters between the top of the writing area and the thin blue line. As soon as you pause, the text is transferred into the text field. If you plan to insert the text as handwriting, there's no need to pause, simply leave a space between words. However, if you are going to have the Writing Pad convert the handwriting to typed text, you should pause to ensure a space is entered between words. That's all there is to using the Writing Pad. Well, at least to the actual writing part. There are, of course, all those buttons to the right of the lined area. Here's what you'll find there:

- ■ **Ink** If you want text transferred from the Writing Pad to the text field to remain in its handwritten form, click the Ink button.

- ■ **Text** To convert handwritten text in the Writing Pad to typed text in the Outlook field, click the Text button.

- ■ **Backspace** Clicking this button moves the cursor back a single space in the text field and deletes any character currently there. When used with handwritten text in the field, it deletes one handwritten entry at a time.

- ■ **Space** Click this button and a space is entered in the text field.

- ■ **Enter** Clicking this button has the same affect as pressing the ENTER key. In a text field, a new paragraph is started. In text fields that are limited to a single line, the cursor moves to the next field.

- ■ **Tab** Works just like the TAB key. It moves the cursor from field to field, or inserts a Tab character when used in a Notes field or message body field.

- ■ **Recognize Now** If the Writing Pad is taking too long in transferring text from the Writing Pad to the text field, click the Recognize Now button to speed things up.

- ■ **Write Anywhere** This button enables the Write Anywhere mode, which allows you to write directly in any field without the use of the Writing Pad. When you select it, the Writing Pad disappears, and the Write Anywhere dialog box (which contains most of the same buttons) appears in its place.

- ■ **Corrections** Place the cursor in a word, or highlight the word (handwritten or typed) in the text field, then click this button to display a drop-down menu of alternate words. Select the word you want used and the correction is made automatically.

- ■ **Clear** Use this button to erase anything currently appearing in the writing area of the Writing Pad. It does not clear text already entered in the Outlook field.

- ■ **Expand** Click this button to display additional Writing Pad buttons. The expanded menu includes a Drawing Pad button, an onscreen keyboard button, and four arrow key buttons.

I almost forgot: There's one more button on the Writing Pad that you might find useful—the Options button. If you look closely, you'll see a small down arrow key to the left of "Writing Pad" in the Writing Pad title bar. Clicking this button displays the same menu that appears when you click the Handwriting button on the Language bar, as well as the Options command and the Help command.

If you click the Options button and then select Options from the menu, you'll discover that the handwriting feature has a number of options you can set (see Figure 20-6).

The Common tab contains options that affect all Handwriting tools. They are fairly self-explanatory. The only one that might need a little explanation is the Recognition Delay slider bar. This setting determines how much time the handwriting recognition engine takes to analyze the text you write. If you find that accuracy is suffering, you might set the speed a little lower.

The Writing Pad tab seen in Figure 20-7, on the other hand, contains options that apply to the Writing Pad only.

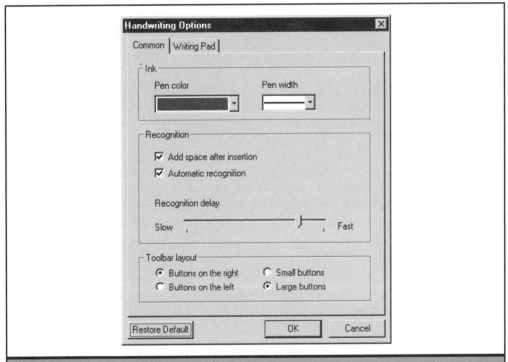

Figure 20-6.   *The Handwriting Options dialog box offers a variety of customization settings*

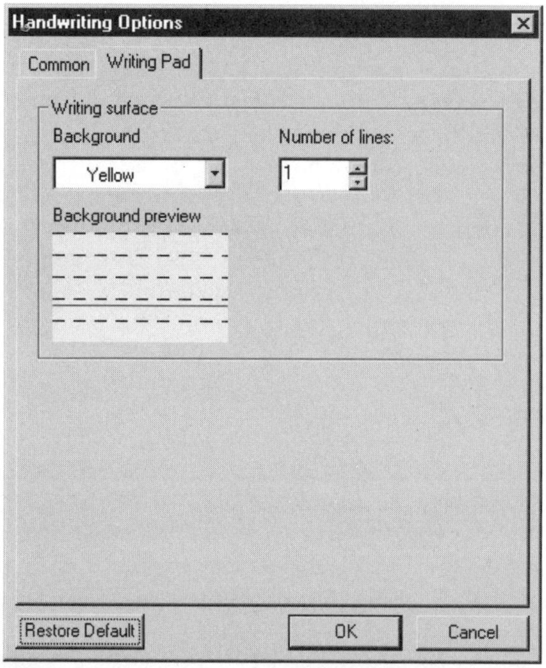

552 Outlook 2002: The Complete Reference

Figure 20-7. *Setting Writing Pad options is easy*

The Writing Pad options are limited to the background color of the writing area, and the number of blue lines it contains. When you're finished setting the handwriting options, click OK to save your changes and return to the active Outlook window.

Writing Anywhere

After you get a little experienced at handwriting in Outlook you may find that you no longer need the structure provided by the Writing Pad to write legibly. When you reach that point, you do away with the Writing Pad and begin using the Write Anywhere mode. To enable Write Anywhere, click the Handwriting button on the Language bar and select Write Anywhere. The Write Anywhere toolbox appears.

As you can see, the Write Anywhere toolbox is almost identical to the expanded Writing Pad toolbox. The only difference is that the Write Anywhere button has been replaced with a Writing Pad button.

With the Write Anywhere mode enabled, you can do just that—write anywhere on the screen. No matter where you write the text, it is added to the Outlook field you're in. Obviously, you'll most often write in the field itself. However, it's not required. As long as the text field is visible on the screen, you can even write over another program window, and the text will still be inserted into the Outlook field. This can result in some unexpected results if you attempt to resize an Outlook window while using the Write Anywhere mode. In spite of the fact that the cursor changes to a double-headed arrow when you reach a window border, the minute you press the left mouse button, the Write Anywhere mode takes over and you begin writing on the screen.

No matter which mode you use, the results are the same. As you can see in Figure 20-8, you can even combine handwritten and typed text in the same Outlook field.

Using the On-Screen Keyboards

If neither your handwriting nor typing skills are up to par, you might consider using the On-Screen Keyboard, which comes in two flavors. The first is the On-Screen Standard Keyboard.

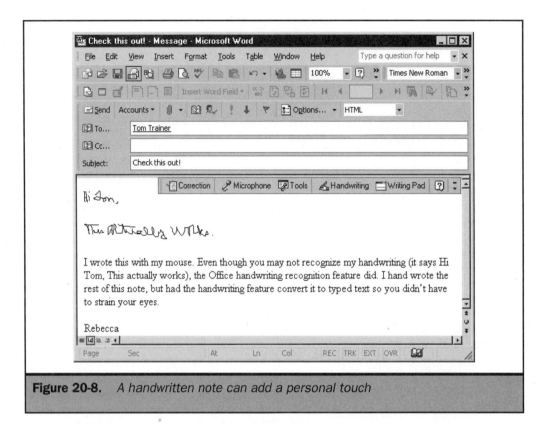

Figure 20-8.   *A handwritten note can add a personal touch*

This keyboard contains letters, numbers, and other basic keys found on most keyboards. You use the On-Screen Keyboard by inserting your cursor in an Outlook text field wherever you want to enter text. Then click each letter, number, or punctuation mark to enter it into the field. You can perform other functions, as well, by using the other keys. For example, you can open the Outlook Help file by clicking the F1 key.

One nice thing about the On-Screen Keyboard is the fact that the SHIFT, CTRL, and ALT keys stay depressed when you click them. This enables you to activate multikey shortcuts without using both hands. For example, if you wanted to move to a previous field, you could click the SHIFT key, then click the TAB key to activate the SHIFT+TAB shortcut.

The On-Screen Symbol Keyboard is similar to the standard keyboard, except the letters are replaced by commonly used symbols.

This works the same way the standard keyboard works. Click the appropriate key to insert the symbol in your Outlook text field.

Creating Drawings with the Handwriting Feature

Not only can you include handwritten text in your Outlook text fields, but hand drawings as well. This is great for adding maps, doodles, and sketches (especially if you have a digital pen and a little artistic talent) to your notes and e-mail messages. To use the feature, click the Handwriting button on the Language bar and choose Drawing Pad from the drop-down menu. The Drawing Pad appears immediately (see Figure 20-9).

Begin drawing anywhere within the blank area of the Drawing Pad by clicking and holding the left mouse button. Release the button to stop drawing. If you make a mistake or don't like something you've drawn, use the Remove Last Stroke button to delete strokes (starting with the last) one at a time. You can continue clicking the button to delete previous strokes. If you decide to start over, you can click the Clear button and remove everything in the drawing area with one fell swoop.

You can even copy the drawing to the Office Clipboard by clicking the Copy to Clipboard button. When you're satisfied with the drawing, click the Insert Drawing button to incorporate the drawing in the text field.

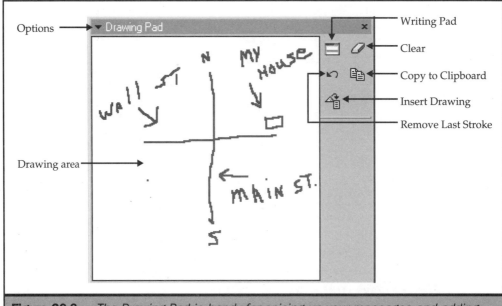

Options ———►

Writing Pad

Clear

Copy to Clipboard

Insert Drawing

Remove Last Stroke

Drawing area

Figure 20-9.   *The Drawing Pad is handy for spicing up your messages and adding graphic information*

If you use the Drawing Pad at all, you'll probably find yourself wishing you could change the color or width of the lines you draw. Well, it just so happens you can. Click the down arrow next to "Drawing Pad" in the title bar to display the Options menu. Choose Options from the menu to open the Draw Options dialog box.

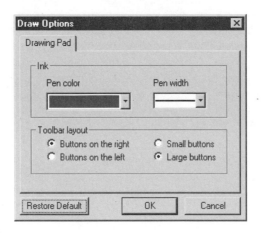

From the Pen Color drop-down list, select the color you want to use in the Drawing Pad. Next, open the Pen Width drop-down list and choose a width for the lines drawn. In addition to modifying the appearance of the lines you draw, you can also change some of the Drawing Pad toolbar options. The Draw Options dialog box lets you choose on which side of the Drawing Pad you want the buttons to appear. It also offers a setting to change the size of the buttons. Both options are self-explanatory. If you modify the settings and later change your mind, you can return to the Draw Options dialog box and click the Restore Default button to return the settings to their original state.

Chapter 21

Using Outlook with
Other Applications

O utlook provides not only a comprehensive set of self-contained e-mail and information management features but also a number of features that offer tight integration with other software applications. Since Outlook is part of the Microsoft Office suite, it naturally plays well with other Office applications. In addition, the import and export feature affords Outlook users the opportunity to exchange information with, and utilize information from, a wide range of other software applications.

Working with Office Applications from Within Outlook

As you might expect, Outlook and its Office siblings are close. So close, in fact, that you can perform various operations from within Outlook that work directly with other Office applications. For example, you can create a single letter or an entire mail merge in Word using the Outlook Contacts folder. In addition, you can use Word as your e-mail editor, even if it's not configured to be the default e-mail editor, by employing the New Mail Message Using command found in Outlook. To take advantage of the ties between Outlook and other Office applications, you must, of course, have the other applications discussed here installed on your computer.

Using the Outlook Contact Database for Mail Merge

 Outlook 2002, like Outlook 2000, includes a true mail merge feature. Previous versions of Outlook required you to access the Outlook contact database and perform the mail merge from within Word. Now you can let Outlook do all the work. Not only that, you can even use the mail merge feature to create personalized e-mail messages and electronic faxes to your contacts.

A mail merge document consists of two basic ingredients, a text document and data fields (either merge or Word fields). The fields are inserted in the document as placeholders for specific information. When the merge is performed, the fields are replaced in each document by specific information from your data source, enabling you to customize each finished document.

To begin, open the Contacts folder. If you don't want to include all the contacts in the mail merge, apply a filter to display only those contacts you want included. For more information on applying filters, see Chapter 23. You can also select individual contacts for inclusion by holding down the CTRL key and clicking the desired contacts. After you've selected the contacts, choose Tools | Mail Merge to open the Mail Merge Contacts dialog box, shown in Figure 21-1.

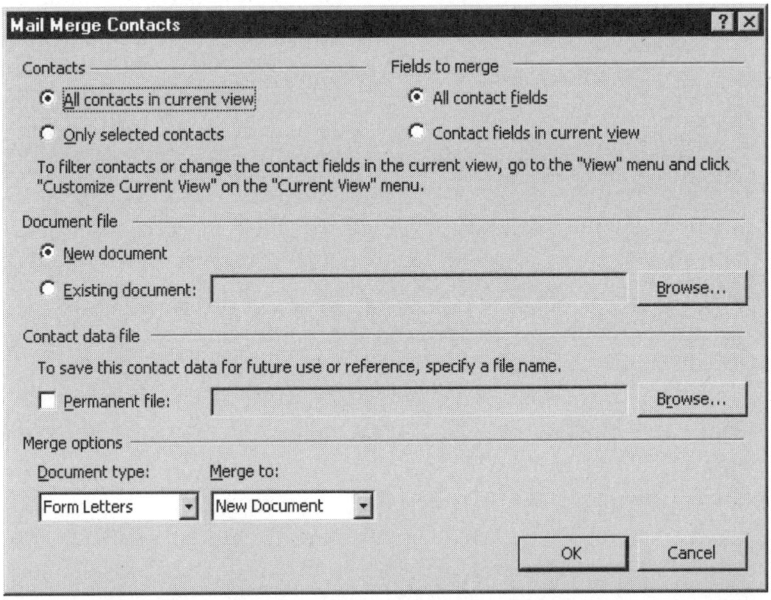

Figure 21-1.   *Mail merge was never this easy*

As you can see in Figure 21-1, the Mail Merge Contacts dialog box contains a number of customization options:

- **Contacts**   Select All Contacts In Current View to include all contacts currently visible. If you've already applied a filter, only those contacts that matched the filter criteria are included. If you applied no filter, all the contacts in the folder are included. If you manually selected contacts to include, choose Only Selected Contacts. Any filter you applied is ignored in favor of those selected contacts.

- **Fields to merge**   Here you can elect to include all contact fields or just those that appear in the current view. If you're thinking this means that the fields you select here are going to be inserted into the mail merge document, don't worry. It simply indicates which fields will be made available for insertion in the merge document. Therefore, you might want to select All Contact Fields to be on the safe side. You may have to scroll a little more to find what you're looking for, but that way you'll be sure not to miss a field you want to include.

■ **Document file**   This option lets you create a new merge document or use an existing document. To create a new merge document from scratch, select New Document. If you already have an existing merge document you want to reuse, select Existing Document, and click the Browse button to locate it. This comes in handy not just for reusing a document created previously but also for modifying an existing document for a different use. For example, if you have an existing document used to notify customers of a change in your pricing policy, you could easily modify it, and create a new merge document to notify vendors of a change in your purchasing policies. Save it with a new name, and you've got a new merge document with a fraction of the effort.

■ **Contact data file**   If you've applied a filter or manually selected individual contacts, you may want to save this particular group of contacts for future mail merges by creating a contact data file and saving it to your hard disk. Enter a path and name for the new file, or click the Browse button to select a location.

■ **Document type**   From the Document Type drop-down list, you can select one of four merge document types: Form Letters, Mailing Labels, Envelopes, or Catalog. The first three are self-explanatory. The fourth, Catalog, is a single document displaying the selected fields for each contact. The catalog type is used to create everything from simple phone or address lists to complex reports detailing a wealth of information about each contact.

■ **Merge to**   This drop-down list provides three or four (if you have a faxing service installed) output options. You can elect to create a new Word document (New Document), send the information to your default printer (Printer), send the information to each contact via e-mail (E-mail), or fax the information to each contact (Fax).

Note   *If you select E-mail from the Merge To drop-down list, an additional field appears, Message Subject Line. The text you enter here appears in the Subject line of each e-mail message created.*

After you set all your mail merge options, click OK to launch Word and complete the mail merge process. No matter which mail merge selections you make, Word opens with a blank document and the Mail Merge toolbar displayed. If you select Mailing Labels or Envelopes, however, the Mail Merge Helper dialog box appears also. You have to let Word know the type of labels or envelopes you want to use by clicking Setup and making your choice. See Figure 21-2.

The next step for any document type is to create the basic document and insert fields in the appropriate places. For the first time, both Contact fields and Word fields are available for all merge documents. Previous versions of Outlook restricted Word fields to Form Letter and Catalog document types. Place your cursor at the location in

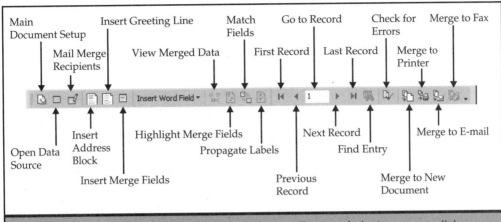

Figure 21-2. *Everything you need to perform a mail merge is just a mouse click away*

your document you want the custom information to appear, and click the Insert Merge Fields button to display a drop-down list of Contact fields. To include Word fields, click the Insert Word Field button. From the list, select the field you want to include in the document. The new field appears in the document at the blinking cursor. Be sure to place the cursor in the appropriate position before selecting a field. For example, if you're including a business address and want city, state, and ZIP code to appear on a single line, add Business_Address_City followed by a comma and a space, then add Business_Address_State followed by a space, and finally, add Business_Address_Postal_Code. The line should appear like this:

<<Business_Address_City>>, << Business_Address_State>>
<<Business_Address_Postal_Code>>

 For adding address and greeting fields, try the Insert Address Block and Insert Greeting Line buttons on the Mail Merge toolbar. They automatically insert all the fields and text necessary for both types of data.

You can intersperse text anywhere you want. For example, you might start a letter with a salutation that looks something like this: *Dear <<Full_Name>>* or *Hi <<First_Name>>*. You can create the body of your letter, e-mail, or fax as you would normally. Again, add fields as needed. Perhaps you're sending a notice to inform your vendors of the new buyers they should contact. If you have a custom field in your contacts database called Buyer, you might add a line to the message that states "In the future <<Buyer>> will be handling your account."

If you want to take a sneak peek at your merge document before completing the merge, click the View Merged Data button. It's a toggle switch that displays the actual data for each field in the document the first time you click it. Click it a second time and the data disappears, and the field names return. While in the data view, you can cycle through all the contacts included in the merge by clicking the various record buttons (First Record, Previous Record, and so on).

The final step is to perform the merge by clicking one of the four merge buttons found on the right side of the Mail Merge toolbar. However, before performing the merge, let's take a quick look at some of the other mail merge commands available on the toolbar.

- **Main Document Setup**   In case you've changed your mind since you started the merge back in Outlook, you can choose a different document type for the merge. As a matter of fact, you'll find even more choices here, including Letters, E-mail messages, Faxes, Envelopes, Labels, Directory, and Normal Word Document.

- **Open Data Source**   Click this button to display the Select Data Source dialog box, which enables you to search for and open the file you're using as the data source.

- **Mail Merge Recipients**   To see the current selection of contacts to be used in the mail merge, click this button. The Mail Merge Recipients dialog box opens, which enables you to view, find, edit, and deselect recipients.

- **Insert Address Block**   This is a great time-saver for inserting address fields in a merge document. Clicking this button displays the Insert Address Block dialog box, from which you select the information and the format in which it's included in the document.

- **Insert Greeting Line**   Similar to the Insert Address Block command, this button enables you to select and enter all the fields and text necessary to create a custom greeting in your merge document.

- **Highlight Merge Fields**   This command is handy for quickly locating all the merge fields (Word fields are not included) in your document. Click the Highlight Merge Fields button, and all of the merge fields in your document are automatically highlighted. Click it a second time, and the highlighting is removed.

- **Match Fields**   If you use a data source other than Outlook contacts, there may be some differences in the field names used by Word and by your data source. Click this button to open the Match Fields dialog box. Here you can designate which data source fields "match up" with existing merge fields.

- **Propagate Labels**   If, while creating labels, you decide you need a full sheet of labels for a particular contact, click this button and an entire sheet of labels is printed with information from one contact. It's great for creating mailing labels for individuals to whom you frequently send correspondence.

■ **Find Entry**   Use this button to open the Find In Field dialog box, with which you can locate a specific piece of information contained in a particular field.

■ **Check for Errors**   Click this button to run an error check on the merge. The Checking And Reporting Errors dialog box opens, offering you several choices. You can simulate the merge and log the errors in a new document, run the merge and simply report the errors as they happen, or run the merge and log any errors that occur in a new document. Since performing a large merge can be time-consuming, you might want to run a simulation first. This is especially true if you're sending the finished documents to the printer, e-mail, or fax. If you elect to run the merge and get a blow-by-blow report, some problems are bound to slip by before you can stop the merge, and you'll have to start all over again. If you choose to run the merge and dump the errors into a log file, you won't know about the problems until the merge is over and it's too late to stop it.

If you're ready to complete the mail merge, you now have the option of selecting one of the last four buttons on the Mail Merge toolbar—Merge To New Document, Merge To Printer, Merge To E-mail, or Merge To Fax. Here's what to expect:

■ **Merge to New Document**   Click this button to start the merge using a new document. The Merge To New Document dialog box opens, offering you the opportunity to modify the current selection of records to be used.

■ **Merge to Printer**   To send the completed merge document to the printer, click this button. The Merge To Printer dialog box appears, offering options for restricting the records included in the merge.

■ **Merge to E-mail**   Clicking this button opens the Merge To E-mail dialog box, which provides a number of options, including the same record restriction options found in the previous two merge commands. In addition, you can select the data source field to use as the To field, add a subject line, and even select the format in which the e-mail is sent (plain text, HTML, or as an attachment).

■ **Merge to Fax**   Clicking this button, which is enabled only if you have faxing installed, displays the Merge To Fax dialog box. Like the others, it offers options for limiting the records included in the merge. In addition, it includes a Fax Number drop-down list from which you can select the fax number field to use.

Note   *When you perform an e-mail mail merge, Outlook alerts you that an attempt to access Outlook e-mail addresses is being made and asks you to approve or decline. If you approve, Outlook also informs you that someone is about to send e-mail on your behalf and requires you to OK it.*

After you set all the merge options, it's time to perform the merge and create the final document(s). Click the merge button of your choice, sit back and relax (with your fingers crossed, of course), and let Word and Outlook do the rest. What you end up with depends on the choices you made along the way:

- **New Document**   If you chose to produce a new document, Word creates a new document containing form letters, labels, envelopes, or catalog entries for each contact.

- **Printer**   If you sent the document to the printer, the Print dialog box appears. Set your printer options, click Print, and your final documents appear in hard copy.

- **E-mail**   An e-mail message is created for each contact and immediately placed in the Outlook Outbox. The next time the Exchange Server does a sweep, or the next time you send e-mail, the messages are dispatched.

- **Fax**   If you performed a fax mail merge, the resulting documents are passed on to the installed fax application and immediately sent to the selected contacts.

If you created a new document, save or print it before closing Word and returning to Outlook to continue working.

MOUS

MOUS EXAM PRACTICE

In this section you learned to use your Outlook contacts to create form letters, mailing labels, and more with the mail merge feature. Unless you have a mail merge project at hand, you'll probably want to start by applying a filter to your contact database to minimize the time it takes to perform your practice mail merge. Perhaps select only those contacts in a certain ZIP code or area code. Next, set the mail merge options and launch Microsoft Word. Take your time in setting up your Word document, and insert the necessary fields where appropriate. Try editing the data source, viewing the merge data, and cycling through the data records before performing the merge. Then perform a merge and use the Print Preview command to see the results.

Using Contacts to Create Letters with Word

In addition to utilizing contact information for creating mail merge documents, you can also use it to create letters in Word. The process is relatively simple. Open the Contacts folder and select the contact to whom you want to write the letter. Next, choose Actions | New Letter To Contact. This opens Word and launches the Letter Wizard shown in Figure 21-3.

Follow the wizard instructions to create the letter. When you proceed to Step 2, the Recipient Info tab, you'll see that the selected contact's name and address have been inserted in the Recipient's Name and Delivery Address fields, respectively.

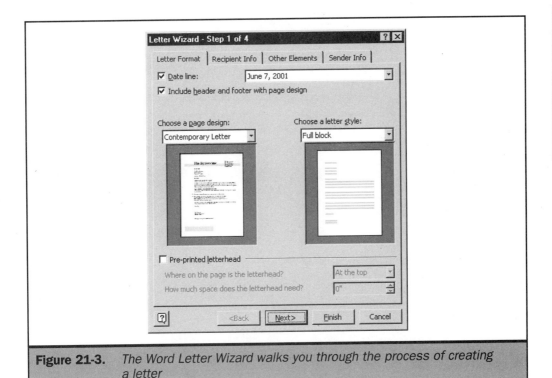

Figure 21-3.   *The Word Letter Wizard walks you through the process of creating
a letter*

When you complete the Letter Wizard, Word creates a letter with the designated
headings, salutation, and closing. Add the contents, perform any necessary
customizing or proofing, and send it on its way.

Using the New Mail Message Using Command

Another handy command you can employ to take advantage of other Office applications
from within Outlook is the New Mail Message Using command. It enables you to create
and send, via e-mail, a document from any of the installed Office applications, without
having to leave Outlook.

To use the command, open the Inbox and choose Actions | New Message Using |
Microsoft Office. This displays the Microsoft Office submenu containing all the Office
applications (except Outlook) currently installed on your system. Choose an application
to launch it with a mail message form opened. You'll see document information of the
type associated with the selected application embedded in the Outlook message body
(see Figure 21-4).

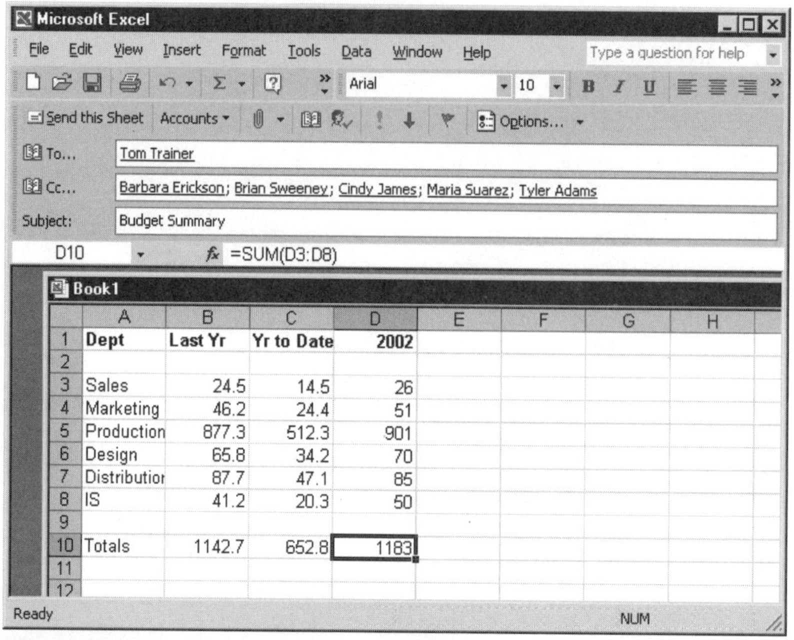

Figure 21-4. *Using the Microsoft Excel Worksheet command opens Excel and embeds a worksheet in the message body*

Note *Only the data from the document is embedded in the message, not the document itself. Therefore, when you receive a message containing such information, you can read it, but you cannot manipulate it as you can a document that's included in a message as an embedded object.*

Enter recipients' addresses in the To and Cc fields, and then enter a brief description of the message in the Subject line. You cannot enter a message to accompany the document data. However, you can set some options. If you take a close look at Figure 21-4, you'll see the message has a toolbar with additional options. You can add an attachment, set the priority, flag the message, and more.

The next step is to add the data to the Office document (worksheet, table, and so forth). Since you're starting with a blank document, you can either add the data manually, or cut and paste it from another document. If you open an existing document, you lose the message form. However, you can still send an existing document by opening it and then clicking the E-mail button on the application's Standard toolbar. This opens another message form containing the document.

When you've addressed the message form and entered the necessary information into the document, you can send the message by clicking the Send button. The name of the

Send button varies depending on the Office application. For example, in Word it's called Send A Copy, while in Excel it's called Send This Sheet. After the message is sent, the Office application remains open with the document still active. However, the message form is no longer available. You can now choose to save, modify, or discard the document.

Using the Office Clipboard

Another nice thing about the closeness of the Office applications is their ability to share the Office Clipboard. Fortunately, in Office XP the Office Clipboard has been transformed from a useful but annoying afterthought to a full-fledged Office tool. Not only does the Office Clipboard enable you to retain multiple items (up to 24), it also conveniently docks itself within the Outlook window (see Figure 21-5) and offers a number of commands and options.

While you can copy from any source that supports copying and cutting, you can only paste items from the Office Clipboard into Office applications (Microsoft Word, Excel, Access, Outlook, or PowerPoint).

The basic operation of the Office Clipboard is no different from that of the Windows Clipboard. The Copy, Cut, and Paste operations can be performed by selecting the text

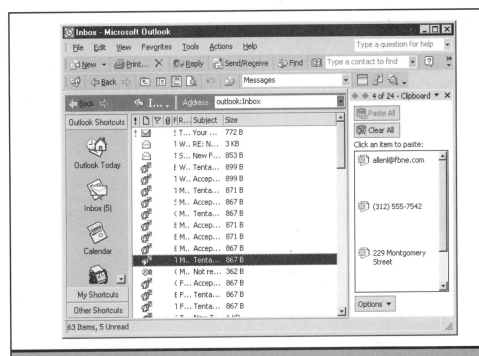

Figure 21-5. *The Office Clipboard stays out of your way and provides easy access to cut and copied items*

or graphic and pressing CTRL+C, CTRL+X, and CTRL+V, respectively. You can also use the Copy, Cut, and Paste commands found on the Edit menu. You'll even find the commands available on a shortcut menu when you right-click selected text or objects.

The Office Clipboard is available not only in the Outlook window but also in all Outlook forms with the exception of the Note form. To display the Office Clipboard, choose Edit | Office Clipboard from the Menu bar.

Tip *You can display the Office Clipboard in an Outlook form by holding the CTRL key and tapping the C key twice.*

By default, the Office Clipboard inserts itself into the bottom-right corner of the window. If you don't like its location, you can turn it into a floating toolbar and move it anywhere you want. Unfortunately, you can no longer dock it anywhere but its original position in the bottom-right corner of the window. To switch between the docked and floating states, double-click the Office Clipboard title bar. To move the Office Clipboard around the window, drag it by its title bar.

Note *The Office Clipboard is not technically a toolbar. The actual toolbar is the Task Pane, which acts as a container for several different features, including the Office Clipboard and the Style And Formatting feature. This is why you won't find the Office Clipboard on the toolbar list that appears when you right-click a visible toolbar. Instead, Task Pane appears. Selecting and deselecting Task Pane displays and hides the current Task Pane feature.*

As you can see in Figure 21-5, the Clipboard maintains a scrollable list of copied items. To paste an item from the Clipboard, place your cursor in a text field and click the item you want to paste. If you want to paste all the collected items, simply click the Paste All button.

Note *If you have the Clipboard displayed in an Outlook folder, double-clicking a Clipboard entry opens a new form of the item type supported by the folder and pastes the entry into the form's Notes field (message body in an e-mail form).*

If you want to remove all data on the Clipboard, click the Clear All button. By the way, the Clipboard can hold a maximum of 24 items. Once you exceed that number, each succeeding item causes the earliest item on the Clipboard to be removed to make room for the new item.

The Office Clipboard also offers several options that become available when you click the Options button:

■ **Show Office Clipboard Automatically** Check this option to have the Office Clipboard display automatically when you perform one of the following three operations: copy a single item twice in succession, cut or copy two different items in any Office program, or copy an item, paste it, and then copy another item.

- **Collect Without Showing Office Clipboard** Check this option if you don't want the Clipboard appearing every time you copy an item.

- **Show Office Clipboard Icon on Taskbar** When you invoke the Office Clipboard, you can have an Office Clipboard icon added to the system tray of the taskbar. Using the icon, you can display the Office Clipboard and access its options.

- **Show Status Near Taskbar when Copying** With this option checked you'll see an indicator near the taskbar each time you copy or cut an item. The indicator displays the number of the item collected (for example, *4 of 24 Clipboard* items collected). If you like hanging on to your copied items, you'll want to enable this option to alert you when you're nearing the limit of 24 items. Remember, after 24, the first item is removed to make room for the new item.

To close the Office Clipboard, click the small X in the upper-right corner, or right-click the Clipboard toolbar and deselect Task Pane from the shortcut menu.

Outlook Commands Available in Office Applications

The integration between Outlook and the Office applications works both ways. In addition to accessing Office applications from Outlook, you can also take advantage of Outlook while working in other Office programs. The two major functions you can perform in other Office applications are sending e-mail and posting documents to Exchange Server folders.

Sending E-mail

While working in most Office applications, you can send the document you're working on with little or no fuss. Rather than open Outlook, create a new message, and attach the document, you might just as well use one of the Send To commands available on the File menu of Word, Excel, Access, or PowerPoint.

Either open an existing document, or create a new one in the application of your choice. When you're ready to send it, choose File | Send To. You'll find two mail commands on the drop-down menu that appears: Mail Recipient and Mail Recipient (As Attachment). Select the one that meets your needs.

- **Mail Recipient** Use this command to open a message form in the application and embed the document information (not the document itself) in the body of the message.

- **Mail Recipient (for Review)** This handy new command enables you to send a document to others for collaboration. A new e-mail message is created with *Please review "document name"* as the Subject, the document inserted as an attachment, and *Please review the attached document* as the message body. The one thing it doesn't do, which it should, is automatically enable Tracking in the attached document.

- **Mail Recipient (as Attachment)**   This command opens a new Outlook e-mail message form with the document already inserted as an attachment.

Enter the desired recipient(s) in the To, Cc, and Bcc fields, and type a brief description in the Subject field. If you don't see the Bcc field and want to use it, choose View Bcc Field from the form's Menu bar or the Options button drop-down list. If you're sending the document as an attachment, type your message. Set any options you want and click the Send button. If you use the Mail Recipient command, the name of the Send button will vary depending on the application you're in.

You can also send e-mail messages from Word by choosing Blank E-mail Message from the New section of the New Document Task Pane. An untitled message form opens. Fill it out and send it. That's all there is to it.

Posting Office Documents to Public Folders

If you use public folders, you'll find this feature quite helpful. It's not uncommon to post documents as well as messages in public folders. You may have a white paper, budget report, or list of ideas you want to get feedback on. Rather than post a message with the document attached, you can post the document itself directly to the public folder. This feature, which is available in Word, Excel, and PowerPoint, also enables you to post Office documents to your Exchange mailbox folders as well. Begin by opening one of the earlier-mentioned Office applications, and opening an existing document or creating a new one. When your document is ready for prime time, choose File | Send To | Exchange Folder to open the Send To Exchange Folder dialog box, shown in Figure 21-6.

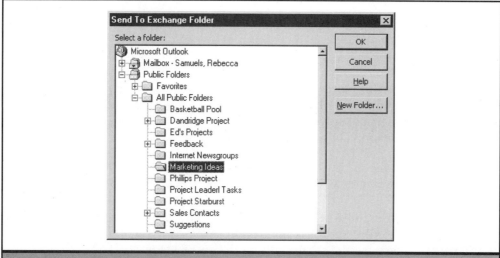

Figure 21-6.   *The Send To Exchange Folder dialog box brings your Outlook Folder List to you wherever you are*

Select the public folder to which you want the current document posted, and click OK. Unfortunately, the folder icons in the Send To Exchange Folder dialog box are all identical. Therefore, you cannot distinguish between the various folder types (mail, contacts, appointments, and so on). So be sure you know the name of the public folder you want to post to before you start out.

While you can post to any folder type, including Mailbox and Personal folders, it doesn't make a lot of sense to post documents to anything other than public folders that contain mail items. When you post to other folder types, the results are generally impractical. For example, nothing appears in a Calendar folder, and a no-name contact record appears in a Contacts folder. No matter where you post it, double-clicking the item launches the associated application and opens the document.

Importing and Exporting Data

The wealth of information that abounds in today's information society is impressive, to say the least, but can easily become overwhelming. Part of the problem is the variety of sources from which that information emanates. Just look at the number of different programs available for handling contact information. Some people use address book software, others use personal information managers, some use spreadsheets or databases, some use contact managers, others use the address books in their e-mail software, and then there are those who use address lists compiled in word processing documents. The same goes for e-mail, appointments, and other bits of information.

In addition, many users today employ both a desktop computer and a hand-held computer (Palm Pilot, Pocket PC, and so on). Using Outlook as your main information management tool enables you to easily transfer information between your desktop and hand-held computer by taking advantage of Outlook's import and export features.

Although Outlook doesn't work directly with most major applications outside the Office suite, you can still make use of Outlook information in other programs, and vice versa. The way to accomplish this is by exchanging data using the Outlook Import And Export feature. When you import information from other programs, Outlook converts it to a format that Outlook can understand. When you export Outlook information, Outlook converts it to a format that other applications can work with.

Importing Data into Outlook

If you happen to be starting out with Outlook and pulling together all your bits and pieces of information from a variety of programs, or if you're gathering information from others who use different software, you'll be glad to know that Outlook has a powerful import feature.

Outlook may be smart enough to convert the data you want to import, but it will need a little help in identifying it. Therefore, the first thing you need to know is the format of the information you want to bring into Outlook. The only other thing you need is access to the file(s) containing the data. Begin by choosing File | Import And Export to start the Import and Export Wizard, shown in Figure 21-7.

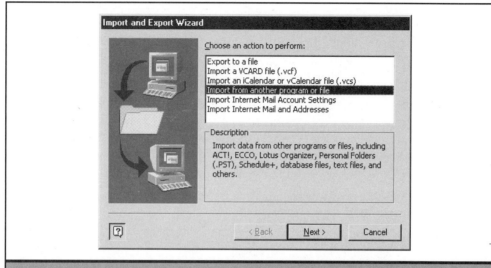

Figure 21-7. *Importing data is child's play when you use the Import and Export Wizard*

The opening screen provides a number of import options, including

- **Import a VCARD file (.vcf)**   vCards have become the standard for sharing contact information in a business card format over the Internet. If you receive and store vCard files from the Internet, you can import them into your Outlook contacts database using this option.

- **Import an iCalendar or vCalendar file (.vcs)**   iCalendar and vCalendar are used to exchange calendar information via the Internet. Use this option to import either format into the Outlook Calendar folder.

- **Import from another program or file**   This is one of the more popular import actions, simply because it enables you to import data from a wide range of programs, including contact managers, PIMs, spreadsheets, databases, text files, and more. As soon as you select this option and click Next, you're presented with a list of file types you can import.

- **Import Internet Mail Account Settings**   If you're switching your Internet e-mail to Outlook from another e-mail client, you can use this option to import the settings from the existing e-mail account into Outlook. Selecting this option and clicking Next launches the Internet Connection Wizard, which searches your hard drive for existing Internet e-mail accounts and lets you select the one whose settings you want to transfer to Outlook. When you finish with the Internet Connection Wizard, Outlook adds the new account to your profile.

- **Import Internet Mail and Addresses**   Often used in conjunction with the previous option, this one makes the transfer of e-mail and recipient addresses relatively painless. Rather than leave all your existing e-mail and recipient addresses behind, this option allows you to bring them into Outlook. There's nothing worse than having to bounce back and forth between two e-mail programs looking for an important piece of e-mail or an address. After selecting this option, click Next to see a list of supported e-mail programs. Before the import completes, Outlook displays an Import Summary dialog box, indicating how many messages, addresses, and distribution lists were imported. Oh yes, one more thing. If you import from Outlook Express, you can also include any mail-handling rules you may have created.

Tip   *Importing third-party file formats such as ECCO and ACT! requires that the original application be installed on your computer. If you're importing data provided by another user who has the application running, ask the user to export the data into a format Outlook can import directly, such as text delimited, Word, Excel, or Access.*

Since most of the Import and Export Wizard screens are self-explanatory, there's no need to go through each one here. However, there are a few things that may need clarification. Those are covered next.

Data Translators

The first time you attempt to import data either from another application or a file (Import From Another Program Or File), you'll run into an error message indicating that the translator is not installed. The dialog box asks if you want to install it now. Since the translator is needed to convert the imported data into a format Outlook can use, it's in your best interest to answer yes. However, before doing so, you should grab your original Office CD and insert it in the CD-ROM drive. All you have to do after that is follow the onscreen instructions.

Since each data type is different, you'll need a separate translator every time you attempt to import information from a different program. Therefore, if you plan to import a variety of different file formats, you might want to install all the translators at once. Insert your original CD in the CD-ROM drive, and start the Office or Outlook setup routine. You can use the Add/Remove Programs applet in the Windows Control Panel (Start | Settings | Control Panel), or double-click Setup.exe on the root of the CD. When the installer is running, go to the Add Or Remove Features section, and expand the Microsoft Outlook For Windows features by clicking the plus sign (+) to its left. Click the down arrow next to Importers And Exporters to display the installation choices for import and export converters. Select Run All From My Computer, and click the Update button. All the converters are installed, and you are returned to the active window.

Mapping Fields

Field mapping is one of the most important, and most confusing (the first time you use it), features of the Outlook import process. It provides an accurate way to import address book and other database information even if Outlook and the source program use different names for the same fields. For example, the ECCO personal information manager calls the field that holds your work phone number *Work #*, while the same field in Outlook is called *Business Phone.* The Outlook file converters are pretty good about recognizing commonly used fields, such as name, company, address, phone number, and so on. However, there's no way the converters can recognize custom fields or obscure fields not used in Outlook. When you run across fields of this nature, you're going to have to give Outlook a hand, which is where field mapping comes in.

When you map fields, you're simply telling Outlook which fields from the incoming file match up with existing Outlook fields. This way, if the imported file has a custom field called *Company URL,* you can instruct Outlook to dump the data from that field into the *Outlook Web Page* field. You get the opportunity to map fields when you reach the Import A File screen, which resembles the one shown in Figure 21-8.

Select the action that requires field mapping, and click the Map Custom Fields button to open the Map Custom Fields dialog box, shown in Figure 21-9.

As you can see in Figure 21-9, fields from the imported file are displayed in the left pane, while fields from Outlook appear in the right pane. The left pane has a single column, Value, which contains the names of the fields in the imported file. The right pane has two columns, Field and Mapped From. Field is the name of the Outlook field, and Mapped From is the name of the imported field that the Outlook converter has matched up with the Outlook field. Your job as a custom field mapper is to ensure that the matching is correct and to match any fields the converter missed. That's not to say, however, that

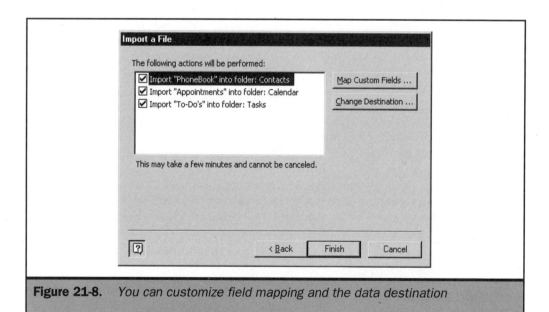

Figure 21-8. *You can customize field mapping and the data destination*

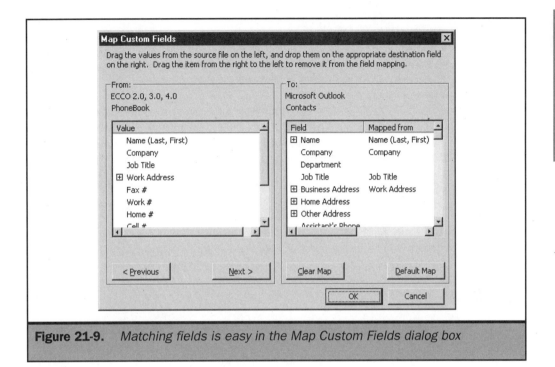

Figure 21-9.   *Matching fields is easy in the Map Custom Fields dialog box*

every field must be mapped. If there's data you don't want to import, you can choose not to map the field or even remove the mapping already done by the converter.

However, for those fields that you want mapped, the task is pretty easy. In the left pane, locate the field you want to map, and drag it to the right pane. Now find the Outlook field you want it mapped to, and drop it on the Outlook field name. The imported field name instantly appears in the Mapped From column. To unmap a field, simply drag the Outlook field name from the Field column in the right pane, and drop it anywhere in the left pane. The association is immediately terminated, and the field name disappears from the Mapped From column in the right pane. You can even change the mapping by dropping a different import field onto an Outlook field without first removing the existing mapped field. The new one replaces the old association.

If you want to see the actual data, rather than the field names, click the Next button. Immediately, the field names in both the Value column on the left and the Mapped From column on the right are replaced by the information from the imported fields. Each time you click Next, you see the data from the next record. When you're finished mapping, click OK to return to the Import a File Wizard. If you're ready to complete the import, click Finish and you're on your way.

MOUS EXAM PRACTICE

In this section you learned all about importing data from a variety of applications into Outlook. The first thing you'll need for this exercise is some data from an outside source. The one thing everyone can obtain is a vCard file. Open the Contacts folder and select a contact. Choose Actions | Forward As vCard. Enter your own address in the To field of the message form that opens. When you receive the message in your Inbox, open it, right-click the vCard attachment, and choose Save As. Save the vCard to any folder you wish. Then start the Import and Export Wizard and import the vCard. You can also export Outlook data to a delimited file and then use the import feature to import back into Outlook. If you have access to other applications supported by the Outlook format, try importing information from them as well.

Exporting Outlook Data

The flip side of importing is, of course, exporting. Exporting Outlook data involves converting it to a format that other programs can utilize or import. It's handy for sharing information with friends and colleagues who happen to use software other than Outlook for their information management needs.

When it comes to exporting Outlook data, the process is similar to importing. You begin by choosing File | Import And Export to start the Import and Export Wizard. However, unlike the import feature, export has only one option, Export To A File.

As soon as you select Export To A File and click Next, the wizard displays a list of file types to which you can convert Outlook information. Your choices include the following file types:

- **Comma Separated Values (DOS)**   Use this type to create a text file (.csv) in which each field is delimited (separated) by commas. The delimiter lets other programs know where one field ends and the next begins. This format uses the ASCII character set, which is compatible with DOS programs as well as with Windows programs.

- **Comma Separated Values (Windows)**   This option is the same as the first, except that the file created uses the ANSI character set compatible with Windows programs, but not with DOS programs.

- **dBase**   To those who were around in the days before Microsoft dominated the desktop software world, dBase is a familiar name. It was, for many years, the most popular database product around. As a result, its .dbf file format is still considered a standard for many database products.

- **Microsoft Access**   Use this option to export Outlook data into the .mdb file format used by Microsoft Access.

- **Microsoft Excel**   To use Outlook data in an Excel worksheet, choose this option. It dumps the Outlook data into an Excel-compatible file with an .xls extension.

- ■ **Microsoft FoxPro**   FoxPro, which has been around for quite a while, uses a variation on the .dbf format. Although the extension is the same, it differs from the dBase .dbf format, so don't confuse the two. Be sure to use this option for exporting Outlook data for use with FoxPro.

- ■ **Personal Folder File (.pst)**   If you want to share your Outlook information with another Outlook user, you can export your mailbox or other folders to a .pst file, which another user can then open in Outlook by adding it to his or her profile. It's also an easy way to create personal folders for yourself from your mailbox folders.

- ■ **Tab Separated Values (DOS)**   This format, sometimes referred to as TSV, is the same as the Comma Separated Values (DOS) format, except that the field delimiter is a tab character (the invisible formatting character created when you press the TAB key) rather than a comma.

- ■ **Tab Separated Values (Windows)**   This is the same as the Comma Separated Values (Windows) format, except that a tab is used as the delimiter instead of a comma.

After you make your selection, click Next to view the export folder screen, which contains a tree-like view of your Outlook folders.

Note *If you haven't installed the necessary translator, you'll encounter an Outlook alert informing you that you must install the appropriate translator before proceeding.*

Select the folder from which you want to export your Outlook information, and click Next. No matter which file type you selected in the beginning, the next screen offers you a chance to locate and name the target file in which you want the Outlook data stored.

If you're exporting to a .pst file, you get added options for handling duplicate records, and you're almost at the end. Clicking Finish creates the .pst file and presents you with a Create Microsoft Personal Folders dialog box in which you can set the configuration options for the new .pst file.

For all other file types, the next step after designating the target folder is to click Next, which brings up the actions screen. Here you get the opportunity to map custom fields. When you're finished with your field mapping chores, click Finish to create the new file.

One last thing: all information from the selected Outlook folder is exported even if a filter is applied at the time the export takes place. For example, suppose you're exporting your Contacts folder to an Access database format, and you decide you only want to export information on your customers. You might think that by first filtering out all the non-customer contacts in the Contacts folder you could limit the export to customers only. Unfortunately, while it is a good thought, it doesn't work that way. Outlook ignores all filters and dumps the entire contents of the selected folder into the target folder. The easiest way to export a subset of one of your folders is to apply a filter and to move or copy the desired Outlook items to a new Outlook folder. You can then export the new folder rather than the original folder.

MOUS Exam Expert Objectives Explored in Chapter 21

Objective	Activity	Heading
OL10E-4-1	Import information into Outlook	"Importing Data into Outlook"
OL10E-4-2	Export information from Outlook	"Exporting Outlook Data"
OL10E-4-4	Use Outlook data as mail merge data source	"Using the Outlook Contact Database for Mail Merge"

The Complete Reference

Outlook 2002

Chapter 22

Using Outlook to Access the Internet

ince the Internet is quickly becoming an inescapable part of everyday life, it's no
surprise that Outlook 2002 provides direct access to the Internet. Its tight integration
with Internet Explorer enables Outlook to associate Web pages with folders, act as
a Web browser, and utilize Internet Explorer Favorites. In addition, Outlook also integrates
with Outlook Express to create the Outlook Newsreader, which lets you access Internet
newsgroups from within Outlook. You can even conduct online meetings over the
Internet from within Outlook by taking advantage of its ability to integrate with
Microsoft NetMeeting.

Viewing Web Pages in Outlook

If you're just noodling around, checking the news, stock quotes, or the latest fashion
trends on the Internet, you can do so without ever leaving the Outlook environment.
You can even associate Web pages with individual Outlook folders by creating a home
page for each folder. (See Chapter 18 for more information.)

Before going any further, there is one thing you should be aware of. When you
connect to a secure Web site, Outlook does not display the Lock icon in the status bar
that usually indicates that your communication with the site is encrypted. Fortunately,
it does display a notice when you enter or leave a secure site, as long as you have the
notice enabled in your Internet Options. In spite of that, it's probably a good idea to use
Internet Explorer or another browser outside of Outlook for conducting sensitive or
financial transactions over the Internet.

*If you've already connected to a secure site in Outlook and want to use your default Web
browser to ensure your communication is encrypted, copy the URL from the Outlook
Address box and choose View | Go To | Web Browser to open Internet Explorer. Now,
paste the URL into the Internet Explorer Address box and click the Go button.*

Using Favorites

Getting on the Web from Outlook is almost too easy. All you need is an Internet
connection, Outlook, and your mouse. When you install Outlook, it searches out and
adds existing bookmarks from Internet Explorer to the Outlook Favorites menu. If you
want to visit one of those links, simply establish an Internet connection, open the Favorites
menu, click the desired link, and you're off. If the Web page is available, it opens in the
Information viewer, replacing the current folder view. You can now view the page,
click links, fill out forms, and do what you would normally do in a Web browser.

*You can follow the progress of a page as it's downloading by keeping an eye on the
Outlook window status bar. The page being loaded is indicated on the left side of the
status bar, and a Loading icon appears on the right side.*

Adding Web sites to the Favorites menu is also quite easy. Open the Web page you want to add, and choose Favorites | Add To Favorites to display the Add Favorite dialog box.

You can change the name for the link and click OK to add the URL to the bottom of your Favorites list. However, simply adding links to the list will eventually create an unmanageable list. Therefore, you may want to click the Create In button on the Add Favorite dialog box to display a list of Favorites folders into which you can place the new link (see Figure 22-1).

Select the folder in which you want to place the Web page shortcut, or create a new folder by clicking the New Folder button in the dialog box.

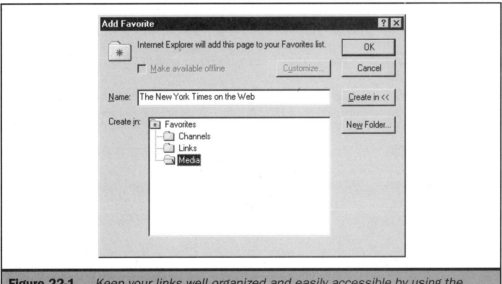

Figure 22-1. *Keep your links well organized and easily accessible by using the Favorites folders*

The name given to the shortcut created when you add a Web page to your Favorites folder is taken from the Web page title, which in many cases is long, drawn out, and often confusing. To give the shortcut a more easily identifiable name, change the file's Name information to something you'll quickly recognize.

Click OK to create a shortcut for the Web page in the selected folder and return to the active window. The next time you want to access the Web page, open the Favorites menu and select the shortcut to return to the associated page.

Using the Web Toolbar and Web Commands

As soon as you open a Web page or Web document in Outlook, the Web toolbar appears.

As you can see, the Web toolbar contains a number of standard browser commands that make navigating the Web easy. The default buttons on the Web toolbar include

- **Back**   Click this button to return to the previously viewed Web page or Outlook folder.

- **Forward**   The Forward button works the same as the Back button. It simply takes you in the opposite direction. It becomes available after you open at least two Web pages and return to one previous page.

- **Stop**   Click the Stop button to halt the downloading of the currently selected Web page.

- **Refresh**   Web pages are constantly being updated. To be sure you're viewing the latest version, click the Refresh button.

- **Start Page**   If there's one thing you can say about Microsoft programmers, it's that they're consistently inconsistent. With the tight integration between Outlook and Internet Explorer, you'd think they would, as a matter of course, name the standard toolbar buttons the same in both programs. But, of course, you'd be wrong. The Start Page button is everyone else's Home Page button. Fortunately, it works the same, and takes you to the home page designated in your Internet Options, which are accessible from the Windows Control Panel or the Internet Explorer Tools menu.

- **Search the Web**   If you don't have a favorite search engine, click this button and Outlook whisks you away to the MSN search page that provides a Web search engine, plus a large selection of Internet links.

- **Address**   Enter the URL of the Web site you want to visit, or view the address of the currently displayed Web page. The drop-down list contains the addresses of recently visited Web pages.

In addition to displaying the Web toolbar, opening a Web page in Outlook also adds several commands to the menu system. The following commands are available when you display a Web page in Outlook:

- **Outlook Bar Shortcut to Web Page**   Choose File | New | Outlook Bar Shortcut To Web Page to add a shortcut to the Outlook Bar for the currently displayed Web page. By default, the new shortcut is added to the My Shortcuts group.

- **Send Web Page by E-mail**   Use this command, found on the Actions menu, to create a new e-mail message that includes the currently displayed Web page. The Web page is inserted into the e-mail message as an HTML file attachment, unless you use the Outlook e-mail editor *and* your default message format is HTML. In that case, the Web page itself is inserted in the document.

Since the Web toolbar is by no means overcrowded, and these commands can be useful when viewing Web pages, you might want to add at least one of them to the Web toolbar for quick access when surfing the Internet in Outlook. You might want to add only one because the Microsoft programmers forgot to add Outlook Bar Shortcut To Web Page to the Commands tab of the Customize dialog box. To add the others, right-click any toolbar, select Customize, and click the Commands tab. Select the File category to locate the Open In Default Browser command. You'll find the Send Web Page By E-mail command in the Actions category. Drag the command of your choice to the Web toolbar, and drop it between two existing buttons.

Caution   *In the event you get wild and crazy and decide to move the Outlook Bar Shortcut To Web Page command from the New menu to the Web toolbar, be careful. If you accidentally drop it along the way, you will not be able to get it back again without running the Detect And Repair command. Losing a command usually isn't a problem since there's (almost) always a permanent copy in the Customize dialog box. However, in this case there is no permanent copy, so you'll be minus the command unless you run Detect And Repair, which requires your original CD and, in some cases, a fair amount of time.*

Opening Web Pages Automatically

Although Outlook can't get your first cup of coffee in the morning, it can make sure your favorite Web site is waiting for you when you return from the coffee room. All you need is an established Internet connection and a URL, and you're all set.

Begin by creating a new appointment. Enter a brief description in the Subject line. If you like to read the *New York Times* with your coffee when you get to work, enter something like **Open NY Times Web site**. Click the Recurrence button on the appointment form toolbar, and fill in the desired information. Using the *New York Times* example, you might make the recurrence pattern Daily, and select Every Weekday. If you get in at 8:00 every morning, you might make the start time 8:05 A.M. Set a start date and click OK to save the recurrence information and return to the appointment form.

Now check the This Is An Online Meeting Using option, and select Windows Media Services from the drop-down list to the right of the option. The Event Address field appears. Enter the URL of the Web site you want to open. In the earlier example, it would be http://www.nytimes.com. The last thing you must do is set a reminder to trigger the action. First check the Automatically Start Windows Media With Reminder option. Then check the Reminder option and enter or select 0 minutes. Click Save And Close and you're done. When the next due date and time arrive, Outlook launches your default Web browser and opens the designated page.

Using the Outlook Newsreader

Newsgroups are specialized forums comprised of messages posted to a news server by users with a common interest in the newsgroup topic. You'll find newsgroups on music, fashion, computers, politics, and much more. If you know how to find and use them, newsgroups can provide a wealth of information. Although Outlook does not technically have its own newsreader, it borrows the one from Outlook Express and uses it as if it were its own. This feature is another example of the tight integration between Microsoft products.

Making Outlook Your Default Newsreader

The first order of business is to make Outlook your default newsreader. You can do this either through the Internet Options applet in the Control Panel or through the Internet Options found in Internet Explorer. From within Internet Explorer, choose Tools | Internet Options to open the Internet Options dialog box. Then click the Programs tab to display the default programs used for Internet access (see Figure 22-2).

From the Newsgroups drop-down list, choose Microsoft Outlook. Click OK to save your settings, and return to the active view. Return to Outlook and choose View | Go To | News to start the Internet Connection Wizard, shown in Figure 22-3.

If your current version of Outlook Express replaced an earlier version, a dialog box may appear informing you that mail will be converted from the old version to the new. Click OK to proceed.

GETTING MORE OUT OF OUTLOOK

Internet Options   [?][X]

General | Security | Content | Connections | Programs | Advanced |

┌─ Internet programs ──┐
│   You can specify which program Windows automatically uses │
│   for each Internet service.   │
│   │
│   HTML editor: [Microsoft FrontPage   ▼]   │
│   │
│   E-mail: [Microsoft Outlook   ▼]   │
│   │
│   Newsgroups: [Microsoft Outlook   ▼]   │
│   │
│   Internet call: [Microsoft NetMeeting   ▼]   │
│   │
│   Calendar: [Microsoft Outlook   ▼]   │
│   │
│   Contact list: [Microsoft Outlook   ▼]   │
│   │
│   │
│   [Reset Web Settings...]   You can reset Internet Explorer defaults for │
│   home and search pages   │
│   [✓] Internet Explorer should check to see whether it is the default browser │
└──┘

                        [OK   ]   [Cancel]   [Apply]

Figure 22-2.   *Outlook must be selected as your default program for Newsgroups*

Enter the name you want to use when you post to any newsgroups using the Outlook Newsreader. Click Next to move to the Internet e-mail address screen. Enter your Internet e-mail address and click Next to continue. The screen that appears asks for the name of your news server. This information is provided by your Internet service provider (ISP) or by your system administrator if your access to the Internet is through a local area network (LAN). Enter the appropriate news server information. If the server requires a user logon and password, check the My News Server Requires Me To Log On option. Click Next to proceed. If you left the My News Server Requires Me To Log On option unchecked, you immediately jump to the final screen informing you that the setup is complete.

If you checked the option, the next screen asks for your account name and password. By checking the Remember Password option, you can instruct Outlook to remember your password so you don't have to enter it each time you log on.

 Caution   *While using the Remember Password option may save you a little time and effort each time you log on, it also means that anyone with access to your computer can log on as you, without having to know your password.*

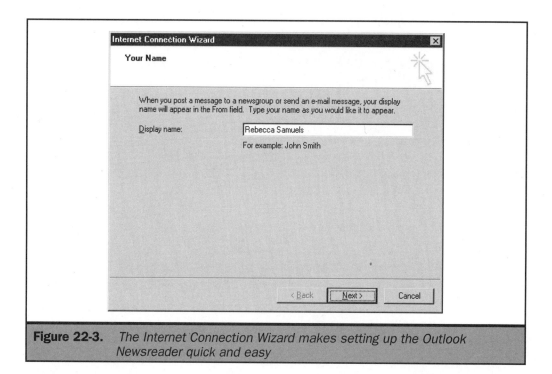

Figure 22-3.   *The Internet Connection Wizard makes setting up the Outlook Newsreader quick and easy*

The final option on the Internet News Server Logon screen is the Log On Using Secure Password Authentication (SPA) option. If your ISP requires SPA, check this option. Click Next to view the final screen, and then click Finish to complete the account setup. Outlook asks if you would like to view a list of the newsgroups available on the account you've just created. If you're connected to the Internet, click Yes to download the list of newsgroups. When you're finished downloading, you should see a Newsgroup Subscriptions dialog box similar to the one in Figure 22-4.

All the newsgroups on the news server are displayed in the All tab of the dialog box.

Note   *While most dialog box tabs appear at the top of the dialog box, the Newsgroup Subscriptions dialog box places them near the bottom of the dialog box.*

To search for specific groups, type a keyword in the Display Newsgroups Which Contain field. You don't have to do anything more. The search is conducted as soon as you stop typing. Select any newsgroups to which you want to subscribe, and click the Subscribe button. Subscribing adds the selected newsgroup(s) to your Outlook Newsreader Folders list. Since most news servers contain a large number of newsgroups, subscribing eliminates the need to scour the entire list each time you want to visit a newsgroup.

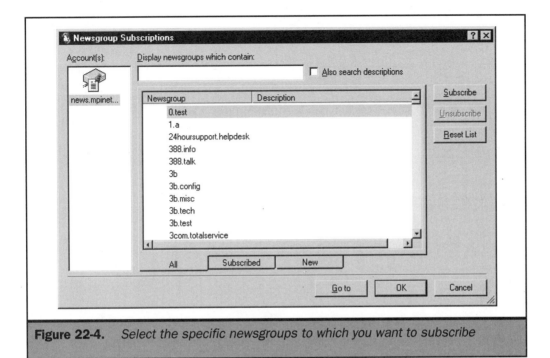

Figure 22-4.   *Select the specific newsgroups to which you want to subscribe*

The Subscribed tab lists all newsgroups to which you are currently subscribed. The New tab lists any new newsgroups added to the news server since the last time you downloaded. When you're done subscribing (or unsubscribing), click OK to close the Newsgroup Subscriptions dialog box and return to the Outlook Newsreader, shown in Figure 22-5.

Reading Newsgroup Messages

After you download and subscribe to newsgroups, the next step is to download messages, read them, and if you're so inclined, post messages of your own. To download messages, click the newsgroup of your choice in the Folders list. As long as you have an Internet connection established, the Outlook Newsreader automatically starts downloading the messages contained in the selected newsgroup. As you can see in Figure 22-6, the top half of the right pane displays the list of messages, while the bottom pane provides a preview of the selected message. It's very much like the Outlook Inbox with the Preview Pane turned on.

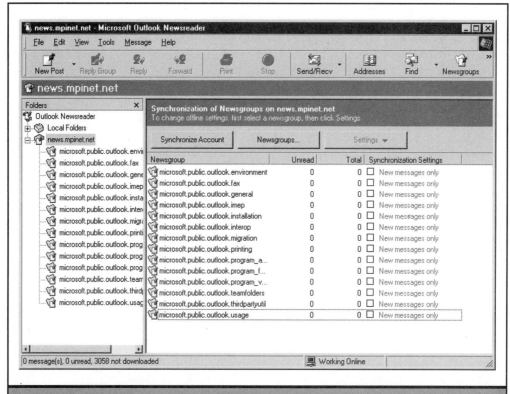

Figure 22-5. *The Outlook Newsreader opens in a separate window*

You can scroll through the messages, displaying them in the Preview Pane as you go, or you can open a message in a separate window by double-clicking the message in the top pane. You can also right-click a message and select Open from the shortcut menu. One last thing about messages: You'll see a plus (+) sign to the left of some messages. This indicates the message has responses, which you can view by clicking the plus sign. This is similar to grouping by conversation in the Outlook Inbox, but it is done automatically when someone responds to a specific message.

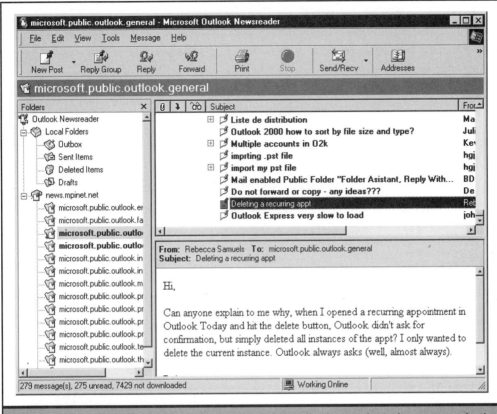

Figure 22-6. *By default, the Outlook Newsreader displays selected messages in the preview pane*

Synchronizing Newsgroups

To make life simple, you can have the Outlook Newsreader automatically synchronize the newsgroups to which you subscribe to keep them up to date. In the Folders list, click the newsgroup account you want to synchronize. The synchronization window appears in the right pane (see Figure 22-7).

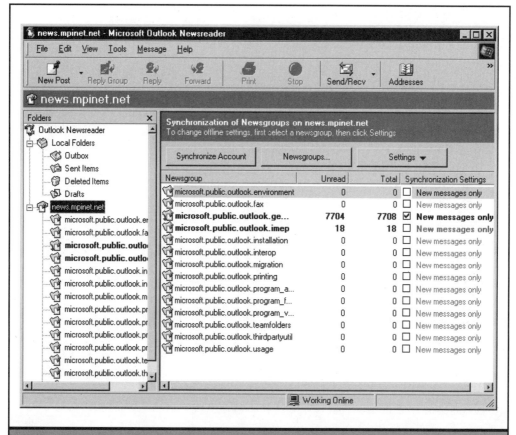

Figure 22-7. *Let the Outlook Newsreader do the work by synchronizing newsgroups automatically*

The synchronization window displays all the newsgroups to which you are subscribed for the selected newsgroup account. In addition, the synchronization window also contains the following three buttons, which appear here in the order they are generally used when performing your first synchronization:

- **Settings** Click the Settings button to set the synchronization options for the selected newsgroup. The Settings drop-down menu that appears contains four options:
  - **Don't Synchronize** This is the default setting. It results in no action on the newsgroup for which it's set. Nothing new will be downloaded during a synchronization.

■ **All Messages**   Select this option to download all messages, including headers and bodies. This will make accessing the messages a little quicker, but will also take up additional disk space since the messages are stored on your local computer. On the other hand, if you can afford the disk space, this is a handy way to access the messages when you're offline. You can always go into the newsgroup properties (right-click the desired newsgroup and select Properties) and delete all the downloaded messages.

■ **New Messages Only**   Rather than clutter up your newsreader with all the messages, you can elect to download only new messages that have been posted since your last download.

■ **Headers Only**   This is the quickest method, and it requires a minimum of local hard disk space, since the message bodies are left on the server and only accessed when you select the associated header.

■ **Newsgroups**   This button activates the Newsgroup Subscription dialog box, where you can subscribe or unsubscribe to newsgroups as you choose.

■ **Synchronize Account**   Click this button to download the most current messages for all newsgroups to which you are subscribed in the selected account. The manner in which the synchronization is performed depends on your selection in the Settings menu, displayed when you click the Settings button.

After you select the setting for each newsgroup, you can turn the setting on and off by checking or unchecking the box next to the setting name in the newsgroup list.

In addition to using the Synchronization window, you can also perform a synchronization by right-clicking the newsgroup account you want to synchronize and choosing Synchronization Settings to display a submenu of choices. Make your selection and the newsgroup is synchronized accordingly. You can also select the newsgroup and choose Tools | Synchronize Newsgroup. The Synchronize Newsgroup dialog box appears, enabling you to choose a one-time setting for synchronizing this newsgroup.

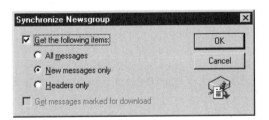

The setting you've chosen for this newsgroup does not change the default. When you return to the Synchronization window, you'll see the default setting is still in effect, regardless of what you selected in the Synchronize Newsgroup dialog box.

Creating News Accounts

Creating a news account is simple. As a matter of fact, that's exactly what you did when you first opened the Outlook Newsreader. To create another news account, choose Tools | Accounts to display the Internet Accounts dialog box.

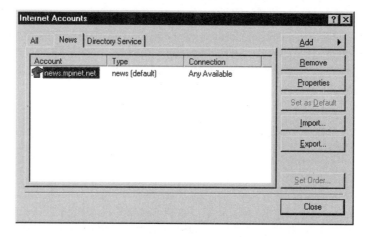

Click the Add button and select News to open the Internet Connection Wizard. Refer to the instructions in the section entitled "Making Outlook Your Default Newsreader," earlier in this chapter. When you return to the Internet Accounts dialog box, click Close to return to the Outlook Newsreader.

Posting to Newsgroups

Subscribing to a newsgroup generally means that the topic covered is of interest to you. Therefore, it's not unreasonable to expect that you may want to post a message of your own to the newsgroup. You may want to ask a question, supply an answer to a question already posted, or simply add your two cents to an ongoing discussion. Whatever your reason, posting to a newsgroup is easy.

The manner in which you post to a newsgroup is very similar to sending e-mail. There are a number of actions you can take to post to a newsgroup. The following Standard toolbar buttons make the most common forms of posting just a mouse click (or two) away.

- ■ **New Post**   Select the newsgroup you want to post to, and click this button to open a new message form addressed to the selected newsgroup. Enter a brief and concise Subject line that makes the message contents clear. Then type your message, and send it on its way by clicking Send.

- ■ **Reply Group**   If you want to respond to a particular message on the newsgroup, select the message and click Reply Group. This opens a new message addressed to the newsgroup, but with the Subject line already filled in, indicating this is a response to the selected message. In addition, the contents of the original message are pasted into the body of your new message, and set off by the greater than (>) symbol, indicating they are not part of your response. Enter your message above the pasted information and click Send. When the message is posted to the newsgroup, it appears as part of the conversation thread beneath the message to which you are responding.

- **Reply** If you don't want to respond to the newsgroup, but would rather reply to the sender of a specific message privately, select the message and click the Reply button. This opens a message similar to the Reply Group message. The difference is that this one is addressed to the sender of the original message, not to the entire newsgroup.

- **Forward** If you find a posting of particular interest, you can forward it to someone else who may share your interest. Select the message and click the Forward button to open a new message form with the Subject line filled in and the contents of the original message pasted in the body. Add the desired recipient(s) and send it on its way.

Note *It's important to always keep in mind that newsgroups are usually very targeted. Therefore, your posts should be relevant to the group. Sharing your favorite Hamburger Helper recipes on a gourmet cooking newsgroup is not going to make you one of the more popular members of the group. Also, keep in mind that it is a public forum, and basic social amenities should be observed.*

In addition to the toolbar buttons, you'll find other commands for posting on the Tools menu. As a matter of fact, there are a lot more commands of all types on the Outlook Newsreader menus. Spend a little time experimenting, and you'll learn all kinds of interesting and helpful things about the program.

MOUS EXAM PRACTICE
In this section you learned to set up and use the Outlook Newsreader. After you configure the Outlook Newsreader, you'll want to practice reading and posting newsgroup messages. Begin by opening one of your newsgroup accounts. Now select a newsgroup of interest to you and view the headers. Use the Preview Pane to read some, and then open others by double-clicking them. Next, find one you can respond to and post a reply. Finally, try your hand at creating and posting your own message.

Using NetMeeting

NetMeeting is a sophisticated piece of software from Microsoft that allows you to communicate in real time with others over the Internet. This means you can place calls over the Internet, chat online, and even conduct virtual meetings online. It's the online meeting part that is of particular interest to Outlook users.

NetMeeting works hand in hand with Outlook to enable you to schedule and conduct online meetings without leaving the Outlook environment. If meeting participants have the requisite hardware installed, you can even include audio and video in your online meetings. In addition to having the necessary audio and video hardware, a fast LAN or Internet connection is recommended for utilizing audio and video in a NetMeeting environment.

NetMeeting enables you to phone, chat, and meet online by using Internet Locator Service (ILS) and Uniform Location Services (ULS). Each meeting participant logs on to an ILS or ULS server, which keeps track of the basic information required to make a NetMeeting connection. The first item it notes is that a user is online. The second piece of information required is the user's IP address. Since most users access the Internet through an ISP, which assigns a different IP address each time, there is no way to determine the IP address until the user logs on. This is where the ILS or ULS server comes into the picture. Once you log on to the ILS/ULS server, it (obviously) knows you're online and takes note of your current IP address. You can then communicate with others who are also logged in.

Since covering NetMeeting thoroughly would require a lot more room than is available here, the sections that follow will take you through the basics of setting up, scheduling, starting, and joining NetMeetings. For additional information, tips, tricks, and more, there are a number of Web sites dedicated to NetMeeting. The following is just a small sample of what's out there. Keep in mind when attempting to use these links that the Internet changes rapidly, and by the time you read this, some of the sites may have changed.

- **Meeting by Wire**   http://www.meetingbywire.com/. This site has a good beginners' overview of NetMeeting as well as tips and tricks for the more experienced user.

- **NetMeeting Zone**   http://www.netmeeting-zone.com/. News, tips, information, and more are what you'll find at the NetMeeting Zone.

- **NetMeetingHQ**   http://www.netmeetinghq.com/. If you're looking for a good listing of ILS servers, check out the NetMeetingHQ site.

- **Microsoft NetMeeting Web site**   http://www.microsoft.com/windows/ NetMeeting/. Surprisingly, most of what you find at Microsoft's site is marketing hype, with a dash of helpful information thrown in here and there.

Configuring NetMeeting

While NetMeeting works with Outlook, it is not part of Outlook. It is a separate Microsoft application provided with Internet Explorer (versions prior to 5.5) or Windows (Windows 2000 and later), which means you must set it up to work with Outlook.

| Tip | *Before you go any further, you should know that Microsoft has closed down all its ILS servers, which means you'll have to find a working ILS server to complete the setup. Access one of the NetMeeting Web sites listed in the previous section, and select an ILS server to use for the NetMeeting configuration. You can always go back and change it after you finish setting up.* |

To configure NetMeeting from within Outlook, choose View | Go To | Internet Call | Internet Call. This launches the NetMeeting Wizard, which walks you through the process of setting up NetMeeting to work with Outlook. The opening screen is purely informational. When you're done reading, click Next, which brings you to the personal information screen. Enter your first and last names and your e-mail address. The remaining information is strictly optional.

| Caution | *If you plan to use NetMeeting for chatting with strangers, do not provide any personal information that may put you at risk. As a matter of fact, most people only list their first names, and use abbreviations, such as MWM35 (a Married White Male who is 35 years old) for their last names.* |

Click Next to proceed to the directory server screen. Enter the address of a working ILS server. If you haven't gotten one yet, check the Web sites listed at the end of the previous section for working ILS servers.

| Note | *The wizard screens described here are found in Windows 98, which comes with NetMeeting 3.0, and in Windows 2000, which comes with NetMeeting 3.01. If you're using an earlier version of NetMeeting, your screens will be somewhat different.* |

To make sure your name does not appear in the directory server indicated in the previous option, check the Do Not List My Name In The Directory option. Displaying your name in the directory enables all other users logged in to the directory server to place calls to you. Click Next to move to the connection screen. Indicate the connection type (and speed, if applicable) and click Next. The NetMeeting Wizard now offers to add a NetMeeting shortcut to both your desktop and your Quick Launch bar. Check the one(s) you want and click Next.

If your computer has a sound card, you'll see the Audio Tuning Wizard. Follow the instructions for configuring your sound card to work with NetMeeting. After you make the adjustments for speaker and microphone volumes, click Finish. NetMeeting starts and you're ready to begin. The remaining sections on NetMeeting assume you've already established an ILS or ULS server to which all users have access.

Scheduling a NetMeeting

Scheduling a NetMeeting in Outlook is practically the same as scheduling any other meeting. Begin by opening a new meeting request form and filling in the basic information. See Chapter 12 for detailed information on scheduling meetings and using meeting request forms. Check the This Is An Online Meeting Using option, and select NetMeeting from the drop-down list. As you can see in Figure 22-8, checking the online meeting option adds a number of new fields to the meeting request form.

The following fields are added to the meeting request form for a NetMeeting:

- **Directory Server** Enter the directory server you want everyone to connect to for the meeting. If you've registered with multiple servers, choose the one for this meeting from the Directory Server drop-down list.

- **Automatically start NetMeeting with Reminder** Check this option to have Outlook automatically connect to the directory server when the reminder activates. If you choose this option, be sure to set the reminder time to 0 minutes so the meeting doesn't start before its scheduled time. Some participants may not be ready. If you use this option, you may want to create a separate appointment for this meeting and set a reminder to go off before the scheduled meeting time.

- **Organizer's e-mail** Outlook automatically completes this field with the address you entered in the personal information screen of the NetMeeting Wizard.

- **Office document** If you want to review or collaborate on an office document, enter the document path here. Use the Browse button to locate the document if you're unsure of the exact path. If you choose this option, the standard NetMeeting application does not open. Instead the office document opens with an Online Meeting toolbar floating in the document.

Complete the rest of the form as you would any other meeting request form, and click Send when you're finished. Each participant will receive an invitation via e-mail.

Starting a NetMeeting

If you set the option to start the NetMeeting automatically when the reminder pops up, there's nothing to do but sit back and wait. At the appointed time, the reminder appears and NetMeeting takes over and logs on to the Internet. Each participant also sees a reminder that provides a Join NetMeeting button.

GETTING MORE OUT
OF OUTLOOK

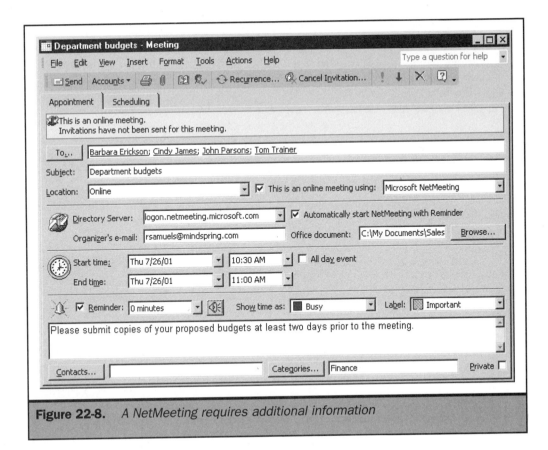

Figure 22-8.   *A NetMeeting requires additional information*

The reminder shown here was generated in Outlook 2002. Reminders appearing in other versions of Outlook will look somewhat different.

As long as he or she has NetMeeting installed and configured, and has established an Internet connection, the participant logs on to the NetMeeting directory server by clicking the Join NetMeeting button.

 Since reminders are handled locally, the clocks on the users' PCs determine when the reminders go off. If all clocks are not set for the same time, participants will be signing on early or late.

To start a NetMeeting manually, right-click the meeting item in the Calendar folder and select Start NetMeeting from the shortcut menu. You can also open the meeting item and choose Actions | Start NetMeeting from the Menu bar.

Joining a NetMeeting

As indicated in the previous section, joining a NetMeeting set to start automatically when a reminder launches is as easy as clicking the Join NetMeeting button on the reminder. To join a NetMeeting in progress, without the help of a reminder, right-click the item in the Calendar folder, and select Join NetMeeting from the shortcut menu. If the meeting item is open, choose Actions | Join NetMeeting.

NetMeeting Tools

As long as all participants have the appropriate hardware installed, audio and video communications are available. However, a NetMeeting can be conducted without either by using the remaining tools, which can replace audio and video communications or enhance them. The following NetMeeting tools enable participants to communicate and collaborate with each other:

- **Share Program**   If you want to make an application on your computer available to others in the meeting, use the Share Program tool. It enables you to select any currently running application and share it with others. In addition, you can even let them take control of the application if you choose. You can start an application during the NetMeeting session and share it.

- **Chat**   If audio communication is unavailable for some or all of the participants, using the Chat feature will certainly come in handy. With this tool you can type instant messages to any or all participants. You can even save transcripts of the messages for future reference.

- **Whiteboard**   This mini paint application provides a way for all participants to share graphical representations with one another. Whether you want to draw a map or sketch a new design, the whiteboard is the perfect tool.

■ **Transfer Files** At any time during the meeting, you may find you want to exchange files with other meeting members. Simply click the Transfer Files button, locate the files, and send them on their way.

All the communication and collaboration features available in NetMeeting make it an ideal tool for conducting important meetings when participants are unavailable for a face-to-face meeting. For some meetings, in which the goal is to review or collaborate on an Office document, NetMeeting may be better than a face-to-face meeting.

MOUS

MOUS EXAM PRACTICE
In this section you learned all about NetMeeting. Now it's time to take it out for a spin and see how it handles. The first thing to do is make sure you've got the latest version of NetMeeting installed. Next, select an ILS server, and configure NetMeeting. Now, open a new meeting request form, and invite some co-workers to an online meeting. You may want to try a couple of meetings—let one start automatically with a reminder, and start another one yourself manually. Try sharing a program you have installed on your computer (Word immediately comes to mind). Then get everyone involved in trying the other tools such as Chat, the Whiteboard, and the ability to Transfer Files.

Communicating with Instant Messaging

Outlook 2002 provides, for the first time, the ability to work with MSN Messenger Service to enable you to communicate in real time via the Internet with other friends and colleagues who are online at the same time. Once the sole province of AOL subscribers, instant messaging is now available to others through the use of Microsoft's MSN Messenger software. While the software can be used alone, it also integrates with Outlook 2002, enabling you to send instant messages while working in Outlook. To take advantage of Outlook's ability to work with MSN Messenger, you must first install MSN Messenger and then enable instant messaging within Outlook.

One more thing: It's not just software you're installing. You're also subscribing to the MSN Messenger Service, which requires a Hotmail e-mail account. Not to worry, they're both free. The only problem you may encounter is the spam generated by the Hotmail account. However, you can always configure Outlook to filter out junk mail. See Chapter 19 for more on dealing with junk e-mail.

Installing MSN Messenger

Installing MSN Messenger, while a little time-consuming, is not difficult. Actually, that's not quite accurate. Installing MSN Messenger is neither difficult nor time-consuming. It's getting the software in the first place (if you don't have it) and setting it up after you install it that are the time-consuming parts.

If you don't have a copy on your system, you'll have to establish a connection to the Internet and download or install the MSN Messenger software from the Web. To find out whether you've got a copy, choose Tools | Options and move to the Other tab of the Options dialog box. Check the Enable Instant Messaging In Microsoft Outlook option, and then click the Options button. If the MSN Messenger software is present on your hard drive (i.e. it's included with Windows Me), the MSN Messenger Service Wizard, which is covered later in this section, opens.

If you don't have a copy of MSN Messenger, an information dialog box appears, asking if you want to download a copy now. Make sure you have a connection to the Internet and click Yes. Your default browser launches and takes you to the Microsoft Office Update Web site. Click your country of choice, and the MSN Messenger Service Web page opens.

The Microsoft Office Update Web site will not let you through to the MSN Messenger Service page unless you have cookies enabled. If you seem to be stuck at the Microsoft Office Update page, check your browser settings and make sure cookies are turned on.

Now, click the Download button located near the top of the page. The next page asks if you have a Passport or a Hotmail account. If you've already signed up for either, click Next to go to the download page. If you don't have either, click Get A Passport to open a wizard that walks you through the process. Follow the steps to set up your Hotmail account or to get your Passport.

When you get to the download page, click the Start Download button located near the bottom of the page to display the File Download dialog box.

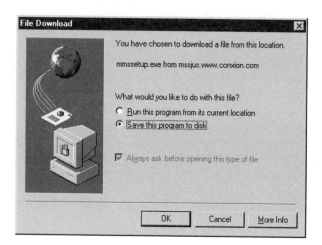

Select Run This Program From Its Current Location to install the MSN Messenger directly from the Web. This is the simplest way to do it. However, if you prefer to handle things yourself, you can save the file to your hard disk and install it from there after the download is complete. Click OK to complete the process. The time it takes to download depends on the speed of your Internet connection. With a 56-Kbps connection (typical modem speed these days) you're probably looking at a few minutes.

As soon as the download is complete, a Security Warning dialog box pops up, asking if you want to install and run MSN Messenger Service. Click Yes to proceed. Now, you have to agree to the ever-popular EULA (End User License Agreement), before going any further. Click Yes to complete the installation.

As soon as the installation is complete, the MSN Messenger Service Wizard shown in Figure 22-9 appears.

Click Next to continue to the Get A Free Passport screen. As indicated earlier, you need either a Hotmail account or a Passport to use MSN Messenger. If you don't have either, click the Get A Passport button and follow the instructions. If you have one or the other, click Next to move to the Provide Passport Information screen. Enter your sign-in name and password and click Next to continue.

Enabling the Remember My Name And Password On This Computer option allows you to access the Instant Messenger Service without having to enter your name and password each time. However, it also enables anyone else who has access to your computer to do the same thing.

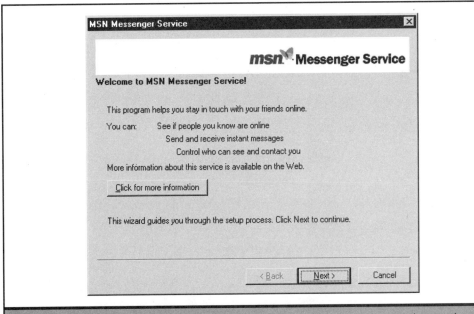

Figure 22-9.   *The MSN Messenger Service Wizard makes setting up the service a breeze*

That's all there is to it. Now click Finish and you're ready to start using instant messaging. As a matter of fact, the service automatically launches (see Figure 22-10) and connects if your Internet connection is still active.

Using Instant Messaging from Within Outlook

Now that we've got that taken care of, it's time to learn how you can utilize instant messaging while working in Outlook. The first thing you have to do is start the MSN Messenger Service. By default, MSN Messenger Service runs every time you start your computer. Therefore, unless you change the default settings, MSN Messenger Service should always be running. You can be sure by checking for the MSN Messenger Service icon in the system tray on the Windows taskbar. If it's not there, choose Start I Programs I MSN Messenger Service to launch the program. One final matter to take care of—log on to the MSN Messenger Service.

Once you're logged on, you can take advantage of integration between Outlook and MSN Messenger Service both in received e-mail and in contacts with MSN Messenger Service accounts. When you receive an e-mail message from an MSN Messenger Service user who is signed on and sending the message from his or her Hotmail account, you can send that person an instant message simply by clicking on the message InfoBar as seen in Figure 22-11.

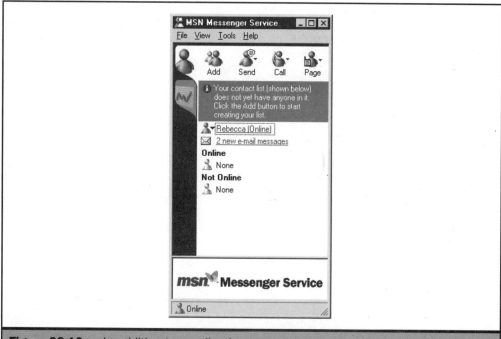

Figure 22-10.   *In addition to sending instant messages, the MSN Messenger Service window also provides access to your Hotmail account*

GETTING MORE OUT
OF OUTLOOK

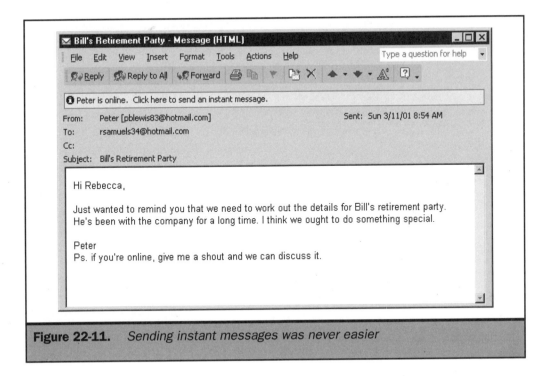

Figure 22-11. *Sending instant messages was never easier*

Note *There's only one catch. The e-mail must be addressed to your Hotmail account as well. For details on adding e-mail accounts, see Chapter 2.*

When you receive a message indicating the sender is online, click the yellow InfoBar to open the Instant Message window similar to the one shown in Figure 22-12.

By default, the cursor appears in the message box near the bottom of the window. Start typing your message and click the Send button when you're finished. As long as the other party is still online and has not blocked you, an Instant Message window appears on his or her screen, displaying the message you just sent. You can now send instant messages back and forth.

There's one more way you can utilize Instant Messaging from within Outlook. If you have an MSN Messenger Service subscriber in your Contacts folder and you've got his Hotmail address listed in the IM Address field, you'll be able to tell if he's online by opening his contact record. As you can see in Figure 22-13, an InfoBar appears in the contact record, indicating the individual is online.

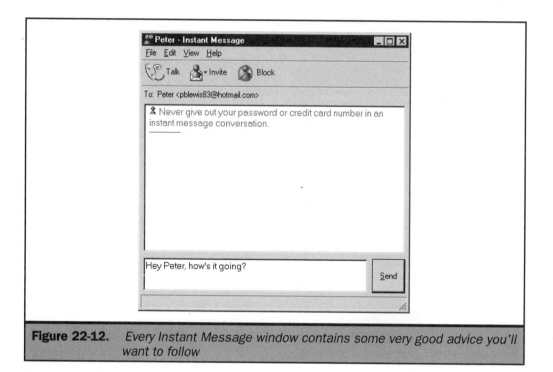

Figure 22-12. *Every Instant Message window contains some very good advice you'll want to follow*

Note *You can also use a contact's sign-in name instead of his or her IM address.*

As with the e-mail InfoBar described earlier, clicking the contact record InfoBar opens the Instant Message window. Enter your message and click Send to send the contact an instant message.

MOUS

MOUS EXAM PRACTICE

In this section you learned to configure the MSN Messenger Service and to send instant messages while working in Outlook. After you establish your MSN Messenger Service account and enable Instant Messaging in Outlook, contact a friend who is also a subscriber and ask him or her to send you a Hotmail message to your Hotmail account. Make sure you add your Hotmail account to Outlook first. Open the message and click the InfoBar to display the Instant Messaging window. Send your friend an instant message. Now, add your friend to your contact folder. Be sure to include the Hotmail address in the IM Address field. Make sure your friend is still online, and open the contact record. Use the InfoBar to send another instant message.

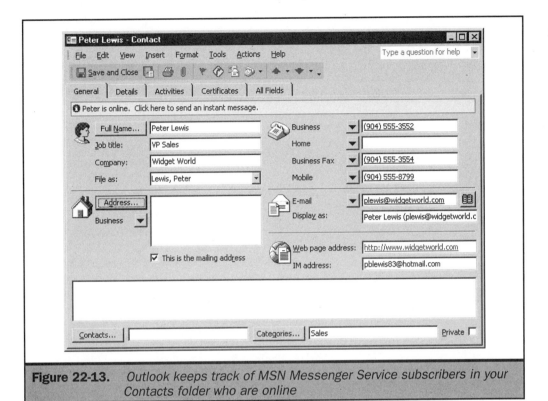

Figure 22-13.   *Outlook keeps track of MSN Messenger Service subscribers in your Contacts folder who are online*

MOUS Exam Expert Objectives Explored in Chapter 22

Objective	Activity	Heading
OL10E-3-5	Schedule and moderate NetMeetings	"Using NetMeeting"
OL10E-6-2	Send and receive newsgroup messages	"Using the Outlook Newsreader"
OL10E-6-3	Send and receive instant messages	"Communicating with Instant Messaging"

The Complete Reference

Outlook 2002

Chapter 23

Working with Views

W ithout folder views, Outlook would be about as useful as a VCR without a television set. All the information might be there, but you'd never be able to see it. Each Outlook folder comes with a number of standard views that present the folder contents in a variety ways. In this chapter, you'll discover not only what types of views are available, but also how you can navigate, customize, and even create your own views.

Understanding Views

Although each Outlook folder has anywhere from five to ten different standard views, they all fall into one of five view types. To use, create, and customize Outlook views, you should understand what a view is, as well as the different types available and their uses.

To begin with, a *view* is the structure within which folder information is displayed. At the minimum, a view consists of at least one piece of information about one or more items or files contained in the folder. Complex views can consist of multiple fields (name, address, phone number, and so on), as well as special sort, filter, group by, and font settings. All Outlook views belong to one of the following types:

- **Icon** An icon view is one in which Outlook items or computer files are represented by their associated icons. The icon and all or part of the item or filename are displayed. The default Notes folder view is an example of an icon view.

- **Day/Week/Month** This type of view, which, not surprisingly, is ideal for Calendar folder items, displays items in a calendar format of the variety you'd find in a daily planner. This is the default view for the Calendar folder.

- **Card** A card view presents information in a format similar to a Rolodex or other address card. As you might guess, Contacts folder information is best suited for a card view.

- **Timeline** For viewing information in relation to time or dates, a timeline view is the answer. Each item in the view is displayed in chronological order along a time scale divided into hours or days.

- **Table** By far the most common view type in Outlook, the table view displays information in a row and column format. Rows represent individual *records* (items), and columns represent *fields* (details about the items).

Some view types, such as day/week/month and card, are almost exclusively used to display specific types of information, while others, such as table views, are versatile enough to display any type of information. The type of view you choose depends on the results you want to achieve. For example, if you want to view detailed information about each of your contacts, you would probably use a card view. However, if you want a simple phone listing of your contacts, you would almost certainly use a table view.

Navigating Views

Utilizing folder views involves two things: switching between views and getting around in a view once you arrive. There are several methods for navigating between folder views—some easy and others even easier. The same goes for navigating within a view. Of course, how you get around in the view depends to some extent on the type of view you're using.

Switching Views

You can switch views by choosing View | Current View to display the submenu of available views. Then select the view of your choice. This method is fine if you only occasionally switch between views. However, if you're an inveterate view switcher, you'll want to add the Advanced toolbar to the Outlook window. The Advanced toolbar provides a Current View drop-down list, which makes changing views a snap.

Current View

To add the Advanced toolbar to all Outlook folders, right-click the Standard toolbar and select Advanced from the shortcut menu that appears. To remove a toolbar, deselect it from the shortcut menu to eliminate the check mark. After you add the Advanced toolbar, you can switch views simply by opening the Current View drop-down list and selecting the view you want to see.

Tip   *If you're a view switcher but don't want to waste valuable real estate by adding the Advanced toolbar to your Outlook window, there's an alternative. You can add a Current View button to your Standard toolbar that displays a menu of all available views when clicked. Right-click a toolbar and choose Customize from the shortcut menu to open the Customize dialog box; then click the Command tab, select View in the Categories list, and drag the Current View command to the Standard toolbar. Drop the command where you want it. See Chapter 24 for details on adding and removing toolbar buttons.*

You can also use the Organize feature to switch views. In any Outlook folder, click the Organize button on the Standard toolbar to display the Organize pane. Click the Using Views link to display the Change Your View list box containing all available views.

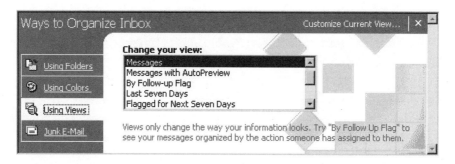

From the Change Your View list box, select the view you want to switch to. When you're through, click the Organize button again or the small *X* in the top-right corner of the Organize pane to close it.

Navigating Within Folder Views

Getting around in a folder view is a snap. The most difficult task is deciding whether to use the mouse or the keyboard. Using the mouse is pretty straightforward. Click an item to select it. Double-click an item to open it. Moving through the view is a simple matter of using the scroll bars. When it comes to the keyboard, you'll find each view type has a variety of keystrokes and shortcuts that enable you to get around without using the mouse at all.

Table, Card, and Icon Views

Although table, card, and icon views are quite different to look at, they have one thing in common: the way you navigate them. Whether you use the mouse or the keyboard, the method is identical in all three—well, almost. The truth of the matter is, there are two types of table views, which complicates things a little. Using the mouse is the same with both types. However, using the keyboard is a little different depending on the view type. Using a shortcut on table views with editable fields sometimes produces a different result than using the same shortcut on a table view with non-editable fields. Card and icon views use the same shortcuts used by table views with non-editable fields.

Note   *Editable fields are those that you can edit in the view, without having to open the item. You can turn editing on or off by checking or removing the check mark from the Allow In-Cell Editing option in the view's Other Settings dialog box (View | Current View | Customize Current View | Other Settings).*

Some keystrokes are obvious, such using the UP ARROW and DOWN ARROW keys to move from one item to the next. The PAGE UP and PAGE DOWN keys also perform as expected, taking you to the item at the top or bottom of the screen, respectively. However, as you can see in Table 23-1, the functions of other keystrokes are not quite so obvious.

Keystroke	Action in Table Views with Editable Fields	Action in Table Views with Non-Editable Fields, Card Views, and Icon Views
CTRL+spacebar	Delete the entry in the selected field.	Select or deselect the active item.
ENTER	Open the selected item.	Open the selected item.
LEFT ARROW	Move one field to the left.	Move to the previous item. In a card view, this moves to the adjacent item in the next column to the left.
RIGHT ARROW	Move one field to the right.	Move to the next item. In a card view, this moves to the adjacent item in the next column to the right.
HOME	Move to the first editable field in the item record.	Select the first item in the view.
END	Move to the last editable field in the item record.	Select the last item in the view.
CTRL+HOME	Move to the first editable field in the first item of the view.	Move to the first item in the view (does not select it).
CTRL+END	Move to the last editable field of the last item in the view.	Move to the last item in the view (does not select it).
SHIFT+UP ARROW	Select the current item and the item above. Continuing to hold the SHIFT key while pressing UP ARROW extends the selection one record at a time. This also deselects records previously selected using the SHIFT+DOWN ARROW shortcut.	Select the current item and the item above. Continuing to hold the SHIFT key while pressing UP ARROW extends the selection one record at a time. This also deselects records previously selected using the SHIFT+DOWN ARROW shortcut.

Table 23-1.   *Shortcut Keys for Navigating Table Views*

Keystroke	Action in Table Views with Editable Fields	Action in Table Views with Non-Editable Fields, Card Views, and Icon Views
SHIFT+DOWN ARROW	Same as SHIFT+UP ARROW except the action moves in the opposite direction.	Same as SHIFT+UP ARROW except the action moves in the opposite direction.
CTRL+SHIFT+HOME	Select all items from the current item to the first item.	Select all items from the current item to the first item.
CTRL+SHIFT+END	Select all items from the current item to the last item.	Select all items from the current item to the last item.
CTRL+A	Select all items in the view.	Select all items in the view.
CTRL+UP ARROW	Move up one item without deselecting the current item(s), but without extending the selection to the next item.	Move up one item without deselecting the current item(s), but without extending the selection to the next item. Use this in conjunction with CTRL+spacebar to select non-adjacent items
CTRL+DOWN ARROW	Same as CTRL+UP ARROW except action moves downward.	Same as CTRL+UP ARROW except action moves downward.

Table 23-1. *Shortcut Keys for Navigating Table Views* (continued)

In case you're wondering, table views in mail, journal, and notes folders contain non-editable fields by default, while table views in calendar, contacts, and tasks folders contain editable fields by default.

If you have Group By settings applied to a folder view, you can use some additional keystrokes for working with the groups. To expand a group, press RIGHT ARROW or ENTER. Once the group is open, press DOWN ARROW to select the first item in the group. To collapse the group, use the LEFT ARROW key or the ENTER key.

Day/Week/Month Views

At first glance, the day/week/month view seems to be rather complex (navigationally speaking) since it contains three different elements to navigate: the Appointment area, the Date Navigator, and the TaskPad. However, once you break it down into its component parts, it's actually pretty simple. To begin with, the Date Navigator relies entirely on the mouse or on actions taken in the Appointment area. Next, the TaskPad is nothing more than a table view with editable fields, which means you can refer to Table 23-1 for keystrokes to use. That leaves only the Appointment area, which does have its own set of shortcut keys. See Table 23-2.

You may find some slight variations in these keystrokes and shortcuts as you move from one subview (day view, week view, or month view) to another.

Timeline Views

Timeline views, which display items in chronological order, also have their own navigational keystrokes. Like table views, Group By settings can be applied to timeline views, which means they also have additional shortcuts that can be used when items are grouped. See Table 23-3 for a listing of shortcuts you can use in a timeline view.

Keystroke	Action
ALT+1	Displays the day view.
ALT+2 through ALT+9	Displays two through nine days in the Appointment area.
ALT+5	Displays the workweek view.
ALT+0	Displays ten days in the Appointment area.
ALT+– (minus sign)	Uses the hyphen or the minus sign to display the week view.
ALT+= (equals sign)	Displays the month view.
TAB	Moves to the next appointment in the Appointment area.
SHIFT+TAB	Moves to the previous appointment in the Appointment area.
CTRL+TAB or F6	Moves between the Appointment area, the TaskPad, and the Folder List. Any of these objects that is not displayed, is skipped.
LEFT ARROW or RIGHT ARROW	Move to the previous or next day.

Table 23-2.   *Day/Week/Month View Shortcut Keys*

Keystroke	Action
LEFT ARROW	Select the previous item.
RIGHT ARROW	Select the next item.
ENTER	Open the selected item(s).
CTRL+spacebar	Select or deselect the active item.
SHIFT+LEFT ARROW	Select the current item and the previous item. Continue to hold the SHIFT key while pressing LEFT ARROW to extend the selection.
SHIFT+RIGHT ARROW	Select the current item and the next item. Continue to hold the SHIFT key while pressing RIGHT ARROW to extend the selection.
CTRL+LEFT ARROW	Move to the previous item without deselecting the current item. Use in conjunction with CTRL+spacebar to select non-adjacent items.
CTRL+RIGHT ARROW	Move to the next item without deselecting the current item. Use in conjunction with CTRL+spacebar to select non-adjacent items.
HOME	Select the first item in the view.
END	Select the last item in the view.
CTRL+HOME	Move to the first item in the view.
CTRL+END	Move to the last item in the view.

Table 23-3.   *Navigational Shortcuts Used in a Timeline View*

The keystrokes used to navigate timeline groups are identical to those used in a grouped table view. Press RIGHT ARROW or ENTER to expand a group. Once the group is open, press DOWN ARROW to select the first item in the group. Press LEFT ARROW or ENTER to collapse the group.

Customizing Folder Views

Folder views, like almost everything else in Outlook, are highly customizable. Although some views are more equal than others when it comes to customization, all views permit you to make some modifications. You can change everything from the fields displayed, to the colors and fonts in which they're displayed. Most customizing in folder views is done using one of five customization features. As you can see in Table 23-4, the available features depend on the view type.

Tip *Outlook 2002 automatically saves all changes you make to views without asking if you want them saved. Therefore, if you plan to make extensive changes to a view but want to retain the original view, your best bet is to create an entirely new view using the selected view as the basis. See the section entitled "Creating New Views" later in this chapter for more information.*

To access the customization options, regardless of the view you're in, you can use the Customize Current View command to open the View Summary dialog box. As you can see in Figure 23-1, the View Summary dialog box contains buttons for each of the different customization features. To open the View Summary dialog box, choose View | Current View | Customize Current View. You'll also find the Customize Current View command on the shortcut menu that appears when you right-click a field header in a table view or a blank spot in any view.

You'll also notice in the View Summary dialog box that a brief description of the feature's current state appears next to each button. Knowing what customizations have already been applied can help you determine additional customizations that need to be added.

Customizaton Feature	Table View	Day/Week/ Month View	Card View	Timeline View	Icon View
Adding and removing fields	X	X		X	X
Grouping	X				X
Sorting	X		X		X
Filtering	X	X		X	X	X
Fonts and other settings	X	X		X	X	X
Automatic formatting	X	X		X	

Table 23-4. *Customization Options Available for Outlook Views*

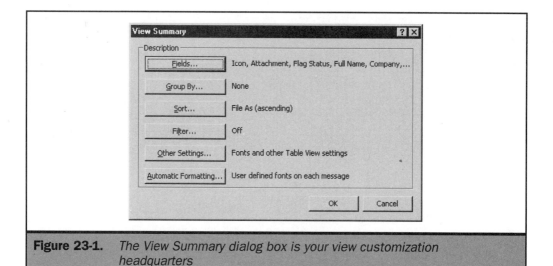

Figure 23-1.   *The View Summary dialog box is your view customization headquarters*

Adding and Removing Fields

In all but the icon view, you can modify the fields that appear in folder views. Table and card views permit you to add and remove as many fields as you choose, while the day/week/month and timeline views only permit minor field changes. Depending on the view type, you may have more than one way to achieve your field modifications. In all views that permit field changes, you can utilize the Customize Current View command to access the dialog box containing the available fields. Table views have an additional feature called the Field Chooser from which fields can be added directly to the view.

Using the Customize Current View Command

To add or remove fields in a view, use the Customize Current View command to open the View Summary dialog box seen previously in Figure 23-1. Depending on the current view type, you may have as many as three options for accessing the Customize Current View command. From any folder view, you can choose View | Current View | Customize Current View, or right-click a blank spot in the Information viewer and select Customize Current View from the shortcut menu. In a table view with column headers, right-click a column header and choose Customize Current View from the shortcut menu.

In the View Summary dialog box, click the Fields button to display the Date/Time Fields dialog box (see Figure 23-2) or the Show Fields dialog box (see Figure 23-3). The dialog box you see depends on the view type from which you invoke the Customize Current View command. From the Day/Week/Month view you'll see the Date/Time Fields dialog box. Accessing the Customize Current View command from a table view displays the Show Fields dialog box.

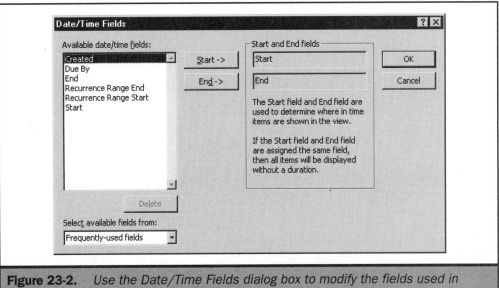

Figure 23-2. *Use the Date/Time Fields dialog box to modify the fields used in calendar and timeline views*

The Date/Time Fields dialog box is simple and straightforward. It only permits you to change the Start and End fields in the view and, naturally, limits your choices to date or time fields. From the Select Available Fields From drop-down list, choose the type of fields you want to use. The fields are then displayed in the Available Date/Time Fields list. Select a field and click the Start or End button to change the associated field. Click OK twice to save the changes and return to the active view.

As you can see in Figure 23-3, the Show Fields dialog box provides not only more fields to choose from, but also more options. The Show Fields dialog box is similar to the Date/Time Fields dialog box in that it contains a drop-down list of field types and a display list of available fields for the selected field type. The remaining options are unique to the Show Fields dialog box.

You can bypass the View Summary dialog box altogether, and display the Show Fields dialog box in table or card view by right-clicking a blank spot in the view and selecting Show Fields.

Begin by selecting the field type from the Select Available Fields From drop-down list. If you want to add a field to the current view, select the field in the Available Fields list and click the Add button. Unlike the Add button in the Date/Time Fields dialog box, this Add button does not replace the existing field, but rather adds the selected field to the list of fields currently included in the view. To remove a field, select it from the Show These Fields In This Order display list and click the Remove button.

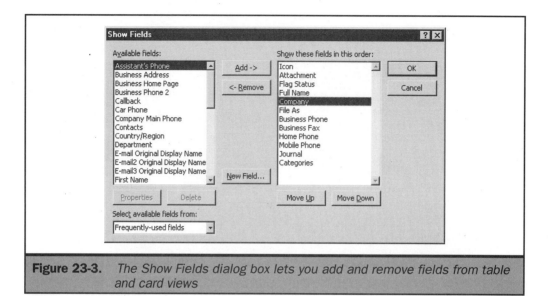

Figure 23-3. The Show Fields dialog box lets you add and remove fields from table and card views

> **Tip** By selecting a field in the Show These Fields In This Order list before adding a field, you can determine the new field's placement (below the selected field).

In addition to adding and removing fields, you can also change the order in which the fields appear in the view by using the Move Up and Move Down buttons. Highlight the field(s) you want to move and click the appropriate button. Moving a field up in the list moves it to the left in the table view itself, and moving it down in the list moves it to the right in the table view. You'll also notice two buttons in Figure 23-3 that are grayed out, Properties and Delete. These options are only available for custom fields. As you might suspect, they show the custom field properties and enable you to delete a custom field. You can even add a new field by clicking the New Field button to open the New Field dialog box.

Give the field a name, select the type of field you want to add, and choose a field format. For more information on creating custom fields, see Chapter 25. When you finish making your selection(s), click OK twice to effect the change(s) and return to the current view.

Using the Field Chooser

Outlook table views have an additional tool available for adding and removing fields, called the Field Chooser. As you can see in Figure 23-4, the Field Chooser is a small dialog box containing buttons (headers, actually) that represent fields. The field type selected in the drop-down list at the top of the dialog box determines the fields that appear.

To access the Field Chooser, right-click a column header in the table view and select Field Chooser from the shortcut menu. You'll also find a Field Chooser button on the Advanced toolbar, which you can display by right-clicking the Standard toolbar and selecting Advanced from the shortcut menu.

By default, Frequently-Used Fields (the most commonly used fields for the folder type) are displayed. If the field you want isn't there, select another field type from the drop-down list. When you find the field you're looking for, drag it to the position on the header bar where you want it to appear and drop it. As you move the field across the header bar, you'll see a pair of red arrows appearing between existing headers you're near. The red arrows indicate the spot in which a new field will land if you drop it. Select the desired position for the new field and let it go. The headers on either side move to make room for the new column.

Tip *You can display (but not modify) a field's properties by double-clicking the field in the Field Chooser.*

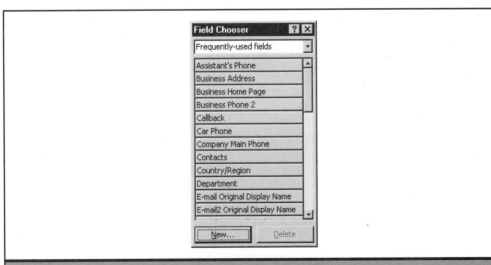

Figure 23-4. *The Field Chooser provides a quick way to add fields to a table view*

The Field Chooser, like the Show Fields dialog box, enables you to add a custom field by clicking the New button and entering the appropriate information in the New Field dialog box. You can also delete custom fields by highlighting the custom field you want to eliminate and clicking the Delete button. When you're finished adding fields to the view, click the X in the top right corner of the Field Chooser to close it.

Working with Fields in Table Views

Table views provide a quick and easy way to rearrange and delete fields without having to bother with the Show Fields dialog box, which is the only way you can move and delete fields in non-table views. In table views you can use drag-and-drop to move field headers from one position to another or to delete them altogether.

Grab the field header you want to reposition, and drag it to a new location. As you move the field over the header bar, red arrows appear at the next spot where you can drop the header. You can release the field as soon as the arrows appear, and the header squeezes into the location indicated by the arrows. Removing a field from the view is even easier. Simply drag the field header into the Information viewer and drop it. It disappears immediately. Of course, it only disappears from the view, not from Outlook. You can re-add it at any time by opening the Field Chooser or the Show Fields dialog box.

Defining the Sort Order

Sorting is one of Outlook's most useful features. It enables you to arrange all the items in the view in a manner that makes finding information fast and effortless. Depending on the type of view you plan to sort, you may have more than one way to perform a sort. All view types that support sorting (table, card, and icon) can be sorted using the Sort dialog box. In addition, table views can be sorted from directly within the view by clicking field headers.

One thing to be aware of is that regardless of which method you employ, some fields cannot be used as sort criteria. When you attempt to sort by Company (in the Task folder only), Categories, Contact (as opposed to Contacts), Notes, or Read, you receive an error message informing you that "You cannot sort by this field." There is no apparent reason for this anomaly.

Using the Sort Dialog Box

The Sort dialog box, seen in Figure 23-5, enables you to sort by as many as four different fields, either in ascending (A–Z) or descending (Z–A) order.

The easiest way to open the Sort dialog box is to right-click a blank spot in the Information viewer and to select Sort from the shortcut menu. If you can't find a blank spot, choose View | Current View | Customize Current View and click the Sort button in the View Summary dialog box.

Once you have the Sort dialog box open, choose the field type for the first sort criterion from the Select Available Fields From drop-down list, located at the bottom of the dialog box. From the Sort Items By drop-down list, select the first field on which you want to base the sort. Click Ascending or Descending to determine the order of the sort.

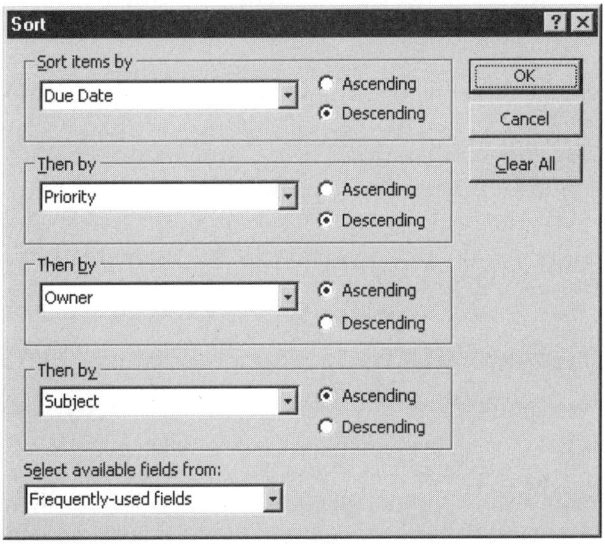

Figure 23-5.   *Applying a sort is easy when you use the Sort dialog box*

If you want to use a secondary sort, repeat the process using the Then By drop-down list. You can add up to four sort criteria using the additional Then By options. When you're finished, click OK (once or twice, depending on how you accessed the Sort dialog box) to apply the sort and return to the current view.

If you've selected fields that are not already in the view, Outlook asks if you want to add them at the same time. Click Yes to add the field and apply the sort, No to leave the field out and still apply the sort, or Cancel to halt the process and start over. To remove the currently applied sort, open the Sort dialog box and click the Clear All button to remove all sort criteria.

Sorting Table Views

Sorting in table views is a breeze. You don't even have to open the Sort dialog box. Simply click a field header to sort the view by the field it represents. The first time you click a field header, the sort order is ascending. Click the header a second time to reverse the order and make the sort descending. Whatever the current sort order is, clicking the header reverses it. You can tell if a field is being used to sort the view by the appearance of a small embossed triangle on the header. The direction in which the triangle points indicates the sort order (up for ascending, down for descending).

You can also sort the view by multiple fields. Set the order for the first field by clicking its header. Then hold down the SHIFT key and select additional column headers to use their fields for subsorts. To reverse the sort order of a secondary sort, click the header again while holding down the SHIFT key. This method, like the Sort dialog box, limits you to four fields for sorting. If you attempt to use a fifth field, Outlook informs you that you're using "Too many sort levels."

The one thing you can't do using the field headers that you can do using the Sort dialog box is sort by fields that are not included in the view. You'll have to add them first. See the earlier section entitled "Adding and Removing Fields."

There's one last method you can use to sort a table view. Right-click the header of the field you want to sort by and choose Sort Ascending or Sort Descending. If a sort is already applied using that field, the appropriate command will already be selected on the shortcut menu.

Adding and Applying Filters

Filters are handy devices that hide (filter out) records that fail to meet search criteria you enter in the Filter dialog box. For example, if you have a ton of messages in your Inbox and you're looking for messages from a certain individual, you can filter out all e-mail messages except those from that person. To access the Filter dialog box, right-click a blank spot in any view type (filtering is supported by all views), and select Filter from the shortcut menu. You can also choose View | Current View | Customize Current View, and click the Filter button in the View Summary dialog box.

The first tab of the Filter dialog box varies depending on the folder in which you happen to be when you open the Filter dialog box. The tab is named for the folder, and the options are tailored to that folder type. The Filter dialog box shown in Figure 23-6 is from the Inbox folder. For information about the opening tab in other folder types, see the chapter that covers that particular folder.

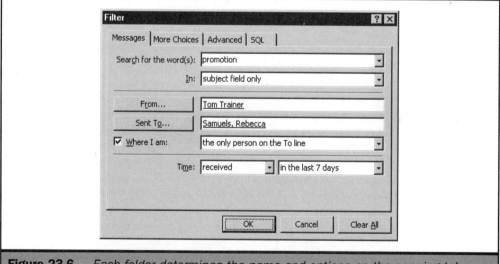

Figure 23-6.   *Each folder determines the name and options on the opening tab of the Filter dialog box*

Using the More Choices Tab

The remaining three tabs are identical regardless of which folder you're in when you invoke the Filter dialog box. The second tab, shown in Figure 23-7, is the More Choices tab.

The More Choices tab offers a variety of filtering options using basic fields common to most Outlook items. These options include

- **Categories**   Anyone who uses categories will appreciate this one. Enter the category you're looking for. Be advised, however, that performing a search that includes multiple categories locates not only messages assigned to both, but also messages assigned to either. Outlook adds an implied *Or* between multiple selections in this field. There's nothing you can do about it, so you'll just have to learn to live with it.

- **Only items that are**   This is a great way to find only items that are marked read or unread. Use the drop-down list to make your selection.

- **Only items with**   If you want to find items based on the fact that they do or do not contain attachments, this is the option for you.

- **Whose importance is**   When time is short and you have a lot to do, you may want to filter out everything but the most important stuff. In that case, use this option to search for those items of high importance.

- **Match case**   If you've entered text in the Search For Word(s) field on the opening tab, you can use this option to search for only those instances of the word(s) that match the exact case of the text you entered. Check the option to enable it.

- **Size (kilobytes)**   This option can be helpful if you know that you received a rather large attachment with your message. Indicate an operator (equals, between, less than, or greater than) and the size.

Using the Advanced Tab

Advanced, the third tab, shown in Figure 23-8, lets you create custom criteria based on almost any field in Outlook. The way it works is simple. You select a field to base the criterion on. Then you enter a condition that must be met by the record(s) you want to see when the filter is applied. All records that do not meet the condition(s) are filtered out, and temporarily hidden from view.

Begin by clicking the Field button to display a drop-down menu of field types. Selecting the field type displays a submenu containing the available fields for that type. Now select the field you want to use for the first advanced filter criterion. The field appears in the textbox below the Field button. The next thing to do is establish the condition to be met. Select a conditional operator from the Condition drop-down list. Depending on the field type you select, the operators vary. For text fields, your choices include operators such as Contains and Is (Exactly) that work on alphanumeric data. Date fields accommodate conditional operators such as Anytime, Yesterday, and Today. Conditional operators for numeric fields include such things as Equals, Is At

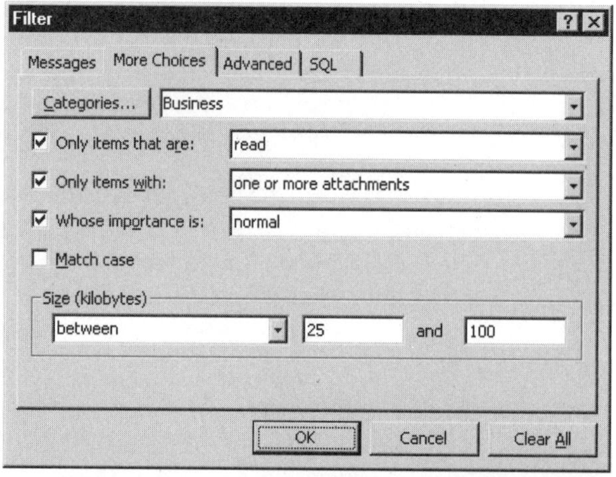

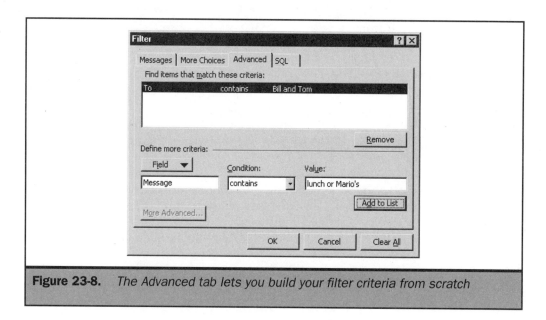

Figure 23-7.   *More choices are just what you get when you click the More Choices tab*

Least, and Is More Than. You'll find even more variations, but as with these, most are self-explanatory.

After you select the condition, move to the Value field. Enter the data you want the conditional operator to evaluate when determining whether the record qualifies. If you

Figure 23-8.   *The Advanced tab lets you build your filter criteria from scratch*

select Is Empty or Is Not Empty, no Value field entry is necessary (or permitted) since the operator is Boolean. Either the condition is met or it's not.

Tip *When entering data in the Value field, you can use And and Or operators between values. For example, to find all messages that contain* lunch *and* Mario's *(Meet Bill for lunch at Mario's) in the subject line, enter* **lunch and Mario's** *in the Value field. However, if you're looking for messages that contain either in the subject line, enter* **lunch or Mario's.**

Once you've entered the information in the appropriate fields, click Add To List to add the new filter criterion to the Find Items That Match These Criteria display list. Add as many conditional statements as you need, and click OK to apply the filter.

Note *If you add multiple conditions, there is an implied And between all statements. Therefore, only those items that meet the conditions of all statements are displayed.*

To remove filter criteria, you can select the statement to eliminate, and click the Remove button. If you want to remove the entire filter, click the Clear All button.

Using the SQL Tab

The SQL tab, shown in Figure 23-9, enables you to enter more sophisticated filtering criteria using SQL-like syntax.

To enter custom filtering criteria, check the Edit These Criteria Directly, All Other Tabs Will Be Unavailable option. This enables the Find Items That Match These Criteria window, which is really nothing more than a rudimentary text editor. Enter your filter criteria and click OK to apply the filter. As the Edit These Criteria Directly, All Other Tabs Will Be Unavailable option indicates, the other tabs in the Filter dialog box are disabled when you use the SQL tab.

Grouping Items

The Outlook Group By feature, which is available in both table and timeline views, enables you to create sets of items that all have one or more things in common. For example, to quickly find vendors, customers, and employees, you might create groups based on categories in your Contacts folder. You could further break down the contacts by creating a subgroup based on the Company field.

As with most Outlook features, there are a couple of ways to create groups, depending on the view you're in. You can create groups in both the timeline view and the table view by setting options in the Group By dialog box. Table views offer two additional methods. You can use the Group By This Field command or the Group By Box command. Both beat the Group By dialog box hands down for quick and easy grouping.

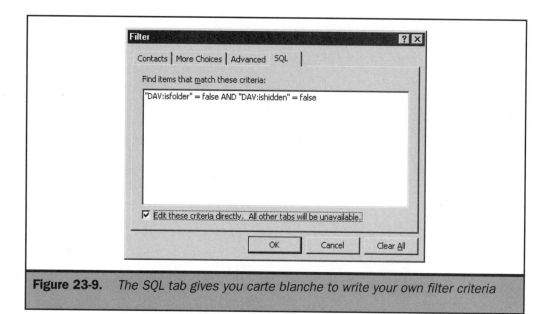

Figure 23-9. *The SQL tab gives you carte blanche to write your own filter criteria*

Using the Group By Dialog Box

To access the Group By dialog box seen in Figure 23-10, in either a timeline view or a table view, right-click a blank spot on the Information viewer and select Group By from the shortcut menu.

Another method you can use in either view is to choose View | Current View | Customize Current View and click the Group By button in the View Summary dialog box. In a timeline view you have one additional method. Right-click the timeline bar or date header, and select Group By from the shortcut menu.

Once you open the Group By dialog box, you'll find it's similar to the Filter dialog box. You can group items by up to four different fields, and you can elect to sort items in the groups either in ascending or descending order. Begin by choosing the field type from the Select Available Fields From drop-down list. Then, from the Group Items By drop-down list, select the field you want to use for the first group. If the field is already in the view, the Show Field In View option appears with a check mark. If the field is not currently displayed in the view, check the option to include the field. Next, indicate whether you want the group sorted in Ascending or Descending order. If you want to create subgroups, repeat the process in one or more of the next three Then By fields.

Note *When you create a group based on a field that can contain multiple values, such as Categories, an item assigned to multiple categories will appear in all groups to which it is assigned.*

GETTING MORE OUT
OF OUTLOOK

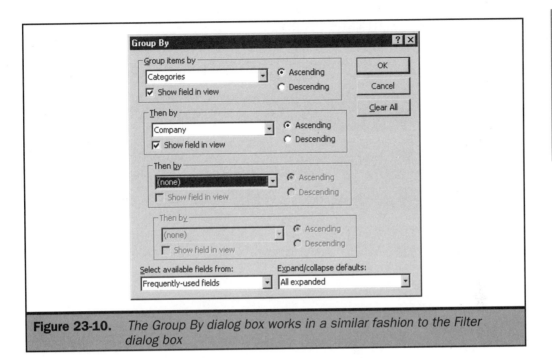

Figure 23-10. *The Group By dialog box works in a similar fashion to the Filter dialog box*

The final option (not counting Clear All) in the Group By dialog box is Expand/Collapse Defaults. This field contains a drop-down list with three choices for the manner in which you want the groups displayed:

- **All expanded**   When you apply the Group By settings, each of the groups is expanded to display all items within.

- **All collapsed**   Select this option to collapse all groups so that none of the items shows.

- **As last viewed**   If you change sort order or Show Field In View options and reapply the Group By settings, the expanded/collapsed state of the view is retained.

Click OK (twice if you accessed the Group By dialog box from the View Summary dialog box) to save the settings and create the groups.

Note   *If you find that you have more than one group with the same name, it's probably the result of grouping by a text field, such as Subject or Company, in which the text entry is followed by one or more (unintentional) spaces. Grouping requires an exact match of characters and considers spaces to be valid characters. Luckily the Group By feature is not case-sensitive, so you can go to town with capitalization, or the lack thereof.*

Working with groups is easy. Click the plus sign to the left of the group header to expand the group. Click the minus sign to collapse the group. To sort groups, use the sort options in the Group By dialog box. To sort items within the groups, use the options in the Sort dialog box. If you want to remove all Group By settings, return to the Group By dialog box and click Clear All.

Alternate Group By Methods

Table views, which are the most prevalent views found in Outlook, provide a couple of alternatives to the Group By dialog box. These alternatives consist of a pair of commands found on the shortcut menu that appears when you right-click a column header. As with many options found only in table views, they are quicker and easier to use than dialog box settings. However, they are also less powerful.

If you have the Advanced toolbar displayed, you can access the Group By box by clicking the Group By Box button. If, on the other hand, you don't want to take up space with the Advanced toolbar but would like to have a Group By Box button on your Standard toolbar, you can add one. Open the Customize dialog box and drag the Group By Box command to the Standard toolbar. See Chapter 24 for more information on customizing toolbars.

Since both commands use the Group By box, the first command to consider is the Group By Box command itself. Right-click any column header and select Group By Box to display the Group By box above the column headers. As you can see in Figure 23-11, the box contains an information box indicating that you should "Drag a column header here to group by that column."

It's that simple. Drag the column header of the field on which you want to base your first grouping, and drop it in the box. To create subgroups, drag another header and drop it in the Group By box. The result, seen in Figure 23-12, is that a copy of each header is placed in the Group By box, and the table view is grouped by those fields.

If you look closely, you'll note that a thin black line connects the headers, indicating the relationship. You can change the relationship by dragging the headers to different positions. Dragging any field to the left and dropping it when the red arrows appear places it higher in the group hierarchy. Moving it to the right demotes it. To remove a grouping altogether, drag the header out of the Group By box and drop it on the Information viewer. Contrary to what you might think, removing a header with subheaders attached does not remove the subheaders as well. They simply move up the ladder. You can sort and re-sort groups by clicking the column headers in the Group By box. To sort items within groups, use the column headers in the view. When you decide it's time to close the Group By box, right-click any column header and select Group By Box again.

You can open the Group By dialog box by double-clicking a blank spot in the Group By box.

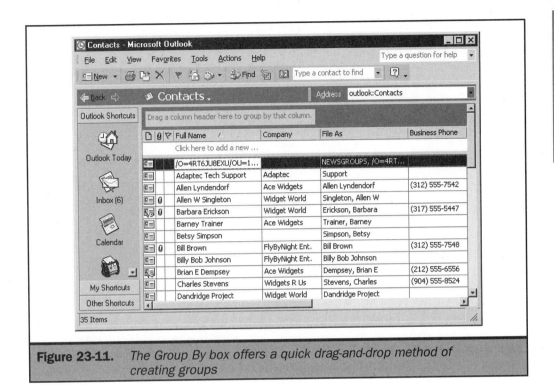

Figure 23-11.   *The Group By box offers a quick drag-and-drop method of creating groups*

Now that you understand how the Group By box works, you're ready to move on to the Group By This Field command. Decide which field you want to use to create a group. Then right-click its column header and select Group By This Field from the shortcut menu. The Group By box opens (if it's not already open), a copy of the column header is placed in it, and the view is grouped by the associated field. To create subgroups, you can either drag additional column headers into the Group By box, or, if you like to do things the hard way, you can choose another column header, right-click, and select Group By This Field again.

Configuring Other Settings

The Other Settings dialog box could be more appropriately named Formatting Settings, since it contains mostly font and formatting options for the view in which it's invoked. Other Settings options range from changing the fonts of headings and item entries to the color of table view grid lines and the width and height of cards in a card view.

You can open the Other Settings dialog box from any view by right-clicking a blank spot in the view and selecting Other Settings from the shortcut menu. You can also access the Other Settings dialog box from the View Summary dialog box.

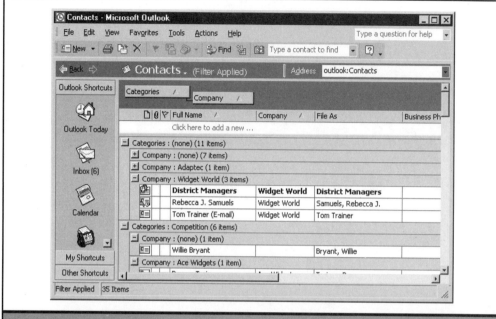

Figure 23-12. The Group By box displays the column headers used, in the order in which they're applied

Table View

Table views, which are widely used throughout Outlook folders, contain an extensive group of Other Settings options. As you can see in Figure 23-13, the Other Settings dialog box options include font options, grid line options, and a handful of options dealing with columns, cells, AutoPreview, and the Preview Pane.

Some table views offer a third method of accessing the Other Settings dialog box. If the table view contains a "new item" row at the top, you can right-click it and select Other Settings from the shortcut menu.

The options available in a table view Other Settings dialog box include the following:

- **Column headings** The Font option in this section changes the font used in the column headings. Click the Font button to display the Font dialog box. Here you can modify the font, font style, and font size used to display header information. The other option found in the Column Headings section is Automatic Column Sizing. This option forces the resizing of all columns to make them fit within the visible Information viewer.

- **Rows**   You can use the Font option in the Rows section to change the font used in the fields contained in each row. One thing to note: font settings applied in the Automatic Formatting dialog box take precedence over font options set here. The other options found in this section include Allow In-Cell Editing, which enables you to modify field contents in the view, and Show "New Item" Row. The Show "New Item" Row option adds a blank row at the top of the view, in which you can enter information to create a new folder item, or which you can double-click to open the item form associated with the folder.

- **AutoPreview**   The Font button here enables you to modify the font used in the AutoPreview feature. The other three options, which are self-explanatory, let you determine if and how the AutoPreview feature works.

- **Grid lines**   Grid lines are the lines separating both fields and columns in some table views. If you check the Phone List view of the Contacts folder, you'll see a table view with grid lines turned on. Now take a look at the Messages view of the Inbox to see what a table view without grid lines looks like. Your Grid Lines choices include the type and color of the grid lines as well as an option to shade (or not shade) group headings. The Shade Group Headings option is checked by default for a good reason. It's much easier to distinguish group headings from group items when the headings are shaded.

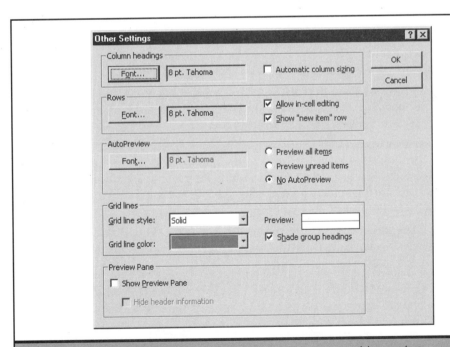

Figure 23-13.   *Other Settings options in table views are wide ranging*

- **Show Preview Pane**   This is a simple option that displays the Preview Pane. It also enables the Hide Header Information option, which displays the Preview Pane without header information.

Once you've set all the Other Settings options, click OK (twice if you used the View Summary dialog box) to return to the active view, which now sports the new "other settings."

Day/Week/Month View

When you access Other Settings from within a day/week/month view, the dialog box that appears is the Format Day/Week/Month View dialog box, shown in Figure 23-14.

The Format Day/Week/Month View dialog box contains font options to change the appearance of time displays as well as information in each of the three subviews (Day, Week, and Month). The font options all work the same for each subview. Click the button to open the Font dialog box and change the font, font style, and font size as needed. In addition to font options, the Format Day/Week/Month View dialog box also contains a number of other options, including

- **Time scale**   The Appointment area in the day view displays appointment blocks based on the Time Scale settings. By default the Time Scale is set to 30 minutes. If most of your appointments are longer or shorter, you can change the Time Scale settings to fit your needs.

- **Show time as clocks**   This field is found both in the Week and Month sections. Besides being unbearably cute, it does offer one advantage. Both the start and end times are displayed in the week and month views.

- **Show end time**   This option also appears in the Week and Month sections. When the Show Time As Clocks option is checked, this option displays the end time of appointments as well as the start time.

- **Compress weekend days**   Figuring that most workweeks are Monday through Friday, Outlook saves space in the month view by forcing Saturday and Sunday to share a single day block, thereby eliminating the need for an additional column. If you want Saturday and Sunday to each have its own column, remove the check mark from this option.

- **Bolded dates in Date Navigator represent days containing items**   With this option checked, any dates for which appointments or events are scheduled appear bolded in the Date Navigator.

When all options are set to your satisfaction, click OK (twice if you used the View Summary dialog box to access the Format Day/Week/Month View dialog box) to save the changes and return to the current view.

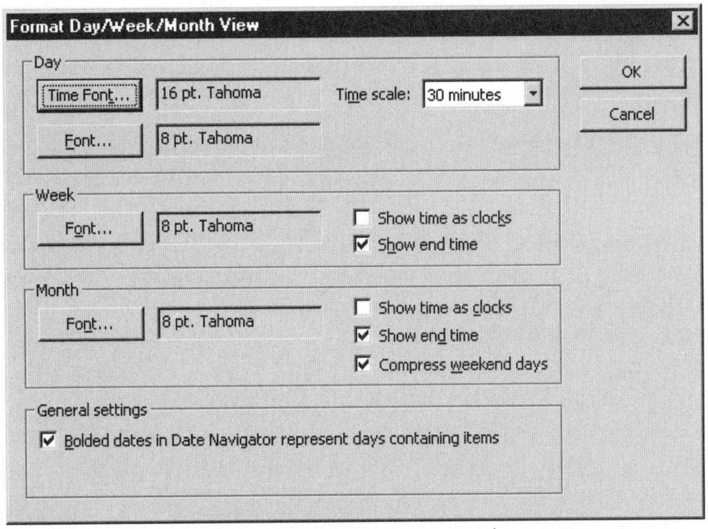

Figure 23-14.   *You can give the day/week/month view a whole new look*

Card View

The Format Card View dialog box seen in Figure 23-15 is displayed when you select Other Settings from the shortcut menu or the View Summary dialog box in a card view.

As you can see, the Format Card View dialog box contains font options for changing both the headings and body of individual cards. These options work like other font options. Click the appropriate Font button to open the Font dialog box. Make the desired changes to the font, and click OK to return to the Format Card View dialog box. Other options for formatting the card view include

- ■ **Allow in-cell editing**   With this option, you can edit individual fields in the card view without having to open the item form.

- ■ **Show empty fields**   By default, Outlook hides fields in the card view that contain no data. If you want to see all fields in the view regardless of their contents (or lack thereof), check this option.

- ■ **Card width**   This option enables you to change the width of cards appearing in the view. In theory you can make the card as small as three characters or as large as 1,000 characters wide. However, neither end of the spectrum is practical. At the low end, only the first three characters of each line appear. At the high end, the width is limited by your window size and display settings. At full screen with a screen resolution of 800×600, the maximum width of a card is around 124 characters (it may vary depending on your video card). If your resolution is higher, the maximum will be higher as well. If your resolution is lower, the maximum will follow suit.

■ **Multi-line field height** This option controls the minimum number of lines displayed in a multiline field such as Address. The number must be between 1 and 20. Be aware, however, that if you raise the minimum to more lines than the field actually holds, blank lines are displayed to make up the minimum, even if Show Empty Fields is disabled.

You can also change the card width by grabbing one of the vertical borders between columns of cards and dragging it to the left to reduce or to the right to increase the card size.

When you're finished setting Format Card View dialog box options, click OK (twice if you used the View Summary dialog box) to save the options and return to the active view.

Timeline View

The Format Timeline View dialog box, shown in Figure 23-16, appears when you select Other Settings from within a timeline view. As you can see, the Format Timeline View dialog box contains Fonts, Scales, and Labels options.

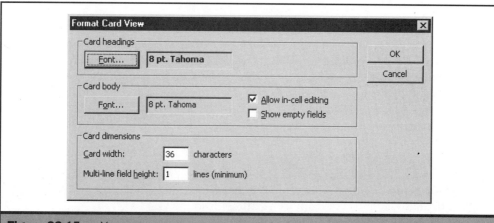

Figure 23-15. *You can spruce up your card views with the Format Card View dialog box*

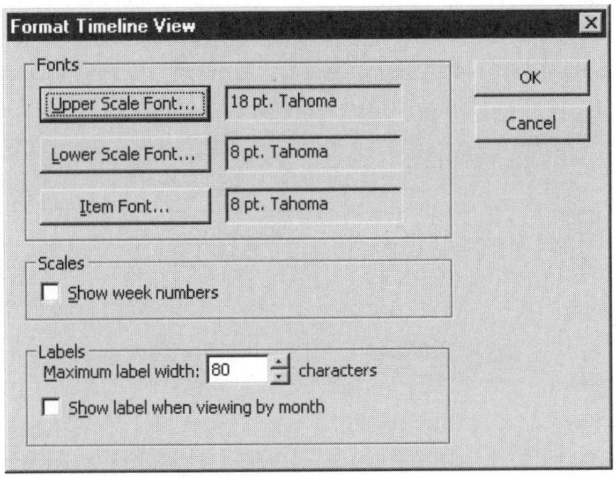

Figure 23-16. *Use the Format Timeline View dialog box to apply custom formatting to your timeline view*

The font options apply both to time scales in the view, and to the items that appear in the view. To change the font options, click the appropriate font button and make the necessary changes in the Font dialog box. The remaining options include

- **Show week numbers** Check this box to add the week number (Week 1 through Week 52) to the view. How this works depends on whether you're in the day, week, or month timeline view. In the day and week views, the week number is added to the upper scale. In the month view, the week number replaces the days of the week in the lower scale.

- **Maximum label width** This option lets you put a limit on the number of characters that can be displayed in an item label that appears in the view. Although the field permits you to enter any number up to 9999, it will not accept anything beyond 132 regardless of your display settings. If you enter a number larger than 132, Outlook automatically resets the option to 132.

- **Show label when viewing by month** By default, item labels are not displayed in the month view. Check this option to turn labels on in the month view.

While you have the Show Label When Viewing By Month option to turn labels on or off in the month view, no such option exists for the day and week views. However, you can get around that by setting the Maximum Label Width option to zero to turn item labels off. If you want to turn them on again, return to the Format Timeline View dialog box and reset the Maximum Label Width to 80 or a length of your choice.

Click OK until you return to the active timeline view. All your changes will be saved and applied to the current view.

Icon View

The icon view is the only view that does not provide font formatting options when the Other Settings command is used. Instead, the Format Icon View dialog box that appears offers options for the size and placement of icons within the view (see Figure 23-17).

There are only two sets of options in the Format Icon View dialog box: View Type and Icon Placement. The View Type options include Large Icon, Small Icon, and Icon List. They are pretty much self-explanatory, but a little additional information might be helpful. It doesn't take a rocket scientist to figure out that the difference between the Large Icon and Small Icon options is the size of the icon. However, the difference between the Small Icon and the Icon List is a little less obvious. Although both use small icons, the arrangement of icons in the Small Icon view is, by default, from right to left, while in the Icon List the arrangement is from top to bottom.

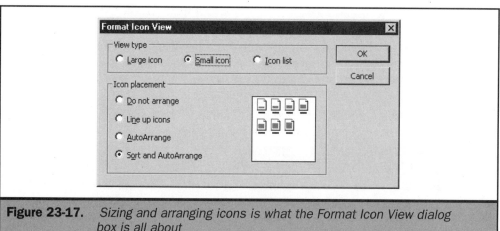

Figure 23-17.   *Sizing and arranging icons is what the Format Icon View dialog box is all about*

The next option, Icon Placement, is available only if Large Icon or Small Icon is selected in the first option. This option enables you to change the arrangement of items in the view:

- **Do not arrange**   Use this option to leave the little critters wherever they fall. No order is imposed on them, unless you do it yourself.

- **Line up icons**   This option imposes a limited amount of order by lining up each item with the nearest grid line of the invisible grid present in all icon views. You can see this option in action by setting the option and returning to the view. Then move an icon and let it go. Unless you happen to be right on a grid line, the icon "snaps" to the grid line closest to the spot where you drop it.

- **AutoArrange**   This feature automatically arranges icons in rows from left to right.

- **Sort and AutoArrange**   Use this option in conjunction with the Sort feature to automatically arrange items in rows based on Sort criteria you specify.

Once you set all the Format Icon View dialog box options, click OK until you return to the active view.

Using Automatic Formatting

Automatic formatting, which is only available for table and card views, enables you to set options that apply formatting to an item when the item meets certain conditions you specify. An example of Automatic Formatting can be seen in the task list. When a task becomes overdue, it automatically changes to red. This is the result of an Automatic Formatting rule that stipulates any task whose due date is earlier than today's date must be dressed in a red font. You might create your own rule to turn e-mail messages from the boss bright blue, to ensure you don't accidentally miss one.

You can create your own rules or modify existing rules. You can do anything you want to your own rules. However, your ability to modify the rules that come predefined with the view is limited to turning them on and off, and to changing the font. What you cannot do is change the conditions upon which these rules are based.

If you want to make sure you don't miss messages from your boss, your bookie, or your spouse, you can take advantage of automatic formatting to highlight only those messages coming from selected addresses.

To create an Automatic Formatting rule, begin by opening the Automatic Formatting dialog box. Right-click a blank spot in the view and select Customize Current View to open the View Summary dialog box. Next, click the Automatic Formatting button to display the Automatic Formatting dialog box. Figure 23-18 shows the Automatic Formatting dialog box from the Simple List view in the Tasks folder. As you can see, the view has a number of predefined formatting rules already in place.

The first thing you'll notice is that all the existing rules have a check box next to them. To turn a rule on, add a check mark. To turn a rule off, remove the check mark. As mentioned earlier, you can only change the font formatting on predefined rules. Until you create a new rule, that's all you have. Therefore, you might as well get to work and create a new rule.

Click the Add button to add a new rule. An "untitled" rule appears in the Rules For This View display list, and all three options at the bottom of the dialog box become available. Enter a name for the new rule in the Name field. Click the Font button to open the Font dialog box. Select the font, font style, font size, font color, and any effects you want the text to have, and click OK to return to the Automatic Formatting dialog box.

Be sure not to duplicate the font formatting already set for an existing rule. If you do, you'll have no way to distinguish items formatted by the old rule from items formatted by the new rule.

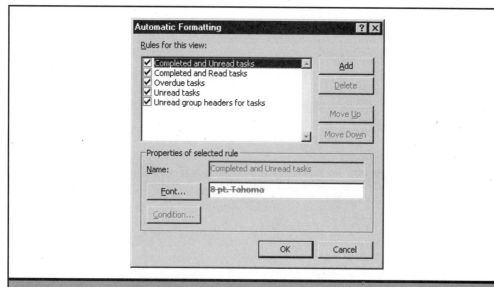

Figure 23-18.   *Let Outlook do all the work for you when it comes to making special items stand out*

The last step in creating the rule is to establish the conditions that will trigger the rule. Click the Condition button and you'll be amazed at what appears—the Filter dialog box. That's right, you use the Filter dialog box to determine the criteria the new rule uses. The filter is not actually applied to the view. When new items are created in the folder or arrive by other means, they are tested against the filter criteria. Those that meet the conditions receive the designated formatting. Those that don't, slide by untouched. For detailed information on creating filters, see the section earlier in this chapter entitled "Adding and Applying Filters."

If you want to modify an existing rule, select it and make the necessary changes using the three options at the bottom of the Automatic Formatting dialog box. You'll find that when editing one of the predefined rules, the only change you can make is to the font used. Deleting a rule is as easy as selecting it and clicking the Delete button. As you might have guessed, you cannot delete predefined rules, nor can you rearrange the order of predefined rules. Since the order in which rules appear in the list determines the order in which they're processed, this means that predefined rules are always processed first. Any rules you create you can reorder by selecting the rule and clicking the Move Up or Move Down button.

When you're finished, click OK until you return to the active view. If you created a new rule or modified an existing rule, you'll see the results immediately.

MOUS EXAM PRACTICE
In this section you learned to apply automatic formatting to messages or to other Outlook items based on criteria you determine. Start by reviewing the existing rules and seeing how they operate. Next, try creating your own rule for highlighting messages from your boss. Perhaps you want those to be bold. Then create a rule that underlines messages from your spouse. After you create the rules, open them up and make changes to both the criteria and the formatting.

Modifying Columns

Columns found in table views can be relocated, widened, narrowed, renamed, and formatted. Moving columns and changing their width can both be accomplished using the column headers. To move a column from one position to another, drag the column header left or right until a pair of red arrows appear. Drop the header, and the column appears at the location indicated by the arrows. To change the width of a column, move your mouse pointer to the right border of the column header, and drag the border left to shrink the column or right to enlarge it.

Format Columns

If you're big on one-stop shopping, you might want to check out the Format Columns dialog box, shown in Figure 23-19.

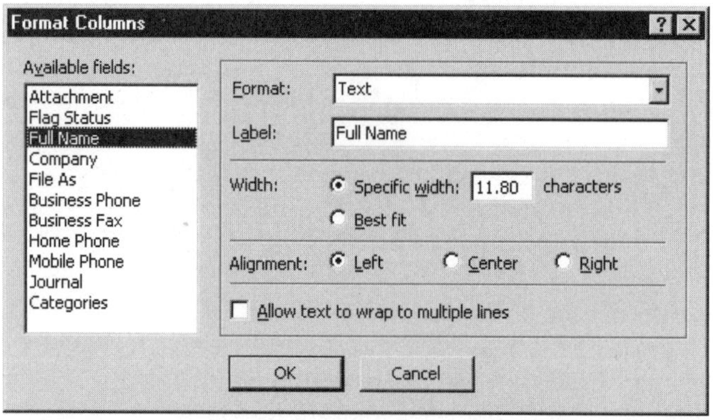

Figure 23-19. *The Format Columns dialog box can fill all your column-formatting needs*

To open the Format Columns dialog box, right-click a field header and select Format Columns from the shortcut menu. As you can see, the Format Columns dialog box has a variety of options for customizing table view columns. To apply the formatting, select a field from the Available Fields list and set the desired options from among the following:

- **Format** If the field is capable of being displayed in more than one format, you can select the format of your choice from the Format drop-down list. For example, the Attachment field can be displayed as an icon (the default), Yes/No, On/Off, or True/False.

- **Label** You can change the text that appears in the column header by using the Label option. This does not change the name of the field nor does it change the label in any other table view in the folder.

- **Width** If you want to set the column to a precise width, you can select Specific Width and enter the number of characters wide you want the column to appear. If you want Outlook to automatically adjust the column to accommodate the longest field entry or the column name, whichever is longer, select Best Fit.

- **Alignment** The Alignment option applies to the text within the column. Setting the alignment to Left forces all field entries to snuggle up to the left side of the cell. Center places the entries in the center of the cell, and Right pushes them up against the right side of the cell.

- **Allow text to wrap to multiple lines** Check this option to enable word wrapping within a cell. With the option unchecked, text that extends beyond the cell borders is hidden from view. When you enable this option, all text is displayed by wrapping to add as many lines to the cell as needed.

You can apply formatting to as many fields as you want. When you're finished, click OK to return to the active view and apply the changes.

Best Fit

The Best Fit command, which appears in the Format Columns dialog box described in the previous section on column formatting, also comes as a stand-alone command. In a table view, right-click the header of the column you want to adjust and select Best Fit. Outlook automatically makes the column wide enough to display the entire column name or the longest field entry in the column, whichever is longer.

Since card views also contain columns, although of an entirely different nature, the Best Fit command can also be accessed in them. Card view columns are simply there to keep the individual cards from spilling over onto one another. All columns are identical in size. Therefore, resizing one automatically resizes all.

The Best Fit command works a little differently in a card view than it does in a table view. Rather than adjusting column size to accommodate the contents, it adjusts column size to prevent partial columns from appearing in the view. If three and a half columns are showing when you apply the Best Fit command, Outlook resizes them to fit three entire columns in the view. To use the Best Fit command, right-click a blank spot in one of the columns (including the partial column) and select Best Fit from the shortcut menu.

Removing Columns

Removing columns from a table view is easy and painless. All you have to do is drag the column header into the Information viewer, and poof! It's gone. Of course, it's not gone for good. You can open the Show Fields dialog box or the Field Chooser and put it back anytime you want. If you're allergic to dragging and dropping, you can always right-click the header of the column you want to delete, and select Remove This Column.

MOUS EXAM PRACTICE
In this section you learned all the ways to customize Outlook views. Begin by sorting a table view using the column headers. Click a column header to sort a field, and then click the header to reverse the sort order. Now, hold down the SHIFT key, and click additional column headers to sort by multiple fields. Next, try your hand at sorting card and other non-table views using the Sort dialog box. After you master sorting, it's time to tackle grouping. Open a table view and use the group by commands found on the shortcut menu that appears when you right-click a column head. Next, display the Group By box and drag column headers into it to create groups. You might also work on setting column widths and using automatic formatting.

Removing View Customizations

If, after customizing a view, you find that you want to remove the customizations and return the view to its original state, you can do so without a great deal of trouble. As a matter of fact, you can do it a couple of different ways. One restores a single view, and the other restores all folder views to their defaults.

To return a single view to its pre-customized state, open the folder where it's used, and choose View | Current View | Define Views to open the Define Views dialog box. Select the view you want to restore and click the Reset button. Outlook immediately wants to know if you really mean it or if you're just kidding around. If you really mean it, click OK and all customizations are removed, and the view returns to its natural state. Click Close to return to the active view.

If you decide it's time to do some serious housekeeping and return everything to its original condition, you'll have to exit Outlook and restart it using a command-line switch.

 Not only does this method remove all customizations to predefined Outlook views, but it also removes all custom views you've created. Therefore, do not use this method unless you either have no custom views or you wish to delete them all.

If you're ready to remove all custom views and all customizations to predefined views, choose File | Exit Now and click Start | Run to open the Run dialog box. Enter **Outlook/CleanViews** in the Open field. Click OK to restart Outlook using the CleanViews switch. Outlook opens with all folder views restored to their original condition.

Customizing Outlook Today

 Outlook Today is a web page that provides a quick overview of your most important Outlook information. By default, Outlook Today displays appointment items due for the next five days, your entire task list, and the number of unread messages in your Inbox, Drafts folder, and Outbox. A quick check here before starting your day can give you a good idea of what's on your plate (see Figure 23-20). To open Outlook Today, click the Outlook Today shortcut in the Outlook Bar.

Using the Customize Outlook Today Page

Of course, your notion of what comprises important information might not coincide with that of the Outlook programmers. Therefore, you may want to take advantage of the customization options available, and make a few changes to your Outlook Today page.

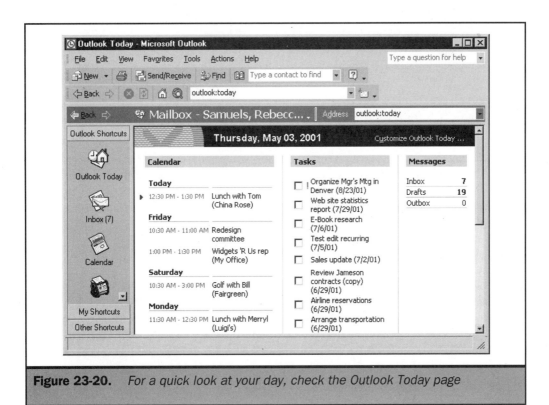

Figure 23-20. *For a quick look at your day, check the Outlook Today page*

Begin by clicking the Customize Outlook Today button in the top-right corner of the Outlook Today page to open the Customize Outlook Today page, shown in Figure 23-21.

As you can see, the Customize Outlook Today page contains five sets of options, which include the following:

- **Startup**   This one's simple. Check it if you want Outlook to open to the Outlook Today page every time you start up. This option actually resets the Startup In This Folder option found in the Advanced Options dialog box (Tools | Options | Other | Advanced Options).

- **Messages**   The name of this option is somewhat misleading since it can apply to any Outlook item, not just messages. In reality, it simply displays the folder name and the number of unread items contained in the folder. Click the Choose Folders button to open the Select Folder dialog box. Then check the folder(s) you want to include in the Messages section of Outlook Today.

- **Calendar** By default, the Calendar section of the Outlook Today page displays appointment items for today and the next four days (for a total of five). You can change this to any number between 1 and 7.

- **Tasks** When it comes to tasks, your options are more extensive:

  - **In my task list, show me** You can begin by deciding whether you want to display all tasks or only those due today. In addition, you can choose whether to include tasks without due dates.

  - **Sort my task list by** You can set a primary sort and a secondary sort to determine the order in which tasks display in Outlook Today. Select the field(s) by which you want the items sorted and then choose Ascending (A–Z) or Descending (Z–A) for each sort you enable.

- **Styles** If you want to gussy up your Outlook Today page, you can select from five different styles. If you choose a style from the drop-down list, you'll see a fair, if somewhat tiny, representation of what the style looks like in the Preview Pane below the option.

After you make your selections, click the Save Changes button in the top-right corner of the page to apply the changes and return to the Outlook Today page. One more thing: if you want to disable Outlook Today, simply right-click the Outlook Today shortcut in the Outlook Bar, and select Properties to open the Mailbox Properties dialog box. Click the Home Page tab, and remove the check mark in the Show Home Page By Default For This Folder option. With this option disabled, the Outlook Today page appears as a blank table view.

Using Advanced Techniques

As with many options in Outlook, you can also change the Outlook Today customization options from within the Windows Registry.

 Only experienced users should edit the Windows Registry. Modifying the Registry can produce unexpected results, including system crashes from which you may not be able to recover. Always create a backup copy of your Registry before making any changes.

You'll find most of the Outlook Today customization options in the HKEY_CURRENT_USER\Software\Microsoft\Office\9.0\Outlook\Today key, and the rest in its \Folders subkey. Well, you'll find them there if you've opened the Customize Outlook Today page and clicked the Save Changes button at least once. The fact that you can change these options in the Registry doesn't necessarily mean you should. With one exception, there's no real benefit to setting the options in the Registry rather than on the Customize Outlook Today page.

The exception is the CallDays value (Show This Number Of Days In My Calendar on the Customize Outlook Today page). Using the drop-down list provided in Outlook,

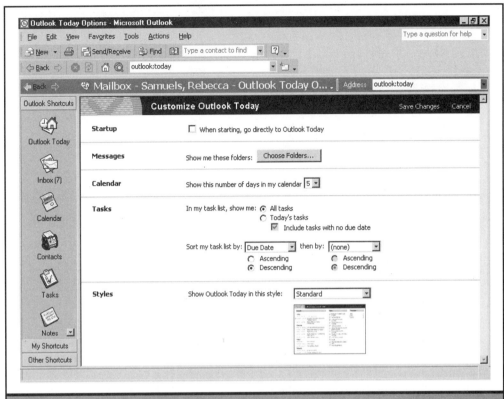

Figure 23-21. *Use the Outlook Today customization options to control the
appearance and content of the Outlook Today page*

the maximum numbers of days you can display in the Outlook Today Calendar section
is seven. By changing the CallDays Value Data in the Registry, you can include as many
days as you want. The only drawback to this method is that it permanently overrides
the option on the Customize Outlook Today page. However, if you reset the CallDays
Value Data to a number between 1 and 7, it returns control to the Show This Number
Of Days In My Calendar option. You can also replace the Outlook Today page with one
of your own. However, it is a much more complex operation, requiring both an Outlook
Today page (outlook.htm) and a Customize Outlook Today page (custom.htm) located
in the same folder. If you're interested in learning more, see the Microsoft Office
Resource Kit web site (http://www.microsoft.com/office/ork/).

Note *The Internet (including Microsoft's web site) is in a constant state of flux. Therefore, by the
time you read this, the URL may have changed or the information may have been removed.*

MOUS EXAM PRACTICE

In this section you learned to customize the Outlook Today page. Begin by opening the Customize Outlook Today page. Since the Startup option is either on or off, there's no need to practice that one. You should, however, change the folders displayed in the messages sections to see how the Outlook Today page is affected. Use the Tasks options to display different information sets from the Tasks folder. Next, do some experimenting with the Styles options to see how you can modify the appearance of the Outlook Today page. If you're feeling up to it, you might also try your hand at some of the more advanced customization options covered.

Creating New Views

While customizing views is great, sometimes you may want to retain an existing view and create a completely new view from scratch. Nothing to it. Open the folder in which you plan to use the view. Next, grab your mouse and head for View | Current View | Define View to open the Define Views dialog box (see Figure 23-22).

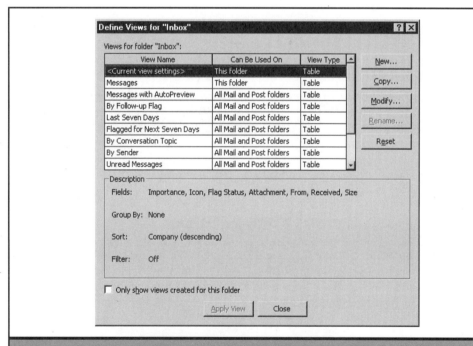

Figure 23-22.   *Create your own custom views in the Define Views dialog box*

> **Tip**
>
> *If you don't use the Define Views command often enough to warrant adding it to a toolbar, but enough to find its default location annoying, you can move it to a more convenient location, such as the View menu. Open the Customize dialog box. Then, while the Customize dialog box remains open, choose View | Current View to display both the View menu and the Current View menu. Now drag the Define Views command from the Current View menu to a spot on the View menu and drop it. You can use this method to move commands from and to any menus.*

To create a new view, you have two choices. You can either create a new view from scratch, or you can make a copy of an existing view and customize it to suit your needs. The advantages of copying an existing view are obvious if the new view will contain a large number of features already found in the existing view.

Creating a View from Scratch

To create a brand-new view, click the New button in the Define Views dialog box to open the Create A New View dialog box, as shown in Figure 23-23.

Give the new view a brief, descriptive name. Then select the view type from the Type Of View list. The Can Be Used On option provides you with the opportunity to restrict or share the new view depending on your needs. To make the new view available to anyone who has access to the folder in which the view is created, choose This Folder, Visible To Everyone. To make it available only in the folder in which it's created but hide it from everyone who has access to the folder except you, select This Folder, Visible Only

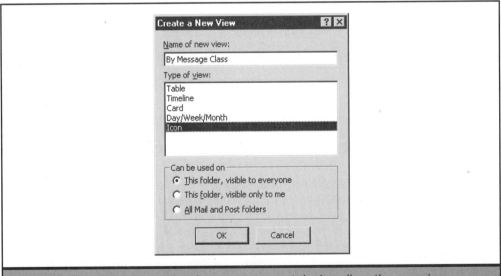

Figure 23-23. *Make sure the view name accurately describes the new view*

To Me. The final choice makes it available in all folders of the type in which the view is being created.

When you've made your selection, click OK to open the View Settings for "insert name of new view" dialog box (really the View Summary dialog box with a new name). Here you can add Fields, and apply Group By, Sort, Filter, Other Settings, and Automatic Formatting (if they're all available) settings to your new view. See the sections on each of these features earlier in this chapter for detailed information.

After you set all the options and return to the Define Views dialog box, you'll find the new view at the top of the View For Folder "[Folder Name]" display list. Click Close and your new creation is ready for prime-time viewing. The next time you open the Current View menu, the new view appears at the top of the menu.

Using an Existing View

Sometimes there's no need to reinvent the wheel. You may have an existing view that's almost right for the job, but not quite. In that case, the simplest method is to make a copy of the existing view and customize it. Before you begin, open the Outlook folder in which you want the new view to appear. Choose View | Current View | Define Views to open the Define Views dialog box seen previously in Figure 23-22. Next, select the existing view on which to base the new view. Now click the Copy button. The Copy View dialog box appears.

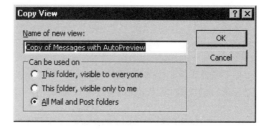

Give the new view an easy-to-identify name. Then select the appropriate Can Be Used On option. The first option makes the view available in the current folder to anyone with access. The second option also makes it available in the current folder, but only to you. The third option makes it available in all folders of the current folder's type and to anyone with access to those folders.

Click OK to open the View Summary dialog box. Here you can customize the existing Fields, Group By, Sort, Filter, Other Settings, and Automatic Formatting settings. See the sections earlier in this chapter on each of those features for more information.

When you return to the Define Views dialog box, the new view appears on the Views For Folder "[Folder Name]" list. Click Close to save the new view and return to the active view. When you access the Current View menu, you'll find your new view listed there as well.

Deleting Views

To ensure you don't do something you may later regret, Outlook permits you to modify but not delete the predefined views that come with it. However, Outlook couldn't care less if you decide to eliminate one of your own creations. All you have to do is open the folder in which the view resides and choose View | Current View | Define Views to open the Define Views dialog box. Then select the offending view and click Delete (if there's no Delete button, it means you've selected a "real" view). Outlook asks for confirmation. If you're sure about your action, click OK, and your view is history.

If you delete the current view, it remains onscreen when you close the Define Views dialog box. Don't worry, it's not really there. Switch views and it disappears, never to be seen again. It also disappears from the Current View menu.

MOUS Exam Core Objectives Explored in Chapter 23

Objective	Activity	Heading
OL10-1-4	Customize views	"Customizing Folder Views"

MOUS Exam Expert Objectives Explored in Chapter 23

Objective	Activity	Heading
OL10E-7-3	Apply conditional formatting to messages	"Using Automatic Formatting"
OL10E-7-4	Customize Outlook Today	"Customizing Outlook Today"

The Complete Reference

Part VII

Building Outlook Applications

The Complete Reference

Chapter 24

Customizing Outlook

If you're a history buff, you'll probably remember Henry Ford's famous proclamation that customers could buy his cars in any color they wanted, as long as it was black. Well, those days are long gone. Today, everything from your toaster to your minivan has a wealth of options. Outlook, like the other tools that help you deal with today's fast-paced life, has more than its fair share of options. Other chapters in this book cover options specific to individual Outlook folders or features. This chapter, on the other hand, is devoted to application-wide options that make Outlook do your bidding at every turn.

Basic Customization

In addition to its many advanced options, Outlook provides a number of basic options both for starting Outlook and for determining how it works after it launches. The startup options let you decide whether you want special commands to run as Outlook opens. The global options affect the way certain features operate throughout all folders within Outlook.

Customizing the Outlook Startup

As you might suspect, the best place to start is at the beginning. In the case of customization options, the beginning starts even before you have Outlook running. In addition to the multitude of options that determines how Outlook performs, there is also a set of options, called *command-line switches,* that determines how Outlook starts. Using command-line switches, you can tell Outlook upon opening to open a certain folder, automatically reset all views to their original state, or even address an e-mail message to a specific individual.

A command-line switch has two components: the path to the Outlook executable file (Outlook.exe) and the command-line switch itself. If you accepted the default target folder for Outlook when you installed it, the path to Outlook.exe is *"C:\Program Files\ Microsoft Office\Office\Outlook.exe".*

Note *When entering the path in a command-line switch, be sure to put the entire path within quotation marks to preserve long filenames.*

Therefore, a command-line switch to start Outlook and automatically open an e-mail message form would appear like this:

```
"C:\Program Files\Microsoft Office\Office\Outlook.exe" /c ipm.note
```

See Table 24-1 for a listing of useful command-line switches.

To Do This	Use This Switch	Example
Hide the Outlook Bar.	/folder	Not applicable
Display the Outlook Bar.	/explorer	Not applicable
Open Outlook to a specific folder displayed.	/select Outlook:<foldername>	/select outlook:calendar
Display the specified file folder.	/select "path\folder name"	/select "C:\My Documents"
Create a new Outlook item using the specified message class. You can use Outlook forms or other valid MAPI forms. This switch does not launch Outlook. It simply creates the form and sends or saves it when you click the appropriate button.	/c <messageclass>	/c ipm.note (e-mail) /c ipm.stickynote (note) /c ipm.appointment (appointment) /c ipm.task (task) /c ipm.contact (contact) /c ipm.activity (journal entry) /c ipm.post (post)
Create and send a message addressed to a specific recipient, without opening Outlook. This switch does not launch Outlook. It simply creates the message and sends it when you click Send.	/c ipm.note /m <full e-mail name>	/c ipm.note /m rsamuels@mindspring.com
Use in conjunction with /c <messageclass> to create a new item with the specified file as an attachment. This switch does not launch Outlook. It simply creates the form and sends it when you click Send.	/a "path/filename"	/c ipm.note/a "C:/My Documents/my.doc" (creates a new e-mail message and attaches my.doc)
Check to see if Outlook is the default program for mail, news, and contacts. If it is, nothing happens. If it's not, Outlook informs you and asks if you want to register it as the default.	/checkclient	Not applicable

Table 24-1.   *Outlook Command-Line Switches*

BUILDING OUTLOOK
APPLICATIONS

To Do This	Use This Switch	Example
Launch Outlook and reset free/busy time for all existing appointments. This command regenerates the .prof file containing free/busy data. Used when free/busy data displays incorrectly.	/CleanFreeBusy	Not applicable
Launch Outlook and regenerate existing reminder data. Use this switch if reminders are not activating at the correct times.	/CleanReminders	Not applicable
Launch Outlook and delete saved searches from the Exchange Server.	/Cleanfinders	Not applicable
Launch Outlook and restore default folder views. Be careful. This one deletes all customizations, including new views.	/CleanViews	Not applicable
Launch Outlook and restore missing Outlook folders. Works on the default delivery location.	/ResetFolders	Not applicable
Launch Outlook and restore the Outlook Bar to the default setting. This removes all customizations.	/ResetOutlookBar	Not applicable
Launch Outlook with the Preview Pane turned off.	/NoPreview	Not applicable
Launch Outlook and launch Outlook in Safe mode. No extensions or toolbar customizations are loaded. This does not remove any of these items; it merely prevents them from loading.	/Safe	Not applicable

Table 24-1. *Outlook Command-Line Switches* (continued)

To Do This	Use This Switch	Example
Launch Outlook and display the Choose Profile dialog box, even if you have the Always Use This Profile option checked on the General tab of the Mail dialog box.	/Profiles	Not applicable
Launch Outlook and use a specific profile, even if another is set as the default. Use quotation marks around profile names that include spaces.	/Profile <profilename>	/Profile "Rebecca Samuels"

Table 24-1.   *Outlook Command-Line Switches* (continued)

There are several methods for using command-line switches:

- **Run**   Open the Run dialog box (click Start | Run), and enter the command-line switch in the Open textbox.

- **Create a desktop shortcut**   Right-click a blank spot on the desktop (not an icon), and select New | Shortcut. Enter the command-line switch (both the Outlook.exe path and the switch) in the Command Line field. Give the shortcut an appropriate name, and click Finish to save it. Since you're using the Outlook.exe file, the shortcut automatically uses the Outlook icon; therefore you don't have to include any reference to Outlook in the shortcut name. The next time you use the shortcut, Outlook starts according to the command-line switch used.

- **Start menu shortcut**   To add a shortcut to the Start menu, begin by right-clicking the Windows taskbar, selecting Properties to open the Taskbar Properties dialog box (Windows 95/98) or the Taskbar and Start Menu Properties dialog box (Windows Me/Windows 2000). In Windows 95/98, click the Start Menu Programs tab, and then click Add to display the Create Shortcut dialog box. Enter the command line, select the folder (menu) in which to place the shortcut, give the shortcut a name, and click Finish. If you're running Windows Me or Windows 2000, click the Advanced tab. The rest of the steps are the same as those for Windows 95/98.

■ **Office Shortcut Bar**   Create a shortcut using either of the previously described methods. Then drag the new shortcut, and drop it on the Office Shortcut Bar.

■ **MS DOS Prompt**   You can open an MS DOS window by using the MS DOS Prompt command. Then type the complete command-line switch at the prompt and press ENTER.

Command-line switches come in handy for dealing with the consequences of electronic mishaps. When certain Outlook files are corrupted due to hard disk or other problems, you can frequently remedy the situation by starting Outlook with one of the command-line switches found in Table 24-1, such as /ResetFolders or /CleanFreeBusy.

In addition, command-line switches can be very useful when incorporated into shortcuts. You can create different shortcuts, each with its own specific command-line switch. This way you can have a shortcut to open Outlook any number of different ways.

> **Tip**   *You can add a desktop (or Start menu) shortcut to the Outlook Bar by dragging it from the desktop to the Outlook Bar. This enables you to add command-line switches to the Outlook Bar. For example, magazine and book editors might create a shortcut to send submission/author guidelines in response to proposals they receive. Simply create a desktop shortcut that opens a blank e-mail message and that attaches the desired file. The command line in the shortcut would look something like this: "C:\Program Files\Microsoft Office\Office\Outlook.exe" /c ipm.note/a "C:\My Documents\ AuthorGdlns.doc". After you create the desktop shortcut, drag it from the Windows desktop to Outlook, and drop it on the Outlook Bar. One caveat: not all command-line switches will run from within Outlook.*

Setting Outlook Global Options

In addition to the many options specific to individual folders or features, Outlook offers a variety of options to customize global features that apply throughout Outlook. You can access the Options dialog box shown in Figure 24-1 by choosing Tools | Options from the Menu bar.

As you can see in Figure 24-1, the Options dialog box contains a tab called Other. This tab is of particular interest to anyone desiring to set global options. It contains a variety of global options affecting numerous Outlook features, including AutoArchiving, tasks, the Outlook startup, reminders, and more.

In addition, there is a Spelling tab that lets you set some rules for how the Outlook spell checker performs its duties.

Setting General Options

Located on the Other tab, the General options include two options and a button. However, as you undoubtedly know, looks can be deceiving and, in this case, certainly are. Begin by choosing Tools | Options to open the Options dialog box. Then click the Other tab to display four sets of miscellaneous options (see Figure 24-2).

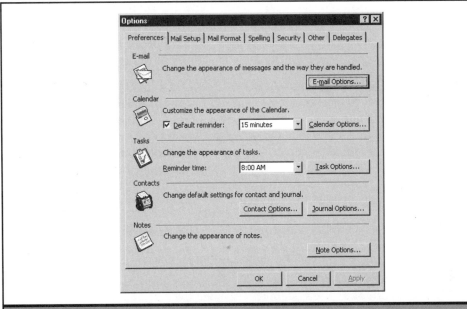

Figure 24-1.   *Outlook options are plentiful*

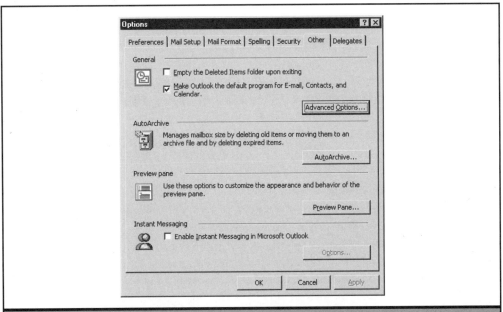

Figure 24-2.   *The General options appear deceptively modest at first glance*

The first General option is Empty The Deleted Items Folder Upon Exiting, which, when checked, causes Outlook to delete everything in the Deleted Items folder when you exit Outlook. This is an easy way to keep your Deleted Items folder uncluttered. But it also means that your access to deleted items will be somewhat limited. Once you clean out the Deleted Items folder, the only way you can retrieve those items is to use the Recover Deleted Items command, by opening the Deleted Items folder and choosing Tools | Recover Deleted Items. Remember, deleted items on the server are periodically eliminated by the administrator to save storage space. Therefore, the deleted items may or may not be there when you go looking for them. The other General option, Make Outlook The Default Program For E-mail, Contacts, And Calendar, does just what it says.

The Advanced Options button opens the Advanced Options dialog box, shown in Figure 24-3. However, in addition to having a number of advanced options, this dialog box also contains five additional buttons, each providing access to another dialog box of options.

The options you can set in the Advanced Options dialog box include

- **Startup in this folder**   From the drop-down list, select the folder you want Outlook to display on startup.

- **Minimize Outlook to the system tray**   When this option is checked, an Outlook icon is placed in the system tray. The system tray icon replaces the taskbar button when the Outlook window is minimized. Double-clicking the tray icon restores the Outlook window.

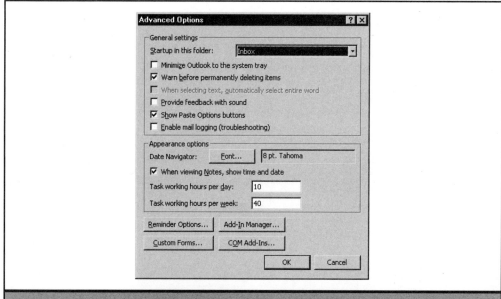

Figure 24-3.   *The advanced options include everything from startup folder options to the COM Add-Ins Manager*

■ **Warn before permanently deleting items**   Check this option if you want Outlook to alert you when you're about to delete an item permanently (as opposed to just moving it to the Deleted Items folder). You will be prompted when you attempt to delete an item from the Deleted Items folder itself, or when you go to empty the Deleted Items folder. You'll also be notified if you use the SHIFT+DEL shortcut key to permanently delete a selected item.

■ **When selecting text, automatically select entire word**   Check this box to change text selection in a textbox from a single character at a time to a single word at a time. Although this is a potentially useful option, it has so many exceptions it's almost worthless. To begin with, it's unavailable if Word is your default e-mail editor. Then, it only works with Rich Text messages. In HTML messages it's always on regardless of the setting, and in Plain Text messages it's always off regardless of the setting. Finally, where it does work (with Rich Text messages), it doesn't kick in until you've selected at least one word. For the first word, selection is one character at a time. After the first word is fully selected, each subsequent word (and its trailing space) is selected as soon as you highlight the first character of the word.

■ **Provide feedback with sound**   If you want Outlook to play a sound when you perform certain actions, check this option. Unfortunately, without the Office 2000 sounds, which you have to download from Microsoft's Web site, this option doesn't work. To download the sounds, establish an Internet connection and choose Help | Office On The Web to go to the Office Update Web site. Choose your country, and then locate the Outlook downloads page. There you'll be able to download the Microsoft Office Sounds for Office. It only takes a couple of minutes, so it's no big deal. Double-click the sounds.exe file after you download it, and a wizard walks you through the installation. One more thing: if you have other Microsoft Office 2002 applications installed, they'll inherit the sounds as well. It's all (well, almost all—Word, Excel, PowerPoint, and Outlook) or nothing. Turn sounds on in one application, and they all have sound. Turn sounds off in one application, and none of them has sound.

■ **Show Paste Options buttons**   Check this option to display a Paste Options button whenever you paste text into an Outlook form text field that permits formatting. Clicking the Paste Options button opens a drop-down menu containing four formatting options. Your choices include keeping the original formatting, applying the formatting of the destination form, pasting the item as plain text, or applying custom formatting.

■ **Enable mail logging (troubleshooting)**   When this option is checked, Outlook maintains a log file of all mail activities. The log file, outitems.log, is stored in C:\Windows\Application Data\Microsoft\Outlook.

■ **Date Navigator**   This option lets you change the font used in the Date Navigator. Click the Font button and select the font, font style, and font size.

■ **When viewing Notes, show time and date**   If you want the date and time the note was created or last modified to appear at the bottom of each note, check this option.

■ **Task working hours per day**   Enter the number of hours your workday comprises. Outlook uses this number to calculate the number of days in the Total Work and Actual Work fields located on the Details tab of task forms. For example, if you enter *8* as the Task Working Hours Per Day, and then enter *16* in either the Total Work or the Actual Work fields, Outlook converts it to 2 days.

■ **Task working hours per week**   This is the same as the previous option except it applies to the workweek. Therefore, if you enter *40* hours here, and *80* hours in the Total Work or Actual Work fields, Outlook converts it to 2 weeks.

■ **Reminder Options**   Click this button to display the Reminder Options dialog box. Here you'll find three self-explanatory options that let you choose whether you want a visual or aural cue when reminders come due.

■ **Add-In Manager**   Click the Add-In Manager button to open the Add-In Manager dialog box, which contains a list of all the add-ins currently installed. To enable an add-in, place a check mark in the box. To disable an add-in, remove the check mark. To install a new add-in, click the Install button.

■ **Custom Forms**   Click this button to open another Options dialog box containing additional buttons that provide access to the Forms Manager, Web services options, and network logon passwords. In addition, the Options dialog box contains a single option for designating the amount of hard disk space available for the storage of custom forms. Reserve as much space as you think you'll need.

   ■ **Web Forms**   Click the Web Forms button to open the Manage Forms dialog box, from which you can copy and delete existing Web forms.

   ■ **Web Services**   The Web Services dialog box that appears when you click this button offers a couple of options for using Outlook Web Access (OWA) to open messages and forms not recognized by Outlook. OWA enables users to connect to the Exchange Server with a browser and is generally employed by non-Outlook users. In this case, Outlook takes advantage of OWA by launching your default Web browser and displaying the unrecognized form in HTML format. Check the first option to enable this feature. Then indicate the location of your Web server. To have Outlook ask before opening such forms, check the Prompt User Before Opening Each Form option. If your administrator has established a Web page library of HTML forms, you can add a Web Form command to the Actions menus of mail folders by checking the Activate Web Forms Link On Actions Menu option. Then enter the URL of the Web page forms library.

- **Password**   This button opens the Change Windows NT Password dialog box, which allows you to change your password to log on to the network. You'll need your username, the name of the domain you log on to, and your current password.

- **Manage Forms**   Clicking the Manage Forms button opens the Forms Manager, which is covered in detail in Chapter 25.

- **COM Add-Ins**   Click this button to display the COM Add-Ins dialog box, which enables you to add and remove COM add-ins that provide added functionality to Outlook through the use of executable (.exe) and Dynamic Link Library (.dll) files. COM add-ins essentially are small programs used to customize the Outlook interface or to provide added functionality to the program. An example is the Personal Folders Backup add-in that automates .pst file backups. You'll find the Personal Folders Backup add-in and other COM add-ins in the download section of the Microsoft Office Update Web site (http://officeupdate.microsoft.com/).

After you finish setting all the advanced options, click OK until you return to the active Outlook window.

Customizing the AutoArchive Feature

The AutoArchiving feature, discussed in detail in Chapters 5 and 18, has several general options that control the way AutoArchiving behaves. After you open the Options dialog box (Tools | Options), click the Other tab. Then click the AutoArchive button to display the AutoArchive dialog box shown in Figure 24-4.

The options in the AutoArchive dialog box work in conjunction with the AutoArchive settings in the individual folders. Before any individualized folder settings work, you must first turn AutoArchiving on here and set the remaining options. Once AutoArchiving is enabled, you can open each folder's Properties dialog box, turn on AutoArchiving for the particular folder, and modify the other settings as needed.

The general AutoArchiving options found on the AutoArchive tab include

- **Run AutoArchive every _ days**   Check this option to turn AutoArchiving on. Then set the number of days between AutoArchiving sessions.

- **Prompt before AutoArchive runs**   Check this option if you want Outlook to ask before it performs an AutoArchive operation.

- **Delete expired items (e-mail folders only)**   If you want to move e-mail messages that have expired to the Deleted Items folder after AutoArchiving is finished, check this option. As you can tell from the option name, this only works on folders containing e-mail messages.

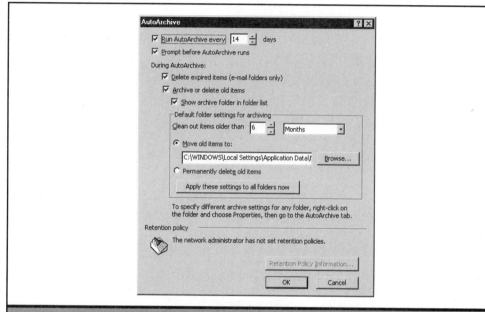

Figure 24-4.   *Use the AutoArchive dialog box to configure the default AutoArchiving settings*

- ■ **Archive or delete old items**   This is the option that turns on full AutoArchiving. Without this setting checked, the only AutoArchive action taken will be the deletion of expired e-mail items (see previous option). When you check this option, the remaining options become available.

- ■ **Show archive folder in folder list**   Enable this option to access the archive folder from the Folder List. It appears as another set of folders, from which you can perform normal operations such as view, move, copy, paste, and so on.

- ■ **Clean out items older than**   Enter the aging criteria for AutoArchiving individual Outlook items.

- ■ **Move old items to**   Check this option and enter the path of the archive folder in which to store items that meet the age criteria designated in the previous option. To locate an existing archive file, click the Browse button.

- ■ **Permanently delete old items**   If you don't want to save items that meet the age criteria, you can select this option and have AutoArchive delete them rather than move them to the archive file.

- ■ **Apply these settings to all folders now**   The name of this button says it all.

- ■ **Retention Policy Information**   Click this button to view the limitations set by your system administrator on items stored in your server-based mailbox.

When you're finished, click OK to save the settings and return to the Options dialog box. Click OK again to close the Options dialog box and return to the active view.

Customizing the Spell Checker

Unless you're a spelling-bee master and unerring typist, you'll probably find the Outlook spell checker quite useful. Since most folks make an occasional mistake or two, whether it's spelling or simply a typo, having a spell checker handy is helpful, especially when preparing important correspondence.

Note *The spell checker is part of the shared Office proofing tools. Consequently, the proofing tools must be installed for the spell checker to work in Outlook. You may have to return to the Add/Remove applet in the Control Panel and install the proofing tools from the Office CD.*

It's important to remember that, as far as the Outlook spell checker is concerned, any word not appearing in either the default dictionary or the custom dictionary is misspelled. Since the combined dictionaries cannot possibly contain every word in the language, you will encounter many correctly spelled words that Outlook considers misspellings.

The Outlook spell checker comes with quite a few options, all of which can be found on the Spelling tab of the Options dialog box, shown in Figure 24-5.

You'll find the following options on the Spelling tab:

- **Always suggest replacements for misspelled words** Check this option to ensure that Outlook not only flags words not found in its dictionary but also offers suggested spellings for the flagged words.

- **Always check spelling before sending** If you want Outlook to remember to perform a spell check even when you forget, check this option. It ensures that a spell check is run automatically before an e-mail message is sent.

- **Ignore words in UPPERCASE** Since words entered in all uppercase letters are frequently acronyms or abbreviations, you can tell the Outlook spell checker to ignore them by checking this option.

- **Ignore words with numbers** Since most words do not contain numbers, you're probably safe in telling Outlook to let words containing numbers slip by without question. However, if you're still using the hunt-and-peck method of typing, you may want to uncheck this one to make sure no mistake gets by unnoticed.

- **Ignore original message text in reply or forward** It's generally considered bad manners to edit another's e-mail message. Unless you're an English teacher and feel compelled to do it, you'll probably want to leave this option enabled. When this option is checked, the spelling checker only reviews for spelling errors in your part of a message containing a reply or forward.

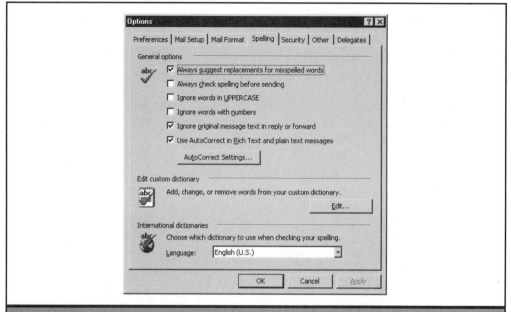

Figure 24-5.   *You can even develop your own custom dictionary for the spell checker*

- **Use AutoCorrect in Rich Text and plain text messages**   Since Word is the default e-mail editor, Outlook now offers the opportunity to take advantage of Word's AutoCorrect feature, which automatically corrects certain common mistakes. For example, if you type *adn*, AutoCorrect immediately changes it to *and*. Check this option if you want Outlook to use the AutoCorrect feature.

- **AutoCorrect Settings**   Click the AutoCorrect Settings button to display the AutoCorrect dialog box. Here you can modify existing entries or add your own.

- **Edit custom dictionary**   Outlook provides a custom dictionary to accommodate those words not found in the default dictionary. This is where those words that Outlook flags end up when you click the Add button. Occasionally, you may hit the Add button accidentally and wish you could remove a misspelled word from the dictionary to ensure it doesn't get by in the future. Well, here's your opportunity. It also comes in handy for adding lists of specialized words. You can cut and paste a list of technical terms so you won't have to deal with each one individually when you use it in an e-mail.

- **International dictionaries**   Outlook comes with dictionaries for several different languages. If you are corresponding in a language different from the default dictionary language, choose the appropriate dictionary from the Language drop-down list.

Just so you don't think you're losing your mind, there's a bug in the Outlook e-mail spell checker that affects certain abbreviations that end with a period, such as *Mr.* and *Mrs.* In HTML messages, they may be flagged as misspelled. If you select the proper spelling from the list and click Change, the spell checker adds an extra period (*Mr.* becomes *Mr..*). If you're using Microsoft Word as your e-mail editor, you will not encounter the problem since Word uses its own spell checker.

Customizing the Outlook Bar

The Outlook Bar is an extremely useful and flexible navigational tool that lets you move between Outlook folders and system folders with a single mouse click. The ability to tailor it to the way you work makes it even handier. You can change its size, hide it, add and remove shortcuts and shortcut groups, and even change the size of the shortcut icons. With a minimum amount of effort you can have it jumping through hoops in no time.

Resizing and Hiding the Outlook Bar

If you find you need more workspace in the Outlook window, one of the things you can do is resize the Outlook Bar by dragging its right border to the left. This increases the space allocated to the Information viewer (and Folder List, if it's displayed). In the event you're an ardent Folder List fan and hardly ever use the Outlook Bar, you can regain all of its space by simply hiding it.

The easiest way to hide it is to right-click a blank spot (not a shortcut) or a program group header on the Outlook Bar, and select Hide Outlook Bar from the shortcut menu. You can also choose View | Outlook Bar from the Menu bar. When the Outlook Bar is hidden, choosing View | Outlook Bar redisplays it.

Tip   *If you discover that you are unable to hide and display the Outlook Bar, or that it is improperly positioned, it may be a Registry problem. Warning! Only experienced users should edit the Windows Registry. All users should back up the Registry before making any changes. To correct display and positioning problems with the Outlook Bar, close all programs and delete the HKEY_CURRENT_USER\Software\Microsoft\Office\9.0\ Outlook\Office Explorer\Frame key from the Registry. After you close the Registry and reopen Outlook, the Registry key is rebuilt, and the Outlook window is restored to its original configuration. Depending on your version of Windows, you may have to reboot before the change takes effect.*

If you're so inclined, you can even add an Outlook Bar button to one of your toolbars so you can hide and display the Outlook Bar with a single mouse click. Here's how: Right-click an existing toolbar and select Customize from the shortcut menu. Click the Commands tab and select View from the Categories list. Scroll down the Commands list in the right pane until you find the Outlook Bar command. Then drag the Outlook Bar command and drop it on the desired toolbar or Menu bar. The next time you want to turn the Outlook Bar on or off, click the Outlook Bar button.

Adding and Removing Shortcuts

As handy as the Outlook Bar is, right out of the box, its real power lies in the ability to customize it, especially by adding and removing shortcuts. You can add shortcuts for new Outlook folders you create, for Web pages, system folders, and more.

To add a shortcut to the Outlook Bar, right-click a blank spot (not a shortcut) on the Outlook Bar and select Outlook Bar Shortcut to open the Add To Outlook Bar dialog box, shown in Figure 24-6.

To add an Outlook folder, scroll through the tree view of existing folders, and select the folder to which you want the new shortcut to point. If, however, you want to add a shortcut to a system folder, select File System from the Look In drop-down list first. This changes the tree view to a listing of the folders on your hard drive and network drives to which you have access. Now select the desired folder. After you select your Outlook or system folder, click OK to create the shortcut. It's automatically added to the bottom of the currently displayed shortcut group.

You can also add shortcuts to Outlook folders and system folders using the drag-and-drop method. For an Outlook folder, you must first display the Folder List. Then simply drag the folder for which you want to add a shortcut to the Outlook Bar, and drop it in the desired group. You can drop the folder anywhere the black, horizontal I-bar appears. The shortcut will then insinuate itself between the shortcuts on either side. To use the drag-and-drop method for a system folder (or file), open Windows Explorer or My Computer, locate the file (or folder), drag it to the Outlook Bar, and drop it where you want the shortcut to appear.

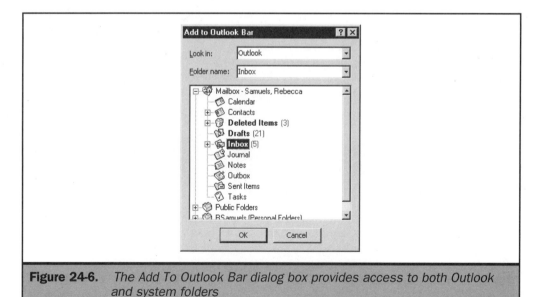

Figure 24-6.   The Add To Outlook Bar dialog box provides access to both Outlook and system folders

You can also open the Folder List, right-click an Outlook folder or a system folder (if you're currently displaying My Computer in the Folder List), and select Add To Outlook Bar from the shortcut menu.

To add a shortcut to a Web page, open the Web page in Outlook, and choose File | New | Outlook Bar Shortcut To Web Page. Outlook adds the new shortcut to the bottom of the My Shortcuts group.

Removing an Outlook Bar shortcut is a simple matter of right-clicking the obsolete shortcut and selecting Remove From Outlook Bar. Just to make sure you're serious, Outlook asks you to confirm the deletion. If you accidentally delete a shortcut, just follow the earlier instruction to re-create it.

Reorganizing Shortcuts

By default, the Outlook Bar is arranged to provide easy access to the most commonly used folders. However, what may be commonly used folders to one user may not be the most commonly used folders to another. For example, suppose you never use the Notes feature, but you're always accessing My Computer. Or perhaps you use Outlook for e-mail and practically nothing else. In either case you'll want to rearrange the shortcuts to suit the way you work. Whether it's to move the Notes shortcut to My Shortcuts and add the My Computer shortcut to Outlook Shortcuts, or to move the Sent Items, Outbox, and Drafts folders shortcuts to the Outlook Shortcuts group, the choice is yours.

If you can drag and drop, you can move shortcuts. Simply drag the shortcut from its current location to a new spot on the Outlook Bar. When you find just the right place for it, drop it. You can drop it anywhere the black, horizontal I-bar appears. To move shortcuts between shortcut groups, use the same drag-and-drop procedure. Without letting go of the left mouse button, hover over the target shortcut group title until the group opens. Then move to the desired location and drop the shortcut group.

Changing the Size of Shortcuts

Once you begin adding shortcuts to the Outlook Bar, you may find yourself spending a lot of time scrolling through all the icons in a shortcut group, looking for a particular shortcut. When this happens, you can start deleting some of the shortcuts you use less frequently than others. However, there's a better way that enables you to keep your existing shortcuts and reduce the scrolling at the same time.

All you have to do is resize the shortcuts in the shortcut group that's getting overpopulated. Start by displaying the shortcut group whose icons you want to resize. Now right-click the shortcut group title, and select Small Icons from the shortcut menu. The shortcut icons are drastically reduced in size, and the text is placed to the right of the icon instead of below it. As you can see in Figure 24-7, both changes result in a dramatic increase in the amount of space available in the shortcut group.

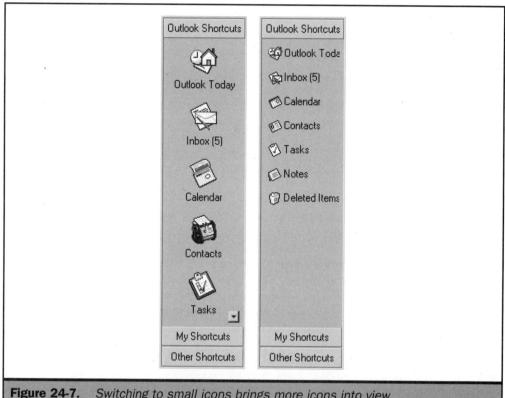

Figure 24-7. *Switching to small icons brings more icons into view*

Returning the shortcuts to their original size is a simple matter of displaying the shortcut group, right-clicking the group title, and selecting Large Icons from the shortcut menu.

Renaming Outlook Bar Shortcuts

There's one more change you can make to shortcuts if you're so inclined: you can rename them. Suppose you're really bored and you decide that Deleted Items is much too tame for you. After a bit of serious consideration, you determine that The Terminator is a more appropriate name for the shortcut. So how do you go about making the name change? Easy. Right-click the shortcut and select Rename Shortcut, which highlights the shortcut name and activates the Edit mode. You can now type an entirely new name over the existing name, or simply edit the existing name. When you're through, press ENTER to save the name change.

Keep in mind that this operation only renames the shortcut icon, not the actual folder the shortcut points to. So even if you change the name of the Deleted Items shortcut to The Terminator, the folder that appears when you click the shortcut is still called Deleted Items.

Adding and Removing Shortcut Groups

In addition to adding and removing Outlook Bar shortcuts, you can add and remove the shortcut groups that hold the individual shortcuts. By default, Outlook 2002 comes with three shortcut groups: Outlook Shortcuts, My Shortcuts, and Other Shortcuts. If you begin to accumulate system folder and Web page shortcuts, you may decide you need additional groups to keep all your shortcuts organized.

If you find yourself in this position, you can add your own shortcut group by right-clicking any shortcut group title and selecting Add New Group. A new group, cleverly entitled New Group, appears at the bottom of the Outlook Bar. The group title box is already in Edit mode, so you can type in a more descriptive name and then press ENTER to save it.

> **Note** On the off chance that you get shortcut-group happy and start adding them indiscriminately, you're probably going to be disappointed to hear that there is a 12-group limit. That's right, you cannot have more than 12 shortcut groups on the Outlook Bar at one time. As soon as you reach the limit, you'll find that the Add New Group command becomes disabled.

To remove a group, simply right-click the group title, and select Remove Group from the shortcut menu. Outlook requests confirmation that you really want to delete the group. If you click Yes, the group is immediately removed. Keep in mind that all shortcuts in the group are also deleted. Therefore, you might want to move any shortcuts before deleting the group.

To rename a shortcut group, right-click the group and select Rename Group. This puts the group title box in Edit mode. You can then enter an entirely new name or edit the existing name. Press ENTER to save the change.

Troubleshooting the Outlook Bar

As powerful a navigational tool as the Outlook Bar is, it can occasionally become cantankerous and start acting a little weird. You may find that shortcuts stop working, error messages start appearing, or Outlook may start crashing when you click a shortcut. If you encounter such behavior, there are a couple of things you can try.

The first thing to understand is that the Outlook Bar settings are contained in two system files. The first is outlbar.inf, which contains all the Outlook Bar basic settings. The second, *profilename*.fav (for example, rebecca.fav), contains any customizations you make to the Outlook Bar. The outlbar.inf file is editable. The .fav file is not. However, only experienced users should edit outlbar.inf, and even they should create a backup copy of it before making any changes.

If your Outlook Bar is acting up, the first thing to try is renaming the .fav file, and letting Outlook rebuild the Outlook Bar by creating a new .fav file upon startup. Close Outlook, and then use the Windows Find feature (Start | Find) to locate the .fav file and rename it.

Note   *If there are multiple profiles, there will be multiple .fav files. Make sure you delete the one associated with your profile.*

A good renaming technique is to change the *.fav* extension to *.old*. For example, if your file is named *rebecca.fav*, change it to *rebecca.old*. Now reopen Outlook, which automatically generates a new .fav file with the same name as the original and rebuilds the Outlook Bar from scratch.

Note   *While it's true that the command-line switch /ResetOutlookBar does the same thing, it's also true that if the .fav file wasn't the problem, all your Outlook Bar customizations are irretrievably lost.*

If this does not solve your problem, you can close Outlook, delete the new .fav file created, and rename the .old file back to .fav. The next time you start Outlook, all your customizations will be back.

If you're not comfortable with renaming files and you don't mind losing (or haven't made) any customizations to the Outlook Bar, you can use the /ResetOutlookBar command-line switch. See the section entitled "Customizing the Outlook Startup" earlier in this chapter for details on using command-line switches.

In some cases, custom views can be the culprits that cause erratic behavior in the Outlook Bar. If nothing else works, you can reset all the Outlook views to their original state by using the /CleanViews command-line switch. Be advised, however, that all custom views are deleted when this switch is used.

Customizing Toolbars

Outlook toolbars are handy items to have around if you use them. They provide quick access to commands you otherwise have to select from a menu or run with a shortcut key combination. The most important thing to remember about Outlook toolbars is that they are there for your convenience. You control which toolbars are displayed, where they appear on the Outlook window, and which commands they contain. If they're not making themselves useful, you can change them, move them, or get rid of them entirely.

Tip   *Outlook toolbar and menu settings are stored in the outcmd.dat file. If you do any customization to toolbars or menus, you should back up this file regularly to ensure against losing your customizations if a problem arises that requires resetting the toolbars and menus. If you have a backup, you'll be able to instantly reapply your customized settings by replacing the outcmd.dat file with the backup copy. Use the Windows Find command to locate outcmd.dat.*

One other thing about toolbars in Outlook: while a toolbar displayed in one folder appears in all other folders, the buttons that appear on the toolbar may change. Since each folder has different features, you'll find that some buttons disappear and others appear as you move from folder to folder. This is also true of changes you make. Only those commands that can be used in the current folder appear on the toolbars.

Showing and Hiding Toolbars

Toolbars, like most tools, are only useful if you have the right one for the job at hand. By default, the Menu bar (which, by the way, is technically a toolbar) and the Standard toolbar are always displayed. While you can hide the Standard toolbar, you cannot hide the Menu bar. The first order of business is to figure out where to find a toolbar when you need it. Fortunately, that's pretty easy. Right-click anywhere on the Menu bar or on an existing toolbar to see a shortcut menu of the available toolbars for the current view.

Once you access the shortcut menu, you can add or remove toolbars by selecting them from the menu. Toolbars with check marks next to them are already visible. Remove the check mark to hide them. Place a check mark next to a currently hidden toolbar and it appears immediately.

You can also display and hide multiple toolbars in one session by using the Customize dialog box, which you can open by right-clicking any toolbar and selecting Customize from the shortcut menu. Then click the Toolbars tab to view the available toolbars. You can also choose View | Toolbars | Customize.

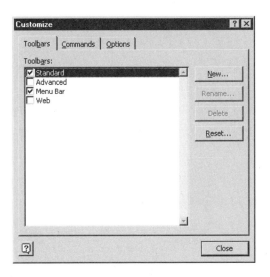

 You can open the Customize dialog box by double-clicking a blank spot to the right of the Toolbar Options button (down arrow), or to the left of the move handle on any visible toolbar except the Menu bar.

Check the toolbars you want to display, and uncheck those you want to hide. The result is immediate, and the toolbar(s) appear even before you close the Customize dialog box. You'll note that the Menu bar appears on the list of available toolbars. However, any attempt to remove the check mark fails. The Menu bar is the one toolbar that must always remain visible, although the menus change with the view. When you're through, click Close to return to the active view.

Repositioning Toolbars

The fact that the Microsoft programmers think that toolbars belong at the top of your application window doesn't mean you have to agree. If you don't, the solution is simple: put them where you want them.

Before rearranging your toolbars, there is one thing you should know about them. You have two options when it comes to the manner in which you position Outlook toolbars in the Outlook window. You can have *docked* toolbars or *floating* toolbars.

Docked toolbars are tightly snuggled up against one of the four sides of the Outlook window or against another docked toolbar. Floating toolbars, on the other hand, are free spirits that hang out wherever you happen to drop them on the screen. As you can see in Figure 24-8, the only problem with floating toolbars is that they invariably get in your way while you're working.

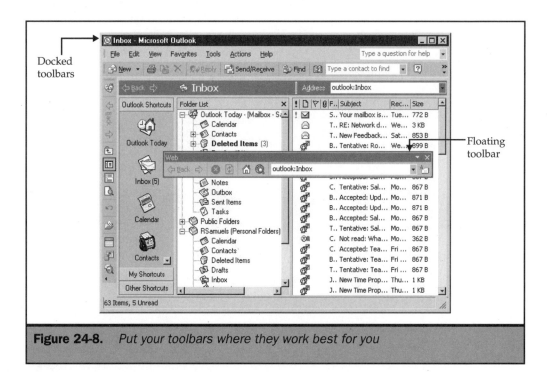

Figure 24-8. *Put your toolbars where they work best for you*

To move a toolbar, position your mouse pointer over the toolbar handle (the raised vertical bar at the left side of the toolbar), and drag the toolbar to a new location. If you want the toolbar docked, drag it to the desired side. As soon as it's in position, it automatically docks itself. If you want the toolbar to float, drop it anywhere on the screen.

You can also change the position of docked toolbars by dragging them around. For example, if you decide that you want the Menu bar to appear below the Standard toolbar, all you have to do is grab the Menu bar handle and drag it under the Standard toolbar. They will immediately switch places.

In addition to the difference in position, floating toolbars contrast with docked toolbars in other ways. As soon as a toolbar changes from docked to floating, it sheds its move handle. Not, to worry, though. You can still move it, only now you have to grab it by its title bar, the gray (unless you've changed your desktop settings) bar that contains the toolbar title.

 You can turn a floating toolbar into a docked toolbar by double-clicking the toolbar's title bar.

Another difference is the shape of the toolbar. When docked along the edge of the window, the toolbar stretches itself out to be as unobtrusive as possible. When it becomes a floating toolbar, it also stretches out. However, to make it more manageable, Outlook lets you change a floating toolbar's dimensions by dragging any of its four sides.

Modifying Existing Toolbars

 The standard toolbars that appear in the Outlook window and in Outlook input forms can be changed to suit your needs or your whims. You can add and remove command buttons, as well as rearrange their position on the toolbar. For example, if you rarely use the Find A Contact box on the Standard toolbar, but are always switching views, you might want to remove the Find A Contact command and add the Current View command.

Adding and Removing Command Buttons

Whether you're adding or removing command buttons from a toolbar, the first order of business is to display the toolbar and open the Customize dialog box. Right-click a visible toolbar and select Customize. If you want to display another toolbar, click the Toolbars tab and check the toolbar(s) you want displayed. To remove command buttons from a visible toolbar, all you have to do is drag them off the toolbar (while the Customize dialog box is visible) and drop them in the Information viewer. Don't worry, removing a command from the toolbar does not remove it from the list of available commands, simply from the toolbar.

Adding a command requires a little more effort. Click the Commands tab in the Customize dialog box to display the available Outlook commands.

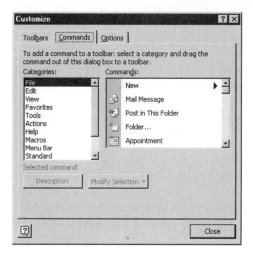

From the Categories list in the left pane, select the type of command you want to add. All the commands available in that category then display in the Commands list in the right pane. Now drag the desired command from the Commands list, and drop it on the toolbar in the location you want it to reside. You can drop the command when the black I-bar appears and when the small square attached to your mouse pointer changes from an *X* to a + (plus sign). If you drop the command too soon, it disappears and you have to repeat the process.

While the Customize dialog box is displayed, you can move toolbar buttons around by dragging them from one location to another and dropping them. You can use this method to move them to a new location on the same toolbar or to a different toolbar (as long as it's displayed).

You can move, remove, and copy command buttons from a toolbar (or a menu) during normal Outlook operations, without opening the Customize dialog box. To move or remove a button, simply hold down the ALT key and drag the button to a new location or onto the Information viewer to remove it altogether. To copy a button, press ALT+CTRL and drag the button from one toolbar to another. When you drop the button, a copy is placed on the target toolbar, while the original button remains on the source toolbar.

Changing Button Icons and Text

Another nice thing about the Outlook toolbars is that you can also modify the individual toolbar buttons. With the Customize dialog box open, you can change a button's appearance, add a keyboard shortcut, and even assign a hyperlink to it.

To modify a toolbar button, display the toolbar containing the button you want to change, and then open the Customize dialog box. Now right-click the button you want to customize to display a shortcut menu similar to the one seen in Figure 24-9.

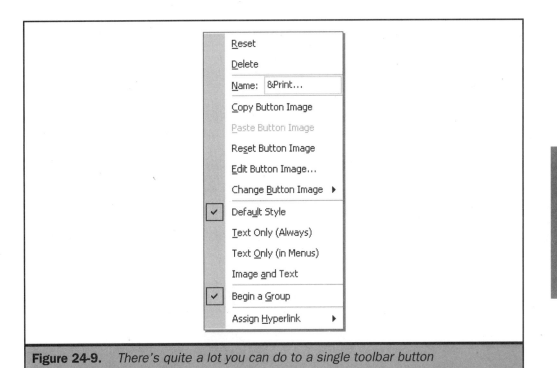

Figure 24-9.   *There's quite a lot you can do to a single toolbar button*

As you can see, there are a number of customizing options available:

- ■ **Reset**   This removes image, text, and hyperlink modifications, and restores the button to its original state. It does not restore style changes to buttons. For example, if you change the style from default to Text Only (Always), selecting Reset does not change it back to Default Style.

- ■ **Delete**   This removes the selected button from the toolbar. It has the same effect as dragging the button off the toolbar and dropping it on the Information viewer.

- ■ **Name**   The current name of the button appears in the Name textbox. This is the text that appears when you select a button style that includes text. You can edit this text to suit your needs. You'll notice an ampersand (&) in some names. When used as part of a button name, it underlines and converts the character that follows to a shortcut for running the command when the text is displayed on the button. As you can see in Figure 24-9, the name for the Print command is &Print.... When you display the name on the toolbar button, it appears as Print.... Any time a command contains an underlined letter in its name, you can activate the command by holding down the ALT key and pressing the underlined letter. Therefore, if the Print name is displayed on the button, you can print the active item or view by pressing ALT+P. You can create your own shortcut keys by placing the ampersand anywhere you want it. Just be sure not to create shortcut keys that conflict with other commands.

- **Copy Button Image** Select a button and use this command to copy the default image (not the button or the command, just the image) used on this button.

- **Paste Button Image** Used in conjunction with the Copy Button Image command, this one pastes the copied image to another button you select.

- **Reset Button Image** If you change your mind about a button image modification you've made, you can use this command to restore the button image to its original state.

- **Edit Button Image** Choose a button with an image you want to modify, and click this menu command to open the Button Editor, a mini-paint program with which you can modify the image. Select a color from the palette, and click a pixel (one square) to change its color. A second click removes the color. Edit the image and click OK to return to the Customize dialog box.

- **Change Button Image** If you don't like the existing image, or if the button doesn't have one, you can use this command to add a new graphic to the button. As soon as you select this command, a submenu of alternative images appears. Click one to add it to the selected button.

- **Default Style** The Default style for most toolbar buttons is graphic only, no text. If you've changed the button style, you can use this command to return the button to its original style.

- **Text Only (Always)** If you find the command button icons confusing or annoying, you can select this command to display the text name on the button and eliminate the icon altogether.

- **Text Only (in Menus)** This command allows the selected command to appear with an icon when used on a toolbar, but with text and no icon when used on a menu.

- **Image and Text** Choose this option to always show both the icon and the text title. This can be helpful for a new user who is just learning the program.

- **Begin a Group** Use this command to add a vertical bar to the left of the button to separate it from other buttons.

- **Assign Hyperlink** This command lets you add a hyperlink to the button. You can link to a Web site, a file, a location in the existing document, or even to an e-mail address. The next time you click the button, the link is automatically activated.

You can also modify the width of toolbar commands that contain drop-down lists, such as Find A Contact and Current View. With the command displayed on a toolbar and the Customize dialog box open (it puts Outlook in the Customize mode), simply drag the command box border to the left or right to change the size.

While you have the Customize dialog box open, you can also copy a command button from one toolbar to another by pressing CTRL and dragging a clone of the button to a new location. When you're through customizing toolbars and toolbar buttons, click Close to exit the Customize dialog box and return to the active window.

Creating New Toolbars

Not only can you customize existing toolbars but you can also create your own. This comes in handy for putting together a toolbar of your favorite commands, or collections of commands you only use occasionally or only in a certain folder.

Creating a new toolbar is a two-part operation. The first step entails creating the blank toolbar. The next step is adding commands to the new toolbar.

To create a blank toolbar, open the Customize dialog box, and click the Toolbars tab. Click the New button to open the New Toolbar dialog box.

Give your new toolbar a unique, descriptive name, and click OK to add it to the Toolbars tab. A blank toolbar one button wide appears next to the Customize dialog box. Look carefully or you might miss it.

Once you've got the blank toolbar, you can start adding commands immediately, or you can move the toolbar to the place you want it to sit before adding commands. Since the process is the same regardless of whether you're adding commands to a new toolbar or an existing toolbar, refer to the earlier section entitled "Adding and Removing Command Buttons" for detailed instructions. The same goes for editing and moving command buttons.

Setting Toolbar Options

In addition to customizing individual toolbars and buttons, Outlook also provides several global options that affect toolbars throughout the application. You'll find these options on the Options tab of the Customize dialog box (see Figure 24-10).

The following Options tab settings pertain to toolbars only (those that affect menus are covered in the later section entitled "Setting Menu Options"):

- **Standard and Formatting toolbars share one row** This option is grayed out unless you are in a form, such as an e-mail message form, that contains a text field which permits text formatting. In that case, you can elect to display both the Standard and the Formatting toolbars on the same row to reduce the amount of space they take up.

- **Large Icons** By default, Outlook uses small icons on the toolbar buttons. This reduces the amount of space each button takes up and provides easy access for most users. However, if you have a difficult time making out the small icons, you can check this option to display large images on those toolbar buttons that contain images.

- **List font names in their font** The Formatting toolbar, which appears in forms that contain textboxes, such as message and note fields, contains a Font drop-down list from which you can select the font of your choice. When the List Font Names In Their Font option is checked, each font name is displayed in the list using the actual font. For example, Comic Sans MS appears on the list in the Comic Sans MS font,

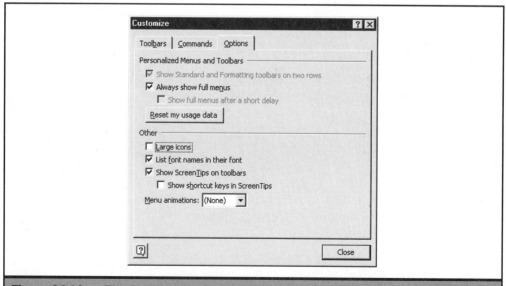

Figure 24-10. *The Options tab offers even more ways to customize Outlook toolbars*

and Impact appears in the Impact font. This enables you to see what the font will look like when selected. Unfortunately, it also requires more memory and takes longer to display the list. If you're familiar with the different fonts, you can speed things up a bit by removing the check mark for this option.

■ **Show ScreenTips on toolbars**   ScreenTips are those little textboxes that appear when you pause your mouse pointer over a toolbar button for a couple of seconds. They contain the toolbar name and can be quite useful for identifying buttons that contain icons only. If you display text in your buttons, you may want to eliminate the ScreenTips by deselecting this option.

■ **Show shortcut keys in ScreenTips**   Some commands have shortcut keys automatically assigned to them. If you want the shortcut key to appear in the ScreenTip along with the command name, check this option.

The remaining options on the Options tab pertain to menus and are covered in the section entitled "Setting Menu Options" later in this chapter.

MOUS   *MOUS EXAM PRACTICE*
In this section, you learned to hide, display, customize, and create Outlook toolbars. Begin this practice session by hiding and displaying toolbars using both methods covered— right-clicking an existing toolbar, and using the Customize dialog box. Next, modify an existing toolbar by adding, removing, and rearranging command buttons. Then try your hand at creating your own custom toolbar and adding new command buttons. Finally, modify some of the toolbar options to see how existing toolbars are changed.

Using Menus

Practically everywhere you go in Outlook you can find menus that make your job a little easier. The Menu bar, which is the only toolbar you can't hide, is always with you wherever you are. Even some toolbar buttons have menus that display a list of commands. Because they disappear when not in use, menus enable you to keep a large number of commands at your fingertips without cluttering up your screen.

The Menu bar is where most Outlook 2002 commands reside. Since the Menu bar is technically a toolbar, it has many of the toolbar properties. You can dock it, float it, change its shape, or customize it just like any other toolbar.

You can move the Menu bar the way you move a toolbar, by grabbing its move handle and dropping it where you want it to go. If you place it at the edge of the screen, it docks itself and rearranges its "buttons" to accommodate its new position.

Drop the Menu bar anywhere on the screen, and like a toolbar, it alters its shape and floats where you place it. You can change its dimensions by dragging any of the four edges. However, unlike the other toolbars, the Menu bar cannot be closed. It must remain visible at all times. Even if you open the Customize dialog box, you cannot remove the check mark next to Menu Bar.

Another thing to note is the shortcut key combinations that appear next to some of the commands. These are generally the more common commands, such as Open, Print, Copy, Paste, and so on. Shortcut keys will save you a lot of time in the long run if you memorize and use them.

Understanding Personalized Menus

While the basic menu system incorporated into Outlook has been around for quite a while, starting with Outlook 2000 a new twist was added: "intelligent" menus. These intelligent menus have been dubbed *Personalized Menus* by Microsoft. They begin by displaying only the most commonly used commands, and hiding those commands that are less frequently accessed. During the initial period of use, Outlook tracks which menu commands you actually use. Based on your usage, Outlook then automatically "personalizes" the menus to display those commands you use most frequently, and hides those you don't use. Depending on the amount of time you spend in Outlook, it can take as little as a couple of days or as much as several weeks before you begin noticing the changes.

While this may sound good in theory, in practice it's more time-consuming and annoying than helpful. It quickly becomes apparent that the changing menus cause confusion since commands are not always in the same place. In addition, there are still enough commands on the menus to ensure a certain amount of hunting for the right command. Finally, when you're searching for a command that happens to be hidden, you have to wait several seconds before the full menu appears. The only way to display the full menu immediately is to click the chevron (») at the bottom of the personalized menu. This of course means an extra action, which is unnecessary if you forgo the personalized menus altogether.

Customizing Menus

Like toolbars, menus are quite flexible, affording you the opportunity to mold them into the power tools that best fit your work habits. You can add and remove commands, as well move, copy, and rename them. In addition, you can reposition and even remove individual menus (but not the Menu bar itself), and add shortcut keys to menu items you use frequently.

The methods used to customize Outlook menus are identical to those used to customize Outlook toolbars. Therefore, you can refer to the section entitled "Customizing Toolbars" earlier in this chapter for detailed information on customizing menus.

Creating New Menus

As with toolbars, sometimes modifying the existing menus just isn't enough. You may have a specialized need that requires a series of commands (from different categories) all grouped on one menu. In that case, you can create your own menu and fill it with exactly those commands that you need. For example, if you do a lot of customizing, you may want to create a Customize menu that contains commands such as Options, Customize Current View, Define Views, Customize, Organize, and others.

To begin, open the Customize dialog box and click the Commands tab. Scroll down and select the last item in the Categories list, New Menu. This displays the New Menu command in the Commands list on the right. As a matter of fact, it's the only command in the New Command category. Drag the New Menu command from the Commands list to the Outlook Menu bar, and drop it next to or between existing menu titles (File, Edit, View, and so on). A new menu immediately appears on the Menu bar.

The next step is to give the new menu an appropriate name. Right-click the New Menu item, and enter the desired name in the Name field. If you want to add a shortcut key to the menu, include an ampersand (&) before the character you want to use as the shortcut. Using the earlier example of creating a Customize menu, you might want to use the C in *Customize* as the shortcut key. If so, you would enter **&Customize** in the Name field. The C then becomes underlined, indicating that you can access the Customize menu by pressing ALT+C. Make sure that your new shortcut key doesn't conflict with any existing shortcut keys.

The final step is to populate the new menu with the desired commands. From the Categories list, select the category containing the first command you want to include. Continuing with the Customize menu example, you might select Tools. Then in the Commands list, select the desired command, such as Options. Drag the command to the new menu, which opens as soon as you move the mouse pointer over the menu title. Drop the command in the box that opens below the menu as soon as the black I-bar appears. Continue adding commands until you have a complete menu.

This works not only for adding new menus to the Menu bar, but also for adding new submenus to existing menus. Suppose, for example, you wanted to have a submenu on the View menu that included all the available commands for defining and customizing views. Drag the New Menu command to the View menu, and drop it among the existing View menu commands. Give it an appropriate name, and then add Define Views, Customize Views, Format Columns, Sort, Filter, and other such commands to the box that opens at the right of the New Menu submenu.

Setting Menu Options

Fortunately, Outlook provides menu options that, among other things, allow you to disable the personalized menus and reset the usage information upon which personalized settings are based. To modify the options, open the Customize dialog box and click the Options tab to display the menu and toolbar options.

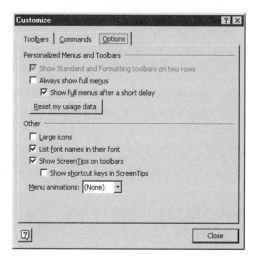

The options that apply to menus include the following:

- **Always show full menus**   Personalized menus are turned on by default. Check this option to disable personalized menus and show all available commands on Outlook menus.

- **Show full menus after a short delay**   If you've elected to use personalized menus, this option automatically displays hidden commands after the menu is open for a few seconds. If you want the hidden commands to remain hidden until you click the chevron (») at the bottom of each menu, remove the check mark.

- **Reset my usage data**   If your personalized menus do not correctly reflect your usage of the menu commands, you can start the usage tracking over by clicking the Reset My Usage Data button. Outlook warns you that this action removes the record of your command usage and restores it to its default state. If you're not sure about taking this action, you might want to make a backup copy of msoutlo.pip that contains your usage data. If you change your mind, you can delete the new msoutlo.pip file, and replace it with the backup copy. Outlook creates two msoutlo.pip files. Use the Find feature in My Computer to locate them both. Depending on the version of Windows you're using, the msoutlo.pip file you want to back up is either in C:\Windows\Application Data\Microsoft\ Office (Windows 95/98/Me) or C:\Documents and Settings\[profile name]\

Application Data\Microsoft\Office (Windows 2000). Just make sure you do not delete or replace the copy of msoutlo.pip in C:\Program Files\Microsoft Office\Office.

■ **Menu animations** If you enjoy computer animations, you can make the Outlook menus a little more lively by selecting an animation type from this drop-down list. By default, the selection is None. With this setting, the menus simply appear when you click the menu title. If you like having the Outlook menus appear by starting at the top left corner of the menu title and "unfolding" toward the bottom right corner of the screen until the menu is displayed, select Unfold. To have the menus appear from top to bottom in a sliding motion, select Slide. Selecting Random makes the menus appear using one of the two animations. However, which animation is used depends entirely on chance.

When you're through setting menu options, click Close to save your new settings and return to the active Outlook view.

MOUS

MOUS EXAM PRACTICE
In this section, you learned to use personalized menus, change existing menus, and create your own custom menus. Start your practice by modifying an existing menu. Add new commands, move them around on the menu, and then remove them. Next, create your own custom menu and add commands to it. Then create a submenu and fill that with commands. Finally, change some of the menu options. Be careful not to reset your usage information unless you're prepared to start the menu personalization tracking over.

MOUS Exam Expert Objectives Explored in Chapter 24

Objective	Activity	Heading
OL10E-7-7	Customize menus and toolbars	"Modifying Existing Toolbars"
		"Customizing Menus"

BUILDING OUTLOOK APPLICATIONS

Chapter 25

Designing Custom Forms and Fields

Although Outlook has an extensive collection of forms and fields right out of the box, there's no way that the Microsoft programmers could anticipate everyone's needs. Therefore, you'll be happy to hear that you can create your own custom forms for inputting and even receiving Outlook information (with the exception of the Notes folder). In addition, you can create new fields to hold data, and add them to your custom forms. In this chapter, you'll discover just how painless creating custom forms and new fields really is.

Understanding Form Basics

Working with and customizing forms is a lot easier if you understand the underlying concepts. The best place to start is at the beginning of the Outlook data chain. Outlook information consists of fields, records, and folders. *Fields* are containers that hold individual pieces of information (Name, Company, Address, and so on). *Records,* more familiarly known in Outlook as *items,* are collections of related fields. For example, the Full Name, Job Title, Company, and other fields that pertain to a single contact in your Contacts folder, together form a record. *Folders* are groups of related records (and views). *Forms* (at last!) are the devices with which you enter, and in some cases, display, Outlook information.

As you can see in Figure 25-1, forms do not contain information; they merely facilitate the input of information into fields and records.

All input forms also display information when you open an individual record. Other forms, such as the Read Pages of mail message forms, exist for the sole purpose of displaying information entered using input forms (Compose Pages of message forms, in this example). One more thing to understand about Outlook forms is that you cannot create a custom form from scratch. You must use an existing form as the basis for new forms.

Planning

The level of success you achieve with form building, as with most projects, is greatly enhanced by forethought and planning. The mechanics of form building is not terribly complex. You open a form in the Design mode, drag a field or a control onto the form, move it around, set its properties, publish the form, and you're done. However, if you want a form that truly meets your needs, you should take a few things into consideration.

Although custom forms are, in theory, backward compatible, it's usually best to design a form for the least common denominator. While the form basics are the same, adding new features to a form for use in a version of Outlook that doesn't support those features means the form won't function properly in that version. Therefore if your form will be used with Outlook 2002, Outlook 2000, Outlook 98, and Outlook 97, you should design for Outlook 97—better yet, design in Outlook 97. Also, be aware that custom Contact forms created in Outlook 2002, 2000, or 98 will not work at all in Outlook 97.

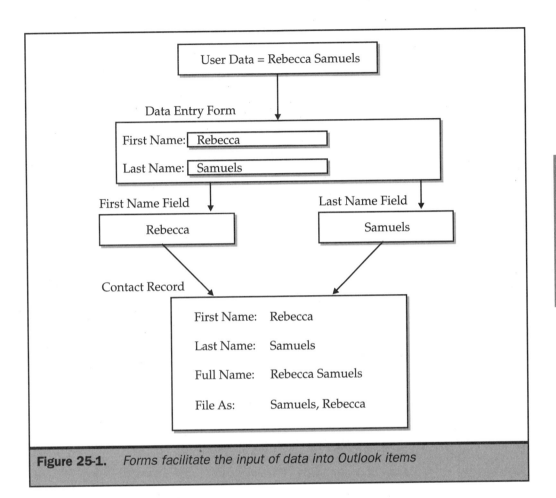

Figure 25-1. *Forms facilitate the input of data into Outlook items*

BUILDING OUTLOOK APPLICATIONS

> **Note**   *The Notes folder form is unavailable for customization, so you're stuck with it whether you like it or not.*

It's also a good idea to think about who's going to use the form and why. Make sure you add necessary fields and eliminate extraneous fields. Too much or too little information can make a custom form ineffective. If you plan to construct a complex, multipage form, you might consider laying it out on paper first. Ask any good craftsperson about the value of working from a plan. Artists may rely on creativity, but an experienced builder won't hammer that first nail without a good blueprint.

One more thing: If you're planning your forms for use within a corporate environment, be sure to take company standards into account before starting.

Pages

Forms consist of one or more pages, which provide the foundation for each form. The page merely acts as a backdrop on which to place controls and fields. Most Outlook forms consist of multiple pages. The Contact form, for example, contains five pages by default: General, Details, Activities, Certificates, and All Fields. Even mail message forms, which appear to have only a single page, consist of two pages: a Compose Page for writing an e-mail message, and a Read Page for reading the contents of a received message. In reality, all forms contain multiple pages. In addition to the page(s) visible when the form is displayed, each form includes blank pages for customization, a Properties page for setting form options, and an Actions page for designating actions available to the user, such as Reply, Reply To All, and so on (see Figure 25-2).

These "hidden" pages become visible when you open a form in the Design mode (Tools | Forms | Design A Form).

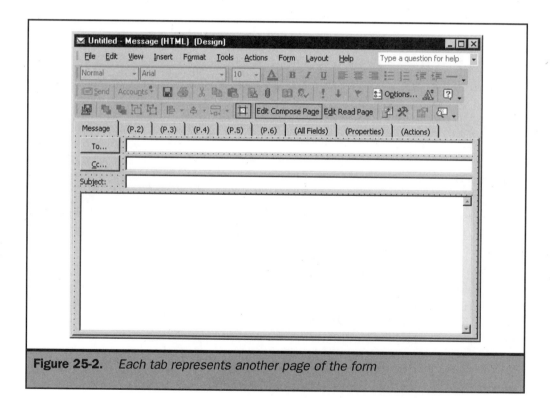

Figure 25-2. *Each tab represents another page of the form*

Objects

Every form must contain objects. Without objects, the form is nothing more than a blank page. There are two types of objects you can use with an Outlook form: fields and controls. *Fields* are the actual storage containers used to hold pieces of Outlook data, while *controls* are objects such as textboxes, scroll bars, and command buttons that enable users to manipulate that data. Some objects simply add informational or decorative items to the form. The Image object, which adds a graphic image to the form, is an example.

Since there's no way to make use of fields without controls, the Outlook fields you can add to a form are, in reality, prepackaged combinations of fields and controls. In other words, each "field" available from the Field Chooser is actually one or more controls, already linked (*bound*) to a specific Outlook field. You can create the same combination yourself by adding the controls and manually linking them to the field. The difference between manually linking controls and fields, and creating new "fields," is simply that "fields" are permanent (until you delete them), reusable combinations.

Layout

The form layout is just what you'd expect—the placement of objects (controls and fields) on the form page. As so many designers of everything from fashion to furniture have pointed out, there is a direct correlation between form (no pun intended) and function. The more organized and aesthetically pleasing your form is, the more effective it will be. Fortunately, Outlook provides a number of tools that make your form layout chores almost effortless. The layout features, which can be found on the Layout menu in the Design mode, include an optional grid (turned on by default) that enables you to easily align objects on the page, plus a wealth of features to automate object alignment, spacing, layering, and more.

Designing Your Custom Form

Now that you've got the basics down, it's time to get to work. The first order of business is to select the existing form on which to base the customized form. Choose Tools | Forms | Design A Form to open the Design Form dialog box, shown in Figure 25-3.

From the Look In drop-down list, choose the forms library containing the form. The first time you create a custom form, you'll probably want to base it on one of the default forms that come with Outlook. You'll find these in the Standard Forms Library. From the list of available forms, pick the one you want to use and click Open to display the selected form in Design mode.

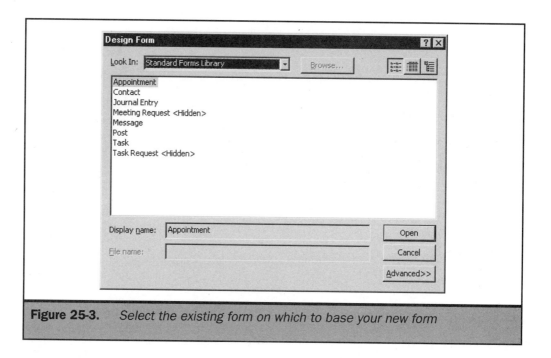

Figure 25-3.   *Select the existing form on which to base your new form*

   You can also double-click the form name to open the form in Design mode.

As you can see in Figure 25-4, the form (the Message form in this case) opens displaying the first page of the form and the Field Chooser.

If you take a close look at Figure 25-4, you'll see that all the tab names except Message are enclosed in parentheses. This indicates the pages are hidden when the form is used. You can choose which pages are hidden and which are displayed when the form is used by opening the page and choosing Form | Display This Page. When the command has a check mark next to it, the selected page will be displayed. Without a check mark, the page will be hidden during normal use.

Using the Grid

If you want to produce a well-organized and professional-looking form, it's important to line up the objects you add to the form. The first line of defense in object alignment is the grid. The *grid* is a pattern of dots on a form page that provides a frame of reference for placing objects relative to one another.

In addition to using the grid as a visual frame of reference, you can also instruct Outlook to force objects to automatically align themselves with the nearest top-left grid intersection. This feature, which is called Snap To Grid, is turned on by default. You can turn it on and off by clicking the Snap To Grid button on the design toolbar, by

BUILDING OUTLOOK APPLICATIONS

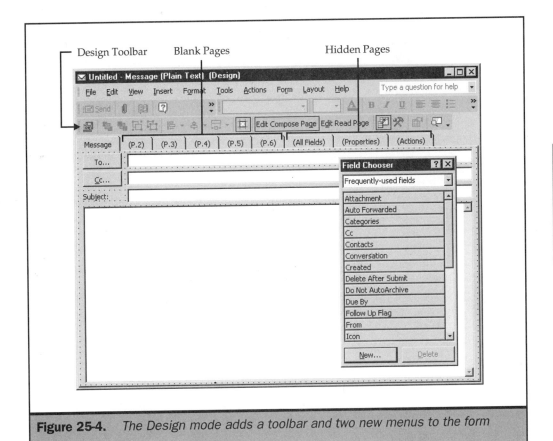

Figure 25-4. *The Design mode adds a toolbar and two new menus to the form*

right-clicking the page (not an object) and deselecting Snap To Grid, or by choosing Layout | Snap To Grid.

If you find the grid too large or small, you can adjust its size by choosing Form | Set Grid Size to display the Set Grid Size dialog box, in which you can manually adjust both width and height dimensions. The larger the numbers, the wider the gap between grid points.

There are a couple of other commands available for working with the grid. The first is Show Grid. This command, found on the Layout menu and on the shortcut menu that appears when you right-click a form page, shows or hides the grid depending on its state. When the command is checked, the grid appears; when the command is unchecked, the grid disappears. One thing to remember is that the Snap To Grid command remains in effect regardless of whether the grid is visible.

The other command that works with the grid is the Size To Grid command. If you have an object with one or more sides that do not extend to a grid line, you can automatically resize the object so that all sides fall on the nearest grid line. Select the object and choose Layout | Size To Grid.

Adding and Removing Fields

Most likely, customizations you perform will involve the addition of fields to the form or the removal of existing fields.

Note   *Before going any further, it's important to remember the distinction between pure fields (data containers alone) and the "fields" you can manipulate with the Field Chooser. The "fields" you can work with are really predesigned field/control combinations, which means that when you add a field to a form, you generally end up with more than one object. For example, many "fields" include a Label control and a TextBox control, both of which are bound to the real [data container] field.*

Removing existing fields is a simple matter of selecting the controls that make up the field and pressing DEL, or right-clicking and selecting Delete from the shortcut menu.

Tip   *You can select multiple objects by holding down the CTRL key and clicking each object. You can also select multiple objects by drawing a selection box around them. Place your mouse pointer above and to the left of the topmost and leftmost objects you want to include. Then hold down the left mouse button and drag the mouse pointer toward the lower-right corner of the page until you've enclosed all the desired objects in the selection box (you can actually start in any corner and drag to the diagonally opposite corner). When you release the left mouse button, any objects completely or partially within the selection box are automatically selected. As long as you touch an object with the selection box, it will be included.*

Adding objects is almost as easy. You'll need the Field Chooser, shown in Figure 25-5, to add fields to your form, so be sure it's visible. If you don't see it, right-click the form page and select Field Chooser from the shortcut menu. You can also display it by choosing Form | Field Chooser.

Once you've got it onscreen, begin by locating the desired group of fields from the drop-down list at the top of the Field Chooser. Although you can use some fields from other item types, you'll generally want to use fields that belong to the same item type as the form you're working on. When you select a field group from the drop-down list, all the fields in that group appear in the Field Chooser. Locate the field you want to

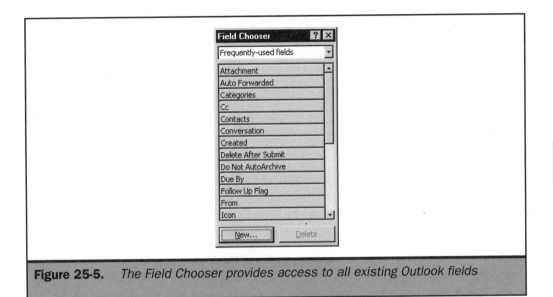

Figure 25-5. *The Field Chooser provides access to all existing Outlook fields*

add to the form, and drag it from the Field Chooser to the location on the form where you want it to appear. When you drop the field on the form, all of its elements are selected. In other words, if the field contains a Label control and a TextBox control, both are selected as soon as they're placed on the form. This lets you work on all the field's elements simultaneously, without disturbing their relationship to one another. If you move the field, you move all the objects; if you resize the field, you resize all the objects proportionally. However, once you select any other object on the form, the focus is transferred, and the objects are treated individually unless you select them manually as a group.

If you decide you need a new field, you can create one on the fly by clicking the New button on the Field Chooser. See the later section entitled "Creating Your Own Custom Fields" for more information.

Working with Controls

Controls are objects that either display information, such as a label or a graphic image, or enable a user to manipulate data in Outlook fields. The Label and Image controls are examples of the first. The TextBox and CommandButton controls are examples of data manipulating controls. Both the Subject title and the Subject textbox on a message form are controls. The title is a Label control providing information only, while the textbox, a TextBox control linked to the Outlook Subject field, lets the user input to, and display data from, the Subject field.

Although there is no official limit to the number of controls or fields you can include on a custom form, you should try to keep the number under 300 to avoid potential problems. While this sounds like a sizeable number, it can be reached more quickly than you might think, especially when you start using multiple pages in a form.

Adding controls is a lot like adding fields. The first thing to do is right-click a blank spot on the form page and select Control Toolbox to open the Toolbox. You can also display or hide the Toolbox by clicking the Control Toolbox button on the form design toolbar.

By default, the Control Toolbox has 14 controls plus a selector tool called Select Objects. You add controls by using one of the two available methods. You can either drag a control icon and drop it on the form, or you can click the control on the Toolbox and draw the control on the form. The difference between the two methods is in the size of the control that appears. Using the drag-and-drop method, you end up with a default-sized control. The default size varies from control to control. If you elect to draw the control on the form, your mouse pointer turns into a crosshairs pointer with an icon of the control attached. Move the pointer to a spot on the form in which you want the top left corner of the control to appear. Click and hold the left mouse button while dragging the pointer toward the bottom right corner of the page (you can start in any corner and drag to the diagonally opposite corner). As you drag, a selector box appears. Drag the pointer until the selector box attains the size you want the control to be, and release the left button to create the control. When you're done, you'll end up with a control planted on the form at the location you specified and in the size you want. As you can see in Figure 25-6, the basic controls provide you with a variety of form elements.

Adding the control to the form is just the beginning. Once you have your control in place, you can set its properties, move it around, resize it, add it to a control group, and more. Since most controls should be bound to fields to make them useful, the decision to use a control or a "field" from the Field Chooser depends on the type of object you're trying to create. For something like a simple textbox (TextBox) with a label (Label), it's generally easier to take an existing field or create a new field and drag it onto the form. However, if you want to create something more sophisticated, such as a drop-down list

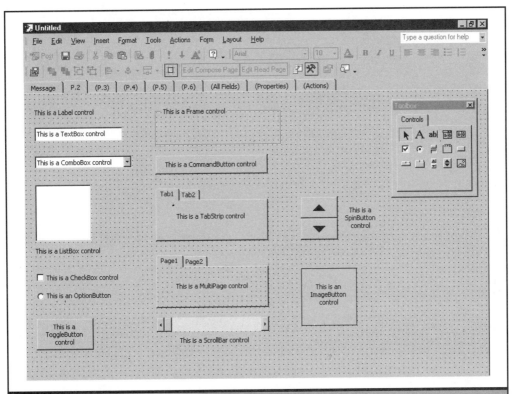

Figure 25-6.   *Controls come in all shapes and sizes*

(ComboBox), a display list (ListBox), or a set of radio button options (OptionButton), you'll have to use a control. The "fields" you can drag off the Field Chooser are rather limited in the default controls they use.

Setting Control Properties

Each control has an extensive set of options you can customize. These options, which can be found in the control's Properties dialog box, include everything from the control name and caption to complex validation rules. To view a control's Properties dialog box, right-click the control and select Properties from the shortcut menu. You can also click the Properties button on the form design toolbar to display the Properties dialog box. Regardless of which control you choose (a combo box control in this example), the Properties dialog box resembles the one shown in Figure 25-7.

The Properties dialog box remains the same for all standard controls with two exceptions: the MultiPage control, which only has a single tab (Display) for each page, and the Frame control, also with a single tab (Display).

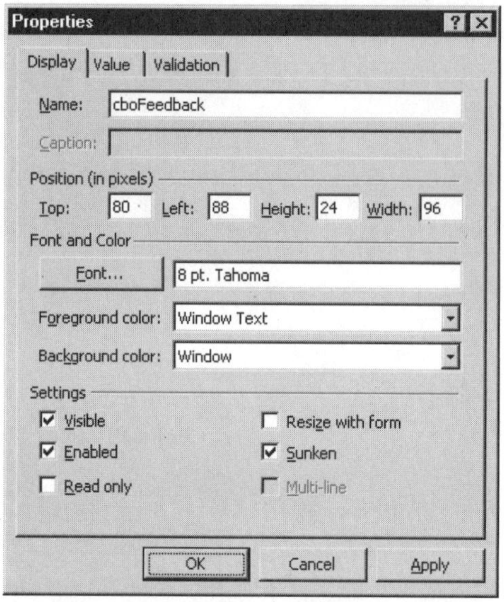

Figure 25-7. *Customizing controls is easy with this extensive collection of options*

Display Properties   The Display tab, seen in Figure 25-7, contains a variety of options that affect the appearance and location of the control, which in this example is a combo box to be added to a feedback post form. It provides the user with a drop-down list of feedback types such as Comment, Suggestion, and Problem. The options you can set on the Display tab include the following:

- **Name**   This field lets you provide a descriptive identifier for the name. If you plan to do any VBA or VBS scripting, you may want to include a control prefix so you can easily identify the control type simply by looking at the name. You can use a standard naming convention such as the one presented in Table 25-1, or create one of your own design. Just make sure you're consistent when using either one.

- **Caption**   The Caption is nothing more than a built-in label for the control. Some standard controls, like Label, CheckBox, OptionBox, ToggleButton, and CommandButton, have captions. The rest do not, which is where the Label control comes in. You add your own caption by placing a Label control next to the captionless control.

- **Position (in pixels)**   If you want to fine-tune the position and size of a control, here's your chance. You can set the control's exact position by indicating the pixel intersection of the top left corner of the control. To set the control's size to within a pixel, set the Height and Width options.

- **Font**   Use this option to open the Font dialog box and change the font, font style, or size used to display text in the control or in its caption.

- **Foreground color**   This option determines the color of the text displayed in the control or in the control's caption. The Foreground Color drop-down list does not contain actual color choices, but rather, Windows styles to which certain colors are assigned. Unfortunately, this is not only confusing but extremely limiting, since most of the choices are white, gray, or black. If you want to pick a color for the text used in a control, open its advanced Properties dialog box and modify the ForeColor setting. You'll still have the option of selecting colors by Window styles. However, by double-clicking the ForeColor property, you can access a color palette from which to select any color you want.

- **Background color**   This option works the same as the Foreground Color option, except it applies to the control's background. If you want to choose a color instead of a style, open the advanced Properties dialog box and double-click the BackColor property to display the color palette.

- **Settings**   The Settings properties are a series of check box options that include the following:

  - **Visible**   If you want the control to appear on the form, check this option. To hide a control, deselect this option.

  - **Enabled**   By default, all controls are enabled. Removing the Enabled check mark disables the control, which means that it no longer functions. For example, a disabled TextBox control becomes totally uneditable, a disabled ComboBox drop-down list will not display, and a disabled CommandButton will not respond to a click.

  - **Read only**   Making a control read-only means you can't edit the visible control in the form. With controls that contain text, such as a TextBox control, you won't be able to change the text, but you will be able to highlight and copy it (which you cannot do if you disable the control using the previous option).

  - **Resize with form**   This option ensures that the size of the control remains relative to the size of the form. If you check this option, the control will shrink when the user reduces the size of the form, and expand when the user increases the size of the form.

  - **Sunken**   If you want the control to have a 3-D appearance that makes it look like it's recessed, this is the option for you.

  - **Multi-line**   With this option checked, a text control such as a TextBox can accept multiple lines of text. If the option is unchecked, the control is limited to a single line of text.

Control	Prefix
CheckBox	chk
ComboBox	cbo
CommandButton	cmd
Frame	fra
Horizontal ScrollBar	hsb
Image	img
Label	lbl
ListBox	lst
OptionButton	opt
TabStrip	tab
TextBox	txt
ToggleButton	tgb
Vertical ScrollBar	vsb

Table 25-1.   *Suggested Control Prefixes*

Value Properties   The Value tab of the control's Properties dialog box, shown in Figure 25-8, which is available for all standard controls except Frame and MultiPage controls, provides quite a bit of power without requiring any coding. For this example we're using the Properties dialog box of a second ComboBox control called Severity, which is to remain hidden unless the user selects Problem from the Feedback combo box.

It offers a number of options that enable you to do more than simply add fields and objects to a form. Here's what you'll find:

- **Choose Field**   Since controls cannot store data, it's necessary to bind (link) a field to any control you want to use for data input or display. Click this button to reveal the menu of available fields you can bind to the selected control. If you want to create a new field, click the New button and enter a name, field type, and field format.

- **Type**   This setting displays the field type of the selected field from the previous option. You cannot change the field type after a field has been created.

- **Format**   Depending on the field type, you may or may not be able to change this option. For example, a text field has but a single format (Text), while a Yes/No field has four possible Format types: Yes/No, On/Off, True/False, or Icon. If the field selected in the Choose Field option has multiple formats, you'll be able to choose the format you want to use.

- **List Type**   If the selected control is a ComboBox, you'll have a choice of list types—Droplist and Dropdown. Although both list types appear to be identical, there is one difference. A *Dropdown* permits the user to select one of the possible values or enter a value by typing it in. A *Droplist* limits the user to only those values that appear on the list.

- **Property to use**   This is the tricky (and powerful) one. It enables you to use the value of a field from one control to customize a specific property in a different control. For example, suppose you have a ComboBox called Feedback, with Comment, Suggestion, and Problem as the possible choices in the drop-down list. You might decide you want an additional drop-down list to appear whenever the user selects Problem. The purpose of the new drop-down list is to indicate the severity of the problem. This ComboBox control might be named Severity. Each control would have a corresponding field to hold the data. Now, the question
  - is, how do you get the second control, Severity, to stay hidden unless the user selects Problem from the Feedback drop-down list? The answer: set the Severity control's Property To Use option to Visible, and then create a formula (in the Set The Initial Value Of This Field To option) that converts the value entered in the Feedback control to something that will turn the Visible property on or off in the Severity control. For the Visible property, –1 (or 1) and 0 (On and Off, respectively) are the magic numbers. Therefore, the formula has to say, *If the value in the Feedback field equals "Problem," make the value for this field (Severity) –1; otherwise make it 0.* When the user selects Comment or Suggestion from the Feedback drop-down list, the Severity control stays out of sight. However, as soon as the user selects Problem, the Severity drop-down list appears. See the Set The Initial Value Of This Field To bullet item in this section for more information on creating a formula.

- **Value**   When this option is available, you can enter a value that is applied to the property selected in the previous option, Property To Use.

- **Possible values**   This option appears only if the selected control is a ComboBox or ListBox. It enables you to specify the choices you want available to the user. Enter each item followed by a semicolon to indicate that the next item belongs on a separate line in the control.

- **Set the initial value of this field to**   Check this option and enter a value or a formula in the associated textbox to be used as the value of the bound field the first time the control appears. Taking the earlier example of the Feedback ComboBox control, you might check this option and enter **Comment**. This would ensure that the Feedback drop-down list displays the Comment choice rather than a blank line when it first appears on the form.

■ **Edit** The Edit button opens a dialog box in which you can create a formula to use in this field. The Field button displays a menu of Outlook fields you can use in the formula. The Function button displays a menu of functions you can use. In the earlier Severity control box option, the formula used was *If the value in the Feedback field equals "Problem," make the value for this field (Severity) –1; otherwise make it 0*. The actual formula is **IIf([Feedback]="Problem",-1,0**. You can enter formula information by using the buttons or typing it manually. Most of the time you'll probably use a combination of both methods.

■ **Calculate this formula when I compose a new form** This calculates the formula only when the form is first created. Thereafter, the formula is ignored.

■ **Calculate this formula automatically** Select this option to instruct Outlook to recalculate the formula every time there's a change in the form. Setting this option in the Severity example ensures that when the user selects Problem, the Severity control appears. If the user changes his or her mind and selects Comment, the formula is recalculated, and the Severity control disappears.

If you want to use the Property To Use option but don't know the values that trigger each of the different properties, there's a way to find most of them. Close the

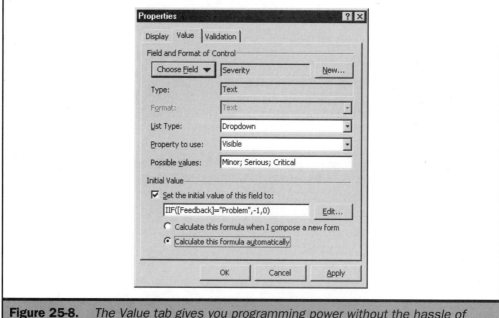

Figure 25-8. *The Value tab gives you programming power without the hassle of learning to program*

Properties dialog box, right-click the control, and select Advanced Properties to display the advanced Properties dialog box. Select a property to view its possible values.

Validation Properties   The final tab of the Properties dialog box, Validation, contains a variety of options for controlling the information a user is allowed to enter into the control. You can choose to let the user ignore the field, or force him or her to enter something before closing or sending the form. In addition, you can determine the parameters for what information the form will accept or reject. The following options let you decide which information can be entered in the selected control:

- **A value is required for this field**   Check this option if you want the user to enter something before closing the form. If the user attempts to skip the field, Outlook displays a message informing the user that "A field on this form requires a value."

- **Validate this field before closing the form**   Check this option if you want to impose restrictions on the values that can be entered into the field to which the control is bound.

- **Validation Formula**   You can use this field to enter a formula against which the user input will be evaluated. If the input fails to meet the formula criteria, Outlook refuses to close the form. For example, if one of your customers recently changed the company name from *Easy Widgets* to *Value Widgets,* you might add a formula that rejects *Easy Widgets* as input in a field that accepts company name information. Your formula would be **<>"Easy Widgets"**. If a user entered *Easy Widgets* in the field and tried to close the form, Outlook would respond with a message stating that the entered data is not valid.

- **Display this message if the validation fails**   If you use a validation formula, it might be more helpful to the user if you create your own message to replace the generic Outlook message that says, "The data you entered for [field name] is not valid." In the Easy Widgets example, you might create a message that says, "Easy Widgets is now known as Value Widgets. Please update your customer information."

- **Include this field for Printing and Save As**   This one means just what it says. If you check this option, the field bound to the selected control appears when you print the form or use the Save As command. If you deselect this option, the field disappears from a printout or a saved file.

When you reach this point, you should be finished setting basic properties for your control. Click OK to close the Properties dialog box and save the new control settings.

Setting Advanced Control Properties

If you want to spruce up your control by modifying more properties than the basic Properties dialog box provides, you might want to try the advanced Properties. Here you'll find an extensive collection of properties. For example, you can add a tool tip, change colors, limit the number of characters that can be entered, change the mouse pointer that appears over the control, and more.

To display the advanced Properties dialog box (see Figure 25-9), right-click the control whose properties you want to modify, and select Advanced Properties from the shortcut menu.

As you can see in Figure 25-9, the advanced Properties dialog box contains two columns of data. The left column holds the property name, while the right column contains the property value. When you select a property, its value appears in the textbox at the top of the dialog box to the right of the Apply button. Depending on the property type, you can enter text, select a value from a drop-down list, or choose a file.

If a property has multiple possible values, you can double-click the property (name or value) to cycle through the choices. If the property uses a file as a value, as does the Picture property, double-clicking the property displays an open (Load Picture in this case) dialog box, with which you can locate and select the appropriate file. Double-clicking a color property opens a color palette from which you can select the color of your choice.

After you change a property's value, you can click the Apply button, and Outlook immediately makes the change to the control. This lets you judge the effects of your changes without having to close and reopen the dialog box.

Rearranging Controls on the Form

As handy as the Snap To Grid feature is, nothing beats auto-aligning tools for really putting controls in their place. The alignment and layering tools Outlook provides let you line up your controls any way you want, with little or no effort.

Properties	☒
Apply	1 - Opaque ▾

AutoSize	0 - False
AutoTab	0 - False
AutoWordSelect	-1 - True
BackColor	80000005 - Window
BackStyle	1 - Opaque
BorderColor	80000006 - Window Frame
BorderStyle	0 - None
BoundColumn	1
ColumnCount	1
ColumnHeads	0 - False
ColumnWidths	
ControlSource	
ControlTipText	
DragBehavior	1 - Enabled

Figure 25-9. *Advanced Properties include a number of properties not found in the basic Properties dialog box*

Alignment is the process of taking two or more controls and lining them up along the same imaginary line, which is determined by two things: the dominant control and the alignment type you select. The *dominant* control is the one to which the other selected controls align themselves. Your method of selection determines the dominant control. If you select by holding down the CTRL key and clicking, the *last* control selected is the dominant control. If you hold down the SHIFT key while clicking, the *first* control selected is the dominant control. If you draw a selector box around multiple controls, the first one selected becomes the dominant control. You can always recognize the dominant control by its white sizing handles.

After you select the controls to align, right-click any one of the controls and select Align from the shortcut menu to display the submenu of alignment commands. The alignment commands you can choose include Left, Center, Right, Top, Middle, Bottom, and To Grid, all of which are self-explanatory, with the possible exception of To Grid. To Grid is really nothing more than a Snap To Grid command that works on multiple fields. If the Snap To Grid feature is turned off or if you've changed the grid size, you can use the To Grid alignment command to snap all the selected controls to the nearest grid intersection.

> **Tip** *You'll find both alignment and layering commands on the form design toolbar.*

There's another feature similar to alignment, called *spacing,* which enables you to position selected objects an equal distance from one another horizontally or vertically. Select the objects you want to space, and choose Layout | Horizontal Spacing or Layout | Vertical Spacing from the Menu bar.

To make form design easier, Outlook permits *layering.* In other words, you can place one control on top of another. This comes in handy for adding other controls to TabStrip and MultiPage controls. Since layering is permitted, it means that one control is positioned in front of or behind other controls. Sometimes this is easy to figure out (when one control partially hides another), and sometime it's not (when the top control is transparent). Fortunately, Outlook provides commands to move objects backward and forward. Right-click the control and select Bring Forward from the Order submenu to move the object one layer closer to the top of the heap (closer to you, the viewer), or Send Backward to move it one layer further away from the viewer. To bring an item to the top layer, even if it's at the bottom of the pile, select it and choose Layout | Order | Bring To Front from the Menu bar. To send it to the bottom of the pile, choose Send To Back.

> **Tip** *You can also use the Bring To Front and Send To Back buttons on the form toolbar.*

Moving and Sizing Controls

No matter how careful your initial placement of an object on the form, you're bound to want to move it sooner or later. You can move all standard controls except Frame and MultiPage controls by dragging them to a new location. Frame and MultiPage controls (along with the other controls) can be moved by selecting the control, and placing your mouse pointer over one of the borders until the pointer turns into a four-sided arrow. You can then drag the control wherever you want. To move multiple controls at once, select them all first, and then drag any one of them. The rest follow, staying in relative position to one another.

There are several ways to resize form objects. You can resize them manually by grabbing one of the sizing handles that appear when you select the object, and dragging the side or corner of the object. You can also open the Properties dialog box or the advanced Properties dialog box and enter the exact dimensions for the control. However, if you want to let Outlook do all the work, use one of these commands:

- **Make Same Size**   Use this command to make one dimension of a control the same as the corresponding dimension of a different control. Select two or more objects, and choose Layout | Make Same Size to display a submenu that contains Width, Height, and Both commands. Select the appropriate command. All selected objects are resized to match the dominant control. See the earlier section entitled "Rearranging Controls on the Form" for more about dominant controls.

- **Size to Fit**   This is a useful command that sizes most controls to the minimum size needed to accommodate the control or its contents. For example, using the Size To Fit command on a Label control shrinks (or expands) the Label control to fit the Caption text. To use this command, choose Layout | Size To Fit from the Menu bar.

- **Size to Grid**   Use this command (Layout | Size To Grid) to resize the control to fit within the closest grid lines. The control will expand or contract depending on which grid lines are closest. One side may expand while the other side contracts.

In case you're wondering, it is possible to resize multiple objects at the same time. Select all the objects you want to resize, and use one of the resizing methods described here.

Grouping Controls

Grouping controls enables you to select two or more controls and temporarily join them together. After you group them, they respond as a single unit. As a matter of fact, you can no longer select them individually. This is great for moving a captionless control such as a TextBox control, and its associated Label control. Group them together and they remain in the same relative position to one another no matter how far or how often you move them.

Select the controls you want to group, and click the Group button on the form design toolbar. You can also right-click one of the selected controls and choose Group from the shortcut menu. To break up a group of controls, select the group and click the Ungroup button on the form design toolbar, or right-click the group and select Ungroup from the shortcut menu. You can also choose Layout | Group or Layout | Ungroup from the Menu bar.

Creating Custom Controls

If you find yourself adding and customizing the same control type over and over, you might want to add it to the Control Toolbox as a custom control. That way the next time you need it, you can just drag or draw it on the form, and all the settings will be taken care of. You can add an existing control to the Control Toolbox by dragging it to the Toolbox. As soon as you drop it on the Toolbox, it appears as an icon. When you move your mouse pointer over the new, custom control, a tool tip appears, containing "New [control type]" (a custom TextBox tool tip would say "New TextBox"). To change the tool tip and the icon image, right-click the icon and select Customize New [control type] to open the Customize Control dialog box.

Begin by entering new text for the tool tip. If you're so inclined, you can modify the icon itself by clicking Edit Picture and editing the icon one pixel at a time. If you have additional icons, you can locate and select one by clicking the Load Picture button.

Tip *You can even add control groups to the Toolbox as custom controls. Just create the group and drag it to the Toolbox.*

In addition to letting you create your own custom controls, Outlook also provides a large collection of additional controls, such as a Toolbar control, an Excel chart control, and more. Right-click the Toolbox and select Custom Controls to display the Additional Controls dialog box. Check the controls you want included, and click OK to add them to the Toolbox. If you start running out of room on the Toolbox, you can add more pages by right-clicking the Controls tab and selecting New Page from the shortcut menu.

MOUS *MOUS EXAM PRACTICE*
In this section you learned to create custom forms. To build and modify forms, you'll need to master working with fields and controls. Begin by using the Field Chooser to add existing fields to a form. Next, display the Control Toolbox and add some controls to the form. Move the fields and controls around on the form, and then use the alignment tools to line them up neatly. Use the resizing handles to change their size. When you're comfortable with field and control basics, try modifying some of their properties.

Setting Form Properties

Forms, like controls, have their own properties you can set. Not surprisingly, you'll find them on the Properties tab of the form in the Design mode (see Figure 25-10).

Some Outlook options set at the time a form is created may become part of the form's properties, even if the options are later changed. For example, creating a custom message form when your E-mail Sensitivity option (Tools | Options | E-mail Options | Advanced Options) is set to Confidential means the new form will have a default sensitivity of confidential. The only way to modify this is to change the original Outlook option and then republish the form.

Most of the options on the Properties tab are self-explanatory. However, there are a few things you should know. To begin with, assigning forms to categories and subcategories can be quite useful, but the only place they're used is in the Forms Manager. It's always a good idea to give the form a version number, and to change it each time you modify the form. This makes it much easier to keep track of the most current iteration of the form, especially if you share it with others. You might want to

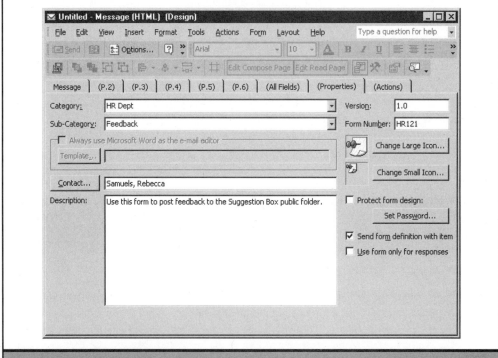

Figure 25-10.   *Setting form properties makes your forms management tasks a lot easier*

use a software version numbering scheme such as 1.0, 1.1, 1.2, 2.0, 2.1, and so on. The fractional increments indicate minor changes; the integer increments indicate major updates. One last thing: You may be tempted to ignore the Description field. Don't. If you create a lot of custom forms, it can quickly become difficult to tell them apart, even with a good naming scheme. A brief description of what the form is used for can eliminate a lot of time wasted searching for the right form.

Testing and Publishing the Form

No matter how strong your design skills, it's always a good idea to run the form before publishing it. All too often, a minor mistake can throw the whole form out of whack. To test a form before publishing, choose Form | Run This Form. A finished form, ready for use, immediately appears. Fill it out and send it or close it to make sure everything works the way you expect. It's also a good idea to get some of your co-workers to test it out before publishing it company-wide.

Tip   *If you plan to use the new form with other versions of Outlook, it's a good idea to test it on those versions before distributing it to others. Some features may not be supported in older versions of Outlook. The time to find out is before everyone starts using the new form.*

After you've tested the form and are satisfied with it, you'll want to publish it. Do not confuse Publish with Save. In the case of forms, the Publish command works more like a standard save command than the Save command does. When you publish a form, you actually are placing a copy of it in the forms library of your choice so you can use, edit, or distribute it later. The Save command, on the other hand, saves only the current instance of the form as an item or one-off form (not a reusable form).

Tip   *Rather than wait until you've finished the form, you should publish it periodically to ensure all your work doesn't go down the drain if a power failure or other mishap shuts down Outlook before you're through.*

To publish your form, click the Publish button on the form design toolbar or choose Tools | Forms | Publish Form to open the Publish Form As dialog box, shown in Figure 25-11.

Note   *Once you create a form, you use the Publish Form command to save changes you make to the form. In the event that you decide to create a new form using the existing one as a template, you then use the Publish Form As command to save the modified version as a completely new form.*

From the Look In drop-down list, select the forms library in which you want to save the custom form. By default, the Personal Forms Library is selected. Depending on

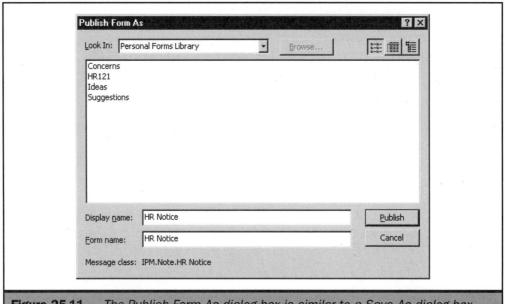

Figure 25-11.   *The Publish Form As dialog box is similar to a Save As dialog box*

your plans for the form, this may or may not be the best location for the new form. When publishing a form, consider the way Outlook searches for the form when you open an item that uses it. The first place Outlook searches is the forms cache on your local computer. If you've used the form during this session, it should be there. The next place Outlook searches for a form is in the folder you're currently in. The Personal Forms Library is the third place Outlook looks. The next place Outlook scans is the Organizational Forms Library.

Therefore, if you're the only one using the form, and you usually create items from within the folder with which they're associated, you might want to publish the form to the folder in which you use it. If you're more inclined to create a new item from anywhere in Outlook, use the Personal Forms Library. If, on the other hand, you plan to share the form with other users, you'll probably want to put it in the Organizational Forms Library to simplify the update process. All users on the Exchange network should have access to the Organizational Forms Library. Therefore, any time you want to change the form, you need only change the copy in the Organizational Forms Library.

After you decide where to put the form, enter a display name in the Display Name field and the name for the file in the Form Name field. Outlook assumes you want them to be the same, so it duplicates the Display Name information in the Form Name field. You can change it if you wish. Click Publish and the form is tucked away for future use.

Creating Your Own Custom Fields

Although Outlook provides an abundance of standard fields, there are going to be times, especially while customizing forms, when you find a need for additional fields. When such a time arrives, you can quickly and easily create a new field to suit your particular needs. From anywhere in Outlook, including the forms Design mode, you can create a new field by opening the Field Chooser and clicking the New button to display the New Field dialog box.

Begin by giving the new field a unique name. Then designate the field type by making your selection from the Type drop-down list. Most of the field types are self-explanatory. A Text field holds text, a Numbers field holds numeric data, a Currency field holds numeric data preceded by a currency symbol, and so on. There are, however, a few fields that might require a little more explanation:

- **Yes/No**   This field type is used to accept simple Yes/No, On/Off, or True/False data. It's most frequently used in conjunction with a CheckBox or ComboBox control. In its Icon format it's also used as a visual indicator in folder views (the Attachment icon in the Inbox).

- **Duration**   A Duration field is used to hold length-of-time information. It is used to record the interval of time that has elapsed or that you expect to elapse (a meeting or phone call).

- **Keywords**   Keyword fields are text fields whose primary purpose is to facilitate grouping and locating items.

- **Combination**   If you've ever wondered how a Full Name field manages to pull data from a First Name and a Last Name field and put them together, here's your answer: by using a Combination field. As soon as you select Combination as the field type, the Format field in the New Field dialog box changes to Formula. You can either enter a concatenation formula here, or click the Edit button to display the Combination Formula Field dialog box, which provides more room to work, and a field selection button, aptly named Field. The formula can be relatively simple, as is the case with the Full Name example, for which the formula is [First Name] [Last Name]. Notice that there is no operator, such as a plus sign, between the two fields. Anything you place between the field names appears in the textbox, which is why you want to make sure you don't add extraneous characters, but do leave a space between them.

- **Formula**   You can use this field type to create a field that can draw information from multiple fields and perform calculations on them at the same time. It can also be used to conditionally draw information from other fields. When you select Formula as the field type, the Format field changes to Formula. Either enter the formula directly, or click the Edit button to open the Formula Field dialog box, which provides both a Field button and a Function button.

After selecting the field type, move to the Format (or Formula) field. Select the desired format for the field or enter a formula. Then click OK to create the custom field. All custom fields are added to the user-defined fields group.

MOUS Exam Expert Objectives Explored in Chapter 25

Objective	Activity	Heading
OL10E-4-3	Create and use Outlook forms	"Designing Your Custom Form"

The Complete Reference

Outlook 2002

Chapter 26

Customizing and Automating Outlook with VBA

O utlook 2002 includes Visual Basic for Applications (VBA), a macro language version of the Visual Basic programming language for customizing Windows applications to work the way you want them to work. A major strength of VBA is that it enables you to customize applications like Outlook 2002 with features specific to your organization. For example, you can add a new option to the Outlook Tools menu or add a custom toolbar button to run the macro. However, unlike many of the other Office XP applications, Outlook doesn't include a macro editor, which captures keystrokes as you execute actions in the application and translates those keystrokes into program code. In Outlook, you create your macros directly with VBA code.

This chapter doesn't teach you how to program in VBA because VBA programming is beyond the scope of this book. Rather, it shows examples of how VBA is used to create Outlook macros that customize Outlook 2002. You don't need to understand VBA code to use the macros presented in this chapter, but if you have a basic familiarity with VBA code, then you should be able to understand the code shown in this chapter.

To learn more about Visual Basic for Applications, consult the Microsoft VBA home page at http://msdn.microsoft.com/vba.

So why do you want to program your own macros? Quite simply, to enhance and customize Outlook 2002, automate frequent and repetitive work tasks, and make Outlook work the way you want it to work. In this chapter, you will learn how to create some useful macros that perform the following:

- Insert time and date stamps and standard disclaimers into e-mail
- Insert the names and e-mail addresses of all members of a distribution list into a table in a Word document
- Import contacts from an Access database

More About VBA

As a macro language, VBA is based upon procedures. A VBA procedure is a named sequence of statements. These statements in turn are associated with constants, data types, and variables to perform a task.

VBA provides two types of procedures, Functions and Subs. *Functions* can return a value to the procedure that calls them, but cannot themselves be macros. In VBA, a macro is defined as a *Sub*. There are two requirements for Subs to be macros. The first is that the Sub is public, which means that it can be seen anywhere in Outlook. The second requirement is that the Sub must not require any inputs, or arguments, when it is called.

If you want to learn more about VBA and VBA programming for Outlook 2002, there are a number of resources on the Web, including the Microsoft Developer's Network (http://msdn.microsoft.com). While the MSDN Web site is primarily for programmers, it does provide a lot of useful examples of VBA programming for Outlook customization and enhancement. Other sites like ZDNET Help& How To (http://www.zdnet.com/zdhelp/filters/home/), VB Explorer (http://www.vbexplorer.com/vbaofficelinks.asp), and Visual Basic World (http://www.vb-world.net) provide information and examples, further resources, and the latest information about VBA development for Outlook 2002 and the rest of the Office XP suite. Slipstick was indeed used in the previous edition of the book but I was looking to break past a consultant's site and use examples that would have a richer variety of Outlook and VBA content.

With the launch of Office XP, and Outlook 2002, there are some new and notable features in VBA you can take advantage of when enhancing Outlook 2002 with VBA. These new additions add refinements to the Outlook 2002 object model, reminders, views, and search.

The object model for Outlook 2002 has an equivalent element for each element in the Outlook 2002 user interface. Some notable additions include

- **A reminders Collection object**   This has been added to the Outlook 2002 object model, enabling you to turn off Outlook reminders (good news if you find the reminders to be a nuisance).

- **The Views object**   This is for altering the existing view options in Outlook 2002.

- **The SyncObject**   This is the programmatic equivalent of Send/Receive Groups.

BUILDING OUTLOOK APPLICATIONS

Using the Visual Basic Editor

So if you can't create a macro using a keystroke recorder, as in Word, how do you create a macro in Outlook? You use the Visual Basic Editor (VBE), a tool available to all Microsoft Office XP programs.

To open the VBE, press ALT+F11. You can also open the VBE from a menu by choosing Tools | Macro | Visual Basic Editor. If you do not have this choice on your Tools menu, use the Office XP installation CD to install this component, which is an optional installation. When it is first opened, the VBE shows *Project1* in the Project Explorer, the window in the upper-left corner of the VBE. When *Project1* is expanded, the VBE looks similar to Figure 26-1.

Tip

Not installing the Visual Basic Editor during your Office XP installation means you won't have access to the range of functionality provided by VBA throughout the Office XP application suite.

If you have ever used the VBE in any of the Office applications—or the similar integrated development environment (IDE) in Visual Basic—the Outlook VBE will look familiar. The VBE has four main windows that you use when creating macros. The top left window is the *Project Explorer*, which is similar to the Windows Explorer and enables you to explore your Outlook project (Outlook only allows one project, and it is always

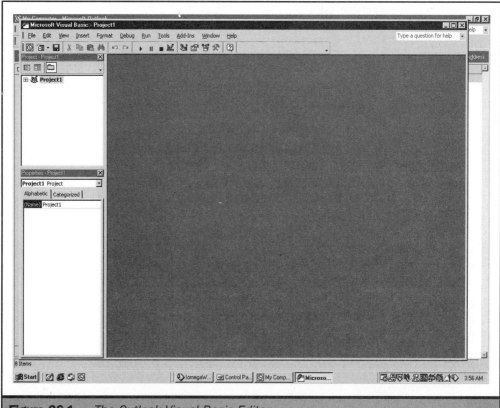

Figure 26-1. *The Outlook Visual Basic Editor*

named VBAProject.OTM). The bottom left window is the *Properties window,* where the properties of the project or selected component of the project are displayed. If you don't see the Project Explorer or the Properties window, you can open them from the View menu. The *Code window* at the top right of the VBE is used to enter and edit code. A Code window opens automatically when a module or class containing code is selected. The *Immediate window* at the bottom right is used to test and evaluate expressions and variables when debugging your macros. The Immediate window isn't shown in Figure 26-1, but can be opened from the View menu.

There are other windows that can be opened, the most important of which is the *Object Browser.* The Object Browser enables you to examine the components of various libraries (DLL files) and object models for Outlook, Word, Excel, and so on. An *object model* is the programming interface that is exposed for you to use in your programs. Any object model or library that is placed in the project's references can be examined in the Object Browser. The *references* for a project are the object models of other programs that you can use in your own code or view in the Object Browser.

Setting Project References

Since you are programming Outlook, a reference to the Outlook object model must be set in the project. Choose Tools | References, and make sure that the Microsoft Outlook 10.0 Object Library is checked. If it isn't, scroll down the list of available references to the Microsoft Outlook 10.0 Object Library and check it. Other macros in this chapter will use the Word and Data Access Objects (DAO) object models, so also check the references to the Microsoft Word 10.0 Object Library and the Microsoft DAO 3.6 Object Library. Click OK to add the checked references. Some references are automatically added for you. When you are finished, the References dialog box should look like Figure 26-2. (Your list of references may be different.) The referenced objects are moved to the top of the list when you close the dialog box.

Looking at the Object Browser

Next, use the Object Browser to show the Outlook object model. Press F2 or choose View | Object Browser to open the Object Browser. In the Project/Library list that

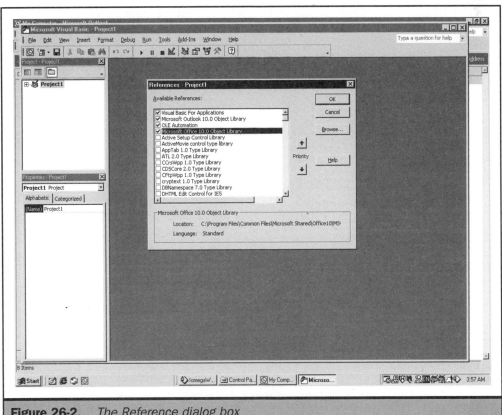

Figure 26-2.   *The Reference dialog box*

shows <libraries>, select Outlook. You can enlarge sections of the Object Browser like any other window, by hovering the mouse over section boundaries and dragging it when it turns into a resizing cursor. The Object Browser now shows the Outlook object model, as seen in Figure 26-3.

We'll return to the Outlook object model later in this chapter, but for now, close the Object Browser by clicking on the Close Window control (the × in the top right corner of most windows). Next, you will insert a code module, where you will create your macros:

1. Choose Insert | Module to insert a new code module into the Outlook VBA project.

2. In the Properties window, change the name from Module1 to **basOutlook2002Macros**. The *bas* prefix indicates that this module is a Basic code module.

3. Return to the Code window.

Figure 26-3.   *The Object Browser interface*

Setting Project Options

Before putting your first lines of code into the project, you should set some options for the project. These settings will make it easier to enter and test your macros. Choose Tools | Options in the VBE and select the Editor tab. It is best to check all the check boxes on the Editor tab, and set a tab width that lets the indented sections of the code stand out without taking too much space. Figure 26-4 shows the Editor tab of the Project Options dialog box.

The Code Setting options on the Editor tab are as follows:

- **Auto Syntax Check**   This checks if a line uses correct syntax when it is entered.

- **Require Variable Declaration**   This option requires that all variables are declared with a Dim statement. This makes it easier to ensure that all variables are of the correct types and spelled correctly in the Sub statements. Checking this option inserts an Option Explicit statement in each new code module that is created.

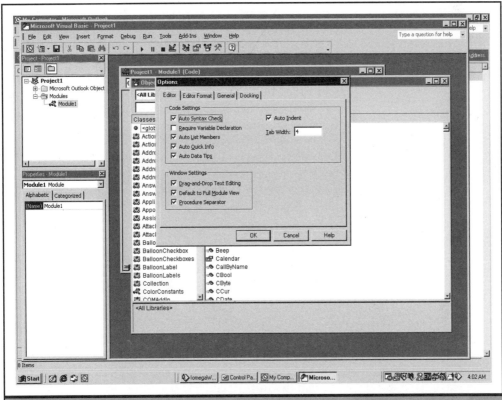

Figure 26-4.   *The Editor tab of the Options dialog box*

- **Auto List Members**   This helps complete code statements by showing a list of permissible entries at the cursor insertion point as you type.

- **Auto Quick Info**   This shows inline help about functions and their parameters as you type.

- **Auto Data Tips**   This displays the value of variables and objects when the mouse cursor is hovered over the variables and objects when testing code.

Each tab has a Help button that explains the meaning of each choice on that tab. Use this help to explain choices you don't understand. Auto List Members and Auto Quick Info are particularly useful when you are entering code. They provide information about the functions you are using while you type and show what entries are needed to complete the code line. Auto List Members provides a list of the possible values that can be supplied to functions, and items from the list can be selected by highlighting them and pressing TAB. This enters the item from the list into your code.

Creating a Macro Template

Click the mouse in the new Code window and enter the following code to create a macro template. You can use this template when you create new macros, customizing it as needed. The first line declares a Sub procedure (also known as a *method*) named MacroTemplate. The Sub is declared to be Private, meaning that it can only be seen by other methods within the same code module. This is to prevent it from appearing in the list of macros. When you are ready to use the template, change the name of the Sub to one that is meaningful, and change the Private declaration to Public.

Tip	*Any text that appears after an apostrophe is considered a comment by VBA. It's good practice to add a lot of comments to your code so later you or others can easily see what the code does. You will see a lot of comments in the macros in this chapter.*

```
Private Sub MacroTemplate()
  ' Change the name and make it Public to use for a macro.
```

The next line creates a variable by using the Dim statement. You should always declare all *variables*, which are containers for values and properties of objects. The template declares a variable for the Outlook Application object, which is required for access to all Outlook properties. You will add other variables as needed for any macro you create, but all your Outlook macros should have this declaration. Following the declaration of the Outlook Application object, the On Error GoTo statement is used to declare an error handler for any errors that might occur when the macro is run. It's a good idea to have such an error handler in your code, to display more meaningful error messages than the system would, and to enable your code to terminate properly if an error occurs.

```
' Add other Dim statements as required.
Dim objOutlook As Outlook.Application

On Error GoTo ErrorHandler
```

The next line uses the CreateObject function to create an instance of the Outlook Application object and assign it to the objOutlook object variable. A common convention is to prefix all variables with an abbreviation that tells what type of variable it is. Table 26-1 shows some commonly used prefixes for variable types.

```
Set objOutlook = CreateObject("Outlook.Application")
```

The next section of the macro template starts with the MacroExit label. Labels are indicated by ending with a colon and are points to which you can direct program execution as needed. It's always good practice to set any object variable declared in the procedure equal to Nothing, which releases it from memory. Not releasing objects is one of the main reasons that programs remain in memory when you close them, so

Prefix	Variable Type
Bln	Boolean (True/False or Yes/No)
Dat	Date
Db	Database
Dbl	Double-precision floating-point number
Int	Integer (16-bit number)
Lng	Long (32-bit number)
Obj	Object
Rst	Recordset
Sng	Single-precision floating-point number
Str	String

Table 26-1. *Variable Type Prefixes*

always release all your object variables. The Exit Sub statement at the end of the exit section terminates the macro.

> **Note**
> *Only variables that are objects can be set equal to Nothing. Other variables that contain values are automatically released when the macro ends. In most cases, object variables are automatically released when the macros in which they are defined end. However, if unhandled errors occur in your code or the object variables are referenced in other code, they may not be released as expected. It's always safest to explicitly release object variables.*

```
MacroExit:
 ' Set all objects equal to Nothing to destroy them and
 ' release the memory and resources they take. Add other
 ' objects that are created.
 Set objOutlook = Nothing

 Exit Sub
```

The error handler displays a message showing the description and error number of any error that occurs. It then clears the error state and tells the program to go to the MacroExit label. Error handlers can be very complex, with tests for different error conditions and different actions to take depending on the results. However, this simple error handler is sufficient for many of the macros you will create. Finally, the End Sub statement tells VBA that the macro ends at that statement.

```
ErrorHandler:
 MsgBox "Error: " & Err.Description & vbCrLf & "Error # " _
    & Err.Number
```

> **Note**
> *The underline character following the space at the end of the preceding line forms what is called a line continuation. The text on the line following the space and underline is considered by VBA to be part of the previous line. Breaking up your code lines with line continuations helps make your code more readable since you don't have to horizontally scroll your code window to read all the code.*

```
 Err.Clear
 GoTo MacroExit
End Sub
```

The error handler is always placed at the end of the macro, after the Exit Sub line. This prevents the error handler from running when there is no error. The GoTo MacroExit line directs the macro execution to the MacroExit label, where the objects created by the macro are released by setting them equal to Nothing, and where other cleanup code may be placed. The flow of code execution for a macro is shown in Figure 26-5.

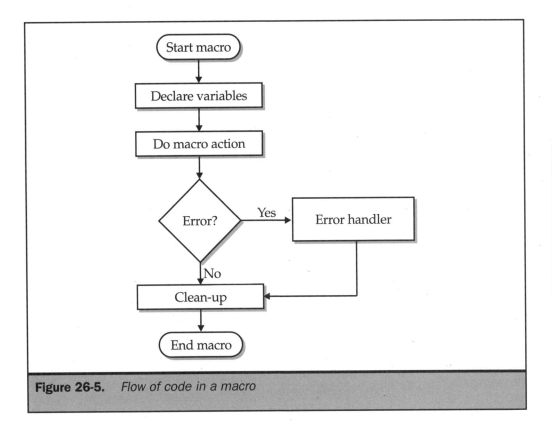

Figure 26-5.   *Flow of code in a macro*

Now that you have seen the environment in which macros are created and have seen how the framework of a macro is organized, it's time to jump in and create your first macro.

Creating a Date/Time Stamp Macro for E-mail

The DateTime macro inserts a date and time stamp at the beginning of an open e-mail message. Figure 26-6 shows the sequence of actions the macro follows. This chart follows the format of the macro template flowchart, with the macro actions performed detailed for the DateTime macro.

To create this macro, use the macro template shown earlier. Change the macro name to **DateTime** and change the visibility (also known as scope) to Public. Additional variables are declared for Outlook Inspector and MailItem objects, and for two string variables, the last of which, strAryDateParts, is an array of strings used for the separation of the date value from the time value. An Inspector is the window that is opened when you open an Outlook item. No Outlook item can be opened without an

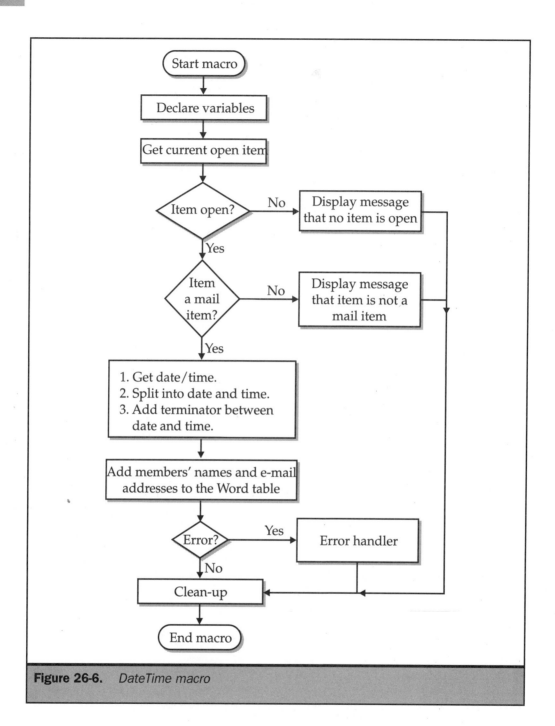

Figure 26-6. *DateTime macro*

associated Inspector being opened. A MailItem is any e-mail item in Outlook. Outlook defines object types for tasks (TaskItem), contacts (ContactItem), appointments (AppointmentItem), and all other special Outlook items.

```
Public Sub DateTime()
 ' This macro requires a reference to the Outlook object model.
 Dim objOutlook As Outlook.Application
 Dim objInspector As Outlook.Inspector
  Dim objMail As Outlook.MailItem

  Dim strDateTime As String
  Dim strAryDateParts() As String
```

After declaring the error handler and creating the Outlook Application object, an Inspector object is declared for the currently open item using the ActiveInspector property of the Outlook Application object. If no items are open, an error will occur and be handled by the error handler.

```
On Error GoTo ErrorHandler

Set objOutlook = CreateObject("Outlook.Application")

' The ActiveInspector is the currently open item.
Set objInspector = objOutlook.ActiveInspector
```

If an item is open, it is checked to confirm it is an e-mail item. If it is not, a message is displayed to that effect. Each item type in Outlook has a Class associated with it; the Class for mail items is olMail. The CurrentItem property of the Inspector is used to check the Class of the item, and if it is a mail item, the objMail variable is assigned to it. Objects are assigned to variables with the Set keyword. Non-object variables do not use the Set keyword. This can be confusing and is often a source of errors in macros.

```
' Check and see if anything is open.
If Not objInspector Is Nothing Then
   ' See if the current item is an e-mail item.
   If objInspector.CurrentItem.Class = olMail Then
     ' Get the current mail item.
     Set objMail = objInspector.CurrentItem
```

The strDateTime variable is set to the current date and time by calling the Now( ) function. Then the date and time are assigned to individual elements of the string array strAryDateParts by the Split function. Split can be used to split up strings at specified characters, called *delimiters*. The delimiter in this case is the space character, and here the date/time string is split into only two elements. This keeps the AM/PM time designator with the time. For example, a date and time string of "7/4/2001 10:00:00 AM" is split into two strings, "7/4/2001" and "10:00:00 AM". The "7/4/2001" string is placed in element 0 of strAryDateParts, and the "10:00:00 AM" string is placed in element 1 of strAryDateParts.

```
' Get the current date and time.
    strDateTime = Now()
    ' Split the date and time at the space separator.
    ' Date goes into one array element and time into another.
    strAryDateParts = Split(strDateTime, " ", 2)
```

Array elements are referenced by a subscript number, which usually starts at 0. In the next section of the macro, the date (element 0) and time (element 1) are combined again into one string variable, this time separated by a new line. Strings are combined by using the ampersand character (&), which is referred to as *string concatenation*. The VBA constant for a new line is vbCrLf, which stands for a combination of the carriage return and line-feed characters. The effect is the same as when you press ENTER when using a word processor.

```
' Combine the date and time, separated on two lines.
    strDateTime = strAryDateParts(0) & vbCrLf & strAryDateParts(1)
```

The effect of combining (concatenating) the date and time strings separated by a new-line combination is to place the date on the first line, followed by the time on the next line. Figure 26-7 shows the result of the macro, with the date and time on two lines.

The big text field in an e-mail item (and most other Outlook items) is called the Body property. The date and time stamp, now consisting of two lines of text, is inserted at the beginning of the body of the objMail item. A bug in Outlook causes any Outlook item to become a Rich Text Format (RTF) item when the Body property is changed. This is no problem when the recipient of the e-mail also uses Outlook, but can cause problems when other mail clients are used. Work-arounds for this problem have been developed, but they use advanced techniques and other object libraries that aren't covered in this book.

```
' Add the date and time stamp to the beginning of the e-mail.
    objMail.Body = strDateTime & objMail.Body
```

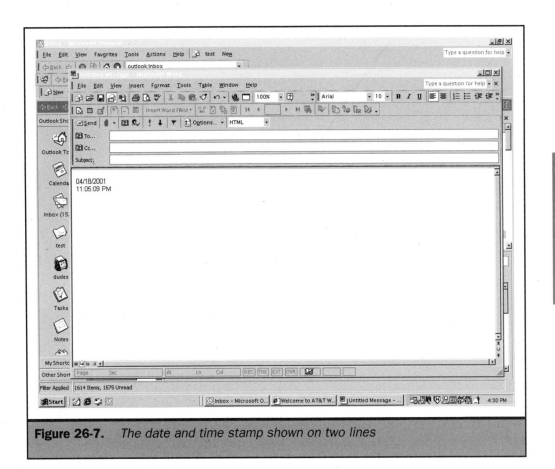

Figure 26-7. *The date and time stamp shown on two lines*

The first Else clause is executed only if the test for the item being an e-mail item fails, and the test displays a message that the item is not an e-mail item. The final Else clause is executed if no item is open. All If statements end with an End If statement. Else and ElseIf statements between If and End If statements are optional and provide alternate paths for program execution when the test for an If statement fails.

```
Else
    ' Show error message with only the OK button.
    MsgBox "This is not an e-mail item"
   End If
  Else
    ' Show error message with only the OK button.
   MsgBox "No item is open"
   End If
```

The remainder of the macro sets all object variables equal to Nothing and exits. Notice that only object variables are set equal to Nothing—strings and other variable types are not. The standard error handler follows the Exit Sub statement.

```
MacroExit:
  ' Set all objects equal to Nothing to destroy them and
  ' release the memory and resources they take.
  Set objOutlook = Nothing
  Set objInspector = Nothing
  Set objMail = Nothing

  Exit Sub

ErrorHandler:
  MsgBox "Error: " & Err.Description & vbCrLf & "Error # " _
    & Err.Number
  Err.Clear
  GoTo MacroExit
End Sub
```

Executing a Macro

Now that you have created your first macro, it's time to test it. Create a new e-mail item by choosing Actions | New Mail Message (or CTRL+N), and choose Tools | Macro | Macros to open the Macros dialog box. You can also use the key combination ALT+F8 to open the Macros dialog box. Highlight DateTime and click the Run button. The current date and time are inserted in the open e-mail item. Congratulations, you have created and executed your first macro.

To save the macro and your work in the VBE, click the disk icon on the toolbar in the VBE, or select Save from the File menu.

Adding a Macro to a Toolbar Button

In addition to running macros from the Macros dialog box, you can put macros that you run frequently on a toolbar or menu. The procedure is similar to the toolbar and menu customizations you learned about in Chapter 24. In the Customize dialog box, select the Macros category in the Commands tab. The available macros appear in the Commands list on the right. Drag the macro you want to add to the toolbar or menu, and it's ready for use.

Tip *When you add a macro, such as DateTime, to a toolbar or menu, it is listed as Project1.DateTime. You can right-click the macro button in Customize mode and change the name to DateTime (or anything else you want).*

Creating the Disclaimer Macro

The next macro is very similar to the DateTime macro. It inserts a standard disclaimer into an e-mail message, but this time the insertion is at the end of the message. Only the sections of the macro that are different from the DateTime macro will be explained.

Here is the macro in its entirety:

```
Public Sub Disclaimer()
  ' This macro requires a reference to the Outlook object model.
  Dim objOutlook As Outlook.Application
  Dim objInspector As Outlook.Inspector
  Dim objMail As Outlook.MailItem

  Dim strDisclaimer As String

  On Error GoTo ErrorHandler

  ' Create the disclaimer string.
  strDisclaimer = "The information contained in this message " _
    & "constitutes privileged and confidential information " _
    & "and is intended only for the use of and review by " _
    & "the recipient designated above."
  ' Add a blank line between the e-mail text and the disclaimer.
  strDisclaimer = vbCrLf & strDisclaimer

  Set objOutlook = CreateObject("Outlook.Application")

  ' The ActiveInspector is the currently open item.
  Set objInspector = objOutlook.ActiveInspector

  ' Check and see if anything is open.
  If Not objInspector Is Nothing Then
    ' See if the current item is an e-mail item.
    If objInspector.CurrentItem.Class = olMail Then
      ' Get the current mail item.
      Set objMail = objInspector.CurrentItem
```

The existing DateTime macro added the text to the beginning of the message. The code for the disclaimer macro adds the disclaimer to the end of the message. The difference is in how the string added by the macro is inserted into the message body. If the string that is combined with the body is first, it appears before the text in the body (objMail.Body = strDateTime & objMail.Body). If the string that is combined with

BUILDING OUTLOOK
APPLICATIONS

the body appears second, it appears after the text in the body (objMail.Body = objMail.Body & strDisclaimer). The ampersand character is used to concatenate (combine) two strings together.

```
' Add the disclaimer to the end of the e-mail.
    objMail.Body = objMail.Body & strDisclaimer
  Else
  ' Show error message with only the OK button.
    MsgBox "This is not an e-mail item"
  End If
Else
  ' Show error message with only the OK button.
  MsgBox "No item is open"
End If

MacroExit:
  ' Set all objects equal to Nothing to destroy them and
  ' release the memory and resources they take.
  Set objOutlook = Nothing
  Set objInspector = Nothing
  Set objMail = Nothing

  Exit Sub

ErrorHandler:
  ' Display the description and number of the error.
  MsgBox "Error: " & Err.Description & vbCrLf & "Error # " _
    & Err.Number
  ' Clear the error.
  Err.Clear
  ' Exit the macro.
  GoTo MacroExit
End Sub
```

Inserting Outlook Data into Word

The DLToWord (Distribution List to Word) macro takes the names of members of an Outlook distribution list and their e-mail addresses and inserts them into a Word table. This macro not only shows a way to get information about the members of a distribution list from Outlook; it also demonstrates one method of exporting formatted information from Outlook to a Word document. Exporting Outlook data into Word tables, bookmarks, and form fields is a common way to present Outlook data formatted in ways that are impossible from within Outlook.

The Word document and table are created by the macro. Controlling one program from within code in another program is called *automation*. Automation is very powerful and can be used to control many programs, including most of the applications in the Office XP suite. Make sure that a reference is set to the Word object library before you enter or test this macro. You always need to have project references set to any object library you intend to use in your code. See the earlier section "Setting Project References" for more information.

Figure 26-8 shows the sequence of actions the DLToWord macro follows.

Two Outlook Application properties that are new to Outlook 2002 are used in this macro: the Explorer object and the Selection collection. An *Explorer object* is what is used to view a folder in Outlook. When you view the Inbox, Drafts, Journal, or any other Outlook folder, you are doing this in an Explorer object. The *Selection collection object* is the one or more items currently selected in an Explorer object. Collections are groups of similar objects. When you look at the Outlook object model in the Object Browser, you will see many examples of collections, such as Selection, Explorers, Inspectors, Items, Recipients, and so on. Figure 26-3, shown earlier in this chapter, shows some other Outlook collections, the AddressEntries, AddressLists, and Attachments collections, in the Object Browser's Classes window.

Many of these collections have corresponding individual items, such as individual Explorer, Inspector, and Recipient objects. This macro uses a Recipient object, declared as objRecipient, and a distribution list item, objDL. A Recipient is a user or resource, usually the person to whom an e-mail is addressed. Here is the content of this macro:

```
Public Sub DLToWord()
    ' This macro requires references to the Outlook
    ' and Word object models.
    Dim objOutlook As Outlook.Application
    Dim objExplorer As Outlook.Explorer
    Dim objSelection As Outlook.Selection
    Dim objDL As Outlook.DistListItem
    Dim objRecipient As Outlook.Recipient
```

The DLToWord macro uses automation to control Word and declares objects for the Word application, including Document, Table, and Range. In addition to the string variables used for the distribution list field values, it also uses two long variables,

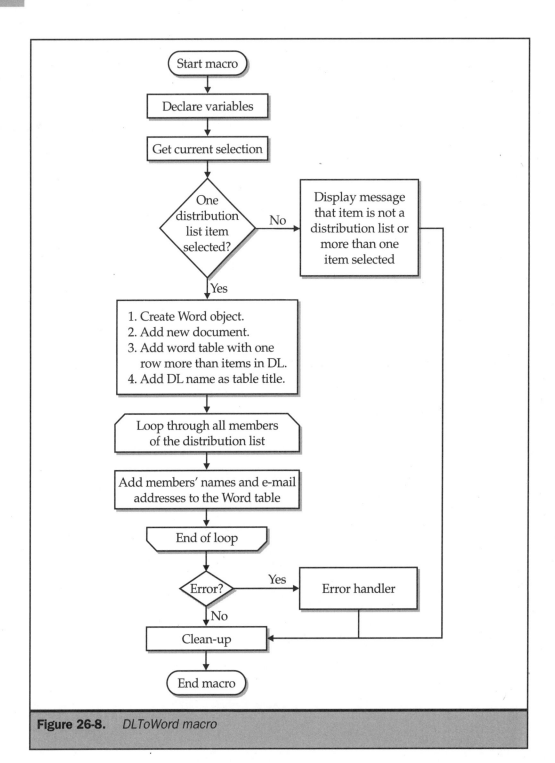

Figure 26-8.   *DLToWord macro*

which can represent numbers ranging from –2,147,483,648 to 2,147,483,647. The long variables are used as counters for the number of items in the distribution list.

```
Dim objWord As Word.Application
  Dim objDoc As Word.Document
  Dim objTable As Word.Table
  Dim objRange As Word.Range

  Dim lngCount As Long
  Dim lngIndex As Long
  Dim strName As String
  Dim strAddress As String
  Dim strListName As String

  On Error GoTo ErrorHandler

  Set objOutlook = CreateObject("Outlook.Application")
```

Similar to the way the currently opened item was *instantiated* (created) from the ActiveInspector property, the ActiveExplorer property is used to get the current folder. The Selection property is used to get the collection of currently selected items in that folder.

```
' Get the currently active folder window.
  Set objExplorer = objOutlook.ActiveExplorer
  ' Get the selected item(s) in that folder.
  Set objSelection = objExplorer.Selection
```

The macro looks for one and only one distribution list to be selected in the current folder. If those conditions are met, the name of the distribution list is stored in a string variable.

```
' Look for 1 distribution list item to be selected.
  If objSelection.Count = 1 And _
    objSelection.Item(1).Class = olDistributionList Then
      ' Get the selection.
      Set objDL = objSelection.Item(1)
      ' Get the name of the distribution list.
      strListName = objDL.DLName
```

If you use the CreateObject function when Outlook is already open, an instance of that open object is used. With Word and other Office applications, however, a new

BUILDING OUTLOOK
APPLICATIONS

instance is created if the application is already open. This requires special handling to avoid having multiple instances of an application created. First, the error handler is disabled by the On Error Resume Next statement, which resumes program execution on the line following the one in which an error occurred. The GetObject function returns an instance of an existing application object if one exists. If no instance of Word exists, CreateObject is used to create a new instance of the Word application object.

```
' Go to next line if there is an error.
    On Error Resume Next
    ' See if Word is already open.
    Set objWord = GetObject(, "Word.Application")
    ' If not, create a new Word application object.
    If objWord Is Nothing Then
       Set objWord = CreateObject("Word.Application")
    End If
```

The next lines first reenable the standard error handler and then add a document to Word. If an existing instance of Word is being used, this prevents the macro from altering any open documents. The new document is then made the active document, and a range is set to the beginning of the document.

```
    ' Now back to the normal error handler.
    On Error GoTo ErrorHandler
    ' Add a new document to Word and activate it.
    Set objDoc = objWord.Documents.Add
    objDoc.Activate
    ' Set the active range to the document start.
    Set objRange = objDoc.range(0, 0)
```

Next, the count of members of the distribution list is acquired, and then a Word table is created at the beginning of the document, with two columns and one more row than the count of distribution list members. The extra row will be used to insert the name of the distribution list.

```
    ' See how many items are in the distribution list.
    lngCount = objDL.MemberCount
    ' Add a Word table, with 1 more row than list members,
    ' use the first row for the list name. Table has 2 columns.
    Set objTable = objDoc.Tables.Add(objRange, lngCount + 1, 2)
```

The With statement is used to allow reference to items using only their properties, in this case properties of the objTable object. With statements not only make your code run faster, but they also make it easier to enter common properties in blocks. The Cell property of the Word table is used to insert the name of the distribution list into the first row in the table. The font for the name is set to boldface.

```
' Use With to make the code faster.
With objTable
  ' Insert the list name in the first row, first column.
  .Cell(1, 1).range.InsertAfter strListName
  ' Make the list name boldface.
  .Cell(1, 1).range.Bold = True
```

A For loop is used to get each member of the distribution list, using the GetMember method of the distribution list object. The index counter of the For loop is used to index the collection of members of the distribution list and to get the name and e-mail address of the list member at that index position. Members of distribution lists are Recipient objects.

```
' Now loop through the members of the list.
For lngIndex = 1 To lngCount
  ' Get a list member
  Set objRecipient = objDL.GetMember(lngIndex)
  ' Get the name of the list member.
  strName = objRecipient.Name
  ' Get the e-mail address of the list member.
  strAddress = objRecipient.Address
```

Note *This code triggers the Outlook Object Model Guard and then displays a prompt for the user to enable access.*

The name and e-mail address of the list member are inserted into the Word table, with the name inserted in column 1 and the e-mail address inserted in column 2. Then the loop is executed again until there are no more members of the distribution list to process. The table is automatically sized to fit the cell contents using the Columns.AutoFit method of the table, and the With block is terminated with the End With statement.

```
    ' Insert the name and e-mail address.
    .Cell(lngIndex + 1, 1).range.InsertAfter strName
    .Cell(lngIndex + 1, 2).range.InsertAfter strAddress
  Next lngIndex
  .Columns.AutoFit
End With
```

Finally, the cursor is moved to the end of the Word document, the document is made visible, and the macro is terminated as usual.

```
      ' Move the cursor to the end of the document.
      objWord.Selection.HomeKey Unit:=wdStory, Extend:=wdMove
      ' Make the document visible.
      objWord.Visible = True
      objDoc.ActiveWindow.Visible = True
   Else
     MsgBox "Not a Distribution List or more than 1 item is
selected"
   End If

MacroExit:
   Set objOutlook = Nothing
   Set objExplorer = Nothing
   Set objSelection = Nothing
   Set objDL = Nothing
   Set objRecipient = Nothing

   Set objWord = Nothing
   Set objDoc = Nothing
   Set objTable = Nothing
   Set objRange = Nothing

   Exit Sub

ErrorHandler:
   MsgBox "Error: " & Err.Description & vbCrLf & "Error # " _
     & Err.Number
   Err.Clear
   GoTo MacroExit
End Sub
```

Importing Contacts from Access

Importing and exporting contact information and other data between Outlook and Access or Excel is a common function that often has problems. Outlook cannot import or export items with custom fields and often misses duplicate items. The ContactsFromAccess macro described in this section demonstrates how to import contacts from an Access table, with code that prevents duplicate contacts from being created.

Figure 26-9 shows the sequence of actions the ContactsFromAccess macro follows.

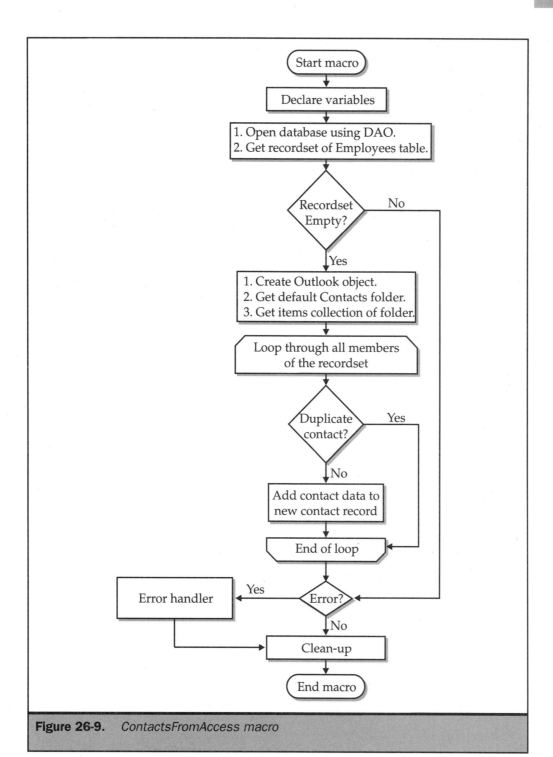

BUILDING OUTLOOK
APPLICATIONS

Figure 26-9.   *ContactsFromAccess macro*

This macro makes use of the Outlook NameSpace object, which is used to get direct access to Outlook folders and items. You can think of NameSpace as the window into the Outlook data store, just as Inspectors and Explorers are windows into the Outlook user interface. The only currently available NameSpace for Outlook is the MAPI namespace. Folders in Outlook are MAPIFolder objects, as shown by the objFolder variable.

```
Public Sub ContactsFromAccess()
    ' This macro requires references to the Outlook and DAO
    ' (Data Access Objects) object models.
    Dim objOutlook As Outlook.Application
    Dim objNS As Outlook.NameSpace
    Dim objFolder As Outlook.MAPIFolder
    Dim objContact As Outlook.ContactItem
    Dim objItems As Outlook.Items
```

Data Access Objects (DAO) are used to work with the Access database. ActiveX Data Objects (ADO) is a newer, more universal data access method, but for working with Access databases and tables, DAO is more versatile and easier to use. The next lines declare DAO object variables for a database and a recordset. If you have worked with Access, you are familiar with recordsets as table objects.

```
' Using DAO to work with the Access database.
    Dim dbEmployees As DAO.Database
    Dim rstEmployees As DAO.Recordset

    Dim strFirst As String
    Dim strLast As String
```

Filters are tricky to set up in Outlook. It's often easier to set up a filter that uses variables with a string declared using the string identifier character ($) than using the usual As String clause.

```
' This string is used for a filter.
    Dim ContactToCheck$

    On Error GoTo ErrorHandler
```

The sample Northwind database is opened using the DAO OpenDatabase method. To run this macro, the sample Northwind database must be installed. The path used is the standard installation path—if you installed the samples to another path, change the path string in the OpenDatabase statement.

```
' Open the sample Northwind database.
' If the install path is different, change the path.
Set dbEmployees = OpenDatabase _
    ("C:Files" _
    & " C:\Program Files\Microsoft Office\Office10\Samples\Northwind.mdb
")C:\Program Files\Microsoft Office\Office10\Samples\Northwind.mdb
```

SQL is a standard database query language, and it is used here to create the recordset of data from the Employees table in the Northwind database. The OpenRecordset method of the database object is used with a SQL statement to get the FirstName, LastName, Address, City, Region, PostalCode, Country, and HomePhone data fields from the Employees table.

```
' Use a SQL statement to get the data from the Employees
' table into a recordset.
Set rstEmployees = dbEmployees.OpenRecordset _
    ("SELECT FirstName, LastName, Address, City, " _
    & "Region, PostalCode, Country, " _
    & "HomePhone FROM Employees;")
```

After the recordset is created, the next statement checks to see if there are any records in it. A newly opened recordset whose record pointer is positioned at EOF (End of File) is an empty recordset. EOF and BOF (Beginning of File) are special locations after and before the records in a recordset. If the recordset is empty, both EOF and BOF will be true. Only one of these conditions needs to be checked, and you can check either one. If the recordset is not empty, the record pointer is moved to the first record in the recordset.

```
' The pointer for a newly opened recordset is EOF
' (End Of File) or BOF (Beginning Of File) only if
' the recordset is empty.
If Not rstEmployees.EOF Then
    ' Set the pointer to the first record
    rstEmployees.MoveFirst
```

After all that housekeeping, Outlook Application, NameSpace, and Contacts folder objects are created with the Set statements. The GetDefaultFolder method is used with the olFolderContacts argument (parameter) to set objFolder to point to the default

Contacts folder. The collection of items in the Contacts folder is then assigned to the objItems Items collection object.

```
Set objOutlook = CreateObject("Outlook.Application")
' Outlook has only 1 NameSpace, named MAPI.
Set objNS = objOutlook.GetNamespace("MAPI")
' Get the default Contacts folder.
Set objFolder = objNS.GetDefaultFolder(olFolderContacts)
' Get the collection of items in the Contacts folder.
Set objItems = objFolder.Items
```

The recordset is looped through (*iterated*) until the EOF condition becomes true. This iterates through the entire contents of the recordset.

```
' Loop through the recordset until the end.
Do While Not rstEmployees.EOF
  ' Extract the first and last names of this entry.
  strFirst = rstEmployees(0)
  strLast = rstEmployees(1)
```

The first and last names of the current record in the recordset are used as part of a filter with the Find method to ensure that no duplicate contacts are created. The first name is compared with the FirstName field in Outlook Contact items, and the last name is compared with the LastName field. The use of quotes in filters or restrictions is tricky; study this filter as an example of how to construct a complex filter string.

```
' Set up a comparison of the first name from the recordset
' and the first name for a Contact item.
ContactToCheck$ = "[First Name] = """ & strFirst & """"
' Add a comparison of the last name from the recordset
' and the last name for a Contact item.
ContactToCheck$ = ContactToCheck$ & " And [Last Name] = """ _
  & strLast & """"
' See if this name already exists in the Contacts folder.
Set objContact = objItems.Find(ContactToCheck$)
```

If no contact is found that matches the first and last names of the current record in the recordset, a new contact item is created using the CreateItem method with the olContactItem argument. The fields from the record are then added to the new contact item. Access database tables may contain Null fields—fields with no value at all. Outlook does not permit Null fields, so a check is made to see if any field is Null before adding it to the contact item. If a Null field is found, that field from the record is not added to the Outlook contact item.

```
If objContact Is Nothing Then
    ' Only add the new contact if it doesn't exist already.
    Set objContact = objOutlook.CreateItem(olContactItem)
    With objContact
        ' Outlook will not accept Null values, so test for that.
        If Not IsNull(rstEmployees(0)) Then
            ' If not Null set the first name.
            ' Repeat for other fields.
            .FirstName = rstEmployees(0)
        End If
        If Not IsNull(rstEmployees(1)) Then
            .LastName = rstEmployees(1)
        End If
        If Not IsNull(rstEmployees(2)) Then
            .HomeAddressStreet = rstEmployees(2)
        End If
        If Not IsNull(rstEmployees(3)) Then
            .HomeAddressCity = rstEmployees(3)
        End If
        If Not IsNull(rstEmployees(4)) Then
            .HomeAddressState = rstEmployees(4)
        End If
        If Not IsNull(rstEmployees(5)) Then
            .HomeAddressPostalCode = rstEmployees(5)
        End If
        If Not IsNull(rstEmployees(6)) Then
            .HomeAddressCountry = rstEmployees(6)
        End If
        If Not IsNull(rstEmployees(7)) Then
            .HomeTelephoneNumber = rstEmployees(7)
        End If
```

The new contact item has no permanent existence until the Save method is used to save it to the Contacts folder. The MoveNext method of the recordset is then used to move to the next record until the recordset has been traversed.

```
    ' Save the new Contact item.
    .Save
End With
```

```
    End If
    ' Go to the next row in the recordset.
    rstEmployees.MoveNext
  Loop ' Until the pointer is at the end of the recordset.
End If
```

The remainder of the macro closes the recordset and database if they exist, and then uses the standard code from the macro template to set all objects equal to Nothing. The rest of the code is the standard exit statement and error handler.

```
MacroExit:
  ' Closing the recordset or database if they do not exist
  ' causes an error.
  If Not rstEmployees Is Nothing Then
    rstEmployees.Close
  End If
  If Not dbEmployees Is Nothing Then
    dbEmployees.Close
  End If

  Set objOutlook = Nothing
  Set objNS = Nothing
  Set objFolder = Nothing
  Set objContact = Nothing
  Set objItems = Nothing
  Set dbEmployees = Nothing
  Set rstEmployees = Nothing

  Exit Sub

ErrorHandler:
  MsgBox "Error: " & Err.Description & vbCrLf & "Error # " _
    & Err.Number
  Err.Clear
  GoTo MacroExit
End Sub
```

Summary

In this chapter, you learned how to create and use Outlook macros. It's a good idea to study the Object Browser to become familiar with the object models for Outlook and other applications you want to customize to meet your specific needs.

As Microsoft Office XP and Outlook 2002 reach store shelves, there will be more books available about VBA programming for Outlook 2002. There are also peer-to-peer newsgroups sponsored by Microsoft that specialize in Outlook programming problems and questions. A newsgroup that specializes in Outlook VBA questions is msnews.microsoft.public.outlook.program_vba.

The Complete Reference

Part VIII

Appendixes

The Complete Reference

Appendix A

MOUS Certification

This appendix explains how to obtain MOUS certification for Microsoft Outlook. Here are the MOUS skills covered in this book, for those of you planning to take the Core certification exam.

Skill Set	Skills	Chapter(s)
Creating and Viewing Messages		
	Opening messages	4
	Printing messages	4, 5
	Inserting signatures	19
	Inserting message attachments	3
	Customizing Outlook views	23
Scheduling		
	Adding appointments to the calendar	11
	Scheduling meetings and inviting attendees	12
	Scheduling resources for meetings	12
	Applying conditional formats to the calendar	12
	Accepting and declining meeting requests	12
	Proposing new meeting times	12
	Printing the calendar	10
Managing Messages		
	Moving messages among folders	5
	Searching for messages	5

Table A-1. *MOUS Core Exam Skills*

Skill Set	Skills	Chapter(s)
	Assigning categories to Messages	19
	Modifying message settings	3
	Modifying delivery options	3
	Archiving messages manually	5
Creating and Managing Contacts		
	Adding contacts	8
	Editing contacts	8
	Organizing contacts using Categories	9
	Sorting contacts	9
	Assigning categories to contacts	9
	Tracking all activities for contacts	9
Creating and Managing Tasks and Notes		
	Creating tasks	13
	Updating tasks	13
	Assigning tasks to one or more contacts	13
	Delegating tasks	13
	Accepting and declining tasks	13
	Creating and editing notes	15
	Assigning contacts to notes	15
	Assigning categories to notes	13, 15

Table A-1. *MOUS Core Exam Skills* (continued)

APPENDIXES

For those planning to move beyond the basics and take the MOUS Expert exam, Table A-2 lists the MOUS Expert skills covered in this book.

Skill Set	Skills	Chapter
Configuring Offline Folders and Remote Mail		
	Creating offline folders	17
	Synchronizing folders	17
	Switching between online and offline states	17
	Specifying a folder for offline use	17
	Downloading messages for remote use	17
Organizing Messages		
	Changing the format for new messages	3
	Filtering and organizing messages	5
	Creating personal folders	17
Scheduling		
	Opening other users' calendars	16
	Flagging appointments as private	11
	Canceling meeting requests	12
	Updating meeting requests	12
	Scheduling NetMeetings	22

Table A-2. *MOUS Expert Exam Skills*

Skill Set	Skills	Chapter
Managing Information in Outlook		
	Importing information into Outlook	20
	Completing a Word Mail Merge using Outlook as a data source	20
	Creating Outlook forms	25
	Assigning categories to Journal entries	14
	Creating new Journal entries	14
	Assigning contacts to Journal entries	14
	Modifying Journal entry types	14
	Setting sharing permissions for a folder	18
	Using Folder Home Pages	18
Managing Contacts and Tasks		
	Assigning tasks to contacts	13
	Sending task requests	13
	Modifying task details	13
	Creating a list of tasks	13
	Tracking assigned tasks using Advanced options	13
	Viewing tasks assigned to other users	13
	Sending task information to other users	13

Table A-2.   *MOUS Expert Exam Skills* (continued)

APPENDIXES

Skill Set	Skills	Chapter
Using E-mail Alternatives		
	Opening a newsgroup message	22
	Using Instant Messaging in Outlook	22
Configuring and Customizing Outlook		
	Setting Word as the mail editor	6
	Specifying startup settings	24
	Specifying mail options	6
	Applying color to mail received from selected addresses	23
	Modifying Outlook Today settings (changing styles, specifying default message folders, ordering tasks)	23
	Modifying security zone settings	19
	Setting up secure e-mail	19
	Configuring dial-up connections	17
	Adding items to Outlook menus	24
	Adding/removing buttons from Outlook toolbars	24

Table A-2.   *MOUS Expert Exam Skills* (continued)

The Microsoft Office User Specialist (MOUS) program is the best way for you to prove to yourself—and your employer—that you have mastered one or more of the programs included in the Microsoft Office suite. By providing a quantified benchmark, the MOUS program gives you a reliable way to measure your strengths and identify your weaknesses. In addition, by following the prescribed coursework and preparing for the exam, you are choosing the best way to improve your skills either in an individual Microsoft Office application or in the overall suite of Office software components.

Currently, there are two levels of MOUS Outlook certification available:

- Core
- Expert

Core certification signifies that you can handle a wide range of everyday computing tasks. Expert certification signifies that you can handle more complex assignments.

Because the MOUS program is dynamic and changes frequently, for details on the most current MOUS certifications available, visit http://www.mous.net for additional information.

How to Get MOUS Certified

The following information details the steps to follow to obtain the MOUS certification for Outlook.

Step 1: Prepare for the Exam

As you begin to prepare for your MOUS certification, you should not only determine which Office product and level of proficiency you want to target but also assess your current skill levels. The specific skill sets required for Core and Expert Outlook certification are listed at the beginning of this appendix, along with the chapters that cover each skill.

The MOUS exams are scenario-based and take place within the application itself. They are not multiple-choice or fill-in-the-blank tests; instead, you will be asked to perform specific real-world assignments. Therefore, as you prepare for the exam, focus on how you will actually work; don't try to memorize information.

We have designed this book to be not only a comprehensive reference but also a complete study guide for both Core and Expert Outlook certification.

Step 2: Register for the Test

All exams are administered by an Authorized Testing Center. To find the testing center nearest to you, either call 1 (800) 933-4493 or check the Web site at http://www.mous.net. Many testing centers require advance registration, but others accept walk-in candidates as well.

Step 3: Take the Test

You will be judged on your ability to complete a task, and on how long it takes you to do it. Using the program's Help system is permissible, but that will eat up your time.

Basic Guidelines for Taking a MOUS Exam

Microsoft provides the following guidelines for taking any of the MOUS exams:

General Tips

- Carefully read the instructions, which will be displayed at the bottom of the screen when you begin the test. Answer each question as if the end result must be shown to the test exam administrator. Do nothing extra; do only what is requested.

- Since all questions have equal value, try to answer all of them, including the more difficult ones.

- Pay close attention to how each question is worded. Responses must be precise, resolving the question exactly as asked.

- Scoring of answers is based on the end result, not on the route or time taken to complete the task. Errant keystrokes or mouse clicks will not count against your score as long as you achieve the correct end result. The result is what counts.

- Remember that the overall test is timed. While spending a lot of time on an individual answer will not adversely affect the scoring of that particular question, taking too long may not leave you enough time to complete the entire test.

- Answers are either right or wrong. You do not get credit for partial answers. If the message "method is not available" displays on your computer screen, try solving the problem a different way.

- **Important!** Check to make sure you have entirely completed each question before clicking the Next button. Once you press the Next button, you will not be able to return to that question. A question will be scored as wrong if it is not properly completed before moving to the next question.

To ensure that a question is properly completed, do the following:

- Close all dialog boxes, toolbars, help windows, menus, and so on. Make sure all of a task's steps are completed. For example, when you select the Copy command, be sure to paste the item being copied rather than leave it on the clipboard.

- Make sure Office has completed the spreadsheet actions before clicking Next to move to the next task.

Don't do the following:

- Don't leave dialog boxes, toolbars, or menus open.
- Don't leave tables, boxes, or cells active or highlighted unless instructed to do so.
- Don't click the Next Task button until you have completely answered the question.
- Don't scroll in the question unless instructed to do so. Leave your answer visible.

Getting Your Test Results

Test results are displayed to each candidate as soon as the test is completed. They are completely confidential. If you pass, you will receive a certificate by mail within four to six weeks. If you fail, you will be informed where you need to focus more attention. You can take the test as many times as you want, but there are no refunds if you don't pass, and you must pay a new fee each time you take the test.

Once you have passed your test, you have proof for the world that you possess specific, relevant skills. Your certification can be invaluable if you are in the job market, as it will show your prospective employer that you have the skills to succeed. It will also show your current employer that they can rely on your knowledge with your demonstrated mastery of Microsoft Office skills.

Index

help
    Answer Wizard, 38
    Ask a Question feature, 31
    customizing the Office
        Assistant, 33–36
    Index, 38–39
    Microsoft Outlook Help, 36,
        37–39
    Office on the Web, 36, 39
    online, 36, 39
    ScreenTips, 36
    using the Office Assistant,
        32, *33*
    What's This?, 36
home pages
    adding a folder home page,
        483–486
    setting for an Outlook folder,
        29, *30*
hyperlinks, 238–239
    syntax used when creating, 238

I

iCalendar, 313
icon view, customizing, 419–420
importing data, 573–577
    data translators, 575
    importing Contacts from
        Access, 738–744
    importing options, 574–575
    mapping fields, 575–577
    from Outlook Express, 575
    See also exporting data

Inbox, *7*, 58
    configuring, 96–99
Information viewer, 14, 16
instant messaging. *See* MSN
    Messenger
items, 690

J

Journal, 8, *10*
    adding attachments to entries,
        403–405
    adding entries, 400–406
    configuring automatic
        journaling, 400–401
    creating entries manually,
        401–403
    creating Journal entries from
        contacts, 248–249
    moving its shortcut, 402
    printing entries, 409–410
    using Outlook items to create
        entries, 405–406
    viewing entries, 406–408
junk mail
    adding senders to the junk
        senders list, 509–510
    color listings, 508
    Exception List, 510
    filtering, 508–509
    moving, 508–509
    viewing and updating the junk
        senders list, 510

V

INTERNATIONAL CONTACT INFORMATION

AUSTRALIA
McGraw-Hill Book Company Australia Pty. Ltd.
TEL +61-2-9417-9899
FAX +61-2-9417-5687
http://www.mcgraw-hill.com.au
books-it_sydney@mcgraw-hill.com

CANADA
McGraw-Hill Ryerson Ltd.
TEL +905-430-5000
FAX +905-430-5020
http://www.mcgrawhill.ca

GREECE, MIDDLE EAST,
NORTHERN AFRICA
McGraw-Hill Hellas
TEL +30-1-656-0990-3-4
FAX +30-1-654-5525

MEXICO (Also serving Latin America)
McGraw-Hill Interamericana Editores S.A. de C.V.
TEL +525-117-1583
FAX +525-117-1589
http://www.mcgraw-hill.com.mx
fernando_castellanos@mcgraw-hill.com

SINGAPORE (Serving Asia)
McGraw-Hill Book Company
TEL +65-863-1580
FAX +65-862-3354
http://www.mcgraw-hill.com.sg
mghasia@mcgraw-hill.com

SOUTH AFRICA
McGraw-Hill South Africa
TEL +27-11-622-7512
FAX +27-11-622-9045
robyn_swanepoel@mcgraw-hill.com

UNITED KINGDOM & EUROPE
(Excluding Southern Europe)
McGraw-Hill Education Europe
TEL +44-1-628-502500
FAX +44-1-628-770224
http://www.mcgraw-hill.co.uk
computing_neurope@mcgraw-hill.com

ALL OTHER INQUIRIES Contact:
Osborne/McGraw-Hill
TEL +1-510-549-6600
FAX +1-510-883-7600
http://www.osborne.com
omg_international@mcgraw-hill.com